本书获得乐施会资助，内容不代表乐施会立场

THE TRANSFORMATIVE
DEVELOPMENT AND AFRICAN
SOUTH-SOUTH COOPERATION IN
AGRICULTURE SECTOR

非洲农业的
转型发展与南南合作

刘海方 宛如 刘均 柯文卿 主编

社会科学文献出版社
SOCIAL SCIENCES ACADEMIC PRESS (CHINA)

序 言
非洲农业的转型发展与南南合作

刘海方

虽然非洲农业有良好的发展条件尤其是其自然条件，但受历史遗产、基础设施和资本积累的限制，其发展仍相对不足。这不仅对本地乃至世界粮食安全造成了重大威胁，也影响了非洲整体经济结构的升级。

非洲农业大体可以分为传统农业和现代农业两种类型，传统农业指自给自足的维生农业，从参与的人口比例来讲仍然是非洲目前的主要生产方式；现代农业则是在城市化进程中纳入政府可控制的国民经济体系、真正的第一产业并创造大量就业机会，同时也为第二、第三产业提供重要支持的商业化的农业。21 世纪以来，非洲的快速发展被认为主要是由世界大宗原料商品价格优势推动的，非洲国家再次意识到当前急需进一步进行整个经济结构的深刻转型升级，以便完成真正的可持续发展。其中，以农业的转型升级尤为重要。对此，非洲的政治经济界精英已经达成共识，正如联合国非洲经济委员会（UNECA）的领导人卡洛斯博士在其最近的文章中所言，"历史证明，成功使人民脱贫的国家都依靠了农业革命，对粮食的生产、仓储、加工、销售和使用都进行了系统的改进。从欧洲工业革命以来，农业生产率的提高对欧洲国家经济结构的快速调整贡献巨大。农业革命影响国家经济的著名例子是巴西、印度和中国等，它们利用农业生产率提高带来的收益促进了经济增长方式的转变。非洲急需学习中国、巴西和印度是如何在农业发展的前提下实现工业化的，而且在不到 30 年的时间里实现大规模人口的减贫。"[①]

[①] Carlos Lopes，"Agriculture as Part of Africa' Structural Transformation"，原文发表在 *Journal of African Transformation* 上，中文见本书第一篇。

1

一 非洲农业发展轨迹：从"结构调整"方案到自主探索

农业是非洲大陆经济转型的关键领域之一，却长期被忽略和误导。获得独立之初，非洲国家急欲摆脱在国际经济体系中的不利地位，于是按照依附论的主张纷纷采取了进口替代战略——国家财政主要支持工业体系建设的同时，也常常忽略甚至牺牲农村和农民的利益。

20 世纪 80 年代初，非洲国家在财政压力之下相继转向接受世界银行和国际货币基金组织主导的《结构调整计划》（Structure Adjustment Programme），尽管对于以往忽视农业的政策有所调整，但更重要的，还是按照新自由主义的药方，重心放在了对于"自由市场"的打造上，即按照经济学教科书塑造一个标准的宏观经济环境。然而这种强调产权保护、保障合同顺利实施的宏观环境，更多的只是有利于外来公司的发展；而对外开放市场使非洲国家刚刚开始萌芽的民族产业受到极大的冲击（1980～2009年，撒哈拉以南非洲国家的制造业占国民生产总值的比重从 16% 下跌到 12%），与此同时，非洲农产品贸易环境急剧恶化，开始更大程度地受到外部市场价格震荡的影响，完全无法与欧美国家政府补贴的经济作物抗衡。[①] 20 世纪 90 年代非洲农产品出口数量增加，收入却在下降，有学者统计，如果 1980 年的单位出口价值为 100 的话，非洲在 1990 年和 2000 年的单位出口价值分别下跌到 81 和 84。[②]

尽管如此，20 世纪 90 年代以来，撒哈拉以南非洲的农业出口还是增加了 30%，例如，肯尼亚的茶叶出口已经占到肯尼亚出口创汇的 20%，花卉种植业也每年增长 15%～20%。南非这样的矿业出口创汇大国，农业也一直占据国民生产总值的 3% 以上，如果再加上中下游的农业加工业，农业总的构成应该达到国民生产总值的 12%。总之，农业成为非洲各国的主要收入来源。马拉维商会联合会（Malawi Confederation of Chambers of Com-

---

[①] 正因为如此，长期以来一直作为世界加工工厂的中国服装行业大企业，一直以来对欧美国家政府大幅度补贴的原材料青睐有加，而不会留意生长在乞力马扎罗山脚下品质优良的棉花。

[②] Michael Barratt Brown, *Africa's Choices: After Thirty Years of the World Bank*, London: Penguin, 1995, p. 28.

merce and Industry，MCCCI）2010 年的报告称，农业是马拉维经济的主要支柱，构成该国经济增长的 33.6%。

近年来，非洲的农业发展更是亮点纷呈。例如，加纳政府引进农业机械，让小农户实现了成片耕作，政府的介入成功地将这个国家变成了"面包篮子"。在乌干达，鱼产量大幅上升，2005～2015 年增长了 35%，水产品从 1999 年的 285 吨猛增到 2012 年的 10 万吨以上。埃及 2013 年的稻谷单产量达到了每公顷 9 吨，名列世界第一，2014 年总产量达到 750 万吨，带来约 5 亿美元的收入。坦桑尼亚在低地地区成功推广了蓄水灌溉系统，从而改善了依靠雨水灌溉的水稻种植。在低成本个体抽水项目的帮助下，尼日利亚农民采用小型灌溉设备，旱季用吊杆或葫芦从河边抽取浅层地下水浇灌蔬菜，供应城市居民。肯尼亚是撒哈拉以南非洲国家中奶制品业最发达的国家，每年产量可以达到 20 亿升。如果综合非洲农业的起点和独立以来的坎坷发展历程以及目前政府体制方面的局限性，非洲的农业已经取得的成绩是必须被承认的，而且也说明其发展潜力是巨大的。

从 20 世纪 60～70 年代开始，世界银行引入支持非洲的农村发展项目，大规模引进现代农业技术，用于种植业和动物饲养，其中包括高产作物、化肥、农业化工、贷款、机械化和灌溉业。令人遗憾的是，因为部门之间缺乏协调，这些项目不但缺少综合收益，而且很多不能持续下去。这个教训被非洲领导人所汲取。2003 年非洲联盟（简称非盟）和非洲发展新伙伴计划批准了"非洲农业综合发展计划"（Comprehensive Africa Agriculture Development Programme，CAADP），[①] 表明了非洲领导人对于农业主导的发展方向的决心。该项目规定，每一个非洲国家的年度预算至少要有 10% 用于发展农业，才能真正完成解决粮食安全和减贫的目标。然而，目标从非盟层面向各个国家落实并不容易，除了少数几国，非洲国家的农业投入一直低于该目标。尽管如此，"非洲综合农业发展项目"作为第一个非洲人自己设计出来的、集体治理农业发展的纲领性文件，仍然具有重要的历史意义，是非洲各国目前制定各自农业发展规划的重要依据和蓝本，而且迄今该项目所发挥的凝聚共识、动员力量、提升能力的作用还是非常显著的。

---

① The Comprehensive Africa Agriculture Development Programme is an initiative of the African Union approved in Maputo in 2003, which is an integral part of the New Partnership for Africa's Development (NEPAD). For more information see http：//caadp. net/.

二 综合治理方案的出台：农业商业—农业加工—工业化的路径

在近代历史上，全球增长最快的经济体主要靠石油、天然气和矿产支撑。然而，可持续的经济增长需要建立在非开采行业的扩大上，特别是那些能够推动创新、满足国内供应链以及促进出口的产业。非洲国家自独立以来，几经摸索实践，经济发展的思路也从原来只专注于进口替代品工业到经济结构调整时期的"自由市场"建设，再到 20 世纪 90 年代中期开始自主探索进行经济治理的新工业化思路，特别是自 2013 年非盟 2063 年议程发表以来，经济转型的概念被不断强调。领导人意识到西方发达国家并不是一开始就专注于建设"自由市场"，国家对本国产业的扶植和保护一直都是需要的。[①] 2008 年世界经济危机的发生并没有使非洲经济发展与欧美世界"共衰退"，而是随着整个亚洲的向好趋势在"共繁荣"，"非洲崛起"也自此成为人们关注的话题，非洲狮子似乎已经真的不可逆转地奔跑在"后发优势"的迅速发展之路上了；但是 2014 年下半年以来的世界大宗商品价格一路走跌，大多数依赖单一资源产品（包括金属和非金属矿业品和农产品）的非洲经济体都遇到明显的困难，这使非洲领导人又一次不得不清醒并痛彻地面对这样的事实：非洲经济的结构必须调整，否则永远被自己不能左右的世界市场价格机制玩弄于股掌之间。

怎么调整呢？20 世纪 60 年代单纯提倡工业化的思路已经有教训摆在那里。显然结构调整需要一个综合治理的思路，非洲国家要明确自身优势，然后找到适合的切入点，迅速跻身并提升自己在世界价值链上的位置。对于大多数还是专业生产主导的非洲国家来讲，从农业产品入手，振兴有优势产品的加工业，利用产业的上下游链条延伸至其他产业，带动运输业、服务业、商业甚至更高端的制造业的发展，正是优势所在。

1989 年在亚的斯亚贝巴召开的非洲统一组织（简称非统）首脑会议上，非洲国家开始认真反思并接受结构调整方案的发展战略，这次会议决定，每年的 11 月 20 日作为"非洲工业化日"，联合国大会也给予承认并

---

① Lin, Justin Yifu and Celestin Monga, "The growth report and new structural economics", *Policy Research Working Paper Series* 5336, The World Bank, 2010.

将其提升到联合国层面。此后，每年的"非洲工业化日"的具体主题有所不同，但都是在非盟和联合国非洲经济委员会的共同努力之下为非洲国家提出的集体发展目标。2013 年，"非洲工业化日"的主题是将工业化与经济转型结合在一起，同时会议报告的封面很有启发意义，表达了非洲国家处在世界大宗商品价格顺风期、希望借机实现完成经济转型的目标，以便继续保持发展的势头。有趣的是，通常所说的资源的概念，不再狭隘地定义为矿产资源，而是被有意地宽泛化为"自然资源"——特别是事关农业生产的自然条件，土地和水源被列为更重要的考量范围。[①] 2014 年"非洲工业化日"的主题不再是以往发挥矿业资源优势。会议提出了发挥非洲农业优势并向工业化方向努力，同时解决粮食安全问题的目标。

上文论述了整体发展战略的逐渐试错并逐步达到全面、各部门协调考虑的过程，它体现了非洲在经济治理方面的认知过程；农业方面的具体政策框架也有一个逐步完善的过程。外来政策干涉是一方面，另一方面非洲领导人也曾经自觉不自觉地长期忽略、牺牲农业发展，无论是公共开支还是政府发展援助，大量资金被错误地分配，没有满足农业的根本需要。例如，2002 年非洲获得了 7.136 亿美元的政府农业发展援助资金，几乎是东亚和南亚国家的两倍，后两者只得到了 4.798 亿美元。然而，非洲获得的援助资金并没有带来更大的回报。

如上所述，非盟和联合国非洲经济委员会 2014 年联合发表的报告提出非洲农业转型关键的第一步：应从商业而非自给自足的农业生产入手来提高生产率。报告认为，非洲绝大多数小农户生产效率低，也不赢利。他们一直只能勉强糊口的主要原因有两个：一是他们生产的农产品产量低、品质差，无法满足市场需要，因为大部分人缺乏了解现代技术和促进生产的信息渠道；二是农民与产品市场脱节——糟糕的基础设施使农产品上游的生产与下游的加工销售几乎不能联系起来。总之，从维生农业向现代农业经济转型，是个系统治理的工程，核心是利用可获得的资源来获取应用技术、提高生产力。这包括培育新的种植作物和动物的种类，实现农业机械化、实施土壤和水源综合治理战略，综合治理病虫害，进行农产品加工以

---

① Fantu Cheru, Renu Modi eds., *Agricultural Development and Food Security in Africa*, London: Zed Books, 2013, Introduction.

提高附加值，以及促进社会和文化行为的变化适应。另外，在发展过程中，有倾斜性地解决大多数农村人口的贫困生活条件，改善农民和农村地区的生活水平。

在自下而上的层面，非洲的有识之士也在积极推动农业的研究和发展。卡罗·B. 汤普森教授的研究涉及南部非洲小农户的贡献，戴安娜·李－史密斯研究员关于《城市农业》的讨论也显示出了非洲国家的社会组织和公众对于这些"本土方案/非洲方案"的不懈努力和巨大贡献。实际上，从 20 世纪 90 年代非洲一些农业科学家在从事援助工作的国际人士的支持下，发起了"非洲农业研究论坛"（Forum for Agricultural Research in Africa，FARA），这个民间组织 1997 年正式成为世界银行研究非洲农业发展在非洲大陆范围内的合作伙伴。在制定"非洲农业综合发展计划"过程中，民间组织也贡献良多。如今，这一论坛已经成为非盟的专门技术机构，其最新的成果就是非洲人自己制定和领导的"农业科学议程"（Science Agenda）的设立。这个论坛能够凝聚非洲知识精英、保持和提升非洲人在农业发展和科学研究方面的能力，从而使非洲的农业发展真正受惠。

2014 年被非盟命名为非洲的农业和粮食安全年，显示了非洲国家振兴农业的决心。非洲农业研究论坛作为协调机构，依照辅助性原则，将非盟的计划分解为次地区的和各国的计划。在执行的过程中，论坛动员非洲大陆范围内的各个相关项目机构，与国际范围内的利益相关方一起，共同针对农业发展过程中的某些机会和挑战采取行动。目前，非洲农业研究论坛在各个国家的合作伙伴包括非洲新农业技术推广（Dissemination of New Agricultural Technologies in Africa，DONATA）、非－欧农业研发伙伴平台（Platform for African－European Partnership on Agricultural Research for Development，PAEPARD）、地区农业信息学习系统（Regional Agricultural Information and Learning Systems，RAILS）、撒哈拉以南非洲挑战项目（Sub－Saharan Africa Challenge Programme，SSACP）、农业创新商学研组织（Universities，Business and Research in Agricultural Innovation，UniBRAIN），等等。对于刚刚设立的"农业科学议程"，论坛也采取类似的流程运作，与已经成立并运作的非洲大陆范围内的农业相关研发机构合作，共同推进科学研究基础上的农业可持续发展。具体已经选定的合作伙伴包括农业适应未来要求组织（Adaptation for Future Demands in Agriculture，AFDA），非洲环境和农业研究特别项目（African Special Progamme on the Environment and Agricultural Research，African SPEAR）、非洲农业集约化纲要（Programme for Agricultural Intensification in Africa，PAINT）、非洲人力资本、科学技术和农业企业家共筑粮食安全框架（Africa Human Capital，Science Technology and Agripreneurship for Food Security Framework，AHC‐STAFF）等。

笔者在加纳调研的过程中了解到，非洲国家的农业科学家在推动农业革新、连接农民的生产和市场中扮演着重要角色，比如加纳的 17 个小型农业研究机构构成了一个大的理事会。加纳甘蔗农多年来苦于田鼠的破坏。在研究机构的实验室里，科学家们将这种偷食甘蔗的田鼠培育、改良成为人们可食用的饲养动物，从而将农业天敌转化为与农作物共生的食用动物蛋白来源——这不能不说是非洲人自己的农业创新技术。该理事会遍布加纳全国的网络将这一技术迅速推广出去，以至于加纳街头很快就可以看到买卖交易这种田鼠的农民了。

三　发展模式之争——小农户还是大公司？

独立以后，大部分非洲国家农业发展迟缓甚至出现倒退，究其原因有一些是殖民时期以来形成的深层观念的影响。为了宣扬殖民占领的合理性，20 世纪上半叶就出现了为白人占地辩护而炮制的"空地说"（其实是非洲人的公社土地在休耕，但被解释为空地）；再如，独立以后，非洲国家的后殖民地土地改革（尤其是坦桑尼亚的国有化改革），被认为是"非理性""短见"的，破坏了粮食安全，因为这些土地改革主张"将土地的种族不平衡作为首要问题置于经济稳定之上"；抑或"白人私有土地经营方式优越于传统非洲人公社土地所有制，应该成为非洲主导方式"；或者"非洲小农户总是破坏土地的生态，而白人大农庄才是有效利用土地的最佳选择""白人农场主的技术整体上远远超过非洲维生农业的农民，后者几乎无助于国民经济的发展"，等等。[①] 归根结底，很多主张源于白人相对于非洲人优越性的心理。这些土地改革贬低了非洲人世世代代积累的本土农业知识。可惜的是，这些深层观念因为欧洲人从

_____

① Fantu Cheru，Renu Modi eds.，*Agricultural Development and Food Security in Africa*，London：Zed Books，2013，Introduction.

历史上延续至今的强势而很难被"解魅"，很多非洲国家独立以后往往不由自主地采取更加倾向于白人大农庄的农业政策，商业、市场、银行信贷等都是向大农庄倾斜，而不是鼓励小农户和传统公社农业的生产方式。[①] 诸如安哥拉等国最终失败了的国有农场的实践，也多少受到这些流行观念的影响。在市场竞争中本来就处于劣势的非洲人小农户，独立以后一直在没有受到政府保护的环境中艰难成长，当然很难与白人农场主抗衡。有长期跟踪研究非洲农业的学者已经指出，历经殖民统治和独立以后的各种危机时期，非洲传统的小农户农业生产方式才是真正养活非洲大多数民众的根本。[②]

是大农庄主模式好还是小农户模式好？关于非洲农业发展模式的争论，显然不仅是有关效率的问题，背后还涉及土地所有权斗争，即谁有权获得更多的土地生产资料从而扩大生产的权力斗争。在白人占有好地、大面积土地的国家，土地所有权仍是长时间困扰这些国家的主要难题。津巴布韦"快车道"土地改革（简称土改），在非洲其他国家激起了很大反响。南非、纳米比亚甚至肯尼亚等国纷纷出现了仿照津巴布韦激进土改做法的声音，而且每次经济不景气都会激发新一轮民族主义式的"非洲人要求土地权利"运动。虽然基本上都是主张不强行没收白人土地一派的政治家占上风，因为强行没收白人土地将加剧非洲的不稳定，并且强行驱逐经验丰富的农场主（他们有时雇佣多达 200 名工人）、把上千英亩的土地交给不熟悉大规模耕种的非洲人也是不切实际的（如津巴布韦土著人商业农场主联盟组织者诺夸姆齐·莫约就说，如果不投资并对非洲农民进行技术培训，重新分配土地很可能会导致农业生产的失败），但是不管大农场主模式还是小农户模式更加有效的争论从来就没停止过。

确实，有效使用土地是发展经济、解决以土地问题形式表现出来的种族问题的关键因素。非洲国家如果想通过重新分配土地来创造财富，必须为非洲人的子女提供教育，使之适应工业化和技术发展，并实行某种有效使用土地的政策和解放市场的措施，以真正扩大非洲的经济基础，从而真

① Fantu Cheru, Renu Modi eds., *Agricultural Development and Food Security in Africa*, London: Zed books, 2013, Introduction.

② 卡罗尔·汤普逊：《比气候变化更可怕的风暴：威胁非洲粮食生产的政策》（Carol Thompson, "Storms More Ominous than Climate Change? Policy Hazards to African Food Production"），北京大学非洲研究中心讲座，2011 年 6 月 29 日。

正解决土地方面的种族问题。然而现实情况是，独立以来，非洲人精英阶层虽然逐渐掌握了更多的土地，但公社土地不允许买卖的习惯法实际上限制了他们的发展。加之这些非洲人农场通常远离交通主干线，一般只能供应本地市场，而且以劳动密集型的方式为主；相比之下，白人农场主占据好地，而且距离交通枢纽很近；同时，非洲国家为了鼓励农业产品出口，基于粮食安全观而采取农业补贴等措施，实际上这些都客观上更能够惠及有实力的白人农场主，而非洲小农户反而更加没有竞争力。①

有意思的是，随着气候变化引发的全球农业活动的减少、生物能源投资兴趣的增加，非洲大陆因为大量尚未使用的可耕土地和具备成为世界粮食中心的潜能而再次吸引了世界各国的主权或者私募投资家。西方跨国公司不断强化全球产业链布局，加大对资源性、战略性农产品市场的掌控力。美国阿彻丹尼尔斯米德兰公司（Archer Daniels Midland，ADM）、邦吉（Bunge）、嘉吉（Cargill）和法国路易达孚（Louis Dreyfus）四大粮商控制了全球80%的粮食贸易，自然不能遗漏非洲市场。在新兴市场国家中，种植大量用于生物能源作物的巴西、韩国和中东的投资者在非洲购地和租地数量较多。最近几年，非洲迅速成为全球农业投资热点。这些投资者都相信，只要扩大耕地面积，或者提高单位面积产量，非洲不仅可以实现粮食自给自足，甚至可以成为人类的粮仓。据不完全统计，许多外国机构已取得或者正在与非洲政府商谈的土地面积达5000万公顷，是英国国土面积的两倍以上，多数以长期租赁或购买的方式取得。

一时间，关于哪种方式能够更好地释放非洲大陆的农业发展潜力又一次成为热门话题：西欧、美国等传统农业出口国坚持大规模商业农业的模式，要求机械化和普遍使用化肥亦即推广所谓奥巴马模式；与此同时，另一派则主要来自非洲各国本土的力量，坚持认为应该投资小农户，因为他们的模式是更加尊重环境，以满足家庭粮食需要为出发点的生产模式。这一派还将大规模工业化农业视作小农户以及他们所依赖的土地和水源的威胁。②

---

① Sam Moyo, "The Politics of Land Distribution and Race Relations in Southern Africa", *Racism and Public Policy*, pp. 242 - 270, p. 8, Geneva: United Nations Research Institute for Social Development (UNRISD) Programme Paper.
② Fantu Cheru, Renu Modi eds., *Agricultural Development and Food Security in Africa*, London: Zed books, 2013, Introduction.

汤普森教授在其为本书撰写的《农业发展与国际政策：非洲的 21 世纪替代方案》一文中指出，今天非洲农业发展的国际合作已成为国际公共政策问题，需要被广泛讨论，因为事关整个人类的未来。

按照达成共识的标准，2 公顷以下土地的小农户（拥有 2 ~ 4 公顷土地的农户被视为中等农户），数量上占非洲总农户的 90%，生产了 80% 的粮食。未来农业必定决定性地影响这个大陆的经济增长和转型的方向，而小农户模式作为非洲农业生产体制的支柱形态，必须得到足够的政策重视和支持，以便为非洲快速增长的城市化提供更充分、更高品质的农产品和食品，同时通过提升小农户生产的农产品的品质使其进入全球市场价值链、增加农民的收入、加快提升非洲自身解决贫困化问题的能力。[①]

当然，来自欧美发达国家的机械化大农业正在积极推进对于非洲农业的投资趋势。虽然大公司模式有弊端，但大公司确实控制着全球价值链的顶端；它们往往从上游到下游在很多领域、很多国家建成了非常完整的产业链条，既分散了投资者的风险，又能快速地产生吸引力，特别是对于缺少生产资料的非洲小农户往往具有很大的吸引力（通过公司 + 农户的模式）；它们通过合同确实发挥了带动小农户技术提升和进入全球价值链的效果。如果要引导更多小农户商业化的倾斜政策，还需要在制定国际政策时邀请这些非洲的小农户加入并全面地参与讨论，承认他们为全球粮食生产和人们更好地获取营养做的贡献，甚至承认保护本土知识培育出的新品种对于更好应对气候变化的积极贡献——显然，影响和转变认知需要很长的道路，并需要有足够的接地气的科学研究和政策公开讨论作为前提。

实际上，讨论大规模商业农场还是小农户的生产模式更优，并不切中问题的根本。非洲农业生产危机的根源主要来自各国的政治经济环境、不健全的农业生产体制、不恰当的农业政策以及欠缺执行能力。另外，当前随着孤立主义和民族经济保护主义在全球的回潮，关于非洲农业的讨论充斥了太多外来投资者"兼并土地"的话语，妨碍了非洲国家制定和实施适宜的农业政策、保护本国国民土地所有权和发展机会，并且妨碍了小农户模式和大商业农场模式互补性地为非洲国家农业发展做出贡献，既无法解决粮食安全问题、创造就业、减贫，也不能成为有利于促进非洲工业化到

---

① 见本书卡罗・B. 汤普森（Carol B. Thompson）教授撰写的文章。

来的引擎。当然，殖民时代以前与土地的亲缘关系、沉重的被殖民的历史记忆以及独立以来扭曲的发展经历，都使得非洲人对于土地问题特别敏感，对外来公司的介入天然地怀有抵触和敌意。这也提醒未来或者当下已经在非洲从事农业国际合作的实践者们，必须特别注意土地的敏感性问题。

四　新兴市场国家对非洲农业的南南合作

出于争取非洲大量新独立的民族国家支持、建设社会主义国际阵营的需求，中国很早就开始了对非洲的农业合作。冷战结束后，中国对非洲的农业合作发生了较明显的变化。1993 年召开的中国共产党第十四届三中全会正式确定建立社会主义市场经济体制，同时也确定了要进一步地扩大对外开放。在此背景下，许多中国企业开始走向海外，如中国农垦（集团）总公司（简称中农垦）、中国水产（集团）总公司等大型企业也进入非洲进行投资。

近年，中国形成了初步的"农业走出去""农业走进非洲"的政策支持体系（详细见本书刘海方和宛如合作的相关章节论述），农业贸易＋援助＋投资的南南合作形式日益形成，并且与巴西、印度等其他新兴经济体一样呈现出很多相似性。

虽然国际上有很多批评的声音，认为新一轮对非合作热潮体现的是大规模购买和租赁土地，是"圈地"，是新的"瓜分非洲"，中国和其他新兴经济体正是激化这一轮"新帝国主义争夺"的罪魁祸首，但是新兴经济体普遍因为政治上"不干涉内政"原则而获得了与非洲国家广泛的合作机会。与此同时，近年来，新兴市场发展的历史显示，成功使人民脱贫的国家都依靠了农业革命，对粮食的生产、仓储、加工、销售和使用进行了系统的改进。非洲领导人开始意识到，自工业革命以来，农业生产率的提高对欧洲经济结构的快速调整贡献巨大，而且巴西、印度和中国等都是重要的成功案例，利用农业生产率提高带来的收益促进了经济增长方式的转变。非洲急需学习中国、巴西和印度是如何在农业发展的前提下实现工业化的，而且要学习它们如何在不到 30 年的时间里实现大规模人口的减贫。

我们之前已经出版了与印度、南非等国学者共同在赞比亚调研农业合作情况的调研报告，因此印度的案例没有收入此书。根据印度学者的调研，印度在非洲的农业投资是与印度当前国计民生的发展休戚相关的，即每年占国家外汇使用第二主要板块的粮食和食用油。印度总理专门组建了农业生产工作组主管此事，鼓励印度公司在海外购买土地进行豆类和食用油作物的生产，要"在海外购买土地种植农作物以满足国内消费需求"并且预计"在15~20年中每年至少生产200万吨豆类和500万吨食用油"。①印度进出口银行为各发展中国家的政府、银行、金融机构及区域金融机构提供优惠信贷的条件是用于国家发展项目——农业发展项目自然可以使印度海外投资者顺理成章地以直接投资的形式赢得优惠信贷和项目合同。这就不难理解塔塔集团等大公司和其他中小公司都竞相涉足非洲商业农业领域，从香料、茶到农用化肥等化学品，范围极广。很多印度公司原来从事建筑行业，现在已经涉足大型商用农场，这些农场分布在埃塞俄比亚、马达加斯加、刚果（布）、乌干达、肯尼亚和坦桑尼亚等国。

值得注意的是，能够让印度在过去十多年不断加强与非洲的农业经济技术合作的是印度已成为一个"高效能、低成本的创新中心"，并且有应对气候变化、自然资源减少、耕地质量下降、粮食需求增加等挑战的国际经验（即作为南南合作中的"价值"不断在各种国际发展合作的交流平台上被广泛传播和宣讲）。为期三年的"印美非三方合作伙伴计划"项目就是一例，美国国际开发署（USAID）粮食安全办公室在美国政府的全球饥饿和粮食安全倡议（Feed the Future）项目下启动了这一合作，预期将把印度的经过检验的创新成果用于解决目标国（利比里亚、马拉维和肯尼亚等国）的粮食安全、营养不良及贫困等问题。类似地，在传统援助国加拿大、德国、日本、荷兰等，类似印美非三方对非合作都在进行。②

类似，2003年卢拉就任巴西总统后，南南合作就成为巴西外交政策的重要工具，并被继任政府所继承。巴西的外交重心转向非洲大陆以来，双边贸易不断增长，促进各种社会和经济部门发展的经济技术合作不断拓展，同时投资性质的商业模式也在不断拓展。巴西在非洲的发展合作在农

---

① Biraj Patnaik, "The New Shifting Agriculture: Shopping for Fields Overseas", *Indian Times*, 9th July, 2010.

② Jamie Morrison, Dirk Bezemer and Catherine Arnold, *Official Development Assistance to Agriculture*, London: DFID, 2004.

业和卫生等领域投入明显。巴西合作署最大的项目"热带草原计划"（20年里预算达到 5 亿美元）与"棉花四国"合作项目（Cotton - 4 program，具体指贝宁、布基纳法索、乍得、马里）吸引了广泛的国际关注——前者以提高受援国种子培育能力为目标，后者则宣称以提升这四个以棉花行业为经济命脉的国家的生产力、基因多样性和棉花行业质量为目标。像印度一样，巴西的对非农业合作经验明显更具有国际化的特点，有很多与日本的三方合作项目，不但利用了作为受援者接受日本的技术援助的经验，同时结合日本经验再创造出对非合作的方式；同时，巴西与联合国系统的各部门也相应设计了向发展中国家传播巴西经验的合作项目。

与此同时，因为大量推进巴西自身从非洲市场获取生物能源方面的投资，巴西的对非农业合作饱受批判，被讥讽为"人没有吃饱之前先去'喂养'汽车"；与此同时，"热带草原计划"虽然在莫桑比克大草原复制了巴西农业发展的经验，但是大豆和玉米的大规模产业化生产，也被认为导致了当地环境恶化和传统村落的消亡。① 巴西国家石油公司、巴西国家社会经济发展银行和私人公司一起，通过巴西与非洲国家达成政府协议的方式促成了这些合作，服务于巴西自己的"乙醇外交"而饱受质疑，批判的声音不仅来自国外，也来自巴西国内的公民社会。这迫使巴西不得不重新调整与非洲国家的农业合作方式。

从本书收录的三篇有关巴西对非农业合作的文章中，读者还可以了解到巴西在安哥拉、莫桑比克和马拉维进行农业合作的不同情况，三个截然不同的案例显示出非洲国家自己的自主能力、对于援助的认知和整个发展战略都大大影响了南南合作的效果。几位巴西学者认为，巴西专业人士应该增加对于非洲不同国情的认知和提高相应的行动能力，相信它们适用于同样是南方国家的中国，这些经验也正是中国国际发展合作署值得参考的经验。

五 中国对非农业合作的新型实践及前景展望

非洲的经济增长曾经长期依靠初级产品出口推动，其直接结果是去工

---

① 《安哥拉全国农民联盟致"热带草原计划"的公开信》，2012 年 10 月 11 日，参见 ht-tp：//www. unac. org. mz/index. php/documentos - de - posicao/38 - pronunciamento - da - un-ac - sobre - o - programa - prosavana。

业化，同时"资源诅咒"风险、长期贸易环境恶化、"荷兰病"、国内上下游产业间联系不密切等问题恶性循环。今天的非洲国家已经形成一个深刻的共识：非洲经济结构调整是非洲摆脱贫困和饥荒的唯一可持续之路，其意义远超越减贫和粮食安全。为了当代，也为了后代，非洲需要设计一以贯之的、战略转型政策，改变世界的认知并确保非洲价值链与世界价值链紧密联系。总之，非洲国家对于农业的认知正在经历重大的变化，因为多数非洲国家政府已不再将农业仅仅理解为农民的谋生手段，而是一种真正有利于国家实现经济转型的活动。根据非盟和联合国非洲经济委员会的探索，前文提到的综合治理的发展战略还赋予农业更多的意义：农业既是创造就业、提高生活水平从而帮助人们自己解决贫困问题的产业，也是非洲避免陷入老的"先污染、后治理"的发展路径的最有可能的重点产业。考虑到联合国 2030 年议程不仅是向发展中国家也是向发达国家提出的新发展议程，今天讨论非洲的农业发展对于人类可持续发展的贡献就格外具有意义。

中国的对非农业合作从 20 世纪 50 年代末完全不求经济回报的单纯援助开始，经历了援建很多大农场的时代，目前已经转向援助、贸易和对外投资并举的阶段。实践不可谓不丰富，教训也不可谓不多。当前中国对非洲的农业合作不像印度那种明确的与本国粮食和食用油安全联系在一起，而是强调"没有从非洲拿回一粒粮食"，但是也不能孤立地在农业领域里面决策——除了塑造国际形象的考虑以外，从实际效益最大化的角度看，农业合作也同样应该具有足够的外交关系和公共政策的视角，并充分考虑到其政治、经济和社会影响。

目前，中非农业合作的主要制约因素来自认知层面，因此已经有的成功案例还有待进行深入的学术研究并作为正面案例广泛传播；课题组在这个研究撰写过程中，尽量完整地收集了中非农业领域的合作实践情况，从援助、商品贸易等各方面分析实施特点和目前的局限，选择的国别案例的考虑是：赞比亚是中国最早进行农业投资的非洲国家，津巴布韦是中国投资比较多且农业合作对于双边关系比较重要的国家，安哥拉是资金技术和当地人脉关系等资源都非常雄厚的大型国有企业进入农业领域的典型案例，而肯尼亚是分析民营企业怎样快速选取优势发展方向占领高端发展空间的案例。坦桑尼亚的剑麻农场打破常规，邀请了多年奋斗在一线的国有农场企业家结合自己的经营经验走进非洲并逐渐立足乃至对当地社会经济发展做出重大贡献。坦桑尼亚的剑麻农场的案例讲述了机遇与挑战，读来非常生动。这几个案例的国别情况和对华关系与目标都非常不同，希望这一组案例呈现的丰富性、差异性能够给下一步深入的学术研究提供足够的经验和知识，也希望为政策决策和实践者提供有意义的参考。

总体而言，对于非洲农业问题，中国政府还必须有作为大国"增加援助但是不能止于援助"的认识。援助目标定位一方面要向非洲人提供尽可能多的知识技术和发展经验，另一方面要扶持和激发中国企业获得在非洲经营的本土化和国际化经验，从而成长为可持续发展的项目，即给当地人带来工作机会的、自主独立的国际化企业。因此，充分调动企业（既包括大的，更应该扶持中小规模的）的能动性，参与新时期的农业合作非常重要。三种合作形式应该有下一盘棋的整体观，要向达到"援助以促进贸易和促进投资"的方向努力。长远来讲，中国对非洲农业领域的介入，还应该有一些更具创新性的介入领域和介入方式，即从双边的角度应该多考虑与非洲本土已经开展的项目和实践的融合；同时从国际经济体系角度多开展一些南南合作层面的新项目和实践，以使中非农业合作的意义更为深远。

对于中国自身而言，讨论中非农业合作，显然既有利于中国更好地实现"十三五规划"中更好利用国内外资源和市场的目标，对于促进非洲发展的意义更为深远。中国的农村正在经历第三次土地改革，只有土地流转、规模经营、集约化经营有序推进，政府、资本、农民才能实现共赢。如果说有哪些中国的发展经验可以贡献于非洲当下正在进行的这场意义深远的农业转型、发挥支持长远国民经济可持续发展的历史重任，政府、资本和个体之间的协调和互动也许可以算是最重要的一条——包容性、可持续发展既需要亚当·斯密所说的"看不见的手"，更需要"看得见的手"，即政府必须起到主导、引导作用，做好规划，提供服务，在资本和民众利益之间搭起沟通的桥梁。中国不但自身在经济转型升级的时候需求非洲承接产能，也需要将自己的经验和教训与更广泛的发展中国家分享，这本身也是中国稳固自身发展的根基。通过与国际发展伙伴的合作，印度和巴西都有了符号性的"价值"可以分享给广大发展中世界，中国在这方面还需要继续努力。

目　录

非洲农业的最新发展与内生动力

新兴市场国家对非洲农业的南南合作

China's Agricultural Cooperation with African Countries

C
H
I
N
A

非洲农业的最新发展与内生动力

A
F
R
I
C
A

农业在非洲经济转型中的作用[*]

卡洛斯·洛佩斯[**] 著

刘 均[***] 译

引 言

数世纪以来,世界许多国家的农业驱动经济增长。农业在欧洲、美洲、亚洲的经济转型和工业化过程中发挥了重要作用。现代经济发展最突出的特点是:在经济结构成功转型的国家中,农业在国内生产总值(GDP)中的比重呈现长期下降趋势,工业和服务业的比重则相应上升。

在非洲,农业提供了近65%的就业机会,农产品交易占国内贸易的70%;未来数年中,它可能继续影响非洲大陆的经济增长。[①] 小农户是非洲农业的支柱。非洲大陆内外的新兴市场都显现出小农户获得更多收益的乐观前景。快速增长的城市人口和中产阶级将需要更多高品质的农产品和食品。将来农产品价值的增加可能会提高农民的收入。

非洲农业转型关键的第一步:应从商业而非自给自足的农业生产入手

---

[*] 本文原文标题为 Agriculture as Part of Africa's Structural Transformation,发表在 *Journal of African Transformation* 杂志 2015 年第一期(Volume 1,No. 1,2015,pp. 43 –61);接到本书的约稿邀请,作者允许将英文翻译成中文以飨中国读者。

[**] 卡洛斯·洛佩斯(Carlos Lopez),几内亚比绍人,发展经济学家,现任联合国非洲经济委员会总干事(Executive Secretary,United Nations Economic Commission for Africa)。

[***] 刘均,北京大学国际关系学院博士候选人,北京大学非洲研究中心助理。

[①] ECA,"Rethinking Agricultural and Rural Transformation in Africa. Challenges,Opportunities and Strategic Policy Options",2013;"Rethinking Agricultural and Rural Transformation in Africa – the Necessary Conditions for Success:The Case of Mauritius";ECA,"The Role of Agriculture,Agribusiness and Value Chains in the Trans-Formation",2014.

来提高生产率。非洲绝大多数小农户生产效率低，也不盈利。他们一直只能勉强糊口的主要原因有两个。其一，他们生产的农产品产量低、品质差，无法满足市场需要，因为大部分人缺乏了解现代技术和促进生产信息的渠道。其二，农民与产品市场脱节。糟糕的基础设施使农产品上游的生产与下游的加工销售几乎不能联系起来。

非洲大约65%的人以务农为生，虽然整个大陆有各种农作物、动物和耕作方式，[①] 但其农业生产率水平全球最低却并不令人惊讶。1965年以来的50年，印度的粮食产量从每公顷0.95吨提高到2.53吨，非洲却停滞不前，粮食产量还是每公顷1.5吨。虽然非洲的耕地总量是中国和印度等国家的3~6倍，但是中国和印度的人均耕地少，分别只有0.6公顷和0.3公顷，它们却成功解决了本国"十亿底层人口"的吃饭问题。

非洲虽然有丰富的自然资源，却是世界上粮食最不安全的地区。非洲大约有2.27亿人（五分之一的人口）长期面临粮食安全问题。事实上，相比其他地区，非洲的人口大约只占世界人口的15%，但是受饥荒影响的人口占世界人口近1/3。当然，尽管有这些挑战，非洲农业毫无疑问还有一些成功的案例。

加纳政府引进农业机械，让小农户实现了成片耕作，政府的成功介入将这个国家变成了"面包篮子"。在乌干达，鱼产量大幅上升，2005~2015年增长了35%，水产品从1999年的285吨猛增到现在的1万吨以上。根据美国农业部商品信息报告（Commodity Intelligence Report, United States Department of Agriculture），埃及2015年的稻谷产量达到了每公顷10.1吨，名列世界第一，2014年总产量有望达到750万吨，带来约5亿美元的收入。坦桑尼亚的低地地区在雨季的集水能力达600~900毫米，从而改善了依靠盆地地区的灌溉水稻种植。在低成本个体抽水项目的帮助下，尼日利亚农民采用小型灌溉设备，旱季用吊杆或葫芦从河边抽取浅层地下水浇灌蔬菜，供应城市居民。

遗憾的是，这些成功案例还不是普遍现象，非洲国家必须提高生产率。虽然已经有很多致力于提高农业技术、更新设备、种子、化肥、农作

---

① ECA, "Rethinking Agricultural and Rural Transformation in Africa: Challenges, Opportunities and Strategic Policy Options", 2013.

物收获加工以及提供农业贷款等的倡议和项目，但是大多数非洲农民没有直接获益。

到目前为止，为什么只取得了极少的成功？答案很简单，农业似乎是非洲大陆经济转型的关键领域之一，却长期被忽略和误导。这也反映在，无论是公共开支还是政府发展援助，大量资金被错误地分配，没有满足农业的根本需要。例如，2002年非洲获得了7.136亿美元的政府农业发展援助资金，几乎是东亚和南亚国家的两倍，后两者只得到了4.798亿美元。然而，这些额外援助并没有带来更大的回报。非洲国家政府的农业开支一直低于非洲农业综合发展计划（CAADP）① 要求的10%的预算目标。

历史告诉我们，成功使人民脱贫的国家都依靠了农业革命，对粮食的生产、仓储、加工、销售和使用都进行了系统的改进。自工业革命以来，欧洲农业生产率的提高对经济结构的快速转型贡献巨大。农业革命影响国家经济的著名例子是巴西、印度和中国，它们利用农业生产率提高带来的收益促进了经济增长方式的转变。

在非洲，农业还没有被真正作为经济转型的工具。非洲自身拥有能力、人民、资源和机会去领导可持续发展。推动农业成为真正的经济转型动力，有几个政策驱动前提。

本文始终强调农业是经济可持续增长的主要引擎，它的成功转型对于包容性的、农业可持续发展的、全面的经济转型至关重要。正如提姆所言：

> 没有农业生产率提高，国家就不可能实现快速脱贫……这个进程与经济结构的成功转型互相交织：其中，农业通过更高的劳动生产率为城市化和工业化提供食物、劳动力甚至资金。②

因此，本文中农业的成功转型是指它与两个发展同步进行：生产率

---

① 非洲农业综合发展计划（The Comprehensive Africa Agriculture Development Programme, CAADP）是2003年在马普托召开的非盟会议上批准的一项新动议，是非洲发展新伙伴计划（New Partnership for Africa's Development, NEPAD）的一部分。详见该计划的网址：http://caadp.net/。

② C. P. Timmer, "Agriculture and Pro-Poor Growth: An Asian Perspective, Center for Global Development", Working Paper, Number 63, 2005, p. 3.

（指单位投入的产出等）持续提高至少二三十年；大多数农民的收入持续增长。① 所以，为了更好地理解当代非洲农业的转型之路，有必要寻找证据观察这两个发展存在与否及其发展规模。②

非洲的表现

1990 年以来，农业生产率、谷物产量、农业人均收入等重点指标显示，非洲农业转型已明显加快。自 2003 年非洲农业综合发展计划公布以来，大多数国家的转型速度已经翻倍。特别是按照每个农业工人的人均农业附加值计算的话，1990~2012 年非洲农业生产率平均提高了约 67%。然而，从生产率水平和进步幅度看，各国间的总体表现差异巨大。就增长幅度而言，有些国家成功地将生产率提高了 326%（如尼日利亚），有些国家却下降了 45%（如布隆迪）。总体上，能找到数据的 48 个非洲国家中，18 个在 1990~2012 年设法将劳动生产率提高了 50% 以上，16 个提高了 1%~49.9%，14 个下降幅度高达 45%。然而，应该提到，相比于 1990~2002 年，非洲国家 2003~2012 年的劳动生产率总体上有大幅度提升，年均增长约 44 美元，而前期仅有 8 美元（见表1）。

表1　1991~2012 年农业生产率（农业工人所获得的农业人均增加值）

	2012 年农业工人所获得的农业人均附加值（美元/工人）	1990~2012 年增长率（%）	1990~2012 年年均变化率（%）	1990~2002 年年均变化（美元）	2003~2012 年年均变化（美元）
非洲	1501.23	66.95	2.91	8.26	44.77
非洲(不含北非)	774.35	52.09	2.26	4.27	20.36
北美	3419.86	64.07	2.79	18.17	75.63
全球	1177.38	31.19	1.36	14.50	7.32

资料来源：作者根据"世界发展指数"（2014 年 9 月）进行的估算。单位以 2005 年不变美元价格计算。

---

① I. Tsakok, *Success in Agricultural Transformation*：*What it Means and What Makes it Happen*，New York：Cambridge University Press，2011.
② 本文甚至进一步倡议，以农商业和农工业为基础的发展才能够真正实现非洲农业和农村革命性发展的转型。

相对于世界其他地区，非洲的表现相当一般。同一时期，东亚和太平洋地区（仅发展中国家）、拉美和加勒比地区（仅发展中国家）、欧洲和中国的劳动生产率都大幅度提高，分别达到115%、72%、130%和133%。非洲的总体进步遮蔽了非洲各地区间的巨大差异。1990~2012年，北非的生产率平均提高了64%，非洲其他地区仅52%。

非洲各国的记录显示的劳动生产率水平差异巨大：2012年布隆迪工人获得的农业人均收入附加值低至129美元，毛里求斯却高达8155美元。[1]

随着农业生产率的提高，1990~2013年的谷物产量[2]从平均每公顷1194公斤提高到1531公斤，年均增长1.17%。总体而言，非洲在2003~2013年增长更快，年均增长13公斤，而1990~2002年只有11公斤。然而，相比其他地区，1990年以来非洲登记的谷物产量28%的增幅实在是表现平淡。

尽管有进步，目前非洲谷物的平均产量仍是全球最低，只有世界平均水平的40%，比1990年的42%还略有下滑。非洲谷物至少还有2~3倍的增长潜力。

如表2所示，1990~2013年非洲国家间谷物的生产水平和提高幅度差异巨大，产量变化幅度大，在负增长70%（圣多美和普林西比）和显著增长175%（科特迪瓦）的区间内。在登记了产量的国家中，1990~2013年有8个增长了101%以上，10个增长了63%~96%。根据生产水平的差异，非洲国家可以分为三类：第一类有22个国家，它们进步很大，生产明显高于非洲平均水平；第二类有12个国家，它们的谷物产量低于非洲平均水平但高于每公顷1000公斤；第三类有16个国家，它们的谷物产量很低，每公顷少于1000公斤。有趣而又可悲的是，这16个国家都名列世界粮食产量最低国家的名单之上（每公顷粮食产量1000公斤及以下）。除了埃及，[3]没有一个非洲国家的粮食产量超过或达到世界平均水平。科特迪瓦的突出成就应被关注：它设法改善了粮食生产，从1990年每公顷1112公

---

[1] 根据2005年美元不变价格计算。
[2] 谷物产量（Cereal yield），是指每公顷土地收获的谷物产量，包括小麦、大米、玉米、大麦、燕麦、黑麦、小米、高粱、荞麦以及其他混合杂粮。
[3] 埃及的产量几乎是世界平均谷物产量的2倍，2013年达到每公顷7200公斤；根据世界银行的统计，中间虽有起伏，2016年再次恢复到7114公斤的高值。——译者注

斤提高到 3054 公斤，增幅达到惊人的 175%，单产仅次于埃及、南非和毛里求斯，高居非洲第四。科特迪瓦的粮食高产部分归功于劳动生产率的巨大提升，估计在 1990~2008 年提高了 47%。科特迪瓦的高生产率有助于提高主要粮食作物的产量。1990~2013 年山药产量增长了 124%，1990~2002 年可可和香蕉产量分别增长了 104% 和 33%，而 1997~2012 年腰果产量增长了 1131%。1990~2013 年，11 个非洲国家粮食产量却持续下滑，这种趋势值得深入探讨。

表2　1990~2013 年非洲的谷物产量

	2013 年谷物产量（公斤/公顷）	1990~2013 年谷物产量增长率（%）	1990~2013 年谷物产量年均变化率（%）	1990~2002 年谷物产量年均变化（公斤）	2003~2013 年谷物产量年均变化（公斤）
非洲	1531.00	28.19	1.17	11.34	13.35
非洲(不含北非)	1426.89	35.49	1.48	6.26	28.65
全球	3850.52	34.28	1.43	15.90	67.11

资料来源：作者根据"世界发展指数"（2015 年 2 月）的数据计算。

　　反思农业转型中收入的持续增长，可以将粮食生产的平均价值视为农村收入的指标。[①] 由此看来，非洲的农村收入总体上稳定增长。进步持续加快，2003 年后年均增长到 1.44 美元，而 1990~2002 年仅 0.17 美元。进步尽管令人鼓舞，但相比其他发展中国家，非洲的粮食产量和收入都还很低。

　　值得一提的是，1990~2002 年马拉维和安哥拉的粮食产量分别提高了 109% 和 162%。另外，同期科特迪瓦的粮食产量增长了 175%，而粮食生产价格仅上涨了 8%，是非洲进步最大的国家。科特迪瓦农业商业的成功显示，在经历了十年的选举和政治危机后，农业的快速成功可能是第二次农工业奇迹和工业起飞，因此小国家农业的成功转型是可能的。尽管入门阶段制造业、农产品加工和农业商业等得分很高，科特迪瓦要想成为新兴经济体，还必须关注非农产业生产力的提高。

---

　　① 粮食生产的平均价值（average value of food production），就是按照联合国粮食及农业组织提供的粮食生产的总价值（the total value of annual food production）除以同样是联合国粮食及农业组织统计数据库（FAOSTAT）的总人口所得出来的单位为国际美元（（International Dollars，I＄）的数值。

表3 1990~2012年非洲粮食的平均价值

	2012年粮食生产的平均价值（美元）	1990~2012年粮食平均价值的年均增幅（%）	1990~2012年粮食平均价值的年均增幅（%）	1990~2002年粮食平均价值的年均增值（美元）	2003~2012年粮食平均价值的年均增值（美元）
非洲	177	12	0.57	0.17	1.44
北非	245	41	1.94	2.50	3.44
非洲(不包括北非)	164	7	0.34	−0.25	1.22
全球	303	26	1.25	2.08	3.78

资料来源：作者根据世界粮食及农业组织发布的"粮食安全指数"数据计算（2014年9月16日首次发布2014年数据）。

使小型农业实现现代化

非洲需要更新观念、发明新产品、创新发展模式和发展平台，以应对各种挑战，力争在包括农业的所有领域中取得进步，通过有效的倒金字塔战略实现笨鸟先飞。在知识经济时代里，非洲靠天吃饭的小农户不能再担当农业生产的主力。决策者虽然进行了政策讨论，但现实和25年前一样，非洲大陆农业的主要模式仍然是小块土地上的自给自足生产，其特点是劳动生产率低、剩余产品少。[1]

非洲农业之所以一直保持自给自足状态的主要原因是：给非洲农业产值贡献了约80%的小农户在发展农产品价值链的过程中一直被忽视、被边缘化。小农户要发展就必须理解他们是如何与国家、地区、非洲大陆和整个国际市场的消费者相关联的。被忽视的环节之一是不理解农产品离开产地后的全球价值链。因此，关键是小农户要以伙伴和贡献者的身份参与价值链的运作。小农户参与其中的好处不仅在于劳动生产率的提高；市场对农产品的需求将使农村需要更多的化肥、改良的种子以及高效实用的农业技术。所以，小农户需要与农资市场联系起来。更重要的是，小农户正是因为农资市场的边缘化和被排斥在价值链之外而受困。使情况变得更糟糕

---

[1] ECA, "Rethinking Agricultural and Rural Transformation in Africa: Challenges, Opportunities and Strategic Policy Options", 2013.

的是，农业本身通常被认为是不盈利、风险高的行业，而农业现代化被认为是大企业的事，因为它们有资本和金融渠道。①

小农户如何才能获得资金？他们生活的大部分农村都没有金融机构网点，即使有也非常有限。甚至在有金融机构的地方，小农户由于信用评级差或有时没有相应的抵押品（比如所有权证），也不能获得资金，从而无法得到金融服务。非洲的商业银行因为前面提到的风险而对农业退避三舍。此外，大多数商业银行一般都设在城市，也不便于服务农民。即便商业银行出现在农村，也是为了吸纳农民的存款。没有金融创新，商业银行对农业也没有一点帮助。

许多非洲国家现在正在成立农业发展银行、制定政策和战略、加强农业金融产品的投入，以扶持小农户，尤其是帮助女性农户获得信贷，推动她们参与到农产品价值链中。这些举措对小农户的金融服务发挥了很强的渗透作用，不仅影响了小农户，而且总体上也影响了整个经济和社会。

非洲的财富创造扎根农业。非洲大多数小农户是妇女，她们经常被排除在普通信贷渠道之外，并且被丢给小微信贷机构或非政府组织，而后者由于资金有限无法推动农业成为增加和创造财富的渠道。获得信贷让小农户能够扩大生产规模，并采用更有效的生产、收割、储存和销售方式，从而扩大生产。小农户获得能够承担的贷款是推动农业发展的关键因素之一，世界其他许多地方也如此。虽然在简化信贷手续方面有了很大进步，但小农户合理取得信贷的渠道仍然有限。强化粮食生产增值链的议程必须得到推动，这是妇女在农业中的作用得到提升的前提。小农户获得信贷的渠道之所以有限，其原因为小型农业在信用评级中属于高风险行业，并且经营规模小、借贷资金回报相对较低。为解决这个问题，很多信贷产品已经被设计并按照顾客要求而量身打造了。就产品类型而言，集体贷款和个人贷款都已经在成功使用了——在非洲许多国家，集体贷款比个人贷款更优惠。为改变有关投资农业的认知，需要首先调查出非洲哪里已经有了成

① ECA, "Rethinking Agricultural and Rural Transformation in Africa: Challenges, Opportunities and Strategic Policy Options", 2013; "Status of Food Security in Africa: A Parliamentary Document", 2013; "Eradication of Food Insecurity in UEMOA: Drivers, Challenges, and the Way Forward", 2013; NEPAD, *African Agriculture, Transformation and Outlook*, South Africa: NEPAD, 2013.

功的小农户金融项目。①

如果不能提高小农户的收入、为农村创造更多非农就业机会，就无法进一步提高农业生产率。② 这就要求将小农户与农资市场和农产品市场联系起来。更重要的是，小农户应该从产品的更大增值中获益，这样他们在创造价值和保有财富时才能摆脱各种限制。③

粮食安全

在非洲，评估显示：1990~2007 年遭受长期饥荒的人口大幅增长，随后的 2008~2009 年经济危机期间问题甚至更严重。④ 政治动荡、战争、恶劣的天气以及缺乏对农业转型的刺激是造成非洲粮食安全问题的主要原因。粮食总产量、农业生产和生产率都没有提高（少数几个国家除外），造成这种局面的其他关键因素有部门之间缺乏联系、主要农作物品种单一。人口的快速增长和气候变化将继续对粮食安全产生负面影响，需要将它们纳入可持续发展战略和政策。北非和西非的社会政治动荡使数千人流离失所，影响了当地经济，也恶化了家庭的粮食安全问题。非洲之角和萨赫勒地区频繁的干旱让数百万人陷入困境。

"全球饥饿指数"（GHI）⑤ 最近对 122 个国家进行的评估报告显示：1990~2012 年，饥饿指数在各地区和国家间变化明显，南亚和撒哈拉以南非洲饥饿指数的分值最高。1990~1996 年，南亚大幅度降低了饥饿指数的分值。虽然撒哈拉以南非洲在 1990 年后的进步比南亚小，但是它已经在世纪之交追赶上来。撒哈拉以南非洲饥饿指数的分值下降了 16%，但比南亚（26%）和中东北非（35%）低了不少。尽管在此期间有 31 个非洲国家的

① AUC and ECA, "Economic Report on Africa: Developing African Agriculture through Regional Value Chains", Addis Ababa: ECA Publications and Conference Management Section, 2009.

② I. Tsakok, *Success in Agricultural Transformation: What it Means and What Makes it Happen*, New York: Cambridge University Press, 2011.

③ AUC and ECA, "Economic Report on Africa: Developing African Agriculture through Regional Value Chains", Addis Ababa: ECA Publications and Conference Management Section, 2009.

④ ECA, "Status of Food Security in Africa: A Parliamentary Document", 2013.

⑤ 全球饥饿指数（GHI）是广泛用来衡量饥饿和粮食不安全程度的指标，包含三个同样加权的指标：a 是营养不良人口的比例，b 是 5 岁以下孩童体重超轻盛行率，c 是 5 岁以下孩童死亡率。

饥饿指数的分值降低了，但只有两个国家：加纳和埃及名列十佳表现者。然而，通过比较 1990 年和 2014 年的饥饿指数，按进步的绝对分值看，全球进步最大的十个国家有 6 个位于撒哈拉以南非洲。可是，根据 2014 年的饥饿指数，世界上被列为"极度危险"和"危险"的 16 个国家中，大部分也位于这一地区。除了伊拉克，1990～2014 年，饥饿状况恶化的国家也都在这一地区。1990 年以来，在那些国家中，部分国家饥荒状况恶化是由长期的冲突和政局不稳所致。①

已有的评估显示，非洲大约 25% 的人口即 2. 45 亿人，没有充足的食物满足他们的基本营养需求，有 30%～40% 五岁以下的儿童长期营养不良。一些非洲国家在反饥饿战斗中确实取得了进步。然而，对大多数非洲国家来说，挑战依旧存在，尤其是东非地区 2006～2008 年闹饥荒的人口估计占了整个非洲人口的 73%。东非地区和萨赫勒地区任何实质性的进步都对非洲大陆遏制饥荒问题有重大影响。

人口的快速增长和难民的大量涌入，是非洲闹饥荒的另一个主要原因。这些问题掩盖了卢旺达、埃塞俄比亚和坦桑尼亚等国在"世界粮食峰会"（WFS）减少饥饿人口的目标方面所取得的进步，那里营养不良人口的数量减少最多、比重减少最大。

为了当代，也为了后代，非洲需要设计一以贯之的战略转型政策，改变世界的认识、确保非洲价值链与世界价值链紧密联系在一起。② 对于农业的认知正在经历重大的变化，因为多数非洲国家政府已不再将农业仅仅理解为农民的谋生手段，而是一种真正有利于国家实现实实在在转型的产业。③

---

① K. von Grebmer, A. Saltzman, E. Birol, et al., 2014 *Global Hunger Index*: *The Challenge of Hidden Hunger*, Bonn, Washington and Dublin: Welthunger-hilfe, International Food Policy Research Institute, and Concern Worldwide, 2014.

② AUC and ECA, "Economic Report on Africa: Developing African Agriculture through Regional Value Chains", Addis Ababa: ECA Publications and Conference Management Section, 2009. AfDB, OECD and UNDP, *African Economic Outlook*: *Global Value Chains and Africa's Industrialization*, Paris: OECD Publishing, 2014.

③ ECA, "Rethinking Agricultural and Rural Transformation in Africa – the Necessary Conditions for Success: The Case of Mauritius", "The Role of Agriculture, Agribusiness and Value Chains in the Transformation", "Strategic Agricultural Commodity Value Chains in Africa for Increased Food: The Regional Approach", FAO, Food and Agriculture Organization of the United Nations Statistics Division, available at http://faostat.fao.org/site/291/default.aspx, accessed 1 August 2014, 2014.

很明显，对于大多数非洲国家而言，如果做好以下各项，农业就可能成为经济转型的催化剂：增加资金投入、加强农业研究和提高农业技术、注重增产活动和技术、提高土地和劳动的生产率以及加强市场准入和基础设施建设。

农业商业的需求

为了实现长期可持续生产、创造财富，非洲的自然资源，包括与农业相关的丰富资源，都应该转化为更高形态的资本，有利于促进贸易发展。[1] 非洲国家在优先发展经济、扩大生产，使产品增值，并对产品进行深加工以满足日益增长的需求。一个深刻的共识是：非洲经济结构调整的关键是生产性部门得以扩展和繁荣，这也是非洲摆脱贫困和饥荒的唯一可持续之路。对自然资源进行加工并使其增值和提升初级产品，可以帮助非洲大陆解决一些问题，如贫困和粮食安全问题。这还能激发出一个更具良性循环的结果：国家通过加强技术创新提高劳动生产率，带来更高的人均收入，使经济更繁荣、更具包容性。

历史上，绝大多数地区和国家的脱贫之路都是对经济结构进行持续调整。这条道路涉及整个经济中劳动生产率的提高：农业和非农产业部门的生产率同时提高，并由此获得产品附加值的大幅度提升。确实，农业生产率提升是整体经济转型的前提，因为经济转型的基础是农业在国民经济中总产值的比重相对下降、农业部门劳动力相对减少，如此才能够惠及其他产业部门，特别是实现工业化。[2] 仔细观察会发现：农业生产率低的国家的工业化

---

[1] AUC and ECA, "Synthesis Paper on the Theme of Agriculture and Food Security: 'Transforming Africa's Agriculture for Shared Prosperity and Improved Livelihoods through Harnessing Opportunities for Inclusive Growth and Sustainable Development' Prepared for Assembly of the Africa Union", 33rd ordinary session, Head of States and Governments Summit, 2014.

[2] I. Tsakok, *Success in Agricultural Transformation: What it Means and What Makes it Happen*, New York: Cambridge University Press, 2011; ECA, "Rethinking Agricultural and Rural Transformation in Africa: Challenges, Opportunities and Strategic Policy Options", "Status of Food Security in Africa: A Parliamentary Document", "Eradication of Food Insecurity in UEMOA: Drivers, Challenges, and the Way Forward", 2013; AUC and ECA, "Synthesis Paper on the Theme of Agriculture and Food Security: 'Transforming Africa's Agriculture for Shared Prosperity and Improved Livelihoods through Harnessing Opportunities for Inclusive Growth and Sustainable Development' Prepared for Assembly of the Africa Union, 33rd ordinary session, Head of States and Governments Summit", 2014.

程度更低，这些国家一般处在发展过程中更初级的阶段。农业是工业化的主要原料（或者剩余产品）来源，是转移到新兴经济活动中的劳动力的来源，也是其他生产性活动的资金来源。此外，农村也是其他产业的主要市场。

虽然农业通过商业化运作能在释放非洲大陆的真正潜力方面发挥作用，但有许多研究和发现已经显示，农业商业化的限制重重，非洲国家必须克服许多瓶颈才能推动农业商业化的发展。[①]

考虑到非洲农业发展环境的多样性，首先有必要讨论一下非洲农业商业经营者面临的最普遍挑战的性质，然后探讨某些特定制约性问题。为此，我们挑选了尼日利亚、肯尼亚、科特迪瓦、加纳、塞内加尔、赞比亚等正在进行快速转型的经济体，探讨它们在提升价值链上遇到的共同挑战。这些经济体的农业商业化经验可以反映其他非洲国家也必须克服的诸多问题。

根据经营者真实经历或认识到的事实，影响价值链上市场投入和产出的问题包括：缺乏创新、政策和法律法规不完善、基础设施和流通渠道问题、融资困难、市场准入和知识信息不足、产品质量和卫生标准限制、生产投入问题、原材料缺乏等。这些众所周知的问题和限制因素长期存在于各个体系和国家中，至今仍未得到妥善解决。

那些问题的负面影响都有研究记录。考虑到各国情况和每一种商品的差异性且问题过多，本文就不过多讨论。尼日利亚的案例可以很好地说明农业商业所面临的大量问题。如调查结果所示（见表4），技术水平低、投资不足、生产成本高、宏观经济问题、基础设施差、政府计划多变、市场渠道少、贷款渠道不足、法律体系不健全、投资回报低等问题被一致认为降低了尼日利亚农业商业公司运营的效率。这些问题导致尼日利亚大量农业经营活动没有效率，还造成了巨大的经济损失，包括粮食收获后的损耗。据《加速农业商业和农业工业化发展倡议》（*African Agribusiness and Agro-industry Development Initiative*）2010年的估计，尼日利亚的谷物损失达30%、根茎类损失达50%、水果蔬菜损失更高达70%。除了宏观经济规模

---

① ECA, "Rethinking Agricultural and Rural Transformation in Africa: Challenges, Opportunities and Strategic Policy Options", "Status of Food Security in Africa: A Parliamentary Document", "Eradication of Food Insecurity in UEMOA: Drivers, Challenges, and the Way Forward", 2013; World Bank, "Growing Africa: Unlocking the Potential of Agribusiness", 2013.

和发展方式这些不应该忽视的问题以外，农业商业的挑战一直令人瞠目，如公司的规模。表 5 的数据来自 2011 年第一季度对"加纳工业协会"管理者们的一次调查，目的是评估管理者的商业敏感性，揭示企业负责人抱怨的挑战和限制因素。表 4 和表 5 清楚地显示，非洲农业和农业商业的真正出路是努力突破小国经济规模和发展方式的限制。

表 4　尼日利亚企业认为阻碍农业商业公司提高效率的限制因素

存在的问题	存在问题的样本公司（%）	因素重要性排名
技术水平低	80	5
投资不足	88.3	4
生产成本高	100	1
宏观经济问题	80	5
政府计划多变	75	7
缺乏安全保障	70	8
市场渠道少	10	11
金融相关问题	100	1
法律体系不健全	30	10
投资回报低	60	9

资料来源：2011 年尼日利亚实地考察。

表 5　不同规模的公司面临的挑战和限制（包括农业商业公司）

企业规模	挑战		
	第一	第二	第三
中小企业	获得信贷	原材料价格高	税率高
大企业	公共设施成本高	原材料价格高	进口商品竞争
非洲超大型企业	公共设施成本高	税率高	当地货币贬值

资料来源：2011 年第一季度对"加纳工业协会"管理者的调查。

实现农业转型的急迫性

2012 年，非洲从其他地区进口了 87% 的粮食，而亚洲发展中国家从其他地区只进口了 34% 的粮食，欧洲从其他地区进口了 63% 的粮食。非洲

87%的高额农产品进口额与它巨大的发展潜力呈现出巨大反差。①

作为经济转型动力的劳动力和城市化

历史上，成功的经济发展都是由不断提高的农村劳动生产率刺激、实现持续发展的。证据显示，农村劳动生产率的提高在更广泛的经济转型过程中发挥了关键作用。在贫穷的农业国，提高农村劳动生产率的绿色革命在更广泛的发展进程中通过发挥多种基础性作用，对经济转型贡献巨大。劳动生产率的提高增加了单位劳动力能获得的食物。首先这意味着减少了用于粮食的开支，其次相对于收入而言也降低了粮食价格，反过来能结余更多的钱，从而增加了农业生产者的实际收入。于是，这又刺激了对粮食之外商品和服务的需求；同时，又将多余的农业劳动力转移到非农产业，从而促进了经济增长和发展。再次，以对非食品类商品和服务的供需增长为基础，工业、服务业和知识革命通过减少劳动力成本和发展规模经济，降低了商品和服务的价格。因此，可以预料农业劳动生产率增长带来的潜在收益将会下降。与之相联系的是，随着商品生产和服务等非农产业劳动力数量的增加和劳动生产率的提高，工业、服务业和知识革命的相对重要性得以提升，这使得消费者开支不断增加，这也是经济转型的最终目标。

关于城市化，1980年约有28%的非洲人生活在城市，相比之下，2010年约有40%的非洲人生活在城市。预计到2030年，非洲将有50%的人生活在城市。虽然从理论上讲，这减少了养活很多农村人口的负担，但也要求农业满足日益增加的粮食消费需求，而且消费方式已经悄然发生巨大变化。另外，城市化有助于增加需求、投资和提高生产率。历史上，工人从生产率低的农业转入被人们广泛认为生产率高的城市产业。很多国家发现，根据农业部门和非农业部门的生产水平，从农村到城市的就业转移使生产率提高了20%～50%。

在城市化进程中，更多的道路、供水和污水处理系统等基础设施建设

---

① AUC and ECA, "Synthesis Paper on the Theme of Agriculture and Food Security: 'Transforming Africa's Agriculture for Shared Prosperity and Improved Livelihoods through Harnessing Opportunities for Inclusive Growth and Sustainable Development' Prepared for Assembly of the Africa Union", 33rd ordinary session, Head of States and Governments Summit, 2014.

可以吸纳非洲额外的 6 亿劳动力，他们预计在 2040 年之前进入劳动力市场。这些劳动力的数量比中国和印度的劳动力数量都多。在非洲，劳动力的增长对 GDP 的影响很大，1990 年以来的 25 年 75% 的 GDP 增长来自劳动力的增长，另外的 25% 来自增长的生产率以及与城市相关的工作。挑战在于，确保非洲城市化不再继续创造贫民窟，而使年轻人具有技能，从而将预期的巨大劳动力转化为发展的主要引擎。

未来之路

过去，非洲的经济增长实际是靠初级产品出口推动的，其直接结果是去工业化。当代历史显示，其他发展中地区特别是亚洲的增长方式是由制造业推动的。依靠初级产品出口的增长方式的负面后果众多："资源诅咒"风险、长期贸易环境恶化、"荷兰病"、国内上下游产业间联系不密切等，从而减少了经济增值潜力。

那些负面后果可以通过农业商业增长战略得以避免，这种战略适合大部分非洲国家的资源禀赋和绝大多数生活在农村地区靠务农维持生计的人口的经济条件。根据创造的工作机会和附加值，农业商业实际上是劳动密集型产业，它加强了产业上下游之间的联系。

需要农业商业而不是农业本身来引领发展的需求是真实的。重要的是从供应推动市场转变为需求推动市场；其中，农业商业价值链将发挥至关重要的覆盖、连接农业、工业和服务业的作用。①

为了推动经济真正转型，本文提出了一个 6 "R" 战略（因英文动词的开头都是 R 而得名——译者注）：

第一，要再次强调农业结构调整的战略和政策。考虑到全面综合的方法涵盖经济、社会和环境等方面，我们需要关注粮食、土地、水、林业安全、生物能源、城乡，以及农业与非洲其他经济部门之间的上下游联系。

第二，要降低高物价和价格大幅波动给无数非洲小农户和消费者带来的风险，提高他们对经济震荡的抵抗力。以减贫替代粮食安全的错误观念必须被抛弃。粮食安全应该通过经济手段而不是作为减贫项目来解决。

第三，认识到非洲的工业化必须以商品为基础的同时，必须再次关注

---

① P. M. Yumkella, et al., *Agribusiness for Africa's Prosperity*, UNIDO, 2011.

全球气候变化。生产加工活动应靠近原料产地，减少原材料的长距离运输，从而大幅度降低碳排放。非洲人必须成为价格的制定者，而不是价格的追随者，特别是当非洲人能够控制生产规模、掌握产品趋势的时候。巧克力巨头美国的嘉吉公司准备收购阿彻丹尼尔斯米德兰公司①的全球巧克力业务，如果交易达成的话，它将控制世界可可交易的60%，但可可的主产区在非洲。

第四，重新制定工业政策，避免国家制定工业蓝图，因为那包含了一套预先设定的政府干预。相反，政策必须立足于私营部门，政策条款和制定流程必须建立在理解和解决日新月异的产业需求之上，学习而不是照搬拉美的进口替代政策和亚洲的出口驱动政策。非洲的工业化应该是由它的资源、商品和不断增长的市场来驱动，同时尽可能扩大与农业部门的联系。

第五，把握非洲绿色增长的机会，它提供了一系列投资机会。非洲必须把自己当作解决气候变化问题的关键参与者，而不是牺牲品。在一个粮食不足的世界里，非洲储备的可耕地最多，因而自然成为领导者。非洲既没有被任何技术限制住，又是全球绿色清洁能源领域发展潜力最大的地区，使它可以实现跨越式发展。

第六，非洲必须坚定地反对不公平的贸易政策和协议。发达国家的农业补贴继续扭曲国际商品市场。发达国家进行倾销，从而压低了农产品价格，使非洲小农户无法盈利。

"农业和粮食安全年"使非洲在国际多边农业谈判中获得领导权，谈判的重点是在国际市场的准入、出口竞争中的补贴、发达国家国内扶持政策和补贴的取消等问题。世界贸易组织促成的《巴厘岛协议》展示了印度的力量，而印度作为一个经济体实力还小于非洲大陆。这里的经验和教训是显而易见的。

---

① 美国阿彻丹尼尔斯米德兰公司（Archer Daniels Midland，ADM）是世界上最大的油籽、玉米和小麦加工企业之一，其大约三分之二的收入来自对大豆、花生及其他油籽的加工。它在大豆、玉米、小麦和可可综合加工工业方面的成就一直名列世界首位。——译者注

农业发展与国际政策：非洲的 21 世纪替代方案

卡罗·B. 汤普森* 著

王筱稚** 译

非洲经常被描绘成一片饱受饥饿的大陆。然而本文将分析非洲成为 21 世纪世界粮食供应者的方法。此外，非洲人正致力于改变当前偏向大规模农业、由少数跨国大企业主导全球食品链的国际农业政策。

关于寻求不同于农业产业化的替代路径的需求，学界已有了相当多的著述，一个简单的概述就足以提醒我们现存农业产业化的通病。产业化农业严重依赖矿物燃料，包括机械运转所需的石油以及化肥、农药中的化学成分。我们在种植的是某种单一农作物的单一品种。全世界的小农户已经培育了超过 5000 种农作物，但是全球产业化农业的食品链只涉及其中 3%的作物。[1] 万亩良田种植同一种农作物通常被描述为呈现了富庶与发达的景象。然而，我们常常忽略这种种植方式背后的基因脆弱性，因为大规模种植的同种农作物会吸引大量的害虫供其大快朵颐。这些农田还面临由每季施撒化肥而带来的土壤退化。产业化农业的发展历史记载了土地所有权的集中，小农户则由于欠债被从自己的土地上驱逐。对农业投入（灌溉、机械种植以及喷洒农药）的规模经济规划证实了土地集中的合理性。在效率与成本节省的名义下，产业化农业"改造"（manufacture）着自然：夷平田地、改变河道、施洒农药和化肥、驾驶昂贵的收割机在农作物茎秆精

---

　* 卡罗·B. 汤普森（Carol B. Thompson），北亚利桑那大学政治学与国际关系学荣休教授。

　** 王筱稚，北京大学 2013 届毕业生，就学期间多次赴非做志愿者、实习生，现在美国创业。

① ETC Group, "Who Will Feed Us? Questions for Food/Climate Negotiators in Rome and Copen-hagen", *Communique*, Issue 102, November 2009, p. 8.

确等高的位置收割并将农作物捆扎成束。大片的产业化农田就像是一座座由程序精确控制的工厂车间。

所谓的全球化农业投入市场与加工食品市场也给农民带来了许多问题。如表 1 所示，市场份额的集中程度在几个粮食相关的企业都非常高。

表 1   全球市场的集中化

单位:%

全球市场	市场份额	跨国公司
种子市场	58	孟山都（美国，Monsanto-USA） 杜邦/先锋（美国，DuPont/Pioneer-USA） 先正达（瑞士，Syngenta-Switzerland） 利马格兰种业集团（法国，GroupeLimagrain-France）
农用化学品市场	57	先正达（瑞士，Syngenta-Switzerland） 拜尔（德国，Bayer-Germany） 巴斯夫（德国，BASF-Germany） 孟山都（美国，Monsanto-USA）
食品加工市场	58	雀巢（瑞士，Nestlé-Switzerland） 百事（美国，Pepsi-USA） 卡夫食品（美国，Kraft-USA） 百威英博（比利时，ABInBev-Belgium）
食品零售市场	56	沃尔玛（美国，Wal-Mart-USA） 家乐福（法国，Carrefour-France） 施瓦兹集团（德国，Schwarz Group-Germany） 特易购集团（英国，Tesco-UK）

资料来源：ETCGroup, *Who will control the Green Economy?* December 2011, pp. 22, 25, 37, 39。

当一个产业如此集中以至于四个卖方可以控制近 60% 的全球销售时，所谓的"市场"就已经不复存在了：这四家企业互相合作决定研究、生产与价格，与供求的互动关系变得十分遥远。四大企业可以为农民制定农业投入的价格，也可以为消费者制定农产品的价格。他们的主要商业目标是为它们生产的农产品创造更多的消费者。因此，此种商业模型的理念将农民作为农业投入品的消费者对待。例如，农民被当作种子的购买者，而非育种者。来自这些公司的种子经过了"优化"（improved），会增加农作物产量。然而，研究已经证明试种是培育新品种的一个非常重要的过程：

试种得到的经验和教训是令人着迷的。我们发现一片农田中基因活动的多变超乎想象，我们先前基于实验室的关于基因工作方式的理解在实际操作田间种群的时候变得非常不足。我们的技术尽管先进，却依旧不足以回答在现实世界中农业生产所遇到的问题。[1]

尽管农民在试种过程中进行了大量的田野实验，从杂交育种到尝试土壤类型与耐水性，他们经历了种子的性能得以最终确定的一切必要过程，但依旧不是被行业认可的育种者。贬低"农民的种子"的最新表现是国际植物新品种保护联盟（International Union for the Protection of New Varieties of Plants，UPOV）通过的种子保护法。种子保护法由商界通过世界知识产权组织（World Intellectual Property Organisation，WIPO）推动执行，它只认可实验室里的育种者，认为他们研制的新品种独特、稳定、统一（Distinct, Uniform, and Stable，DUS），却否认农民通过育种试验栽培新变种的权利。[2]

那些改变、调整并分享种子这种关键生产投入品的农民被商业种子公司看作"糟糕的消费者"。例如，当一个高粱的人工变种作为"改良品种"推入非洲市场时，只有不到 10% 是被购买的。[3] 在南部非洲，大约 80% 的种子是之前储存的或互相分享的种子。跨国企业将这些储存种子的农民看作"未开发的"市场，想象这些农民能够从卡特尔垄断企业（先锋 Pioneer、孟山都 Monsanto、先正达 Syngenta 等）购买商业化的种子，而非共享农民自己培育的种子。跨国种子企业想为广大市场提供同一个品种，而在社区层面育种者则希望在小范围内培育与分享更多的品种。二者之间的目标相去甚远：一方希望为全球大规模的农民提供同一品种，另一方则希望为一小部分本地农民提供不同的品种（为不同生态环境区域提供不同的生态上更加多样的种子）。南部非洲的农民们依旧在培育不同的种子，拒

① Richard Jefferson, "Science as Social Enterprise – the Cambia BiOS Initiative", *Innovations*: *Technology, Governance and Globalization* 1, no. 4 (2007), pp. 17 – 18.

② UPOV (International Union for the Protection of New Varieties of Plants), *International Convention for the Protection of New Varieties of Plants of December* 2, 1961, as revised at Geneva on November 10, 1972, on October 23, 1978, and on March 19, 1991 in Geneva, Switzerland.

③ Alliance for a Green Revolution for Africa (AGRA), *Africa Agriculture Status Report-Focus on Staple Crops*, Nairobi: AGRA, 2013, p. 63.

绝退化成被动的种子消费者，接受由种子企业为他们决定什么是下一个
"符合潮流的"（fashionable）农作物品种。

农业生态学

与之相对的是，21世纪的农业趋势是农业生态学。在此只能简单概括
这个复杂的系统：农业生态学指的是（在种植农作物之前）首先种植可以
给土地补充营养（例如氮）的农作物的种植方式。农民交叉种植各种农作
物以达到最大化灌溉利用率、驱赶害虫、提供需要的荫凉等效果。例如，
将高粱与花生在一公顷土地上交叉种植，它们的产量会多于（即"超产"）
单独种植半公顷高粱与半公顷花生的产量。[1] 农业生态学关注与自然的互
动，将生物多样性视为最重要的生产目标之一。为达到这一目标，农民注
意、尊重并且使用本土关于耕作、授粉、植物互动、种子选择以及水土流
失的知识。

本文着重研究南部非洲的社区育种者把农业生态学作为其农业系统的
组织与活动。我们的分析反映了他们二十年来在选择及培育种子方面的经
验，以及保质保量地供给本地小型种子企业的经历。研究的成果基于社区
育种者在农民中创造与维系合作网络的努力（在津巴布韦已有30余年，
在马拉维、莫桑比克、坦桑尼亚、赞比亚等国也持续了不同时间），[2] 以共
同克服挑战，并寻求发展壮大的机会。这种努力不同于媒体所展示的"非

---

[1] Miguel Altieri, "Agroecology, Small Farms, and Food Sovereignty", *Monthly Review* 61, no.3, 2009, p.5.

[2] 非洲在定期（一年数次）举办工作坊与信息共享会议的小农户宣传组织数量众多，因此
不全部列举。在此列出的几个网络都已经有15年以上与农民社区合作的经验。有些是在
特定国家内部的，有些是区域化的，还有一些横跨整个非洲大陆。Participatory Ecological
Land Use Management（PELUM, http：//www.pelumrd.org/index.html，该网络包含230个
成员机构）；Regional Agricultural and Environmental Initiatives Network（RAEIN-Africa,
www.raein-africa.org，该网络的总部位于南非）；Réseau des Organizations Paysanneset de
Producteurs d'Afrique de l'Quest（ROPPA, http：//www.roppa.info/? lang = en）；Eastern
and Southern Africa Farmers' Forum（ESAFF, http：//www.esaff.org，成员分布在12个国
家）；African Biodiversity Network（ABN, http：//www.africanbiodiversity.org/content/home，
该网络包含36个成员机构）；Tanzania Alliance for Biodiversity（TABIO, http：//envaya.
org/tabio，它是一个拥有15个成员机构的全国性网络）。Community Technology Development Trust（CTDT, www.ctdt.co.zw）该网络在南部非洲地区的三个国家都有办公室）。

洲崛起"，即高耸入云却只惠及少数（而且常常是外来者）的摩天大楼的画面，而是一幅"植根土地的非洲人"的画面，农民们植根田野，根据本土知识与积年累月的经验，发展生物多样性，并组织起来保护种子、践行农民的权利。

基于社区的种子生产

基于社区的种子生产开始于鼓励全民参与，通过参与式植物育种（Participatory Plant Breeding，PPB）并采用最佳的理念，让农民选择科学证明的最优种子。长期的讨论促进了更多的田野实验，实验者将种子分配到土壤湿度、营养与光照不同的地点进行实验。组织和参与同最终的种子选择与分配一样重要，因为经过分享的知识会呈指数增长，就像一株植物可以繁殖大量种子一样（例如，一株苋菜可以产出大约 5 万颗种子）。不同的观念既丰富了相关的知识，也促成更多的知识分享。随着参与式植物育种的发展，有时社区会选择两三个育种者专门在田地中较大规模地培育种子，而且往往是在公共土地中。这些选出的育种者是社区中最好的种植者，并为整个社区增加福祉。

基于社区的种子培育的确始于田间，以就地种子贮存为原则，进行本地种植。不同于矿物等其他商品，种子并不会越用越少，反而会越用越多并分享给更多的人。参与式植物育种者也会选择并非原位（即在此田间以外）的种子来贮存，即放置于罐子里储存在温度合适的小屋里，这种小屋就是社区专门指定的种子银行。根据本地知识选择的进行干燥处理过的叶子也与种子存放在一起，起到驱虫的效果。如果一个农民失去了一种农作物，或者想要实验一种新农作物，他可以向种子银行索要种子，唯一的要求就是他需要在收获后用新的种子来替换。这些种子可以自由交换以鼓励知识的分享。那些借过种子的农民可能会培育出新的品种，或者为其找到一个新的落脚点——一个更合适的种植环境。

这些社区拥有能力培育足够数量与质量的种子以卖给小型的种子公司（例如，种业公司 AgriSeeds）。这些种子被标以高质量的标识，并且在本地和区域市场里销售。这些当地的种子销售量很高，因为它们满足了当地农民对种子品种多而数量小的需求。与之形成对比的是上文讨论过的大型跨国种子公司，它们根据规模经济而希望为市场提供品种少而数量多的种子。但在气候变化的大背景下，大型跨国种子公司提供的种子并不能满足农民应对当地微型气候的需要。能够维系未来粮食所需的生物多样性的是农民培育的非正式种子，而且农民的合作网络抵制来自外界对主要生产投入品的控制。跨国公司与它们的同盟（美国农业部、G8 峰会、盖茨基金会、世界经济论坛、世界银行）拒绝了农民们提出的路径，因为它暴露了产业化农业的弱点：推广极少数农作物的少数品种（例如，大豆的一两个品种）使得粮食很难抵御旱涝虫病等自然灾害。农民们的育种社区仍然被国际的"农业合作"与"农业发展"论坛排除在外，但农民们已经在改变关于这些议题的论述，并且还在继续努力改变国际农业政策。

国际农业政策转型一：转变概念

最令人困惑的概念就是被随意使用的"小农户"（smallholder），因为这个概念既可以指拥有 50 ~ 150 公顷的农民，也可以指仅拥有一公顷土地的农民。非洲绿色革命联盟（Alliance for a Green Revolution for Africa, AGRA）与其盟友①用"小农户"指代小型的商业农户，他们拥有足够的土地、工具、水资源还有其他的投入品使其既能够快速购买种子与肥料，也能快速地将其产品销售至全球市场。当然，南部非洲的小型商业农户拥有补贴，特别是交通方面的补贴，但是他们出口的主要是经济作物。大型的产业化农业综合企业对只种植 1 ~ 5 公顷的小农户并不感兴趣，因为这些农户们无法提供规模经济，他们的农作物"太多样"，他们也可能负担不起所需的化肥。这些农户被称为自给（subsistence）农户，尽管他们并非只为自己的家庭提供食物，还为本地的其他人（尽管可能只是一公里以外的人）提供食物。联合国环境署（United Nations Environment Programme,

---

① Rajiv Shah 在成为美国国际开发署（USAID）署长之前曾在盖茨基金会（Gates Foundation）担任多个领导职务，而美国的千年挑战公司（Millennium Challenge Corporation）资助 AGRA 的粮食生产方式。世界银行也共同资助 AGRA 的项目。一个直接对非洲的影响是，新非洲伙伴关系（NEPAD）项目开始实施的非洲农业综合发展计划主要接受盖茨基金会的资助以引导"战略性的农业投资"。

UNEP）强调，小农户（自给农户）正在喂养全球超过 80% 的人口。[1] 南部非洲的种子培育社区的农户是"小农户"，而且他们为"农民"（peasants）这个称呼而感到自豪。这些农民意识到，跨国公司的意图是将他们从土地上驱逐出去，而将土地集中以供给那些在苛刻的合同下购买企业的种子与投入品的小型商业农户们。那些国际农业政策的制定者需要理解这些概念中的混淆之处，根据育种者社区的定义来区分小农户与小型商业农户。

另外，南部非洲的育种者社区正在改变的重要概念是"价值"（value）。他们反对将价值仅看作交换价值，即由那些确定农业投入与产出的跨国公司给予的定义。交换价值通常是指自由市场中的"愿卖愿买"。但是农业投入与农产品的全球市场不同于教科书上的情况。经常的情况是，价格由那些只通过电脑操作就在瞬间完成买进和卖出种子、玉米与棉花的投机商决定。"交换价值"（即价格）反映的是投机贸易而非真实的食品市场的供求情况，当然价格就不是由供求关系所决定的了。

育种者社区所指的价值随着时间以及种子、农作物所在的区域而变化。一个人工基因变种可能被认为是"没有价值的"，如果它不能带来收益或者可能带来损失。但是对于参与式育种者来说，通过知识的交换分享，他们可能会发现这些变种中的重要遗传特性能对抗某种新型害虫，也能在全球气候变化的背景下对降雨的变化性更加耐受。"时间"改变遗传资源的价值；"新发现"也会改变遗传资源的价值。当一种新用途被发现的时候，不管新的变种是进入全球市场还是保留在当地，它的价值都会增加。"地点"也深刻地影响着价值，因为种子是被培育成针对不同环境的。它们并不提供"规模经济"的效益，除非这些种子是针对某种被控制的环境（"改良的种子"），包括特定数量的水源、肥料与农药。若要使种子的表现如广告所说的一样好，这些"改良的种子"必须在特定的时间投以特定数量的农业投入品（肥料与水）。与此相反，针对不同环境的种子则会导致生物多样性，是保障未来粮食安全的关键。当有上百种高粱、小米、水稻与小麦的变种时，粮食产量才能适应全球气候变化的影响。小农户证

---

[1] United Nations Environment Programme （UNEP）, *Towards a Green Economy – Pathways to Sustainable Development and Poverty Eradication*, DTI/1353. GE, 2011.

明"价值"由时间、新发现以及地点所决定而非由伦敦或者纽约的金融师通过敲击电脑键盘来决定。

国际农业政策转型二：转变衡量标准

小农户一直不同意每公顷产量是衡量一种农作物是否"成功"的唯一指标：他们还考量产量的稳定性、农作物的质地、成熟的变化性、抗虫性以及味道和口感。产业化农业制造出的玉米和大豆不需要有任何的口味，实际上，美国大部分玉米品种是完全没有味道的，因为在加工的过程中生产者会把化学添加剂加入玉米粉和即食谷物中（家乐氏的玉米片之所以有玉米味是因为在麦片的加工过程中加入了化学增味剂）。将提高农作物的每公顷产量置于种子的其他特征之上，抹杀了种子的其他特征的重要性。南部非洲的种子培育社区正致力于制定一种新的衡量标准以挑战"每公顷产量"的唯一标准，即推广"每公顷的营养浓度"（nutrition density）。一个农民一季在一公顷土地上种植20～25种不同的农作物，相比于产业化农业的农田只有一种农作物的一个品种，谁才是更"成功"的农作物种植者是显而易见的。每公顷的营养浓度这一指标注重农作物生物多样性的价值，因为不同农作物需要的可利用的水资源使用量、成熟期、防虫、吸引授粉媒的方式都不同，在遭遇突然而至的暴雨等自然灾害而损失了一两种农作物时土地依旧可以产出食物。在一公顷土地上具有生物多样性的生产方式可以减少一切可能的脆弱性：遗传、天气、虫害甚至是当地市场价格。在非洲、南美洲以及亚洲正在进行的一个计划（2014～2016年）是向小农户征集每公顷营养浓度的具体衡量标准。这个具体的标准并非由坐在办公室中的专家和学者决定，而是由那些在田野中的农民来选择每公顷营养浓度这一衡量标准中的具体指标。这一标准的制定来自实践，并且是自下而上的。小农户正在要求那些国际农业政策制定者关注并采用"每公顷营养浓度"作为衡量农业生产成功的标准之一。

这个计划还有一部分会具体衡量小农户自己食用的食物中的营养成分。预期的结果是，他们的饮食会比大多数食用深加工食物与快餐（高糖、高脂、高盐）的城市居民更具有生物多样性。未来的饮食习惯将是生物多样的食品消费，更注重健康，也更注重对自然的合理利用。学会与自然和谐共处，不同地区的不同食品作物将会更好地满足人们的饮食需要。住在沙漠里的人并不需要每日食用热带水果，仙人掌就已经提供了丰富的营养。

拓宽资本的含义而非仅狭隘地把现金流或金融资本作为衡量投资的标准，这会改变国际农业政策。小农户总是因为"缺乏现金"而被认为"贫穷"并因此受到贬低。然而，现金是对投资最狭隘的衡量，小农户聪明地采用其他资本形式来改善生产方式与提高农作物产出。自然资本对于粮食生产比现金要更加珍贵，而小农户如前文所述，擅长调动从吸引授粉媒、减缓水流失到增加土壤有机肥力的各种自然资本。他们增加自然资本投资的方式不只交叉种植，还有将种植与动物饲养、养蜂以及养鱼结合起来。不同于产业化农业试图指挥和控制自然、将自然看作有害的做法，小农户计划并利用与自然的互动以改善农业生产。作为现金资本和自然资本的补充，第三种投资的衡量标准是社会资本，指的是例如参与式植物育种这类的活动——可最佳调动可用资源的创新与组织的人类互动。农业是一种可通过参与及分享而改善的集体活动。人力资本作为第四种衡量标准认可人力劳作在农业中的作用，而农业生态学比产业化农业更倾向于人力密集。通常劳动力——不管是家庭单位还是集体模式——是对现金的有效替代，因为田野中的人最清楚他们的工作并可以互相学习。最后，知识资本是第五种投资的衡量标准，而且社区在种子、农作物、气候模式（经常比官方天气预报更加准确）、防虫等本土知识层面拥有丰富的知识资本。

每一个农民，无论是大规模农户还是小农户，总需要更多的现金，但是将金钱作为唯一的投资衡量标准抹杀了其他的资本形式：自然、社会、人力以及知识。小农户正在改变这些投资衡量标准，或者更加准确地说，根据联合国粮食及农业组织（Food and Agriculture Organisation of the Unitecl Nations，FAO）认可的数据，它们是 85% 世界粮食生产投资的来源。投资引导粮食的未来，因此国际农业政策需要包括全部五种资本的衡量标准（金融、自然、社会、人力与知识），而不是其中一种。如果把五种资本衡量标准列成表格，那么小农户多样化的财富（与安全的不同种类组合相类似）就会变得显而易见。他们只是"现金贫穷"，在其他方面都是富裕的，且非常富裕。

国际农业政策转型三：促进国际条约签订

在基层田间工作的小农户的经验证明，高高在上的国际政策会怎样严重影响他们的工作。不仅在南部非洲，而且在全球范围内，小农户的合作网络对于促进《粮食和农业植物遗传资源国际条约》（*International Treaty for Plant Genetic Resources for Food and Agriculture*，IT PGRFA。以下简称《条约》）与 2014 年 10 月刚刚生效的《名古屋议定书》（*Nagoya Protocol*）都具有关键作用。[①] 这两个协议都详细叙述了资源使用与收益共享（Access and Benefit Sharing，ABS）的原则，该原则促进了遗传资源获得，同时要求认可交叉育种以及利用基因获得的收益以及收益共享。

企业持续获得植物遗传材料的资源，却不将收益与培育出早期人工变种的个人与机构共享。尽管《条约》中有一个约束企业与个人获得遗传材料后必须将所得利益共享的《标准材料转让协议》（*Standard Material Transfer Agreement*，SMTA），但此协议并没有付诸实施。此协议生效 10 年之后仍未被执行的主要原因是缺乏运作基金。各国政府开始拒绝开放本国基因银行供外部获得遗传材料，并非表示那些政府正式从《条约》中退出，而只是不再开放遗传材料而已。要改变协议"开放"（access）的部分直至同样尊重"收益共享"（benefit sharing），需要完善协议使之不只是纸面上的原则，并变为认可和补贴最初培育出遗传母体材料的机构或个人的实践。这些协议认可小农户几个世纪以来为具有生物多样性的粮食的遗传财富做出的贡献，并且农户的合作网络正在要求一种新的"最佳实践"，将收益共享作为资源公开的交换条件，实施收益共享原则在开放资源前签订收益共享合同（Benefit Sharing Contracts，BSA），通过并执行物资转让协议（Material Transfer Agreements，MTAs）。

---

① Food and Agriculture Organization of the United Nations（FAO），*International Treaty on Plant Genetic Resources for Food and Agriculture*，Rome：FAO，2004（http：//www. planttreaty. org/content/texts-treaty-official-versions，accessed 5，August 2014）．"Convention on Biological Diversity"，*Nagoya Protocol on Access to Genetic Resources and the Fair and Equitable Sharing of Benefits Arising from their Utilization to the Convention on Biological Diversity*，Montreal：Secretariat on the Convention of Biological Diversity，2011（http：//www. cbd. int/abs/doc/protocol/nagoya-protocol-en. pdf，accessed 2，February 2015）．

　　虽然《名古屋议定书》主要强调国家间的收益共享，但也同样将"事先知情同意"（Prior Informed Consent，PIC）视为神圣不可侵犯的，即要求在去除某种遗传资源前必须咨询并得到当地社区的同意。该议定书在政府之外确定了社区参与在决定本地知识使用、本地动植物遗传材料等方面的合法性。它为最初培育人工变种的社区提供了保有其生物多样资源的权利的方法。2009 年，津巴布韦政府颁布了《第 61 号法规》，这部非洲大陆的第一步相关法规，既规范了遗传资源的开放，又规定在消除某种遗传资源时必须征得当地社区的同意。因为这部法律，南部非洲在制定《名古屋议定书》的过程中至关重要，并且各种工作坊在继续培训人员，研讨其他的非洲政府如何采用津巴布韦这个法律模型。①

结　论

　　南部非洲的小农户正在努力改变粮食生产的国际政策。由于他们的生产正在为全球提供 80% 的粮食，并且他们根据本地知识培育出的新品种能够更好地应对气候变化，他们有足够的资格全面参与政策转型的讨论。然而，当前制定国际农业政策的过程通常忽略这些南部非洲的农民，并且不经这些育种者的同意而随意取用他们的遗传资源与知识。这种不共享收益的获取方式违背了国际法的规定。

　　小农户已经取得的重大成果强调了将他们带至会议圆桌与工作坊中的急迫性，他们应当全面参与新国际政策的制定。正如本文所讨论的，南部非洲的小农户提出了新的概念与新的衡量标准，这些概念和标准可以被广泛采纳以理解具有生物多样性的粮食生产。农民的合作网络还参与推广两项维系并保护他们的遗传宝库与本土知识的国际条约。对这些条约的全面执行将会认可农民作为创新的育种者，持续将他们的遗传财富通过种子分享出去。因此从很多层面来说，南部非洲的小农户是 21 世纪维系生物多样性粮食生产的真正领导。

---

① Chishakwe，Nyasha and Regis Mafuratidze，*Access to Genetic Resources，and the Sharing of Benefits Arising from their Use*（ABS），*Trainers' Manual*，Harare：Southern Africa Biodiversity Policy Initiative，2010.

非洲的城市农业：错过的发展机会？

戴安娜·李-史密斯[*] 著

杨逸凡[**] 译

政策与现实——城市粮食的维度

大多数国际农业政策分析忽视了城市层面，因此错失了充分阐明相关政策的机会。城市人口对粮食的需求巨大，但为了使农业能有效地解决城市粮食及营养安全问题，还需要考虑城市问题的其他方面。本文系统地阐述了这些内容，并在此过程中揭示了粮食安全委员会对此议题的贡献的重要性，特别是因为粮食安全委员会通过公民社会的全球进程将农民自己的观点纳入其中。

纵观国际农业政策的发展过程，围绕着"城市粮食"（其内涵包括供给、消费乃至生产）一词，相关的概念尚未形成完整的体系。本文旨在填补这一空白，使得政策与现实更好地接轨。现在世界各地的一些公民社会组织已经开始质疑由"粮食安全与营养新联盟"（the New Alliance for Food Security and Nutrition）和"非洲进步小组"（Africa Progress Panel）提出的国际农业政策模式。这些普遍性的质疑是重要的，但同时需要在"城市"话语体系中对他们进行进一步的阐述。

"粮食安全与营养新联盟"于2012年成立，主张通过巨型农业综合企业解决饥饿问题；而以科菲·安南为主席的"非洲进步小组"则提出以解决日益悬殊的贫富差距问题的方式来达到同样的目的。针对二者政策模式

---

* 戴安娜·李-史密斯（Diana lee-Smith），肯尼亚环境研究院高级研究员。

** 杨逸凡，北京大学国际关系学院毕业，现在莱顿大学非洲研究中心攻读硕士学位。

的批评认为，它们的策略和相应的资金投入过于侧重"粮食生产"，却没有给予"营养安全"以足够的关注。一份关于影响营养安全因素的调查引导人们关注小型家庭农场这一主导非洲农业生产的企业，与之相关的建议也被2014年10月的联合国第二次国际营养会议采纳。① 尽管如此，在国际农业政策领域城市的维度仍需更多的关注。

我们接下来讨论非洲的城市农业（Urban Agriculture）这个经常被忽视的对象。数据表明，城市农业为非洲城市居民的营养安全做出贡献，而营养安全对城市中脆弱的低收入人群至关重要。本文关注的一个焦点是位于城市及其周边地带的小型家庭农场企业；而更大的关注范围则是从外围理解非洲的城市居民们如何获取粮食，以及粮食的可获取性和可购买性。

在粮食和营养安全概念中，"可获取性"和"可购买性"已是定义明确的概念。尽管如此，在国际农业政策制定中，它们也并不总是被放入本土语境中。这造成了它们被过度简化甚至被忽视的后果。另外，人们习惯性地把"城市"和"农村"作为两个严格对立的概念进行区分，认为城市的标志是消费者和非农业生产。事实上，从农村到城市周边再到城市，是互相衔接、逐渐过渡的，并且非洲家庭所采取的混合型谋生手段通常也包括粮食生产。

本文描述非洲的城市农业和城市饥饿的现状，可持续发展因其与城市农业的特殊关系也被涵盖其中（尽管这种关系需要在政策和实践中加以解决），同时需要得到充分的概念化。简要来说，城市地区存在着一些可以作为农业资源的多余营养素。本文的结尾会检验非洲的城市粮食政策正在发生的转变，并展示内罗毕这个城市的案例。结论是这些政策转变也会影响非洲整体的国际农业合作。

---

① Food and Agriculture Organization of the United Nations（FAO）and the World Health Organization（WHO），"Conference Outcome Document：Rome Declaration on Nutrition," in FAO and WHO, Second International Conference on Nutrition, Rome, 19 – 21 November 2014. Public Interest Civil Society Organizations, "Public Interest Civil Society Organizations Statement to the ICN 2 Open Ended Working Group", in FAO and WHO, Second Internatioal Conference on Nutrition, Geneva, 22 September 2014. Sandrine Dury and Anne Bichard, "Identifier et limiter les risques des interventions agricoles sur la nutrition", Working Paper CIRAD, UMR MOISA, France, 2014.

非洲城市农业的范围和影响

截至 2020 年，撒哈拉以南非洲将有 40% 的城市家庭、约 2 亿人口部分依赖城市农业。① 尽管相关数据收集还比较支离破碎，给相关解读留下很多困难，但可以确定地说，在南部非洲的 11 个城市，截至 2008 年约 22% 的贫困家庭从事城市农业生产；在西部非洲的 21 个城市，截至 2006 年有 20% ~50% 的家庭从事城市农业生产。② 城市之间存在着的较大数据差异可归结于城市的规模和政策两个因素。以坦桑尼亚为例，2002 年，在两个人口规模为 20 万 ~30 万的城镇，进行农业生产的家庭的比例达 90% 以上。③ 但在首都达累斯萨拉姆，其人口在 1995 年就已经达到 250 万人，同样从事农业生产的家庭只占 36%。④ 坦桑尼亚被认为在两个时间段里均对城市农业采取了较为有利的政策。

乌干达首都坎帕拉是调研过程中唯一对两项数据——从事城市农业生产的家庭和人口总数——保持长时间跟踪和记录的城市。坎帕拉的城市农业保持着增长的趋势，由 1991 年的 30% 增长至 2003 的 49%。⑤ 当然调研

① Denninger Mats, Bertil Egero and Diana Lee-Smith, "Urban Food Production; A Survival Strategy of Urban Households", in Regional Land Management Unit (RELMA) and Mazingira Institute, *Workshop series.* vol. 1, 1998, Nairobi. S. Staal. and D. Lee – Smith, "Livestock and Environment in Peri-urban Ruminant Systems", presented to seminar on Livestock, Environment and Development (LEAD) /International Livestock Research Institute(ILRI), Nairobi, 2002. Food and Agriculture Organization (FAO), "Growing Greener Cities in Africa. First Status Report on Urban and Peri-urban Horticulture in Africa", FAO, Rome, 2012.

② Bruce Frayne, et al., "The state of urban food insecurity in southern Africa", Urban Food Security Series, no. 2, Queen's University and AFSUN, Kingston and Cape Town, 2010.

③ Dick Foeken, Malongo Mlozi and Michael Sofer, "Urban Agriculture in Tanzania: Issues of Sustainability", ASC Research Report, vol. 75/2004, ASC, Leiden, 2004.

④ Ophelia Mascarenhas, "Kigogo and Hananasif in Dar-es-Salaam, Tanzania: Gender Aspects of Urbanization and Natural Resource Management", in D. Lee – Smith. ed, *Women Managing Resources: African Research on Gender, Urbanization and Environment*, Mazingira Institute, Nairobi, pp. 52 – 79.

⑤ D. Lee-Smith, G. Prain and O. Cofie et al. "Urban and Peri-Urban Farming Systems (UP-UFS): Feeding Cities and Enhancing Resilience", in *Farming Systems and Food Security in Sub – Saharan Africa: Priorities for Science and Policy under Global Change*, Eds. John Dixon, Dennis Garrity, Jean-Marc Boffa, Tim Williams and Tilahun Amede, London, Earthscan Series, Routeledge, 2019.

方法也可能会对数据产生影响。2003 年调研的重点是城市周边地区，并将其与城市进行对比；而从城市到城郊地带，从事农业人口的比例和用地规模肯定会增加。[①] 一项关于南部非洲若干城市中饥饿问题的研究表明，超过3/4 的贫困人口遭遇粮食危机，而城市贫民窟的居民属于最营养不良的人群。就业不足导致他们买不起粮食，这是造成这一人群营养不良的重要原因。[②] 有些贫困人口将自给自足的粮食生产作为权宜之策。

人们经常想当然地以为主要是穷人在从事城市农业生产，但若把从业人员划分成不同的收入群体并计算城市农业从业者在其群体中所占的比例，那么就会发现其实中等收入和高收入人群的从业比例反而比低收入群体更高。[③] 各收入群体中的城市农业从业者也有共同点——农业生产首先是为了食物自给，当然也可以用于售卖。目前看来，低收入者的粮食威胁是居住在人口密集的贫民窟中且缺乏粮食生产空间。事实上，应该区分两种不同类型的城市农民——"后院农民"和"空地农民"；前者拥有生产空间和土地所有权，而空地农民则总体上贫穷并缺少这样的安全保障。[④]

相反地，城市农业被证实可以为从业者带来明显的收益。这种收益既体现在财富上，又体现在粮食安全和营养质量的提高上。尽管绝大部分城市农民为了自给自足（而且就连以商业为目的的生产者也会把一部分产品用于家庭消费），城市农业还是可以为家庭带来相当可观的收入。大多数城市农民的收入高于城市平均水平；把废水作为灌溉利用的农民，其收入是官方公布的最低薪资的十倍。[⑤]

---

① Sonii David et al., "Changing Trends in Urban Agriculture in Kampala', in G. Prain, N. K. Karanja and D. Lee-Smith (eds): *African Urban Harvest: Agriculture in the Cities of Cameroon, Kenya and Uganda*, Springer, New York, NY, 2010. pp. 97 – 122.

② African Population and Health Research Center, "Urban Health in Kenya, Key Findings: The 2000 Nairobi Cross – Sectional Slum Survey", *Fact Sheet*, June 2012, Nairobi. Bruce Frayne et al., "The State of Urban Food Insecurity in Southern Africa".

③ Dick Foeken, and Samuel Ouma Owuor, *To Subsidize my Income: Urban Farming in an East African Town*, University of Nairobi, 2006.

④ D. Lee-Smith et al., "Urban and Peri-Urban Farming Systems (UPUFS): Feeding Cities and Enhancing Resilience".

⑤ Van Veenhuizen, René and George Danso, *Profitability and Sustainability of Urban and Periurban Agriculture*, Food & Agriculture Org., vol. 19, 2007.

城市农业与家庭粮食供给安全、营养安全之间存在正相关关系；动物性食品消费量同儿童健康水平和营养水平之间也有正向联系。这表明在城市饲养牲畜可以保证粮食和营养安全，因此它应得到支持和鼓励。[1] 但是城市农业对家庭粮食安全的贡献更主要集中在生鲜食物，而非卡路里上——淀粉类的日常主食的获取渠道是购买由农村生产的谷物或块茎。[2]

鸡、奶牛等牲畜在东非城市家庭中最为常见。坎帕拉和内罗毕的小规模乳业蒸蒸日上，这里的孩子和大人喜欢在吃早餐时在茶中加奶来摄入蛋白质和微量元素。然而，这种习惯在西非并不常见。在喀麦隆首都雅温得，尽管人们也养牲畜，低收入人群获取蛋白质和微量元素（特别是钙）的主要方式却是将花生和绿叶类蔬菜一起食用。低收入家庭食用的27%的传统蔬菜由他们自己种植。一些家庭会通过卖蔬菜增收，但基本所有家庭20%的蔬菜来自亲友间的相互赠予。城市农业高比例地为达累斯萨拉姆市提供保质期短的时鲜，保守估计90%的叶类蔬菜和60%的牛奶都来自城市农业。[3]

1985年，内罗毕20%的人口在城市中种植农作物，其经济价值每年约800万美元；其中30%的人使用以废物为主的有机肥料。[4] 2013年，已经有超过20万户家庭在这个城市中从事农业生产，牲畜为：55000头牛、35000只绵羊和47000只山羊（2009年的统计数字）。尽管和其他城市一样，内罗毕城市农民生产的首要目的也是供给家庭内部消费，可是相当多的人还是会出售生产剩余，特别是农副产品。在过去十年，内罗毕环境、食品安全、农业和家畜论坛（NEFSALF）一直与政府的服务机构合作，为

① Donald Cole, Diana Lee-Smith and George Nasinyama (eds.), *Healthy City Harvests: Generating Evidence to Guide Policy on Urban Agriculture*, CIP/Urban Harvestand Makerere University Press, Kampala, Uganda and Lima, Peru, 2008.

② Pay Drechsel, Sophie Graefe and Michael Fink, "Rural – Urban Food, Uutrient and Virtual Water Flows in Selected West African Cities", *International Water Management Institute (IWMI) Research Report*, no. 115, Colombo, Sri Lanka, 2007.

③ Gordon Prain and Diana Lee-Smith, eds., *African Urban Harvest: Agriculture in the Cities of Cameroon, Kenya and Uganda*, Springer, New York and International Development Research Center (IDRC), Ottawa, 2010.

④ Diana Lee-Smith and Pyar Ali Memon, "Urban Agriculture in Kenya", in A. G. Egziabher et al., *Cities Feeding People: An Examination of Urban Agriculture in East Africa*, International Development Research Center (IDRC), Ottawa, 1994.

城市农民提供相关的培训，帮助他们提高产品附加值。[1]

可持续性：废物作为营养素

虽然土壤肥力是非洲农业生产的主要限制因素，但城市的固态、液态废物可以产生大量富余的营养素（氮、磷、钾等）。[2] 因此在农业生产力方面城市反而具有相对优越的区位条件，并在保证操作安全合理的前提下，可以通过土壤改良实现营养素循环，并促进可持续生产。

废水灌溉在非洲城市开阔的空地上得到了大面积的应用，灌溉区一年可以产出三茬至十茬农作物。相反固体废物的利用程度却比较低——其年产出尽管在百万吨的水平，营养素循环的潜力巨大，但目前还没太被利用。以内罗毕为例，固体废物每年可以产生2233吨氮元素、2223吨磷元素和3700吨钾元素，其经济价值达两百万美元，但利用不佳。[3] 将城市的过剩营养素转移到农村起码现在并不现实，这需要完善的市场和附加值，可能也需要政策补贴，以便使废物运输业具备像食品运输业一样的经济可行性。[4]

更何况城市农民（尤其是后院农户）倾向于小规模利用营养素。"种植—畜牧"混合农业的农户后院，其实就是一个理想的生态循环单元。对东部和中部非洲的研究表明，在上述模式中，90%粮食废物可以通过牲畜喂养而被循环利用，另外10%用作有机肥。[5]

对于过剩的城市营养素的使用，可以通过城市、社区和家庭这三个层次完成，每一个层次都可以对农业政策产生影响。现阶段，尽管小规模后

① Mazingira Institute, *Nairobi and Environs Food Security*, *Agriculture and Livestock Forum*, NEF-SALF Bulletin, Nairobi, Issue no. 2 March 2005.
② Diana Lee-Smith et al., "Urban and Peri-Urban Farming Systems (UPUFS): Feeding Cities and Enhancing Resilience".
③ Mary Njenga et al., "Recycling Nutrients from Organic Wastes in Kenya's Capital City", in G. Prain, N. K. Karanja and D. Lee-Smith eds., *African Urban Harvest: Agriculture in the Cities of Cameroon, Kenya and Uganda*, Springer, New York and International Development Research Center (IDRC), Ottawa, 2010.
④ Pay Drechsel, Olufunke Cofie and George Danso, "Closing the Rural-Urban Food and Nutrient Loops in West Africa: A Reality Check", *Urban Agriculture Magazine*, vol. 23, 2010, pp. 8 – 10.
⑤ Gordon Prain and Diana Lee – Smith, "African Urban Harvest: Agriculture in the Cities of Cameroon, Kenya and Uganda".

院农民们在"种植—畜牧"混合农业中已经开始利用城市垃圾，但在相对宏观的层面上，剩余城市营养素尚未被列入城市管理或农业部门政策规划的框架内。①

人类文明之初，城市与农业关联，在施肥过程中使用营养沉积物是人类与生俱来的。② 墨西哥、加尔各答和中国的许多城市很早就开始在生产方式中合并使用自然资源的环流（包括废水农业）。相反，西方城市在工业革命时期（1850～1950 年）后的一百年里产生、壮大，甚至呈现爆发式增长趋势，可是在这些城市进行基础设施建设时，却没有考虑如何回应自然物质的循环过程。欧洲城市将公共卫生政策作为优先目标，要消除微生物携带的病菌。非洲城市建设倾向于模仿欧洲模式。直到 20 世纪中期，在环境保护运动的引导下，人们才逐渐重视生态系统在城市废物管理系统中的作用和机制。③

21 世纪将废物中可利用的营养素应用于农业的生产方法再次流行起来。早些时候，直到其他来源的肥料更加经济实惠以前，④ 欧洲粮食生产曾大规模运用废水作为灌溉系统，如今这种方法重回生产领域。非洲尼罗河流域国家是最典型的案例，这些国家将营养素作为自然馈赠的"礼物"并利用它们发展城市和文明，可如今这一带城市对营养素的利用还不够充分。然而，研究仍在推进，另外一些城市（如科托努等）通过城市园艺大量循环生活垃圾和动物排泄物。2006 年，世界卫生组织与联合国粮食及农业组织、联合国开发计划署合作共同发布了农业中安全利用废物（包括人

① Nancy Karanja et al. , "Crop-Livestock-Waste Interactions in Nakuru's Urban Agriculture", in G. Prain, N. K. Karanja and D. Lee – Smith eds. , *African Urban Harvest*: *Agriculture in the Cities of Cameroon*, *Kenya and Uganda*, Springer, New York and International Development Research Center (IDRC), Ottawa, 2010.
② Jac Smit and Joe Nasr, "Urban Agriculture for Sustainable Cities: Using Wastes and Idle Land and Water Bodies as Resources", *Environment and Urbanization*, vol. 4 no. 2, October, 1992, pp. 141 –152.
③ Donald Cole, Diana Lee-Smith and George Nasinyama eds. , "Healthy City Harvests: Generating Evidence to Guide Policy on Urban Agriculture". Carolyn Steel, *Hungry City*: *How Food Shapes our Lives*, Random House, 2013.
④ Donald Cole, Diana Lee-Smith and George Nasinyama eds. , "Healthy City Harvests: Generating Evidence to Guide Policy on Urban Agriculture". Carolyn Steel, *Hungry City*: *How Food Shapes our Lives*, Random House, 2013.

类排泄物）的相关指南。①

在邻里社区层次，有机垃圾可收集起来与粪便混合，共同进行堆肥。这样既保证居住环境整洁，又通过社区动员和鼓励粮食生产。现在内罗毕的部分贫民窟已采用这种做法。规划者可以为城市农民修建一些仓库，用于粪便的收集，而社区的清扫活动则能为堆肥提供原料。

在个体家庭层次，基于肯尼亚纳库鲁地区的研究发现，绝大多数家庭将全部的生活有机生活垃圾用于牲畜喂养，而且接近一半的牲口粪便又循环使用，投入生产。其中，中等收入者的城市后院农业中，废物再利用比例高达88%；但在人口密集的城市空地农业区，仅实现了17%的废物再利用。

上述例子清楚地显示，本地农业政策只需要将粪便从牲畜棚移到农户处这样简单的措施，就可以发挥干预和管理营养素流动的作用。② 其实很多城市（包括开普敦和纳库鲁）的地方政府已经实施了类似政策。更早些时候也有类似的政策干预，如二战时期英国家庭须对所有食品垃圾进行分类，之后放到街角的"猪桶"处，然后由当地农户收集。

非洲城市粮食政策的转变

正如城市的维度没有被纳入农业政策的考量，在20世纪，城市农业也不在城市政策、机制的框架内，尽管"花园城市"的概念已经是现代城市规划的根基。③ 20世纪90年代非洲就业结构的调整却使城市农业备受重视，并且由国际发展研究中心（International Development Research Centre，IDRC）支持的相关研究表明，城市农业成为非洲显著的区域特征。④

极少数国家支持城市园艺。比如坦桑尼亚，从20世纪60年代就开始了自给自足运动。这场运动并不代表完全意义上的官方政策，相反，它更

---

① World Health Organization（WHO）and United Nations Environemnt Programme（UNEP），"Wastewater Use in Agriculture"，*WHO Guidelines for the Safe Use of Wastewater，Excreta and Grey Water*，vol. 2，Geneva. 2006.

② Nancy Karanja et al.，"Crop-Livestock-Waste Interactions in Nakuru's Urban Agriculture".

③ Jac Smit，Joe Nasr and AnnuRatta，*Urban Agriculture：Food，Jobs and Sustainable Cities*，New York，The Urban Agriculture Network，Inc.，1996.

④ AG. Egziabher，*Cities Feeding People：An Examination of Urban Agriculture in East Africa*，International Development Research Center（IDRC），Ottawa，2014.

像是政府对在城市进行农业活动采取的宽容姿态。内战通常有助于促进这类非正式的城市农业政策的产生，比如，世纪拐点的塞拉利昂和利比里亚，以及更早些时候的乌干达和莫桑比克。莫桑比克当时建造了环首都马普托的绿带区。

直到 21 世纪，正式的政策、机构才开始有真正的作为。在城市农业这一新领域，2002 年非洲之角发布的《关于解决城市温饱问题的声明》、2003 年关于城市和城郊农业政策的《哈拉雷声明》都为非洲政府提供了政策指南。乌干达的坎帕拉等地更有能力将"城市农业"的理念落地，因为20 世纪 90 年代后，其行政结构开始开展"从中央向地方让渡权力"运动，这意味着地方政府接管了原中央政府的权力，所以坎帕拉市政府才能够设立本市的农业部门。[①]

这些举措为坎帕拉带来一系列引人注目的成就，包括对城市及周边地区进行系统的农业区域划分，与各社会组织合作进行农业推广服务网络的部署和相关文件的出台，如 2006 年关于城市农业、家畜的新法案等。[②] 可惜好景不长，来自首都的政治变动影响了坎帕拉市政府的创新举措。此外，城市中的农业从业者缺乏自己的组织，因此无力自下而上向政府施压。与城市农业相关的、有效的法律法规和机制的研究发现，如阿克拉（加纳首都）和弗里敦（塞拉利昂首都）一般，将城市农业从业者及其协会整合入与当地政府谈判的机制能够对机制建设产生更明显的影响。[③]

"从中央向地方让渡权力"也为另一个首都城市内罗毕的城市农业带来政策和管理上的变化。2013 年以前，内罗毕市政府反对城市农业，新宪法颁布后却把它列入了发展计划。内罗毕市之所以能支持城市农业的发

① Prain, Gordon, and Diana Lee-Smith, "Urban agriculture in Africa: What has been learnt?" in G. Prain, N. K. Karanja and D. Lee-Smith eds., *African Urban Harvest: Agriculture in the Cities of Cameroon, Kenya and Uganda*, Springer, New York and International Development Research Center (IDRC), Ottawa, 2010.

② Prain, Gordon, and Diana Lee-Smith, "Urban agriculture in Africa: What has been learnt?" in G. Prain, N. K. Karanja and D. Lee-Smith eds., *African Urban Harvest: Agriculture in the Cities of Cameroon, Kenya and Uganda*, Springer, New York and International Development Research Center (IDRC), Ottawa, 2010.

③ Yves Cabannes, *Pro-poor Legal and Institutional Frameworks for Urban and Peri-urban Agriculture*, Rome, Food and Agriculture Organization of the United Nations, 2012. Prain et al., *African Urban Harvest: Agriculture in the Cities of Cameroon, Kenya and Uganda*.

展，一方面归功于市区政府收回了行政自主权，另一方面也离不开市民（包括城市农民自己）对政府施加的压力。这些压力不仅包括来自内罗毕环境、食品安全、农业和家畜论坛这一城市农民的活动联络平台，在内罗毕市政府政策调整前的整整十年间，它就已经和中央政府相关农业部门合作，进行农业推广活动。①

市民的施压也推动了 2010 年的肯尼亚新宪法出台，其中包含了提升立法的公众参与度的要求条款。作为宏观的改革成果，"城市农业"开始出现在一系列政策文件和立法中，包括 2009 年的《土地政策》和 2011 年的《城区和城市法案》，后者要求每个城区都出台城市农业的发展方案。

积极的改变仍在继续，内罗毕和肯尼亚其他城市是否可以比坎帕拉更成功地将城市农业涵盖在公共政策和城市规划中还有待观察。从 2013 年开始，内罗毕的市政府不仅接收了原中央政府农业、畜牧部门进行农业推广的人员，还新设立农业、畜牧和渔业部门。另外设立的市协调会召集了相关领域的各利益相关方负责人，包括了内罗毕环境、食品安全、农业和家畜论坛，这样它就可以继续现有的培训项目。内罗毕农业发展的优先项是：机制的优化、能力提升、环境承受力、社会包容性以及价值链升级。

在整个国际农业合作领域，本文所描述的趋势和动力尚未引起足够的重视。"本地环境倡议国际委员会"这一机构一直将城市农业作为关注点，就如何提升城市环境承载力的问题提供政策建议。国内、地区和国际层面还有相当数量的公民社会组织，对城市粮食安全（包括城市农业）进行了积极的研究、宣传和推广教育，其中，有很多涉及城市之间的经验交流。

全球粮食安全委员会（CFS）有一套公民社会机制（http：//www. fao. org/cfs/cfs - home/cfs - about/en/）。在这个联动机制中，世界各地与粮食安全相关的各利益相关方都派代表参与其中。这些参与者身份各异，包括小农户、传统维生渔民以及女性农民等。"城市"的代表也列席在这个机制中，他们通过"国际生境联盟"（Habitat International Coalition）组织发声。该联盟强调粮食安全是住房、安居的重要方面，粮食安全包括了城市粮食生产（城市农业）。正如本文开头提到的，这些是已具备影响全球决策过程（包括国际声明）能力的公民社会组织（http：//www. csm4cfs. org/）。

---

① Mazingira Institute, Nairobi and Environs Food Security, Agriculture and Livestock Forum.

总之，可以得出这样的结论，在国际和本地（城市）两个层面，一个由城市农民推动的自下而上的进程已对城市农业、城市的粮食和营养安全产生了政策性影响；但这些进程和机构仍需影响国际合作中农业政策的主流观点。国际农业合作政策应当支持城市低收入者、照顾他们的营养需求。在国际发展合作议程中，城市农业只在20世纪90年代和21世纪初期得到过国际发展研究中心的研究项目支持，除此以外就一直没有受到国际发展领域的机构的足够关注。几乎所有关于"城市农业""城市粮食安全"的机构、运动都来自基层。与之相似，营养安全也从未成为国际农业合作的目标；与之相反，因为受到商业驱动，食物生产却总处于优先地位。国际农业政策现在是时候应当与联合国粮食安全委员会及其国际粮食、营养安全机制携手同行了。

津巴布韦的土地改革：增产与减贫

珍妮特·曼珍格瓦博士* 著

沈晓雷** 译

引　言

津巴布韦人口刚刚超过1300万人，其中有67%生活在农村地区，那里的贫困水平非常高，超过了70%。[①] 农业主宰了人民的生活，在国民经济中发挥着关键性的作用。如此，土地在津巴布韦成为一个存在很大争议的问题就丝毫不令人奇怪了。土地引起了津巴布韦国内外学者的兴趣。本文以《津巴布韦收回自己的土地》[②] 一书、《谁将"更好地"利用非洲的土地？以津巴布韦为例》[③] 一文以及大量关于津巴布韦土地改革的学术研究为基础，介绍最近一次土地改革——2000年"快车道"土地改革与重新安置计划（Fast Track Land Reform and Resettlement Programme）实施十多年来所发生的事情，并探讨人们是如何利用土地来增加农业产量和降低贫困的。

土地的本土化势在必行，但仅此还不够。土地是一种宝贵的资源和一

---

* 珍妮特·曼珍格瓦博士（Dr. Jeanette Manjengwa），津巴布韦大学环境研究所副所长（jmanjengwa@ies. uz. ac. zw）。

** 沈晓雷，北京大学国际关系学院博士，北京大学非洲研究中心成员，现任中国社会科学院西亚非洲研究所助理研究员。

① *National Census Report*，Harare：ZIMSTAT，2013；*Poverty Analysis Poverty Datum Lines*，Harare：ZIMSTAT，2013.

② Joseph Hanlon, Jeanette Manjengwa and Teresa Smart, *Zimbabwe Takes Back its Land*, Kumarian Press, VA 2013.

③ Jeanette Manjengwa, Joseph Hanlon and Teresa Smart, "Who will make the 'best' use of Africa's land? Lessons from Zimbabwe", *Third World Quarterly*, 35：6, 2014, pp. 980 – 995.

种重要的国家资产，应该得到可持续利用以促进经济增长和实现社会公平。本文首先回顾过去 120 多年来围绕土地所展开的斗争，以求将土地问题置于更广阔的背景之中。接下来，本文将对重新安置农场的所有权、生产和劳动力等方面的实际情况进行考查。最后，本文将在更广阔的津巴布韦和国际背景下考查土地改革问题，并探讨如何才能促进津巴布韦以农业为基础的增长。

土地斗争的历史

19 世纪 90 年代，赛西尔·罗德斯（Cecil Rhodes）占领了现在津巴布韦的大部分地区。他认识到农业所具有的潜力，将大片广阔的土地交给了获胜的欧洲士兵——正是他们赶走了非洲原住民。

1930 年的《土地分配法》明确划定了欧洲人和土著的土地区域，巩固了白人对南罗得西亚（津巴布韦共和国的旧称）的控制。根据这项法规，51% 的土地（最好和农业潜力最大的土地）被交给了 1.1 万名欧洲人，100 万非洲人则只能分配 30% 的干旱与贫瘠的土地。[①]

时任总理戈弗雷·哈金斯（Godfrey Huggins）在 1935 年写道："1930 年《土地分配法》的颁布无疑是南罗得西亚历史上的一个里程碑，它标志着南部非洲第一次尝试在欧洲人和非洲人之间推行种族隔离制度。"[②] 这要比南非引入正式的种族隔离政策早十多年。

在接下来的 20 年里，并没有足够的白人农场主来实际利用这个国家一半的土地，成千上万津巴布韦黑人仍然在他们祖先的土地上耕作与生活。第二次世界大战之后，这些土地被分给了罗得西亚白人老兵，欧洲白人老兵也被鼓励到这里定居并获得了一系列激励政策，其中包括免费接受两年的农业培训。为了给这些新农场主腾出土地，在 1945 ~ 1955 年短短十一年的时间里，超过 10 万名非洲人被赶到了保留地和（或）条件恶劣与遍布采蝇的地区。[③] 他们没能

① Arthur Cyril Jennings, "Land Apportionment in Southern Rhodesia", *African Affairs*, 1935, pp. 308 - 311.

② Arthur Cyril Jennings, "Land Apportionment in Southern Rhodesia", *African Affairs*, 1935, p. 296.

③ Robin Palmer, *Land and Racial Domination in Rhodesia*, University of California Press, 1977.

带走耕牛，他们的房屋被烧毁，并且他们失去了对自己农场的一切投入。

在白人农场主中有位在二战中驾驶喷火式战斗机的老兵，名叫伊恩·史密斯（Ian Smith），他在回忆录中讲述了自己是如何将黑人农场主赶出他的土地的。① 史密斯后来成为罗得西亚的统治者，在 1965 年脱离英国单方面宣布独立，并最终为保住白人在罗得西亚的统治而进行了一场残酷的战争。战争最终失败，因为那些在二战结束后的十年里被白人老兵驱逐的黑人的孩子成了 20 世纪 70 年代独立运动的中坚力量，他们不仅为独立而战，还为土地而战。与邻国莫桑比克和南非的解放运动由城市精英所领导不同，津巴布韦解放运动的领袖重视土地和农业。当那些获胜的解放战士在 1980 年赢得战争和实现独立后，他们渴望得到土地。②

独立之后不久的 20 世纪 80 年代初，津巴布韦进行了初步的土地改革。在独立后的十年间，7.5 万户家庭获得了津巴布韦 11% 的可耕地。但这次土地改革为两方面的因素所阻碍。一方面，《兰开斯特大厦协议》规定，只能在愿买和愿卖的基础上将土地从白人农场主转到黑人农场主的手中。政府以可负担的价格收购的土地，基本都是不太成功的农场主所拥有的更贫瘠的土地。另一方面，津巴布韦处于国际压力之下。20 世纪 80 年代，南非种族隔离政权的蓄意破坏和公开的军事攻击使津巴布韦的交通运输和经济陷于瘫痪；③津巴布韦欠下了国际债务，从而导致世界银行强迫其进行经济结构调整，并最终给其经济带来了严重损害。津巴布韦的贫困率从 1990 年的 26% 上升到 1995 年的 55%。老兵变得越来越不安分并开始采取行动；2000 年 3 月和 4 月，共强行占领了 1000 多个农场。④ 占地运动被称

---

① Ian Douglas Smith, *The Great Betrayal：The Memoirs of Ian Douglas Smith*, London, UK：Blake, 1997. Joseph Hanlon, Jeanette Manjengwa and Teresa Smart, *Zimbabwe Takes Back its Land*, Kumarian Press, VA 2013.

② Zvakanyorwa Wilbert Sadomba, *War Veterans in Zimbabwe's Revolution*, Woodbridge, Suffolk, UK：James Currey, 2011.

③ Collin Stoneman, "Zimbabwe：The Private Sector and South Africa", in Joseph Hanlon, *Beggar Your Neighbours*, James Currey,1986.

④ Government of Zimbabwe, *Zimbabwe* 2003 *Poverty Assessment Study Survey Main Report*, Harare：Ministry of Public Service, Labour and Social Welfare, 2006；Admos Chimhowu, Jeanette Manjengwa and Sara Feresu, *Moving Forward in Zimbabwe：Reducing Poverty and Promoting Growth*, Harare：Brooks World Poverty Institute, the University of Manchester, UK and the Institute of Environmental Studies, University of Zimbabwe, 2012.

为"贾姆班加"（jambanja，绍纳语，意为"暴力"或"愤怒行为"），该词很快便在占地者、媒体和大众中流行开来，学者在研究"快车道"土地改革的时候，也使用了这个词。参与解放斗争的老战士们，利用他们的军事才能，将城市的失业者和人口拥挤的村舍地区的无地者组织起来，然后以井然有序的军事方式组织了占领农场的运动。

罗马天主教主教多纳尔·拉蒙特（Donal Lamont）在白人政权时期曾因在教会医院医治解放斗争的游击队员而被判有罪，他在 1976 年的演讲中警告："如果这个国家出现一个非洲人的政府——这事实上似乎不可避免，而且很快就将出现，到时这些为保护白人特权而制定和实施的现行法律可能会得以保留并被反过来用到欧洲人的身上，你觉得他们能去抗议吗？……成千上万的白人将会被赶出他们的家园和农场，而不会得到任何补偿。"[1] 这确实发生了，而且如主教所预言，抗议又有何用。

这种有组织的占地运动并非仅发生在津巴布韦。无地人民运动（Landless People's Movement）在巴西以相同的方式进行，运动的组织者首先将那些想要农场的人招募和组织起来，然后在约定的日子去强占土地。

津巴布韦仍然有一半的农田在传统的村社地区，有80%的农民在那里从事自给农业生产。现在已有40%的农田被重新安置给了24.4 万个家庭。表1是萨姆·莫约（Sam Moyo）2010 年估计出来的土地分配模式：20 世纪80 年代有7.5 万个家庭获得了土地。[2]新的"快车道"土地改革机制建立了两种模式的农场。第一种是 A1 农场，其中每个前白人农场被分割成40～45 个小农场，每个小农场有 6～10 公顷可耕地。A1 农场总数约为 14.6 万个，大部分被占地者所拥有，许多占地者来自城市或村社地区。另外一种是 A2 农场，其中每个白人农场被分割成 3～5 个农场，A2 农场的总数约为 2.3 万个，需要正式申请才能获得。在申请的时候，申请人需证明自己拥有农业知识和充足的资金来启动农场。这一要求意味着大多数 A2 农场主来自精英阶层，且通常在政府部门任职或在做其他生意。

① Donal Lamont, *Speech from the Dock*, Leigh-on-Sea, Essex, UK: Keven Mayhew, 1997.

② Sam Moyo, "Three Decades of Agrarian Reform in Zimbabwe", *Journal of Peasant Studies*, 38, no. 3, (2011), pp. 207 - 208.

表1 津巴布韦在 2010 年的农田占有状况[①]

	2010 年的农场数量		2010 年的农场面积	
	数量（个）	占农场总量的比例（%）	百万公顷	占农场总面积的比例（%）
小型农场				
村社农场	1100000	81	16.4	50
20 世纪 80 年代重新安置农场	75000	6	3.7	11
A1 农场	145800	11	5.8	18
小　计	1321000	98	25.8	79
中型农场				
非洲人购买的农场	8500	0.6	1.4	4.3
小型 A2 农场	22700	1.7	3	9.1
小　计	31200	2.3	4.4	13
大型农场				
大型 A2 农场	217		0.5	1.6
黑人大型农场	956	0.1	0.5	1.6
白人大型农场	198		0.1	0.4
小　计	1371	0.1	1.2	3.5
农业种植园	296		1.5	4.5
总　计	1354000	100	32.9	100
土地改革总计	243717	18	13	40

注：农场的面积取决于其所处的农业生态区。小型农场的面积最大可达近 50 公顷；中型农场的面积为 50~200 公顷；大型农场的面积为 200 公顷以上。

资料来源：Sam Moyo, "Three Decades of Agrarian Reform in Zimbabwe", *Journal of Peasant Studies*, 38, no. 3, (2011), p. 512。

　　对"快车道"土地改革最主要的批评是大量土地流入了所谓执政党领导人亲信的手中。虽然 A1 农场的分配并不存在政治倾向，但在分配 A2 农场和所有大型农场的时候，政治倾向却很明显。[②] 还有一些人拥有多个农场，或农场的规模远远超过最高限额。据估计，在 2000~2004 年的土地转移中，有 10% 的土地被可称为亲信的人也就是那些被认为与执政党津巴布

---

① 表1 中的数据与实际加和后的数据略有出入，译者查对了本文作者的英文原著，数据如表所示。表中的数据疑为原作者错误计算所致。特此说明。——译者注

② Joseph Hanlon, Jeanette Manjengwa and Teresa Smart, *Zimbabwe Takes Back its Land*, Kumarian Press, VA 2013.

韦非洲民族联盟－爱国阵线关系密切的人以及高级公务员和高层军官所取得。①虽然这一比例并非很高，但也凸显了进行土地审查的重要性。

土地的重要性

土地总量有限且通常供不应求，因此必须建立一种将土地分给一些人而非另外一些人的制度。在许多国家，这一制度是市场价格，而在殖民时期的罗得西亚，则是种族。这种土地转让与剥夺通常使人们将土地视为历史上不公平与压迫的重要象征，尤其是在遍布贫困和不平等的地方更是如此。②

土地拥有不同的价值与意义，虽然人们在传统上将其视为农业生产的资料，但它同时还具有象征性的价值。土地在经济方面的价值，并非仅限于经济赋权与粮食安全，因为它还被视为安全的居所和生计的来源。对于绝大多数农村居民和越来越多从事城市农业生产的城市居民而言，土地首先是一种谋生的资源。

所有土地改革都伴随产量与社会福利之间的紧张关系。应该将土地分配给最贫穷和最需要的人以向他们提供直接的帮助，还是将土地分配给那些能够增加产量和创造就业以及通过乘数效应来促进经济增长的人？毕竟出售新产品的所得可以被用来在当地购买商品，并因此在农场和城市创造就业机会。津巴布韦土地改革的方式拥有两方面的潜力：一是可以提高生产率，二是可以降低贫困。

产量与生产率

农业产量与生产率是衡量土地改革成功与否的一项重要指标。就津巴布韦而言，唯一现实的参照系是被土改后的新农场主所取代的白人农场主。一般而言，新农场主需要一代人的时间来掌控土地和实现最高水平的

---

① Joseph Hanlon, Jeanette Manjengwa and Teresa Smart, *Zimbabwe Takes Back its Land*, Kumarian Press, VA 2013.

② Bridget O'Laughlin, Henry Bernstein, Ben Cousins and Pauline E. Peters, "Introduction: Agrarian Change, Rural Poverty and Land Reform in South Africa since 1994", *Journal of Agrarian Change*, vol. 13 no. 1, January 2013, pp. 1 – 15.

生产率，这既适用于二战后的白人农场主，也适用于 20 世纪 80 年代的土改后的新农场主。"快车道"土改后的新农场主只耕种了 10 ~ 12 年的时间，且与其他津巴布韦人一样，在经济危机期间受到了恶性通货膨胀的沉重打击。[1]因此我们预计"快车道"土改后的新农场主还需要一些时间来实现最高生产率。[2]

支持也是问题。20 世纪 80 年代土地改革和"快车道"土地改革后的新农场主，只从政府那里获得了很少的支持，因此他们是靠自己的努力或所谓底层积累，即将利润进行再投资，或利用其他家庭成员的工资收入来实现增长。[3] 与之相比，新的白人农场主获得了免费培训，而且罗得西亚政府从 1940 年开始投入巨资以提高他们的产量和生产率。大量的研究培育了现代杂交种子，有保证的市场使白人农场主出售相同的农作物，价格要比黑人农场主高很多，此外还有包括补贴和信贷在内的其他一系列支持措施。[4]

比较的第一步是考察土地的使用情况，而我们最好从一段关于马绍纳兰省的引文开始，因为该省拥有津巴布韦 75% 的基本农田。

> 只要登上飞机并飞越马绍纳兰欧洲人的农业区，你就会发现每个农场都有成片的土地被闲置在那里……如此多的土地被闲置，这是国家的耻辱。[5]

这段话所批评的不是土地改革，它是农村土地委员会主席在 1965 年说的。在接下来的 1976 年，罗格·里德尔（Roger Riddell）估算出欧洲人潜在的可耕地只有 15% 得到了耕种[6]（到 1982 年，津巴布韦在制定的《国家

---

① Joseph Hanlon, Jeanette Manjengwa and Teresa Smart, *Zimbabwe Takes Back its Land*, Kumarian Press, VA 2013.

② Joseph Hanlon, Jeanette Manjengwa and Teresa Smart, *Zimbabwe Takes Back its Land*, Kumarian Press, VA 2013.

③ Ian Scoones, Nelson Marongwe, Blasio Mavedzenge, Jacob Mahenehene, Felix Murimbarimba and Chrispen Sukume, *Zimbabwe's Land Reform*, *Myths and Realities*, Woodbridge, Suffolk, UK and Harare: James Currey and Weaver Press, 2010.

④ Joseph Hanlon, Jeanette Manjengwa and Teresa Smart, *Zimbabwe Takes Back its Land*, Kumarian Press, VA 2013.

⑤ Malcolm Rifkind, "The Politics of Land in Rhodesia", *MSc Thesis*, Edinburgh University, 1968.

⑥ Roger Riddell, *The Land Question*, *From Rhodesia to Zimbabwe*, Pamphlet 2, Gwelo: Mambo Press, 1978.

转型发展计划》（*Transitional National Development Plan*）中指出："大型与小型商业农场所利用的潜在可耕地比例分别约为 21% 和 18%。"①）。罗得西亚全国农场主联合会（The Rhodesian National Farmers' Union）在 1977 年发现，有 30% 的白人农场已陷入破产的境地，它们完全依靠贷款、价格支持和补贴来维持运转。在 1975 ~ 1976 年农业季，有 60% 的白人农场主所赚取的利润不足以缴纳所得税，而仅 271 个白人农场主就占据了应纳税收入总额的 52%。②确实有些白人农场主从很小的规模开始，通过几十年的努力和当地政府的大力支持取得了巨大的成功。但这样的人并不多，白人农场主从未成功地占领他们在南罗得西亚的那一半土地。

土地改革后的非洲人农场主也没有利用他们全部的土地，而且主要由于资源的限制，他们也没有进行足够的集约化耕作。但值得注意的是，他们现在所利用的土地要比此前的农场主多很多。

重新安置农场的产量正在持续增长。表 2 列出了 20 世纪 90 年代（即"快车道"土地改革之前的十年）包括大型白人商业农场在内的农业平均产量、小型农场在 2014 年收获时的农业产量。总体而言，津巴布韦正在接近土地改革之前的十年的平均粮食产量，而其 2014 年的谷物产量则超过了预计的需求量（见表 2）。此外，烟草与棉花的出口量马上就要超过土地改革之前。

表 2　津巴布韦农业产量

农作物	农业产量（千吨）		2013 ~ 2014 年农业季的占比（%）	
	20 世纪 90 年代平均值	2013 ~ 2014 年农业季的产量	20 世纪 90 年代平均占比	2013 ~ 2014 年农业季的需求量占比
粮食作物				
玉米	1686	1456	86	118
谷物	165	224	136	
花生	86	135	157	145

---

① Government of Zimbabwe, *Transitional National Development Plan* 1982/83 – 1984/85, vol. 1, Harare：1982, p. 65.

② Roger Riddell, *The Land Question, From Rhodesia to Zimbabwe*. Pamphlet 2, Gwelo：Mambo Press, 1978, pp. 11 – 13.

农作物	农业产量（千吨）		2013～2014 年农业季的占比（%）	
	20 世纪 90 年代平均值	2013～2014 年农业季的产量	20 世纪 90 年代平均占比	2013～2014 年农业季的需求量占比
大豆	93	84	90	
出口作物				
烟草	198	193	97	
棉花	207	200	97	
种植园作物				
甘蔗	439	488	111	
茶叶	11	24	218	

资料来源：20 世纪 90 年代的数据，Sam Moyo, "Three Decades of Agrarian Reform in Zimbabwe", *Journal of Peasant Studies*, 38, no. 3, (2011), p. 519；2013/14 *statistics-Ministry of AgricultureMechanisation and Irrigation Development* (2014)；*except* ＊ = *industry estimates*。

表 3 列出了 2014 年各类农场玉米和烟草产量的比例。我们从中可以看出重新安置农场的农场主生产了一半以上的玉米和 63% 的烟草。

表 3　各类农场玉米和烟草产量的比例

	玉米		烟草
	2014 年产量（千吨）	百分比（%）	2014 年百分比（%）
重新安置农场	739	51	63
其中			
A1 农场	323	22	28
A2 农场	285	20	35
老重新安置农场	131	9	
村社地区的农场	636	44	27
商业农场	47	3	10
城郊农场	19	1	
总　额	1441		

资料来源：*Ministry of Agriculture, Mechanisation and Irrigation Development* (2014)；*Tobacco Industry and Marketing Board* (*TIMB*) (2014)。

土改后新的农场主正在变得越来越有效率，他们生产的农作物的产量也随之不断提高。与此前的白人农场主相比，他们正在耕种更多的土地，但这些土地集约化耕作的程度仍然较低。尤其需要指出的是，他们的灌溉率要低很多。但尽管如此，重新安置农场的农场主正在达到原来白人农场主的生产水平，相信再过十年，尤其是在提升灌溉率和改进机械的情况下，他们将会做得更好。

降低贫困与创造就业

土地改革可以降低贫困和创造就业机会。单就更多的人获得土地并生产更多的粮食而言，土地改革对降低贫困就具有明显和直接的影响。但这些获得土地的人的收入和生活水平还有更大的提升空间。比尔·金赛（Bill Kinsey）用近 30 年的时间跟踪 400 个 20 世纪 80 年代的重新安置家庭，从而获得了独特的视角。他与他的同事在 1997 年总结道，"这些家庭的农产品收入急剧增长"和"这些家庭积累了大量财产"。[1] 伊恩·斯库恩斯（Ian Scoones）及其研究团队也发现，在 2000 个重新安置农场的农场主当中，出现了类似的收入增加和财产积累情况。[2]

同样重要的是就业问题。农业是津巴布韦最大的就业部门，在 1999 年提供 26% 的就业岗位。2011 年，非洲农业研究所（African Institute for Agrarian Studies）的瓦尔特·查姆巴蒂（Walter Chambati）估计，重新安置土地的全职农业工人的数量增加了 5 倍，从 16.7 万人增加到 100 多万人。[3] 这是因为与它们所取代的农场相比，重新安置农场的机械化程度较低，劳动密集程度更高。

2000 年土地改革具有很强的破坏性，成千上万的（农业）工人失去了工作和家园。这与 20 世纪 90 年代经济结构调整所导致的大规模失业相类似。在独立后的前 20 年，全职农场工人稳定地保持在 16.7 万人。虽然我

---

① Bill Kinsey, "Zimbabwe's Land Reform Program: Underinvestment in Post-Conflict Transformation", *World Development*, 32, no. 10 (2004), p. 1682.

② Ian Scoones, Nelson Marongwe, Blasio Mavedzenge, Jacob Mahenehene, Felix Murimbarimba and Chrispen Sukume, *Zimbabwe's Land Reform, Myths and Realities*, Woodbridge, Suffolk, UK and Harare: James Currey and Weaver Press, 2010.

③ Walter Chambati, "Restructuring of Agrarian Labour Relations after Fast Track Land Reform in Zimbabwe", *The Journal of Peasant Studies*, 38, no. 5, 2011, pp. 1047 – 1068.

们很难确定全职工人的具体人数，但有一项研究表明，在 2006 年仍然有 9.8 万人受雇于种植园和剩余的大型农场。如此看来，剩余的种植园、大庄园和大农场保住了大约 7.5 万~10 万全职工人的工作，另有 7.5 万~10 万人失去了全职工作甚至家园。在那些失业者当中，或许有 15% 的人获得了土地，有些人重新回去耕作村社土地，另外一些人则在农场工作或去淘金。[①] 这确实造成了严重且极具破坏性的失业。

然而据查姆巴蒂估计，截至 2011 年，A1 农场有 24 万全职工人，A2 农场有 11.5 万全职工人。[②] 但同样重要的是，A1 农场主家庭中有 51 万人是全职"自我雇佣"，A2 农场的大家庭则有 5.5 万人。这些自我雇佣的农场主不仅是自给自足的生产者，还是小型商业农场主。鉴于还有近 10 万人仍然在（农业）企业和其他大型商业农场工作，这意味着现在有超过 100 万的人在土地上全职劳作，而土地改革之前则仅为 16.7 万人。

2012 年的一项调查出人意料地表明，人们正在迁回农村地区，其原因主要包括两个：一是土地改革，二是因结构调整和恶性通货膨胀而导致城市缺少工作机会。[③]烟草属于劳动密集型农作物，其产量在查姆巴蒂的研究之后快速增长，这表明季节性农业劳工的数量也在不断扩大。

这些数据背后是一些重大的变化。例如，在 2000 年之前，仅 1500 名白人商业农场主就生产了 97% 的烟草，现在则有超过 10.6 万名注册烟草种植者。女性从烟草乃至从整个土地改革中获取了重大收益。据津巴布韦女性烟草农场主联合会（Zimbabwe Association of Women Tobacco Farmers）披露，有三分之一新的烟草种植者为妇女，她们生产了津巴布韦约四分之一的烟草。事实上，在 2000 年土地改革期间，共有 17 万个家庭获得了土

---

① Ian Scoones, Nelson Marongwe, Blasio Mavedzenge, Jacob Mahenehene, Felix Murimbarimba and Chrispen Sukume, *Zimbabwe's Land Reform, Myths and Realities*, Woodbridge, Suffolk, UK and Harare: James Currey and Weaver Press, 2010; Walter Chambati, "Restructuring of Agrarian Labour Relations after Fast Track Land Reform in Zimbabwe", *The Journal of Peasant Studies*, 38, no.5 (2011), pp.1047 – 1068; Sam Moyo, "Three Decades of Agrarian Reform in Zimbabwe", *Journal of Peasant Studies*, 38, no.3, (2011), pp.493 – 531; Joseph Hanlon, Jeanette Manjengwa and Teresa Smart, *Zimbabwe Takes Back its Land*, Kumarian Press, VA 2013.

② Walter Chambati, "Restructuring of Agrarian Labour Relations after Fast Track Land Reform in Zimbabwe", *The Journal of Peasant Studies*, 38, no.5 (2011), pp.1047 – 1068.

③ *National Census Report*, Harare: ZIMSTAT.

地，其中18%的A1农场被分配给了女性户主家庭；与之相比，白人农场只有4%在女性手中，20世纪80年代土地改革也只有5%的农场分给了女性。女性已经逐渐能够继承土地，这是将夫妻双方的名字都写在授予他们农场的分地函上的直接结果。如此一来，土地改革既降低贫困，又创造就业，还提高妇女的地位。

如果这些土地改革农场能够在投入、灌溉、机械和更好的市场方面获得支持的话，它们可能还会具有更高的生产率和创造更多的就业机会。

资本、信贷与促进增长

大部分土改后的新农场主都是商业农场主，在为市场生产农产品。商业玉米产量正在增长，但增长速度没有期待中的那么快，其中一个原因是成千上万的农场主正在种植烟草而非玉米。因此，津巴布韦出口烟草却从国外进口玉米，这是一个重要的教训。

津巴布韦正在利用杂交种子、化肥、杀虫剂、机械耕作和雇佣劳工发展高科技农业。每公顷的最低投入成本为100美元，但要想取得较高的产量，每公顷玉米和烟草的投入则分别要增加到500美元和800美元。玉米产量直接取决于化肥的使用量；少用40美元一袋的化肥就会减少500公斤玉米产量，从而损失200美元的收入。[①]

相较于白人农场主和二战老兵获得的巨额支持，20世纪80年代和2000年重新安置的农场主获得的支持非常少。如上所述，大多数重新安置农场的农场主只能通过利润再投资来进行积累和建设自己的农场。那些最为成功的土改后的新农场主都是在出售农产品之后，马上便购买下一年的农业投入品。他们带回家的，不是成沓的10美元纸币，而是成袋的化肥。他们必须在购买化肥、为孩子买鞋或修葺漏雨的屋顶之间做出艰难的选择。许多农场主在农业季开始的时候，根本就凑不够几千美元。

超过一半的烟草农场主现在靠订单劳作。[②] 烟草公司以信贷的方式为

① Joseph Hanlon, Jeanette Manjengwa and Teresa Smart, *Zimbabwe Takes Back its Land*, Kumarian Press, VA 2013.

② Joseph Hanlon, Jeanette Manjengwa and Teresa Smart, *Zimbabwe Takes Back its Land*, Kumarian Press, VA 2013.

他们提供种子、化肥等投入品和农业支持。农场主必须将烟草卖给订单公司，他们通常都会接受这种安排，因为这相当于保证了他们的市场。世界银行在2012年的一项研究中指出，出口作物的订单种植产量实现了快速增长，当时已有28万多名生产棉花的订单农场主，1.5万名园艺订单农场主，以及少量生产茶叶、咖啡、甘蔗、牛肉和雪豆的订单农场主。[1]

世界银行指出，在那些因订单农业而比较容易获得贷款的地区，出口作物产量的增长最为迅速。与之相比，"玉米及其他农作物的产量仍然远未实现其潜力"。"显而易见，并不是农业技术落后、土地使用权缺乏保障，抑或无法将土地作为抵押品限制了产量的增长。产量较低的真正原因是缺乏资金。"[2]

世界玉米价格较低，当前价格为每吨390美元——与烟草相比，利润似乎要低不少，这是驱使农场主转而种植烟草的另外一个因素。事实上，玉米与烟草的利润相当。如果一个农场主有6公顷土地，他只能全力以赴地种植1公顷烟草；如果种植5公顷玉米，每公顷产量为3吨，他也能获得相同的收入。种植这两种作物都需要农业技术，且投入相当，但烟草种植获得了支持，种玉米则没有得到支持。

土改后的新农场主的能动性也不能被低估。有一个因素使津巴布韦非比寻常：解放战争是为土地而战，津巴布韦人对农业有真实的情感。2000年占地者都是希望务农的人，他们主动占领土地并在土地上种植农作物。这创造了一个全新的农村市场结构，与此前几十年所存在的市场结构完全不同，且在2009年美元化之后出现了爆炸式的发展。该市场结构的最顶层为大型订单企业，而最底层则是成千上万的小商贩和小商人，这些人通常自己就是农场主，他们将牛出租给邻居耕地，或许还会从邻居那里购买农产品。农业商人正在重新安置地区开设商店。前白人农场主已经进入商业领域并成为重要的中间商，他们还在从事屠宰牲畜等加工业务。此外，鸡肉的产量也在上升。

信贷与技术支持尤其重要。信贷可以帮助商人启动小型加工设施，购

---

① Hans Binswanger-Mkhize and Sam Moyo, *Zimbabwe from Economic Rebound to Sustained Growth*: *Note II*: *Recovery and Growth of Zimbabwe Agriculture*, Harare: World Bank, 2012.

② Hans Binswanger-Mkhizeand Sam Moyo, *Zimbabwe from Economic Rebound to Sustained Growth*: *Note II*: *Recovery and Growth of Zimbabwe Agriculture*, Harare: World Bank, 2012.

买卡车和获得流动资本，并且可以帮助农场主购买化肥、小型拖拉机和小型灌溉设施，尤其由于气候变化，降雨变得越来越不稳定，小型灌溉设施可以在干旱的时候提供灌溉用水。而来自农业技术与推广服务中心（Agricultural Technology and Extension Services，AGRI TEX）和企业的技术支持则有助于更好地发挥信贷的作用。

欧洲联盟已经取消了对津巴布韦大多数政治领导人的制裁，但其对17.4万名"快车道"土改后的新农场主的制裁仍然尚未取消，这就意味着他们无法从任何接受欧洲资助的非政府组织那里得到援助。如此一来，土改后的新农场主只能依靠私人资本，如通过出口作物订单种植获取的资金和海外津巴布韦人日益增长的侨汇，抑或津巴布韦政府动用矿业收入来支持他们。

粮食生产更为复杂，且通常还需要补贴。津巴布韦在过去成功地做到了这一点。

• 在独立之后不久的20世纪80年代，政府决定将玉米生产从白人商业农场主转移到村社农场主的手中。政府为此设定了较高的玉米保障收购价格，并让农业技术与推广服务中心提供种子、化肥和技术援助方面的支持。这最终取得了巨大的成功，一些村社农场主变成了真正的小商业农场主。[1]

• 粮食收购管理局（Grain Marketing Board）近年来允许用玉米换购补贴化肥和种子。[2]

• 单就2013～2014年农业季而言，包括A1农场主和村社农场主在内的160万户家庭从政府那里获得了10公斤装的谷物种子和100公斤装的化肥。[3] 这可能解释了为何接下来一年的产量会比较高。

伊恩·史密斯与罗得西亚白人政权在一个方面是正确的——新农场主需要大量补贴，如果没有补贴，就不要指望他们生产多少粮食。据估计在独立之前，白人农场主平均获得的补贴折合成当前的货币相当于每年4万

① Mette Masst, "The Harvest of Independence: Commodity Boom and Socio-economic Differentiation among Peasants in Zimbabwe", *Ph. D. Thesis*, Roskilde University, 1996, available at http://www. open. ac. uk/technology/mozambique, accessed November 1, 2011.

② John Kachembere, "Legal Instrument Stalls Grain Exchange", *Daily News*, 13 December 2013, Harare.

③ Government of Zimbabwe, *National Budget Statement for 2014. Towards an Empowered Society and a Growing Economy*, Harare: Ministry of Finance and Economic Development, 2013.

美元，[①] 这还不包括对市场营销机构和相关研究的支持。美国与欧洲也对农产品生产提供了大量的补贴。第二次世界大战之后，新成立的欧洲共同体实行"共同农业政策"（Common Agricultural Policy），旨在使欧洲实现粮食自给。该政策建立在两个支柱之上——补贴小农和保障市场，它如此成功，以致欧洲成了粮食出口者。欧盟对其农场的补贴一直没有间断，现在每公顷耕地还可获得750美元的补贴。泰国通过对其东北部地区农民进行广泛的支持，成为世界上最大的稻米出口国之一。津巴布韦也可以通过土改后的新农场主养活自己并成为重要的玉米出口国。

有人认为，农业补贴会在津巴布韦导致所谓的依赖综合征（Dependence Syndrome）。但在美国和欧洲，对农场主的补贴已经实行了好几代人的时间。从泰国到罗得西亚白人政府，补贴都是再正常不过的行为。没有人谈论所谓的依赖综合征，因为政策制定者知道，粮食自给依赖于补贴小商业农场主。

因此，土地改革的成功依赖于政治决策。津巴布韦政府需要挪用大笔矿业收入来支持农业。土改后的新农场主需要信贷和补贴，商人和加工业者也需要信贷和技术支持。

津巴布韦土地改革表明了如下事实：与他们所取代的大型农场主相比，拥有耕作热情的小型商业农场主能够生产更多的农作物和创造更多的就业机会。但这需要政府的大量投资。

---

① Joseph Hanlon, Jeanette Manjengwa and Teresa Smart, *Zimbabwe Takes Back its Land*, Kumarian Press, VA 2013.

解析赞比亚农业发展框架及其
对小农户的影响

西蒙·恩戈纳*

李家福** 译

农业是赞比亚农村经济的支柱，所以发展农业是赞比亚减贫的有效途径之一。虽然人们普遍认为农业发展与减贫的关系密不可分，但是在过去的十多年里，农业领域的公共投资一直不足，小农户长期挣扎在贫困之中。赞比亚政策的主要目标是加速农业发展、提高农业竞争力，但除非保证在这一领域有充足的公共资源投入，否则这些目标便不可能实现。公共资源在研发领域、推广服务部门、农村基础设施建设领域、食品安全和质量系统的长期投入成效显著，而且是促进农业发展、提高其竞争力的最重要驱动力之一。大多数情况下，农产品商品化的制约因素对小农户的影响很大。在这种情况下，有必要了解赞比亚农业发展框架在何种程度上帮助小农户改进了生产，并最终改善其生计状况。

农业对赞比亚的国民收入做出了积极贡献，目前约占 GDP 的 21%。尽管如此，有一点仍然让人担忧：虽然近些年赞比亚雨水丰沛，但是农业相较其发展潜力而言表现一般。农业的持续增长可以帮助农民增加收入并改善生活。赞比亚的大部分人从事农业生产，尽管农业为 GDP 做出了积极

---

* 西蒙·恩戈纳（Simon Ng'ona），赞比亚商贸与工业部官员，负责由欧盟赞助的南部非洲发展共同体（SADC）贸易相关项目。此外还担任 CUTS（Consumer Unity & Trust Society，国际非营利性组织）赞比亚卢萨卡分部的中心协调员。本篇文章是乐施会赞比亚分部（OXFAM Zambia）的报告，由 CUTS 承担这项研究，西蒙·恩戈纳为研究报告的撰写人。——译者注

** 李家福，北京大学国际关系学院研究生，非洲研究中心成员。

的贡献，但是赞比亚的贫困率仍然居高不下。联合国开发计划署（The United Nations Development Programme，UNDP）发表的《2011 年赞比亚人类发展报告》证实了这一点。报告涉及如下数据：

- 2006 年，赞比亚 58.3% 的人口生活贫困。2004 年则有 56.3% 的赞比亚人生活贫困；
- 2006 年，穷人平均贫困的指标权重是 44%，2004 年则是 42.8%；
- 2006 年，多维贫困指数（MPI）①（根据被剥夺的强度核算）为 0.257，2004 年则是 0.241。

这一报告说明，赞比亚农业部门表现不佳，未能显著创造就业机会、保证粮食安全，具体表现为赞比亚居高不下的贫困水平，这一点在农村地区尤为突出，因为那里的大多数人以农业为生。由此可见，要想让赞比亚经济实现更公平的增长，还有许多工作要做。

表 1　减贫项目资金分配比例（2006 ~ 2010 年）

单位：十亿瓦查，%

项目	2006 年		2007 年		2008 年		2009 年		2010 年	
单位	赞比亚克瓦查	减贫项目资金分配比例	赞比亚克瓦查	减贫项目资金分配比例	赞比亚克瓦查	减贫项目资金分配比例	赞比亚克瓦查	减贫项目资金分配比例	赞比亚克瓦查	减贫项目资金分配比例
支持灌溉	2.0	0.7	9.2	2.4	5.8	2.0	60.0	1.0	0.45	0.1
农业的商品化	6.0	2.2	10.1	2.6	6.4	2.2	0.0	0.0	0.0	0.0
动物疾病控制	4.0	1.5	6.5	1.6	9.7	3.3	24.0	4.2	13.5	2.5
畜牧业发展	0.0	0.0	3.4	0.9	1.8	0.6	3.2	0.6	2.0	0.4
化肥支持项目	199.0	74.0	150.3	38.2	185.0	62.2	435.0	75.6	430.0	78.0
战略粮食储备	50.0	18.6	205.0	52.1	80.0	26.9	100.0	17.4	100.0	18.1

---

① 多维贫困指数（MPI）是衡量个体在健康、教育和生活水平等方面多重被剥夺状况的指标。——译者注

续表

项目	2006 年		2007 年		2008 年		2009 年		2010 年	
单位	赞比亚克瓦查	减贫项目资金分配比例	赞比亚克瓦查	减贫项目资金分配比例	赞比亚克瓦查	减贫项目资金分配比例	赞比亚克瓦查	减贫项目资金分配比例	赞比亚克瓦查	减贫项目资金分配比例
合作教育及培训	1.0	0.3	2.6	0.7	0.5	0.2	0.1	0.0	0.0	0.0
其他	6.0	2.2	6.2	0.7	7.9	2.7	0.1	0.0	5.1	0.9
总 计①	269.0	100	393.3	100	282.9	100	575.1	100	551.05	100

资料来源：联合国开发计划署《赞比亚人类发展报告（2011）》②

表 1 说明，2006~2010 年，减贫项目在各项目的分配资金（包括支持灌溉、化肥支持项目等上表中提及的项目）都呈持续上升态势。其中，大部分资金流向化肥支持项目和战略粮食储备项目。2010 年，这两项的拨款共占减贫项目资金总额的 96.1%，而其余六项只占 3.9%。虽然赞比亚的玉米产量有所增加，但是伴随而来的可能是不平等的加剧，因为价格政策事实上使收益从玉米消费者向从事规模生产的商业农场主转移。提高产量的关键领域，如农业科学、推广计划、基础设施建设、稳定的政策扶持环境等，都没能得到应有的支持。

如果进一步看农业部门对粮食安全和营养安全的贡献，近年来农作物产量的增加，至少在宏观层面上改善了赞比亚的粮食安全状况。然而在微观层面，粮食安全还取决于其他因素，如从事粮食作物生产和非粮食作物生产农户的比例、出口倾向和家庭层面上权力的性别分配等。这些因素交织在一起，使赞比亚在微观层面的粮食安全问题不容乐观。

---

① 此栏百分比总计均为 100，但是计算表格中各项目所占百分比之和并非 100，这是因为联合国这份报告在计算时四舍五入，只保留了小数点后一位，所以出现误差，可对照表格中的资金分配数额理解。

② 原作者使用的数据来源是联合国开发计划署的《赞比亚人类发展报告（2011）》，但是这些数据和联合国的报告有出入，此处数据替换为联合国的原始数据。具体报告参见：http://hdr.undp.org/sites/default/files/nhdr_zambia_2011_en.pdf。——译者注

小农户的参与和贡献

赞比亚的小农户在种植业和部分经济作物生产领域所占比例较高。根据《2011~2012年度农产品收成预测》，大多数小农户主导了玉米、籽棉、高粱、大米、小米、向日葵、花生、豇豆、甘薯、班巴拉豆、辣椒、混合豆类等作物的生产；而大型农场主主要生产烟草、白马铃薯、小麦和大豆等。这表明，作为整个国家粮食生产的支柱，小农户也拥有一定的机会。

小农户占到农业生产人口的70%。根据《2011~2012年度农产品收成预测》，小农户主导了下列作物的生产：玉米（95%）、小米（99.9%）、高粱（93%）、花生（99.5%）和籽棉（99.4%）。这表明，小农户为整个农业生产做出了巨大贡献。

除此之外，《2011~2012年度农产品收成预测》还表明，小农户生产了100%的大米、98%的向日葵和99%的混合豆类，而大型农场主则在烟草（74%）、小麦（100%）和大豆（93%）的生产中占据着主导地位。虽然农民在扩大生产和增加销售方面存在巨大的潜力，但是整个农业部门仍然处于落后状态。由于促使小农户生产迅速提高的多个要素仍然发展缓慢，因此政府和捐资者资助的各项计划都未能让小农户提高产量和生产效率，小农户无法转变为中型农户。只有当赞比亚政府设法降低小农户在获取资金和信息、农业技术培训和推广，以及粮食收获后的管理和销售等方面的难度时，农业才能实现显著的增长。除此之外，政府还应该提供必要的基础设施（支线道路等），以降低农村社区农业生产的成本。

赞比亚农业发展框架

（一）主要政策

1. 国家农业政策（2004~2015年）

国家农业政策（NAP）的总体目标是支持和促进农业部门实现可持续、有竞争力的发展，以此保障赞比亚的粮食安全。

在投入阶段，其中一项规定旨在防治害虫和农作物及牲畜的疾病。为实现这一目标，政策规定：在优先发展区域，对于会对经济产生重要影响的疾病，要加强对疾病和传疾生物控制项目的监管、规范与促进工作。保证农作物和牲畜免受疾病的影响十分重要，因为这决定着农业活动能在多大限度上转化为生产成果。

推广灌溉也是该政策在投入阶段帮助农业转型的一项关键举措。由于赞比亚时常发生的大旱也是造成农作物产量下降和牲畜损失的原因之一，政府提供的这项政策可以全面而有效地开发全国丰富的地表和地下水资源。推广灌溉能够保证农业生产在全年都可进行。这项政策对小农户有着特殊的意义，他们将成为改善家庭粮食安全和收入状况的优先对象。

2. 灌溉政策（2004 年）

灌溉政策的总体目标是建立一个规范化、营利性的灌溉部门，以吸引私人投资者和赞比亚的发展伙伴。这一目标的最终实现将会面临大量与小农户相关的挑战。例如，该政策表明，赞比亚的法律执行不力，无法公平和经济地管理和分配水资源，因此小农户很难积极地参与其中；如果相关的政策和法律能得到有力执行，小农户就可以参与到灌溉农业中，并且能够从中获益。

为了实现建立规范化、营利性的灌溉部门这一总体目标，灌溉政策也设定了一系列中期目标，其中包括建立诸多需求驱动型服务机构，它们高效清明，富有服务精神，方便满足农户需要。小农户所面临的主要挑战之一是如何与那些愿意回应其需求的机构建立联系。因此，如果能够建立需求驱动型的服务机构，那么小农户作为赞比亚农民的主体，其需求将得到满足。

3. 国家种业政策（1999 年）

种子的有效供应对政策目标的实现和赞比亚的粮食安全至关重要。赞比亚国家种业政策因此而制定，其总体政策目标是保证将各种农作物的优质种子以高效便捷的方式供应给农民，从而增加农作物产量、提高农业生产力。这一目标可以通过其他有利于小农户的中期目标来实现。其中包括保证一个可行、高效、可持续的优质农作物种子生产和供应体系的发展，用以满足全国的种子需求。由于种子短缺会导致种子价格过高，农民主要依靠传统方式获得种子，这对农民而言是很严重的问题，这一政策的实施有助于提高赞比亚农业生产率。

国家种业政策还旨在建立一个包含正式和非正式制度的一体化种业。由于使用往年收获留存的种子或者向其他农户借用种子是农民之间常见的非正式渠道，所以对种业非正式制度的认可是保证种子供应的一则良策。

4. 国家发展合作政策（2011 年）

合作社的成立是一个关键战略，小农户可以通过这一举措实现转型。例如，以下根据这一政策建立的服务型合作社，可能会为整条市场链上的小农户提供有效帮助。

- 市场营销和供应合作社。合作社销售其社员生产的谷物。这一点很重要，因为相比于每个农民单独销售和通过剥削农民的中间商销售，由合作社销售可以增加农民的议价能力。

- 运输合作社。合作社运营交通设施，运输其社员的农产品。由于基础设施网络落后，农民在运输他们的产品时经常面临困境，并且经常被迫支出大量运输费用。因为农民之间相互信任，通过运输合作社运输农产品，可以大幅削减运输费用和经常造成成本陡增的中间商费用。

- 储蓄和信贷合作社。合作社成员相互集资贷款。鉴于农业需要一定程度的投资，所以农民应该获得信贷融资活动的支持。很多农民经常因为无法获得农业投资需要的资金，而无法进行大规模生产。因此，这些合作社会有效帮助农民比较轻松地获得更加优惠的贷款。

制定措施来鼓励合作社成立并规范其运营变得十分重要。因此，农牧业部于 2011 年 11 月制定了国家发展合作政策。这一政策的总体目标是，为建立自主、透明、可行和需求驱动的合作社创造有利的制度和法律环境，从而为社会经济发展和减贫做出贡献。

如果上述政策的配套措施能够顺利实施，那么将非常有助于提高小农户的生活水平。因此，如果这些政策能够得到很好的执行并根据小农户目前的需求进行修正，它们就有很大的空间对小农户和传统农民产生益处。此外，要让这些政策更有效地实现其所承担的目标，还存在一些亟须解决的重大问题。

（二）组织机构

农牧业部（MAL）是上述既定政策的主要执行机构，此外还需要其他机构来辅助政府的工作。其中包括：

种子管理和认证协会（SCCI）。它负责向农民提供优质种子、种子质量管理和贸易监控、部门协调等方面的工作，以弥补农牧业部在这些工作上的不足。

国家植物基因资源中心。它负责基因资源的采集和保存，其他研究机构负责品种的开发和改良。私营种子公司、非政府组织和社区组织也深入参与其中，因为它们负责种子的生产、销售和分配。

农牧业部的土壤和作物研究司。它在农业生态区谷物的比较优势基础上，开展土壤和谷物研究。

私营部门和非政府组织。现有的政策框架为它们的参与提供了空间，例如，提供技术推广以及种子的生产、营销、分配等服务。

其他主要成员是：研究基金、赞比亚大学、科学部，提供技术与职业培训的国家科学与技术委员会（NSTC）、国家科学与工业研究院（NISIR），还包括一些进行农作物研究的种子公司。

总而言之，这些机构在实现各种农业政策所制定的农业发展目标中起到关键作用。它们之间协调合作的能力对促进农业发展十分重要。

政策局限性对小农户的不利影响

赞比亚看上去有很多旨在广泛促进农业发展的宏伟政策。但是，这些政策的内容和措施与它们对农业生产尤其是对小农户的实际影响相去甚远。例如，灌溉是铜带省、奇帕塔省（东部省）和南部省大多数小农户共同面临的巨大挑战之一。对于这些省份的小农户而言，汲取地下水仍然是遥不可及的梦想。那里大部分生产棉花、花生、玉米的小农户仍然将丰收的希望寄托于使用降雨和人工灌溉系统。

这些省份的绝大部分小农户没有任何形式的灌溉设施可以使用。只有南部省的少数小农户在使用脚踏泵灌溉他们的田地。但是，这种灌溉形式只是专门用于他们的园艺作物，所以这些小农户也没有对他们的棉花、花生和玉米采取任何灌溉措施。

十分有趣的是，现有的灌溉政策在承认存在诸多问题的同时，提供了一些补救措施，来努力实现它建立一个规范化、营利性的灌溉部门的总体目标。灌溉政策的实施可以为解决小农户面临的困境提供很大的帮助。但是，让人担心的是：这些政策自 2004 年实施以来，在深入落实政策方面所做的努力十分有限，灌溉面临的挑战依旧明显存在。这可以归因于农牧业部的能力不够或者政府实施这些政策的决心不足。如果能够重新对农牧业部的工作人员进行技能培训，将更多的预算资源分配到农业领域，那么政府就能为解决政策实施困境提供很大的帮助。

另一个限制小农户发展的关键性政策因素是信贷的获取。国家农业政策为小农户获得资金提供帮助，包括通过相应的金融机构和非政府组织为小农户建立基金。此外，这一政策鼓励团体贷款以保证良好的贷款回收率，同时在提供信贷和动员储蓄方面很好地促进了私营部门和公共部门的合作。虽然这些建议与措施同政策挂钩，但是没有真正开始实施，所以信贷的获取仍然是一个问题。虽然小农户中存在一部分团体贷款，但是规模很小而且难以持续。研究显示，所有农民都因为金融机构的担保要求而面临获取信贷的困难。除了金融机构的严格要求以外，赞比亚高额的借贷成本也同样不利于小农户。

另一个值得关注的问题是推广服务和投入的获取。通过推广服务人员向农业人口提供推广服务是政府的职责所在，同时也是国家农业政策的规定。虽然国家农业政策在提供推广服务方面存在局限性，但是它似乎并没有为克服这些局限性做出多少努力。例如，在铜带省、东部省和南部省，1 名推广人员平均要负责 1000 家农户。研究显示，推广人员平均 1 年只能和农民见 3 次面。研究结果还表明，距离对推广服务的交付和获取也有一定影响。地方农业协调员（DACO）表示，他们的人手十分缺乏，在面对农民日益增长的需求时，很难频繁向农民提供农业推广服务。

小农户面临的问题

研究表明小农户面临很多问题。由于饲料成本过高，牛羊养殖户不得不依靠天然草场来饲养他们的牲畜。他们采用不花钱的饲养方式，利用现成的牧场来饲养他们的牲畜，并且没有任何正规的饲养方案。大部分小农户确实具有一些保护牧场的知识，但是研究发现，由于落后的存储技术，他们保存的牧场质量存在严重问题。所以，通过良好的管理来改善牧场质量，是更好地养殖奶牛的基础。因此，对这些小农户进行牧场质量保护知识的培训十分重要。

国家农业政策承认政府在提供农业推广服务上存在很多局限性，所以鼓励私营部门和非政府组织参与提供推广服务的工作，但是并不包括对这些参与者的协调和监管政策。轧棉厂提供信贷支持、推广服务和市场营销服务，这是一个很好的变化，对这些运行良好的措施应该给予一切必要的支持。但是，轧棉厂和小农户之间的关系应该受到严格监管。从不久前小农户和轧棉厂的冲突可以看到，小农户在冲突中往往处于劣势。以下是一个发生在 2012 年的典型例证，当时农民和轧棉厂之间因为棉花价格产生了分歧①。

赞比亚的小农户和代表着主要棉花买家的赞比亚棉花轧棉协会之间（ZCGA）爆发了一次激烈的对峙。小农户要求的价格是 4000 克瓦查，但是轧棉厂只愿意给出一半的价格。面对这一状况，赞比亚棉花轧棉协会坚持认为，由于国际棉花价格大跌，因此它的成员无法提供更高的棉花收购价。

2011 年，利物浦指数的国际棉花价格远远超过 150 镑（120 万克瓦查）每千克，创造了近年来棉花价格的新高，这使小农户相信他们应该得到一个可以反映国际价格水平的棉花收购价。虽然现在的国际棉花价格早已不在这一水平，但是农民们仍然认为，国际棉花交易价格处于一个较高水平，并且应该以较高水平反映在当地价格上。

通过这一例证可以清楚地看到：农产品价格的议定确实缺乏来自农牧业部或其他类似于"竞争和消费者保护委员会"（CCPC）等法定机构的有效监管。从竞争政策的角度考虑，价格的议定应该受到这些机构的严密监控，以免再出现此类情况，从而避免这种勾结行为造成的市场失灵和扭曲。

缺乏理解大量花生品种的知识和能力是小农户面临的重要挑战之一。研究显示，小农户更愿意使用回收的种子，而很不情愿使用新品种和改良品种。对于种植玉米的小农户而言，他们可以从小农户投入

---

① Cotton News："Zambia cotton farmers burn lint as local prices dip by 50%"，http：//cottonmar-ketnews.com/2012/07/03/zambia-cotton-farmers-burn-lint-as-local-prices-dip-by-50/，Last vis-it，03 - 07 - 18.

支持项目（FISP）获得投入。但是，大多数小农户并不能从 FISP 得到充足的支持，所以他们只能从农资经销商处花钱购买化肥和除草剂，以弥补 FISP 投入的不足。

总而言之，赞比亚各种农作物生产力水平的提升空间还很大，有必要进行适当的技术整合以提高农作物产量。至于生产率（产量/公顷），铜带省的表现比东部省和南部省更好，因此有必要对复制铜带省做法的范围进行评估，以提高其他省份的生产率。东部省棉花和花生的产量比铜带省和南部省更高（见表2）。

表2　2011~2012年度农产品收成预测

农产品	省份	种植面积（公顷）	收获面积（公顷）	预期产量（吨）	生产率（吨/公顷）	预期销量（吨）
玉米	铜带省	89501	79329	205542	2.30	122306
	东部省	276288	245319	572760	2.07	214265
	南部省	303429	227076	554275	1.83	257126
花生	铜带省	8709	8447	5399	0.62	2892
	东部省	56903	54793	30895	0.54	10223
	南部省	22874	20420	9514	0.42	2040
棉花	铜带省	605	605	785	1.30	—
	东部省	190607	184472	160956	0.84	—
	南部省	40380	36460	33417	0.83	—

资料来源：《2011~2012年度农产品收成预测》。

根据赞比亚中央统计局的数据，截至2010年，赞比亚全国黄牛的存栏量是3038000头，山羊是758501头。不可否认的是，从多产价值方面考虑，山羊是赞比亚仅次于猪的第二大牲畜。有必要从商业化的角度来审视山羊生产，因为山羊肉是一个可以通过卡松巴莱萨（Kasumbalesa）和纳孔德（Nakonde）的边防哨所，并且具有庞大和专门出口市场的产品。山羊肉等畜牧产品的需求不断增加，能为小农户提供更多的市场参与机会。但是，现有的山羊肉销售市场很大程度上是非正式的，并且缺乏完善的投入和服务支持。

小农户正在使用的存储设施没有得到很好的改进，这导致小农户收获后的损失增加。那些使用传统存储设施的小农户，在病虫害防治、堆垛、记录保存、消防安全等方面都存在严重问题，首先是存储空间不足。

销售问题

玉米市场的最大参与者是通过粮食储备署（FRA）行事的政府。虽然粮食储备署提供了一个现成的市场，但是农民都因其拖延付款而对它的运作感到不满。这制约了小农户有效规划他们下一季的生产。赞比亚政府通过农牧业部制定的最低收购价并不能对部分小农户产生吸引力。然而，来自小农户的强烈意愿表明，政府也应该允许私营部门参与到采购链中来，因为这样可以提供一个替代市场。解除玉米的出口禁令，同样能允许小农户开拓诸如刚果（金）与马拉维这样的区域性市场。

棉花行业很大程度上受到那些向小农户提供承包种植计划的私营部门的控制。轧棉厂通过向小农户提供资金等预订棉花，从而使小农户必须把产品卖给它们。该研究发现，三家轧棉厂（杜纳万特、嘉吉和联盟）保持着这一行业的主导地位。根据订单农业项目，轧棉厂会给予小农户一定的贷款，在对棉花定价时通常也会考虑贷款因素。最大的问题是，小农户被捆绑在一个预先确定的价格上，但是很多小农户最终都会抱怨这一定价。

花生销售渠道并不发达，很大程度上是因为其大部分市场是非正式的。这一领域的问题是，小农户不能根据花生的品种和品质进行分类，如果他们能够分类，就可以最大限度地提高花生种植的回报。小农户对花生收获后的处理也存在问题，这导致了花生中黄曲霉素含量的增加，使其达不到国际标准。

另外，大多数小农户对畜牧业利润丰厚这一特点认识不足。大多数小农户并没有将畜牧业看作一个利润丰厚的产业。国家农业政策承认畜牧业的重要性及其国内外的需求，同时提供政策支持以保证牲畜生产和销售的增加。但是，实地调研清楚地表明，政策意图和现实情况脱节。唯一的希望是，经过重新评估之后，国家农业政策能够为保证政策的实施提供更好的策略。

农业投资法规和举措

从《2012年赞比亚投资者指南》可以看出，赞比亚政府已经出台多项措施鼓励农业领域的投资，具体措施如下：

- 在农业生产经营之前，保证免征 4 年投资税；
- 农产品和农用物资出口零关税；
- 延期征收部分农业设备和农业机械的进口增值税；
- 所得税税率为 10%；
- 为修建栏杆、砖墙或石墙提供 100% 的农场改善补贴，给获得农场的农场工人补贴 1000 万克瓦查；
- 为农场改造提供 100% 的补贴，如清除树桩、防止水土流失、钻孔打井、航空和地球物理调查、水资源保护等工作；
- 分销公司经营农场的前 5 年，对农场收益的红利免税。

从上述针对大规模投资者、尚未完全列举的激励和免税措施可以清楚地看到，这些激励措施给了大规模生产者扩大经济规模的机会。为保证小农户也能从中获益，这些措施中的大部分可以追溯到 1993 年的《投资法案》（1996 年修订），将对小农户的发展产生很大的推动作用。这样的尝试反映在 2012 年的财政预算案中，该预算案指出，在致力于发展外国直接投资刺激计划的同时，赞比亚政府需要对这些政策进行重新评估，以使其更合算，并使它有利于更大范围内的赞比亚人口，这也会对小农户带来益处。

在赞比亚，投资者可以通过多种不同的方式获取土地，这取决于土地是国有土地还是社区公有土地。对于国有土地，他们可以联系赞比亚发展署（ZDA），后者可以引导投资者找到可以用于投资的土地。此外，潜在的投资者也可以联系现有的国有土地持有者，进行商业基础上的土地转让协商。投资者在寻找土地时，也可以通过直接接触村长和酋长获取社区公有土地。但是，社区公有土地在被收购之前必须转化为国有土地。

未来发展的政策建议

1. 灌溉和生产效率

此项研究表明，农业仍有很大的发展空间，特别是应当更多关注小农户。小农户约占农民的 70%，主导了玉米、小米、高粱、花生和棉花的种植。本研究确认了一些迫切需要解决的问题，以保证提高小农户的生产力。例如，灌溉条件差，这可以从小农户使用水桶和水罐进行灌溉得到证明。如果农民使用其他的灌溉措施，如安装水泵、收集存储雨水，便可以提高生产力。

灌溉政策也存在执行不力的问题。虽然政府更新了灌溉工程规划、设计和建设方面的标准和指导原则，以便惠及小农户，但仍未开始大规模地付诸实施。事实上，在铜带省、东部省和南部省，分别约有76%、62%和50%的小农户没有实行任何形式的灌溉，这一现象令人担忧。正如前面提到的，有必要促进灌溉政策的实施，以提高小农户的生产力。

2. 种子的使用

国家农业政策规定，将通过种子实验、种子作物检验、品种登记、品种保护和实行种子质量标准等举措，对种子行业进行规范，以促进种子的贸易、检疫及其他相关事宜。虽然种植棉花的小农户表示他们通过轧棉厂商的订单农业项目得到了优质种子，但在这方面花生行业仍存在问题。种植花生的农民表示他们使用主要是从非正规渠道获得的回收种子，所以政策没有得到有效的落实。虽然国家农业政策通过提供研究的种畜/种子为非正规种子行业的发展创造条件，但调查结果显示，由于技术方面缺乏分拣的能力，农民无法根据花生的品种和档次进行分拣。另外，种植花生的小农户都不愿意采用新改良的品种，这可能是由信息不对称导致的，因而需要对使用提高产量的新改良品种的小农户进行基层培训，并加强技术推广服务。这也需要开设省级"种子银行"。此政策的实施对于上述问题的解决大有帮助。

3. 推广服务

组织农民团体和农民田间学校、使用电子和纸制媒体被国家农业政策视为战略性举措，作为传播工具以支持服务信息的推广，但仍未付诸实施。正如本研究指出的，农民表示推广服务人员在一年内只来访了三次；在铜带省、东部省和南部省，分别只有约71%、78%和84%接受采访的农民表示他们有机会获得推广服务。地方农业协调员证实了这一点，将其归因于人手不足。显而易见，政策的实施需要加强，以使更多的农民获得推广服务。为了提供有效的推广服务，需要配置足够的人员，提高业务效率。为增加推广服务的覆盖面，需要地方农业协调办公室在每方圆10千米的范围内设立一个分支机构。

4. 资金的获取

国家农业政策也尚未解决资金方面的问题，尽管国家农业政策的确提议成立一个基金会，使农民能够通过适宜的金融机构获得资金，并鼓励集体贷款。所有接受采访的农民都表示，他们无缘获得金融机构提供的计划贷款，这是由于在赞比亚借贷成本高。因此，建议政府根据国家农业政策，采取措施，保证小农户更容易获得贷款。政府应通过合作制度和鼓励建立自助团体来促进小额贷款的提供。需要鼓励私营部门投资订单农业，而政府发挥监管作用。

5. 市场支持

虽然国家农业政策承诺采取措施，促进市场信息在各地区利益相关方之间的流动，包括促进如道路、储存设备等农村基础设施建设，发展市场中心等，但小农户仍然面临市场营销方面的问题。花生行业的营销渠道基本上是非正规的。调查结果还显示，三省农民使用的存储设施落后，造成了收获后的损失。在病虫害防治方面，记录保存和消防安全举措也存在问题。在畜牧行业，小农户面临的问题源于他们没有冷藏设施（政府应采取措施并鼓励私人投资建设存储设施），这使小农户难以连续生产山羊肉和牛肉。因此，国家农业政策在市场营销方面的措施迫切需要贯彻落实。在实施中，有必要建立省级召集中心或信息单元，也有必要由国家及其他重要的利益相关方开设能力建设工作坊，以传播市场信息。

6. 合作社的发展

国家合作社发展政策制定的策略也将提高小农户的生产能力。完善法规和制度体系，以促进合作组织的重新定位和改革，通过实地工作人员直接处理合作社方面的问题，保证农牧业部在全国所有地区切实承担起在合作社发展方面的责任。应鼓励发展合作种植，以保证农民的收益。考虑到人员配置和运营效率方面的问题，需要重构现有的合作组织。

7. 畜牧业发展

如果想提高赞比亚的牛羊肉产量，那么也有必要转变行业观念。所有的小农户都表示，他们让山羊自己寻找食物，没有正规的喂养计划。牛肉生产也一样，投入在很大程度上依赖于传统牧场。有必要为小农户指明方向，并帮助他们提高技能，让他们把山羊和肉牛的养殖当作一门生意来对待，这就需要一些投资。政府的支持将对提高生产力起很大的推动作用。

目前的推广服务政策没有覆盖畜牧业，因此也需要制定一个能同时涵盖种植业和畜牧业，全面、清晰并且能得到有效实施的推广服务政策。

8. 投资者的投资与土地购置

应保证投资符合"负责任农业投资原则"。有必要保证对土地及相关自然资源现有的权利得到承认和尊重，保证小农户不会在违背意愿的情况下失去土地。在征收农民的土地时，需要保证告知当事人所有的信息。被迁移农户在新投资的区域占地过少的情况也许意味着投资危及到了粮食安全，因为农民的生产将低于投资前的情况。应进一步采取措施，以保证征询所有因大型投资而蒙受物质损失的当事人的意见，并履行协商达成的协议。

另外一个明显的问题是农民土地所有权制度的脆弱。赞比亚土地所有权的主要形式是传统的土地所有权，只有37.5%的受访者表示拥有土地所有权契据。其中70%来自铜带省，这是一个以城市为主的省份。土地所有权契据对农民获得贷款有很大的帮助，因为它可以作为抵押品。政府需要重新审视土地所有权制度，以保证更多农民拥有自己土地的所有权契据。

C H I N A

新兴市场国家对非洲农业的南南合作

A F R I C A

兄弟齐心？ 巴西在非洲的贸易、投资与合作[*]

保罗·德·伦齐奥　朱理克·塞弗特　乔凡纳·佐科·戈麦斯

曼纳拉·阿辛卡奥[**]　著

贾　丁[***]　译

巴西加快介入非洲

　　由于历史纽带和共同的殖民地经历，巴西与非洲历来保持着密切关系，特别是与葡语非洲国家的密切关系。伴随二战后的非洲非殖民化浪潮，巴西同非洲国家之间的关系越发紧密，尤其是在 1974 年葡萄牙殖民政权倒台后。2003 年卢拉政府上台之后，由于在任总统与其"总统外交"的推动，巴西和非洲之间的互动增加，主要表现扩大的贸易额、政治对话与双边合作上。

　　无论是通过企业、政府机构还是公私合作伙伴关系，巴西在非洲大陆的存在都被纳入推动非洲国家重大经济和社会发展的话语体系中。巴西不仅推动成功经验的交流，还加强了贸易、文化和外事活动，并增加农业、卫生等领域对非洲的技术输出。与此同时，巴西和非洲之间日益增进的关

---

　　[*]　本文是"巴西南南合作和金砖国家：改变在非洲的战略"研究项目（SSC 项目）发表在巴西金砖国家政策中心（BPC）的政策简报的更新版本，该研究项目由英国国际开发署和里约热内卢天主教大学国际关系研究院合作，更多信息请参见 www. bricspolicycenter. org。

　　[**]　保罗·德·伦齐奥（Paolo de Renzio），里约热内卢天主教大学国际关系研究院教授；朱理克·塞弗特（Jurek Seifert）和乔凡纳·佐科·戈麦斯（Geovana Zoccal Gomes）都是里约热内卢天主教大学国际关系研究院的博士候选人。曼纳拉·阿辛卡奥（Manaíra Assunção）里约热内卢天主教大学国际关系研究院的硕士研究生。

　　[***]　贾丁，北京大学国际关系学院硕士毕业，现供职于中国国际问题研究院，工作邮箱：jiading@ ciis. org. cn。

系，遵循了前者在这一时期的外交主旋律，即提高巴西的国际存在感。① 卢拉总统的亲自参与和他强调将南南合作作为横向合作的一种形式，是巴西"团结外交"② 这一外交政策的缘起，这一外交政策尤其针对非洲国家。

罗塞夫总统自 2011 年上台之后，没有展现出与前任同样的在巴非关系上的参与热情。2011 年 10 月，罗塞夫总统首次访问非洲，到访了南非、莫桑比克和安哥拉，之后长达一年多都没有踏上这片大陆，直到 2013 年 2 月才出席了在赤道几内亚举行的"南美—非洲峰会"，并访问了尼日利亚。同年 3 月，她出席了在南非德班举行的金砖国家峰会，5 月又参加了在埃塞俄比亚举行的非盟成立 50 周年的庆祝活动。虽然这些外事活动可以被解读为罗塞夫总统对非洲关注的显著提升，但相较于前任总统，她对待非洲大陆持一种明显的实用主义态度。虽然这可能同她强调国内政治的个人风格有关，但存在这样一个事实：对于相对可用于合作的资源，卢拉向非洲伙伴做出的承诺是一个大难题。然而，无论如何，罗塞夫继承了卢拉政府开创的南南合作的话语，强调非洲作为巴西外交政策平等伙伴的重要性。

> 巴西认为非洲大陆是兄弟和近邻……我们的共同利益有很多：我们寻求发展，这要求我们推动将人民纳入国家利益和财富中的进程。③

同时，罗塞夫总统继续鼓励巴西企业在非洲发展。在她出访埃塞俄比亚期间，罗塞夫总统宣布减免非洲 12 国共计 8.977 亿美元的债务。④ 尽管这一债务减免行为被冠以"团结"的标签，它还是被批评受到贸易和投资动机的驱动。有人指出，巴西国家社会经济发展银行（BNDES）只支持在与巴西没有债务关系的国家内的企业活动。

---

① J. F. S. Saraiva, "The New Africa and Brazil in the Lula Era: The Rebirth of Brazilian Atlantic Policy", *Revista Brasileira de Política Internacional*, vol. 53, n. 2, 2010, pp. 169 – 182.

② Cristina Yumie Aoki Inoue University of Brasilia & Alcides Costa Vaz, "Brazil as 'Southern donor': Beyond Hierarchy and National Interests in Development Cooperation?" *Cambridge Review of International Affairs*, 25 (4), pp. 507 – 534.

③ 参见 http://noticias. band. uol. com. br/mundo/noticia/? id = 100000601265&t = 。

④ 坦桑尼亚、赞比亚、刚果共和国、塞内加尔、科特迪瓦、刚果民主共和国、加蓬、苏丹、毛里塔尼亚、几内亚、圣多美和普林西比、几内亚比绍。安哥拉和莫桑比克是巴西在非洲的两个最重要的合作伙伴，巴西免除了安哥拉 315 万美元的债务，免除了莫桑比克 330 万美元的债务。参见 http://www. revistaconstrucaoenegocios. com. br/materias. php? FhIdMateria = 277。

巴西与非洲贸易的增长

巴西因为将非洲作为外交政策的重点，与非洲的贸易自 2001 年以来实现了持续增长。根据英国皇家国际事务研究所的数据，巴非贸易额由 2001 年的 42 亿美元增长到了 2013 年的 285 亿美元，自 1990 年以来年均增长 16%。这使巴西成为金砖国家中非洲的第三大贸易伙伴国，排在中国和印度（贸易额为 320 亿美元）之后，俄罗斯（只有 35 亿美元）之前。①

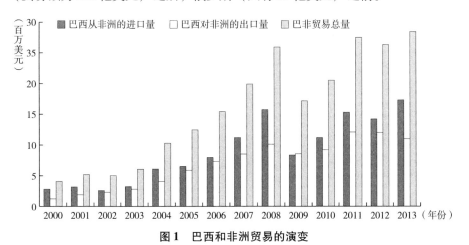

图 1 巴西和非洲贸易的演变

资料来源：巴西发展工业外贸部（MDIC）①。

巴西最重要的非洲贸易伙伴国是尼日利亚（2009 年占巴西对非贸易总量的 32%）、安哥拉（占 16%）、阿尔及利亚（占 12%）和南非（占 7%）。②而就贸易总量而言，非洲仍然只是巴西的普通伙伴。自 2001 年以来，巴西对非出口量占其出口总量的比重从 4% 提高到 5.7%，进口量占其进口总量的③比重从 5.7% 提高到 9.8%。④ 在出口方面，工业制成品占巴西对非出

---

① H. B. Barka, "Brazil's Economic Engagement with Africa", *Africa Economic Brief no. 5*, Tunis: African Development Bank, 2011.

② H. B. Barka, "Brazil's Economic Engagement with Africa", *Africa Economic Brief no. 5*, Tunis: African Development Bank, 2011.

③ 参见 http: // www. desenvolvimento. gov. br/sitio/interna/interna. php? area = 5&menu = 576。

④ MRE, Comércio Brasil-África, 2012.

口份额的一半以上，初级产品出口主要包括糖及糕点糖果（2008～2010年占出口总量的 26.4%）和肉制品（占 12.2%），此外资本商品（机器设备、客车、卡车和轻型商用车）的出口自 2001 年以来也显著增加。巴西从非洲进口的产品以初级产品为主，其中占最大份额的是矿物燃料（2008～2010 年矿物燃料进口占进口总量的 85.4%）。这些数据不仅表明了双方商业议程上的不平衡，也显示了巴西自 2001 年以来如何不断地提高其与非洲的经济相关性，从而增强其在该地区的经济影响力。

在非洲的巴西企业

2003 年之后巴非经济关系的一大变化，是巴西企业的国际化。虽然巴西的私营企业自 20 世纪 80 年代就来到了非洲，但在过去十年中出现了巴西大公司进入非洲大陆的第二次浪潮，这次浪潮在很大程度上源于非洲经济的增长以及对原材料的需求和发展它们所需的基础设施之间的关系。[①]一般而言，在非洲的巴西企业分为两类：一类是巴西的大型企业，另一类是最近才进入非洲的巴西中小型企业。[②]

包括巴西国家石油公司（Petrobras）、安德拉德古铁雷斯建筑公司（Andrade Gutierrez）、淡水河谷公司（Vale do Rio Doce）、卡马戈科雷亚建筑公司（Camargo Correia）和欧德布莱克特建筑公司（Odebrecht）在内的大型企业是巴西在非洲投资的主要参与者。规模较小的投资者则瞄准了非洲的消费品市场，较早进入该领域的中小型企业有打入埃及和南非市场的马可波罗客车制造公司（Marcopolo），以及打入安哥拉市场的波缇卡丽奥化妆品公司（Boticário）和诺贝尔公司（Nobel）。在非洲，共有 22 个国家有巴西企业的身影。

比较巴西的贸易和投资活动，我们并未发现一个清晰的本地化战略，因为高投资、低贸易的情况与具有合理贸易量但没有巴西企业的情况并

---

① Iglesias and Costa, Investimento Estrangeiro Direto na A frica. Rio de Janeiro, Brazil (2011). Retrieved from http://www.cebri.org/midia/documentos/katarinacosta.pdf.

② Banco Mundial/IPEA (2011) Ponte sobre o Atlântico. Brasil e África Subsaariana：Parceria Sul-Sul para o Crescimento, Washington：World Bank. 巴西出口机构（APEX）也为最近巴非贸易的发展做出了贡献，例如，通过组织商务票价。

存。巴西的投资主要集中在南部非洲，特别是南非、安哥拉和莫桑比克三国。巴西企业倾向于使用当地劳动力，如欧德布莱克特建筑公司就是安哥拉最大的雇用当地人的企业。① 尽管如此，巴西企业还是因为区别对待巴西籍雇员和非洲籍雇员，即"同工不同酬"问题受到批评。巴西企业另一个饱受指摘的问题在于其与非洲当地政府之间的关系缺乏透明度。在淡水河谷公司在莫桑比克的大型煤炭开采项目中，该公司就一直遭受着严厉的批评和抗议，尤其是在将居住在矿区附近的几个传统村落搬迁之后。②

在非洲的巴西企业主要由其自身的直接投资（2009 年达到 100 亿美元）和主要金融机构援助支持，而后者重点支持大型跨国公司。巴西政府在 2008 年实施的"生产力发展政策"（Productive Development Policy，PDP）③ 和 2011 年的"大巴西计划"（Bigger Brazil Plan），目标都是提升巴西工业的国际竞争力，并通过这些政策确保巴西国家社会经济发展银行发挥更大的国际影响。因此，该行针对拉丁美洲和非洲设立了新的理事会，并试图在南非约翰内斯堡开设新的办事处，以回应其在非洲日益扩大的状况。④ 自 2007 年起，该行就向非洲的巴西企业提供了大量贷款，如安哥拉作为巴西在非洲最大的投资接受国，就获得了 50 亿美元的信贷。除了巴西国家社会经济发展银行之外，在非洲活跃的巴西金融机构还有巴西联邦储蓄银行（Caixa Econômica Federal）、巴西银行（Banco do Brasil）和巴西布拉德斯科银行（Bradesco）。

金融机构的财政支持和其对非洲的日益重视，是巴西和非洲之间贸易显著增长的关键因素。大型公共融资项目的存在表明了巴西外交政策对巴西企业在非扩张的积极扶持；而集中在基础设施、自然资源开采和能源领域的融资也反映了巴西在该地区的主要利益。

---

① Banco Mundial/IPEA（2011）.
② 参见 http：//www. bbc. co. uk/news/world-africa-22646243 和 http：//www1. folha. uol. com. br/mundo/2013/04/1266520-megaprojeto-da-vale-e-alvo-de-protestos-em-mocambique. shtml。
③ 生产力发展政策（PDP）于 2008 年推出，旨在促进和维护国内经济扩张的周期，甚至在全球金融危机期间，为巴西国家社会经济发展银行的国际干预提供指导和支持，例如，为加强商业关系和巴西对非洲的直接投资建立实际的渠道。
④ 参见 http：//brazilafrica. com/negocios/bndes-tera-escritorio-na-africa/。

巴西与非洲的发展合作

不可否认，南南合作作为巴西外交政策转型的产物，在过去几年中史无前例地迅猛发展。① 认识到促进国际发展的能力，新兴国家明确表达了不同于传统南北合作的话语。在这种背景下，巴西推出的技术合作模式表明，巴西从受援国的需求出发，强调没有附加条件，采取水平方式，且不干涉非洲国家内政。

在与巴西的投资合作中，不管从项目数量看还是从资金量来看，非洲和拉丁美洲都是获益最多的地区。巴西与非洲的技术合作集中在葡语非洲国家（莫桑比克、圣多美和普林西比、安哥拉和佛得角）。巴西强调与这些国家的文化相似性和共同的殖民地历史，这是巴西与上述国家实现合作的重要原因。2013 年，作为巴西的主要合作受援国，莫桑比克共有 14 个在建项目，排在之后的是圣多美和普林西比与佛得角，圣多美和普林西比分别有 12 个在建项目，佛得角有 11 个。② 除了非洲葡语国家，阿尔及利亚、贝宁、博茨瓦纳和坦桑尼亚也受益于同巴西的合作。巴西的技术合作已表现出了多样性，巴西在非洲的合作重点是卫生（占 22%）、农业（占 19%）和教育（占 14%）领域，除此之外，还有环境、公共管理、城市建设、社会发展、国防、体育、文化等领域。③

如图 2 所示，为非洲项目提供的财政资源在 2003 ~ 2010 年显著增长，但在过去几年里由于巴西的财政预算削减政策而有大幅减少。根据巴西合作署（ABC）主任费尔南多·德·阿布雷乌（Fernando de Abreu）大使的报告，该机构为 2012 ~ 2015 年在非活动的预算拨款是 3600 万美元。④

---

① 可参见另一近期发表在巴西金砖国家政策中心的政策简报 http：//bricspolicycenter. org/homolog/Job/Interna/5992。

② "Fernando de Abreu, Diretor da Agência Brasileira de Cooperação（ABC）", 2013 年 7 月 28 日发表在巴西金砖国家政策中心，参见 http：//bricspolicycenter. org/homolog/Event/Evento/596。

③ IPEA, *Cooperação Brasileira para o Desenvolvimento Internacional* –2010, Brasília: IPEA, 2013, 参见 http：//www. ipea. gov. br/portal/images/stories/PDFs/livros/livros/livro _ cooperacao _ brasileira02. pdf。

④ Abreu, 2013 年 7 月 28 日发表在巴西金砖国家政策中心，参见 http：//bricspolicycenter. org/homolog/Event/Evento/596。

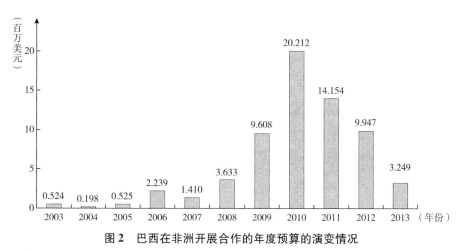

图2　巴西在非洲开展合作的年度预算的演变情况

资料来源：2013年6月28日，费尔南多·德·阿布雷乌大使在金砖国家政策会议上的报告。

卫生合作

　　巴西与非洲的卫生合作，很大程度上是在如下几方面展开的：派遣巴西专业的医护人员提供专业教育和培训、结构性援助及机构能力建设、分享巴西在公共卫生政策方面的经验以及赠送药品和物资。巴非合作项目重点针对艾滋病防治，其中一个最突出的例子就是提高抗反转录病毒药物的生产能力。莫桑比克有十分之一的人口携带艾滋病病毒，巴西合作署与奥斯瓦尔多·克鲁兹基金会（the Oswaldo Cruz Foundation）共同努力，在莫桑比克建立了一家制药厂，旨在加强当地专业人员药物生产的能力，抗击疫情。该药厂由一家国有企业运行，意图为整个地区提供抗艾滋病药物。虽然该项目于2008年启动并已经建成，但至今还没有开始生产。为了建设该厂，莫桑比克政府提供了部分财政拨款，但还是需要来自巴西淡水河谷公司的资金支持。

　　此外，为了建立集临床、防疫、实验和诊断为一体的研究中心，奥斯瓦尔多·克鲁兹基金会从2009年就开始在莫桑比克和安哥拉开设公共卫生硕士课程。非洲学生将收到来自巴西高等教育人员促进会（CAPES）的资助，前往巴西完成他们硕士学位。

　　奥斯瓦尔多·克鲁兹基金会积极参与国际卫生合作，并在莫桑比克首都马普托建立了它在巴西之外的第一个办公室。该基金会主要以加强能力建设和改善当地医疗系统的方式推进巴西与莫桑比克的卫生合作。①

毫无疑问，莫桑比克是奥斯瓦尔多·克鲁兹基金会在非洲开展卫生合作的重点国家。巴西对非洲葡语国家很重视，该基金会还加强了同安哥拉的合作。莫桑比亚和安哥拉两国都被纳入该基金会的"母乳银行网络"（Human Milk Bank Network）中。巴西还与日本携手在安哥拉提出了名为"安哥拉卫生部门人力资源开发项目"的三边倡议，该倡议针对安哥拉卫生部门的个人和机构能力建设问题，引起了安哥拉卫生机构的注意。

农业合作

根据巴西农业部下属的国有研究机构——国家农业研究所（EMBRA-PA）给出的专业意见，在过去的几十年中，热带农业已成为巴西与非洲合作的主要领域。2010 年，国家农业研究所在 11 个非洲国家进行了 12 个项目和 1 项独立活动。"热带草原计划"是目前巴西合作署最大的对外合作项目。根据巴西塞拉多地区（cerrado）的发展经验，通过与日本和莫桑比克的三边合作，该项目旨在提高纳卡拉走廊［纳卡拉走廊（Nacala Corridor）主要包括莫桑比克的热带草原地区］的种子培育水平。

"热带草原计划"由三个部分组成，未来二十年的预算将达 5 亿美元。该计划的第一个部分由国家农业研究所负责，其任务是提高莫桑比克农业研究所（IIAM）的培训和研究能力，促进技术进步。第二个部分由另外两家巴西机构负责，它们分别是农村技术援助与推广机构（EMATER-DF）和国家农村学徒服务机构（SENAR），为推进该计划建立模型。第三个部分由格图里奥巴尔加斯基金会的农业产业化研究中心（GV Agro）和一家

① Giuliano Russo, Lícia de Oliveira, Alex Shankland and Tania Sitoe, "On the Margins of Aid Orthodoxy: The Brazil-Mozambique Collaboration to Produce Essential Medicines in Africa", *Globalization and Health* 10 (20), 2014; CéliaAlmeida, Rodrigo Pires de Campos, José R. Ferreira, Paulo Buss and Luiz E. Fonseca "A concepção brasileira de 'cooperação Sul-Sul estruturante em saúde'", *Revista Eletrônica de Comunicação*, Informação & Inovação em Saúde-RECIIS 4 (1): 25 – 35, 2010.

日本咨询机构负责，它们为纳卡拉走廊的农业发展设计总体规划蓝图，[①] 这也是该计划中被一些研究人员和民间社会团体视为最有争议的部分，并导致了莫桑比克国内舆论对巴西的批评。

在贝宁、布基纳法索、乍得、马里开展的"棉花四国"项目（Cotton–4 program）于2009年开始，吸引了广泛的国际关注。棉花行业是这四国的经济命脉所在。以提高生产力、基因多样性和棉花行业质量为目标，国家农业研究所旨在加强和发展"棉花四国"的生产能力和整体经济。

棉花行业是巴西、贝宁、布基纳法索、乍得、马里的经济命脉所在。该项目也是由国家农业研究所负责的，旨在提高这些国家棉花行业的生产力，进而发展经济。现阶段的任务是在马里建立区域的基因资源中心，在五国开展研究人员能力建设、技术转移，建立试验和示范单位以及开展昆虫饲养实验室的活动，并为非洲各国提供棉花病害防治技术的培训。

2004～2008年，巴西与非洲国家签订了22个关于生物燃料项目的合作协定。[②] 根据这些双边或三边协议，巴西通过援助专业技术和基础设施的方式，帮助合作伙伴建立了生物乙醇的生产线。一些非洲国家在土地和气候方面的适宜性同巴西的土地和气候条件的相似性，为这些项目的开展提供了有力的支持。除了巴西外交部的新能源和可再生能源司，许多巴西的能源、工业和农业部门以及科研机构也参与了这些生物燃料项目的制定和实施。

理论上，这一过程分成两个阶段：第一阶段，国家农业研究所将围绕生产力和乙醇与粮食生产进行可行性研究；如果可行性研究的结论是可以继续实施项目，则在随后的阶段中筹集资金和启动实施。在某些情况下，巴西的私营企业会与非洲企业成立合资公司，从事与巴西国家社会经济发展银行资助项目有关的设备与机械出口业务。2011年，巴西国家石油公司

---

① "草案初稿零版"参见 http：//prosavana. gov. mz/index. php？ p = biblioteca&id = 27。

② John Wilkinson，"Brazilian Bio-diplomacy in Africa. The Case of Biofuels"，*Report for Action Aid within the Framework of the Project：Impact of Biofuels on Food，Farmers and the Environment* （《"生物燃料对粮食、农民和环境的影响"项目框架内的行动援助报告》），2014，available at：http：//www. actionaid. org. br/sites/files/actionaid/biodiplomacia_en_web. pdf。

计划在莫桑比克建立一个乙醇工厂以供应本地市场。一年后，巴西国家社会经济发展银行与非洲开发银行（African Development Bank）签署了合作备忘录，探讨在生物能源方面的投资合作。公私合作伙伴关系符合巴西的"乙醇外交"战略，一方面，政府间协定为公私合作提供政策支持；另一方面，私人公司进行技术转让。[①]

然而，自 2010 年以来，很多国家纷纷减少对生物燃料的投资。"乙醇开发"作为政策首选在巴西遭遇挫折，巴西农业部的预算被削减了一半。[②]投资项目没有达到初始目标，还处于种植和原料加工的阶段。2013 年，莫桑比克只有 3% 的总预期地区在种植原料，而 6 个乙醇项目实施了 3 个，12 个生物柴油项目实施了 10 个。[③]

虽然巴西对非投资上一直强调水平方式和团结，但是其在非洲开展的技术合作项目还是受到了批评。对巴西在非洲最大的合作项目"热带草原计划"的常见批评，在于该计划虽然在莫桑比克大草原复制了巴西农业发展的经验，但是大豆和玉米的大规模产业化生产导致了当地环境恶化和传统村落的消亡。[④]

尽管如此，巴西合作署声明，将农业作为优先事项不仅是莫桑比克政府国内政策的责任，也是莫桑比克民间社会与国家力量相互作用后的选择，这一优先事项不应该受到巴西、日本或其他项目合作伙伴的干预。

因此，为了推动有效合作和可持续项目，巴西不能忽视与当地参与者的关系，还要提高适应不同社会和政治环境的能力。正如最近的评论所强

---

① Afionis et al.，"Unpacking Brazil's Leadership in the Global Biofuels Arena：Brazil Ethanol Diplomacy in Africa"，Sustainability Research Institute Paper no. 74，2014，available at：http：//www. see. leeds. ac. uk/fileadmin/Documents/research/sri/workingpapers/SRIPs – 74. pdf.

② Afionis et al.，"Unpacking Brazil's Leadership in the Global Biofuels Arena：Brazil Ethanol Diplomacy in Africa"，Sustainability Research Institute Paper no. 74，2014，available at：http：//www. see. leeds. ac. uk/fileadmin/Documents/research/sri/workingpapers/SRIPs – 74. pdf.

③ Boris Atanassov，"The Status of Biofuels Projects in Mozambique"，*ODI & Green Light Research*，2014，available at：http：//www. odi. org/sites/odi. org. uk/files/odi-assets/publications-opinion-files/8799. pdf.

④ 安哥拉全国农民联盟致"热带草原计划"的公开信，2012 年 10 月 11 日，参见 http：//www. unac. org. mz/index. php/documentos-de-posicao/38-pronunciamento-da-unac-sobre-o – programa-prosavana。

调的,① 巴西与非洲国家开展合作的主要限制因素是解决发展中国家面临挑战的"技术途径"以及巴西专业人士在国际环境下缺乏行动经验。

未来的巴非关系

巴西与非洲的合作及贸易和投资都沿着卢拉政府一开始制定的道路推进。虽然罗塞夫政府保持了这样的态势，但是上一届政府的热情和个性化的做法已经被更务实甚至有时矛盾的政策所取代。

巴西政府将继续推动技术合作作为其更广泛的国际战略的一部分，将自己定位为"南方国家"的一员，并与发展中国家紧密团结在一起。但与此同时，与其他公共机构一样，巴西合作署也经历了大幅的预算削减。

另外，巴西公司在非洲的扩张仍然是通过巴西国家社会经济发展银行由政府支持的，并取得了贸易和自然资源方面实实在在的利益。更清楚界定"巴西在非洲所扮演的角色""合作、贸易与投资之间的关系"的必要性变得更加迫切，特别是关于巴西合作署可能的机构改革的辩论。

2013 年 3 月，罗塞夫总统在埃塞俄比亚宣布，"巴西将成立一个不隶属于外交部的新机构，该机构将是一个贸易机构，鼓励在拉丁美洲和非洲的合作和投资"，但没有明确说明该机构的体制结构以及它将如何有助于实现巴西外交政策的目标。虽然总统表示要成立一个独立机构，但巴西合作署主任仍然捍卫其与外交部的关系。他还指出，有一个团队正在研究其他国家的机构建立适当监管框架的模型，其研究成果将帮助巴西合作署提高独立性和技术能力。

巴西与非洲国家双边关系最重要变化，集中在合作与投资的整合趋

---

① I. Leite, et al. , "Para além do tecnicismo: a Cooperação Brasileira para o Desenvolvimento Internacional e caminhos para sua efetividade e democratização", *Policy Brief*, São Paulo: Articulação Sul, 2013, available at: http://blogbrasilnomundo. files. wordpress. com/2013/08/policy_briefing_para-alec2b4m-do-tecnicismo. pdf; L. Cabral et al. , "Brazil-Africa Agricultural Cooperation Encounters: Drivers, Narratives and Imaginaries of Africa and Development", *IDS Bulletin*, 44 (4), 2013, pp. 53-68.

势。2015年3月，巴西政府与莫桑比克政府签订了《合作和投资促进协定》（*Cooperation and Investment Facilitation Agreement*）①，4月，又与安哥拉政府签订了相似的协定。② 正如前文所强调的，莫桑比亚和安哥拉两国是巴西在非洲的主要伙伴国，莫桑比克是巴西发展合作项目的主要目的地，而安哥拉则是巴西私人投资的主要接受者。

在莫桑比克，淡水河谷公司自2004年就开始在太特省（Tete）开采煤矿。该公司还投资修建了连接纳卡拉港和莫桑比克北部煤炭产地的铁路。该铁路也将服务于"热带草原计划"的大豆生产运输。虽然巴西政府的国际发展合作不涉及私人投资，但是公私项目在同一地区的重叠则引起了争论和批评，特别是跨国公司使用土地为大豆生产服务。③

独立的机制改革目前正在讨论中，巴西介入非洲所面临的最大挑战是如何协调贸易和投资的目标与实践，并权衡涉及非洲国家优先事项和必需事项的方式。如上所述，虽然技术合作和巴西公司的行动总体受到非洲国家的欢迎，但是它们也受到主要来自民间社会团体的批评，"热带草原计划"和淡水河谷公司在莫桑比克的项目就是例证。在正确方向上迈出的第一步是建立一个国际合作的监督框架（这可能需要设立一个新的机构），以及为巴西介入非洲的各种形式制定一个具体的战略。

---

① 葡文版协议可参见 http：//www. itamaraty. gov. br/index. php？ option = com_content&view = article&id = 8511：acordo-brasil-mocambique-de-cooperacao-e-facilitacao-de-investimentos-acfi-maputo-30-de-marco-de-2015&catid = 42&Itemid = 280&lang = pt-BR。

② 葡文版协议可参见 http：//www. itamaraty. gov. br/index. php？ option = com_content&view = article&id = 8520&catid = 42&Itemid = 280&lang = pt-BR#mou-econ。

③ Ana Garcia, *O novo acordo de cooperação e facilitação do investimento entre Brasil e Moçambique：Algumas Considerações*, 2015, https：//grupoemergentes. wordpress. com/2015/04/12/o-novo-acordo-de-cooperacao-e-facilitacao-do-investimento-entre-brasil-e-mocambique-algumas-consider-acoes/#_ftn2.

巴西在安哥拉卫生与农业领域里的南南合作[*]

约翰·莫拉·丰塞卡 乔凡纳·佐科·戈麦斯 保罗·埃斯特维斯^{**} 著

贾 丁 邹雨君^{***} 译

安哥拉的发展与国际合作

在安哥拉内战期间，由联合国机构、双边捐助国、国际非政府组织和宗教组织提供的发展合作项目大量进入该国。这些项目主要是针对政府力量难以涉及的地方所开展的应急和人道主义救援。国际机构提供资金支持国际和安哥拉本土公民社会组织在安哥拉建立、发展，并在协助战区内项目人员安全流动上也发挥了重要作用。[①]

内战结束后，安哥拉政府的一个优先事项就是组织捐助者会议，希望提高和调整资金用于安哥拉的基础设施和经济重建。然而国际货币基金组织和安哥拉政府无法在治理和透明度问题上达成协议，也无法调和双方的统计数据，这

---

* 本文是"巴西南南合作和金砖国家：改变在非洲的战略"研究项目（SSC 项目），是在发表于巴西金砖国家政策中心（BPC）的政策简报《巴西与安哥拉的卫生与农业合作》一文基础上的更新与升级版本，该研究项目是英国国际开发署和里约热内卢天主教大学国际关系研究院合作支持的，更多信息请参见 www. bricspolicycenter. org。

** 三位作者分别为里约热内卢天主教大学金砖国家政策中心研究员，2014 年获里约热内卢天主教大学国际关系研究院国际关系专业硕士；里约热内卢天主教大学金砖国家政策中心研究员，里约热内卢天主教大学国际关系研究院博士候选人；里约热内卢天主教大学金砖国家政策中心研究员，2003 年获政治科学博士。

*** 贾丁，北京大学国际关系学院硕士毕业，现供职于中国国际问题研究院，工作邮箱：jiading@ ciis. org. cn；邹雨君，北京大学国际关系学院博士研究生，北京大学非洲研究中心成员。

① 2014 年 9 月在罗安达采访。

阻碍了会议的召开。① 由于双方都没有实质性的让步，会议被一再推迟，一直没能举行。此外，安哥拉政府一直没有通过"巴黎俱乐部"的批准对其债务进行重组。② 笔者就此议题采访了多位知情者，其中几位提到，很多安哥拉的高层官员都表现出对北方捐助国家的怨恨，认为它们在"安哥拉需要帮助的时候没有施以援手"。③ 正是在这个时期，南方国家，特别是中国，开始巩固其在安哥拉的存在。还有一位受访者指出，他不止一次听到安哥拉政府的高层官员在谈及中安关系时说，"当你快要淹死的时候，你不会关心是谁扔给你救生衣的"。

2004 年，中国向安哥拉提供贷款换石油的合作，这使得安哥拉可以驳回国际货币基金组织所说的"实施将使安哥拉得到更好治理"的改革方案。布拉蒂加姆（Brautigam）和很多受访者一样，认为除了一些细微的差别，在与安哥拉签订协议前后，中国政府的所作所为并非迥异于任何西方银行［如法国巴黎银行（BNP Paribas）、德国商业银行（Commerz bank）、法国兴业银行（Societé Générale）、英国巴克莱银行（Barclays）和渣打银行（Standard Chartered）］。只是中国的条件对安哥拉更有利，包括较低的利率和更长的宽限期、还款期。在此之后，安哥拉凭借蓬勃发展的石油产业收入开始偿还债务，同时提升透明度。④

在安哥拉内战结束后，很多公民社会组织随着传统发展合作项目的退出而消失。除了资金极度紧张之外，这些社团还要面对飞升的物价和政府越发严厉的管制。这种趋势在罗安达特别明显，战争年代曾有大批人口涌入这里寻求庇护。⑤ 鉴于罗安达畸高的物价，尽管其仍旧是安哥拉的行政中心，但一些非政府组织还是将总部迁到了本格拉（Benguela）。另外，安哥拉的受访者纷纷指出，有关公民社会组织的监管框架，包括"14 号法令第 11 号"⑥

---

① "No Donors' Conference for Angola on Horizon"，2003，http：//afrol. com/html/News2003/ ang006_donors. htm. Oct. 6 2014.

② Deborah Brautigam，*The Dragon's Gift*：*The Real Story of China in Africa*，Oxford University Press，2009.

③ 2014 年 9 月在罗安达采访。

④ Deborah Brautigam，*The Dragon's Gift*：*The Real Story of China in Africa*，Oxford University Press，2009，pp. 273 – 277.

⑤ 2014 年 9 月在罗安达采访。

⑥ http：//www. rjcplp. org/sections/informacao/anexos/legislacao – angola/outra – legislacao – ango-la/lei – das associacoes/downloadFile/file/Lei _ das _ Associacoes. pdf？ nocache = 1365699390. 02， 10 October 14，2014.

在内的社团法使内战后公民社会组织减少了。因此多数受访者认为安哥拉的公民社会组织力量薄弱，只有少数非独立的社团能发挥作用，其中很多是执政党安哥拉人民解放运动（MPLA）的喉舌。但这些受访者也指出，政府在民主治理和透明度方面不断改善。

安哥拉在地区事务中日益活跃，在非洲联盟、"非洲发展新伙伴计划"（NEPAD）和南部非洲发展共同体（SADC）等区域组织中扮演着重要角色。《安哥拉 2025 年：未来远大之国》设定了安哥拉的长期发展目标。为实现这一目标，安哥拉确定了中期规划——《安哥拉 2013～2017 年国家发展规划》，这是 2010 年安哥拉修改宪法后的首个国家发展规划。该规划定义了以下六大国家目标：（1）维护国家团结和凝聚力；（2）确保发展所必需的基本原则；①（3）提高生活质量；（4）保障青少年积极生活；（5）推动私营企业发展；（6）提高安哥拉的国际竞争力。

表1　《安哥拉 2013～2017 年国家发展规划》在农业和卫生领域的目标和优先事项

农业	
目标	优先事项
为了保证粮食安全和国内供应以及更好地利用安哥拉在国际和地区市场的优势，要推动农业部门的综合可持续发展，推动自然资源生产潜力和农业竞争力的充分发展	1. 发展竞争性农业，家庭生产以市场和商业发展为导向
	2. 恢复和扩大农业和畜牧业生产的基础设施
	3. 在发展农业生产的综合战略框架下，推动联合生产和商业化
	4. 实现基本粮食自给自足
	5. 发展利润高和传统的农作物，提高生产者的收入和国家出口
	6. 减少进口，促进经济活动的多样化
	7. 发展灌溉农业，提高生产力和竞争力，有效缓解气候变化的影响
	8. 通过科学技术手段完善土地调查制度
	9. 积极创造就业，有效推动家庭农业收入增长和企业发展
卫生	
目标	优先事项
持续提升安哥拉人民的卫生条件和寿命，扶持社会低收入群体，对抗贫困	1. 提高出生预期寿命
	2. 提升人类发展指数和千年发展目标的指标
	3. 降低孕产妇、青少年和儿童的死亡率，降低国家整体的发病率和死亡率

① 基本原则为：保持宏观经济稳定发展、推广国家人口政策、促进积极就业和国家人力资源定价的政策、提高生产力以及国家经济结构的转型、实现多元化和现代化。

续表

卫生	
目标	优先事项
持续提升安哥拉人民的卫生条件和寿命，扶持社会低收入群体，对抗贫	4. 完善全国卫生系统的组织、管理和运作，引导所需资金，采取规范流程，提高全国卫生系统的效率和质量
	5. 在宣传、预防、治疗和康复方面改善医疗保健服务，加强初级卫生保健和医院治疗之间的衔接工作
	6. 积极推进旨在降低孕产妇、儿童死亡率和防治地方病的国际合作
	7. 运用足够的人力资源来实现目标，并采用新的卫生技术
	8. 提高个人、家庭和社区的保健能力
	9. 通过绩效考核和专项研究，对卫生部门的表现进行监测和评估

《安哥拉 2013～2017 年国家发展规划》显示了一个稳健和现代的发展观，重点强调了经济增长的重要性。虽然安哥拉的经济在过去几年中实现了大幅增长，但各项社会指标仍然偏低，安哥拉人口的预期寿命是 51 岁，低于撒哈拉以南非洲地区的平均值，36.6% 的人口仍生活在全国贫困线以下。[1]

这样的背景也表明了发展合作的潜力与挑战。不难想象，总数为 2 亿美元的净官方发展援助资金尚不到安哥拉国民总收入 0.3%，该发展合作基金在国民总收入中将继续扮演一个边缘角色，但是它在改善社会指标以及减少贫困和不平等方面发挥了重要作用。2011 年，官方发展援助提供者中，美国是发展援助委员会中提供援助资金最多的国家（约 6300 万美元），其后是欧盟（2600 万美元）、日本（2500 万美元）、韩国[2]（1800 万美元）和葡萄牙（1800 万美元）。这些援助主要针对安哥拉的社会部门，特别是教育、卫生和人口[3]三个部门。

根据安哥拉政府的需求，联合国机构与公民社会组织和官方捐助者一样，重新界定了作用区域，对安哥拉的援助预算在 2003～2013 年中也大幅削减。联合国机构的行动基于《2009～2013 年联合国对安哥拉发展援助框

①　The World Bank Data：Angola, http://data.worldbank.org/country/angola, Mar. 10th 2014.
②　值得注意的是，虽然是发展援助委员会的成员，但韩国认为自己是南方国家。
③　根据经济合作与发展组织的定义，人口部门活动通常包括人口与发展政策、普查工作、人口登记、统计迁移数据、人口研究与分析、生殖健康研究以及其他未特指的人口活动。

架》（UNDAF – Angola），旨在协调和整合在安哥拉活动的联合国系统各部门，新的计划尚未发布。世界银行也重新修改了其介入安哥拉的战略：国际复兴开发银行（IBRD）、国际开发协会（IDA）、国际金融公司（IFC）和多边投资担保机构（MIGA）在 2013 年 8 月发表了《2014～2016 年国家合作战略》。

正如世界银行《2014～2016 年国家合作战略》所呈现的，受访者普遍认为安哥拉政府一直保持着"自己管理发展议程的良好记录"。双边和多边的发展合作伙伴如果希望参与发展政策的制定和实施，都必须遵守安哥拉政府的规则。因为安哥拉政府已与本国石油和石油提炼工业的发展有了内在联系，所以对于"新的政治和经济杠杆不再感兴趣"；① 此外，传统和新兴大国已经被吸引参与到石油和石油提炼工业的扩张中。尽管与莫桑比克等国相比，安哥拉仍然高度依赖自然资源和国际大宗商品价格，但这种依赖使安哥拉在发展中找对了位置。依赖援助使莫桑比克的国家主权受到限制，而尽管从中短期来看石油依赖在财富集中和巩固民主方面起着消极作用，但安哥拉则可以自行决定其发展议程。正如下将讨论的，随着越来越多的新兴大国进入安哥拉，安哥拉政府执行发展政策和计划的能力得到了提升。②

巴西与安哥拉关系的发展

巴西与安哥拉的关系可以追溯到 17 世纪，两国同属葡萄牙的殖民地，在三角贸易中安哥拉向巴西输送了大量的奴隶。此外，安哥拉的高级官员在中高层会议中经常提起 1975 年巴西是第一个承认安哥拉为主权国家的西方国家。同年，巴西在安哥拉设立了大使馆。

巴西国家社会经济发展银行资助了巴西公司在安哥拉的一些项目，特别是在基础设施领域。巴西联邦储蓄银行（Caixa Econômica Federal）、巴

---

① Lucy Corkin, Christopher Burke and Martyn Davies, "China's Role in the Development of Africa's Infrastructure", *Documents de travail du SAIS dans African Studies* 04 – 08，2008.

② 然而，这种背景分析并不意味着与莫桑比克这样的援助依赖国相比，安哥拉正在取得更好的发展成果。相反，在依赖石油和自然资源的国家，专注于静态比较优势和围绕特定部门造成的经济集中会产生负面影响。

西银行（Banco do Brasil）和巴西贴现银行（Bradesco）也进入了安哥拉。与中国一样，巴西政府也将商品和原材料作为信用抵押。①

安哥拉是巴西在非洲投资的主要国家。目前，巴西是安哥拉第四大进口国和第十九大出口国。② 与安哥拉的贸易量占巴西总贸易量的0.4%。相关数据显示，巴西从安哥拉的发展中收益颇多。2000~2010年，巴西和安哥拉之间的双边贸易额大幅度增长，并于2008年达到了42.1亿美元的历史最高纪录。2010年，巴西向安哥拉主要出口的货物有肉和鱼（均占对安哥拉出口总额的23.7%）、工业制品和精制糖（均占对安哥拉出口总额的13.0%），从安哥拉主要进口的商品是石油与天然气（均占对安哥拉进口总额的73.7%）以及石油衍生产品（占安哥拉进口总额的25.9%）。③ 2009~2013年，巴西对安哥拉的出口下降4.6%，进口增长427.6%，这表明贸易正朝着有利于安哥拉的平衡方向发展。④

安哥拉也是巴西私人公司投资的主要目的国之一，在所有非洲国家中安哥拉聚集了最多的巴西中小企业。从2007年起，巴西国家社会经济发展银行，为在非洲的私人投资提供了28亿美元的贷款，其中安哥拉占96%。⑤ 表2列举了巴西跨国公司在安哥拉开发的一些主要项目。

表2 巴西跨国公司在安哥拉的投资项目

公司	起始年份	领域	投资项目
巴西石油公司	1980	能源/油气	石油和生物燃料的开发。该公司是安哥拉六个石油区块开发的合作者、四个石油区块开发的执行者。2013年6月，与巴西百达投资银行（BTG Pactual）成立合资企业（1500万美元，各占50%的股份），在包括安哥拉在内的几个非洲国家进行石油和天然气的勘探

① Ana Saggioro Garcia, Karina Kato and Camila FONTES, "A históriacontada pela caçaoupelocaçador", *Perspectivas do Brasilem Angola e Moçambique*, Rio de Janeiro: PACS, 2013.
② Victoria Waldersee, "Chinese and Brazilian Private Firms in Africa", BRICS Policy Center, 2015.
③ http://www2. apexbrasil. com. br/exportar – produtos – brasileiros/inteligencia – de – mercado/estudos – sobre – paises/perfil – e – oportunidades – comerciais – angola – 2012.
④ http://www. brasilglobalnet. gov. br/ARQUIVOS/IndicadoresEconomicos/INDAngola. pdf.
⑤ Victoria Waldersee, "Chinese and Brazilian Private Firms in Africa", BRICS Policy Center, 2015.

续表

公司	起始年份	领域	投资项目
淡水河谷公司	2005	矿产	通过合资公司进行矿产（主要是镍和铜）勘探和开发
安德拉德古铁雷斯建筑公司	2005	建筑/基础设施	与一家葡萄牙公司合作，得到欧盟资助。修建了多条道路以及通往罗安达国际机场的高速公路，改造班戈国际机场。2011年取得改造罗安达港集装箱码头的合同
卡马戈科雷亚建筑公司	2005	建筑/基础设施	修建威热省马克拉杜宗布的道路。在本格拉，同一家葡萄牙公司和一家安哥拉公司共同建设水泥厂
欧德布莱克特建筑公司	1984	建筑/基础设施/农业/能源/零售/房地产	持有房地产、生物燃料、矿产、农业和能源等领域的25份合同。修建了马兰热的卡潘达水电大坝和坎班贝的水电工程。拥有安哥拉一家生物能源公司40%的股份和安哥拉国家石油公司20%的股份。与安哥拉政府合资开办连锁超市，全国共有37家店铺。有一个农业产业化项目。欧德布莱克特建筑公司负责工农业生产管理、工厂建设和能力建设
安吉维克公司	2005	能源	与安哥拉企业合作，参与环境工程、电力和水电等方面的项目
费登公司	2009	建筑/基础设施	修建卡托卡机场跑道
阿斯帕拉斯公司	2007	房地产/基础设施	参与经济特区建设，涉足房地产、住宅公寓、灌溉系统、商用车等领域
奎罗斯加尔旺公司	2005	房地产/基础设施	从事房地产、道路建设和改造
斯帝芬尼公司	2004	信息和通信技术	涉足技术与信息产业

资料来源：Deborah Vieitas e Isabel Aboim，África：oportunidades para empresasbrasileiras，https：//www. bcgbrasil. com. br/Imprensa/Documents/Africa% 20 – % 20oportunidades% 20para% 20empresas% 20brasileiras% 20_Revista% 20Brasileira% 20de% 20Comercio% 20Exterior. pdf。

巴西与安哥拉的发展合作可以追溯到安哥拉内战期间，当时合作的重点是职业发展和专业培训。1998年，在巴西"国家工业培训服务"（SENAI）项目的支持下，卡赞卡职业培训中心（CFPC）在罗安达郊区启

图1 巴西在安哥拉的投资分布图

资料来源：Victoria Waldersee，"Chinese and Brazilian Private Firms in Africa"，BRICS Policy Center，2015。

动，该中心每年培训2500名专业人士。至今合作范围已遍及从体育运动到消防的多个领域。[①] 国家农业研究所和奥斯瓦尔多·克鲁兹基金会分别在安哥拉开展农业和卫生的合作项目。

2012年，安哥拉是巴西第五大技术接收国，相比其他的葡语发展中国家，它的技术接收的规模最小。巴西合作署的材料表明，巴西与安哥拉双边合作仍然处于低水平，据说，这是因为安哥拉企业的执行机构在决策方面水平较低，且一直有较高的离职率。因此，巴西企业很难与安哥拉的合作方开展对话。

巴西与安哥拉在卫生领域的合作

巴西与安哥拉在卫生领域的合作始于1996年，在葡语国家共同体

---

① http：//luanda. itamaraty. gov. br/pt – br/cooperacao_tecnica_e_cientifica. xml.

（CPLP）已经确定的战略框架内，巴西合作署组织医疗专家团讨论前瞻性的项目。自此，包括安哥拉在内的非洲葡语国家开始为构建本国的卫生体系寻求支持。20 世纪 90 年代卫生领域的重点是培训和能力建设，十年之后，各葡语国家的卫生部部长们在卫生领域制订了"2009～2012 年战略计划"。该战略计划的主要目标是完善国家卫生体系，以保证优质的医疗服务得到普及。① 该计划包含七个战略支柱和四个结构网络。除了葡语国家共同体卫生计划构建的结构网络，巴西卫生部和奥斯瓦尔多·克鲁兹基金会也把"母乳银行网络"扩展到了非洲国家。表 3 就葡语国家共同体卫生计划以及"巴西南南合作和金砖国家：改变在非洲的战略"项目在安哥拉和莫桑比克的开展情况进行了比较。

表 3　葡语国家共同体的战略支柱和结构网络及巴西在安哥拉和莫桑比克的南南合作项目

CPLP 的战略支柱和结构网络	CPLP 战略支柱内的巴西南南合作项目		结构网络中的参与者	
	安哥拉	莫桑比克	安哥拉	莫桑比克
SA1—培训和卫生领域人力发展	×	×		
SA2—卫生领域的信息与交流		×		
SA3—卫生领域的科研		×		
SA4—健康产业园区的发展		×		
SA5—流行病学监测和健康状况监管		×		
SA6—突发事件和自然灾害				
SA7—促进和保持健康	×	×		
SN1—国家卫生局				×
SN2—国家公共卫生学院			×	×
SN3—卫生技术院校			×	×
SN4—设备安装和技术维护中心				×

资料来源：Paulo Buss，"Brazil：Structuring Cooperation for Health"，*The Lancet*，377：9779，pp. 1722－3，2011。

---

① COMUNIDADE DOS PAÍSES DE LÍNGUA PORTUGUESA（CPLP），"Plano Estratégico de Cooperação em Saúde da CPLP（PECS/CPLP）Reunião Técnica de Avaliação do PECS－2009－2012，"*Secretariado Executivo da CPLP Lisboa*，*RelatoResumido da Reunião*，17 e 18 de Abril de 2013.

根据巴西驻安哥拉大使馆提供的文件，截至2013年7月巴西与安哥拉在卫生领域仅开展了两项合作项目，分别是"镰刀型细胞贫血病试点项目"和"安哥拉卫生系统能力发展项目"。"镰刀型细胞贫血病试点项目"旨在通过完善与疾病斗争的公共政策、推广新生儿筛查实验与显像诊断的手段，来降低镰刀型细胞贫血病的发病率和死亡率。"安哥拉卫生系统能力发展项目"目标是提升在科学、技术和教育领域的公共卫生培训能力。①该项目在实施初期遇到了很多困难，②但后来培训了30名获得了公共卫生硕士学位的安哥拉专业人员，③该项目被认为是一个成功的经验。此外，同在其他国家遇到的情况一样，由于巴西外交部和协作署的预算被大幅削减，巴西与安哥拉处于谈判阶段的技术合作项目被叫停。

　　巴西在安哥拉最知名的卫生合作项目是"安哥拉卫生部门人力资源开发项目"，这是一个由巴西、日本和安哥拉共同推动的为期三年的合作倡议，旨在提高安哥拉卫生系统、机构和个人的能力。虽然该项目是公认的巴西在安哥拉最著名的卫生合作项目，但不同利益相关方对于该项目的具体认知有着显著的不同。该项目源于2004年巴西坎皮纳斯大学（UNI-CAMP）和日本国际协力机构（JICA）在安哥拉卫生能力发展领域的交集与共同兴趣。日本国际协力机构原本在安哥拉开展医院的基础设施修复和针对员工的卫生培训的活动，考虑到巴西的语言优势及其带来的大量好处，该机构通过"第三国培训计划"（JICA – TCTP）使巴西团队加入培训活动中。官方与民间的评价都认为，这个项目大大提高了安哥拉的初级卫生保健普及程度和质量，对于改善卫生系统和指标具有关键作用。在此之前，由于得不到基本的治疗，大量本不必转诊的病人被迫转入中央医院，这造成安哥拉卫生医疗体系中心部分的超负荷。"安哥拉卫生部门人力资源开发项目"正是为解决这一问题而设计的。

---

① 该项目的目的是支持安哥拉卫生部在公共卫生学校开展的教学、科研和技术合作方面的培训工作。该项目还致力于建立一个网络卫生图书馆、调整卫生技术学校的结构，并加强国家公共卫生研究所的实力。
② 巴西的卫生工作人员报告称，虽然他们充分合作，但与安哥拉同行之间反复出现的问题导致项目在执行过程中多次出现延滞和步调不一致。研究小组无法跟踪项目的实际情况，根据受访者提供的信息，虽然没有完成实施的活动，但该项目可能在2013年结束。
③ 该项目在第一阶段就遇到困难，包括学生无法或按时完成学业。然而，安哥拉政府认为公共卫生硕士学位课程是非常成功和重要的，并随后支持了该项目第二期的实施。

表4　"安哥拉卫生部门人力资源开发项目"的初始预算分配额

单位：美元,%

国　家	份　额	
巴　西	970415	24
日　本	2500000	61
安哥拉	630000	15
共　计	4100415	100

随着 2011 年"安哥拉卫生部门人力资源开发项目"的开展，奥斯瓦尔多·克鲁兹基金会通过国家公共卫生学院和一家卫生职业技术学校，成为该项目的领导机构。综合考虑被筛选医院的条件、转入中央医院的病人数量，以及项目的重点是提高医院的服务和护理质量（如妇幼保健领域），该基金会最终在罗安达筛选出了四家医院，项目致力于提升这四家卫生机构[①]的能力。

在"安哥拉卫生部门人力资源开发项目"中，对初级卫生保健的管理是急需解决的主要问题，因此在 3 年时间里该项目团队设计并实施了一个划分为 10 个模块的能力发展计划和一个初级卫生单位专业化的管理课程。在研究团队访问罗安达期间，该项目的安哥拉团队正在进行参与性评估，并回复建议。有关基本结构问题的建议，如对注册表和临床过程记录的系统整合，已被普遍接受。事实上，这些整合已被 2010 年安哥拉卫生部发布的法令所反复强调。但消息指出，该法令并没有系统地实施，部分原因是卫生工作者缺乏对手头基本问题进行整合的理解力和执行力。

在这个意义上，"安哥拉卫生部门人力资源开发项目"是一个多方共同开发的建设性项目。该项目致力于为卫生部门基础公共政策的实施提供必要培训，包括对健康和临床过程记录的管理和组织培训。因为安哥拉卫生系统在很大程度上被认为是无效的，是公共政策需要治理的对象，该项目把协商一致、系统化和具体情况具体分析的诊断方式作为指导原则。

根据受访者提供的信息，项目的管理模式和实施流程受安哥拉卫生部颁布指令的指导，安哥拉卫生部会定期与监管机构，如国家公共卫生局和

---

① 据受访者的叙述，日本国际协力机构之前也给这四家卫生机构捐赠设备。

罗安达省卫生局讨论。对关键管理人员的培训在巴西进行，但受访者反复强调，所有用于诊断和实施解决方案的信息都是在本地收集的。总之，这样的做法保证了安哥拉国家对于项目的自主权。

一个受访者强调，奥斯瓦尔多·克鲁兹基金会恰当地提高了安哥拉卫生系统的利益相关者对基本问题的理解。同一个受访者批评了自上而下的措施，项目方在没有与卫生工作者讨论的情况下，便实施了新的管理规则、指令和措施，有些措施是由私人卫生咨询公司来实施的，其中一些公司是来自巴西的。"安哥拉卫生部门人力资源开发项目"也存在相似的问题。虽然最近通过卫生咨询公司，在实施项目的医院建立起了管理系统，但巴西坎皮纳斯大学和日本国际协力机构都认为有必要在与医院工作者讨论的基础上建立一个更简单的管理系统。虽然受访者纷纷指出，"安哥拉卫生部门人力资源开发项目"带来的收益可能产生显著和持续的影响，很多受访者也从中受益。访谈也表明，"安哥拉卫生部门人力资源开发项目"的执行在具体操作、财政以及政治文化环境等方面仍然面临一些挑战。

巴西与安哥拉在农业领域的合作

如上所述，安哥拉一直是巴西私人投资的理想国家。在农业领域，位于马兰热省（Malanje）的占地 36000 公顷的蓬戈安东戈（Pungo Andongo）农场是巴西在安哥拉的精品农业项目。该农场是一个农业商业化项目，欧德布莱克特建筑公司主要负责玉米面粉和动物饲料厂的建设和运作以及农场的能力建设和工农业生产的管理。2007 年，欧德布莱克特建筑公司与国家农业研究所非洲分公司（Embrapa‒Africa）签署协议，为玉米、大米和大豆的实验提供技术支持。来自安哥拉公民社会组织的受访者正面评价了巴西私人企业对于安哥拉农业的参与，认为蓬戈安东戈农场是一个学习巴西经验的例子。

根据巴西驻安哥拉大使馆提供的文件，截至 2013 年 7 月在农业技术合作领域，巴西与安哥拉仅开展了一项双边项目，即"支持安哥拉农村职业培训和社会推广计划"。在巴西合作署网站上还列出了一个由巴西合作署、日本国际协力机构和国家农业研究所三方共同推出的蔬菜可持续生产课程。该项目旨在通过提高生产者的知识和能力改善蔬菜生产过程，进而改善非洲葡语国家的食品安全状况。

与农业利益相关的受访者们指出,在安哥拉农业和粮食安全领域的其他合作倡议中,其中一人身处巴西官方合作的灰色区域,涉及对安哥拉农业研究和创新系统的制度支持。相关的巴西受访者认为,"支持安哥拉农村职业培训和社会推广计划"的成功有赖于招募专家参与重要的规划环节,它是国家农业研究所的独特的国际合作项目。一位受访者指出,该项目主要由安哥拉政府通过联合国粮食及农业组织的单边信托基金(UTF)资助,不涉及技术转让和检验评估。

根据巴西政府工作日志的记录,"支持安哥拉农村职业培训和社会推广计划"的预算超过 300 万美元。安哥拉的合作方包括农学研究协会(IIA)和兽医研究所(IIV),它们都位于安哥拉中西部的万博省(Huambo)。本项目第一阶段的主要目标是促进双方机构的协调,更好地衔接研究、推广活动和技术转让,这包括制订一项战略管理和人力资源建设的计划。

受访者还提到了"巴西与安哥拉的粮食安全能力建设"项目,由加拿大瑞尔森大学的食品安全研究中心(CSFS)同里约热内卢联邦农村大学(UFRRJ)的营养与食品安全研究中心(CERESAN)共同领导。加拿大国际发展署(CIDA)从 2004 年开始支持这个为期 6 年的项目。其主要目标是促进葡语国家在食品安全教育上的国际合作。该项目通过线上葡萄牙语课程提升巴西和安哥拉学生的能力,同时还有讲习班和研讨会等学习模式。

尽管可能不会被列为官方技术合作,另两项在食品安全领域的倡议值得关注。第一个倡议旨在支持多部门参与的安哥拉食品与营养安全问题的管理机制的创新。虽然不是官方发展合作,即该倡议并没有来自巴西政府的正式承诺,但巴西国家食品和营养安全委员会(CONSEA)的专业人士在这项合作倡议中发挥了核心作用。巴西国家食品和营养安全委员会创立于十多年前,是沟通政府与公民社会组织的主要机构,负责提出有关巴西食品和营养安全的指导原则和结构化倡议。虽然该机构是咨询协商性质,但巴西国家食品和营养安全委员会对食品和营养安全领域的公共政策有重大的影响力,并能够与巴西最高级别的行政部门取得直接联系。

据参与该倡议的受访者的消息,巴西的参与来自联合国粮食及农业组织罗马总部的要求。这一倡议与联合国粮食及农业组织第一个官方战略的目标有关：帮助消除饥饿、粮食不安全和营养不良。联合国粮食及农业组织聘请了一位巴西顾问参与该倡议，国家农业研究所和农业发展部（MDA）也参与了这一倡议项目。安哥拉政府方面的主要合作方是农业部，具体是戴维·通加（David Tunga）领导的食品安全小组。安哥拉非政府组织"农村发展与环境行动"（ADRA）参加该倡议项目，主要负责与安哥拉公民社会组织的对话。该倡议始于 2013 年在安哥拉举行的一次会议，各参与方在会议中阐述了初步的工作计划。虽然没有巴西机构参加，2014 年还是举行了几次会议。

虽然大部分的筹备工作似乎已经完成，但该倡议项目尚未正式开展。据一位受访者提供的信息，该项目在几个月一直处于停滞状态，原因是与巴西国家食品和营养安全委员会相比，安哥拉在粮食安全政策方面难有质的提高，双方难以协调。另一位受访者指出，整合过程中出现问题的一个原因在于外贸部，[①] 机制的合作意味着从"纵向隶属变成水平合作"，机构隶属关系的变化改变了各部委影响公共政策的机制。

第二项倡议是 2013 年在埃塞尔比亚首都亚的斯亚贝巴的非盟会议上，推出的"非洲零饥饿计划"。该计划是在《统一行动结束非洲饥饿的新伙伴关系宣言》框架下，非盟、巴西卢拉学院和联合国粮食及农业组织之间的一次合作。该计划的主要目的是到 2025 年消除饥饿和贫困，在此之前还有 5 个目标，如到 2017 年，在全面实施本计划的国家减少 40% 的饥饿人口以及在 10 年内减少对外部粮食援助的依赖。该计划的部分资金来自包括安哥拉在内的很多非洲国家支持的非洲国家粮食安全信托基金（2012 年联合国粮食及农业组织在非洲地区会议上启动）。受访者指出，该计划得以在安哥拉实施，关键是因为巴西倡导的"零饥饿计划"适合安哥拉的国情。

结　论

经济和政治之间的相互依赖往往意味着较高的脆弱性和较低的弹性。

---

① 据当地受访者提供的信息，事情发展到这一步是因为之前推动该进程的、担任总统社会问题秘书的罗莎夫人成了外贸部部长。

虽然利用各自的比较优势、自然资源禀赋和资源，政府在努力改善社会经济系统的可持续性，减轻依赖的相关风险。然而，对不同的资源、机构或外国援助的依赖会对国家发展政策的制定和实施产生不同的影响。在这个意义上，管理依赖是开发管理的一个重要方面，特别是对发展中国家的政府而言。

安哥拉自 20 世纪 90 年代末的社会经济轨迹显示了安哥拉政府的优先事项是发展采矿业和石油工业而非吸引外国援助。南北合作所附加的严格政治条件以及安哥拉丰富的自然资源，促成了安哥拉政府的决定。本调研表明，在安哥拉发展合作的项目有更好的协调一致和结果管理。随着金砖国家在安哥拉参与度的不断增加，石油和援助依赖模式受到的影响更加复杂。

与南北合作相比，巴西与安哥拉的卫生与农业合作，无论在援助规模还是数量上都要小得多。然而，巴西在安哥拉和莫桑比克两国最新和最重要的项目都是基于本国经验并强调"结构化"维度的。这不仅符合巴西政府的外交政策，还增强了巴西合作署和国家农业研究所等相关机构在国际和国内工作中特殊的地位和工作原则。这进一步表明，在巴西南南合作问题上，有必要推广"自下而上"和"自上而下"研究方法，不仅要分析巴西合作署在巴西发展合作体系中的作用，还要分析每个参与机构在南南合作中的利害关系。

国内体制和南南利益：巴西与马拉维和莫桑比克农村发展合作的成果

卡罗莱娜·米朗斯·德·卡斯特罗* 著

贾 丁** 译

近年来，来自新兴经济体的公共和私营部门越来越多地在非洲出现，这一现象引起了全世界学者和政策制定者的关注。在一些多边环境中，这些国家已经发挥了积极作用，它们在非洲国家的政治支持下推动了规范和操作上的变革，[①] 并成为非洲大陆重要的投资者。[②] 在对外直接投资方面，中国扮演着重要角色，但其并非是唯一的主角。凭借持续增加的政治和经济存在，巴西与非洲国家的关系在过去十年不断加强。关于这些国家不断扩大的在非洲的利益和战略，以及它们对非洲的影响，最近有很多研究都提出了相关见解。[③] 对于巴西等国对非洲的不断介入，一个流行的观点是：来自新兴世界的国家对非洲国家发展面临的类似挑战更为熟悉，因此可以

---

* 卡罗莱娜·米朗斯·德·卡斯特罗 (Carolina Milhorance de Castro)，巴西大学可持续研究中心 (Center for Sustainable Development, University of Brasilia) 博士后。

** 贾丁，北京大学国际关系学院硕士毕业，现供职于中国国际问题研究院。

① Monica Hirst, "Emerging Powers and Global Governance", Universidad San Andrés, Buenos Aires, 2012, http://www.udesa.edu.ar/files/UAHUMANIDADES/EVENTOS/PAPERHIRST11112.PDF.

② Marin A. Marinov and Svetla T. Marinova, "International Business and Emerging Economies", *Impacts of Emerging Economies and Firms on International Business*, eds. Marin Marinov and Svetla Marinova, Basingstoke: Palgrave Macmillan, 2012.

③ Chris Alden, *China in Africa: Partner, Competitor or Hegemon?* Zed Books, 2007; Jean-Jacques Gabas and Jean-Raphaeël Chaponnieère, *Le Temps de La Chine En Afrique: Enjeux et Réalités Au Sud Du Sahara*, GEMDEV (Group), Hommes et Sociétés, 2012; Lidia Cabral, *Cooperação Brasil-África Para O Desenvolvimento: Caracterização, Tendências E Desafios*, Texto Cindes 26, Rio de Janeiro: Cindes, 2011.

根据自身经验更好地提出解决方案。①

然而，非洲国家的国内体制和政治利益在非洲与中国、巴西等国的关系及其自身发展轨迹中所扮演的角色，却没有引起足够重视。本文旨在探讨非洲国家的国内体制如何与来自新兴国家的援助和投资互动，并在一定程度上改变其影响。根据巴西公私部门在非洲，特别是在莫桑比克和马拉维两国的活动，本文对非洲国家的国内体制和国际机构在对外直接投资和技术合作方面的互动进行了评估。本文基于两个案例进行研究，一是巴西在莫桑比克和马拉维两国农村推广的"非洲粮食采购计划"（PAA Africa）发展合作项目，二是淡水河谷公司在纳卡拉走廊修建铁路的发展项目。在巴西公私部门促进该地区经济一体化的能力方面，本文也提出了一定见解。国内体制是指在具体政策之外，国家、社会和国家社会关系具有的制度特征。②

巴西与马拉维和莫桑比克关系的背景

卢拉总统时期（2003～2010年），巴非关系显著发展。在卢拉的两个任期内，政治对话、技术合作、投资和贸易促进了巴西与非洲国家关系的深化，其中技术合作得到了越来越多的财政支持。③ 新设立的几座大使馆使巴西在非洲的大使馆数量升至世界第五位。此外，卢拉政府出台了旨在加强与非洲经济关系的战略，不仅要巩固贸易关系，还要发展巴西在非洲的公司。④ 这些与巴西国内抗击贫困和饥饿的努力有力结合，共同支持集中在社会问题和经验分享上的外交议题。⑤ 2011年，罗塞夫当选巴西总统，

---

① Iara Costa Leite, Bianca Suyama and Melissa Pomeroy, *Africa-Brazil Co-Operation in Social Protection: Drivers, Lessons and Shifts in the Engagement of the Brazilian Ministry of Social Development*, WIDER Working Paper, 2013.

② Thomas Risse-Kappen, *Bringing Transnational Relations Back in: Non-State Actors, Domestic Structures and International Institutions*, Cambridge University Press, 1995.

③ Carolina Milhorance de Castro and Frédéric Goulet, "L'essor Des Coopérations Sud-Sud: Le Brésil En Afrique et Le Cas Du Secteur Agricole", *Techniques Financières et Développement*, no. 105, December 2011.

④ Matthew Flynn, "Between Subimperialism and Globalization A Case Study in the Internationalization of Brazilian Capital", *Latin American Perspectives* 34, no. 6, November 1, 2007, pp. 9 – 27.

⑤ Iara Costa Leite, Bianca Suyama and Melissa Pomeroy, *Africa – Brazil Co – Operation in Social Protection: Drivers, Lessons and Shifts in the Engagement of the Brazilian Ministry of Social Development*, WIDER Working Paper, 2013.

虽然与卢拉出自同一政党并继承了前任大多数的政令，但她的外交风格和外交政策倾向都有些许不同。新总统面临一个不太有利的国际经济环境，经济议程已经成为后金融危机时代的重要议程。

如前所述，新兴经济体的崛起不仅增加了其对外国直接投资流入的吸引力，而且使本国企业在全球对外直接投资市场中更具竞争力。[①] 在本国企业高度国际化的过程中，巴西巩固了自身地位。[②] 巴西政府曾试图出台一项战略，使其在商品和服务出口方面更具竞争力，并同政治承诺和长远规划联系起来，2013 年其主动免除几个非洲国家的债务，就是一个例证。[③] 对商品出口领域的公共资助机制，被认为是巴西对非洲商业政策的重要抓手，巴西国家经济社会发展银行（BNDES）是出口信贷方面最为活跃的公共机构。[④] 这些机制有利于商品出口和国有大型企业的服务出口。为了探究并克服巩固经济关系方面的瓶颈，巴西发展工业和贸易部（MDIC）还成立了"非洲贸易战略研究"（GTEX Africa）工作小组。巴西国家经济社会发展银行也与非洲多边金融机构建立了更为紧密的关系，旨在建立共同筹资机制，并促进信息交流。另外，为了创造支持对外投资和出口方面更灵活的条件，该行自 2007 年以来经历了重要的机构改革。

葡语非洲国家，特别是莫桑比克和安哥拉，是巴西在非洲的主要伙伴，这很大程度上是因为语言和历史纽带。就技术合作而言，莫桑比克是巴西的头号伙伴，同时，莫桑比克也是巴西企业国际化的一个重要目的地，尤其是采矿行业和基础设施建设行业的企业。虽然两国外交关系的建立可以追溯到莫桑比克独立伊始，但直到 21 世纪两国关系才真正得到加深。两国的贸易关系也在这一时期显著增强，2008～2012 年，巴莫两国之

① Marin A. Marinov and Svetla T. Marinova, "International Business and Emerging Economies", *Impacts of Emerging Economies and Firms on International Business*, eds. Marin Marinov and Svetla Marinova, Basingstoke: Palgrave Macmillan, 2012.

② Matthew Flynn, "Between Subimperialism and Globalization A Case Study in the Internationalization of Brazilian Capital", *Latin American Perspectives* 34, no. 6, November 1, 2007, pp. 9 – 27.

③ Alessandra Scangarelli Brites et al., "Os BRICS na África: a diversificação das parcerias e a contribuição da cooperação sul-sul para o desenvolvimento do continente", Século XXI 3, no. 2, January 14, 2013, pp. 95 – 116.

④ 巴西开发银行（Brazilian Development Bank, BNDES），也被称为巴西国家经济社会发展银行，它是一个与巴西发展、工业和贸易部相关联的联邦上市公司。——译者注

间的贸易增长超过了 300% ，巴西的进口规模也扩大了十倍以上。在莫桑比克的官方合作员工数量和国际伙伴数量证明，莫桑比克对于巴西以农业、教育和卫生为主的国际合作有极大重要性。[①] 此外，两国合作正从一次性的培训方式向机制化转变，在这个意义上，双方关系也得到了加强和深化。

在卢拉政府亲近非洲的背景下，马拉维等非洲国家也在最近与巴西建立了关系。2013 年 6 月，巴西正式设立驻马拉维大使馆，这既遵守了两国于 2009 年马拉维前总统宾古·瓦·穆塔里卡（Bingu wa Mutharika）访问巴西期间所共同立下的约定，也符合巴西在该地区不断增长的利益。双边关系包括了多方面共同利益，如生物燃料行业潜力的探索、消除饥饿政策的经验分享和淡水河谷公司的私人投资等。淡水河谷公司正在修建将横穿马拉维、连接其在莫桑比克的矿业投资地太特（Tete）和印度洋纳卡拉港（Nacala Port）的铁路。马拉维前外交部部长埃弗拉伊姆·丘梅（Ephraim Chiume）也曾表示，该国的利益正被纳入在莫桑比克进行的合作项目中，比如，由日本、巴西、莫桑比克三方在莫桑比克北部纳卡拉走廊共同开发的商业性农业项目"热带草原计划"。有些项目，如由三方合作的在马拉维和莫桑比克的棉花项目，在巴西大使馆设立之前勘查阶段就已经完成了。[②]

虽然莫桑比克和马拉维是邻国并有着广泛的社会经济联系，但两国在历史上一直相互仇恨，甚至在近代促进双边合作的努力下依然如此。[③] 拉尔巴哈指出，这种关系起源于 20 世纪 70 年代末 80 年代初莫桑比克内战期间马拉维对莫桑比克反对派游击运动的支持。早在 60 年代，纳卡拉（Nacala）铁路就是该地区的争论焦点：当时南非种族隔离政府愿意以"软贷款"的形式向马拉维提供金融援助以修建铁路，在这样的背景下，马拉维政府选择了反对莫桑比克解放阵线领导的反葡萄牙殖民的独立斗争，即使

① Sérgio Chichava et al. , "Brazil and China in Mozambican Agriculture: Emerging Insights from the Field", *Ids Bulletin* 44, no. 4, 2013, pp. 101 – 115.

② SERE/MRE, "Encontro com o Ministro de Negócios Estrangeiros do Malaui. Entrega de cópias figuradas. Relato. ", Circular Telegráfica, April 7, 2013, Itamaraty.

③ Aditi Lalbahadur, *Mozambique and Malawi: Recalibrating a Difficult Relationship*, Policy Briefing, SAIIA Policy Briefings, Johannesburg: South African Institute of International Affairs, June 2013.

在莫桑比克独立后仍然保持着对莫领导人的怀疑。

20世纪70年代，马拉维前总统伊斯·班达（Joyce Banda）通过推动区域一体化，使两国关系得到了和解。[①] 莫桑比克内战期间，反对派"莫桑比克全国抵抗运动"（RENAMO）破坏了本国的运输通道，这对于马拉维的影响很深[②]：纳卡拉铁路虽然仍可以通行，但路况恶劣，运力极其有限。在20世纪90年代的民主化后，两国关系尽管实现了正常化，但一直保持冷淡。进入21世纪，两国在贸易和基础设施领域达成多项重要协议，如2005年的《双边优惠贸易协定》（*Bilateral Preferential Trade Agreement*）、2007年的《夏尔—赞比西河航道发展备忘录》（*MoU on the development of the Shire-Zambezi Waterway*）和2010年的《纳卡拉走廊发展备忘录》（*MoU on the Nacala Development Corridor*）。

莫桑比克、马拉维两国在基础设施方面都面临着紧迫的挑战，电力和交通项目被投资者和发展机构视为应对这些挑战的必由之路。[③] 此外，马拉维对出海口的需求和近期的基础设施项目也有助于增加两国的相互依存性。但一些边境和外交事件，如一艘运往马拉维恩桑杰港（Nsanje Port）的驳船被莫桑比克当局扣留，弱化了本就脆弱的和解努力。恩桑杰港是夏尔—赞比西河航道工程的一部分，该工程使夏尔—赞比西河与印度洋之间可以实现通航。2012年以来，马拉维前总统乔伊斯·班达积极推动两国关系改善，强调与莫桑比克双边关系的战略重要性，并在两国共同面临发展挑战的领域开放合作。

共享农村公共政策：因地制宜的倡议

巴西的技术合作依赖于这样一种思路：新兴世界的伙伴与巴西面临着

---

① David Robinson, "Renamo, Malawi and the Struggle to Succeed Banda", *Eras*, no. 11, November 2009.

② David Robinson, "Renamo, Malawi and the Struggle to Succeed Banda", Eras, no. 11, November 2009.

③ Aditi Lalbahadur, *Mozambique and Malawi: Recalibrating a Difficult Relationship*, Policy Briefing, SAIIA Policy Briefings, Johannesburg: South African Institute of International Affairs, June 2013.

相似的发展挑战，因此可以根据巴西的经验，制定出合适的应对之策。[1]
巴西的发展战略在一定程度上减少了贫困和不平等，这引起了世界的关
注，特别是在 2007 年到 2008 年的国际粮食和经济危机期间。顺利渡过这
次危机后，巴西在外交、技术和政策方面得到了肯定，成为农业和粮食安
全领域政策对话和合作的重要参与者。[2] 从人口增长的角度来看，粮食危
机使农业和粮食安全重新成为国际议程的首要议题。在 2010 年的 "巴
西—非洲：粮食安全、抵抗饥饿和农村发展对话会"（Brazil-Africa Dialogue
on Food Security，the Fight against Hunger and Rural Development）上，巴非
领导人讨论了巴西与撒哈拉以南非洲的农村合作政策。 "零饥饿计划"
（Zero Hunger Strategy）是国际公认的经验之一，不管是巴西国内还是国际
社会都督促其与撒哈拉以南非洲国家分享该计划框架。受巴西 "粮食采购
计划"（PAA）的启发，"非洲粮食采购计划"成为这一合作倡议的主要渠
道。[3] 该计划由巴西政府、联合国粮食及农业组织（FAO）、世界粮食计划
署（WFP）联合发起，旨在 "提高非洲国家农民和弱势群体的粮食安全及
营养摄入"。[4] 其他合作伙伴还有提供知识共享支持的英国国际发展部
（DFID）。

　　巴西的 "粮食采购计划"展示了一个新农业政策模型，该模型在提高
小农户收入的同时，还能帮助陷入粮食不安全状况的人口。凭借巴西社会
发展部（MDS）和土地开发部（MDA）的资源，以及国家粮食供应公司
（CONAB）、各州和直辖市的共同努力，该计划为家庭农场产品的商业化创
造了一个新的市场，产品在该市场通过买卖进入社会援助网络，这使公共
储备、价格监管以及采购制度（基于粮食安全网的采购）得以建立，而不
需要一个公开的招标程序。虽然缺乏对该方案具体结果和其对人们生活影
响的研究，但是 "粮食采购计划"已经展示了一个国家驱动的结构性需求

---

[1] ABC/MRE, *Manual de Gestão Da Cooperação Técnica Sul-Sul*, Versão externa, Brasília：
Agência Brasileira de Cooperação/Ministério das Relações Exteriores, 2013；Costa Leite, Suyama and Pomeroy, *Africa-Brazil Co-Operation in Social Protection*.

[2] F. Pierri, "How Brazil's Agrarian Dynamics Shape Development Cooperation in Africa", 2013.

[3] Iara Costa Leite, Bianca Suyama and Melissa Pomeroy, *Africa – Brazil Co – Operation in Social
Protection*：*Drivers, Lessons and Shifts in the Engagement of the Brazilian Ministry of Social Development*, WIDER Working Paper, 2013.

[4] PAA Africa, "PAA Africa：Purchase from Africans for Africa", PAA Africa Website, 2013.

模式。① "公立学校供餐计划"（PNAE）是另一个结构性需求的主要来源，其 30% 的食物来源于家庭农场。②

"非洲粮食采购计划"包括在埃塞俄比亚、马拉维、莫桑比克、尼日尔和塞内加尔的五个子项目。该项目将农业恢复和粮食援助的紧急措施同小农户结构化需求的发展战略结合了起来。③ 其目的是促使政府在援助粮食的公共采购问题上采取更长的过渡战略。在莫桑比克，三个试点项目都在太特省（分别在 Angonia、Cahora Bassa 和 Changara），包括农业投入的分布、生产系统的培训和采收后的处理。鉴于粮食采购计划本地采购项目在国内不同地方实行，"非洲粮食采购计划"试图借参与"公立学校供餐计划"（PRONAE）的机会，建立一个模板，以供全国借鉴本地采购项目的经验。包括园艺在内的多样化生产将在第二阶段开始实施。此外，为了与世界粮食计划署的直接采购项目形成互补，地方政府需评估测试并加强政府的采购能力。

试点的第一阶段就遇到了一些挑战。联合国粮食及农业组织莫桑比克办公室为期五个月的参与—观察—研究、在太特地区进行的实地调研、个人访谈以及"粮食采购计划"工作小组内的争论证实了如下情况：位于太特省的产粮区远离粮食不安全区（约 400 千米），这意味着粮食运输造成的高额后勤成本，并导致一个问题，一旦试点项目关闭，当地组织是否有能力继续该计划？此外还有其他的一些制度瓶颈，例如，莫桑比克的采购框架要求农民组织在行政审批、财政登记、创建银行账户方面通过各种繁复的官僚程序，这对于文盲率高、经济条件差的农民来说，是难以完成的。

此外，小农户很难参与强制性的投标流程，这使其无法同大、中型农场主和当地商人竞争。另外，与其他社会政策对话的不足，也加大了实施跨产业政策的挑战。然而，在莫桑比克的项目已经算得上是参与进程的开

① Fabio Veras et al., *Structured Demand and Smallholder Farmers in Brazil*: *The Case of PAA and PNAE*, IPC Technical Paper, Brasília: International Policy Centre for Inclusive Growth（IPC-IG）/WFP Centre of Excellence Against Hunge, October 2013.

② Joseé Graziano da Silva et al., *The Fome Zero（Zero Hunger）Program*: *The Brazilian Experience*, Brasília: Ministry of Agrarian Development, 2011.

③ PAA Africa, "PAA Africa: Purchase from Africans for Africa", PAA Africa Website, 2013.

始，与民间社会团体的合作将继续深化与国家机构的政策对话，并促进当地采购理念的发展。这种合作也来自莫桑比克组织同参与"粮食采购计划"的巴西组织建立的关系，这些组织从该计划中受益，并认同该计划在发展家庭农业这一领域中发挥的作用。

皮耶雷认为，巴西的家庭农业政策框架是一个基于国家领导的特定公共政策和规章的实施过程。因此，在分享经验时，金融能力、民间社会的作用以及非洲农民与巴西农民之间的差异性和相似性等因素必须被考虑进去。农业和粮食安全策略依赖于强有力的制度化过程，以及实现财政可持续化的过程的财政能力。[1] 同样，现金转移方案被认为是昂贵且复杂的。[2]即使是在巴西，除了政治滥用的风险，该计划也面临着一些挑战：最弱势的生产者和运输、支付机制及扩大规模等因素造成的操作障碍。[3]

在这种情况下，了解国际项目所有权的动态的政治经济学是至关重要的。[4] 有学者认为，所有权是期权、优先权、内容和发展机会相互竞争和影响的结果。社会和经济的发展意味着对所有权的持续纷争，或是对发展动力、机构、经济和社会影响的争夺。因此，所有权本身的意义不如社会和政治互动，因为影响政治选择的权力往往在互动中形成。在不同的社会经济和政治背景下，不同的社会主体由于目的和利益不同对所有权概念的看法也存在差异。例如，放弃所有权的实践已在受援国实现，这使得由援助者承担改革的高社会成本的责任成为可能。

在制度化市场和学校供餐计划的案例中，对国家主导的投资和社会保障政策的要求水平是非常高的，这可能引起政府在这类项目上的退缩。另

---

① Francesco Maria Pierri, "How Brazil's Agrarian Dynamics Shape Development Cooperation in Africa", *IDS Bulletin*, Volume 44, Issue 4, 2013, https：//doi. org/10. 1111/1759 – 5436. 12043.

② Iara Costa Leite, Melissa Pomeroy and Bianca Suyama, *Africa – Brazil Co – Operation in Social Protection*, 10 November 2015, https：//doi. org/10. 1002/jid. 3191.

③ Maya Takagi, "Food and Nutrition Security and Cash Transfer Programs", *The Fome Zero（Zero Hunger）Program*：*The Brazilian Experience*, Joseé Graziano da Silva et al. , Brasília：Ministry of Agrarian Development, 2011；Ryan Nehring and Ben McKay, *Scaling up Local Development Initiatives*：*Brazil's Food Acquisition Programme*, Working Paper, International Policy Centre for Inclusive Growth, 2013.

④ Carlos Nuno Castel-Branco, *Aid Dependency and Development*：*A Question of Ownership? A Critical View*, Working Paper, Colecção de Workin G Papers Do IESE, Maputo：IESE, February 2008.

外，莫桑比克政府对投资高农业潜力地区给予优先，包括扶持在生产和服务领域活跃的私人企业，同时专注于使用大规模畜力牵引，采用成套技术，推广机械化、加工和销售。①

相反，在马拉维的试点项目则依赖于政府部门的大力支持。该项目计划将学校供餐计划扩展到马拉维南部的曼戈切（Mangochi）和帕隆贝（Phalombe）。学校将直接采购，而农民组织则将向附近 30 千米以内的学校提供农产品，以缩短粮食运输的距离及减少由此产生的费用。② 值得注意的是，马拉维是一个人口稠密的国家，全国 1500 万人口中有 85% 生活在农村，并从事与农业相关的工作。与莫桑比克相比，马拉维的大多数人口和生产活动集中在开展项目的中部和南部地区。③ 自 2010 年起，马拉维政府通过一系列公共政策拨款来支持学校供餐计划。

推动"粮食采购计划"在马拉维顺利实施的因素包括：集中的生产和消费区；行政机构保证学校供餐计划的批准和预算；简化采购规则，使小农户可以参与，学校可以直接采购。此外，在目标地区的一些权力下放举措也有助于快速动员公众和非政府行为体，以找到合适的解决方案。然而，项目的持续成功仍面临一定障碍，如马拉维对化肥和杂交种子的使用政策就使其无法像莫桑比克那样有效地讨论可持续农业系统。

在推广服务上缺乏流动性的弱点限制了马拉维和莫桑比克生产力和生产率的提高。同样地，在这种背景下，两国也都面临着援助依赖的约束和社会保障政策带来的挑战。但在地理位置、领土规模和矿产资源等方面，莫桑比克拥有一些战略优势，这些因素会影响其与援助者谈判时的地位。

马拉维的学校供餐计划始于 1999 年。世界粮食计划署资助了 24 所学校。2007 年内阁决定扩大这个计划，并确定应该制定一个战略以保证这一扩张。巴西方面，根据笔者对该计划一位知情者的访谈，世界粮食计划署

---

① Ministry of Agriculture, *Strategic Plan for Agriculture Developmen-PEDSA* 2010 – 2019, Republic of Mozambique, 2010, http://www.safi – research.org/wp – content/uploads/2015/10/2010_PEDSA_FINAL – English_22_Nov.pdf.

② PAA Africa, "PAA Africa: Purchase from Africans for Africa", PAA Africa Website, 2013.

③ Jacob Ricker-Gilbert, Charles Jumbe and Jordan Chamberlin, "How Does Population Density Influence Agricultural Intensification and Productivity? Evidence from Malawi," *Food Policy* 48, October 2014, pp. 114 – 128.

反饥饿卓越中心（Centre of Excellence against Hunger）在提供有关巴西经验的信息方面发挥了重要作用。在马拉维前总统正式访问巴西期间，学校供餐计划是其优先议程，马巴两国领导人的会谈也推动了起草一份国家公共政策提案的目标，以保证学校供餐计划的可持续性。制订国家计划和政策是从援助国甚至政府预算中吸引资金的关键。根据笔者对该计划另一位知情人的访谈，该提案草案应在 2014 年总统选举后提交内阁。除了"非洲粮食采购计划"，该国也在实施其他基于采购、学校菜园推广和市场准入这三大不同模型的试点方案。

此外，一个独立的、由教育部部长主持的部门正主导着一项旨在提高马拉维学生健康和营养水平的工作。但就执行情况而言，负责管理的是地区级政府，而来自不同部门的地方工作人员则直接参与其中。马拉维对该计划的实施比莫桑比克顺利，因为其所需的生产规模远低于后者。在被选为项目试点的地区有很多合法化的、强化的农民协会，以及满足学校市场需求的足够生产供给品。

由于马拉维的学校在之前已经被授权进行材料采购，"粮食采购计划"利用相同的结构，培养学校的粮食采购能力。学校直接从当地进行食物采购，是该计划在马拉维的一项概念创新。鉴于采购量不大，采购程序被简化为直接协商和购买，由地区议会负责。虽然有这样的有利因素，但马拉维市场还是受到了生产量和价格不稳定的影响。对于更广泛的体制化市场产生的影响，需要一个更深入的分析。

托马斯·里瑟－卡彭（Thomas Risse-Kappen）① 研究了国家和跨国关系在各领域的互动，认为国内体制和国际体系在国际社会的非国家行为主体网络中起到了居中调和的作用。国内体制有可能决定了跨国行为体是否有进入政治系统的渠道及其为争取联盟而改变政策的要求。根据文献，我们认为，国内体制会调解、过滤和折射国际行为体（在本案例中为巴西的公共和私人联盟）的努力，影响不同领域的政策。其影响政策变化的能力取决于国内联盟的构建进程和建成的制度结构，正如在马拉维和莫桑比克推行学校供餐计划的案例中观察到的。文章将继续以这两国为案例，说明

① Thomas Risse－Kappen, *Bringing Transnational Relations Back In: Non－State Actors, Domestic Structures and International Institutions*, Cambridge University Press, 1995.

除了国内联盟的构建进程，监管框架和对话机制也可能改变外国投资的影响，并影响政策变化。

基础设施投资：区域整合的机会和挑战

巴西对非洲出口商品和服务能够在多样化的地区展开，依赖于公众的支持，即便大公司也是如此。巴西对非投资主要集中在基础设施、能源和矿产领域，这使资金流向对政府间的决策非常敏感。[1] 自21世纪以来，巴西对莫桑比克的投资大幅上升，淡水河谷公司在其中起到了重要的作用。该公司投资的莫阿蒂泽（Moatize）煤矿和塞纳走廊（Sena Corridor）项目已投入运营，莫阿蒂泽2号煤矿和纳卡拉走廊项目则正在开发中。

淡水河谷公司的存在已被媒体、民间社会团体和学术界广泛讨论，特别是针对居民因莫阿蒂泽煤矿搬迁的问题。[2] 淡水河谷公司投资了44亿美元来翻新和扩建连接莫桑比克和马拉维的纳卡拉走廊铁路以供其煤炭运输。[3] 这条912千米铁路的海上终端位于纳卡拉港，那里正在建设一个深水港口。该铁路每年可以运输1800万吨的煤炭。

淡水河谷公司正在修建纳卡拉铁路马拉维段137千米长的铁路。2011年，其子公司通过与马拉维政府签署铁路修建特许权协议进入该国。这些位于莫桑比克和马拉维境内的铁路由北部走廊发展公司（CDN）和中东非洲铁路公司（CEAR）所有，而这两个公司都是纳卡拉走廊发展公司（SCDN）占51%股份的子公司。该铁路还将为赞比亚卢巴姆贝（Lubambe）铜矿的运输发挥重要作用。

莫桑比克政府的期望是，除货运外，该铁路还可用作客运；而对于马拉维，考虑到其内陆国的性质，铁路是货物进出口和乘客运输的新选择；但这些期望还没有实现或得到具体讨论的迹象。值得注意的是，由于国际

①　World Bank and IPEA, *Ponte Sobre O Atlântico*: *Brasil E Africa Subsaariana-Parceria Sul-Sul Para O Crescimento*, Brasilia, 2011.

②　Sergio Chichava, et al., "Brazil and China in Mozambican Agriculture: Emerging Insights from the Field", *IDS Bulletin*. 44（4）, 2013, pp. 106 – 107.

③　VALE, "Vale Highlights Its Projects in Mozambique at an Event in Africa", *VALE*, February 17, 2014, http://www.vale.com/mozambique/EN/aboutvale/news/Pages/vale-destaca-proje-tos-em-mocambique-em-feira-na-africa.aspx.

市场的矿产品价格下跌，淡水河谷公司不得不出售其在纳卡拉走廊的部分资产，该公司最近就宣布日本三井公司将参与其煤矿—铁路的复合投资。

针对淡水河谷公司带来的影响，巴西、加拿大、智利和莫桑比克的非政府组织联合创立了一个国际网络来批评该公司的可持续发展政策。它批评淡水河谷公司在莫桑比克的投资，并指责该国采矿业对社会发展特别是农村地区的发展①无所作为。莫桑比克政府为此制定了一个新的采矿规范方案，包括国家优先采购，并要求采矿权和股权的转让需要得到莫桑比克法律和政府部门审批。

此外，淡水河谷公司 2012 年的年度报告显示，"更严格的要求可能导致成本增加和项目实施的延迟"。② 对莫桑比克矿业企业财政激励的减少，意味着生产成本的增加，在国际市场矿产品价格疲弱的情况下，这几乎使得矿业投资无利可图。虽然已出售部分资产，但是控制纳卡拉走廊物流基础设施的战略依然符合淡水河谷公司的利益。其他公司如力拓公司（Rio Tinto）则决定以低于当前市场价格的价格，将其在太特省的项目出售给一家印度集团。

经历了莫阿蒂泽项目的批评后，淡水河谷公司在其纳卡拉走廊项目中改变了居民安置工作的做法。因为当地社区问题具有长期性、持续性，该公司行动的连续性极为重要。莫桑比克近期公共意识的觉醒和《土地法》等法律框架的推进也是巴西公司面对的新情况。在莫桑比克，随着近年来采矿业的急速发展以及如何权衡社区公共土地权与私人投资间的激烈争论，土地问题也关乎政治利益。

1997 年 7 月，莫桑比克通过了《土地法》（*Law 19/97*），之后又通过了《农村土地法令》（*Decree 66/98*），其目的在于支持农村社区的土地权益，并鼓励私人投资。法律体系在一定程度上为当地社区提供了土地使用权保障，但是，大多数农村居民并不了解他们的权利或缺乏资金和技术支持去登记土地权。自殖民地时期开始耕地分配就没有发生过显著变化。在

---

① João Mosca and Tomas Selemane, "Mega-Projectos No Meio Rural, Desenvolvimento Do Territorio E Pobreza", *Desafios Para Moçambique* 2012, Maputo: IESE, 2012, pp. 231 – 255, http://www.iese.ac.mz/lib/publication/livros/des2012/IESE_Des2012_12. MegRur. pdf.

② VALE, *Delivering Value through Capital Efficiency*: *Annual Report* 2012, VALE SA, 2013, p. 74.

此背景下，自《土地法》批准以来，民间社会团体就开始帮助农民和社区行使这些被赋予的权利。①

与莫阿蒂泽项目相比，纳卡拉走廊项目使用了不同的安置方法，由于采取线形轴运作，每平方千米需要被转移的家庭数目相对较少。在已经举行的补偿协商会中，大多数人选择了经济补偿。此外，企业也经常给当地领导提供补贴来处理社区期望解决的问题，这样往往先行解决了企业与社区的一些利益冲突，因为在大部分受到铁路发展影响的地区，当地传统的领导者是非常强大的。此外，在农民并不拥有土地所有权的情况中，他们也收到了约定的经济补偿，补偿范围是"土地以上的东西"：房屋、设施和一些果树，但并不包括全部财产。这种模式已经在修建铁路的纳卡拉和贝拉地区实施。除去"不拥有土地所有权"的部分，根据国家法律，该模式是有效的。

在马拉维，土地问题还没有得到相同程度的认识。淡水河谷公司刚刚开始在该国的移民安置工作，而这个过程预期将由当地政府主导。马拉维的土地制度基于1967年的土地法，该法受到殖民地时期英国法律的影响。法案将土地分成三种法定类型：传统土地、私人土地和公共土地：第一种不承认永久所有权，但保证使用权是不可剥夺的；私人土地是由个人或机构独占、持有和占用的；公共土地归政府所有，并用于公共用途。因此，独立后马拉维在土地使用权和产权的制度安排以及土地治理的内在目标方面并没有重大变化。

在这种背景下，私有制和法律保障是众望所归，习惯法下传统土地则应被视为保留地，可在之后建立私人和公共所有权。② 当地社区有义务通过社区协商证明待租赁土地没有被有效利用或兼并，但只有少数投资者能够承受土地收购和加工的高成本。在土地租赁方面，当地酋长往往分为支持和反对两派，这导致对于传统土地是否可以被占用或空置问题的看法呈现高度分化的态势。③ 母系社会和土地权力下放是大多数马拉维人的传统规范，特别

① João Mosca, *Políticas Agrarias de（em）Moçambique*（1975 - 2009），1ª ed.，Lisboa：Maputo：Escolar，2010.

② Blessings Chinsinga，"Seeds and Subsidies：The Political Economy of Input Programmes in Malawi"，*IDS Bulletin* 42，no. 4（2011），pp. 59 - 68.

③ Blessings Chinsinga，"Seeds and Subsidies：The Political Economy of Input Programmes in Malawi，"*IDS Bulletin* 42，no. 4（2011），pp. 59 - 68.

是在中部和南部地区，然而正式的土地制度是仿照英式父系制度建立的；但对于大多数人尤其是小农户来说，在土地权属关系上还是遵照传统。①

面对马拉维国内情况的挑战，淡水河谷公司分析了一些该国政府与莫桑比克政府的差异，考虑到马拉维政府增加投资并建造另一条印度洋道路的愿望，设计了让马拉维政府更多参与的模式。土地供应仍然是一个重要的问题，特别是在农村人口密度非常高的南部地区。高人口密度还是会影响农业集约化和农户，因为信息流要增加、市场和机构要发展、交易成本要降低，供给能否满足这些需求面临挑战。但研究表明，在马拉维农村人口密度高的地区，农场规模和实际农业工资率在降低，玉米价格较高，每公顷的化肥使用量在增加。② 因此，虽然需要安置的家庭数量相对较少，社区的可持续发展仍应被考虑到项目运作进展中。

另一个亟待解决的重要问题是铁路沿线社区搬迁对当地商品生产和销售的影响。当地商品的生产和买卖活动是农村社区的重要经济来源，但这一问题在项目可行性方案中还未得到完全解决，马拉维政府也没有制订任何安置计划。与莫桑比克相比，马拉维没有明确的指导方针和相关立法，这将在根本上阻碍谈判进程，也使得地方政府与地方领导人在执行移民安置活动时有更多的自主权。该公司的工作人员认为，在马拉维比在莫桑比克更容易联系当地政府和社区。在其他方面，该公司可以在任何工作时间与矿业部协商，这恰恰显示了快速完成项目的利益所在。马拉维政府希望能通过降低运输成本受益，但淡水河谷公司尚未讨论过同意政府使用铁路来运送产品的可能性。

淡水河谷公司的物流项目满足了区域在地理上整合的需要，包括世界银行与其伙伴共同推动的纳卡拉走廊开发项目（Nacala Corridor Development Project）。其目的是改善从赞比亚到莫桑比克的道路交通和贸易便利性，以及这些国家的运输服务。从马拉维到海港的高额长途运输费是其在地区和国际贸易中面临的一个主要障碍。同样在莫桑比克，非洲开发银行（AfDB）、日本

---

① Erling Berge et al. , "Lineage and Land Reforms in Malawi: Do Matrilineal and Patrilineal Land-holding Systems Represent a Problem for Land Reforms in Malawi?" *Land Use Policy* 41, November 2014, pp. 61 – 69.

② Ricker-Gilbert, Jumbe and Chamberlin, "How Does Population Density Influence Agricultural Intensification and Productivity?".

国际协力机构（JICA）和韩国进出口银行共同出资，在马拉维和莫桑比克的边界修建了一条从楠普拉（Nampula）经祈朋得（Chiponde）到利欣加（Lichinga）的公路。当被问及这些举措是否巩固了纳卡拉走廊的农业项目时，"热带草原计划"的工作人员只肯定了一体化在运输基础设施方面的努力。

在马拉维运作的跨国机构与东道国的民间社会保持着一定的互动，特别是一些涉足采矿领域的机构在这方面很有经验。如孟祖贝（Mzembe）和米顿（Meaton）所举的例子，作为澳大利亚一家跨国矿业公司的子公司，经营马拉维第一个铀矿的非洲帕拉丁公司（Paladin Africa）就在企业社会责任问题上受到民间社会团体及当地社区等外部压力的强烈影响。[1] 对于投资者而言，马拉维的这种情况显示了该国的"司法不安全"。在马拉维和莫桑比克，矿区周边的社区、民众及一些民间团体希望跨国公司可以扮演政府缺失的角色。然而，尽管这些非洲东道国的法律框架相对复杂且并非总能充分考虑到社区的土地权利和福祉，跨国公司还是应该在不对社区产生偏见或是代替国家的角色的基础上解决这些问题。

最后，巴西在外交上建议将纳卡拉走廊铁路及其参与的巴西、马拉维、莫桑比克三边倡议作为加强区域一体化的工具。这项三边倡议包括一份目前正在定稿阶段的备忘录，旨在支持马拉维和莫桑比克在采矿、运输、物流、能源、农业和林业领域开展经济、贸易和投资项目——这是一份一揽子合作协议，而不是要建立一个自由贸易区。但马拉维官员指出，该协议无法解决本国的具体需要，且其无法预见协议效益。除了上述领域，马拉维还对农业发展和乙醇制造有着浓厚的兴趣。在采矿业方面，虽然进行了矿产勘探研究，但矿业部官员表示还没有找到合适的投资地点。

因此，在莫马两国，与巴西的双边协定都处于优先地位。目前，巴莫两国正就一份谅解备忘录展开谈判，这是由巴西政府在合作和投资领域提出的协议。该协议由巴西发展工业和贸易部出面协商，旨在通过简化商人流动和资本转移等促进投资。在这一点上，从巴西进货的莫桑比克个体商人将从这些关于跨国迁移的协议中受益。

---

① Andrew Ngawenja Mzembe and Julia Meaton, "Driving Corporate Social Responsibility in the Malawian Mining Industry: A Stakeholder Perspective: Driving CSR in the Malawian Mining Industry: A Stakeholder Perspective," *Corporate Social Responsibility and Environmental Management* 21, no. 4 (July 2014): 189 – 201.

结　论

　　2003～2013 年，新兴经济体与非洲国家的关系持续升温，这令学术圈、政界和媒体对这些关系动机、方法和后果开始争论。巴西在这波国际浪潮中发挥了关键作用，尤其是对莫桑比克这类国家；不过，从卢拉政府开始，通过政府和私人的多样化尝试，巴非伙伴关系已扩展到葡语国家或有历史关系的国家以外，如马拉维。而国内体制所起的作用，已被确定为研究议程的一个重要补充。本着为这场争论贡献初步成果的目的，本文试图展示在受到巴西相似的介入时，马拉维和莫桑比克体现出不同的国内体制以及两国对公私部门互动的回应。尽管有着不同的历史关系，但巴西选中了这两个相邻的国家，并在两国推行一些类似的综合性项目。

　　本文分析的项目和协议都是由同一巴西机构在莫桑比克和马拉维两国提出的。"非洲粮食采购计划"作为一个试点项目，旨在分享巴西在对抗饥饿和提高家庭农业部门效率的经验。莫桑比克和马拉维都将学校供餐计划作为市场制度化的优先事项。但是，在试点执行和扩大公共政策讨论的过程中，两国的制度条件和政策路线都是不同的。马拉维的农业、政治和体制条件以及更灵活的采购流程有利于"非洲粮食采购计划"的实施。这些条件可以与地区政府在学校供餐计划中的政治利益、社区的强势介入和政府对这些行动的预算分配相结合。

　　在莫桑比克，企业采取了不同的路径，从制定一个国家方案开始，这同时也是对试点模式的检验。莫桑比克的农业政策试图把农民与市场联系起来，并扶持私人部门，但帮助农民应对市场的行动和社会保障政策需要大量的财力和人力资源，这是莫桑比克政府无法提供的。另外，在莫桑比克的项目有较多的民间社会团体参与，这源于莫桑比克组织与巴西组织建立的关系，这种参与有助于在全国推进制度化的市场举措。

　　具体到淡水河谷公司，纳卡拉走廊铁路项目承诺运输旅客和货物，并为区域一体化做出努力。由于其内陆国性质及与邻国恶劣的历史关系，马拉维是最受影响和最有兴趣促进一体化的国家之一。土地治理和使用方面的问题应得到足够重视。多年来，莫桑比克一直面临着大型项目的挑战，而现在，应对这些投资的制度条件已逐步建立。此外，为回应民间社会的努力，社会控制体制也已经建立。

　　在马拉维，自殖民时期以来，土地权利一直未实现，社区权利也不是很清晰。为实现国家利益利用铁路的可能性和条件尚未确立。同时，巴西也在通过其他三边倡议拓展其在非洲的存在和影响力。然而，合作伙伴在领导权上的矛盾也使协议能否得到全面执行成为问题。因此，尽管巴西可能采取相似的政治战略，且同巴西资本相比，非洲国家均处于非对等地位，但是非洲国家的内部体制，包括监管框架、制度结构、社会动态和政治利益仍在互动中发挥重要作用。

非洲崛起叙事与农业发展：深化中非关系

萨义德·阿德朱莫比

盖迪翁 G. 加拉塔* 著

聂 晓** 译

进入 21 世纪以来，非洲大陆经济增长势头强劲，非洲国家首脑发表了《马普托宣言》，致力于促进农业发展。笔者认为，非洲崛起并非空穴来风，但非洲发展确实存在挑战。虽然中国对非洲农业的援助不断增加，但较之其他领域仍显微不足道。发展非洲农业的重担仍应落在非洲人民自己的肩上。同时，应当慎重考虑包括中国在内的新兴大国在非洲农业发展方面所能发挥的作用，这一作用应符合非洲大陆以及相应国家的特殊国情。

非洲崛起叙事：故事与证据

自 20 世纪 80 年代中期开始，非洲国家开始加大措施振兴经济。这也反映在一些重要文件当中，如《非洲经济复苏优先方案 1986 ~ 1990 年》《联合国非洲经济复苏与发展行动方案》《实现社会—经济复苏与转型——替代结构调整方案的非洲框架》，以及近期的 "非洲发展新伙伴计划"（NEPAD）。它们体现了部分非洲国家经济治理能力的提升。例如，联合国非洲经济委员会在 2005 年发表的首份《非洲治理报告》调查了 25 个非洲

---

* 萨义德·阿德朱莫比（Said Adejumobi）教授，联合国非洲经济委员会南部非洲办公室主任。盖迪翁 G. 加拉塔（Gedion G. Jalata），伊拉斯谟大学博士候选人，联合国非洲经济委员会能力建设处顾问。

** 聂晓，北京大学国际关系硕士毕业，现任永新专利商标代理有限公司商标代理人助理，联系方式 niexiao92@163.com。

国家，其中 17 国降低了预算赤字，其余 8 国在 1980～1990 年经济情况恶化。经济状况改善最为显著的国家包括埃及、赞比亚和莱索托，情况最为恶化的国家包括乍得、纳米比亚和加纳。不过，除博茨瓦纳的经济增长率水平堪比东亚国家，大部分非洲国家的经济增长率不高。同时，博茨瓦纳的收入差距较大、贫富悬殊。

20 世纪 90 年代中期，部分非洲国家出现的经济复苏扩展到大部分非洲国家。非洲大陆的国内生产总值增长率从 1990～1994 年的 1.5% 上升至 1995～1997 年的 4.5%，出口增长率从 1990～1994 年年均增长 3.9% 上升至 1995～1997 年的 7.8%，翻了一番；并且非洲地区的平均增长率在 1998～2002 年上升至 3.4%。26 个非洲国家在多个方面取得了切实的进步，包括经济治理、公共财政管理与问责以及健全的货币与金融制度。非洲国家同时通过提供财政奖励和其他支持性措施努力加强私营部门的发展。因此，非洲较之十年之前取得了长足的进步。

2007 年，超过 39 个非洲国家取得了三年以上年均 3% 的持续增长，其中 15 国的增长率达到 5% 甚至更高水平。人力投资也有所增加，大中小学总体注册率以及结业率都出现了增长。2009 年非洲国内生产总值增长率有所下降，不同国家下降程度不一，但也有部分国家较之 2007 年和 2008 年出现了上升。在此背景下，29 国出现了 3% 及以下的增长，17 国增长率成功实现了 3% 到 5% 的水平。埃塞俄比亚和刚果（布）甚至出现了 7% 及以上的增长。[1] 2014 年，非洲国内生产总值增长率达到 3.3%，这一数字低于东亚和南亚，但高于拉丁美洲和加勒比地区。东南亚地区受到出口以及内需的驱动，保持 6% 左右的高增长。

总之，非洲国家在经济治理和公共财政管理方面取得了巨大的成就。进入 21 世纪以来，非洲实现了相对较高的经济增长，较之 1992 年低至零的增长率，1998～2014 年的平均增长率是 4.7%。图 1 显示了 1998～2014 年非洲的国内生产总值的增长情况。非洲成为世界上仅次于东南亚的经济增长第二快的地区。非洲在诸多方面取得了改善：1）税收制度和财政动员；2）预算管理；3）更适合私人投资和私营部门增长的宏观经济环境；

---

① Said Adejumobi，"Adjustment Reforms and its Impact on Economy and Society"，in S. Adejumobi and A. Momoh，eds.，*The Political Economy of Nigeria under Military Rule*：1986–1993，1995，Harare：SAPES Trust.

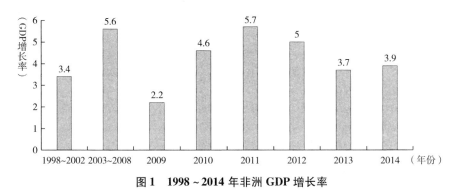

图 1　1998～2014 年非洲 GDP 增长率

资料来源：UNECA，*Economic Report on Africa*，Addis Ababa：ECA Printing Press，2015。

4）消费者价格通胀率维持在个位数；5）政府预算更趋平衡且经常账户状况改善；6）非洲大多数国家债务与 GDP 比率显著下降。

虽然非洲取得了上述经济增长，但是非洲在 21 世纪的经济发展依然面临很多挑战。过去几年非洲实现了经济增长，但多数非洲国家未能长期维持高达 7% 的增长水平，从而不能有效提高非洲大陆的人均收入水平。非洲大陆的经济增长还被批评是未能实现繁荣的增长。非洲在提高边缘群体的地位方面存在挑战，包括农村人口、妇女、青少年和残疾人等的经济和社会条件有待改善。与其他地区相比，非洲社会发展的各项指标还很滞后。许多非洲经济体正在经历转型，不过转型速度没有快到能够解决失业问题，尤其是青年人的失业问题。例如，为了跟上本地区劳动适龄人口的增长，非洲在接下来的二十年里需要创造 4.5 亿个工作岗位，以期满足本地区适龄劳动人口的增长。[①] 同时，在加快工业化、提高附加值以及结构性调整以实现多元化的增长方面也存在挑战。此外，非洲经济还面临着来自外部的挑战，如商品价格震荡、全球货币政策收紧和全球经济增长放缓，其内部风险则包括天气引发的动荡。

同时，对非投资在管理和财务方面遇到了较大阻碍。很多非洲国家不能把合理的政策转变为切实的行动，无法执行合同，国内企业家很难成功贷款，产权保护不足，人员流动不够，以及难以开发土地，这些都对非洲经济发展带来了挑战。例如，政治动荡、恐怖主义和暴力活动影响了数个

① Pauline Bax，"From Burkina Faso to Burundi，Jobless Young Africans Rise Against Corrupt and Failed Rule"，*fahamu：networks for social justice*，05. 14. 2015.

非洲国家，包括中非共和国、刚果（金）、肯尼亚、莱索托、利比亚、埃及、马里、尼日利亚、索马里和南苏丹，而且南非的民众骚乱、劳工动乱以及仇外心理令人担忧。鉴于非洲大多数经济体农业生产活动仍是靠天吃饭，天气状况恶劣也是一大威胁。

正是在这一背景下，近年来非洲许多国家取得共识，即调整经济结构以提高增长质量。总之，非洲不仅需要实现增长，而且需要有深度的增长，即生产和出口多元化，出口竞争力和收益增加，生产力提高，技术升级，以及通过正式就业和增加收入提高经济福祉。[①]

非洲农业发展的努力：区域、次区域和国家

非洲拥有丰富的自然资源。非洲大陆可耕地面积占全世界的12%，但其中60%的土地尚未开垦，而且，只有7%的耕地经过灌溉，远远低于亚洲40%的获得灌溉的比例。2013年，撒哈拉以南非洲已经开垦1.83亿公顷土地，还有近4.52亿公顷适合种植的土地尚未开垦。已开垦土地中的大部分为小农户所有，他们在农业生产中占相当大的份额。例如，肯尼亚、坦桑尼亚、埃塞俄比亚和乌干达超过75%的农业总产出是小农户创造的，其平均农场规模为2.5公顷。[②] 非洲65%～70%的劳动力从事农业活动。图2显示了非洲11国农业的GDP产值占比、就业人数占比和相对生产力水平（1960年、1990年以及2010年）。本次调查的国家有博茨瓦纳、埃塞俄比亚、加纳、肯尼亚、马拉维、毛里求斯、尼日利亚、塞内加尔、南非、坦桑尼亚和赞比亚。

如图2所示，本次调查的非洲11国中，各国农业在国内生产总值中的占比不断下滑，在1960年、1990年以及2010年分别为37.6%、24.9%和22.4%。农业生产率也从1960年的0.5%降至2010年的0.4%。同时，从事农业活动的人数也不断减少，1960年、1990年以及2010年农业领域就业人数占比分别为72.7%、61.6%和49.8%。不过，农业在促进非洲经济

① African Centre for Economic Transformation (ACET), 2014 *African Transformation Report: Growth with Depth*, ACET, 2014.

② United Nations, Economic Commission for Africa (ECA), *Frontier Markets in Africa – Misperception in a Sea of Opportunities*, ECA, July 18, 2014.

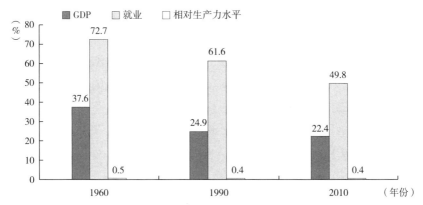

图 2　非洲 11 国农业的 GDP 产值占比、就业人数占比和相对生产力水平
（1960 年、1990 年以及 2010 年）

资料来源：Gaaitzende Vries，Marcel Timmer and Klaas de Vries，"Structural Transformation in Africa：Static Gains，Dynamic losses"，*Research Memorandum* 136，University of Groningen，Groningen Growth and development Centre，The Netherlands，2013：6，p. 11。

增长和转型上仍有相当大的潜力。农业关乎非洲大部分国家的粮食安全、就业、经济增长和发展。农业能够提升农村地区收入、扩大出口和增加用于进口机器的外汇，并且政府通过释放农业劳动力使其进入制造业和其他产业，加大对工业的投入。另外，农业还能扩大其他产业提供的必要农业投入、消费品和服务。①

农业带动的增长能够最大限度降低贫困的深度与广度，这可能源于主食作物与经济增长之间的密切联系。主食作物的增长通常被视作有利于穷人，因为出口农作物可能创造更高的价值和增长潜力。在价值链开发之前的最初阶段，粮食作物在促进经济广泛增长和减除贫困方面更有效。非洲的一项发展议程就是实现农业每年至少 6% 的增长率，以期在 2015 年之前达到联合国千年发展目标中设定的任务。② 然而仅有 9 个国家能够实现农业 6% 的年增长率，分别是安哥拉、埃塞俄比亚、布基纳法索、刚果

① Henley David，"The Agrarian Roots of Industrial Growth：Rural development in South-East Asia and Sub-Saharan Africa"，*Development Policy Review*，30（1），pp. 25 – 47；African Centre for Economic Transformation（ACET），2014 *African Transformation Report：Growth with Depth*，p. 107.

② Economic Commission for Africa（ECA），The Organization for Economic Co-operation and Development（OECD），*The Mutual Review of Development Effectiveness in Africa：Promises and Performance*，ECA and OECD，November，2014.

（布）、冈比亚、几内亚比绍、尼日利亚、塞内加尔和坦桑尼亚；埃塞俄比亚、卢旺达和加纳取得了高速的经济增长，并且迅速改善了农村地区的贫困状况，这都受惠于农业领域的增长。然而，整体上非洲的农业生产力很低，远远落后于其他大洲，非洲人民依然身处极端贫困的条件下，这仍是非洲大陆发展的主要障碍。①

20 世纪 50～70 年代，非洲国家通过干预手段资助农民，如合作社发放信贷、发展援助、政府拨款以及中央银行提供贷款，然而由于财政限制和缺乏效益，这些措施并未达到效果。20 世纪 80 年代实施结构调整方案（SAP）的一项内容就是政府取消补贴以及废除银行为农业提供的贷款配额。20 世纪 90 年代，这一时期出现了小额融资，成为拯救农业银行和金融自由化的灵丹妙药。事实证明小额融资对于城镇和乡村的穷人更为有效，其利率由市场决定，贷款偿付机制专为贫困家庭设计。但批评人士指出农业领域并未从小额融资中获得丰厚收益。② 关于非洲农业综合发展计划的《马普托宣言》发表于 2003 年，即非洲国家承诺划拨 10% 的预算用于农业领域，自此非洲农业发展状况出现明显改善。埃塞俄比亚和马里自 2004 年起开始划拨 10% 及以上的预算用于农业，马拉维和赞比亚则分别是从 2005 年和 2007 年开始拨款用于农业发展。表 1 显示了非洲部分国家农业支出占全部支出的比重。

虽然撒哈拉以南非洲国家在农业生产力上面临挑战，但是近期取得的成就表明该地区有望实现可持续的农业增长。在这方面值得注意的经济体包括肯尼亚、马拉维、赞比亚、乌干达、坦桑尼亚、埃塞俄比亚、马里和布基纳法索。多方面因素促进了此种增长：1）统一汇率，减少工业保护，大幅降低出口税额，从而增加对生产者的价格激励；2）国际商品价格提升，为进口替代和地区农业贸易创造了更多机会；3）非洲政府、地区机构以及开发伙伴大力投入农业和农村发展。

---

① Economic Commission for Africa (ECA), African Union (AU) and African Development Bank Group (AfDB), *MDG 2104 Report*: *Assessing Progress in Africa toward the Millennium Development Goals*: *Analysis of the Common African Position on the Post-2015 Development Agenda*, 2014, pp. 13–17.

② Alliance for a Green Revolution in Africa (AGRA), *Africa Agriculture Status Report*: *Focus on Staple Crops*, Smart Printers, 2013, p. 25; Xiayun Li, et al., "What Can Africa Learn from China's Experience in Agriculture Development?" *IDS Bulletin*. 44 (4), 2013, pp. 31–41.

表 1　非洲部分国家农业开支份额（占全部开支的百分比）

国家	2000	2001	2002	2003	2004	2005	2006	2007	2008	2009	2010	2011	2012
布基纳法索	25.0	18.0	23.0	33.0	20.0	12.0	20.0	16.0	14.0	9.0	11.0	—	—
埃塞俄比亚	10.4	4.0	5.6	8.4	13.6	16.5	17.5	14.6	11.7	17.5	21.2		
加纳	3.2	4.7	6.9	5.8	8.8	9.8	10.3	9.9	10.2	9.0	9.1		
肯尼亚	6.8	6.6	5.4	4.1	5.1	6.6	5.9	4.4	4.8	3.9	4.6	8.7	6.8
利比里亚	—	—	—	—	—	—	4.0	5.5	8.6	2.3	2.9		
马拉维	8.8	4.9	8.7	6.6	7.0	11.1	11.0	13.2	31.6	24.7	28.9		
马里	8.9	12.8	8.9	9.6	11.4	15.5	10.6	11.0	12.7	16.9	13.9	23.9	
莫桑比克	—	—	—	—	6.2	4.4	3.4	3.9	5.4	5.8	5.5		
尼日尔		15.8	16.6	16.4	19.5	14.5	15.1	15.4	12.2	13.9	12.7		
尼日利亚	1.6	6.0	3.5	1.9	3.1	3.4	4.1	4.4	4.6	5.3	5.7		
卢旺达		6.2	8.6	3.9	4.0	3.4	3.3	5.5	5.6	6.4	6.6		
塞拉利昂	—	2.4	2.3	3.1	3.0	2.3	2.9	2.5	2.2	2.0	1.7	0.2	
南非									1.4	1.9	1.4	1.9	
坦桑尼亚	—	—	4.5	6.8	5.7	4.7	5.8	5.7	2.5	6.7	6.8	6.8	
乌干达	2.6	1.6	2.6	2.3	2.1	2.0	3.9	3.0	3.2	4.5	3.8	3.1	4.5
赞比亚	8.6	6.2	5.2	6.1	6.1	7.2	9.3	13.2	12.5	9.3	10.2	—	—

资料来源：Regional Strategic Analysis and Knowledge Support System, ReSAKSS, 2015, available at http：//www. resakss. org。

非洲国家把农业发展置于优先地位。非盟于 2003 年通过"非洲发展新伙伴计划"为非洲农业综合发展计划提供指导和支持，其目标在于通过农业消除饥饿、减少贫困。该计划调动了大笔资金来实施具体项目，如让市场为穷人服务（项目筹集了 380 万美元）、致力于支持土地和水资源可持续管理的"非洲土地"（Terre Africa）（项目筹集了 10 亿美元）、非洲化肥融资机制（项目筹集了 3500 万美元）、增加畜牧地区生计（项目筹集了 1980 万美元），以及东南非地区粮食安全与风险管理（项目筹集了 1000 万欧元）。① 尼日尔、埃塞俄比亚、马里、马拉维和赞比亚是依照 CAADP，

① NEPAD, 2015, available at http：www. nepad. org/foodsecurity/agriculture/about, last visit on Oct. 6, 2016.

完成了农业在全国年度预算中的占比达到 10% 目标的国家。另外，非洲国家还承诺增进区域内农业贸易往来，并且调整化肥政策以降低采购成本。

非盟把 2014 年定为非洲农业和粮食安全年。2014 年《马拉博宣言》提出加快农业增长与转型，从而创造共同繁荣与改善生活，并重申了《马普托宣言》。非洲各国政府承诺到 2025 年至少要让目前的农业生产率翻番，并且动员私人和公共投资。非盟大会（AUC）和"非洲发展新伙伴计划"计划与协调处（NPCA）努力为农业增长与转型规划出一张路线图，同时通过非洲农业综合发展计划的成果框架评估进展。

非洲还出现了其他地区性的农业发展战略。《2063 年议程》关于农业的愿景是更高产、更有活力的。2015 年非盟发表关于 2015 年之后发展议程的《非洲共同立场》（*Common African Position*），重申提高农业生产力对非洲经济转型的成功至关重要。这份文件进一步表明，多元化的现代农业能够提升农业生产力，通过可持续发展的农业能够确保粮食自足和营养达标，从而改善劳动力的体质，提高生产能力，并且最终促成经济和社会的结构转型，实现更具包容性和以人为本的发展。该文件还呼吁建立多边合作伙伴关系，以加速可持续农业的发展，保障粮食自足和营养达标。

非洲农业发展面临的挑战

虽然非洲国家努力提高农业生产力，但政府对农业的重视依然不够，大部分非洲国家没有践行马普托承诺。参加非洲农业综合发展计划的 37 国中，仅有半数国家的农业预算占财政预算的 5%，整个非洲大陆农业预算平均占比为 4%，非洲仅有 5 个国家能够持续实现农业预算占比 10% 及以上。贸易监管和关税壁垒也阻碍了经济往来，区域内谷物交易额低于非洲进口总额的 5%。这些都不利于非洲的粮食安全。①

农业是非洲大多数经济体的支柱产业，占国内生产总值的 30% 以上。

---

① Economic Commission for Africa（ECA），The Organization for Economic Co-operation and Development（OECD），*The Mutual Review of Development Effectiveness in Africa：Promises and Performance*，2014，pp. 14 – 15.

尽管如此，非洲农业并未取得快速发展，这是多个因素综合作用的结果，如支持农业的政治意愿较弱、价格风险和不合适的政策，以及国际开发伙伴的关注不够。除此之外，土壤退化、灌溉土地盐碱化、年轻人移居城市、气候变化、基础设施问题以及市场准入制度都对非洲国家的农业生产潜力造成了不利影响。如许多非洲国家的国内种子管理政策削弱了整个种子价值链的作用。根据生产力水平，谷物产量一直不高，平均每公顷产出一吨。这仅是世界平均生产水平的四分之一。虽然通过开垦新的土地增加了粮食总产量，但人均粮食产量一直下滑。加上近期的粮食危机，除南非以外的非洲国家成为粮食净进口地区。非洲每年进口的谷物总量，从 20 世纪 60 年代初的不到 500 万吨猛增到 21 世纪第一个十年中期的 5000 多万吨。亚洲的情况迥然不同，该地区同期人均粮食产量几乎翻番。[1] 这是因为亚洲迅速采用了高产的小麦和水稻品种，使用了化肥和灌溉系统，并为农业提供补贴。因此生产投入的单位成本降低，土地和农民的生产力提高。

调查发现，非洲"通过改善道路交通基础设施降低 10% 的运输成本，能够增加 25% 的交易额，并且减少经销差额，从而使生产者和消费者双双获利"。[2] 这说明了较差的交通基础设施对农业生产而言造成的严重制约。另外，人员技能水平较低、土地管理能力不够，以及缺乏技术支持部门，这些因素也解释了非洲部分国家农业发展的相对滞后。缺乏资本和可用资金、无法获得额外资本进行融资，这些使非洲农业面临的问题进一步加剧。资金匮乏还表现在没有货真价实的农业投入，如高产的种子品种、合适的化肥以及低息信贷。[3]

撒哈拉以南非洲的农业研发不足。这一地区的农业科学家数量比印度

---

[1] Economic Commission for Africa (ECA), African Union (AU), *Economic Report on Africa 2007: Accelerating Africa's Development through Diversification Africa*, Addis Ababa, Ethiopia, 2007, p. 48; Deborah A. Brautigam and Xiaoyang Tang, "China's Engagement in African Agriculture: Down to the Countryside", *in China Quarterly*, November 199, 2009, pp. 686 – 706.

[2] Alliance for a Green Revolution in Africa (AGRA), *Africa Agriculture Status Report: Focus on Staple Crops*, p. 86.

[3] Hans P. Binswanger-Mkhize, "Challenges and Opportunities for African Agriculture and Food Security: High Food Process, Climate Change, Population Growth and HIV and AIDS", *Expert Meeting on How to Feed the World in*, vol. 2050, 2009.

多出 50%，比美国多出三分之一，但该地区所有国家在农业研发上的全部支出仅为印度的一半，不到美国的四分之一。只有五国从国家资源中支付农业研发系统的预算，分别是尼日利亚、南非、博茨瓦纳、埃塞俄比亚和毛里求斯。[1] 只有肯尼亚和乌干达两国的农业研发费用持续占国内生产总值的 1% 以上。笔者认为非洲国家应当增加农业研发预算，并且使其至少占国内生产总值的 1%。[2]

另外，需要大量的融资是非洲农业发展的另一挑战。如上所述，农业占非洲大多数国家国内生产总值的 30% 以上，而政府在农业领域的开发不到其三分之一。尽管各国在非洲农业综合发展计划中承诺农业优先，政府部门却并未大量增加对农业研发的投入。[3] 同时，非法资金流动也消耗了非洲发展的可用资源。根据联合国非洲经济委员会和非盟 2015 年关于非法资金流动（IFFs）的报告，仅贸易往来错误定价一项，非洲每年就会损失500 亿美元。1970 ~ 2008 年，非洲大陆因非法资金流动损失了近 8540 亿美元。2000 ~ 2010 年资金外流总额几乎相当于非洲大陆接受的政府开发援助（ODA）总额，本可投入非洲发展的巨额资金大量流失。正是因为包括上述原因在内的多个因素，非洲农业依然难获投资青睐。

总之，尽管农业对非洲极其重要，非洲农业仍然存在"政府重视程度不够、资源分配不足、政策环境不佳"等问题。[4]

中非农业开发合作

中国政府从政策层面十分重视与非洲国家的农业合作。正如 2013 年

---

① Hans P. Binswanger-Mkhize, "Challenges and Opportunities for African Agriculture and Food Security: High Food Process, Climate Change, Population Growth and HIV and AIDS", *Expert Meeting on How to Feed the World in*, vol. 2050, 2009.

② Alliance for a Green Revolution in Africa (AGRA), *Africa Agriculture Status Report: Focus on Staple Crops*, p. 25.

③ Economic Commission for Africa (ECA), The Organization for Economic Co-operation and Development (OECD), *The Mutual Review of Development Effectiveness in Africa: Promises and Performance*.

④ Hans P. Binswanger-Mkhize, "Challenges and Opportunities for African Agriculture and Food Security: High Food Process, Climate Change, Population Growth and HIV and AIDS", *Expert Meeting on How to Feed the World in*, vol. 2050, 2009, p. 46.

《中非经济和贸易合作白皮书》所示，"中国政府十分重视与非洲的农业互惠合作，努力帮助非洲国家把资源优势转变成发展优势，并且提高农业持续发展能力"。①需要注意的是，中国对非洲农业的参与长达半个世纪。不过，直到2005年，中国政府才对来自最不发达非洲国家的产品和其他非洲国家的部分产品实行零关税政策，非洲对华农业出口从2009年的11.6亿美元增加到2012年的28.6亿美元，增长了146%。而中国对非洲农业出口从15.8亿美元增加到24.9亿美元，仅增长57.6%。非洲对华出口最多的农产品是非粮食类农产品，如棉花、大麻、丝绸和含油种子。尤其是在采取零关税政策之后，中国进口芝麻的总值从2005年的9700万美元增加到2011年的4.41亿美元，年均增长28.7%，远远高于同期从非洲进口产品的平均增长率。②

中国对非洲农业的直接投资同样增长迅速。例如，投资额从2009年的3000万美元增加到2012年的8247万美元，主要原因在于中国企业在非洲投资培育良种、种植谷物和经济作物以及农产品加工。③

中国对非洲农业的支持体现为现金和实物两种形式，主要用于支持非洲粮食生产、饲养、仓储和交通运输，基础设施建设、培训、建立农业技术示范中心，以及派遣高级农业专家和技师。中国银行还为非洲农业提供融资服务。乍得是这种援助的受惠者之一，它从中国获得农业开发援助，用于发展高产量和高品质的农作物，数千名农民获得了培训。因此，该国的农作物产量提高了25%。④农业在中国自身的经济发展中发挥了关键作用，中国在非洲一直致力于分享这些经验。中国与非洲的农业合作集中在技术管理、能力建设以及提供杂交种子。同时，中国自身的发展经验对此

① Information Office of the State Council, The People's Republic of China, *White Paper on China-Africa Economic and Trade Cooperation*, 2013.
② Information Office of the State Council, The People's Republic of China, *White Paper on China-Africa Economic and Trade Cooperation*, 2013; Lila Buckley, "Chinese Agriculture Development Cooperation in Africa: Narratives and Politics", *IDS bulletin* 44.4, 2013, pp. 46–47.
③ Information Office of the State Council, The People's Republic of China, *White Paper on China-Africa Economic and Trade Cooperation*; Lila Buckley, *Chinese Agriculture Development Cooperation in Africa: Narratives and Politics*, pp. 42–45.
④ Information Office of the State Council, The People's Republic of China, *White Paper on China-Africa Economic and Trade Cooperation*; Lila Buckley, *Chinese Agriculture Development Cooperation in Africa: Narratives and Politics*, pp. 42–45.

也有影响。中国和非洲国家合作发起了 30 个农业技术合作项目。除此之外，中国还向非洲派遣了五百名农业专家和技师。[①]

国别案例研究 1：埃塞俄比亚

历史上中国与埃塞俄比亚已有联系，两国都是文明古国。不过包括正式援助在内的中国和埃塞俄比亚的经济合作始于 20 世纪 70 年代初。1991年，自从现任执政党埃塞俄比亚人民革命民主阵线（EPRDF）上台之后，中国和埃塞俄比亚的经济合作有所发展，尤其是在 1995 年之后，双边经济合作在各个方面进步显著、发展迅速。一方面，1995 年埃塞俄比亚总理梅莱斯·泽纳维访问中国，两国签署了经济技术合作协议，梅莱斯还与中国著名的企业和公司达成共识。另一方面，1997 年，时任中国国家主席的江泽民正式访问埃塞俄比亚，两国签署了关于贸易、投资与合资经营企业以及科技方面的协议。[②]

中国对埃塞俄比亚 92% 的开发援助流向了能源生产和供应（65%）以及交通运输和仓储（27%），农业的开发援助仅占援助总额的 3%。自2008 年起，中国开始支持埃塞俄比亚农业发展。2008~2015 年，中国为埃塞俄比亚农业提供了近 1100 万美元的优惠贷款（准确数字是 11374700 美元）。2013 年和 2014 年，中国还为埃塞俄比亚农业项目拨款约 97000 美元（准确数字是 97355 美元）。上述贷款和拨款针对的中埃农业合作有两个主要特征，一是建立农业技术示范中心，二是在农业技术示范中心传授农业技术，并在埃塞俄比亚执行中国—埃塞俄比亚农业职教项目（ATVET），教授农业知识。图 3 展示了从 2005 年到 2015 年（4 月）中国对埃塞俄比亚的援助领域（实际拨款）。

埃塞俄比亚政府向其他国家和私人投资者提供多种刺激政策，促进对

---

① ChinAfrica, "A Good Story to Tell: China-South Africa Relations Reach Strategic Milestone", *Africa Report*, vol. 7, 2015; Lila Buckley, "Chinese Agriculture Development Cooperation in Africa: Narratives and Politics", *IDS bulletin* 44. 4, 2013, p. 45.

② Gamora Gedion and M. Venkataraman, "An Analysis of Ethio-China Relations during the Cold War", *China Report at Siege Publications in New Delhi* 45, 2009, pp. 17 – 22; Dawit Alemu and Ian Scoones, "Negotiating New Relationships: How the Ethiopian State in Involving China and Brazil in Agriculture and Rural Development", *IDS Bulletin*. 44 (4), 2013, pp. 91 – 100.

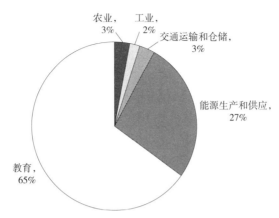

图 3　从 2005 年到 2015 年（4 月）中国对埃塞俄比亚的援助领域（实际拨款）

资料来源：埃塞俄比亚财政和经济发展部（MOFED, 2015）。

本国的投资。不过，中国对其农业的直接投资相当少。2015 年，中国对埃塞俄比亚的投资总额近 160 亿美元，然而，实际投资仅为 20 多亿美元，其中农业投资占比仅为 0.024%。中国在埃塞俄比亚最大的投资领域包括交通、能源、技术、房地产和农业。[①] 自 2008 年以来，经过注册的中国农业投资项目超过 32 个，其中：1）18 个项目是蔬菜种植项目；2）4 个是食用油的生产和加工项目，包括对棕榈油种植园的投资；3）3 家公司获得了甘蔗种植和加工的许可证；4）3 家公司获准从事养猪和猪肉加工；5）还有 2 家公司获准饲养家禽；6）1 家公司种植蘑菇；7）1 个投资橡胶种植园。尽管中国对埃塞俄比亚的农业投资很少，但是一直在持续增长。2005 年之前中国在这方面的投资接近于零。

埃塞俄比亚借鉴了其他新兴经济体的经验，如印度（重组农业研究系统）、巴西（推进生物能源战略）和韩国（组织农民采取集体行动）。埃塞俄比亚也从中国的农业政策和措施中获取了经验[②]：

（1）建设农业技术职业学校；

---

① American Enterprise Institute（AEI）and the Heritage Foundation, *The China Global Investment Tracker*（*CGIT*）, 2015.

② Future Agricultures, "Can China and Brazil Help Africa Feed Itself?", *Comprehensive Africa Agriculture Development Programme*（*CAADP*）*Policy Brief*.

（2）在大型城镇附近建设农用工业带；

（3）采取集体行动的方式组织农民。

国别案例研究2：莫桑比克

1975 年，莫桑比克从葡萄牙统治下独立之后，迅速与中国建交。莫桑比克是中国开发合作、贸易与投资最主要的目的地之一。2007 年 2 月，时任中国国家主席胡锦涛正式访问莫桑比克，他和莫桑比克时任总统阿曼多·格布扎承诺开展技术、农业和教育合作。时至 2012 年，中国在莫桑比克的开发合作项目共计 53 个，中国还修建了公共建筑和设施。中国进出口银行提供了 5000 万美元的贷款，其中 3000 万美元用于修复和开发重要的农业基础设施，以及建立三家棉花、水稻和玉米等农产品加工工厂，剩下 2000 万美元用于从中国进口农业设备。2012 年，莫桑比克从中国获得 6000 万美元的优惠贷款，用于发展农业加工业。该产业涵盖了加工、包装、储存和水稻处理等多个领域。根据 2006 年中非合作论坛上的承诺，中国在莫桑比克首都马普托的西南部建立了农业技术示范中心。其主要目标是进行农业展示、农村技术推广和技术培训，从而提高农业生产力，保障粮食安全。①

中国企业对莫桑比克的投资飞速增长。例如，中国在下林波波河的雷加迪奥（Regadio do Baixo Limpopo）投资了约 2 亿美元，不过也有信息显示投资额是 9500 万美元，这就是有名的赛赛（Xai-Xai）灌溉工程。该工程致力于为当地农民提供灌溉系统和转让水稻生产技术，从而提高水稻产量。自此，当地农民发现每公顷水田能够生产 5 吨水稻，比之前的产量整整多出了 2 吨。不过，批评人士认为莫桑比克农民对此项目的投入不够，因此技术转让实际上失败了。中方的投资也被认为是在"攫取土地"，甚至有报道称当地百姓因此流离失所。批评人士进一步指出中方落实项目时并未征询当地人民意见。②

---

① Sergio Chichava, et al., "Brazil and China in Mozambican Agriculture: Emerging Insights from the Field", *IDS Bulletin.* 44 (4), 2013, pp. 106 – 107.

② Cecilia Anesi and Andrea Fama, "China Accused of Stealth Land Grab over Mozambique's Great Rice Project", *The Ecologist* 30, 2013.

中国政府对此回应说，农业投资是基于莫桑比克政府的要求，旨在使该国的水稻产量从 10 万吨增加到 50 万吨。中方企业和中非发展基金联合投资了棉花种植和加工项目，该项目是采取企业与从事该行业的农户合作的方式推进的，数万名当地农民参与其中，有效提升了当地的棉花加工能力。同时，这个项目还拓展到了马拉维和赞比亚。[①]

国别案例研究 3：加纳

1960 年，中国和加纳建立了外交关系。自此之后，加纳通过提供外交支持，回报中国给予加纳的物质支持、贷款和拨款。2007 年，温家宝总理访问加纳，两国签订经济合作协议。两国合作主要领域包括基础设施、能源、通信、农业、贸易、教育和培训。中国还把合作领域扩展到了修建水坝和道路，资助教育、贸易、通信、能源和审计等培训课程，并且目前已经教授 700 名加纳人农业和渔业操作。同时，中国也不断加强与加纳在石油产业的开发合作，最近加纳同中国进出口银行签署了价值 130 亿美元的协议。[②]

在农业领域，中国为支持加纳渔业和水稻项目，提供了 9900 万美元的无息贷款，并且不断促进灌溉、农业加工、农业技术和基础设施发展方面的交流，由中国政府发起的志愿者们也在加纳大学教授农业课程。中国为了推进在次区域的投资，还在阿克拉设立了中非发展基金（CAD Fund）西非地区办公室。然而，中国在农业领域的投资依然很少——仅占对加纳投资的 4%。农业投资中占比最大的是灌溉工程，该工程名为阿非非工程，也叫维塔工程（Afife or Weta Project），占地 880 英亩，是加纳最大的水稻

---

① Jean-Jacques Gabas and Frederic Goulet，"South-South Cooperation and New Agricultural Development Aid Actors in western and Southern Africa，China and Brazil Case Studies"，in Agence Française de Développement and Agricultural Research for Development（CIRAD），*Working Paper*，no. 134，May 2013.

② Austin Strange，et al.，"China's Development Finance to Africa：A Media-Based Approach to Data Collection"，in Center for Global Development（CGD），*Working Paper* 323，Washington DC，2013；Kojo Sebastian Amanor，"South-South Cooperation in Africa：Historically, Geopolitical and Political Economy Dimensions of International Development"，*IDS Bulletin*，44（4），1013，pp. 80 – 81，84，85.

灌溉工程。同时，中国企业还投资了化肥和农药工厂，这可能与加纳发现了更多的石油资源有关。①

深化中非农业合作的挑战与互利

虽然中非双方为推动农业开发合作付出了诸多努力，但农业领域的合作依然是低水平的。如上所述，较之贸易关系、投资水平和开发合作等，中国对非洲农业的支持依然不够。

批评人士认为，中国开发援助和对外直接投资可能会导致中国和非洲国家之间出现潜在的粮食安全冲突。特别是中国为非洲数个水稻生产国提供农业支持，如莫桑比克的水稻最终是要出口到中国市场。然而，相关证据表明，中国在非洲农场生产的粮食仅供应当地市场或是出口到全球市场。不过学者也担心，未来在中国人口压力可能导致耕地紧缺，从而威胁粮食安全，因此中国会像日本和韩国一样选择在海外大量生产粮食。②

如上所述，中国对非洲农业的投资主要是农业技术和种子培育，并且为此建立了一批农业技术示范园。示范园主要传授杂交水稻技术，较之亲本水稻，杂交水稻抗倒伏、产量高。但是杂交水稻囿于无法复制亲本水稻的遗传特征，需要持续购买种子。而杂交水稻种子又被跨国种子公司所控制。非洲农民失去了传统种子，未来这可能会造成麻烦。除非延长合同期限，中国专家通常只在非洲待两年，这可能也不利于非洲农业实现持续盈利的目标。③

另外，中国的农业支持"主要通过示范、教学和维修实现技术转让，

---

① Austin Strange, et al., "China's Development Finance to Africa: A Media-Based Approach to Data Collection", in Center for Global Development (CGD), *Working Paper* 323, Washington DC, 2013; Kojo Sebastian Amanor, "South-South Cooperation in Africa: Historically, Geopolitical and Political Economy Dimensions of International Development", *IDS Bulletin*, 44 (4), 1013, pp. 80 – 81, 84, 85.

② Ian Scoones, Lidia Cabral and Hennry Tugendhat, "New Development Encounters: China and Brazil in African Agriculture", *IDS Bulletin*, 2013, 44 (4), pp. 1 – 18; Lila Buckley, "Chinese Agriculture Development Cooperation in Africa: Narratives and Politics", p. 48.

③ Sergio Chichava, et al., "Brazil and China in Mozambican Agriculture: Emerging Insights from the Field", pp. 101 – 115; Deborah A. Bräutigam and Tang Xiaoyang, "China's Engagement in African Agriculture: Down to the countryside", pp. 700 – 706.

然而没有调查非洲经济状况，如市场、交通、分配，以及支持杂交水稻的系列机制。非洲国家希望中国人展现出的工作精神和个人实践能够激励当地村民"。①

另一个挑战在于中非之间的文化差异带来的障碍。例如，并非所有的中国专家都会说英语，所以他们一般通过示范传授实用技能，而这导致中国专家和他们的非洲同事在交流上存在困难。同时，中非农业存在巨大差异。中国采取密集型种植，而非洲则是轮种制度。轮种制度会让土地休耕，因而可能导致中非之间的误解，从而出现中非互不理解的情况。进而，中国实施开发援助项目时，很可能因此疏远非洲人民。②

虽然上述观点认为目前中非关系在农业发展方面存在一些问题，但农业仍是中国参与非洲发展的新兴领域。现在，对非洲农业的参与被称作"南南合作"，强调双边关系的平等互惠。农业领域由于以下几点有光明的前景。

第一，正如非洲需要中国一样，中国同样需要非洲，包括土地、廉价资源、劳动力和市场等对经营农业和贸易往来至关重要。非洲大片耕地尚未开垦，这关乎着全球长期的粮食安全，尤其是对于包括中国在内的人口密集的亚洲更是如此。

第二，中非关系不断深化，这将有利于双方未来的农业合作。2013 年中国发表了《经济与贸易合作白皮书》，文件表示中国计划将在多个方面加强与非洲的农业协作。

> 未来，中国将在各个方面加强与非洲的农业合作，并且确保在此种合作中，双方平等、互惠，实现共同发展。通过确立和改善双边农业合作机制进一步巩固中非合作，共享农业技术、资源和信息，开展农产品加工和贸易、农业基础设施建设以及人力资源培训。中国将继续鼓励和支持中方企业对非洲农业和技术合作的投资，按照实际需求

---

① Sergio Chichava, et al. , "Brazil and China in Mozambican Agriculture: Emerging Insights from the Field", pp. 101 – 115; Deborah A. Bräutigam and Tang Xiaoyang, "China's Engagement in African Agriculture: Down to the countryside", p. 703.

② Sérgio Chichava, et al. , "Brazil and China in Mozambican Agriculture: Emerging Insights from the Field", pp. 110, 112; Lila Buckley, "Chinese Agriculture Development Cooperation in Africa: Narratives and Politics", p. 48.

在非洲国家设立数个农业示范中心，并且中国还将在联合国粮食及农业组织和国际农业发展基金框架[①]内深化中非合作。

第三，非洲国家和地区不断加强关于发展农业的政治承诺，这尤其体现在非洲国家承诺制定合适的农业政策，提高农业预算比重。如上所述，中国一直基于需求提供开发援助，非洲要求中国加强对非洲农业领域的投入。尤为重要的是，非洲国家可以从中国服务小农户的农业政策中汲取经验，从开发合作中提高政府机构能力。未来的中非农业合作也可能发展到修建灌溉系统和大坝，供应农用机械、化肥和农药，从而超越目前集中在农场管理、提供种子和农业用品方面的援助。[②]

第四，农业开发援助与中国在能源和矿产项目上的利益相辅相成，这也符合中国外交政策关于"取予两得"的原则。正如中国农垦总公司负责人所言："中国在非洲越来越多的能源和矿产项目很可能带来负面影响。"就此，他建议"中国在开采他国资源的同时，应当帮助促进农业发展"。[③]正是如此，中国通过中非合作论坛和联合国粮食及农业组织等多边和双边平台，不断增加对非洲国家的农业援助。

最后同样重要的是，其他新兴国家也在参与非洲的农业发展，最引人瞩目的就是巴西，和中国在农业领域的成就一样显著，两国都有兴趣支持非洲农业。中国和巴西在参与非洲农业时展开了竞争，这在加纳和莫桑比克体现得尤为明显，而这也将影响中国对非洲的农业支持。因此，非洲国家需要最大限度地利用新兴国家竞相支持非洲农业的优势。同时，也要注意新兴经济体在支持非洲国家农业时关切不同。例如，中国主要投入小型密集型农业，且已取得巨大成功。而巴西在改造稀树草原方面有着丰富的经验和先进的技术，改造之后，稀树草原成为上佳的谷物和牛肉生产地区，并能畜养大批奶牛。[④]

---

① 国际农业发展基金框架（The International Fund for Agricultural Development，IFAD），联合国专门致力于提高农村人口的粮食安全和营养能力的机构，成立于 1977 年。——译者注

② Kojo Sebastian Amanor, "South-South Cooperation in African Agriculture: China, Brazil and International Agribusiness", *Great Insights* 4.3, 2014, pp. 53 – 55.

③ Deborah A. Bräutigam and Tang Xiaoyang. "China's Engagement in African Agriculture: Down to the Countryside", p. 689.

④ Kojo Sebastian Amanor, "South-South Cooperation in African Agriculture: China, Brazil and International Agribusiness", pp. 53 – 55; Kojo Sebastian Amanor, "Expanding Agri – business: China and Brazil in Ghanaian Agriculture", *IDS Bulletin* 44.4, 2013, pp. 80 – 90.

结论：中非关系的前景

非洲农业正处在蓄势转型的节点上。推进农业转型和提高农业生产力是非洲人民的核心要务。要实现非洲大陆的发展，需要农业领域率先实现全面持续的增长，同时在基础设施、管理和其他社会指标上要有巨大的改善。因此，促进农业发展并使其成为非洲经济转型的引擎，这样一种政治意愿、决心和承诺是恰逢其时、切合实际的。

然而，这并不意味着非洲不需要他国的帮助，以解决自身的贫困问题，以及开发农业生产的潜力和实现转型，从而满足不断增长的人口的粮食需求。非洲要从其他新兴经济体，如中国、印度和巴西的农业发展中借鉴相关经验，把更多的资源投入农业科学、教育、研究和技术当中。非洲要认识到中国农业的发展并非通过开发援助来实现，而是借助市场改革、贸易和外国直接投资。同样，各种开发援助并不能从根本上帮助非洲国家实现农业转型。就此而言，非洲各个国家必须意识到农业对经济发展的重要性，并且实施合理的农业政策和战略，即帮助穷人和农村地区持续发展的政策，这一政策需聚焦生产力驱动和主要农作物引领的农业发展，政策还应把农业效应和工业化联系起来，并且要求中国和其他新兴国家支持这一政策。

正如中国改革开放的总设计师邓小平所言，农业发展需要政策和科技先行。与此相应，农业生产力的提高要求政府为小农户提供技术革新、输入—输出市场、融资渠道、政策环境、机制建设和能力培养。对灌溉系统、农村基础设施和农业技术研发的投资能够提高农业生产力，同时小农户和妇女亟须特别关注。提高非洲国家、次区域和大陆的能力，从而生产和掌握对非洲农业综合发展计划进行规划与评估的知识，这一点尤为关键。

中国农业模式来自中国自身的经验，人们对于其能否在非洲复制依然存在争议。应当注意的是农业的成功取决于本土科技水平，即能否发明适应非洲大陆和相应国家特定环境的新技术。例如，水稻和小麦引领了亚洲的绿色革命，但它们对非洲并不重要，而这也是为什么非洲的水稻和小麦的产量均占该种农作物世界总产量的2%。非洲的主要农作物是小米和高粱，分别占世界总产量的40%和18%；山药、大蕉和木薯则分别占95%、70%和44%。因此，非洲绿色革命和中国对非洲的农业开发援助应当重视这些作物。

这表明要实现非洲粮食的安全、繁荣与可持续性，必须采取独一无二的绿色革命。因此，可以对技术研发和基础设施进行投资，为私人企业创造适宜的环境，以及帮助农民从事经营活动，并且还可以考虑建设一条涵盖供应、生产、需求和消费渠道的农业价值链。

如上所述，非洲农业转型存在巨大的资金缺口。在这方面，应当鼓励各种人员参与非洲农业领域。如公共投资有助于克服挑战，还可借助外国私人或是国有企业投资，农民也能成为金融家，小农户也能为撒哈拉以南非洲的经济发展和减少贫困做出巨大贡献。农业是非洲人最主要的谋生手段，非洲农村地区80%以上的人口靠此吃饭，因此必须要有农业政策和发展干预的支持。

毫无疑问，亚洲绿色革命是由国家推动和市场调节的，是一种服务小农户的战略。为填补非洲农业领域的资金空缺，来自外国私人企业的直接投资被视作重要资源。实施各种新颖的融资方式对非洲农业的发展也极为关键。因此，可以采取私人、国有和公私合营等多种投资方式。

同时，也要认识到中国的对非开发合作本质上是一个长期规划的战略性目标。就此而言，中国也从支持非洲的农业发展中获益。一方面，中国技师积累了关于非洲农业情况的专门知识，因而能够影响非洲大陆的后续发展。另一方面，中国企业通过投资，收回了对非洲国家农业基础设施的投入。

中国开发合作基于自身的战略政策考量、受援国的要求、受援国执行政策的官僚体制以及在每三年一次的中非合作论坛上做出的承诺。每个非洲国家都能在中非合作论坛中通过进一步协商获得属于自己的一份承诺。"一个中国"原则要求非洲国家在获得中国的开发援助前，必须承认台湾是中国领土不可分割的一部分。因此，非洲国家需要制定相应的农业政策和战略，增进中国与非洲农业领域的联系。非洲国家还要加强行政管理能力，使政策落到实处。此外，鉴于中国和非洲在农业转型方面面临相似的困境，非洲国家还需从中国农业发展失败的案例中汲取教训。毋庸置疑，中国仍在进行农业改革。

　　综上所述，中国和非洲的农业存在系统性差异。在这方面，中国政府必须大力支持中国企业和农业专家，不断增进对非洲农村文化、社会和历史的了解。进而，为支持非洲的低端研究和农业发展中心，欢迎和鼓励中国通过非洲各地的示范中心提供农业研发领域的开发援助。不过，这也需要非洲当地的积极参与，尤其是在农业项目的设计和实施方面。

中国对非洲农业合作的新型实践

从援助到开发：中非农业合作的
支持体系研究

刘海方　宛　如[*]　著

非洲农业资源丰富，中非农业有诸多的显著互补性，因此中非之间开展农业国际合作的潜力很大。中非农业合作已有50多年的历史，大体经历了纯粹的无偿援助时期、改革调整时期、市场经济体制时期以及中非合作论坛框架下新型合作四个时期，当前保持着贸易、援助和投资开发三位一体的合作形式。与其他业界近年来快速增长的合作相比，农业合作显得过于保守。本文通过梳理中非农业合作变迁的过程，讨论目前中方对非洲农业合作的战略定位及政策和资金支持体系是否充足，回答为何中国对非洲的农业投资的进展相对缓慢。

中国对非农业合作的变迁

在冷战、美苏两大阵营对立的大背景之下，新中国成立后选择了"一边倒"地站在社会主义阵营。出于争取非洲大量新独立的民族国家支持、建设社会主义国际阵营的需求，中国很早就开始了与非洲的农业合作。这种合作起源于1959年中国对几内亚提供的农业合作，其形式主要为一般的物资援助和粮食援助、派出农业技术专家、培训以及援建农场、农业技术试验站、推广站和农业技术示范中心等。[①] 其中，援建农场、试验站和技术推广站是中

---

* 刘海方，北京大学非洲研究中心执行主任；宛如，北京大学国际关系学院硕士毕业，现任中国工商银行迪拜国际金融中心分行法律合规部。

① 徐秀丽、徐莉莉：《国际发展话语的重塑：中国与非洲国家农业合作的方式与反思》，《中国农业大学学报》（社会科学版）2011年第4期，第27页。

国最早向非洲提供农业合作的方式。到20世纪70年代末，中国先后在非洲的十多个国家建设了技术试验站和农业技术推广站，规模种植的农场面积达4.34万公顷，项目总数近180个。① 在这个时期，虽然官方说法是与非洲进行农业合作，但是实际上合作多是以援助的形式展开的。

随着20世纪70年代末中国第二代领导人开启一个新的历史发展阶段，中国政府的工作重点转换到了经济建设上来，外交也转向更加独立自主的和平外交战略。在各原因综合影响下，这一时期中国的对非援助及经济合作一度下滑。② 但波动只持续了很短的几年，1983年1月13日赵紫阳访问坦桑尼亚时，宣布了与非洲国家进行经济技术合作的新四项原则，即"平等互利、形式多样、讲求实效、共同发展"，重振了中非合作，包括农业方面合作的信心。

在这一时期，除了国内领导人的更迭对中国与非洲的农业合作造成了一定的影响外，中国国内开始实行改革开放、引入市场机制的经济变化也反映到了对外的经济合作方式上。改革开放后，中国的经济逐渐活跃，经营的手段和方式也丰富起来，具体到与非洲的农业合作，原先以无偿援助形式为主的合作模式增加了新的方式和内容。例如，从20世纪80年代起，部分援外项目在实施时就开始实行投资包干制，而非过去的行政部门负责制。1983年，中非合作四项原则公布后，中国政府开始鼓励和推动中国公司到非洲开展工程承包和劳务合作业务。1986年，中国还通过联合国的多边计划，为非洲的42个国家"提供了水稻种植、淡水养殖、蔬菜栽培、农业机械等方面的技术帮助"。③

进入20世纪90年代，中国对非洲的农业合作又一次发生了较明显的变化。1993年召开的中国共产党第十四届中央委员会第三次全体会议上通过了《中共中央关于建立社会主义市场经济体制若干问题的决定》，正式确立社会主义市场经济的新体制，同时也确定了要进一步地扩大对外开放

---

① 齐顾波、罗江月：《中国与非洲国家农业合作的历史与启示》，《中国农业大学学报》（社会科学版）2011年第4期，第11~17页、第12页。

② 李安山：《全球化过程中的南南合作：中国对非援助的理念与行动》，2008年北京论坛讲话，人民网2008年11月12日，http://theory.people.com.cn/GB/136457/8326945.html，2015年4月15日访问。

③ 齐顾波、罗江月：《中国与非洲国家农业合作的历史与启示》，《中国农业大学学报》（社会科学版）2011年第4期，第12页。

的方针。在此背景下，1995~2000 年"走出去"战略逐渐成形。1997 年的中国共产党第十五次全国人民代表大会上，第一次明确提出了"鼓励能够发挥我国比较优势的对外投资。更好地利用国内国外两个市场、两种资源"。[①] 1998 年 2 月的中国共产党第十五届中央委员会第二次全体会议，江泽民更指出"在积极扩大出口的同时，要有领导有步骤地组织和支持一批有实力有优势的国有企业走出去，到国外去，主要是到非洲、中亚、中东、中欧、南美等地投资办厂"。[②] 除了在这一时期开始鼓励中国企业投资非洲农业外，中国政府对非洲的农业合作也有别的新举措，其中最明显的一条就是开始推动采用政府贴息优惠贷款方式对非洲国家进行援助。1995 年 7 月 25 日，时任副总理的朱镕基在访问津巴布韦时对津工商界发表的演讲中也特别提到了这种扶持措施。[③]

有了这些政策的支持，许多中国企业开始走向海外，如中国农垦（集团）总公司（简称中农垦）、中国水产（集团）总公司等的大型企业也走向非洲进行投资。成立于 1980 年的中农垦，自 1990 年开始先后在赞比亚、坦桑尼亚、加蓬、加纳、多哥、几内亚等九个国家创办了农牧业生产和加工项目，从事种植业和养殖业。由于进入时间早、覆盖国家多，中农垦是目前在非洲从事农业投资的中国企业中规模最大的之一。[④] 当然，从中国企业开始走进非洲开始，农业方面的投资在所有中国对非投资中，无论是规模还是数量都相对较少。

2000 年之后，中国"走出去"战略的正式提出以及中非合作论坛的创立，给中国与非洲的农业合作尤其是中国对非的农业投资带来了新的机遇。历届中非合作论坛部长级会议都强调了加强中国与非洲农业合作以及中国对非洲的农业投资的重要性，虽然大多是宏观政策方向上的论述，未必能够直接使中国企业在对非投资的具体行为上受益，但客观上中非合作

---

① 《高举邓小平理论伟大旗帜，把建设有中国特色社会主义事业全面推向二十一世纪（2）——江泽民在中国共产党第十五次全国代表大会上的报告（1997 年 9 月 12 日）》，人民网，http://news.xinhuanet.com/ziliao/2003-01/20/content_697207.htm，2015 年 4 月 15 日访问。

② 中国国际贸易促进委员会经济信息部：《我国"走出去"战略的形成及推动政策体系分析》，2007 年 1 月，http://www.ccpit.org/Contents/Channel_1276/2007/0327/30814/content_30814.htm，2015 年 4 月 15 日访问。

③ 《中国与非洲关系大事记（1949—2003）》，中国网，http://www.china.com.cn/chinese/HIAW/445819.htm，2015 年 4 月 15 日访问。

④ 韩相山：《中垦集团在非洲》，《世界知识》2000 年第 19 期，第 50 页。

论坛对投资非洲农业的重视有助于增强中国企业投资非洲的信心和动力，振奋投资市场；借中非合作论坛这一平台成立的许多机构和机制也都促进了中国投资非洲的农业，如中非发展基金的成立、中非企业家大会和中非地方政府合作论坛的召开等；同时，政府和相关部门提供了一系列投资非洲农业的政策、资金和信息支持，鼓励中国企业进入非洲农业领域。

中非农业合作的三种形式

农产品贸易

近十年来，中非农产品贸易发展迅速。从总体上看，中非农产品贸易的互补性明显提高，中国从非洲主要进口烟草、棉麻毛、油籽等资源密集型农产品，向非洲出口的主要是蔬菜、茶类、水果等劳动密集型农产品。[①] 2004年，中非农产品贸易总额为1517.93万美元，其中，中国对非洲的农产品出口额为595.82万美元，从非洲的农产品进口额为92211万美元。2017年，中非农产品贸易总额达到了60.2亿美元，其中，中国自非洲国家进口农产品30.8亿美元，向非洲国家出口农产品29.4亿美元。十三年间中非农产品贸易额增加得非常明显。[②] 就贸易种类来看，中非农产品贸易的种类趋于稳定，主要是产业间贸易，产品集中度高且互补性强。目前，中非农产品贸易还存在着贸易规模较小、产品结构与市场结构过于集中等问题，着力解决这些问题，应成为今后中非农业合作中的重点。

发展援助

在援助方面，自1959年向几内亚政府无偿提供粮食援助以来，中国对非洲的农业援助获得长足发展，至2011年6月，中国在非洲的农业援助项目达100多个。[③] 无论是中国援建的坦桑尼亚姆巴拉利农场和鲁伏农场、索马

---

① 杨军等：《中非农产品贸易结构变化趋势、比较优势及互补性分析》，《中国农村经济》2012年第3期，第46~54页、第69页，转引自拉非克《中非农产品贸易发展与问题研究》，大连理工大学硕士学位论文，2013。

② 农业农村部对外经济合作中心，"中非农业合作概况"，中国农村网，http://journal.cnews.net/ncgztxcs/2018/dsqq/jj/103454_20180904101753.html，2018年9月30日最后访问。

③ 参见迟建新《助力非洲粮食安全》，《人民日报》2011年11月30日。

里费诺力农场、乌干达奇奔巴农场、几内亚科巴甘蔗农场、马里两个甘蔗农场、毛里塔尼亚姆颇利水稻农场、塞拉利昂甘蔗农场、多哥甘蔗种植园、刚果（金）甘蔗农场等，还是建设水利灌溉配套设施，抑或提供生产技术指导，均是配合非洲国家农业发展战略与规划、解决非洲国家农业发展面临的问题。在长期的发展过程中，中国对非洲的农业援助已经从早期的单边援助到双边经济技术合作，发展到了今天的多渠道、宽领域的合作。总体而言，中国对非洲的农业援助对于非洲经济社会的发展、人民生活的改善做出了很大贡献。

对非洲的农业援助的一大重心是帮助非洲国家提升农业技术水平，提高其自身农业发展能力，因此中国对非洲的农业援助始终注重农业技术的分享，大致可分为3种形式：援建农业技术试验站和推广站、建立农业技术示范中心、开展农业管理与技术培训。

援建农业技术试验站和推广站。中国曾先后帮助几内亚、马里、坦桑尼亚、刚果（布）、索马里、乌干达、塞拉利昂、尼日尔、多哥、刚果（金）、毛里塔尼亚等十多个国家建设了农业技术试验站和农业技术推广站。中方向这些援非农业技术试验站、推广站提供资金与派驻农技人员，通过研究、试验、推广和扩散等农业技术传播途径，[①] 如中国农业专家帮助受援国提高农作物种植技术、繁育技术和管理技术，畜牧、水产养殖技术以及农产品初加工技术，并使这些技术转化为生产力。

建立农业技术示范中心。这是自中非合作论坛建立以来中非农业合作的新举措。至2012年年底，中国已在坦桑尼亚、赞比亚、莫桑比克、乌干达、津巴布韦、苏丹、利比里亚、刚果（布）、贝宁、多哥、卢旺达、喀麦隆、埃塞俄比亚和南非建立了14个农业技术示范中心，均已进入技术合作期。马拉维、安哥拉、刚果（金）、南苏丹、马里和毛里塔尼亚拟新建的农业技术示范中心现已完成项目考察。在运作模式方面，项目的投资主体是政府，运行主体是企业（即由地方政府推荐的农业技术示范中心的承办企业，如陕西农垦集团负责喀麦隆项目等），因此每个项目的运行管理均主要由懂农业的经营主体来承担，以期实现项目的可持续发展。

结合非洲农业规划，开展农业管理与技术培训。中国结合发展中国家

① 李小云等：《小农为基础的农业发展：中国与非洲的比较分析》，社会科学文献出版社，2010，第209页。

农业发展的特点和实际需要，举办近 300 期形式多样、内容丰富的研修和培训项目，培训了近 7000 名农业官员和技术人员。农业培训项目领域广泛，既涵盖种植业、林业、畜牧业、渔业等农业管理领域，也涉及农村发展与减贫、粮食安全、农业南南合作等宏观政策制定问题，同时关注农业技术推广、农产品加工、储藏、销售与流通等产业链发展议题。

2003 年出台的非洲农业综合发展计划中，第四大支柱即推动农业研究、促进农业技术推广。因此，农业技术示范中心在提供各类实用农业技术服务方面，内容因国而异，关切非洲农业综合发展计划国别投资计划中关于农业技术合作方面的需求。如在卢旺达，农业技术示范中心项目主要开展水稻、旱稻、菌草、蚕桑、水土保持 5 个领域的技术示范与推广，这与该国非洲农业综合发展计划关注的重点（发展粮食作物、特色农业、农业自然管理等）相一致。但是对于非洲以小农户为主的技术需求而言，能力建设不仅是种植和养殖技术的学习，还有整个农业商业化的知识和管理能力的提升。而目前的农业技术示范中心很难把能力建设设计到项目中，这是农业技术示范中心发挥更大作用需要思考的方向。

农业投资

总体上讲，中国对非的投资额持续增多。2009 年以来，非洲地区吸收外国直接投资连续下滑，但中国对非洲的直接投资不减反增。2009～2012 年，中国对非洲的直接投资流量由 14.4 亿美元增至 25.2 亿美元，年均增长 20.5%，存量由 93.3 亿美元增至 212.3 亿美元，增长 1.3 倍。[①] 2016 年中国流向非洲的对外直接投资为 24 亿美元，同比下降 19%，占当年对外直接投资流量的 1.2%。截至 2016 年年末，中国在非洲地区的投资存量为 398.8 亿美元，占中国对外投资存量的 3.0%。[②]

农业方面，近些年来中国对外的农业投资发展势头很快。2003 年至 2011 年，中国农林牧渔对外直接投资存量从 3.32 亿美元增加到 34.17 亿

---

① 《中国与非洲经贸合作（2013）白皮书》，中华人民共和国国务院新闻办公室，2013，http：//www.scio.gov.cn/ztk/dtzt/2013/9329142/329145/Document/1345040/1345040.htm，2015 年 6 月 2 日访问。

② 中华人民共和国商务部：《中国对外投资合作发展报告 2017》，http：//fec.mofcom.gov.cn/article/tzhzcj/tzhz/upload/zgdwtzhzfzbg2017.pdf，第 100 页，2015 年 6 月 2 日访问。

美元，增长 9.3 倍，年均增长 33.8%；该领域的对外直接投资流量从 0.81 亿美元增长到 7.98 亿美元，增长 8.8 倍，年均增长 33.1%，其中 2005 年之后的对外直接投资流量增速更是超过了 40%，快速增加。① 这表明中国农业"走出去"政策的正式提出，对于企业发展战略的指导性意义巨大，中国企业纷纷响应号召，向外开拓农业市场、进行投资。但目前主要的投资地区仍然是离中国更近的欧洲（尤其是俄罗斯远东地区）和亚洲，二者加起来占到了对外总投资的近 68%。当然在非洲的农业投资也不容小视。截至 2012 年年底，中国对外农业累计投资总额达到了 37.13 亿美元，其中对非洲累计投资 5.8 亿美元，占总额的 15.5%。在中国对非洲的农业投资的目的国中，莫桑比克、马达加斯加和南非排名前三，投资额分别为 1.35 亿美元、1.1 亿美元和 7476 万美元。② 另外，截至 2012 年 5 月，中华人民共和国商务部统计的境外投资企业（机构）名录中共有中国境外农业企业 598 家，其中在非洲的农业投资企业 78 家，占 13%。这 78 家投资非洲的企业分布在 54 个非洲国家中的 33 国中，覆盖率达 61%。③ 虽然对非农业投资增长迅速，但在中国对外农业直接投资总量中所占的比重仍偏小，与中国对非洲地区的其他领域相比还有很大差距，如 2016 年存量分布的前 5 个行业领域依次为建筑业（28.3%）、采矿业（26.1%）、制造业（12.8%）、金融业（11.4%）以及科学研究和技术服务业（4.8%）。④ 2017 年年底，中国对非洲的投资存量达到 1000 亿美元，为 2003 年的 40 倍，农业被认为是基础设施投资热潮之后的一个重要领域之一。⑤

农业"走出去"战略的提出

"走出去"实际上即指中国对外直接投资。正如前文所说，"走出去"

① 数据来源：2013 中国境外农业投资分析报告概要，中商情报网，http://www.askci.com/news/201401/04/041126135281.shtml，2015 年 4 月 25 日访问。
② 中华人民共和国农业部国际合作司、农业部对外经济合作中心编著《中国对外农业投资合作报告（2012）》，第 7 页。
③ 数据来源：2013 中国境外农业投资分析报告概要，中商情报网，http://www.askci.com/news/201401/04/041126135281.shtml，2015 年 4 月 25 日访问。
④ 中华人民共和国商务部：《中国对外投资合作发展报告 2017》，第 102 页。
⑤ 中国商务新闻网：《中非双向投资迈向更高水平》，http://news.comnews.cn/top/20180830/10555.html，2015 年 4 月 25 日访问。

战略的提出经过了 1995 年至 2000 年这一段酝酿草创的阶段。2000 年在全国人大九届三次会议上，江泽民提出随着中国经济的不断发展，"要积极参与国际经济竞争，并努力掌握主动权。必须不失时机地实施'走出去'战略，把'引进来'和'走出去'紧密结合起来，更好地利用国内外两种资源、两个市场"。① 同年 10 月，中国共产党第十五届中央委员会第五次全体会议上通过的《中共中央关于制定国民经济和社会发展第十个五年计划的建议》中，首次明确提出了"走出去"战略。②

　而对于农业领域来说，步入新世纪后"走出去"的时机也逐渐成熟。2004 年 1 月，中央下发《中共中央国务院关于促进农民增加收入若干政策的意见》，成为自 1986 年以来，时隔 19 年再一次将农业问题作为"一号文件"的内容。"一号文件"是指中共中央每年发出的第一份文件，因其作为"第一份文件"的特殊时间和位置，所涉及的问题往往也是每年中共中央最重视、最急于解决的问题。2004 年至今每年的"一号文件"都聚焦"三农"问题，表明了中央对农业的重视空前之高。2006 年，我国商务部、农业部和财政部联合下发了《关于加快实施农业"走出去"战略的若干意见》，随后农业部还专门制定了《农业"走出去"发展规划》。③ 2010 年中央"一号文件"提出，要加快国际农业科技和农业开发合作，制定鼓励政策，支持有条件的企业"走出去"。党的十八届三中全会和 2014 年中央"一号文件"，进一步提出加快农业"走出去"步伐。2014 年中央农村工作会议强调，要"善于用好两个市场、两种资源，适当增加进口和加快农业走出去步伐"。2015 年《关于加大改革创新力度加快农业现代化建设的若干意见》的"一号文件"也提出，要"提高统筹利用国际国内两个市场两种资源的能力。加强农产品进出口调控，积极支持优势农产品出口"。④

---

① 陈扬勇：《江泽民"走出去"战略的形成及其重要意义》，人民网，http：//finance.people.com.cn/GB/70392/8313311.html，2015 年 6 月 2 日访问。

② 中国国际贸易促进委员会经济信息部：《我国"走出去"战略的形成及推动政策体系分析》。

③ 《农业"走出去"，企业如何走稳走好？》，中国农业新闻网引《农民日报》2014 年 5 月 1 日，http：//www.farmer.com.cn/xwpd/nbyl/yl/201405/t20140501_958113.htm，2018 年 4 月 16 日访问。

④ 中共中央国务院《关于加大改革创新力度加快农业现代化建设的若干意见》，新华网，http：//news.xinhuanet.com/politics/2015-02/01/c_1114209962.htm，2015 年 5 月 21 日访问。

　　除了中央的政策和文件逐渐提出和完善农业"走出去"的规划和相应政策，各省份也根据自身的农业发展优势，制定本省份的农业"走出去"规划方案，许多省份有多家企业在外国投资农业。截至2012年，对外农业投资企业数排名前6的省份和企业数量如表1和表2所示。

表1　2012年中国各省（自治区、直辖市）对外农业投资存量排名

单位：万美元,%

各省对外农业投资存量前六名			
排名	省（市）	投资存量	比例
1	黑龙江	1444483	38.9
2	天津	30645	8.3
3	四川	24763	6.7
4	山东	23285	6.3
5	云南	20196	5.4
6	重庆	17147	4.6

　　资料来源：中华人民共和国农业部国际合作司、中华人民共和国农业部对外经济合作中心编著《中国对外农业投资合作报告（2012）》，中国农业出版社，2014，第12~14页。排名以各省对外农业投资企业数量计。

表2　中国各省（自治区、直辖市）对外农业投资企业数量及排名

单位：个,%

各省对外农业投资企业数量前六名			
排名	省份	企业数量	比例
1	云南	57	15.0
2	黑龙江	55	14.5
3	山东	47	12.4
4	四川	20	5.2
5	江苏	19	5.0
6	辽宁	19	5.0

　　资料来源：中华人民共和国农业部国际合作司、中华人民共和国农业部对外经济合作中心编著《中国对外农业投资合作报告（2012）》，中国农业出版社，2014，第12~14页。排名以各省对外农业投资企业数量计。

中国对赴非农业投资企业的支持体系

随着农业"走出去"政策的制定和实施、中非合作论坛的创设，以及中国对非洲投资的不断攀升，为鼓励企业走进非洲进行农业投资、解决对外投资中存在的一些问题，中国政府的相关部门制定了很多优惠政策和措施。

政策和平台支持

中国对企业到外国投资农业的政策支持主要体现在前文提到的农业"走出去"这一系列政策和中央"一号文件"的支持上。此外，2013 年中央经济工作会议上还提出了要"加强对走出去的宏观指导和服务，提供对外投资精准信息，简化对外投资审批程序"。[①] 这些政策有利于各级政府重视农业海外投资，加大对外农业投资的扶持力度，创造有利于投资农业的企业"走出去"的条件。

中国与非洲不同国家的合作以双边协定形式表现出来，比如赞比亚，早在 1996 年就签订了《中华人民共和国政府和赞比亚共和国政府关于鼓励和相互保护投资协定》。2004 年国务院制定的《对外投资国别导向目录》中，对赞比亚的优先支持领域第一项就是农业（具体为农作物种植），这意味着政策上投资种植业的合格企业将优先享受国家在资金、外汇、税收等多个方面的优惠政策。[②] 此后赞比亚高层领导多次访华时，中国也对赞比亚表达了在农业领域合作的意愿。例如，2015 年 3 月 30 日新任赞比亚总统埃德加·伦古访华时，习近平同志就表达了要与赞比亚加深农业等领域互利合作的愿望，表示鼓励和支持更多中国企业赴赞比亚投资兴业，同时希望赞方为中国企业创造更加有利的条件。[③]

---

① 中华人民共和国农业部国际合作司、农业部对外经济合作中心编著《中国对外农业投资合作报告（2012）》，第 2 页。

② 中华人民共和国商务部：《对外投资国别导向目录（一）》，2004 年 7 月 21 日，http：//www. mofcom. gov. cn/aarticle/bi/200407/20040700252005. html，2015 年 6 月 2 日访问。

③ 《习近平主持仪式欢迎赞比亚总统访华》，人民网，http：//pic. people. com. cn/n/2015/0330/c1016 - 26772468. html，2015 年 6 月 2 日访问。

资金支持

中国政府对中国企业在非洲进行农业投资的资金支持主要有财政专项资金和中非发展基金两种。

财政专项资金指"附加条件和政府间财政转移支付"，拨款者规定了资金的用途，接受者必须按照规定的方式使用资金，做到专款专用。[①] 2014年以前，中央鼓励企业进行境外投资的专项资金包括对外经济合作专项基金的资金、外经贸区域协调发展促进资金、中小企业国际市场开拓资金、进口贴息资金、境外经济贸易合作区发展资金、服务外包资金等。各地方再根据每年相关部门贴出的具体重点领域，结合本地的实际情况，制订自己的配套资金计划。

以对外经济合作专项基金为例，该资金是为了实施"走出去"发展战略、鼓励有比较优势的企业开展各种形式的对外经济合作，于2005年设立的国家专项资金。[②] 该资金涉及的业务包括境外投资，境外农业、林业和渔业合作等，但是具体的重点支持领域每年都会由财政部和商务部再次通知确定。它提供的支持为直接补助或者贴息，但是对于申请的企业也有一定的要求。企业不仅需要满足一系列在中国和投资国的投资资格条件和注册条件，投资规模上也有要求，例如，中方投资境外项目的投资额原则上不能低于100万美元。但是，该专项资金的种类和规模过于庞大、资金用途被过分限制、资金分配的不合理、资金落实情况欠佳等问题长期存在，影响了实际使用效果。

鉴于上述情况，2014年党的十八届三中全会做出了"构建开放型经济新体制"的决定，在2010年《外经贸发展专项资金管理办法》的基础上，修改制定了新的外经贸发展专项资金管理办法。[③] 而根据新的专项资金管

---

① 马海涛、冷哲：《新外经贸发展专项资金对我国外经贸的影响研究》，《国际商务财会》2014年第10期，第30页。

② 《财政部商务部关于印发〈对外经济技术合作专项资金管理办法〉的通知》，中华人民共和国财政部网站，2005年12月，http：//www.mof.gov.cn/zhengwuxinxi/caizhengwengao/caizhengbuwengao2005/caizhengbuwengao200511/200805/t20080525_42849.html，2015年4月21日访问。

③ 中华人民共和国商务部：《关于印发〈外经贸发展专项资金管理办法〉的通知》，2014年5月6日，http：//www.mofcom.gov.cn/article/cwgongzuo/huiyjl/201405/20140500573030.shtml，2015年4月21日访问。

理办法指定的申报指南，"农业、林业、牧业、渔业投资合作"成为境外投资的重点支持领域。①

另一项资金支持来自 2006 年成立的中非发展基金。中非发展基金于 2007 年正式运行，是纯市场化运作的，通过直接投资推动中非双方企业实现合作的目标。中非发展基金为企业提供的融资服务主要是"投资＋贷款"的形式，基金会为发现投资机会但缺乏资金的企业提供资金，反过来也为有资金但缺乏投资机会的企业寻找投资机会，对拥有项目和资金但不愿意独立承担风险的企业，基金提供了分担风险的服务。此外，基金还可以为非洲项目寻找中国投资人。② 具体的投资方式有股权投资、准股权投资和投资其他非洲基金等方式。例如，中非基金与青岛瑞昌、青岛汇富合作在马拉维、莫桑比克、赞比亚等国开展的棉花种植加工项目中非棉业，总投资约 3500 万美元，采用"公司＋农户"的模式进行棉花的生产、收购与加工。其中在马拉维的项目由中国开发银行与中非发展基金通过"投资＋贷款"的融资模式，由基金阶段性大比例投资控股该项目，中国开发银行配套提供贷款资金支持。③

中非合作论坛的推动作用

2000 年，中非合作论坛（Forum on China – Africa Cooperation, FO-CAC）第一届部长级会议召开，中国与非洲的合作进入了一个新的阶段——论坛通过的《中非经济和社会发展合作纲领》提到了农业合作的重要性。④ 论坛成立的近二十年来，农业合作的进展虽然相对缓慢，但通过时间线可以看出，其战略意义越来越高，政策上的重视明显推动了更大规模的实际合作。

---

① 中华人民共和国商务部：《关于 2014 年度外经贸发展专项资金申报工作的通知》，2014 年 5 月 6 日，http：//www. mofcom. gov. cn/article/cwgongzuo/huiyjl/201405/20140500573026. shtml，2015 年 4 月 21 日访问。
② 《中非基金宣传手册（2013 年 11 月版）》，中非发展基金网站，http：//www. cadfund. com/Article_List. aspx？columnID＝16，2015 年 4 月 21 日访问。
③ 《中非棉业》，中非发展基金网站，http：//www. cadfund. com/NewsInfo. aspx？NId＝781，2015 年 6 月 2 日访问。
④ 《中非经济和社会发展合作纲领》，中非合作论坛网站，http：//www. focac. org/chn/ltda/dyjbzjhy/hywj12009/t155561. htm，2015 年 4 月 16 日访问。

● 2003 年在亚的斯亚贝巴召开的第二届部长级会议上，不仅将农业放在《中非合作论坛——亚的斯亚贝巴行动计划（2004～2006 年）》中经济领域的第一部分进行强调，还提出"中国将继续通过金融等优惠政策，支持和鼓励有实力的中国企业在非洲开展农业合作项目"。①

这不仅体现了中国对与非洲开展农业合作的重视，还通过中非合作论坛这个平台鼓励企业与非洲国家在农业领域进行合作与投资。

● 2006 年，北京峰会暨中非合作论坛第三届部长级会议召开，非洲多国政要齐聚北京，震撼了世界，也展示了中国与非洲合作的信心。胡锦涛在北京峰会开幕式上的讲话中就提到了增加农业合作中的技术转移，派遣农业技术专家、建立农业技术示范中心。②

此次峰会通过的《中非合作论坛北京行动计划（2007～2009 年)》更是将"鼓励和支持中国企业扩大对非农业投资"写入其中，并表示要"进一步参与非洲农业基础设施建设、农机生产和农产品加工业"。另外，投资与企业合作也成为经济领域合作中的一个重点部分，被列在农业合作之后。③

● 2009 年的中非合作论坛部长级会议通过的未来三年行动计划中首次将以往放在经济领域合作第一项的农业改为"农业与粮食安全"，并明确表示这是双方"合作的优先领域"。当然，鼓励中国企业加大对非的农业投资再次被列入其中。④

● 2012 年第五届部长级会议不仅对以往基于中非合作论坛这一平台的中非农业合作给予了积极的评价，还为未来的发展进行了规划。在《中非合作论坛第五届部长级会议——北京行动计划（2013～2015 年)》中，除了重申推动中国企业投资非洲之外，还首次表示要鼓励国内的金融机构对这些投资非洲农业的企业进行支持，并且进一

① 《中非合作论坛——亚的斯亚贝巴行动计划（2004～2006 年)》，中非合作论坛网站，http：//www. focac. org/chn/ltda/dejbzjhy/hywj22009/，2015 年 4 月 16 日访问。
② 《胡锦涛主席在中非合作论坛北京峰会开幕式上的讲话》，中非合作论坛网站，http：//www. focac. org/chn/ltda/bjfhbzjhy/zyjh32009/t584768. htm，2015 年 4 月 16 日访问。
③ 《中非合作论坛北京行动计划（2007～2009 年)》，中非合作论坛网站，http：//www. focac. org/chn/ltda/bjfhbzjhy/hywj32009/t584788. htm，2015 年 4 月 16 日访问。
④ 《中非合作论坛—沙姆沙伊赫行动计划（2010～2012 年)》，中非合作论坛网站，http：//www. focac. org/chn/ltda/dsjbzjhy/bzhyhywj/t626385. htm，2015 年 4 月 16 日访问。

步明确了优先合作的农业领域。①

● 2015 年在南非召开的第六届中非合作论坛部长级会议升格为峰会，农业现代化再一次被加强并列入中国对非洲"十大合作计划"。实际上早在 2015 年 4 月，中国外交部部长王毅在南非比勒陀利亚与南非外长马沙巴内举行会谈，提出了包括推进在现代农业等重点领域的产业合作。加大农业合作与投资规模，是中非经济合作转型升级中的组成部分，是又一次新的战略提升。

历届中非合作论坛部长级会议和峰会都强调了加强中国与非洲的农业合作以及中国对非洲的农业投资的重要性，虽然大多是宏观政策方向上的论述，未必能够直接使中国企业在对非投资的具体实践上受益，但客观上中非合作论坛对投资非洲农业的重视有助于增强中国企业投资非洲的信心和动力，振奋投资市场。

中非合作论坛机制下成立的许多机构和机制也促进了中国投资非洲的农业。例如，2006 年北京峰会上宣布成立的中非发展基金。2007 年正式挂牌运行的中非发展基金不同于对非经济援助，采取自主经营、市场运作、自担风险的方式进行运作和管理。农业被中非发展基金视为"对非洲国家恢复、发展经济具有重要作用，能够帮助其提高自身'造血'机能"的产业，是重点支持的领域之首。目前中非发展基金支持青岛瑞昌、青岛汇富两公司在马拉维、莫桑比克、赞比亚三国展开了棉花种植项目"中非棉业"，投资约 3500 万美元，仅 2011 年就已收购棉花 4.5 万吨，带动三国约 11 万农户、60 多万农民增收。②

中非企业家大会是中非合作论坛的配套会议，2003 年 12 月的第二届中非合作论坛上举行了第一次中非企业家大会，目前已经召开了四届。历届企业家大会不仅有中非双方的重要领导人出席，还会在会议上设置企业洽谈的环节，供有投资意愿的中非企业进行接触和沟通。作为中非企业家

① 《中非合作论坛第五届部长级会议——北京行动计划（2013~2015年）》，中非合作论坛网站，http://www.focac.org/chn/ltda/dwjbzzjh/hywj/t954617.htm，2014 年 4 月 16 日访问。

② 《中非棉业》，中非发展基金网站，http://www.cadfund.com/NewsInfo.aspx? NId=781，2015 年 4 月 16 日访问。

大会通常的"压轴大戏"，闭幕式的环节往往还附带有签约仪式。近年来，在各个领域中的合作协议中，农业签约也日益增多。① 这样的安排使得国家的相关部委需要寻找和支持可以合作的中非双方企业，以便在大会上进行签约，间接促进了中国企业投资非洲。

2012 年 8 月 27 ~ 28 日，中非地方政府合作论坛作为首个在中非合作论坛框架下设立的中非地方政府领导人集体对话平台召开了，为中国企业投资非洲地方提供了平台。该论坛专门设立了中非经贸论坛，在"推动地方合作，促进共同发展"的主题下，促进双方基层和民众的相互了解、相互学习，并为双方的地方政府和企业寻求更多的合作机会提供广阔平台。② 来自中国 29 个省、市、直辖区和来自非洲的 40 个国家，以及许多国际组织的 1700 余名人士参与此次中非地方政府合作论坛。首届中非地方政府合作论坛的承办方之一是北京温州商会，更有 200 多名温州商人参加该论坛，北京温州商会会长吴家齐表示"介入承办这次论坛就是希望以后有更多机会走入非洲"，并希望通过成立"非洲风险发展投资基金"，更好地帮助企业投资非洲。③ 2015 年、2018 年，中非地方政府论坛召开第二、第三届，目前中非地方政府合作论坛已经成为中非合作论坛下面机制化的分论坛。

类似的论坛近年来越来越多，例如，中国政协下设的一个机构也举办过促进中国企业和非洲地方政府的官员对接的活动。再有，在非洲经营多年的华人华侨联合中非双方政府和企业界组织的活动，如 2015 年在赞比亚组织的"中国经验，非洲共享——首届中非农业合作与发展高峰会"助推非洲农业发展。④ 论坛一般邀请多国驻北京使馆的经济参赞或直接来自该国的官员与中资企业代表、相关领域的专家学者一起，了解非洲国别投资政策和投资环境、讨论中资在非洲的实际运作经验和教训，甚至直接搭建平台和渠道洽谈合作，并为相关业界人士预留问

---

① 中华人民共和国商务部对外投资与合作司：《第四届中非企业家大会在北京召开》，http：//hzs. mofcom. gov. cn/aarticle/xxfb/201207/20120708247815. html，2015 年 5 月 1 日访问。

② 《首届中非地方政府合作论坛》，新华网，http：//www. bj. xinhuanet. com/zt/2012zflt/，2015 年 4 月 16 日访问。

③ 《中非地方政府合作论坛闭幕，非洲或成民资下一站》，新华网，http：//www. bj. xinhua-net. com/zt/2012 - 09/02/c_112930180. htm，2015 年 4 月 16 日访问。

④ http：//www. china. com. cn/aboutus/2017 - 08/08/content_41370240. htm.

答时间，帮助中国地方资本走入非洲、充分了解优惠政策和投资环境。

结论：信息和其他农业商业服务体系的不足

农业作为"走出去"战略中较晚一个产业，目前的支持体系还严重不足。上面的政策和资金体系的支持还相当有限。上面的各种论坛活动的受欢迎程度恰恰显示，企业实际上极其需要这类信息和平台，而实际落地的相关信息很缺乏。课题组在赞比亚调研中国企业时候发现，2011年中华人民共和国商务部、中华人民共和国国家发展和改革委员会和中华人民共和国外交部联合发布的《对外投资合作国别产业指引（2011年）》（以下简称《指引》）① 虽然内容较为简略，与很多成熟的国际商业机构的农业投资指南还有很大差距，但已经成为中国企业手中的"圣经"。一些中国驻非使馆做了很多有针对性的努力。如中华人民共和国驻赞比亚共和国大使馆经济商务参赞处在官网上发布了他们翻译的赞比亚发展署的《赞比亚投资指南》（以下简称《指南》），对赞比亚的概况、投资环境、投资须知及在赞比亚生活的基本需求进行了简要介绍。同时，指南的最后还附上了许多常见机构（如银行、使馆、政府和行业机构等）的联系地址和方式，并列举了申请投资许可的要求以及申请多功能经济区许可证或执照的程序。② 对于中国投资者来说，绝大多数很难直接获取英文信息，中国驻赞比亚使馆翻译的这份中文版的《指南》为他们在赞比亚进行农业投资提供了很大的便利。与中国三大部委联合编写的《指引》相比，这本《指南》显然更符合当地实际，内容也更加具体，其中列举的很多投资须知和激励政策，都能直接为中资企业所用。虽然《指引》和《指南》两个文本存在很多差别，但不可否认的是这些信息政策方面的指导、翻译并公开发布特别有助于中国企业获取投资非洲国家农业的信息，做好前期投资评估和准备

---

① 《指南》扼要介绍了115个国家。以赞比亚为例，《指引》列出了赞比亚的主要产业发展目标、优先发展和重点发展的产业领域、外资准入规定、主要进出口产品和在赞比亚开展业务的中国企业。2013年发布了新一版《对外投资合作国别产业指引》，覆盖全球165个国家和地区。

② 中华人民共和国驻赞比亚共和国大使馆经济商务参赞处：《赞比亚投资指南》，http：//zm. mofcom. gov. cn/article/ztdy/201209/20120908334277. shtml，2015年4月21日访问。

工作。

除了这些对各国投资的国别指南外，中华人民共和国农业部国际合作司和对外经济合作中心还响应国家政策号召，出版了《中国对外农业投资合作报告》（简称《报告》）。《报告》搜集了中国进行对外农业投资企业的名录，并根据企业申报填写的所属省份、投资情况、经营状况等信息，结合统计的农业总投资存量等信息，汇总编撰而成。《报告》专注于农业对外投资，有利于中国政府和投资者从宏观上把握当前中国企业对外农业投资的整体状况，并对生产合作经营方式、产业区域布局、产品结构等信息有初步了解。但显然，《报告》连续出版了几年，非洲地区都不是重点，这既反映了中国在非洲农业领域对外投资的局限，也说明了相关部门研究力量的薄弱。据笔者了解，中华人民共和国农业部国际合作司的人员编制极为有限，特别是覆盖两个大洲的亚非处，直到 2018 年还是只有几个编制，显得与中国政府的大农业"走出去"战略极不相称。

2017 年，《中国对外农业投资合作报告（2016）总篇》（简称《报告（2016）》）出版。[①] 该报告一方面认为中国农业对外开放的推进是为维护全球和区域粮食安全做出的积极贡献；另一方面强调伴随世界经济的深度调整、不确定因素增多和国内农业发展不平衡、不协调、不可持续问题的突出，中国应该加快构建开放型农业新机制、统筹利用好两个市场两种资源。可以把《报告（2016）》视为中国农业振兴战略的一个新里程碑，它将国内、国外的农业发展和全球的粮食安全问题做通盘考虑，与以往的农业"走出去"的认知相比，《报告（2016）》更具时代性和战略高度。当然，推进新一轮战略落地的各种动力机制和支持体系亟待建设。显然，作为中国全球战略部署推进双边关系基础最为坚实的地区，非洲在新一轮农业开放战略里面理应发挥更大的作用。目前的首要工作是全面、综合、前瞻性地研究、认知中国和非洲的资源、优势和发展条件，知己知彼，相应地充分搭建好中非农业现代化合作的支持体系。

---

① 中华人民共和国农业部国际司、农业部国际经济合作中心：《中国对外农业投资合作报告（2016）总篇》，中国农业出版社，2017。

安哥拉的农业发展和中国的角色

周瑾艳* 著

作为南部非洲地域面积最大的国家，安哥拉的政策重点主要体现在两点：一是经济多元化，二是外交伙伴多元化，力图摆脱对石油资源的依赖。在对外关系上，与中国发展战略合作伙伴关系的同时，安哥拉也一直努力拓展多元的外交伙伴，以获得更广泛的世界认同。除了与欧美国家开展合作，安哥拉与世界银行、国际货币基金组织等国际组织的关系也逐渐改善。

安哥拉的多元化战略与战后农业的发展

作为非洲第二大产油国，2004～2008 年，安哥拉的经济高速增长，国内生产总值（GDP）的年均增长率达到17%。受金融危机的影响，安哥拉的 GDP 在 2009 年骤降至5%以下，但在之后的五年又逐渐反弹。由于农业发展的恢复和非石油行业的发展，GDP 增长率达到6.3%。①

安哥拉的劳动人口为 620 万，其中一半从事农业和渔业，但 2010 年，农业和渔业只贡献国内生产总值的11%。② 长期的独立战争和内战造成教育中断，导致安哥拉大部分人口文化和技术水平低下，缺乏有技术的劳动力。石油价格的剧烈下跌让安哥拉政府充分认识到促进经济多元化、公平分配石油财富、提供公共产品的重要性。促进非石油行业的增长成为安哥拉政府的优先任务，农业是安哥拉实现经济转型的关键。在安哥拉政府经济多元化政策的指导下，石油和非石油行业对 GDP 的贡献比例发生了一定变化（如表1

---

* 周瑾艳，中国社会科学院西亚非洲研究所助理研究员。
① World Bank (2014)，"Angola Economic Update 2"，June 2014.
② World Bank (2014)，"Angola Economic Update 2"，June 2014.

158

所示)。2008 年金融危机以来,农业和渔业对 GDP 的贡献从 6.8% 增长到
2011 年的 12% ,而石油和天然气对 GDP 贡献的比例则从 57.9% 下降到 43%。
安哥拉政府发起 2010～2011 年农业运动,粮食产量比上一年提高了 19.3%。
2015 年之前的十年,安哥拉农业部门的年均增长率达到 13% ,只有 2012 年
受干旱的影响农业增长率下降到 7.3%。[1] 2015 年 6 月,在意大利召开的联合
国粮食及农业组织大会第三十九届会议上,安哥拉因实现在 2015 年之前将贫困
人口比例减半、积极完成联合国千年发展目标而获得粮农组织奖。

表 1　安哥拉国内生产总值的行业构成比例变化（2008～2011 年）

单位:%

行　业	2008 年	2009 年	2010 年	2011 年
农业和渔业	6.8	10.0	11.0	12.0
石油、天然气	57.9	46.7	48.4	43.0
钻石和采掘业	1.1	1.1	1.1	1.0
转型工业	4.9	6.0	6.2	8.0
电力	0.1	0.1	0.1	0.2
建筑	5.2	7.5	6.2	6.2
服务业	17.9	21.0	20.0	21.6
其他	6.1	7.6	7.0	8.0

资料来源: Ministério do Planeamento, INE e estimativas do MINFIN, 转引自 UNFAO, Angola
Country Programming Framework, 2013 – 2017。

安哥拉自然条件优越,雨水充沛,河流密布,农业资源丰富。现有耕
地 670 万公顷,待开发耕地超过 3000 万公顷,[2] 潜力巨大。战前的安哥拉
曾经是世界上第四大咖啡生产国和最大的甘蔗、香蕉、剑麻和棉花出口国
之一。由于战争的破坏,基础设施遭到毁坏,技术和投资缺乏,安哥拉的
农业发展较为缓慢。当前安哥拉的土地只有 30% 得到耕种,当地农民以耕
作小面积土地为主,靠天吃饭。粮食不能自给,每年的粮食缺口达 300 万
吨,近一半的粮食供给依赖进口。安哥拉的农业生产力水平低下,即使与
非洲其他国家相比,粮食单位面积产量也比较低(如表 2 所示)。尽管近

---

① World Bank (2013), *Angola Economic Update*, June 2013.
② 《商务部部长介绍中国与安哥拉经贸合作情况》,中华人民共和国商务部网站,http://
www. gov. cn/xinwen/2014-05/10/content_2676852. htm,2014 年 5 月 10 日访问。

年粮食产量逐年增长，但产量的提高还主要是因为耕地面积的扩大，农业生产力并无显著的提高。

表 2　安哥拉单位面积粮食产量

单位：千克/公顷

	2000 年	2005 年	2010 年
安哥拉	572	599	644
肯尼亚	1375	1646	1613
马拉维	1676	778	2206
莫桑比克	868	741	1006
尼日利亚	1172	1422	1413
南非	2755	3315	4162
赞比亚	1682	1902	2547
撒哈拉以南非洲	1131	1174	1336

资料来源：世界银行 2015 年公布的数据。

内战结束后，安哥拉政府立刻将减贫设为工作重点。2003 年安哥拉政府制定《减贫战略（2003～2005 年）》，以粮食安全和农村发展作为农业发展的核心目标。安哥拉政府充分认识到农业的重要性，在所有的政府战略中，农业和粮食安全都是重中之重。在解决了内战后人口重新安置的问题之后，安哥拉政府已经将社会政策的重点转移到粮食安全、对贫困和脆弱人口的扶助。对于农业发展的落后，安哥拉政府分析了几大原因：多年战争、人口变迁、被破坏的社会和经济基础设施、宏观政策条件难以推动农业市场化和教育、医疗健康和保障体系的不足，以及人力资源缺乏。[①] 因此，安哥拉政府试图从生产、加工、资金投入以及市场环节来解决农业难题。

发展农业不但是安哥拉政府的优先任务，也是人民的迫切希望。安哥拉通讯社在首页上发起关于"为了实现国家经济的多元化应主要进行何种投资"的调查，农业以 62% 的支持率高居榜首。[②] 由于安哥拉大部分的贫

---

① 《商务部部长介绍中国与安哥拉经贸合作情况》，中华人民共和国商务部网站，http：//www. gov. cn/xinwen/2014-05/10/content_2676852. htm，2014 年 5 月 10 日访问。

② "Survey Points to Investment in Agribusiness, Family Farm", 15 May, 2015, http：//www. portalangop. co. ao/angola/en _ us/noticias/economia/2015/4/20/Survey-points-investment-agri-business-family-farm, 147b613b－0e71－40f3－b9c3－329df81b8d86. html.

160

困人口在农村，农业和农村发展可以提供更多的就业机会。在安哥拉政府2007～2008 年的发展大纲里，预计农业将会带来 2.8 万个就业岗位。[1] 农业还是减少贫困、提高粮食安全、刺激增长和促进财富公平分配的关键。2009 年，安哥拉政府更把粮食安全上升到一级国家战略的高度。[2] 2010 年，安哥拉政府将上述减贫战略和粮食安全战略整合为《农村发展和减贫的综合战略》，并设定了总目标：消灭安哥拉尤其是农村地区的极度贫困，促进公共服务，使安哥拉成为一个社会公正的繁荣国家。[3] 这与安哥拉政府出台的 2025 愿景、国家发展战略（2013～2017 年）以及减贫计划（2010～2015 年）一致。[4] 2015 年 5 月起，安哥拉开始在罗安达兴建一座每日可处理小麦 1200 吨的面粉厂，实现安哥拉自主生产面粉的突破，延伸农业产业链。安哥拉的中期发展规划（2013～2017 年）规定了农业部门的四大战略目标：（1）通过更广泛的专业培训和转让技术优化农业生产和生产力；（2）在家庭农业、合作社和公私伙伴关系的基础上实现农业转型；（3）建立不同行业之间以及其他利益相关者的紧密协调和协同机制，强调社会对国家发展过程的参与；（4）为国家工业化做贡献。[5] 安哥拉农业和农村发展部具体制定了安哥拉农业发展的五大优先任务：（1）提高农业的总产量和生产力；（2）建立农民（尤其是小农户）与市场之间的联系，增加农民的收入；（3）增强灌溉系统、交通、电力等农村基础设施建设，提高土地质量；（4）创造非农就业机会；（5）增强农村社区组织的能力。2016 年，安哥拉宣布农业、渔业和矿业为促进经济多样性发展、短期内重点发展的三大产业。

安哥拉发展农业、实现经济多元化的政策得到了多国政府和国际组织的支持。从 2011 年开始，联合国粮食及农业组织在安哥拉平均每年投入

① 刘海方：《从因资源"被诅咒"到以资源求繁荣——新世纪增速最快国家安哥拉发展研究》，李安山主编《非洲梦：探索现代化之路》，江苏人民出版社，2013。
② 刘海方：《从因资源"被诅咒"到以资源求繁荣——新世纪增速最快国家安哥拉发展研究》，李安山主编《非洲梦：探索现代化之路》，江苏人民出版社，2013。
③ UNFAO, Angola Country Programming Framework, 2013－2017, ftp：//ftp. fao. org/TC/CPF/Countries/Angola/CPFAngola_FirstDraftNov2012. doc.
④ Estrategia de Combate a Pobreza, ECP, 2010－2015.
⑤ UNFAO, Angola Country Programming Framework, 2013－2017, ftp：//ftp. fao. org/TC/CPF/Countries/Angola/CPFAngola_FirstDraftNov2012. doc.

300 多万美元，用于帮助建立农业框架、跟进农业政策，支持安哥拉政府消除贫困。欧盟在安哥拉的农业项目未来五年的预算是 2.2 亿欧元，① 主要用于完善安哥拉的土地使用登记系统，为小农户提供农业技术的培训和营养学方面的教育。联合国粮食及农业组织和世界银行在指导安哥拉制定农业和农村发展战略时，均以家庭农业作为重点。世界银行在安哥拉的农业项目主要是通过培训小农户提高农作物的平均产值，从而提高粮食安全，增加农村收入，消除极端贫困。世界银行的"农产品市场计划"，目标是使小农能够通过集中的销售点直接把农产品卖给农业加工者，从而克服在无数分散场所通过中间商交易的现行体系的低效。② 美国进出口银行在 2014 年向安哥拉企业推出一种无额度限制的贷款，支持农业和能源等领域的发展。③ 英国政府也表示打算支持安哥拉的经济多元化过程，重点是农业部门。④ 国际组织和西方国家主要支持安哥拉的家庭农业，而巴西、中国等南方国家更重视大型农商业综合项目。巴西的最大建筑承包商欧德布莱克特公司在安哥拉马兰热省投资了面积达 36000 公顷的篷戈安东戈农场。巴西不但负责农场的基础设施建设，经营玉米粉厂和饲料厂，还对玉米、大豆和大米的试种提供支持。阿根廷在 2013 年宣布提供 1 亿美元信贷资助安哥拉农业项目。⑤

综上，安哥拉农业发展的优势在于良好的政策框架、国际组织的政策和技术支持，以及双边合作伙伴的资金和技术支持。不足则在于基础设施建设的落后、农业技术和生产力的落后，以及安哥拉政府的执行能力与其抱负之间的鸿沟。在宽扎急剧贬值、人民生活成本畸高的情势下，农业投资面临的另一大挑战是安哥拉日益恶化的安全环境。

---

① 2014 年 4 月在罗安达与欧盟驻安哥拉代表团农村发展部项目经理 Vincent Rodrigues van Halsema 的访谈。

② World Bank，"Country Partnership Strategy（FY 14 – FY16）for the Republic of Angola"，August 15，2013.

③ 中华人民共和国商务部网站，http：//www. mofcom. gov. cn/article/i/jyjl/k/201402/20140200494635. shtml。

④ 《英国拟支持安哥拉农业发展》，https：//macauhub. com. mo/zh/2015/02/25/uk-intends-to-support-agricultural-development-in-angola/。

⑤ 中华人民共和国商务部网站，http：//www. mofcom. gov. cn/article/i/jyjl/k/201308/20130800226243. shtml。

中国在安哥拉农业发展中的角色

中安两国的双边贸易自 2002 年以来稳步增长。安哥拉是中国在非洲仅次于南非的第二大贸易伙伴，中国是安哥拉第一大贸易伙伴国、第一大出口目的地国、第二大进口来源国，中安贸易额约占安哥拉对外贸易额的 37.6%。自 2006 年起，安哥拉连续 8 年位居中国全球第二大原油进口来源国，仅次于沙特。2012 年，中国给予原产于安哥拉的 95% 的输华产品实施免关税待遇。[①]

中安合作以资源、信贷、基础设施一揽子的模式为起点，如今已经深入农业等民生领域。2009 年，中国国家开发银行（简称国开行）向安哥拉首次提供了价值 15 亿美元的商业贷款，该笔贷款与以往进出口银行提供的贷款不同，不以石油作为担保，[②] 主要用于安哥拉的农业领域，成为中安合作的亮点。目前国开行的第一期 15 亿美元贷款额度已经全部安排使用完毕。[③]

2010 年，时任中国国家副主席习近平访问安哥拉，两国签署了关于建立战略合作伙伴关系的联合声明，鼓励和支持两国企业和金融机构扩大双边贸易和投资，重点加强在农业、工业、基础设施建设和能源等领域的互利合作。2014 年 5 月李克强总理首次出访安哥拉期间，与安哥拉签署新的融资贷款合作协议，由中国国家开发银行向安方提供新一期 25 亿美元贷款，用于交通、农业、医院、学校、水电等领域。[④] 此间，中国商务部部长高虎城表示，中方将加大对安哥拉农业投资合作的力度和深度，尽早实施农业示范中心项目，开展农作物良种推广和示范种植，同时推动企业深入参与安哥拉农垦种植、仓储加工等重点环节。[⑤] 2014 年下半年以来安哥

---

① 《中国与非洲的经贸合作（2013）白皮书》。
② 姚桂梅：《中国对非洲投资合作的主要模式及挑战》，《西亚非洲》2013 年第 5 期，第 109 页。
③ 中国驻安哥拉使馆经商处，http://cccla.mofcom.gov.cn/article/i/jyjl/k/201405/20140500590705.shtml。
④ 中国驻安哥拉使馆经商处，http://ao.mofcom.gov.cn/article/sqfb/。
⑤ 中华人民共和国商务部新闻办公室：《高虎城：中安经贸合作蓬勃发展前景广阔》，2014 年 5 月 9 日，http://www.mofcom.gov.cn/article/ae/ai/201405/20140500580214.shtml。

拉经济陷入油价大幅下跌的困境，农业更成为实现经济多样化的关键。中国与安哥拉的农业合作形式主要是农业基础设施建设、技术培训和信贷支持。自 2009 年以来，在中国国家开发银行和中国进出口银行的信贷支持下，中国在安哥拉开始实施七个农业综合开发项目（如图 4 所示）。基本的模式是由中国企业与安哥拉农业部签署为期五年的承包工程合同，由安哥拉国有农业公司伊斯戴尔（Gesterra）代表安哥拉农业部作为项目的业主方。项目是一站式的，中国企业不仅负责农场、灌溉设施、谷物烘干、粮食仓储和加工厂、办公室和员工宿舍等基础设施建设，还负责帮助安哥拉培训农业技术和农场管理人才。农场种植水稻、玉米或大豆，以满足安哥拉当地市场的需求。农场的规模在 1500 公顷到 12000 公顷，土地属于安哥拉所有，由伊斯戴尔公司提供给中国企业使用。在目前中国支持的七个农场中，除即将开工的库茵巴农场外，其他六个农场都获得国开行贷款的支持。中安农业合作项目中规模最大的是中信建设有限责任公司（简称中信建设）和新疆生产建设兵团组成农业联合舰队共同开发的马兰热黑石农场，于 2010 年 8 月开始建点垦荒，总占地 12000 公顷，项目合同总额超过 1.2 亿美元，目前已开垦超过 4500 公顷。黑石农场是中信建设安哥拉国家大区正式签约并实施的第一个非工程类项目，标志着中资企业在安哥拉的业务由建筑工程领域向农业等领域的拓展。黑石农场主要种植粮食作物玉米和大豆，基本模式是由中资企业与安哥拉农业部签署为期五年的承包工程合同，前三年由中信建设负责开荒、基建和试种，后两年农场正式运营和中方对安哥拉农业技术人员培训。项目集种植、仓储、加工为一体，粮食收获后全部转交安方，五年合同期满后农场和所有设备也移交安方。

表 3 中国国家开发银行和中国进出口银行在安哥拉承建的 7 个大型综合农场项目

农场名称	地理位置	承建公司	公司类型	开始日期	信贷来源	信贷额度（百万美元）	农场规模（公顷）	经营内容
黑石	马兰热省	中信建设	国有企业	2011	国开行	160	12580	玉米、大豆
桑扎蓬勃	威热省	中信建设	国有企业	2012	国开行	87.5	1050	水稻、养牛

164

农场名称	地理位置	承建公司	公司类型	开始日期	信贷来源	信贷额度（百万美元）	农场规模（公顷）	经营内容
隆格	库安多古邦戈省	中国国际工程股份有限公司（简称中工国际）	国有企业	2012	国开行	77.6	1500	水稻
卡玛库巴	比耶省	中工国际	国有企业	2012	国开行	88.64	4500	玉米
库茵巴	扎伊尔省	中国电子进出口有限公司（简称中电子）	国有企业	2015	中国进出口银行	68	3000	玉米、大豆、养殖
嘎马洋噶拉	墨希科省	中电子	国有企业	2013	国开行	79	16000	玉米、大豆
芒哥特	库内内省	中电子	国有企业	2014年年底	国开行	85.5	45000	水稻

资料来源：周瑾艳：《中国在安哥拉：不仅仅是石油——以农业合作为例》，《亚非纵横》2014年第5期。

现阶段的中安农业合作具有如下特点：第一，与中国在坦桑尼亚、莫桑比克等国的农业投资中民营资本发挥主导作用的情况不同，与安哥拉农业合作的中国企业中，国有资本起到了主导作用，私人资本对农业的投资仍然处于初始阶段。一方面，安哥拉战后重建的十多年，大量中国国有企业通过框架合作协议进入安哥拉从事基础设施建设，在工程结束后继续留下来寻找商机。目前，在安哥拉已经承揽项目的中国国有企业主要有中国水电建设集团国际工程有限公司、中国机械设备工程股份有限公司、中国机械对外经济技术合作有限公司、国华国际工程承包公司、广西水利电业集团有限公司、中国中铁四局集团有限公司、中铁二十局集团有限公司、中国电子进出口有限公司、中国工程与农业机械进出口有限公司、中江国际集团公司、中国江苏国际经济技术合作集团有限公司等。国有企业进入安哥拉较早，对当地的情况比较熟悉，加上中国政府的信贷支持，国有企业在安哥拉开展农业合作具有天时地利的优势。另一方面，安哥拉的基础设施状况和投资环境也制约了中国很多民营企业去安哥拉投资农业。

以 2016 年为分水岭，中国在安哥拉的农业合作模式正在发生逐渐转变。第一，中安合作正从大型农业综合项目向以市场为导向的农业投资项目转变。表 3 中的项目刚刚启动时，中国尚未成为安哥拉农业的主要投资者，主要是以农业工程承包商的身份与安哥拉合作——这些任务主要是国家层面的合作，中安农业合作更多承担了维护中国国家形象、提高软实力、夯实中安战略伙伴关系的任务。2016 年以来，农业合作已逐渐向以市场为导向、以企业（包括国有企业和民营企业）为主体的方向过渡。越来越多的中国民营企业看到了在安哥拉投资的商机。娃哈哈集团有限公司董事长宗庆后呼吁浙江商人抱团投资非洲，在实地考察期间与安哥拉签订合作备忘录，"希望整合浙江生产各类型产品的企业到该国兴建经济开发区，同时组织渔民、农民去远洋捕捞及进行农业开发，建设钢铁厂、开铁矿、开发地产"。① 这项合作意向得到了中非发展基金和国开行浙江分行的资金支持。

2012 年起，国内承包商、分包商看到安哥拉农业的巨大潜力，将企业发展重点转向农业投资。通过参与七大农场项目的建设，他们获得了在安哥拉经营农业的宝贵经验，在签订的五年合同即将到期之际，纷纷开辟新的农业投资项目。江苏省江洲农业科技公司（简称江洲农业）曾分包承包中工国际在卡玛库巴的综合农场项目，根据分包工程获得的经验，江洲农业在 2016 年获得了万博省嘎啦（Caala）农场的开发项目，拟签订 10000 公顷的农业合作协议。

第二，除了中国中央政府主导中安合作，中国地方政府正逐渐成为中安农业合作的重要推动力。2013 年，库内内省省长访问中国寻找合作方时，安哥拉库内内省与中国江苏省讨论了结对项目。2015 年 7 月，江苏省南京市政府宣布拟与安哥拉库内内省在两省的结对项目框架下开展农业合作项目。② 2016 年 5 月底，由安哥拉万博省副省长率领的安哥拉代表团一行 10 人来到江苏农牧科技职业学院，并为"安哥拉万博省农牧人才培养基地"揭牌。有 15 名安哥拉留学生来江苏农牧科技职业学院接受为期 3 年

---

① 娃哈哈集团董事长宗庆后在 2014 世界杭商大会上的发言，http：//finance. people. com. cn/n/2014/1022/c1004 - 25886872. html。

② 澳门荟萃新闻（Macauhub）：《中国江苏希望加强与安哥拉库内内合作》，2015 年 7 月 3 日。

的全日制学历教育。江苏农牧科技职业学院也在讨论与万博省在农业、科技、教育等领域展开更深远的合作。

除了双边农业合作外，中国还积极参加联合国粮食及农业组织实施的粮食安全行动特别计划，在"南南合作"协议框架下向安哥拉派遣专家，帮助安哥拉发展农业生产，培训农业技术人员。

中安农业合作的作用与前景展望

中国在安哥拉的农业项目有助于改善安哥拉的农业基础设施，提高农业生产技术和产量，从而实现减贫和粮食安全。

中国最大的优势在于改善基础设施。基础设施掣肘安哥拉经济发展，也是促进经济多元化、吸引投资的最大障碍。在一揽子合作框架下，中国在安哥拉建设了大量交通网络和公用设施，有效地改善了安哥拉工农业的基础设施条件。安哥拉已成为中国在非洲的第三大承包市场。基础设施的长远影响在于改善投资环境，提高私营部门的竞争力，从而促进经济的长期发展。中国建造的基础交通和公用设施不但为两国投资合作从石油领域向农业等领域拓展打下了良好的基础，也减少了其他国家在安哥拉投资的成本，为私人投资提供更多机遇，创造了更多就业和收入机会。以中铁二十局集团有限公司修建的本格拉铁路为例，西起安哥拉最大港口洛比托，东至与刚果（金）毗邻的边境城市卢奥，铁路时速90公里，规划年运送货物2000万吨。本格拉铁路通车后与周边国家铁路网接轨，实现南部非洲铁路的互联互通，形成大西洋与印度洋之间的国际铁路大通道。由于安哥拉巨大的农业发展潜力，本格拉铁路的通车有助于农产品在安哥拉境内和赞比亚、刚果（金）的运输，促进安哥拉的农业贸易，从而吸引私人投资，提高整体经济竞争力。

另外，在合作框架协议下，中国水电建设集团国际工程有限公司还为安哥拉修建了对农业升级发展至关重要的大量农业灌溉项目，包括卢纳（Luena）灌溉重建项目、甘德杰拉思（Gandjelas）灌溉修复和升级项目、卡西吐（Caxito）灌溉重建和升级项目，以及马吐布（Wako-Kun-go）灌溉项目。安哥拉的土地面积为3500万公顷，目前只有约五分之一被开垦。安哥拉有很大的农业发展潜力，但因为土地贫瘠，土地需要前期大量的拓荒和投资才能进行耕种。中信建设、中工国际、中电子等国有企业自 2010 年起在安哥拉开发七大农业综合项目，计划开荒近 10 万公顷土地，通过建设农场、农业培训中心、农产品加工工厂和仓储设备帮助安哥拉进一步改善农业基础设施，提高生产力，并且将农产品输送到市场上。2014 年 11 月，中信建设宣布 2015 年在安哥拉投资 5 亿美元开发面积为 50 万公顷的大型农场。2017 年中信建设进行农场评估和前期商务谈判，决定以股权投资的形式部分收购中信建设在安哥拉建设运营的马兰热农场和威热农场。收购农场后中信建设利用投资增加和改善现有农业设施，建设安哥拉的农业技术示范中心、农业制种育种中心、种牛繁育中心、区域农业加工中心，它们成为中信建设在安哥拉大农业全产业链投资的起跑道。

另外，中国通过农作物良种推广和示范种植，帮助安哥拉提高农业技术，提高产量，延伸产业链，对安哥拉减贫和实现粮食安全做出贡献。安哥拉的农业耕作灌溉方式以喷灌为主，新疆生产建设兵团把在以色列学到的节水型滴灌方式带到了安哥拉。通过示范种植的方式，极大地提高了安哥拉粮食的单位产量，中国目前在安哥拉开展的农业综合项目的另一亮点是建设农业加工工厂，以帮助安哥拉延伸农业产业链，提高农副产品附加值，促进农业增效。目前黑石农场的玉米加工厂已投入运营，每小时可生产玉米粉 12 吨。中国在安哥拉的农业项目引导安哥拉增强农作物收获后的加工业和服务，提高生产力。

除了基础设施落后，制约安哥拉农业生产力提高的阻力还有缺乏掌握农业技术的劳动力。因此，中国现阶段的农业综合项目均以传授农业科技和农业管理知识作为重点，主要通过"培训培训者"的方式进行能力建设。中国电子进出口有限公司委托黑龙江八一农垦大学培训了首期 17 名安哥拉籍学员，中信建设资助 19 名安哥拉学员在新疆石河子大学进行为期一年的学习。在中国接受农业技术和农场现代管理的安哥拉农业人才，将被安哥拉农业部派遣到全国其他农场培训和管理更多农业技术人才。

中安合作已经走过了粗放发展的最初十年，通过国家信贷获取基建承包工程和进行石油贸易的合作方式在安哥拉战后重建初期这一特殊时期是成功的，实现了中安双方政治经济利益的双赢。但随着安哥拉发展多元化经济，安哥拉政府与中国企业的合作热情已然减退，导致模式本身运转平缓。① 中国与安哥拉在农业领域的合作对中国来说，最大的意义在于拓展新的合作方式，夯实与安哥拉的战略合作伙伴关系，深化中安合作。

对安哥拉来说，国际石油价格骤降倒逼安哥拉在国内真正推行经济多样化改革。安哥拉政府将农业列为整个国家的优先目标，重视农业和农村发展对社会和经济发展的重要作用。农业不但能够帮助安哥拉减少贫困，提高粮食安全，也是安哥拉摆脱对石油的依赖、实现多元经济政策成败与否的关键。对中国来说，与安哥拉的农业合作不仅是中国农业企业"走出去"战略的一部分，更是夯实与安哥拉战略合作伙伴关系的关键。2015 年6 月，安哥拉前总统多斯桑多斯访华期间，习近平主席在与其会谈时强调中安合作共赢、共同发展、互有需要、互有优势、互为机遇。中安两国领导人达成了推动中安合作转型升级的共识。② 具体的转型就是从过去以工程承包和贸易为主的合作模式转向兼顾传统合作领域同时开辟投资合作领域。中资企业投资农业可成为中安合作转型的先行军。通过基础设施建设、提高育种选种和技术人才培训等，中国实际尚在帮助安哥拉解决粮食危机，稳定世界粮食价格；客观上这也有利于对中国从世界市场上以稳定的价格获取粮食并对中国的粮食安全有间接的促进作用。

在世界银行等国际组织的指导下，安哥拉政府已经制定了很多好的战略，但问题的关键在于政策的执行。安哥拉农业发展潜力巨大，但是农业资源未被充分利用，基础设施落后和技术人才短缺成为制约农业发展的最大瓶颈。促进非石油行业的发展对安哥拉的基础设施要求很高。安哥拉政府有望进一步改善投资环境，为外来投资提供便捷、安全的投资环境，为农业投资制定减免税收等优惠政策。由于农业投资是长期的，安哥拉政府需要致力于保障投资者的人身安全，减少投资者的结构性风险，吸引更多的中国投资者。由于目前在安哥拉的农业投资短期内很难获利，大部分民营企业难以承受三年至五年的开荒和准备期，中国的国有企业充分利用国家信贷支持的优势，有效地帮助安哥拉改善基础设施。同时，随着中安合

---

① 姚桂梅：《中国对非洲投资合作的主要模式及挑战》，《西亚非洲》2013 年第 5 期，第 109 页。

② 《驻安哥拉使馆临时代办李翀接受安媒体专访》，中国驻安哥拉大使馆网站，2015 年 6 月 20 日，http://ao.china-embassy.org/chn/sghd/t1274791.htm。

作的首期七大农业综合项目的五年合同期接近尾声，中资企业正在从农业基础设施工程承包商的角色，努力转变成真正的农业投资者。未来的中安农业合作应逐渐过渡到市场模式，提高农业投资的利润，吸引更多中国企业的投资。同时，安哥拉农业的可持续发展不仅需要资金，更需要宏观政策和规划的指导、知识和经验的交流。中国应在现有的农业技术培训、基础设施配套、农业投资的基础上增强在安哥拉农业规划制定领域的影响力。

中国应进一步促进企业（包括国有企业和民营企业）去安哥拉投资农业，不但要注重当前的农业综合开发项目等大规模农业投资，也要将中国的优势——小农户生产模式推广到安哥拉。通过培训小农户、向小农户直接下订单等方式连接农户和市场，这不但有利于提高安哥拉的农业科技水平和市场协作机制，改善粮食安全，也有利于更多的普通民众从中安合作中获利，改变外界对中安合作集中于资源领域的印象。

中国在最危急的时候成为安哥拉"硕果仅存"的战略伙伴，支持了其最为紧迫的战后重建工作；如今中国与安哥拉全面合作面临着转型升级的挑战和契机，未来还需在双方共同努力下探索适宜的合作方向，农业合作无疑是双方迈出的重要一步。安哥拉经历战后重建和金融危机洗礼，国内景观和国际地位均已今非昔比，在与中国继续发展战略合作伙伴关系的同时也在积极地"向西看"，通过发展多元伙伴关系提高自身的信誉评级，拓展国际空间，实现自身国家利益的最大化。自 2009 年以来，安哥拉与国际货币基金组织（IMF）和世界银行的关系逐步改善，在宏观和具体政策方面接受布雷顿森林组织的指导。2009～2012 年，安哥拉接受 IMF 提供的14 亿元备用贷款计划（SBA）。IMF 在安哥拉首都罗安达设有代表处，除了通过正式途径对安哥拉的政府政策和宏观经济发展进行"监督"，IMF还通过与安哥拉官员的日常交流影响安哥拉政府的经济政策。国际货币基金组织驻安哥拉的总代表认为，外界对安哥拉的印象有很大改善与成功开展国际货币基金组织的三年备用安排计划（SBA）项目有很大关系。[1] 安哥拉财政部部长则澄清说，与国际货币基金组织的合作主要是技术层面

---

① Interview with Nicholas Staines, IMF Resident Representative, December 9, 2014, www. imf. org/external/country/AGO/rr/2014/120914. pdf , accessed 27 May 2015.

的，并非援助。类似地，世界银行与安哥拉的合作方式主要是提供咨询和指导。21 世纪以前，世界银行曾为安哥拉制定的唯一一份国家战略报告是 1991 年发布的《安哥拉国家援助战略》。2013 年，安哥拉政府明确表达了加强与世界银行合作的强烈意愿。① 世界银行首次制定新的"与安哥拉伙伴关系战略"。从过去自上而下的"援助"到如今平等相待的"伙伴关系"，世界银行对安哥拉的态度发生了翻天覆地的变化。在准备和撰写 2013 年战略报告的过程中，世界银行也一改居高临下的态度，充分尊重安哥拉政府的自主权，共同撰写报告，并将撰写报告的过程视作与安哥拉重新建立强劲合作的契机和基石。对今天的安哥拉来说，经验、技术和政策指导远比资金更加重要。正如安哥拉政府一直对世界银行强调的："（我们）需要（你们的）大脑，而不是（你们的）钱。"②

---

① World Bank（2013），"Country Partnership Strategy（FY14 - FY16）for the Republic of Angola"，August 15，2013.

② World Bank（2013），"Country Partnership Strategy（FY14 - FY16）for the Republic of Angola"，August 15，2013.

中国在赞比亚的农业投资情况及建议

宛 如* 著

20 世纪中叶以来，赞比亚一直是中国援助和投资非洲的重点国家之一。随着赞比亚经济的自由化和中国农业"走出去"政策的实施，越来越多的中国企业来到赞比亚投资农业。本文将概述赞比亚自身的农业发展条件和引资情况，介绍中国在赞比亚的农业投资，并通过对三家不同农场的对比和分析，思考中国在赞农业投资所存在的问题，提出发展建议。

赞比亚的农业发展和引资情况

赞比亚位于南部非洲海拔 1000～1500 米的高原之上，农业自然条件良好，适宜农耕。然而与优越的农业生产条件所不相称的是赞比亚农业生产的发展水平。在英国殖民时期，赞比亚中北部发现的铜矿成为其支柱产业和主要的财政收入来源，很长时间农业只是作为采矿业的补充，支持城市和矿业工人生活而存在，农业生产水平不高。在获得对赞比亚土地的管辖权后，英国殖民当局将赞比亚的土地按照种族和用途划分为皇家土地、白人居住区、赞比亚本地人居住的保留地、托管地四类，并对不同类型的土地采取不同的规划和政策。这样的土地管理方式为独立后的农业发展埋下了隐患。

1964 年赞比亚独立之后，卡翁达政府面临快速恢复国民经济、改善人民生活的压力，因此具有一定实力和基础的铜矿业成为赞比亚经济发展的重点。而在农业方面，卡翁达政府出于用统一全国的玉米市场价格增加黑

---

* 宛如，北京大学国际关系学院硕士毕业，现任中国工商银行迪拜国际金融中心分行法律合规部经理。

人农场和农民的收入的考虑，出台了玉米"平价政策"，导致许多本不适宜种植玉米的地方盲目扩大种植规模；但随着 20 世纪 70 年代石油危机来袭，国际铜矿价格大跌，赞比亚政府收入也随之骤减，无力维持原来的玉米生产的财政补助，极大地影响了农民种植玉米的积极性，全国范围内粮食产量大幅下降。

为了保证赞比亚自身的粮食安全，卡翁达采取了一系列措施试图发展农业。土地方面，卡翁达于 1975 年 7 月 1 日颁布了《土地法令》（*Land Conversion of Title Act 1975*），宣布赞比亚的土地国有化，禁止私人拥有土地，对殖民时期白人占有的土地实行 99 年租期的租赁制，其他的土地则分为城镇土地和城镇外土地，实行不同的土地政策。土地法案还保留了酋长管辖区内酋长对土地的决定权，只是不能买卖和出租。[1] 1985 年通过的《土地法令修正案》再次对土地的获得增加了限制，规定在没有总统的批准时，非赞比亚人不允许获得土地。《土地法令》本来的意图是改变白人拥有大片土地而当地人无地可耕的状况，让赞比亚人获得更多的土地进行农业生产。激进的措施反而导致外国投资赞比亚农业的动力骤降。[2] 农业生产方面，卡翁达允许多种经济存在，但是重点强调发展国有农场和农民集体生产组织。具体的措施包括推动合作化、仿效坦桑尼亚"乌贾马"运动改造农村、建立农业复兴中心和国有农场等。[3] 当然，客观地看，这一阶段政府支持农业发展的动机和主要目的是供给国内市场，保证国内粮食安全，做到粮食自给，而非出口农产品进行创汇。粮食（尤其是玉米）价格过高导致了社会的动荡和多党化、自由化呼声的兴起，间接导致了 1991 年 10 月 31 日奇卢巴领导的"多党民主运动"（Movement for Multi-party Democracy）通过选举获得政权。

奇卢巴上台后，以农业市场自由化手段来复苏农业，从改革土地制度、提供有利的投资环境等方面吸引外国对赞比亚农业的投资。一直以来，赞比亚实行的是传统土地所有制和官方登记租赁制土地所有制双轨并行的土地制度，独立后 93% 的土地为传统土地所有制，只有 7% 的土地属

---

[1] 刘静：《赞比亚农业及其面临的问题》，《西亚非洲》1988 年第 3 期，第 36 页。

[2] Bastiaan van Loenen，"Land Tenure in Zambia"，University of Maine，http：//www. spatial. maine. edu/ ~ onsrud/Landtenure/CountryReport/Zambia. pdf.

[3] 刘静：《赞比亚农业及其面临的问题》，《西亚非洲》1988 年第 3 期，第 36 ~ 37 页。

于国有土地，可以通过官方租赁给农民或企业使用。1995 年新的《土地法》颁布（*Land Act 1995*），为将土地租给外国人提供了可能，并设立了两个专门的机构：土地法庭（Land Tribunal）和土地发展基金（Land Development Fund），分别负责处理所有土地相关的案件和鼓励对新近开辟出来的土地进行开发使用。

除了 1995 年制定的《土地法》，赞比亚还通过了许多别的政策及规划方案来保证农业的发展。《国家农业政策（2004～2015 年）》（*National Agriculture Policy*，NAP）① 中提到，农业的工作重点是：发展和推广适当的农业机械、工具、设备、零件和捕鱼方法；发展和推广适宜的种子、树苗和牲畜品种；发展和推广适宜的鱼种及水产品品种；研究病害防治方法；发展可持续的工作方法和推广适当的生物科技技术。2006 年 12 月发布的《赞比亚远景规划 2030》（*Zambia Vision 2030*）中，农业的远景是在 2030年农业发展为一个高效、有竞争力、可持续、以出口为导向的产业，并能保障赞比亚的粮食安全，提高国民收入。《赞比亚远景规划 2030》还提出了具体领域的增长和改善目标，最终使农业产量和生产力得以提升并实现农业发展多样化，并使农业部门在 GDP 中所占的比重达到 20%。② 最近一次赞比亚政府出台的关于农业的重要政策举措，便是 2013 年 12 月公布的《赞比亚国家农业投资计划（2014～2018 年）》（*National Agriculture Investment Plan 2014–2018*，NAIP）。该投资计划认为，赞比亚政府以往的农业发展计划和规划对农村地区的贫困问题和农业抗风险能力建设重视不够，这使赞比亚整体的贫困水平仍然很高，且大部分贫困人口依然集中在农村地区；农业整体呈现增长的态势，但是波动很大，2005 年和 2007 年因受暴雨影响农业呈现了负增长。《赞比亚国家农业投资计划（2014～2018 年）》将减贫纳入了农业发展的日程中，使农业发展真正实现包容性的增长。③

① Ministry of Commerce, Trade and Industry, Policy Documents, "National Agriculture Policy (2004–2015)", http：//www. mcti. gov. zm/index. php/quarterly–newsletters/cat_view/37–policy–documents，2015 年 4 月 21 日访问。

② "Zambia Vision 2030", http：//www. mcti. gov. zm/index. php/quarterly–newsletters/cat_view/37–policy–documents，2015 年 4 月 21 日访问。

③ Ministry of Agriculture and Livestock, Government of the Republic of Zambia, *National Agriculture Investment Plan*（*NAIP*）2014–2018, online available http：//www. gafspfund. org/sites/gafspfund. org/files/Documents/6. %20Zambia_ investment%20plan. pdf，2015 年 4 月 28 日访问。

赞比亚吸引农业投资的政策

对于赞比亚政府来说，农业有着特殊的意义。第一，赞比亚人民生活与农业息息相关。根据联合国粮食及农业组织的统计，2013 年赞比亚人口总数为 1453.9 万人，其中 872 万人居住在乡村，353.6 万人从事农业经济活动，占从事经济活动总人口的 61.37%，可以说，农业是赞比亚大部分人民赖以生存和发展的主要手段。第二，广大的农业人口也是赞比亚选举中的宝贵"票仓"，有着重要的政治意义。第三，农业是赞比亚摆脱对矿业部门的依赖、发展经济多元化过程中的重要一环。此外，发展农业也与保障本国的粮食安全有关。因此，赞比亚政府近年来非常重视农业的发展。

赞比亚目前本土农业生产和发展中仍然存在很多不利因素。首先，生活在农村的人口大多为贫困人口（83%），其中 71% 的人口极度贫困，他们从事的农业主要以自给自足为目的，很少能生产出剩余农产品或将农产品拿到市场售卖，甚至还需要政府对他们进行补贴。其次，虽然赞比亚可耕地面积占国土面积 58%，但目前只有 14% 的可耕地被开发利用了起来。而在这不多的已利用土地上，大部分农业人口以家庭为单位，耕作一块面积很小的土地。据赞比亚中央统计办公室估计，72.7% 农户的耕地面积不到 2 公顷。生产规模小也使得很多有利于提高农业生产效率的工具（但多用于大规模生产）难以普及，且农业生产更容易受到不良自然因素的影响，抗打击能力差。最后，广大的农村地区交通不便、离主要市场（城市）远、缺乏农业生产的基本设施如灌溉、电力等，小农户也很难获得贷款，自行扩大农业生产规模非常困难。因此，无论是从开发更多的可耕地、提高农业生产效率的角度，还是从保证国内粮食供给和粮食安全的角度，发展大规模的商业农场是支撑赞比亚农业生产和商品粮市场的重要选择之一。

但是由于本国的资金和实力有限，赞比亚政府更多的是选择了开放农业部门的投资市场，鼓励外国的企业和个人在赞比亚进行农业投资，并通过一系列的机构和政策支持来激励外国投资者进入农业部门。其中最主要的支持部门是创立于 2006 年的赞比亚发展署（Zambia Development Agency，

ZDA)。赞比亚发展署的主要职能是通过推进赞比亚的投资和出口，深化经济发展，主要手段包括：提供投资服务、发展市场和商业、对中小型企业提供支持等。① 发展署设立的初衷就是将投资赞比亚的手续和资讯集中起来，方便投资者以较短的时间和较便捷的程序进入赞比亚的经济部门中。虽然并不是所有投资都必须要通过发展署完成，但是由于发展署为通过其申请投资并成功的投资者提供了一系列的优惠措施，因此绝大多数投资者愿意在发展署申请投资。

中国在赞比亚的农业投资情况

在非洲 55 个国家中，赞比亚一直是中国外交中极为重要的非洲伙伴，两国的友好关系可以追溯到 20 世纪 60 年代赞比亚独立之时。中国与新独立的赞比亚建立了外交关系，赞比亚也成为第一个与中国签署建交协定的南部非洲国家。而 20 世纪 60 年代末赞比亚与南罗得西亚（现津巴布韦）对赞比亚—罗得西亚铁路的使用权产生纠纷，无法通过铁路将主要经济来源——铜矿运出时，中国决定援建立一条新铁路，支持赞比亚和坦桑尼亚两国的地区独立斗争和经济发展。至今，坦赞铁路仍然是中非、中赞友谊的象征。

除坦赞铁路之外，中国对赞比亚进行了长期的援助。随着中国的改革开放和赞比亚 1991 年后的经济改革，中国和赞比亚的经济交往不再只是贸易和援助；作为特殊友好的国家，赞比亚成为较早吸收中国投资的非洲国家。但是总体来说，中国在赞比亚投资的主要领域是矿业部门。1993～2009 年，中国对矿业的投资总额占到了所有投资的 88.03%，而农业仅有 0.2%，投资比重非常小。② 中国对赞比亚的农业投资有着极大的发展空间。

根据驻赞比亚使馆经济商务参赞处的中资企业名录，中国在赞比亚投资的农业企业共有 36 家。③

---

① Zambia Development Agency, Backgrounds, http：//www. zda. org. zm/? q = content/background, 2015 年 4 月 28 日访问。

② 玄兆娟：《中国企业对赞比亚投资研究》，浙江师范大学硕士毕业论文，2011 年，第 16 页。

③ 《赞比亚中资企业名录》（截至 2015 年 4 月），中华人民共和国驻赞比亚共和国大使馆经济商务参赞处，http：//za. mofcom. gov. cn/，2015 年 5 月 22 日访问。

表 1　中国在赞比亚农业投资名录

企业名称	负责人	英文名称（如登记）
中垦农场有限公司	段昌龙	Johnken Estates LTD
中赞友谊农场	宋国强	China Zambia Friendship Farm
喜洋洋农场	姜建	
阳光农场	斯肃	Sunlight Farm
求华农场	黄向高	
东阳（董杨）公司	杨庆宪	
威马农场有限公司	胡洪毅	
仲一农场	冯轲红	
百信农业有限公司	周斌	
中华农场	田文秀	
特吉农业发展有限公司	韩志伟	
隆平新西农场有限公司	姜庆文	
赞钦农场	周顺生	
华丰农场	田峰秀	China Havest Farm
兴达投资有限公司	李刚	
荣合公司（老胡农场）	胡合荣	
赞比亚农业科技有限公司（AST）	杜丹	Agriculture Science and Technology Co. Ltd.
SUNUP AGRIFARMS AND INVESTMENTS	霍树仁	Sunup Agrifarms And Investments
天翔公司	刘长明	
路遥农场（路明理农场）	路明理	
张振生农场	张振生	
华盛东方农场	刘清华	LZ Easter
开封农业投资有限公司	贾世国	
华非畜禽（赞比亚）股份有限公司	孙德金	
华星公司	张振生	
丹慧农场	王安	
吉林农业大学（援赞农业示范技术中心）	包和平	
江泉国际公司		
兴华农业投资公司		
赞荣公司	翟光华	
安雅投资有限公司	李志杰	Agriyana Investment Co. Ltd.

企业名称	负责人	英文名称（如登记）
快乐兄弟农场有限公司	黄建华	
大西洋木业有限公司	魏志彬	
赞比亚吉海农业有限公司	姚允武	Zambian Jihai Agriculture Co. Ltd.
原始生态产品有限公司	袁广杰	Pristine Ecological Products Co. Ltd.
师诺农业发展有限公司	杨劲	

虽然驻赞比亚使馆将该名录放在使馆网站上并请企业核实信息和联系方式，但是从表1可见，许多在赞的中国农业企业信息并不完整，更难获得它们实际经营的农作物种类、生产状况等信息。因此，需要更加详细的实地调查。

赞比亚中国农场及案例分析

笔者在田野调查中发现，中国在赞比亚投资的农场种类繁多，情况复杂，不能一概而论。例如，从农场属性来看，可以分为国有农场、承包制农场和私营农场等；从规模上来看，又可以分为大型农场和中小型农场等。因此在研究赞比亚中资农场的情况时，需要考虑到不同农场之间的差异性，寻找共同问题的同时也照顾到个体差异。由于时间和空间上的局限，笔者尽量选择了不同类型的中资农场进行了实地考察和访谈，分别是：中垦农场有限公司（简称中垦农场）、喜洋洋农场及开封农业投资有限公司（简称开封农场）。根据与三家农场经营者的访谈，笔者总结了三家农场的性质、经营者（或是公司）选择进入赞比亚投资农业的原因、经营活动中使用了哪些中赞双方的优惠政策，以及生产经营面临的困难和问题。

根据总结的表格，不难看出根据农场的性质、经营者自身的技术和交流水平、农场规模，农场日常生产中使用的中赞双方的优惠政策或激励措施也不同。三家农场面临的困难也不同，虽然总结起来大致为市场、管理、技术、设备和资金这几方面的问题，但仍需根据具体情况进行具体分析。

表2　中垦农场、喜洋洋农场和开封农场的比较

农场	农场性质	经营者进入原因	使用优惠政策		面临的问题
			中国	赞比亚	
中垦农场	国有农场	*响应国家政策号召 *总公司派遣 *自身有农业知识（如前经理王驰）	*国家贷款 使领馆重视	*加入 ZNFU[①]	*中方管理层管辖权不统一 *大额资金使用不自由 *国有企业决策链长，反应慢 *当地员工对工资有争议
喜洋洋农场	国营转承包	*响应江苏省政府政策号召 *总公司派遣 *自身有农业技术知识 *在赞比亚从事过农业生产相关活动		*加入 ZNFU * ZDA 的税收优惠 * ZDA 的农具进口优惠	*农作物市场价格波动 *设备老旧，更新成本高 *难以获得资金
开封农场	私营农场	*响应开封市农业厅的政策号召 *开封市农林局有优惠补贴 *领导亲自到赞比亚考察过	*开封市农林局的工资补贴	* ZDA 的签证办理	*难以进入主流市场 *缺乏养殖和防病技术 *社会不稳定 *赞比亚政府效率低 *难以获得资金

中国在赞比亚农业投资的不足与问题

（一）中国优惠政策和鼓励机制存在很多不足

第一，中国的许多鼓励农业"走出去"的政策在实际操作上很难为在赞比亚进行投资农业的企业所用，尤其是非国有的私人农场。以下为几个鼓励政策在实际运作中可能存在的问题举例。

（1）《中非合作论坛第五届部长级会议——北京行动计划（2013 ~ 2015 年）》中，除了重申推动中国企业投资非洲之外，还首次表示要鼓励国内的金融机构对中非企业开展农业种植、农产品加工、畜牧业养殖、渔

---

① 赞比亚国家农民联合会（ZNFU）。

业捕捞和养殖等领域的合作进行支持。① 但是行动计划中同时明确了支持的是"有实力、信誉好"的企业，这个标准就非常模棱两可，但可以肯定的是拥有国有企业背景、国家贷款支持的国有农场受到支持的可能性要远远大于私人投资、小规模的农场。

（2）虽然中国对中国企业在非洲的农业投资有专项资金，但是对于申请的企业也有一定的要求：企业不仅需要满足一系列在中国和投资国的投资资格条件和注册条件，投资规模也不能小，中方投资境外项目的投资额原则上不能低于 100 万美元。这使得许多私人企业投资的小型农场很难申请到专项资金补贴。

（3）虽然随着中非发展基金的设立和多次中非合作论坛行动文件出台，中非发展基金可以为在非洲投资的企业提供贷款或其他融资服务，但是中非发展基金对于投资的标准和要求中规定合作伙伴必须是"在非洲的投资项目或在非洲以外但直接投资、服务于非洲的项目；投资项目市场前景良好，有快速、稳定增长的潜力，能够产生良好的现金流；投资项目能够促进当地经济发展和有利于改善民生"② 的企业。很显然，农业尤其是粮食种植和畜牧业受市场波动的影响较大，且许多小规模企业无法达到中非发展基金所要求的潜力和现金流，很难申请到投资或贷款。中非发展基金目前投资的其中一个重点农业项目——中非棉业是目前"中国在非洲最大的农业投资项目"，③ 在赞比亚的其他中资农场显然达不到这个规模。

因此，中国政府和相关部门在制定的政策时需要更加"接地气"，既要有好的意图，也要有好的执行力，而且应该鼓励相应的商业服务机构成长起来，配套企业"走出去"，使优惠政策和激励措施能够被"走出去"的农业企业切实利用起来、带来效益。

第二，国内行之有效的激励政策还没有转化为对于农业企业"走出去"的"推力"。中国本身的"三农"问题长期存在，在治理过程中已经

① 《中非合作论坛第五届部长级会议——北京行动计划（2013～2015 年）》，中非合作论坛网站，2012 年 7 月 23 日，http：//www.focac.org/chn/ltda/dwjbzzjh/hywj/t954617.htm，2015 年 5 月 1 日访问。

② 《投资标准与要求》，中非发展基金网站，http：//www.cadfund.com/NewsInfo.aspx？NId = 27，2015 年 4 月 21 日访问。

③ http：//www.ca-cotton.com/index.htm（中非棉业发展有限公司网站），2015 年 5 月 1 日访问。

总结出了许多鼓励和支持国内农业投资、扶持国内农业企业发展的行之有效的激励措施和优惠政策。然而这些优秀的政策很多没能延伸到已经"走出去"的中国农场上。例如，国家给予国内的农业企业30%的农机购置补贴，鼓励企业购置农机具进行机械化、规模化生产。访谈中笔者了解到，投资赞比亚农业的中国企业也存在着购买农机具的资金短缺问题，但是对于这些投资赞比亚农业的中国企业，国家却没有类似的政策。中国政府可以考虑将国内已经实践有效的优秀政策推广到海外的企业当中，鼓励和支持对外的农业投资。

第三，即使对于容易使用中国优惠政策和激励措施的国有企业（如中垦农场）来说，优惠政策和资金也存在种种限制与约束。身为国有农场可以较便利地获得国家的贷款和其他优惠政策，但是大额资金的使用和重要的运营决定需要向上级企业或者国家申报审批通过，手续多、流程长、效率低，在适应变幻莫测的国际市场方面存在一定的障碍；反倒是私营或者承包制的农场不受这些制度性规定的约束，可以更自主地根据当时当地的情况制定生产经营的目标和方式。优惠政策、专项资金和贷款的使用如何做到宏观监管与经营自主权的平衡，也值得相关部门做进一步的探究。

总结来看，对于国有农场来说，使用中国对外农业投资优惠政策时主要存在的问题是受到国有企业体制的制约，难以灵活地应对农业生产和经营中瞬息万变的市场实际情况，一定范围内的经营决策权亟待下降到一线的企业行为主体。而对于私营企业来说，没有国有企业的背景往往使它们较难获得政策决策层的注意和支持，但是存在很高的生产经营的自主度和灵活度。私营企业中大规模的农场比起小型农场理论上更容易申请到专项资金支持，但是实际操作起来几乎不可能；小型投资的私人农场无论从资金，还是从基础设施上来看，都是最脆弱的且抗风险能力较弱，有关优惠政策框架的适用度很低——或者说，这些小型私人农场根本不被考虑——但是真正与当地人融合在一起、很大程度上创造了当地人心目中的中国人、中国文化形象的正是这些中小规模的、非政府的、稳扎稳打的中小农场。因此在未来制定相关扶持农业"走出去"政策时，除了对国有企业放松管制、加大其经营决定的灵活性之外，还应当加强对中小型企业和农场的帮扶。

（二）经营者自身的不足之处

第一，虽然来自投资母国和当地的优惠推动政策有助于企业进入农业领域投资，但是一个企业或者农场能否长远稳健地发展下去，很大程度上也取决于经营者自身的经营能力。如果农业企业的经营者事先对赞比亚的农业有所了解、熟悉赞比亚发展署提供的优惠政策并妥善运用、自身也有在相关农业领域生产经营的经验，毋庸置疑将会比没有这些能力的企业更容易将投资落地。此外，对赞比亚当地官方语言（英语）和其他通用语种的掌握程度也影响农业企业和农场是否能与当地雇员、传统酋长和政府官员进行及时有效的沟通，更好地推进自己的生产。例如，采访中笔者发现，拥有英语优势是喜洋洋农场对当地政策的了解和使用多于其他两个农场的原因之一。

中国企业选择了"走出去"对赞比亚进行农业投资，就意味着不可避免地会受到全球层面和赞比亚国内层面的客观问题制约。一般来说，企业的性质很难更改，但是经营者个人能力层面可能产生问题的空间较大，不同农场的表现也会根据不同的经营者而产生巨大的差距。但同样，这个层面的问题也是最容易解决的。客观上，在了解已有法律法规、克服语言障碍之外，经营者可以根据自己实际的知识漏洞有针对性地"查漏补缺"；对于动态的农业消息、市场动态、政策变更等，经营者可以加强对实时信息的关注，提升自己的敏感度；对于主观的农业投资经营决策，短时间内经营者很难取得很大进步，但可以通过咨询专家和合作者意见、总结经验教训，提升自己的经营管理水平。

第二，笔者还发现，中国投资赞比亚农业的企业大多在经营农场，以生产初级农产品为主，种植的作物或蓄养的牲畜种类相对单一。在20世纪90年代刚刚进入赞比亚投资时，如此谨慎的经营行为可以理解；然而二十余年过去了，许多农场除了生产规模较当时有所扩大，产品种类和涉及的产业变化甚少，在扩大自身经营规模、进行本土化生产、向高端和其他产业价值链发展时显得踟蹰不前。然而，经营农场、生产初级农产品不但成本高、风险大、耗时长、生产辛苦，且最终产品的附加值低、价格随国内市场和国际市场波动大、与其他企业竞争激烈，综合来看经营农场、生产初级农产品并不是农业投资中最理想的选择。同时，由于缺乏相关产业链，中国农场的农产品很难通过加工进入更广阔的市场。例如，开封农场的经营者在访谈中曾提道，由于缺乏活鸡屠宰的设备和冷链，他只能在当地市场上卖活鸡，无法将屠宰处理好的鸡肉供应给附近超市，扩大生产。反观其他国家在赞比亚投资的农业企业，投资的领域和具体的生产方式要比中国企业丰富得多。例如，英国企业在赞比亚发展署登记的农业类型中，除了混合型农业、种植业、养殖业外，还有种子生产、家禽业、生物柴油生产、野生动物猎场、农产品加工、商业渔场等多种类型，种类更丰富、产业链更长，产品附加值也就越大。如果农业投资不能很好地融入上游和下游的当地农业市场的话，那么这种投资只能供应城市中心，而非为当地社区带来有利影响。如果农业投资与当地社区密切合作的话，通过投入、加工和仓储，可以形成规模经济。

因此，在赞比亚从事农业生产的中国企业在制定未来发展的目标时，应当考虑增加自身产品的附加值，打入更广阔、更高端的农业市场，避免初级农产品受市场价格波动影响大的问题，更多元化地进行生产。

第三，在采访中，笔者发现中资企业之间的交流和沟通很少。作为在赞比亚最著名的中资农场，中垦农场的大名许多农场主都知道，也知晓其经营中比较广为人知的故事。然而规模越小、越晚进入赞比亚农业领域的中资农场，越不为人所知。因为缺乏相互沟通和信息交流，即使有的农场了解赞比亚政府的最新优惠政策，也很难将这个信息普及给其他农场。

针对这个问题，一方面，赞比亚的中资农场可以自行成立一个商会或者中国农场主联合会性质的组织，有效地将在赞比亚投资的农业企业团结在一起。这样中资农场不仅能够相互交流农业生产经验，还能相互传达政策措施，更加有效地进行生产。另一方面，驻赞比亚使馆的经济商务参赞处也应当发挥自身的协助功能，多为企业提供所需要的经商信息、商业资源、政策指引等服务。

建立平台和渠道、增加企业间的信息交流和沟通也是有效解决经营者自身能力有限而导致困难和问题的途径之一，尤其有利于动态信息的传达和交流，克服中国企业在外投资对当地政策和信息不敏感的问题。

总结与建议

在目前市场经济的浪潮下，企业既是国际认可的投资主体，又比个人有投资实力，因此应当是中国开展农业"走出去"的重点扶持对象。然而"走出去"政策实施已有十余年，政府和企业的关注目标不应再集中在如何架设渠道、鼓励对外投资之上，而应考虑在已有大量企业进行海外投资的情况下，如何让这些企业在海外发展得更稳定、更有前景。

赞比亚中国农场的例子也正反映了这一点：中国企业已经投资赞比亚农场二十余年，但是现在仍然面临着来自国际市场、赞比亚国内、国内母公司制度和资金审批、自身能力等方面的问题。要想把握时机、建设产业链，成为实力不断壮大的农业跨国公司，还需要来自政府和企业双方的努力。企业需要转变思想、丰富投资领域和产业链建设，并通过行业联合的方式"抱团取暖"；政府也需要转变思路，鼓励企业走出去，更需要提供政策支持，让企业"稳下来"，做到"走稳、走好"。政府需要从顶层设计和战略谋划的角度着眼，制定有利于向海外投资的企业扎根当地、持续发展的政策和规划。另外，中国政府还需要不断对企业在海外的发展情况进行跟踪调查，及时总结经验和教训，鼓励企业在良性竞争的环境中不断壮大自身。同时，国内也需要针对海外投资农业企业的特殊需求进行相关部门的改革。例如，对企业融资难的问题，中国政府应当适时改善对外投资的金融服务，提供专项的资金；对农业投资风险大的问题，中国政府应当建立一定的海外农业投资保险，为企业在海外的"行稳致远"提供"保护伞"。

津巴布韦农业国际合作与中资企业的
粮食作物种植

沈晓雷[*] 著

  自 2000 年 "快车道" 土地改革以来，土地问题就成了津巴布韦最受国际社会关注的问题。很多学者认为，正是 "快车道" 土地改革的暴力与无序，以及新农场主的技术落后等，导致了津巴布韦近年来的农作物产量大幅下降及粮食安全问题。[①] 虽然《津巴布韦的土地改革：神话与现实》[②]和《津巴布韦收回自己的土地》[③] 在 2010 年与 2012 年相继出版后，国际社会开始转变对津巴布韦土地改革的态度，并逐渐接受将土地分配给小农户有助于增加农业产量和降低贫困的观点，但土地改革导致国际社会降低对津巴布韦农业援助与投资的局面，在短期内难以发生重大改变。津巴布韦因欧美国家的制裁而在 2003 年实施 "看东方" 政策，向以中国为主包括马来西亚、新加坡、印度和俄罗斯在内 "东方国家" 寻求帮助，中国则在 2000 年之后加大了与非洲各国合作的步伐。正是在这一背景下，中国与津巴布韦的农业合作得以在援助与投资等各个领域逐步展开，而皖津公司是安徽省农垦集团有限公司（简称安徽农垦）和安徽天瑞生态科技有限公司（简称安徽天瑞）先后在 2010 年和 2013 年进入津巴布韦从事粮食作物

---

* 沈晓雷：北京大学国际关系学院博士，北京大学非洲研究中心成员，现任中国社会科学院西亚非洲研究所助理研究员。

① International Crisis Group, *Blood and Soil*：*Land*, *Politics and Conflict Prevention in Zimbabwe and South Africa*, 2004；African All Party Parliamentary group, *Land in Zimbabwe*：*Past Mistakes*, *Future Prospects*, 2009.

② Ian Scoones, Nelson Marongwe, Blasio Mavedzenge, et al., *Zimbabwe's Land Reform*：*Myths and Realities*, James Currey, 2010.

③ J. Hanlon, J. Manjengwa & T. Smart, *Zimbabwe Takes Back Its Land*, Jacana Media (Pty) Ltd., 2013.

185

种植，既开拓了中津农业新的领域，又使中国区别于其他国际合作方。

津巴布韦农业发展概况

农业在津巴布韦的国民经济中占据着重要位置。据津巴布韦农业、机械与灌溉部的数据，农业为80%的人口提供了生活来源，创造了23%的正式就业岗位，贡献了14%～18.5%的国内生产总值。① 从农业内部的国内生产总值占比来看，玉米占14%，烟草占25%，棉花占12.5%，蔗糖与园艺占7%，牛肉与鱼占21%，其他牲畜占20%，剩余0.5%为自给作物。②

从资源禀赋来看，根据土壤类型和降雨量的大小，津巴布韦的耕地被划分成五类农业生态区（见表1）；根据土地占有与使用的情况，可分为A1农场、A2农场、村社农场、老重新安置农场③、小型商业农场和大型商业农场等类型（见表2）。

表1　津巴布韦农业生态区

类型	分布	年降雨量	占比	特征	农业活动
I	马尼卡兰省	1050毫米以上	2%	降雨量高，专业化和多元化经营	林业，生产茶叶、咖啡豆、水果以及集约畜牧养殖
II	中马绍纳兰省、东马绍纳兰省、西马绍纳兰省、马尼卡兰省和哈拉雷市	750～1000毫米	15%	降雨量高	生产玉米、烤烟、棉花、雪豆，从事园艺活动、集约畜牧业，生产咖啡豆、小麦、大麦、高粱、花生
III	马尼卡兰省、中部省	450～650毫米	19%	阶段性干旱，雨季开始日期不定且时有干旱发生	半集约农业，集约牛场以及种植勉强维生的玉米、小米、高粱

---

① 见津巴布韦农业、机械与灌溉部网站主页：http://www.moa.gov.zw/。

② "Zimbabwe Agricultural Investment Plan（ZAIP）2013－2017：A Comprehensive Framework for the Development of Zimbabwe's Agriculture Sector"，p.14.

③ 老重新安置农场，是指20世纪80年代重新安置的农场，官方文件里面都写作farms resettled in 1980s。

类型	分布	年降雨量	占比	特征	农业活动
Ⅳ	马斯温戈省、南马塔贝莱兰省、北马塔贝莱兰省、马尼卡兰省、中部省、布拉瓦约市	450~650毫米	37%	非常干旱,需要灌溉才能获得好的产量,雨季期间有较长时间的干旱期	种植勉强维生的小米、高粱,创立放型牛场、休闲牧场
Ⅴ	马斯温戈省、南马塔贝莱兰省、马尼卡兰省、布拉瓦约市	低于450毫米	27%	非常干旱,需要灌溉才能获得好的产量,雨季期间有较长时间的干旱期	种植勉强维生的小米、高粱,创立粗放型牛场、休闲牧场

资料来源:Ministry of Agriculture, Mechanization and Irrigation, "Zimbabwe Agricultural Investment Plan(ZAIP)2013–2017", p. 15。

表2 2011年津巴布韦各类农场的具体情况

农场类型	面积(公顷)	个 数
A1农场	5759153.89	145775
A2农场	2978334.08	16387
村社农场	16000000	1200000
老重新安置农场	3667708	75569
大型商业农场	648041.27	1154
小型商业农场	1400000	8000
其他	1695220.93	630
总 计①	32148517.17	1447523

资料来源:Prosper B. Matondi, *Zimbabwe's Fast Track Land Reform*, Zed Book Ltd., 2012, p. 9。

津巴布韦曾被誉为南部非洲的粮仓,但2000年"快车道"土地改革后,由于政府在市场和价格管控等方面的错误政策、农业投入不足、恶性

---

① 此处涉及的两个数据,是把以上两列数据加和后的总计,应分别为32148458.2,1447515,表中数据略有出入。本篇作者查对了所引述的英文原著作品,也是如表格所示。疑为原作者错误计算所致。特此说明。

通货膨胀、国际制裁及新农场主缺乏农业技术与管理经验,[1] 其农业产量严重下降,最重要的两种农作物玉米和烟草,相较于 1990 年的平均产量,最高曾分别下降 65.8%（2007～2008 年农业季）和 72.2%（2005～2006 年农业季）。[2] 粮食安全也自此成为津巴布韦所面临的严重问题。[3]

为恢复农作物产量和提高农业生产率,津巴布韦政府先后出台了一系列农业政策文件,其中包括《农业部门 2011～2015 年中期计划》和《津巴布韦 2013～2017 年农业投资计划》,以从宏观层面指导津巴布韦农业发展。就具体措施而言,主要包括以下几个方面:自 2004 年开始实行烟草订单种植,允许烟草企业直接与烟农签署订单种植协议,此举极大促进了烟草产量的大幅回升;粮食收购管理局（Grain Marketing Board）放开私人粮食收购市场,[4] 设定最低保护价格,并允许农场主用玉米换购化肥,以此鼓励粮食作物生产;扩大订单种植范围,纳入大豆、芸豆、花生、高粱、小米、球形玉米和向日葵等农作物;鼓励农业投资,向国内外投资者提供税收和非税收优惠政策,其中包括出口 50% 以上产品的农业加工企业可享受 20% 的优惠税率,对升级农场和修建烤烟房等提供特殊启动津贴,对化肥、种子、农药和机械设备等农业投入征收零增值税和推迟征收进口农业物资的增值税等。[5]

津巴布韦政府所采取的上述政策取得了一定的成效,从 2009 年开始,其农业生产逐渐走出低谷,并在 2010 年获得 33% 的增速。[6] 到 2013～2014 年农业季,玉米、谷物、烟草和棉花等主要作物的产量已经达到甚至超过

① Prosper B. Matondi, *Zimbabwe's Fast Track Land Reform*, Zed Book, 2012, p. 134; Hanlon, et al., *Zimbabwe's Fast Track Land Reform*, pp. 93 – 96.
② Sam Moyo & Walter Chambati, eds., *Land and Agrarian Reform in Zimbabwe: Beyond White – Settler Capitalism*, CPDESROA 2013, p. 212.
③ T. S. Jayne, etc., "Zimbabwe's Food Insecurity Paradox: Hunger amid Potential", in Mandi-vambaRukni, etc., *Zimbabwe's Agricultural Revolution Revisited*, University of Zimbabwe Publications, 2006, pp. 525 – 541.
④ "Zimbabwe: No winds of change at the Grain Marketing Board", http://www.irinnews.org/report/85092/zimbabwe – no – winds – of – change – at – the – grain – marketing – board, accessed 2005 – 04 – 26.
⑤ "Zimbabwe Agricultural Investment Plan (ZAIP) 2013 – 2017: A Comprehensive Framework for the Development of Zimbabwe's Agriculture Sector", pp. 54 – 56.
⑥ "Zimbabwe Agricultural Investment Plan (ZAIP) 2013 – 2017: A Comprehensive Framework for the Development of Zimbabwe's Agriculture Sector", p. 3.

20世纪90年代的平均水平，而其中重新安置农场生产了一半以上的玉米和烟草。农业生产的恢复不但正在为"快车道"土地改革正名，而且表明以家庭为单位的小农业生产符合津巴布韦当前的国情，具有更高的生产率和能够提供更多的就业机会。①

然而尽管如此，从当前津巴布韦的农业发展来看，其仍存在诸多不利因素，这其中包括农业生产的机械化和集约化程度不高、灌溉设施落后和灌溉率较低，以及化肥和农药等基本农业生产资料投入不足等。要解决这些问题，一方面需要政府加大对农业部门的财政支持，另一方面则需要扩大国内外对农业部门的投资。而从当前津巴布韦经济发展陷入停滞和财政收入不足的情况来看，加大政府的财政支持显然不太现实，如此一来，开展农业国际合作，获取援助和吸引投资，就成为津巴布韦政府的当务之急。②

农业国际合作

津巴布韦在1980年独立后，以英国为首的西方国家曾向其提供大笔资金用于土地重新安置和农业发展项目，但2000年之后，因"快车道"土地改革和此后选举中出现暴力等因素的影响，美国、欧盟和澳大利亚先后在2002年和2003年对津巴布韦进行制裁，国际社会与津巴布韦在农业领域的合作也相应减少，尤其是对土地改革农场主而言，欧盟和美国都禁止对其进行援助。③尽管如此，国际社会还是从以下两个方面与津巴布韦开展了农业合作：一是农业援助，二是农业投资。

农业援助

农业援助的主体仍以英国、美国、瑞士和联合国的相关机构等西方传

① Jeanette Manjengwa, Joseph Hanlon and Teresa Smart, "Who will Make the 'Best' Use of Africa's Land? Lessons from Zimbabwe", *Third World Quarterly*, vol. 35, No. 6, 2014, pp. 980–995.

② 为更好地吸引投资，津巴布韦投资局专门列出了18个存在投资机遇的项目，主要涉及灌溉设施维修、畜牧业（牛、猪和家禽）、肉类与奶制品加工、农产品深加工、冷藏、内陆渔业开发、棉花和马铃薯种植、花生和球形玉米等订单种植，以及农业机械化等领域。见"Opportunities in the Agricultural Sector", http://www.investzim.com/index.php? option = com_content&view = article&id =251&Itemid =688, accessed 2005 –04 –26.

③ J. Hanlon, J. Manjengwa and T. Smart, *Zimbabwe Takes Back Its Land*, Jacana Media (Pty) Ltd., 2013.

统援助者为主，近年来巴西等新兴经济体也开始加入进来。从农业援助的具体内容来看，包括三个方面：一是粮食援助，二是修复和援建灌溉设施，三是恢复农业生产。而农业援助的着眼点主要是解决津巴布韦的粮食安全问题。

1. 粮食援助

2011年，瑞士发展合作署向津巴布韦拨付230万瑞士法郎的粮食援助资金。2012年，瑞士发展合作署又向联合国粮食计划署（WFP）提供100万瑞士法郎并委托其将现金和粮食分配给贫困人民。① 加拿大国际开发署在2009~2010年向津巴布韦提供了700万美元的粮食援助。② 世界粮食计划署也通过粮食援助计划小组，向津巴布韦提供了一定数量的粮食。③

2. 修复和援建灌溉设施

2013年10月，巴西政府向津巴布韦提供9800万美元贷款，用于支持津巴布韦农业机械化和修复部分灌溉项目。④ 2014年年底，瑞士承诺出资630万美元修复马斯温戈省的6个灌溉项目，项目完成后将灌溉农田700公顷。⑤ 日本国际集团也在马斯温戈省的古图县援建了灌溉项目。⑥

3. 恢复农业生产

美国国际开发署在2010年10月启动《津巴布韦农业收入与就业发展计划》，旨在通过提高农业产量和深化农业加工等方式增加15万户津巴布韦农村家庭的收入和粮食安全，该项目在2015年9月结束。⑦ 英国国际发展署牵头17个机构共同组织实施《延续性救助计划》，旨在帮助津巴布韦提高粮食安全、提供农业投入和促进农业生产，该计划已先后在2003~

① 中国—发展援助委员会研究小组：《农业发展的有效支持——津巴布韦实地调查报告》，第7~8页。
② 张军：《浅谈西方国家援助津巴布韦农业发展的方式与特点》，《援津巴布韦农业技术合作项目简报》2014年第12期，第17页。
③ "Zimbabwe Agricultural Investment Plan (ZAIP) 2013-2017: A Comprehensive Framework for the Development of Zimbabwe's Agriculture Sector", p. 40.
④ "US $ 98m Loan for Mechanization, Irrigation Development", http://www.herald.co.zw/us98m-loan-for-mechanisation-irrigation-development/, accessed 2005-04-27.
⑤ "Zimbabwe: Switzerland Avails U.S. $6,3 Million for Irrigation", http://allafrica.com/stories/201412190556.html, accessed 2005-04-27.
⑥ 张军：《浅谈西方国家援助津巴布韦农业发展的方式与特点》，《援津巴布韦农业技术合作项目简报》2014年第12期，第17页。
⑦ 参见《津巴布韦农业收入与就业发展计划》官方网站，http://www.zim-aied.org/。

2007 年和 2008～2012 年完成两期，均取得了较好的效果。① 联合国的一些
机构，尤其是联合国粮食及农业组织和联合国粮食计划署也通过不同渠
道对恢复津巴布韦的粮食生产进行了援助。它们通过协调捐助者和非政
府组织等，组建了一些捐助工作小组，涉及农业协调、市场联系、畜牧
养殖和保护性农业等。从援助重点来看，它们最初侧重紧急粮食援助，
当前的援助重点则为农业恢复与转型。据统计，它们在 2008～2009 年农
业季和 2009～2010 年农业季的援助额分别为 2500 万美元和 7400 万美
元。② 此外，2011 年，巴西与津巴布韦签署《非洲粮食增产计划》谅解备
忘录，希望通过向津巴布韦提供农业机械、培训和技术支持，以此增加津
巴布韦的粮食产量。③

农业投资

就投资而言，由于美国和欧盟等的制裁，国际社会对津巴布韦的农业
投资也受到了很大的限制。从津巴布韦投资局公布的数据来看，2009 年、
2010 年、2012 年和 2013 年四年农业领域的外资项目只有 7 个，④ 而且津巴
布韦农业部的官员指出，这些项目基本都没有成功。

从当前来看，国际社会对津巴布韦农业领域的投资主要集中于烟草和
棉花等经济作物。2014 年，在津巴布韦开展订单种植或烟草采购的国家和
地区共有 50 多个，除中国外，其他处于前列的国家还包括比利时、南非、
阿联酋、俄罗斯、印度尼西亚、苏丹、德国、英国和法国等。⑤ 就企业层
面而言，英美烟草集团、环球公司和联一国际公司等均长期在津巴布韦开
展业务，并通过在当地的分公司进行订单种植。在棉花方面，南非是津巴
布韦棉绒最大的购买方，其在 2007 年和 2008 年购买的棉花分别占津巴布

① Mary Jennings, Agnes Kayondo, et al., *Impact Evaluation of the Protracted Relief Programme* Ⅱ, Zimbabwe, April 22, 2013.
② "Zimbabwe Agricultural Investment Plan (ZAIP) 2013 – 2017: A Comprehensive Framework for the Development of Zimbabwe's Agriculture Sector", pp. 40 – 41.
③ Langton Mukwereza, "Zimbabwe – Brazil Cooperation through the More Food Africa Programme", China and Brazil in Africa Agriculture Project Working Paper, No. 116, p. 5.
④ 津巴布韦投资局的年度报告上只列出了这些项目的数量，而没有列出具体的项目名称。见 Zimbabwe Investment Authority, 2009 *Annual Report*, p. 17, 2010 *Annual Report*, p. 24, 2013 *Annual Report*, pp. 33 – 34。
⑤ Tobacco Industry and Marketing Board, *Annual Statistical Report* 2014, p. 18.

韦出口棉花总量的 39.9% 和 36.4%。[①]

需要指出的是，目前尚没有国际合作方在津巴布韦购买和租赁土地，也就是说，在津巴布韦还没有出现所谓的"圈地"的现象。

中津农业合作：粮食作物种植[②]

中国与津巴布韦的农业合作始于 20 世纪 80 年代，当前主要从三个方面开展合作，一是进行农业援助，包括派遣农业技术专家、[③] 援建农业技术示范中心，[④] 以及捐赠粮食和农业机械等；二是在经济作物，尤其是在烟草和棉花种植领域开展合作，其中从事烟草业务的主要是天泽烟草有限责任公司，[⑤] 从事棉花业务的主要是中非棉业发展有限公司；[⑥] 三是安徽农垦和安徽天瑞自 2010 年开始的粮食作物种植。中国与津巴布韦的农业合作同其他国际合作方相比，既有相同点又有不同之处：相同点为强调农业援助和对烟草等经济作物的投资，不同点为在解决津巴布韦的粮食安全这一问题上，其他国际合作方仍主要以改善农业基础设施和提供粮食援助为主，而中国的农业企业则开始走进津巴布韦开展粮食作物种植，也就是

① Langton Mukwereza, *Chinese and Brazilian Cooperation with African Agriculture: The Case of Zimbabwe*, China and Brazil in Africa Agriculture Project Working Paper 048, March 2013, p. 7.
② 本部分所引资料和数据主要为笔者在津巴布韦采访所得。
③ 中国自 2009 年开始向津巴布韦派遣农业技术专家，截至 2016 年已经派遣三批共 25 人，他们的专业主要包括畜牧业、园艺、水产、农作物、兽医和农机维修等。
④ 农业技术示范中心位于津巴布韦奎比农校，占地 109 公顷（其中种植面积 90 公顷），2012 年 6 月正式投入运营，现有农业专家 7 名，主要任务为开展农作物种植、农产品加工、畜禽养殖技术示范推广、实验研究工作，并就地培训津巴布韦地方技术人员。
⑤ 天泽烟草有限责任公司成立于 2005 年 4 月 1 日，为中国烟草总公司全资子公司。该公司通过向订单农户提供无息贷款和提高烟草收购价格等方式，自 2008 年起成为津巴布韦烟草最大的买家之一并为津巴布韦烟草产业的迅速恢复做出了重要贡献。See Longton Mukwereza, "Situating Tian Ze's Role in Reviving Zimbabwe's Flue – Cured Tobacco Sector in the Wider Discourse on Zimbabwe – China Cooperation: Will the Scorecard Remain Win – Win?", China and Brazil in Africa Agriculture Project Working Paper, No. 115, February 2015, p. 8.
⑥ 该公司由中非棉业发展有限公司 2014 年在津巴布韦并购 2 家棉花公司后成立，设有 2 个轧花厂，年产能力约 8 万吨，为津巴布韦第二大棉花企业。参见《中非农业跨越式发展的开拓者——中非棉业津巴布韦有限公司》，http://zimbabwe.ca – cotton.com/Index.asp?id = 10，2015 年 4 月 28 日访问。

说，其他国家援助方仍主要强调"授人以鱼"，而中国的农业企业则已经开始实践"授人以渔"。

中资农业企业进入津巴布韦种植粮食作物存在一个相互矛盾的背景：一方面，"快车道"土地改革之后，由于缺乏资金、技术和基础设施等，津巴布韦仍有大量土地闲置或未能得到充分利用，[①] 这为外资进入津巴布韦经营农场并从事粮食作物种植提供了机会；另一方面，津巴布韦政府禁止出租和买卖国有土地，要想获取土地进行农业种植，必须同土地所有者进行合资，土地所有者以土地作为资本入股，且根据本土化法规要占51%以上的股份，此举无疑大大限制了外资的进入。[②] 正是在这一背景下，安徽农垦和安徽天瑞走进津巴布韦，先后于2010年和2013年成立津—中皖津农业发展有限公司（简称皖津公司）和津—中皖津天瑞食品加工（私人）有限公司（简称皖津天瑞）并开始以玉米为主的粮食作物种植。

皖津公司

皖津公司是安徽农垦为贯彻农业"走出去"战略，在安徽省政府与津巴布韦政府的支持下，于2010年1月与津巴布韦国防部合资成立的公司。根据合资合同，安徽农垦与津巴布韦国防部各占50%的股份并按股投资，其中津巴布韦国防部投资部分由安徽农垦垫付。公司经营利润按照五五分成，但津巴布韦国防部要将分红的70%先用于偿还安徽农垦的垫付款。公司董事长和总经理由安徽农垦委派。安徽农垦提供资金和设备。津巴布韦国防部则提供土地供公司经营，使用权为99年。

2011年，皖津公司在西马绍纳兰省成功开发首期1800公顷土地，2015年后开展二期1万公顷土地的开发种植，所涉地块以西马绍兰省为中

---

① 中国援津农业技术专家估计土地利用率仅为10%左右，萨姆·莫约（Sam Moyo）等人在2006年的调查中也发现津巴布韦耕地利用的情况不乐观。见张安平《试论津巴布韦土地撂荒的解决方案》，《援津巴布韦农业技术合作项目简报》2014年第12期，第18页；Sam Moyo, et al., *Fast Track Land Reform Baseline Survey in Zimbabwe: Trends and Tendencies*, 2005/06, Harare: African Institute for Agrarian Studies, 2009, p.55。

② 津巴布韦2007年通过的《本土化与经济授权法》规定，无论现有企业还是新成立企业，津巴布韦本地人必须控股51%以上。由于看到了该政策对外资进入的限制，包括现任副总统姆南加古瓦在内的政府高官在2014年年底相继表示要调整本土化政策，但迄今为止津巴布韦政府并未付诸行动。

心，辐射首都哈拉雷、中马绍兰省、东马绍兰省部分地区，主要集中在津巴布韦降雨量较为丰沛的农业生态二区。2014～2015年农业季，皖津公司共种植3000公顷玉米、500公顷大豆、700公顷小麦和150公顷高粱。

在项目实施过程中，皖津公司遵循"统一规划、分步实施、滚动发展、稳步推进"的原则，优先加大农场基础设施建设，特别是水利设施建设，根据当地土壤条件和耕作方式确定农作物种植和农业机械使用的品种，制定切实可行的生产方案，加大科技培训和技术方案的落实，从而做到"开发一块、建成一块、收效一块、带动一块"。

在投入方面，为节省资金，皖津公司从中国国内采购农业机械，从当地采购种子、化肥、农药和燃油等。在粮食销售方面，它们并没有将粮食运回中国以帮助中国解决"粮食安全"问题，相反，它们将粮食出售给津巴布韦综合实力最强的粮食加工企业——国家粮食有限公司，并因质量较高，以每吨高于当地市场价20美元的价格售出。

2014年，皖津公司种植的玉米、大豆和小麦每公顷的平均产量分别为6吨、2.5吨和6吨，每吨销售价格分别为390美元、520美元和430美元，扣除生产成本，每吨利润分别为1040美元、400美元和880美元（见表3）。

2013年6月，安徽农垦为贯彻安徽省政府抱团"走出去"战略，牵头成立"皖企赴津巴布韦开发合作联盟"，以皖津农业为平台吸引其他中资企业赴津巴布韦共同投资与发展。现已有3家企业加盟该合作联盟，投资领域为建材生产、食品加工和物流运输。此外，为进一步提升农业利润空间，打造以农产品存储和加工企业为龙头的农业产业链，皖津公司拟在奇诺伊市建立农产品加工经贸园区，如能成功，将为津巴布韦现代农业发展做出更大的贡献。

皖津天瑞

2013年1月，经安徽农垦推荐，安徽天瑞应津巴布韦国防部邀请，赴津巴布韦参观考察当地矿产、建材、农业及食品加工等项目。通过综合考察当地政治、经济、文化、人口和地理环境等因素，在结合公司实际的情况下，2013年5月，安徽天瑞与皖津公司签订战略合作协议，接手后者从津巴布韦国防部获得、位于奇古图市西北的卡萨马、奇沃卢和尤瑞卡三个农场，总面积为3228公顷，用以发展现代农业、木材加工和食品加工。7

月，安徽天瑞在津巴布韦注册成立皖津天瑞，安徽天瑞与安徽农垦分别占50%的股份，但其全额投资并独立经营。

皖津天瑞经营的这三个农场只有少量为熟地，大部分土地长期闲置，从地里的树木、灌木、蚁丘和废弃的灌溉设施看，基本已闲置10年以上，有些地块甚至闲置长达30年。2013～2014年农业季，皖津天瑞克服了各种困难，共种植320公顷玉米，其中70公顷为复垦。2014～2015年农业季，皖津天瑞继续扩大复垦面积，玉米种植面积已增加到600公顷。

就产量而言，由于缺乏农业种植经验，且土地因长期闲置，土壤已不适合耕种，至少需要三年的时间才能变成熟地，因此皖津天瑞在2013～2014年农业季的玉米产量不高，320公顷土地只收获800多吨玉米，平均每公顷产量还不足3吨，远远低于当地大农场的平均产量。有一个地块没有做好施肥和除草工作，玉米穗小得可怜，因产量不够租用收割机的成本，最后没有收获。但这也为公司积累了经验，2014～2015年农业季耕种的玉米，由于赶在来迟的雨季之前播种，且施肥和除草均做得比较好，在笔者2015年1月前去考察的时候，玉米长势明显要好于周边的农场。皖津天瑞总经理张恒习告诉笔者，因为雨水充足且降雨规律，每公顷玉米产量达到5吨左右。

皖津天瑞已从中国和南非购置了20余台大型农业机械设备，并继续清理土地和扩大复垦面积。2015～2016年农业季，总种植面积扩大到1000公顷。但由此也带来了另外一个问题，即因土地基本为沙性土壤，大面积清理树林和灌木丛后，如果在此后的耕作中保护不善，土壤可能有出现沙漠化的风险。笔者在调查中发现，皖津天瑞在规划中已开始注意到这方面的问题，在2014～2015年农业季开垦的地块周边，保留了10～30米的防风林，以此防止风沙的侵袭。

成效与困难

当前，皖津公司与皖津天瑞主要在津巴布韦开展粮食作物种植且进展顺利，已经取得了一定的成效，但仍然面临一些困难。

从成效来看，主要表现在三个方面。

1. **为津巴布韦粮食安全做出了贡献**

津巴布韦近年来一直粮食短缺，每年都需要从国外进口几十万吨粮食。以最主要的粮食作物玉米为例，2014 年雨季以来旱涝不均，导致 2015 年玉米产量下降 35%，需进口 70 万吨玉米以填补供应缺口。① 皖津公司和皖津天瑞虽然在津巴布韦种植玉米等粮食作物的时间还不长，但还是从三个方面为其粮食安全做出了贡献：首先，它们在 2015 年共种植了 3600 公顷玉米，每公顷的产量为 5 吨，总量达到 1.8 万吨，相当于 2015 年进口总量的近 3%，而且，它们还会继续增加产量和扩大种植面积；其次，它们生产的全部粮食，不是运回中国，而是出售给当地的粮食公司，直接为当地人所用；最后，它们接手的农场此前大多已经长期闲置，进行复垦本身就是一件对粮食安全有益的事情。

2. **带动了当地的发展**

皖津公司和皖津天瑞已经因它们先进的管理经验和现代化的耕作方式，在当地发挥了示范效应并带动了当地经济发展。在农业技术培训方面，皖津公司将其中一个农场开辟为奇诺伊大学的教学与实验用地，以及周边农民进行技术交流和展示农产品的平台；皖津天瑞则利用农场的大型机械，培养了十几名司机和机械师。在创造就业方面，它们共雇用了 1000 多名农业工人，每个工人从农场所赚取的工资，基本可满足一个四口之家的日常花销。笔者曾前往皖津天瑞所属卡萨马农场附近的村子参观，发现青年壮大多在农场工作，而有些房屋明显刚刚修建不久。农场还向周边农户提供农业机械租赁服务，并以批发价向他们出售买来的种子、化肥和农药。此外，皖津公司和皖津天瑞还带动了当地其他产业的发展，如自皖津天瑞 2013 年进驻奇古图省以来，当地的建材业、服务业和银行业等都有了较大的发展。

3. **构建了良好的社会关系**

皖津公司注重履行企业社会责任，免费为当地群众解决用电和饮水等生活问题，为周边的学校捐资助学，为边远地区修建道路，这些举措密切了其与当地社区的关系。皖津天瑞专门在农场辟出一块土地，免费让农场

---

① "Zimbabwe to Import 700000 Tonnes of Maize after Poor harvest", http：//thezimbabwemail.com/zimbabwe－to－import－700000－tonnes－of－maize－after－poor－harvest/, accessed 2015－05－08.

工人耕种以解决他们的粮食问题；还为周边村庄失学的儿童成立了足球队，让他们在农场驻地的空地上玩耍。笔者在卡萨马农场调研的时候，还看到有村民前去租借拖拉机运输建筑材料，这无疑表明皖津天瑞已经与当地人建立了良好的关系。

至于他们面临的问题，主要与津巴布韦政府的土地政策、投入和产出以及自然因素等有关。

1. 在土地政策方面存在不利因素

根据津巴布韦政府禁止出租和买卖国有土地的政策和本土化政策的要求，安徽农垦和安徽天瑞只占皖津公司和皖津天瑞50%的股权，这无疑给它们的经营权，以及收回投资并盈利带来了一定的风险。此外，津巴布韦"快车道"土地改革后，此前的白人大型商业农场基本被分配为A1农场和A2农场，在适合耕作的前三类农业区，A1农场的最大面积为20公顷，[①]A2农场情况较为特殊，但即使其中的大型商业农场，在前三类农业区的最大面积也仅为400公顷。[②] 这就意味着这两家公司在以后的发展中要想扩大耕作面积，只能从政府拿地，因为与农户直接合作，土地面积小，合作主体多，经营和管理的难度肯定会增加。目前它们经营的农场周边已经有不少农户希望与它们合作，但正是受制于以上两方面的因素，合作无法开展。

2. 资金投入大，回报期长

由于津巴布韦农业基础设施落后，皖津公司和皖津天瑞在前期农业开发中，需要清理土地，修建道路、储存间和灌溉设施，再加上购买农业机械、种子、化肥和农药等基本农业投入，投资额之大可想而知。[③] 截至2014年年底，皖津公司已对二期项目投资2000多万美元，皖津天瑞的投资额也达到了400万美元。但从产值来看，相较于烟草和棉花经济作物，粮食作物的产值要低很多。以皖津公司2013～2014年农业季种植的烟草为例，其每公顷产量为2.5吨，每吨销售价格为3000美元，扣除4000美元成本，利润为3500美元，为玉米与小麦的三倍多（见表3）。而皖津天瑞

---

① Prosper B. Matondi, *Zimbabwe's Fast Track Land Reform*, Zed Book, 2012, p. X.

② J. Hanlon, J. Manjengwa and T. Smart, *Zimbabwe Takes Back Its Land*, Jacana Media（Pty）Ltd. , 2013, p.140.

③ 以清理土地为例，皖津天瑞清理灌木丛和蚁丘的成本每公顷高达600～800美元。

2013～2014 年农业季种植的玉米，因产量较低，还没有收回成本。鉴于此，为充分挖掘农场潜力，皖津公司在 2014 年拟定"种植 + 养殖 + 烟草 + 其他高效经济作物"的现代农业架构，并在当年种植了 100 公顷烟草；皖津天瑞也在 2014～2015 年农业季试种了 15 公顷烟草，并准备在 2015～2016 年农业季除扩大烟草种植面积外，再试种土豆和洋葱等高效作物。

表3 皖津公司玉米、小麦、大豆和烟草的产值（2013～2014 年农业季）

农作物品种	产量（吨/公顷）	价格（美元）	成本（美元）	利润（美元）
玉米	6	390	1300	1040
小麦	6	430	1700	880
大豆	2.5	520	900	400
烟草	2.5	3000	4000	3500

3. 受降雨等自然因素影响严重

津巴布韦虽然拥有丰富的水力资源，但因为缺乏灌溉设施及管理不善，可灌溉用地在 2009 年仅为 13.5 万公顷。[1] 对于玉米等粮食作物而言，基本是"靠天吃饭"，对气候和降雨等自然因素的依赖非常大，一旦雨季推迟或雨量不足，产量就会大幅降低。皖津公司和皖津天瑞虽然开始修建灌溉设施，但由于资金和电力等方面的原因，短期内很难改变这种"靠天吃饭"的现状。2014～2015 年农业季，由于雨季来迟、元旦前后降雨过多及干旱，它们的粮食产量都受到了影响。据估计，皖津公司的粮食要减产 20% 左右，[2] 皖津天瑞的玉米产量，每公顷仅为 2 吨，远低于 5 吨的预期。[3] 据津巴布韦气象专家介绍，由于全球气候变暖，津巴布韦正常的雨季时间正在逐年缩短甚至消失，取而代之的是不可预测且反复无常的季节，这无疑将给包括皖津公司和皖津天瑞在内的津巴布韦粮食种植企业带来重大的挑战。此外，麻雀、白蚁、狒狒，甚至周边村民的偷窃行为，也在一定程度上造成了粮食的减产。

---

① "Zimbabwe Agricultural Investment Plan（ZAIP）2013 - 2017: A Comprehensive Framework for the Development of Zimbabwe's Agriculture Sector", p. 19.
② 皖津公司总经理何宏顺在 2015 年 4 月 26 日发给笔者的电子邮件。
③ 对皖津天瑞总经理张恒习的微信采访，北京，2015 年 7 月 30 日。

皖津公司和皖津天瑞在津巴布韦开展的以玉米为主的粮食作物种植，无疑开拓了中国与津巴布韦农业合作的新领域，并为中国其他农业企业前往津巴布韦投资提供了经验与创建了平台。它们已经取得了一些成效，但还面临着诸多问题。在采访中，皖津公司的何宏顺总经理和皖津天瑞的张恒习总经理均提出，他们赴津投资农业存在单打独斗的局面，且在资金和政策方面都无法享受中国国内的惠农政策。为此他们建议，中国政府应出台相关政策支持农业"走出去"，如对农业机械和化肥等农资出口减免关税，为创建农业加工企业和修建灌溉等农业基础设施提供优惠贷款，以及支持建立现代农业经贸园区等。张恒习曾在采访中提出一个颇有见地的观点，笔者以此作为本文的结尾：为解决津巴布韦的粮食安全问题，中国政府已多次向津巴布韦提供粮食援助，并提供了其他多种形式的援助，但如果能从资金和政策方面加大对赴津粮食种植企业的支持力度，相信将会取得事半功倍的效果，因为企业为了获取利润而扩大种植面积和提高粮食产量，才是解决津巴布韦粮食安全问题的根本之道。

中国与肯尼亚农业合作现状和除虫菊投资案例启示

胡　姣* 　汪段泳** 　著

肯尼亚的农业现状和发展政策

独立后肯尼亚实行以私营经济为主体的"混合经济"体制，私营经济在整个经济中占70%。[1] 农业是肯尼亚经济的支柱产业，约70%以上的人口直接或间接从事农业生产，农业占肯尼亚GPD的比重在逐年上升。2016年，肯尼亚农业产值占GDP的比重由2012年的26.2%攀升至2016年的32.6%。毫无疑问，农业成为肯尼亚第一大产业。[2]

肯尼亚是全球红茶的最大出口国，也是欧洲的第三大花卉供给国。农业产品占肯尼亚出口总额的65%，茶叶、园艺产品（以鲜花和蔬菜为主）和咖啡是其三大主要创汇农产品。肯尼亚的粮食作物主要为玉米，还有小麦、水稻、粟类、豆类和薯类等。正常年景玉米基本自给，小麦和水稻则严重依赖进口。经济作物除了茶叶、园艺产品和咖啡之外，还有除虫菊、

---

* 胡姣，中山大学管理学学士，青年研究员和社会创业者，哈佛社会创新种子社区2014年成员。2014年起常驻肯尼亚，足迹遍布埃塞俄比亚、坦桑尼亚、乌干达、卢旺达和刚果（金）等多个非洲国家，关注中国海外投资可持续发展议题，具体议题包括企业社会责任、本土化、技能转移、创造就业和非洲大陆企业家精神等。

** 汪段泳，副教授，上海外国语大学国际关系与外交事务研究院副研究员，中国海外利益研究中心主任。毕业于武汉大学经济系，获经济学博士学位。

① 中国驻肯尼亚大使馆经济商务参赞处网站，http://images. mofcom. gov. cn/ke/201604/20160427091609875. pdf。

② Kenya National Bureau of Statistics, *Economic Survey* 2017, https：//www. knbs. or. ke/download/economic-survey-2017/.

甘蔗、剑麻、棉花、马卡达姆坚果（即夏威夷果）等。

表1　肯尼亚农业产值及农业对 GDP 的贡献率①

单位：百万肯尼亚先令

项目	2012 年	2013 年	2014 年	2015 年	2016 年
农业产值	1115198	1254813	1482840	1900965	2334147
GDP 总产值	4261370	4745143	5402410	6260646	7158695
GDP 增长率（%）	4.5	5.9	5.4	5.7	5.8
农业占 GDP 比率（%）	26.2	26.4	27.4	30.4	32.6
农业的增长比率（%）	2.8	5.4	4.3	5.5	4.0
农业对 GDP 增速的贡献率（%）	14.3	20.9	18.2	21.2	15.2

农业是肯尼亚 2030 远景规划中 GDP 增长加速的主要领域之一，农业发展的首要目标是通过农产品附加值的提高来增加收入。同时，肯尼亚政府也期望通过促进主要粮食如玉米、小麦和大米的生产，来结束国家对于进口的依赖。肯尼亚政府制定土地管理政策，让中高潜力的土地的价值更好地发挥，增强供应链管理，让小农户更好地对接市场，并对接本地、区域和国际市场以提升农林渔业产品的附加值。据不完全统计，自 2030 远景规划公布后，肯尼亚官方颁布了至少十九项规范和指导农业各个领域发展的法案和政策文件，其中多数面向种植业。② 2010 年，肯尼亚政府发布了《农业发展战略（2010~2020 年）》，这是在之前曾产生重要影响的指导性文件《农业振兴战略（2004~2015 年）》基础上，依据 2030 远景规划修订。③具体而言，肯尼亚政府通过修改农村生产合作社制度、扩大生产规模、普及农业技术、提供财政支持等提高本国中、小农户的生产效率与国际竞争能力，并通过整顿交通运输、加强农业基础设施建设、制定相关的制度等吸引更多的民间与国际资本进入肯尼亚的农业。

---

① Kenya National Bureau of Statistics, *Economic Survey* 2017，根据第 45~46 等页数据计算。

② Ministry of Agriculture, Livestock and Fisheries of Kenya, *Strategic Plan* 2013 – 2017, revised 2015, p. 10, http://www.kilimo.go.ke/wp-content/uploads/2015/05/MoALF_Strategic-Plan_2013 – 2017. pdf.

③ Carol N. Kamau, "Kenya's Agricultural Sector Reforms", *Global Agricultural Information Network Report*, USAID, Foreign Agricultural Service, 2013.

然而肯尼亚农业基础设施薄弱，缺乏资金、技术和管理人才，信息交流不畅通，农业产品附加值低。总体而言农业生产粗放，人们基本靠天吃饭，尤其是广大中小型农场主和普通农户。普通农户个体更是在农药、种子等基本的农资投入方面，由于资金所限面临捉襟见肘的困境。[①] 另外，农业发展受外部环境影响较大，如 2016 年肯尼亚的农业增长率为 4.0%[②]，低于 2015 年 5.5% 的记录，[③] 2016 年农业表现不佳的主要原因是干旱，尤其是 2016 年下半年降水量稀少。外部环境变化对普通农户影响较大，由于收入来源单一，农户整体抗风险能力也比较低。

中肯农业合作：贸易、援助与投资

中国和肯尼亚的双边投资和经贸关系自两国 1963 年建交开始。目前中国对肯尼亚投资以及双边贸易飞速发展，是肯尼亚第一大直接投资来源国和最大工程承包商。[④] 自 2015 年起，连续多年中国成为肯尼亚第一大贸易伙伴。[⑤] 根据中国海关统计，中国从肯尼亚进口货物中的重要类别为农业产品，包括生皮（毛皮除外）及皮革，咖啡、茶、马黛茶及调味香料，植物纤维，鲜花等。

建交以后，中肯的农业合作主要集中在政府层面，主要为援助项目，包括高级别官员互访、推动农业科研合作、中方培训肯尼亚农业技术人员等形式。2002 年 4 月，中肯两国签署《中华人民共和国农业部与肯尼亚共和国农业与农村发展部农业合作谅解备忘录》，为深化两国农业合作奠定了基础。此后，中肯高层互访频繁，大力推动在农业领域的合作。2014 年 5 月，中国国务院总理李克强访问肯尼亚，双方签署包括农业合作在内的 17 项合作协议和谅解备忘录。其中《中华人民共和国科学技术部与肯尼亚共和国教育科学技术部关于共建中国和肯尼亚作物分子生物学联合实

① 对当地华人农产品经销商的访谈，2015 年 8 月 13 日，肯尼亚纳库鲁。
② Kenya National Bureau of Statistics, *Economic Survey 2017*，根据第 24 页数据计算，https：//www.knbs. or. ke/download/economic – survey – 2017/。
③ Kenya National Bureau of Statistics, *Economic Survey 2017*，根据第 24 页数据计算，https：//www.knbs. or. ke/download/economic – survey – 2017/。
④ 中国驻肯尼亚大使馆官网，http：//www. fmprc. gov. cn/ce/ceke/chn/xw/t1493715. htm。
⑤ 中国驻肯尼亚大使馆官网，http：//www. fmprc. gov. cn/web/dszlsjt_673036/t1337078. shtml。

验室的谅解备忘录》即是其中的重要文件之一。2017 年 5 月，国家主席习近平在"一带一路"国际合作高峰论坛期间会见肯尼亚总统肯雅塔，建议将中肯关系升级为全面战略合作伙伴关系，深化包括农业在内的多领域合作。中肯农业合作的另外一个重要内容是人力资源开发合作。其中，由南京农业大学支持的肯尼亚埃格顿大学孔子学院是全球首家具有农业特色孔子学院，在中肯农业合作和人力资源开发合作中扮演了重要作用，为肯尼亚累计培养了成百上千名的农业人才。此外，中国政府也通过相关部委为肯尼亚提供农业援外培训，如 2015 年中国政府拟培训的534 肯方人员就涵盖了农村可持续发展等肯方重点关注的领域。[①] 此外，中肯双边的农业代表团也积极开展互访，且随着近些年两国关系的加强，互访频率也在不断增加。

根据笔者在肯尼亚的实地调研了解，目前中国在肯尼亚的农业投资还处在起步阶段。与莫桑比克、坦桑尼亚、赞比亚、埃塞俄比亚等国不同，中国国有企业在肯尼亚的农业领域鲜有投资，仅有的几家企业均为私营企业。从中华人民共和国商务部网站名单看，最早投资肯尼亚农业生产的大中型中资企业注册于 2012 年，迄今也仅有 5 家，占全部注册企业总数的3.1%。根据在肯尼亚的访谈，目前在肯尼亚个别中方私营企业开始关注农业投资，且多从农业贸易开始。如天津的聚龙集团 2014 年 5 月进入肯尼亚市场设立办事处，最初从贸易起步，向肯尼亚出口橄榄油，目前仍没有正式的农业投资项目。肯尼亚的鲜花出口总额位列非洲第一，目前也有少数几个在肯尼亚的企业从事鲜花贸易把鲜花直销中国，凯景国际鲜花（非洲）有限公司就是其中一个，到 2016 年，该公司销往中国的鲜花已经达到 320 吨，以玫瑰花、水仙百合、绣球花、大飞燕、火龙珠等鲜切花为主。[②] 笔者实地走访发现，中国商人在纳库鲁（Nakuru）郡投资建驴皮加工厂，从事驴产品贸易，把驴肉出口到中国和越南等国，驴皮进行加工，为中国国内东阿阿胶生产提供原材料。此外，还有部分个体工商户在肯尼亚从事中国农场经营，种植菠菜、豆角、黄瓜、辣椒

① CRI 国际在线，《中国与肯尼亚人力资源培训合作日益密切》，http：//gb.cri.cn/42071/2015/09/16/3245s5104976.htm。

② 王小鹏：《肯尼亚玫瑰香飘中国》，新华网，http：//news.xinhuanet.com/world/2017-09/17/c_1121676990.htm。

等中国蔬菜，为在肯尼亚的中国公司、超市和餐厅供货。此外，也有私营投资者关注辣木籽、除虫菊等经济作物的种植和投资。后面案例提到的除虫菊投资项目是中国目前在肯尼亚最大的私营农业投资项目之一。

中国在肯尼亚农业投资案例：除虫菊项目

据定居当地的中国资深农业专家指出，肯尼亚适宜农业发展的面积有限，占国土近三分之二面积的东北、西北部地区常年干旱，南部又有大面积地区处于高原，传统上适宜耕作的地区比较集中，因此谷物等大宗农产品根本没有能力和大型外资企业生产的农产品展开竞争，缺乏国际竞争力。肯尼亚本土具有竞争优势且有出口创汇能力的作物主要是一些经济作物。[1] 除虫菊就曾是肯尼亚主打出口的农产品之一。

除虫菊素是除虫菊的提取物，一直是国际公认的无公害的生物农药，2005 年，中国农业部已经把除虫菊素列为高毒农药的首选替代品种之一。除虫菊素只能从除虫菊中提取，无法人工合成，更神奇的是除虫菊素能够麻醉冷血动物的神经，而对恒温动物没有毒副作用，打在瓜果上面，雨水可以将其分解，没有残留。正因为除虫菊素的天然优势和不可替代性，随着人们对健康产品的认识越来越多，对除虫菊素的需求也越来越大，经过 2000 年前后的低谷后，国际市场对除虫菊素的需求一直以每年 15% 的速度在增长，2013 年对除虫菊素的国际需求在 450 吨左右，折合成除虫菊干花约 24000 吨。目前正在种植除虫菊的国家有中国、肯尼亚、澳大利亚、坦桑尼亚和卢旺达等国。肯尼亚曾是世界上除虫菊适种面积最大的国家。

事实上，早在 1928 年，肯尼亚就开始种植除虫菊。自 20 世纪 30 年代起，肯尼亚即成为全球除虫菊的主要生产者。40 年代，肯尼亚的除虫菊干花的年生产量已经超过 6000 吨，60 年代超过 10000 吨。从 20 世纪 60 年代到 90 年代末期，肯尼亚占世界市场的份额都在 90% 以上。直至 2003 年，肯尼亚除虫菊干花年产量还超过 1 万吨。[2] 除虫菊不仅长期以来是肯尼亚

---

① 笔者对定居当地的中国农业专家的访谈，2015 年 8 月 13 日，肯尼亚纳库鲁，埃格顿大学。

② Justus M. Monda（Chairman of Pyrethrum Growers Association of Kenya），*Pyrethrum Sector in Kenya: Current Status*，30th October，2014，http：//projects. nri. org/options/images/Current_status_of_py-rethrum_sector_in_Kenya. pdf.

出口创汇的重要来源，而且对肯尼亚普通农户的生活至为重要。在正常年份，约有20万户农村家庭种植除虫菊，带动100万人直接或间接以该作物为生。一个典型的种植户，通常要拿出自家所拥有耕地（一般是2~4公顷）的一半面积来种植除虫菊以换取现金，非如此则不能维持正常的家庭生活支出。通常一户农家从除虫菊种植中所获得收入相当于一个小学教师的工资，这足以支持家庭成员的学费、医药费、养老钱和其他日常必要开支。种植除虫菊投入不高，而收益较高，因而对农村发展一直做出重要贡献。因除虫菊产业的重要性，早在殖民时期的1934年，肯尼亚就设立了一个官方机构"肯尼亚除虫菊委员会"（Pyrethrum Board of Kenya，PBK）来负责该产业的事务，[1] 这家机构事实上成了垄断除虫菊全产业链的国有企业。但从2004年起，肯尼亚的除虫菊生产突然开始断崖式剧跌，当年就比上年减少50%，此后产量继续一路下降，到2011年产量仅为250吨，短短八年间就下降了98%，占世界市场额已不足2%。[2] 除虫菊产业的崩溃不仅使肯尼亚国家和所有种植户整体的绝对收益遭受重大损伤，留在行业内农户的相对收益也大不如前了。至于产业崩塌的原因，肯尼亚官方一方面认为是国际市场供给过剩，另一方面也承认是肯尼亚的管理机构肯尼亚除虫菊委员会对种植户支付拖延所致。[3] 实际上，通过实地走访肯尼亚除虫菊委员会，笔者认为后者才是主要原因，指出有些地方的农户被拖延付款长达四年。[4] 作为第三方的一些地方农业部门也持近似观点。[5] 从塔斯马尼亚、坦桑尼亚等国后来居上取代肯尼亚传统的除虫菊产业霸主地

---

① 肯尼亚除虫菊委员会官网，http：//www.kenya-pyrethrum.com/。

② Justus M. Monda（Chairman of Pyrethrum Growers Association of Kenya），*Pyrethrum Sector in Kenya：Current Status*，30th October，2014，http：//projects.nri.org/options/images/Current_status_of_pyrethrum_sector_in_Kenya.pdf.

③ Justus M. Monda（Chairman of Pyrethrum Growers Association of Kenya），*Pyrethrum Sector in Kenya：Current Status*，30th October，2014，http：//projects.nri.org/options/images/Current_status_of_pyrethrum_sector_in_Kenya.pdf.

④ Justus M. Monda（Chairman of Pyrethrum Growers Association of Kenya），*Pyrethrum Sector in Kenya：Current Status*，30th October，2014，http：//projects.nri.org/options/images/Current_status_of_pyrethrum_sector_in_Kenya.pdf.

⑤ Barnabas Bii，"Farmers in Rift Valley Return to Pyrethrum Production"，June 29，2014. http：//www.nation.co.ke/counties/eldoret/Rift-Valley-pyrethrum-farming/-/1954186/2365558/-/e93hea/-/index.html.

位的现实来看，① 关键制约因素是肯尼亚传统形成的高度垄断的国家管理
体制造成的管理者低效的工作习惯：一方面，肯尼亚政府漠视国际市场变
化，不能及时调整政策；另一方面，更为严重的问题是，肯尼亚政府完全
漠视除虫菊种植户利益，不尊重产业生态和价值链基本规律。这两方面的
原因都说明，导致除虫菊产业遭遇厄运的主要症结在于当地政府存在严重
的治理不善问题。无论如何，重振除虫菊产业，不仅是推动肯尼亚农业发
展和国民经济增长的必然要求，更是帮助农户个体增加收入、减贫、脱贫
的有效途径。而中国农业投资企业也参与了肯尼亚除虫菊产业的复兴。根
据中国外交部发布的信息，在肯尼亚至少有两家中资企业专营除虫菊的种
植生产及产品的开发和销售。② 其中，联合国环境署与同济大学在肯尼亚等
东非国家开展除虫菊种植项目，并生产有机化学杀虫剂，此项目有云南一家
环保公司参与。另据外媒报道，一家中国公司通过设立培育基地向当地种植
户提供材料和技术培训，以此帮助当地种植户将除虫菊产量提高了43%。③

2013 年以后，肯尼亚的除虫菊生产量和产值都有大幅回升，整体行业
在逐渐恢复。

表2　肯尼亚除虫菊产业 2012～2016 年年销量及产值表④

	2012 年	2013 年	2014 年	2015 年	2016 年
除虫菊销量（精加工）（吨）	1.0	4.2	3.6	3.7	3.3
除虫菊生产量总值（百万肯尼亚先令）	17.0	52.6	61.6	51.0	37.9

本文案例的公司正是在肯尼亚除虫菊行业处于低迷时期进入肯尼亚

① 2012 年，塔斯马尼亚生产的除虫菊在国际市场上占有 65% 的份额，坦桑尼亚、卢旺达、
中国等合计占有 33%，肯尼亚仅占 2%。参见 Justus M. Monda（Chairman of Pyrethrum
Growers Association of Kenya），*Pyrethrum Sector in Kenya：Current Status*，30th October，
2014，http：//projects. nri. org/options/images/Current_status_of_pyrethrum_sector_in_Kenya.
pdf。

② 《美丽中国与绿色非洲期待再次握手》，中华人民共和国外交部官网，http：//www. fmprc.
gov. cn/zflt/chn/jlydh/dfwl/t1316403. htm。

③ Samuel Gebre，"Kenya Plans Pyrethrum Industry Comeback with Chinese Help"，March 4，
2016，https：//www. bloomberg. com/news/articles/2016-03-04/kenya-plans-pyrethrum-industry-
comeback-with-chinese-help。

④ Kenya National Bureau of Statistics，*Economic Survey 2017*，根据第 170、第 175 等页数据汇总
而得。

的。肯尼亚鼎立国际贸易有限公司是 L 先生于 2009 年在肯尼亚成立的公司，主要从事农产品的收购和出口，主要出口市场是中国大陆，在中国有广泛的客户基础和良好的口碑。同时也在继续开拓美国和欧洲的市场。为了减少投资风险，L 先生把贸易与生产分开，于 2012 年成立了肯尼亚亦善农业种植有限公司，专门进行农产品的种植和加工。目前通过租地的方式全资拥有基加贝（KIJABE）种植园和基罗梅（KILOME）种植园，注册资金 100 万肯尼亚先令（按 2017 年 9 月末汇率合约 1 万美元），总投资额约为 1500 万元。

肯尼亚亦善农业种植有限公司已从肯尼亚林业部门在基加贝地区长期租赁了 12000 亩荒山土地，租期 45 年，目前已经开发了约 1000 亩，试种了除虫菊、蓖麻、辣木籽、芦荟、玫瑰、麦冬、夏威夷果树等多种经济作物，并从中找到适合种植、经济效益优且可以轮作互补的品种辣木籽和除虫菊。种植公司采用了"公司＋政府＋农户"的订单农业的方式种植除虫菊，即以政府为中介（在肯尼亚的除虫菊管理体制下，官方机构"肯尼亚除虫菊委员会"的介入是不可回避的），公司和种植户之间签订贯穿整个种植环节的合作协议。

这家以大规模集约化方式来运营的中国在肯投资的农业企业，在管理本地化和价值链打造上面临着挑战，同时也积累了一手的实践经验。

关于经营管理模式

L 先生认为，在他的企业中管理面临的问题是，肯尼亚人力资源市场不完善，要在当地找到足够数量的中高层管理人才是不容易的；另外，除虫菊的种植和加工都需要一定的技术，而旨在提升产品附加值的企业化运营方式，与传统的小农户生产也有很大不同，相比之下，小农户直接转变为企业员工，在专业技能与职业素养方面需要一个提高的过程。但是，要完全依靠中国人来担任企业各级管理工作，在成本和管理落地方面显然都极不可行。而完全依靠当地人来经营，除前述人力资源不足外，还很有可能使投资人面临严重的信息不对称，出现管理失控的风险。因此，在本土化这个必然要求的前提下，中方管理层和本土员工融合到位，往往是企业生存的关键。同时，如果使管理有效发挥作用，并让占企业人员多数的基层员工适应公司运营，避免文化冲突，是公司日常管理中最为基本而重大的问题。

L先生的公司在2011年开始种植除虫菊，最初仅是给农户开会宣讲，免费发放种子，定点收购，经营形式类似合作社。但从2012年开始，随着种植园开始承担科研职能，公司逐渐增加雇佣当地的劳动力从事育苗、试种工作。2013年7月，公司开始发展自营种植，需要更多的劳动力充当农业工人。由于农业生产存在季节性，公司对种植园雇工采用灵活的弹性雇佣方式。最多的时候雇工超过200人，最少时也不低于30人，雇工大多是当地农民。由于他们原有的生产习惯与企业要求不完全一致，因此与公司在技能培训、人员管理等方面存在着一个相互适应的过程。双方经过两年多的磨合，相互融合与适应基本是成功的，其间从没有发生过罢工等当地较为常见的劳资冲突事件。

L先生总结管理上的成功经验主要包括：减少管理冲突环节、缩短管理反馈流程、管理过程透明可见、充分发挥管理激励作用。

公司管理层中的中方人员极少，各级经理特别是中基层管理岗位都由本地人担任。中方高层通常不会涉足非常具体的、基层的、事务性工作的管理工作，而是由本地管理人员直接管理。管理层一方面关注最终结果，另一方面关注组织建设。当组织机构中的某些环节出现流程不畅时，说明管理层的本土化对接出现了问题，这是涉及企业管理的根本性问题，就需要不惜代价，进行必要的岗位或职能调整。

在肯尼亚工作的中国人，语言能力普遍存在问题，这就更需要与本土员工加强面对面的沟通，以解除一些不必要的误会。公司在实践中发现，当有问题发生时，应即时将有关人员召集起来，当场协调，使相关人员厘清问题的症结和提出解决方案，是化解沟通不畅的有效方式。这样直接、充分的交流即使当时不能让所有员工都完全理解，但先理解的本地员工也会以自己的言行去影响其他本地员工，这样做比单纯的说教要有效得多。

公司与农户之间、管理层与员工之间，在订购协议和劳动合同签订后，就构成了严肃的法律关系，双方事先协商同意的业务内容和工作计划必须得到绝对尊重，绝不能动摇和迁就。L先生认为，对于当地人的工作方式、习惯、信仰等，他和公司管理层已充分给予尊重。在企业的范畴内，L先生认为最好的表达尊重的方式是在管理过程中相互理解、相互信任、充分授权。管理层对作业流程保持常态化的跟踪、控制、协调，通常是以周为时间单位来设置工作目标和核查工作进度，保证每周在作业现场与中层经理和基层组长会商，检验上周工作进度，了解下周工作安排，听取意见和建议，在此基础上管理层形成下周生产计划。这样透明和充分参与的管理方式让本地管理人员感到得到最大限度的尊重，从而激发出他们最大的主观能动性。

农业种植对人员技能要求不高，但对作业的规范有严格标准。从组织管理的角度，制度的严肃性也必须得到维护和尊重。因此，公司管理的有效需要配合奖惩制度来发挥学习效应。对于员工中破坏管理有效性的"害群之马"，公司会给予机会修正，但若多次犯规，公司只能予以解雇，以防止产生"破窗效应"；同时，对于勤奋、做出突出贡献的员工，公司也会在适当场合给予奖励。这些有效地形成示范效应。

总之，通过基于相互深入了解的四年多的磨合改造、人才培养、本土化运作，L先生的种植园的日常管理已经非常顺畅，基本解决了令中国海外企业非常头疼的中外员工磨合的问题。前期的融合成功为后来合作开发者加快种植园的建设步伐提供了可能，减少了投资周期。

关于培育和延伸价值链

发展农业，需要相关配套的基础设施的支持，可以最大限度地节约成本，而出口导向型的农业种植对配套设施的要求更甚。种植园离首都仅50千米左右，开车约1小时，全程都是路况非常好的高速公路和高等级公路。肯尼亚电力短缺，但离该种植区域30千米左右，中国公司在此援建了地热发电站，因此，该区域的电力比首都内罗毕还稳定，停电的状况很少发生。农业当然离不开水，但不可能统一灌溉，因此雨水显得非常重要，经过仔细考察和资料分析，公司最终选定的种植区域是肯尼亚雨水最充沛的地区之一。同样，种植园对劳动力在数量和职业素质上也提出一定要求。而在肯尼亚，降雨量大的地方，往往形成传统的农业种植区域，不仅劳动力数量充足，而且劳动者有丰富的技能和经验。

公司采用订单农业的形式可最大限度地降低管理当地劳动力的成本，育苗、移栽、采摘、晾晒的整个过程都交给了农户自己完成，公司要做好的就是对除虫菊采割的监控和质量的控制。从种植起点开始，公司免费向农户提供除虫菊种子；在生长过程中，公司派技术人员指导农户育苗、移栽、采收和晾晒；在收购环节，签订协议时即商定好最低保护价，由公司指定的代理商进行收购，向农户直接支付现金，不打白条，不拖欠收购款。公司还把种植园作为育种和培训农业技术人员的基地，同时承担向当地农户转移技术的科研职能。值得一提的是，公司派出指导农户的技术人员越来越多的是由这个基地培训出的本地人。

在产品出口销售方面，肯尼亚长期以来对除虫菊实行国家高度垄断的管理方式。2012 年以前，在肯尼亚从事除虫菊的任何业务都需要许可证，除"肯尼亚除虫菊委员会"之外，其他公司拿到许可证的可能性基本没有。2012 年除虫菊市场有限度地放开后，历经近 3 年，L 先生的公司花了大量的人力、物力拿到了除虫菊的加工出口许可证。截至目前，肯尼亚仅颁发了 3 个这样的许可证，L 先生的公司是其中唯一有中资背景的公司。由于肯尼亚政府目前仍然对除虫菊产品出口有较严格的管理规定，L 先生设计了分步实施的产品加工出口方案。由于肯尼亚政府不允许除虫菊干花出口，但把除虫菊加工成粉末后可以出口。因此，在现阶段公司将除虫菊干花简单加工粉碎后出口销售；下一阶段，L 先生在肯尼亚建立工厂，经过精加工，可自行生产除虫菊精油等成品，再行出口。为此，L 先生设法使价值链尽可能地延长至国际市场终端。L 先生已与中国公司在上海合资成立了一家高新技术企业，专门从事有关除虫菊加工的技术研发和国际贸易。这样，就形成了一条从种植源头开始延伸至海外销售终端的完整价值链。

在肯尼亚，发展除虫菊种植的前景非常巨大，通过政府的引导支持，发动农户开始种植，L 先生的公司完全可以做到一年收获 3000 吨以上的除虫菊干花。在肯尼亚政府的政策支持下，届时该公司将有可能成为仅次于澳大利亚公司的全球第二大除虫菊供应商。如果远期能建成加工能力超过 1 万吨的加工厂，凭借肯尼亚低成本、高含量的优势，L 先生的公司完全有可能帮助肯尼亚超过澳大利亚，帮助肯尼亚恢复在除虫菊领域的历史荣光。

结　论

肯尼亚除虫菊产业突然崩塌的直接原因是国际市场需求发生变化和作

为唯一收购方的国有企业拖欠支付对除虫菊农户生产积极性的严重挫伤（还可能有国内经济困难的因素）。① 肯尼亚官方对农户等基本经济单位的生存和国家整体发展之间的关系缺乏足够清醒的认识。因此，要重振除虫菊茶产业，推动整个国民经济的健康增长，应该从最基本的个体经济单位（小农户）入手，着眼于人的生存状况的改善和发展的可持续。

本案例中的 L 先生和他的种植公司，对肯尼亚的产业结构、经济传统和发展走向有较为准确的理解，在此基础上对可能的市场机会进行了有价值的尝试。肯尼亚除虫菊产业的崩溃并非其要素禀赋或比较优势发生了重大变化，而是来自产业外部的风险所致。一方面，产业本身的核心竞争力并未丧失，经注入资源后有可能恢复其传统优势；另一方面，传统上完全控制该产业的国有垄断力量因难以为继开始逐渐退出，从而为私营部门腾出了一定的市场空间。

因此，准备长期运营的外来企业应对投资的远期收益超出即期收益形成强烈信心，在一定程度上愿意将部分即期收益转化为远期收益的投资，或将利益让渡理解为风险折现。为降低即期风险、强化交易合作，较好的解决途径是与东道国伙伴形成风险共担关系。在前两条因素作用下，外来企业往往可能将即期收益转化成对东道国伙伴或利益相关者的投资。在发展中国家，外来投资与发展合作形成密不可分的关系。从这个角度，可以较方便地理解外企的社会责任问题。

在这个案例中，L 先生首先是对肯尼亚除虫菊产业的振兴抱有信心，着眼点主要放在远期收益。另外，注入资金、订单农业、培训人力资源等让渡部分即期收益的行为，可以理解为对远期收益的投资或规避风险。整体来看，L 先生企业的运营模式是与种植户建立起共生关系，通过绑定双方利益来激励合作行为，在帮助当地伙伴培育自生能力的同时，公司自身也获得了生存、发展、壮大的机会，这是一种典型的合作博弈模式。实际上，这是以融入产业价值链的方式来参与重塑除虫菊价值链。

---

① Justus M. Monda（Chairman of Pyrethrum Growers Association of Kenya），*Pyrethrum Sector in Kenya：Current Status*，30th October，2014，http：//projects. nri. org/options/images/Current_status_of_pyrethrum_sector_in_Kenya. pdf.

中国农业"走进非洲"的机遇与挑战

——国有企业经理人的视角

刘　均　管善远　汪路生*　著

现有针对中国农业"走出去"的研究中，有的从经济学的视角分析了中外资源禀赋的互补优势，有的从发展人类学的视角分析了在农业投资过程中存在的文化差异，有的从社会责任的角度分析了企业需要承担的四重责任；① 也有文章总结了中国对外农业投资所取得的重要成果和经验，还有文章则突出了中国企业包括农业企业在对外投资过程中存在的诸多问题。② 以上都是从旁观者的角度进行研究，优点是"旁观者清"，比较客观中立；但可能对于中国农业企业"走进非洲"的理解失诸全面。本文尝试从长期实际参与中国农业"走出去"的国有企业经理人的角度，结合国家政策的制定和具体落实情况，从政治经济学的角度对坦桑尼亚这个国别个案进行历史和现状分析，使读者经由"局内人"的分析获得一个新的理解视角。

中国从 1990 年开始，以中国农垦为代表的大型国有企业开始尝试在非洲创办农场，从援建过渡到小规模投资，到 2000 年，在赞比亚等 9 个非洲

---

*　刘均，北京大学国际关系学院博士候选人，北京大学非洲研究中心助理；管善远、汪路生，中非农业投资有限责任公司坦桑尼亚公司经理。

① 施勇杰：《中非农业合作模式创新研究》，石河子大学 2009 年博士学位论文；韩璟：《中国海外耕地投资》，华中科技大学 2014 年博士学位论文；刘靖：《摸着石头越洋：国家资本走出去——以坦桑尼亚中资国有资本为例》，中国农业大学 2014 年博士学位论文；张晓颖、王小林：《坦桑尼亚中资企业履行企业社会责任评估》，《中国外交》2016 年第 2 期，第 113 ~ 131 页。

② 韩相山：《如何开发非洲农业市场》，《瞭望新闻周刊》2000 年 10 月 2 日第 40 期，第 41 页；唐晓阳：《劳资关系问题影响中非外交大局》，《非洲研究》2015 年第 1 卷（总第 6 卷），第 193 ~ 205 页。

国家创办了 12 个农牧业项目,经营总面积只有 25 万亩(1.6 万公顷)。[①] 投资进展相对缓慢。2000 年中国的"走出去"战略逐渐形成,中国以政府 贴息优惠贷款方式对非洲国家进行援助,这给中国对非洲的农业合作特别 是中国对非的大规模投资带来了新的机遇。[②]

随着"走出去"呼声一浪高过一浪,继中国在坦桑尼亚投资矿业、工 程、贸易、加工业之后,投资的目光开始转向坦桑尼亚的农业。[③]

投资坦桑尼亚农业的有利条件

坦桑尼亚政局稳定

自独立以来坦桑尼亚政局稳定,堪称非洲国家的典范,按照中国 大使的说法,三方面关系(即部族关系、宗教关系和政党关系)处理 得很好。"坦桑尼亚民众对国家认同度很高,各部族和睦往来,基督教 和伊斯兰教和平共处,政党互动也比较理性、克制、守法。"[④] 在坦桑 尼亚,社会政治稳定为经济发展打下了坚实基础,而且基尼系数小也能说 明发展相对均衡。[⑤] 在日常生活工作中作为中国的农场经营者对此感同身 受:农场周围社区有不同政党活动,基督教和伊斯兰教和谐相处,农场的 工人来自十六个大区,其方言各不相同,但丝毫不影响他们对国家的 认同。

农业优先的发展政策

坦桑尼亚国土总面积为 947300 平方公里,农业用地约为 4000 万公顷, 占总面积的 42%。2013 年,耕种面积为 1565 万公顷,占全国的 17%,其

① 韩相山:《开发非洲农业的市场前景》,《西亚非洲》2000 年第 3 期,第 59 页。
② 刘海方:《中非农业合作现状、问题与对策建议》,中非联合研究与交流计划 2015 年课题 研究报告(内部资料),第 25 页。
③ 魏建国:《此生难舍是非洲:我对非洲的情缘和认识》,中国商务出版社,2011,第 221 ~ 240 页;《农业"走出去"重点国家农业投资合作政策法规及鼓励措施概况》,中国农业 出版社,2011,第 1 ~ 3 页。
④ 中国驻坦桑尼亚大使馆官方网站,使馆动态,中国驻坦桑尼亚大使吕友清在使馆接受了 英国《金融时报》驻非洲记者凯特琳娜的采访,2013 年 8 月 28 日。
⑤ 黄承伟等:《国际减贫理论与前沿问题 2012》,中国农业出版社,2012,第 316 ~ 317 页。

中耕地面积 1350 万公顷。① 农业在坦桑尼亚经济中扮演着重要角色，在整个国民产出中占有很大的份额，1990~2007 年，坦桑尼亚农业对 GDP 总量的平均贡献率约为 48.5%。

根据联合国统计，坦桑尼亚总人口在 2017 年为 5966 万人，其中 69%是农村人口。2005 年以来人口年增长率约为 3.2%，68.1%的人口居住在农村。② 农业产值 2014 年达到 139 亿美元，对于国民生产总值的贡献率达到了 30%。③

坦桑尼亚农业经济是由小农户主导的。最新的农业地区综合调查显示：约 462 万农户在从事农业生产，平均每个农户耕种 1.78 公顷土地。坦桑尼亚农业技术极为落后，农民使用简单的农具，在依赖降雨的农业系统中，约 70%的土地都依靠锄头耕种，20%依靠畜力耕种，10%依靠拖拉机耕种。机械化水平低是农业发展的制约因素之一。

坦桑尼亚有 7 个农业生态区，每个生态区都有各自的优势农作物，不过所有生态区都种植主要的粮食作物。按照坦桑尼亚种植业分类，农作物主要为 3 大类：粮食作物、传统出口作物和非传统出口作物。主要粮食作物包括玉米、水稻、小麦、马铃薯、甜薯、香蕉、大蕉、甘蔗、木薯、高粱、粟米。主要传统出口作物为咖啡、棉花、腰果、烟草、茶叶、剑麻、除虫菊、丁香。非传统出口作物包括各类油料作物、豆类、香料、可可和装饰花卉等。④

2009 年 6 月，坦桑尼亚宣布实施"农业第一"政策，实施该政策的具体措施包括：增加政府对"农业第一"政策的预算拨款，成立坦桑尼亚农业开发银行（TADB），建立"农业第一"的特别基金，提高农业部门开发

---

① Food and agriculture organization of United Nations (FAO), AQUASTAT, "United Nations of Tanzania", 2016, http：//www. fao. org/nr/water/aquastat/countries_regions/TZA/, 2018 - 08 - 24.

② Worldometers, *Tanzania Population*, available online：http：//www. worldometers. info/world - population/tanzania - population/, last visit on September 30th, 2018.

③ Tanzania Agriculture, TanzaniaInvest, https：//www. tanzaniainvest. com/agriculture. last visit on September 30th, 2018.

④ 陈宗德等：《非洲各国农业概况（1）》，中国财政经济出版社，2000，第 607~643 页；郝风等：《中国援坦农业专家组专家》，《坦桑尼亚联合共和国农业国别调研报告（内部资料）》；商务部国际贸易经济合作研究院：《对外投资合作国别（地区）指南：坦桑尼亚（2014）》。

项目一揽子资金,支持实施"农业第一"政策,鼓励大、中、小型私营部门对农业投资,养老基金和其他基金团体提供一定比例的资金用于农业生产,为小农户建立社会保险,成立专门的土地银行从事农业商业化投资,有效利用政府及政府机构目前拥有的土地,取消农产品市场的壁垒,加强农业转型中的农村地区的电力供应。

2011 年 1 月,坦桑尼亚政府又推出"南方农业走廊"(SAGCOT)开发计划。"南方农业走廊"又称"坦赞铁路走廊"(TAZARA Corridor),是进一步贯彻落实坦桑尼亚"农业第一"政策所规划的可操作性较强的计划,其目标是将这一区域建成高产农业转型的典范并成为经济增长的"引擎"。"南方农业走廊"的具体构想是:建设 3 ~ 4 个由可获利的大、中、小型农场和农业综合企业构成的农业集群。农业集群位于极具农业高产潜能区的中心,由核心商业性农场以及种植、加工和仓储、基础设施维护和改善等支持机构组成。在基础实施、价值链、农业系统和人力资本的协调投资和支持下,实现收益性农业和农业服务集群化发展。在 2012 年 11 月 27 ~ 28 日举行的"坦桑尼亚农业投资推介会"上,水稻、甘蔗被列为发展的首选作物(还有畜牧养殖业)。该推介会还重点推出了三块区域,提供土地、政策、资金支持。

品质领先世界的作物——剑麻

剑麻是仅次于天然橡胶、棕榈油的不可替代的热带作物,因为剑麻纤维在制作高档电梯用钢丝绳内芯和不锈钢抛光布上具有"两个不可代替"的特性,市场潜力巨大。目前,全球剑麻纤维年产量仅维持在 30 万吨左右,但远不能满足 80 万吨的市场需求。这几年,剑麻纤维价格一路上扬,从 2008 年的出厂价(UG 级,下同)700 美元/吨上涨到 2015 年第一季度的 1700 美元/吨。

因纤维色泽洁白,剑麻被称为"白色的金子",坦桑尼亚素有"剑麻王国"之称,非常适宜剑麻生长。沙性黑棉土和气候条件都特别适合喜温热、耐干旱的剑麻生长,剑麻的品质一直名列世界前茅。[①] 自 1893 年从墨西哥引种以来,二战期间由于战争的需要,剑麻产业得到了飞速发展。

---

① 孙屹:《坦桑尼亚种剑麻 合作开发求发展》,《经济日报》2007 年 11 月 10 日第 008 版。

1950～1970 年，坦桑尼亚一直是世界最大的剑麻生产国，高峰时期年产量达到 23 万吨，20 世纪 60 年代每年出口剑麻制品 10 多万吨。[①] 剑麻产业属劳动密集型产业，从育苗、取苗、定标、种植、田间管理、割叶、刮麻、晾晒、收麻、抛光、分级、打包，等等，无不需要大量的劳动力，而坦桑尼亚人民较为勤劳，这个产业在坦桑尼亚成为"领军"产业。世界上最好的剑麻纤维产于坦桑尼亚。巴西剑麻纤维未经水洗，胶质含量高，无法纺织高等级麻纱，无法用于高档电梯用钢丝绳内芯；同样，中国广东、广西生产的剑麻纤维因受气候、土壤等因素影响，其品质亦不如坦桑尼亚纤维，中国仅广东、广西、海南等局部地区可种植剑麻，且规模极为有限。

较大的成本优势

在国内种植热带作物地区，农村土地租赁价格平均在 6000 元/公顷/年，而在坦桑尼亚平均约为 600 元/公顷/年（当然汇率还在不断变化，只能是大概数字，下同）。若仅指国家的租金，在坦桑尼亚远离城镇的农业用地租金平均为 10 元/公顷/年，靠近城镇的农业用地租金平均为 100 元/公顷/年。从劳动力成本方面分析，广西剑麻产区农民工资为 140 元/日，坦桑尼亚剑麻行业协议工资最高（割麻工）为 25 元/日。在坦桑尼亚的劳动力成本优势明显。

中坦友谊为经济合作开路

1996～1998 年，中国农垦总公司（简称中国农垦）先后 4 次派团赴坦桑尼亚考察剑麻种植加工项目，并顺利完成了《项目可行性研究报告》，随后经两国有关部门批准，该项目被推荐给中国进出口银行，成为中坦两国政府框架协议下的优惠贷款项目，获得了中国进出口银行 900 万美元的授信。1999 年，时任坦桑尼亚总统的姆卡帕来华访问，两国签署了《中国政府向坦桑尼亚联合共和国政府提供优惠贴息贷款的框架协议》，十分顺利地促成了第一家中国农业企业赴坦桑尼亚投资，这就是"中国农场"项目。当年，中国农垦在坦桑尼亚成立了分公司，并开始寻找合适的项目。要在异国他乡找到一个非常合适的项目并不容易，可谓"踏破铁鞋无觅

[①] 黄艳：《世界剑麻生产现状及未来展望》，《中国热带农业》2008 年第 5 期，第 26 页。

处"。然而"柳暗花明"的是，2000年项目组人员在路上偶遇在此援建的中国农垦老同事，经他牵线搭桥，很快就找到了合适的农场。这个农场的老板是总统顾问，本来已经谈好价格即将把农场卖给英国人，听说中国人要买，立刻就将农场卖给了中国人，而且要价比英国的报价还低5万美元。整个交易过程非常顺利，项目组利用前期贷款120万美元就将农场买下，取名为"中国农场"（也称剑麻农场），使中国农垦总公司在非洲投资的农牧业用地面积增加了近一半。可以说，农场也完全是中国政府"走出去"战略相关政策支持的产物。农场是独立经营，自负盈亏。中国农垦总公司购买农场看似偶然，但如果没有中坦人民的深情厚谊，如果没有中国政府、中国农业专家在当地长期援助建立的人力资源网络，中国农垦不能如此顺利地购买农场。

得益于坦桑尼亚人对于中坦友谊的珍视，中国农业企业才顺利地"走进非洲"。国有企业也需要国家的支持力度再大一些，步伐才能迈得更大，成果也会大得多。姆巴拉利农场是中国援建时间较早、规模较大的综合性机械化农场，1977年建成投产后，坦桑尼亚政府把它誉为"模范农场""坦桑尼亚农业发展的榜样"和"第三世界经济合作的典范"。该农场的水稻生产经历了前兴后衰的过程，最好年份种植水稻2700公顷，产量为2万吨。在中国农垦收购剑麻农场的同时，姆巴拉利农场也开始私有化，当时灌溉和排水设施依然发挥作用，而且水源条件好，农田基础设施完善，加之双方人员都非常熟悉，农场职工委员会也希望中国人接手农场，而且价格也不高。如果中国农垦当时能买下姆巴拉利农场，很容易取得经营效益。但是，中国农垦当时的银行贷款是专门用于剑麻项目的，确实没有多余的资金用来从事其他项目，错失了良机。

中坦友谊在企业运营中一直发挥保驾护航的作用。从坦桑尼亚中央政府到各级地方政府都曾给予中国企业大力支持和帮助，一直非常支持和关心"中国农场"。2003年，在剑麻农场成立初期，时任坦桑尼亚总理苏马耶及夫人就到农场来视察，包括省长、县长及各政府管理部门领导60多人随行。苏马耶总理先后参观了剑麻农场的两块苗圃和剑麻大田，并详细询问了剑麻的种植和管理情况，对中国专家先进的工作方法和丰富的经验表示赞赏。苏马耶总理一行的访问给了正处于资金链条困难中的农场极大的鼓励。农场在2007年遇到大规模罢工时，当地县乡政府坚决与公司站在一起，派联合工作组来农场调解，同时县警察局也派警察到现场维持秩序，帮助农场妥善解决了罢工事件，恢复了农场的正常生产。2009 年，坦桑海关总署又因为赞赏剑麻农场对当地社会发展的贡献而返还了农场因为遗失《进口物资免税清单》而缴纳的大笔税款。

中坦农业合作面临的挑战

坦桑尼亚经营环境的局限

坦桑尼亚的水利设施十分落后，丰富的水资源白白浪费，其根本原因是国家无力支持个体农户修建水利工程。虽然有个别水坝工程竣工，但配套的灌渠又难以兴建，导致水坝工程难以发挥作用。在中国农场所在的莫罗戈罗省基洛萨（KILOSA）县的鲁代瓦（RUDEWA）乡，这种情况很常见。

物流、运输、仓储发展滞后，电力保障能力弱

在坦桑尼亚物流主要靠公路，成本很高，大型粮仓很少。坦桑尼亚政府已经意识到这个问题，所以在"南方农业走廊"计划中把物流、仓储等作为优先发展项目。同时，以水电为主的电力缺乏，电力供给满足不了需求，且电线杆多为木质，易遭白蚁危害，在雨季电线杆倒伏导致断电是常事，电力保障能力弱。

发展农业的科技力量薄弱，经费不够，科研转化程度低

笔者走访了剑麻农场附近的翼龙噶研究所（主要研究玉米、高粱、大豆新品种）和武陵岗研究所（主要研究剑麻、土壤、气象），其科研能力及设备与中国县级农科所不相上下，研究人员普遍老龄化，新生代不愿从事这种待遇低、条件较为艰苦的工作。

疾病影响劳工效率

坦桑尼亚是疟疾、艾滋病、肺结核高发区，农业劳动力受害严重，每年与疟疾相关疾病导致的死亡人数约为 10 万人。此外，一些地方病如萃萃蝇传播的嗜睡病、丝虫病等发病率比较高，由于卫生设施落后，几乎每年雨季都会出现伤寒、霍乱高发期。在雨季剑麻农场每天平均 40 人请病假，约占职工总数的 4%，得病的职工最多约占职工总数的 8%。

优惠政策落实难

为了促进农业发展，坦桑尼亚也制定了一系列优惠政策，如资本项下货物免关税与增值税；农业机械与设备免关税或可享受增值税豁免；农用工具免关税或可享受增值税豁免；外资企业可享受 100% 资本返还；外国股东所得股息和红利可自由汇出；在资本投资回收（即公司利润与资本投资相抵）前，免缴所得税；外汇管制较宽松；获得土地只需 30 天时间（"A"类居留许可只需 14 天）等。

实际执行起来，这些政策往往是"南辕北辙"。[1] 例如，土地获取政策的执行。坦桑尼亚所有土地均属国家所有。土地取得方式分三种：政府给予该土地入住权；坦桑尼亚投资中心所拥有衍生权的土地；从私人手上转租的土地。土地入住和衍生权分为短期和长期。长期使用的土地期限为 5~99 年，可更新，但不超过 99 年；长期衍生土地和租赁期限通常在 5~98 年；每年需向政府交纳土地使用费，而费用与地域和用途相关，目前远离城镇的农用地的土地使用费为每英亩 1000 坦桑尼亚先令。对坦桑尼亚政府处事缓慢的抱怨不仅来自中资企业。日本国际协力机构（JICA）首席代表曾经通过坦桑尼亚媒体指出坦桑尼亚注册公司程序官僚化严重，不利于投资者前来投资，特别是日本投资者。坦桑尼亚必须减少处理商业登记的机构，简化商业注册流程，以吸引更多的日本投资者。[2]

为了吸引投资，坦桑尼亚政府设立了投资中心，这就意味着申请土地本来由土地事务部主管，而申办工作证则由移民局和劳工部负责（现在主要由劳工部负责），但现在都要经过投资中心，简化流程的目标无法实现。

另外，不同的政策执行者对具体政策条文的理解往往不同。比如，对于征收剑麻类农产品的"地方发展基金"，农场主协会认为应按剑麻类农产品总产量扣除直接成本后的毛利的 0.3% 稽征基金，而地方政府认为剑麻纤维属工业产品，须按售价的 5% 稽征基金，二者相差极大。对此，目前双方仍处在僵持状态，具体征收的数额往往取决于农场与当地政府是否

---

① Pius Rugonzibwa, "New Act to ensure stricter work permit issuance", Dar es Salaam：*DAILY NEWS*, Oct. 4th, 2013.

② Dar es Salaam：The *Guardian*, March 13th, 2015.

存在良好的互动关系。

同样，不同的政策执行者关于农用土地问题也存在理解偏差。在2012年11月26日召开的"坦桑尼亚农业投资推介会"上，平达总理和土地事务部长分别提到，虽然坦桑尼亚土地归国家所有，但70%的土地属村级主导，28%的土地属国家自然保护区，仅2%的土地属私有化农场和被中央政府土地部门掌控。坦桑尼亚政府对国土面积的10%进行了勘察、图绘和颁证。农村土地流转过程分六步，从申请用地到颁证耗时6～12个月或更长时间，这取决于与村级组织的谈判、补偿、土地勘测等。

政策执行者对农用工具的理解也存在极大偏差。如关税部门认为农用拖车也可"商用"，无法限定其在农场，所以，必须征收关税和增值税。

总之，坦桑尼亚的投资政策难以吸引投资者，主要因为社会化服务体系极为落后。产前的化肥、农药不仅依赖进口，而且被极少数商家掌握，量少、品种少、价格高，进而影响应用；产中的技术指导更是无从谈起；产后的物流与仓储也落后，达市港口一个仓储容量达6万吨的粮仓闲置多年却无人问津。

民主制与工会文化的负面作用

与这些营商环境的初级状态不相称的是，参照欧美的标准，坦桑尼亚作为非洲民主化进程相对比较好的国家之一，规定了极为详细的劳工权益保护。[1] 公司必须为员工提供相应的福利保障，如为其配偶和4个18岁以下的孩子提供免费的医疗服务，员工每年享受28天的带薪年假，公司要负担职工亲属的丧葬费等。劳工职业安全与健康方面的要求也极为苛刻，劳工部下属的劳工职业安全与健康局每年都要对员工进行身体健康检查，高额的费用（相当职工两周工资）由企业负担。[2]

坦桑尼亚工会势力强大，这在国内难以想象。法律倾向保护工人的权益，这在一定程度上大大降低了劳动效益，无形中增加了生产成本，降低

---

[1] 这里关于非洲民主化、民主、人权与经济发展阶段之间的关系的看法，是在非洲工作的中国国有企业经理人以及其他层面的管理人员的普遍看法，并不代表本书主编和北京大学非洲研究中心的观点。特此说明。——主编

[2] Times Correspondent，"Agricultural Council Berates New Agro - texes in Budget"，Dar es Salaam：*The Guardian*，May 13[th]2015，p. 3.

了农产品的国际市场竞争力。坦桑尼亚沿用英国劳工法体系，规定标准工作时间为每周 45 个小时，超时属加班，平时加班雇主须按标准工资的 1.5 倍支付工人加班费，周日和节假日加班雇主须按标准工资的 2 倍支付工人加班费；雇主还应支付工资总额 6% 的技术培训税、10% 的社会保障基金。工会与雇主常常就工资、加班费、福利产生分歧，而工会常号召工人罢工或消极怠工。

追求短期效益，中国对非洲农业合作支持严重不足

虽然国务院批准建立了以农业部部长为总召集人、由 21 个部级单位共同组成的"农业对外合作部际联席会议"制度，但与矿业等比较，落到实处还有一段路要走。目前，农业走出去企业在咨询费、法律费用、评估费、论证费等方面可以得到政府补贴；企业员工的境外人身意外保险可得到一定的补贴；此外，中国政府对境外人员的培训也给予每人 500 元的补贴。但这些补贴与农业的弱质性和艰苦条件相比，吸引力不强。与之相对应的是，来自国内的投资者更关注短期利润，普遍追求"短平快"的项目和"有影响力"的项目。

"中国农场"项目的起步非常艰难。中方管理团队的住房是原有农场留下的几间破砖房，宿舍连玻璃窗也没有，偶尔还有蝮蛇溜进来，周围杂草丛生，也没有水电，住宿条件非常差。但相比于当时农场的生产条件，这都不算什么。由于农场陆续停产十多年，土地早已荒芜，有的地方布满荆棘和大树；剑麻纤维加工厂的机器老化生锈，仓库和加工车间都破败不堪。就是在这样的艰苦条件下，中方管理团队逐步组建起剑麻农场的生产和管理体系。中方管理团队从开荒种苗、招聘当地工人、组建当地的管理层开始，与当地工人一道辛勤劳作，逐步恢复了闲置多年的剑麻农场的生产和经营。由于当时资金有限、机械设备落后，也没有推土机和挖掘机，中方人员就带领当地工人，完全靠手工艰苦开垦了八个多月，终于在 2000 年年底开垦出第一批田地，当年就种下了 96 公顷的剑麻。2001 年，农场又开荒栽种了 236 公顷剑麻，到 2005 年一共开荒栽种了 1218 公顷剑麻，为农场后来 8 年的生产奠定了坚实的基础。

按照项目安排，农场在 2001 年可以继续申请贷款，加强生产投入，扩大生产规模。中国进出口银行到农场实地考察后认为，对农场的贷款存在

重大风险，要求中国农垦的母公司用实物抵押后才能贷款。但是，由于中国农垦本身没有可以抵押的东西。从 2002 年起，中国进出口银行单方面终止协议，停止了项目的剩余贷款，还要求中国农垦在规定的时间内连本带息偿还第一笔贷款，这简直是釜底抽薪，几乎给农场带来了灭顶之灾，整个项目面临夭折。① 之所以遇到这样的问题，并非是国家的政策不好，而是政策落实不到位。首先是因为农业不是中国进出口银行关注的重点。如它在 2002 年、2003 年的对外优惠贷款业务中，重点支持的是合作开发和高新技术项目，带动机电产品和成套设备的出口，推动中国企业到国外投资建厂、承包工程。② 整体上，中国进口出银行的优惠贷款有力地支持了中国这些产业部门"走出去"，但因为不关注农业，给农业项目提供的贷款也不多；同时，中国进出口银行在坦桑尼亚没有派驻人员，不了解当地情况，更缺乏对农业特别是剑麻行业的了解，走马观花式的考察一番就草率地认为"中国农场"项目没有前途，这实际上是对中国进出口银行自己前期审批决策的否定。中途停止贷款意味着项目可能破产，国家前期的投入可能彻底打水漂。归根结底，这一切还是局部利益与短期利益的矛盾所致。中国对外发展的整体战略还有待加强研究，协同效应还有待提升。

中国农场之所以能坚持下来，首先因为母公司中国农垦的竭力支持。尽管自身面临窘境，但中国农垦不惜变卖国内资产或暂时拆借其他项目经费来支持农场的运作，将赞比亚中垦农场的资金暂时挪借到"中国农场"项目，后来又设法贷款 50 万美元，使农场的耕种得以坚持下来，保证了第一批剑麻的栽种。农场管理人员更是经常四处借贷，寻找资金，苦苦支撑，耗费了大量的精力。在最困难的时候中方管理团队只留下一人，其他人都回国筹集资金。虽然经过大家的共同努力，农场挺过了那段艰难的日子，但还是很影响管理人员的积极性。从经济效益来看，如果不是资金链断掉，农场每年至少可以多开发 300～500 公顷土地，剑麻种植面积至少可

① 刘靖：《摸着石头越洋：国家资本走出去——以坦桑尼亚中资国有资本为例》，中国农业大学博士学位论文，2014 年，第 43～44 页。

② 2002 年《中国进出口银行年度报告》，第 18 页，2003 年《中国进出口银行年度报告》第 2003nb007 号文件，http://www.eximbank.gov.cn/tm/report/index_27_14082.html，2016 年 10 月 23 日访问。

以扩大一倍以上。

中国农垦的剑麻农场开发进度的延缓，使农场在前五年的种植规模受限，远远落后于预期安排；从大处来看，这直接影响了中国农业"走出去"的步伐，因为像"中国农场"这样的优质农业项目尚且如此，这也基本可以反映中国农业企业"走进非洲"的总体情况。今天中国农业企业在国外的经营规模不仅落后于欧美国家，也远远落后于印度等发展中国家。根据渣打银行 2012 年的研究，中国在非洲租用约 10 万公顷土地，中资企业的农业投资似乎没有超过 1 万公顷，超过 5000 公顷的也不多（剑麻农场占地 6900 公顷，截至目前已经开发约 1500 公顷）。[①]

中方长期经营之道： 本土化发展和企业社会责任

依法经营并及时了解最新政策

坦桑尼亚政府、组织、人民对法律的遵从相对较为重视，中国的农场经营者必须重视这一点，特别是涉及雇工、税务方面的法律。如剑麻农场按照法律要求，与 65% 的工人签订了劳动合同，为 85% 的合同工人缴纳社会保障费，依法兴办职工医院，定期为员工进行健康体检，依法组建工会，定期听取工会意见。剑麻农场按时、照章、足额纳税。辞退员工均按法律要求的程序进行。即便是每月的生产与销售情况，剑麻农场也按坦桑尼亚统计法的要求及时、完整地上报主管行业协会。

信守承诺，常态沟通，赢得当地工人的心

中国进出口银行撤资后，中方员工的工资就开始被拖欠，直到 2007 年年底才开始补发。但就是在资金如此紧缺的情况下，剑麻农场也严格遵守当地法律法规，按时给当地员工发工资和缴纳各种社会保障费，可谓勒紧腰带支持农场建设。这也让剑麻农场在当地获得了极好的声誉，当地人都说"中国农场，不欠薪"。中方管理者要一如既往地关心爱护当地员工，只有通过爱心的传递，才能缩小文化差异，同时，也能增加当地员工对农

[①] 《港媒：中国人投资非洲农业进展缓慢》，新华网，http://news.xinhuanet.com，2016 年 10 月 23 日访问。

场的向心力与凝聚力。

彼此沟通是消除误会的首选途径。在很多跨文化的误解案例中，事件之所以能最终圆满解决，归根到底就是中非方面有效、即时的沟通的结果。在企业内部，在中方管理团队与当地管理团队之间的沟通与交流应保持常态化，尤其是针对容易引起误会的事项，更应增加沟通的频率。

常态的进行制度建设

随着农场经营规模的扩大，农场的管理模式也需日益完善，相关规章制度的建立也需细化，每个岗位应该有一套与之衔接的规章制度。中方管理团队应该多层面地向当地相关部门或律师了解或咨询相关的法律法规，尤其是涉及劳资管理方面的政策与法规，以此完善与丰富自己企业内部的管理方式。健全公司内部管理制度，用制度管事、制度管人、制度管物、制度管财，在公司制度面前，人人平等。此外，公司应倡导"忠诚、勤奋、细致、制度、合作、尊重"的企业文化，规范公司中国员工和坦桑尼亚员工的行为；让员工牢记"公司是所有员工生存与发展的平台"的理念，员工对公司的财产要爱惜，对公司的规则要遵守，对任何欺诈行为给予强烈谴责；培养员工勤奋工作才能改变现状的认知；让员工认真对待每一个岗位、每一道工序，否则会给公司和所有人带来灾难的认知；公司也应将"众志成城，团结才有力量"的中华文化理念融入企业经营管理之中，在分工的同时强调合作，既发挥员工的专长又形成团队的战斗力。

剑麻农场特别强调中坦人员之间的彼此尊重；充分发挥当地管理层的协调作用和工会的缓冲作用；组建业余足球队，恢复职工俱乐部，丰富职工的业余生活，培植公司团队精神；与此同时，与当地社区友好相处，力所能及地回报当地社会，逐步建立一种和谐的社区关系；积极与坦桑尼亚相关政府部门沟通，营造有利于公司经营与发展的氛围。对于外界的不实指责，应该欢迎本地媒体的采访。2014 年 3 月 21 至 23 日，坦桑尼亚 MWANANCHI 报社两名记者来公司采访，并在 4 月 17 日出版的报纸上的 20~21 版通栏刊登报道，对农场依法纳税、为员工缴纳社保、支持妇女平等就业、为残疾人提供就业机会、职工医院造福当地人民、与周边社区和谐相处等给予赞许，在坦桑尼亚当地获得较大反响。

总之,在非洲的中国企业和公民要牢记,自己每时每刻都在展示中国的形象。每个人都要自觉遵守当地法律法规和风俗习惯,每家企业都要加强自律、自觉承担社会责任,大家都要自觉践行习近平主席提出的正确义利观,彻底摒弃"一切向钱看""捞一把就走"等短视行为。剑麻农场不仅在依法经营、照章纳税、提供就业机会、丰富职工文化生活、解决残疾人就业等方面付出努力,还在当地人民健康与减贫方面创造性开展工作。公司兴办职工医院,高薪聘请具备坦桑尼亚卫生部相关资质的医生2名、助产士2名、化验师2名、护士4名,为公司员工及家属、公司所在地居民近万人提供了医疗救助与服务。医院设有诊疗室、妇幼保健室、检查室、注射室、化验室、药品房等,化验室可以从事疟原虫、伤寒、血糖、血压等方面的检测。这样的配备几乎可以解决当地社会所有常见疾病问题。对剑麻农场这种劳动密集型小企业而言,负担远远超出其承受能力。但考虑能服务当地民众,服务国家政治外交,公司还是有决心坚持办下去。

另外,因为剑麻农场长期致力于坦桑尼亚社会的减贫工作,2012年中国国务院扶贫办主任与莫罗戈罗省省长共同为"中坦村级减贫学习中心"揭幕。该中心落成以来,开展了大量的减贫项目,影响越来越大,对于当地社会的贡献明显。非洲研究机构"非洲晴雨表"(Afrobarometer)发布题为"坦桑尼亚民众对中国的看法"的问卷调查,结果显示自2012年以来坦桑尼亚民众对中国的好感度不断提升。

结论: 作为中资企业一线经营者的反思

中共中央总书记习近平在一份调研材料上批示:推动农业"走出去",既有利维护粮食安全,又能服务于国家外交战略全局。要组织力量,认真研究农业"走出去"面临的机遇、存在的问题和相应的对策措施,积极稳妥地推进这项工作。与任何事物一样,机遇与挑战在不断变化,这就要求企业经营者紧跟时代的步伐,关注经营环境,可持续地经营。

目前很多国内管理层已经意识到在非洲一线经营的中方人员也存在着很多自身需要反省和提高的地方,首先就是法律风险。"当前,中央企业'走出去'过程中面临的投资环境日趋复杂,法律风险大幅增加。""中央企业一定要高度警惕'走出去'过程中国际投资环境发生的最新变化，决不能对所在国和地区法律政策的规制掉以轻心，决不能因为短期投资收益而忽视长期潜在的法律风险。""企业在对外投资时，不仅要关注硬环境，更要关注软环境。要弄清吃透当地的法律规定、政策要求、交易习惯和文化传统。""企业境外投资一旦发生法律风险，其处理难度往往大于国内。"① 由于法律意识淡薄、语言沟通问题、短期行为、"潜规则"处事等，在非洲经营的中方人员已经出现很多违法行为。这造成的损失与影响是巨大的。② 一个实例就是在阿曼注册的中国台湾籍渔船"TAWARIQ 1 号"在坦桑尼亚专属经济区被东南非洲国家联合缉私舰拦截，涉嫌无证非法捕捞、将剔除的鱼杂抛入海洋污染环境而被起诉，而中国大陆籍人士赵汗青以该船船务代理身份，和台胞一同涉案、被捕并被提起诉讼。③

另外，中方以"我"为主的文化观造成的负面影响。很多中方经营人员往往一厢情愿把国内政治文化下形成的做事方式和逻辑搬到非洲来。坦桑尼亚政治存在着复杂的政府与议会的关系、执政党与反对党的关系、预算收支的权限等，坦桑尼亚政府发挥作用的方式与中国政府大相径庭。中方经营管理团队的人员因为成长经历、文化程度、所处社会地位等因素，很难深入认知和理解非洲社会，例如，有的中方管理人员坚持认为给工人缴纳社保只会增加企业的负担；再如中方管理人员对当地员工的称谓，有时会出现歧视性语言；另外，中方管理人员往往对当地员工的信仰不尊重，还不时质疑。

国内公司管理制度的局限

中国国有企业对境外物资采购的基本程序是：境外企业仓储部门或物资使用部门提出采购计划，境外企业负责人批准后报境内投资者总经理办公会议审议；境内投资者物资采购部门发出订购单，物资到货后，经境内

---

① 黄淑和：《为转变经济发展方式提供坚强法律支撑努力推动中央企业法制工作再上新台阶：在中央企业法制工作座谈会上的讲话》，国务院国有资产监督管理委员会网站，2010年11月26日。

② Issa Yussuf, "Chinese firm blasted for shoddy work", Dar es Salaam：*DAILY NEWS*, August 6th, 2013.

③ 《矢志不渝五载营救，重刑"犯人"终获自由：曾在坦桑尼亚被判重刑的中国公民近日获免于起诉》，中华人民共和国驻坦桑尼亚联合共和国大使馆网站，2014年8月30日。

投资者质检部门检验合格后才可根据需要向境外企业发送。这种程序貌似严谨，实际上往往令企业无法落实，特别是日常使用的柴油等物资的价格天天在变。更严重的问题是，这样僵化的管理制度，令一线经营者难以应对瞬息万变的市场，审批流程的漫长，常常使得必需经费和物资等到位的时间太久。

中坦农业有实质的交流和互动尚付阙如

坦桑尼亚政府比过去更加重视农业。由坦桑尼亚农业部、投资中心、南方农业走廊项目中心共同主办，坦桑尼亚 NMB 银行协办的"坦桑尼亚农业投资推介会"于 2012 年 11 月 27～28 日在达累斯萨拉姆召开。来自美国、英国、日本、韩国、泰国、赞比亚、伊朗、印度、南非、毛里求斯、澳大利亚等 80 多个国家和国际组织的投资机构、农业企业、非政府组织代表共约 400 人到会。坦桑尼亚总理平达出席会议并致词，强调这是继 2012 年 9 月 6 日召开的主题为"加快坦桑尼亚农业发展"会议的重要后续行动。坦桑尼亚农业部部长、畜牧水产部部长、土地事务部部长、交通部部长、能源与矿产部部长、水利部部长出席会议并就相关政策做了阐述。据会议主办方介绍，这种高规格、大规模的农业投资推介会在坦桑尼亚属首次，表明坦桑尼亚政府在推进农业优先政策方面的决心与行动路径。

在这种情况下，中国作为新兴大国，不仅可以并且应该在坦桑尼亚农业的发展中扮演恰当的角色，然而，坦桑尼亚政府极力推崇的"南方农业走廊"计划，得到了联合国粮食及农业组织、联合国开发计划署、美国国际开发署、孟山都公司、挪威基金等若干国际机构和公司的积极响应，却鲜有中国的声音，这不能不让坦桑尼亚怀疑中国是否真诚地愿意按照坦桑尼亚人的愿望发展自己的农业并提供力所能及、恰到好处的计划。[①]

中方管理者的政策失误

战略布局上，一些中方经理人好大喜功，出现了追求大规模占地的行为。在中国企业"走进非洲"的过程中，也出现了以大举占有土地为出发

---

① Abdulwakil Saiboko, "Japan fertilizer aid to up food production", Dar es Salaam: *DAILY NEWS*, Oct. 2nd, 2013.

点和首要目标的思潮。^① 对坦桑尼亚而言，这种行为实在并非明智之举。

首先，按照坦桑尼亚的土地法规，即便取得了土地证，若土地3年闲置则政府可收回。其次，大举占有土地，即便资金到位，开发的劳动力从何而来？如何严格遵照《劳动法》解决对劳工权益的保护问题？再次，如上所述，有限的基础设施条件，如水利、道路、电力、仓储等都是目前大规模农业开发的制约，有地何用？最后，未曾建立完善的社会化服务体系，农业开发之后续保障能力极弱，如油料全部依赖进口，一旦供应链条断裂，公司将如何运转？

反过来看，国际上的四大粮商都没有在中国"买地"，但他们几乎把中国的食用油市场"一网打尽"了，他们靠的是规模经营和品牌战略。这种现代企业运作方式才是值得中国认真分析和借鉴的。

---

① 中国—发展援助委员会研究小组：《经济转型与减贫：中国的经验和对非洲发展的启示综述报告》，中国财政经济出版社，2012，第46页。

228

C
H
I
N
A

Recent Development of African Agriculture & Its Endogenous Dynamics

A
F
R
I
C
A

Agricultural Development and International Policies: African Alternatives for the Twenty-first Century

Carol B. Thompson

Most often the continent of Africa is depicted as a continent of hunger. In contrast, this paper analyses ways in which Africans are providing the future of food for the twenty-first century. In addition, they are working to change international agricultural policies that favor large scale farming linked in a global food chain by a few corporations.

The need for alternatives to industrial agriculture is well documented. Only a brief summary here will remind us of the endemic problems. Industrial agriculture remains fossil fuel addicted, not only for petroleum for machinery, but for inputs to fertiliser and pesticides. What is grown is a monoculture within a monoculture or a single variety of a single crop. Smallholder farmers around the world have domesticated over 5000 plants, but the global food chain of industrial agriculture uses only three per cent. [1]Often depicted as a sign of wealth and development, these thousands of hectares covered with one crop instead representgenetic vulnerability, because vast tracts of the very same plant attract pests and provide a banquet for them to flourish. The fields also represent soil degradation, with chemical fertiliser applied every season.

The history of industrial agriculture documents consolidation of land ownership,

---

[1]　ETC Group, "Who Will Feed Us? Questions for Food/Climate Negotiators in Rome and Copenhagen", *Communique*, Issue 102, November 2009, p. 8.

removing smallholder farmers as they fall into debt, or in many cases, removing them by force. Planning for economies of scale in the use of inputs (irrigated water, use of machinery, spraying of pesticides) validates the land consolidation. In the name of efficiency and cost-savings, industrial agriculture "manufactures" nature, by leveling all fields, diverting whole river systems to change watersheds, spraying chemically derived pesticides and fertilizers, and driving expensive harvesting machines that not only cut the crop at the same exact spot on the stalk, but bundle it. The extensive fields of industrial agriculture are as programmed and controlled as a factory floor.

The so-called global market for industrial agricultural inputs and for processed food also present problems to farmers. As seen below (table 1), the degree of concentration is very high across several food related sectors. When an industry is concentrated to this extent, with just four sellers controlling almost 60 percent of global sales, a "market" no longer exists: decisions about research, production, and prices are made by collaboration among the four, only remotely related to the interaction of supply and demand. The big four can set prices for the farmers for their inputs and for the consumers for the outputs. The major business goal is to create more customers for the products they produce. The rationale of this business model, therefore, treats farmers as consumers of agricultural inputs. The farmer is not seen as a seed breeder, for example, but as a buyer of seeds. Seeds coming from the corporations are "improved" and will increase yields. Yet it has been shown that field trials by farmers are a very necessary step in breeding new varieties:

> The lessons of the field trial were fascinating. We found innovations that geneactivity in a field is extraordinarily variable, and our preconceived laboratory based notions of how genes worked would turn out to be very inadequate whendealing with field populations. *Our technology, though cutting-edge, was not up to the questions that real-world agriculture presents* (emphasis added). ①

---

① Richard Jefferson, "Science as Social Enterprise – the Cambia BiOS Initiative", *Innovations: Technology, Governance and Globalization* 1, no. 4 (2007), pp. 17 – 18.

Table 1   global market concentration

global	market share (%)	by
seed market	58	monsanto-usa dupont/pioneer-usa syngenta-switzerland groupelimagrain-france
agrochemical market	57	syngenta-switzerland bayer-germany basf-germany monsanto-usa
food processing	58	nestlé-switzerland pepsi-usa kraft-usa abInbev-belgium
food retailers	56	wal-mart-usa carrefour-france schwarz group-germany tesco-uk

Source: compiled from ETCGroup, *Who will control the GreenEconomy?* December 2011, pp. 22, 25, 37, 39.

Although farmers' seeds are cultivated, and the farmers themselves conduct extensive experimentation in the field through cross-breeding, trying different soil types, and testing water tolerance-all very necessary steps for final acceptance of seed performance-these farmers are not considered breeders by the industry. The latest expression of this derogation of "farmers' seeds" is the UPOV91 (International Union for the Protection of New Varieties of Plants) seed law the commercial sector is trying to impose via the World Intellectual Property Organisation (WIPO). It recognizes laboratory seed breeders whose new varieties are distinct, stable, and uniform (DUS), while denying farmers' rights to experiment with all seeds for new cultivars.[1]

---

[1] UPOV (International Union for the Protection of New Varieties of Plants), *International Convention for the Protection of New Varieties of Plants of December* 2, 1961, as Revised at Geneva on November 10, 1972, on October 23, 1978, and on March 19, 1991, Geneva, Switzerland. UPOV *Explanatory Notes on the Definition of Breeder under the Act of the UPOV Convention*, Geneva, Switzerland, 2011, http://www.upov.int/edocs/expndocs/en/upov_exn_brd_1.pdf, accessed 19 September 2014.

Farmers who change, transform, and share a vital productive input-the seed-are not "good customers" of commercial seed companies. For example, when a new strain of sorghum is placed on the African market as "improved", less than ten percent of what is made available is purchased. [1] About 80 percent of the seeds in Southern Africa are saved or shared seeds. The global corporations view those who save seeds as a large "untapped" market, if only the farmers would purchase commercial seeds from the cartel (Pioneer, Monsanto, Syngenta), instead of sharing their own farmer-bred seeds. Global corporate seed sellers want to offer one variety for a very wide market, while seed communities expect to propagate and share many varieties among a few. The goals could not be more different: one variety for large-scale farmers around the globe, versus many varieties for a few local farmers (biodiverse seeds for widely varying ecological zones). Farmers in Southern Africa continue to breed and propagate their diverse seeds, refusing to be reduced to a passive consumer of whatever the corporations decide is the next "fashionable" seed of one variety.

Agroecology

In contrast, the farming approach that leads into the twenty-first century is agroecology. A complex system that can only be summarised here, agroecology refers to farming methods that first "feed the soil", with crops that replenish nutrients (for example, nitrogen). The farmer intercrops various grains and vegetables to maximise water efficiency, to deter pests, and to provide use of shade or wind breaks. For example, when sorghum and groundnuts are intercropped on one hectare, they produce more ("over-yielding") than if half a hectare were planted in sorghum, and the other half groundnuts. [2] Agroecology works with nature, valuing biodiversity as a top production goal. To achieve it, the farmer notices,

---

[1] Alliance for a Green Revolution for Africa (AGRA), *Africa Agriculture Status Report-Focus on Staple Crops*, Nairobi: AGRA, 2013, p.63.
[2] Miguel Altieri, "Agroecology, Small Farms, and Food Sovereignty", *Monthly Review* 61, no. 3, 2009, p.5.

honours and uses indigenous knowledge about husbandry, pollinator and plant interactions, choice of seeds, and water runoff.

This brief paper focuses on the organisation and activities of Southern African seed production communities who are engaged in agroecology as a farming system. The analysis reflects more than 20 years of their experience in selecting and propagating seed, at the quality and quantity necessary to supply local small commercial seed companies. The findings are based in their work to create and sustain farmers' networks (for three decades in Zimbabwe, for various other periods in Malawi, Mozambique, Tanzania, Zambia), [1] to overcome challenges and to take opportunities to expand. It is not the media cliché of "Africa Rising", with pictures of soaring skyscrapers that enrich the very few, often outsiders; rather, it is a picture of "Africans Grounded", in the soil, and in their indigenous knowledge and long experience, as they cultivate biodiversity and organise to conserve seeds and exercise farmers' rights.

Community-based Seed Production

Community-based seed production begins by encouraging the participation of all, in participatory plant breeding (PPB), to mobilise the best ideas, to scientifically choose the best seeds. Discussions are long and lead to further experimenta-

---

[1] African smallholder farmers' advocacy organizations that hold regular (several times a year) workshops and information-sharing conferences are too numerous to list. The ones here are selected because each has a record of over 15 years of working in farmers' communities. Some are country specific, some regional, and other span the continent. Participatory Ecological Land Use Management (PELUM, http://www.pelumrd.org/index.html, a network of 230 member organizations); Regional Agricultural and Environmental Initiatives Network (RAEIN-Africa, www.raein-africa.org, based in Southern Africa); Réseau des Organizations Paysannes et de Producteurs d'Afrique de l'Quest (ROPPA, http://www.roppa.info/? lang = en); Eastern and Southern Africa Farmers' Forum (ESAFF, http://www.esaff.org, with members in twelve countries); African Biodiversity Network (ABN, http://www.africanbiodiversity.org/content/home, a network of 36 member organizations); Tanzania Alliance for Biodiversity (TABIO, http://envaya.org/tabio is an example of a national network of fifteen organizations). Community Technology Development Trust (CTDT, www.ctdt.co.zw) is an example of an organization with three country offices in one region, Southern Africa.

tion in the fields, with seeds distributed to specific locales that differ in soil moisture or nutrients or sunlight. The organisation and participation are as important as the final selections and seed allocations, for shared knowledge multiplies exponentially, just as one plant can propagate many seeds (for example, one amaranth plant can produce as many as 50000 seeds). Diverse perspectives enrich the knowledge, leading to more sharing. As the participatory plant breeding advances, sometimes the community chooses two or three in the group to specialise in propagating larger amounts of seed, often on land that is recognized as communal. These propagators are the best growers and enrich the whole community.

The community-based seed production does begin in the fields, with *in situ* conservation of seeds, by planting it. Unlike many commodities, such as minerals, seeds are not depleted when used, but multiply to be shared among even more people. The participatory plant breeders also choose which seeds to conserve *ex situ* (outside the fields), kept at the appropriate temperature in jars or tins in a small building designated as the community seed bank. Dried leaves, chosen by indigenous knowledge from local trees and herbs, are added to the seed to deter pests while they are in storage. A farmer who has lost a crop or wants to experiment with a new one can request seed and the only requirement is to replace it after the harvest. The seeds are freely exchanged, encouraging sharing of knowledge. The farmer who borrowed the seed may breed a new variety or may find a habitat that is more conducive to a flourishing crop. [1]

These communities have the capacity to propagate sufficient quantity and quality of seeds to sell to small seed companies (for example, AgriSeeds). The seeds are certified high quality and sold in the local and regional markets. This local system of commercial seed sales are successful because they provide varieties desired by the local farmers: diverse seeds in small quantities. In contrast, as discussed above, the large global seed corporations want to provide very few varieties of seeds in large quantities, following the logic of economies of scale. But this

---

[1] Author observations based on multiple fields trips in several Southern African countries, from 2000 – 2015.

approach does not provide seed biodiversity necessary to adapt to micro-climates during climate change. It is the farmers' informal seed systems that sustain the biodiversity for the future of food, and the farmers' networks resist outside control of this vital input to their production. The global corporations and their allies (US Department of Agriculture, Gates Foundation, World Economic Forum, G8, the World Bank) reject the farmers' proposed alternatives, for they expose the weakness and frailty of industrial agriculture: marketing a few varieties of very few crops (for example, one or two varieties of soya) renders the food source vulnerable to natural disasters of flood or drought and to pests or diseases. The farmers' seed communities are not yet at the table at international forums about "agricultural cooperation" or "agricultural development", but they are already changing the discourses and continue to work to change international agricultural policies.

Transforming International Agricultural Policies I: Changing Concepts

The most confusing concept is the loosely used term "smallholder", for it is used to refer to a farmer with 50 to 150 hectares, as well as to one cultivating only one hectare. The Alliance for a Green Revolution for Africa and its allies[1] use "smallholder" to refer to small commercial farmers who either lease or own enough land, tools, water, and inputs to quickly link the purchase of seeds and fertilizers to their selling of crops to the global market. Certainly, small commercial farmers in Southern Africa could use subsidies, especially transport links, but they will export mainly cash crops. The large industrial agriculturalist are not

---

[1] Rajiv Shah held various leadership roles at the Gates Foundationprior to becoming director of US-AID, and US Secretary of Agriculture Thomas Vilsack isa strong advocate of the Gates Foundation. Across Africa, the US's Millennium Challenge Corporation finances AGRA's approach to food production. The World Bank isjointly funding AGRA projects. For Africa directly, a NEPAD initiative, the ComprehensiveAfrica Agriculture Development Program (CAADP), receives major Gates Foundationfunding to direct "strategic investments in agriculture".

interested in the smallholder who is cultivating one to five hectares as she offers no economy of scale; her crops are "too diverse"; she cannot always afford the fertiliser at the time it may be needed. They call her a "subsistence" farmer, when in fact, she is feeding not only an extended family but many others in the local area.

The United Nations Environment Programme (UNEP) affirms that smallholders ("subsistence") farmers are feeding over 80 percent of the world's population. [1] The seed communities in Southern Africa are "smallholders" and are proud of the term "peasants". These farmers realise that the global corporations would like to remove them from their lands, with the goal of consolidating land to create more small commercial farmers who will buy corporate seeds and inputs under harsh contracts. Those working in international agricultural policies need to recognise the confusion in concepts, following the lead of the seed communities to differentiate small scale commercial farmers from smallholder farmers.

Another major concept that the Southern African seed communities are changing is the important term, "value". They are refusing the idea that value is only exchange value, one determined by the global corporations that set input and output prices. Exchange value usually refers to "willing seller, willing buyer" in a free market. But the global market for agricultural inputs and for sales of commodities does not reflect that textbook theory. Prices are often determined by speculators who only buy seed, maize, or cotton for a few seconds and then sell it immediately, with the flick of a computer key. The "exchange value" (price) reflects speculative trading, not a functioning food market, and certainly not prices determined by supply and demand.

Value for seed communities varies with time and location of the seed-of the crop. A genetic strain may be considered "valueless" and thus of no interest. But participatory seed breeders, ones sharing knowledge with each other, may discover genetic traits of importance against a new pest, or traits more tolerant of

① United Nations Environment Programme (UNEP), *Towards a Green Economy-Pathways to sustainable Development and Poverty Eradication*, DTI/1353. GE, 2011.

rain variability in this time of climate change. "Time" changes the value of genetic resources, "discovery" changes the value of genetic resources. As a new use is discovered, the value increases, whether the new strain enters the global market or stays in the community. "Location" also profoundly affects value as-seeds are site specific. They do not provide "economies of scale" unless they are manufactured for the controlled environment ("improved seeds") of the exact a-mount of water, fertiliser, and pesticide. To perform according to what is advertised, these "improved seeds" must have those inputs (fertiliser, water) at the exact time and in exact amounts. Yet site specificity of seeds breeds diversity, the key to the future of food. With hundreds of different strains of sorghums, of millets, or of rice, of wheat, food production can adapt to climate change. Smallholders are demonstrating that "value" depends on timing, discovery, and location-not on the flick of a keyboard among financiers in London or New York.

Transforming International Agricultural Policies II: Changing Measures

Smallholder farmers never agreed that yield per hectare was the only indicator of "success" of a crop: they plant for yield stability, for textures, for maturation variability, for pest resistance, and for taste. The manufactured maize and soya of industrial agriculture do not need to have any taste; in fact, the major varieties of maize grains in the US have no flavour, because it is added chemically to the maize meal or cereal during processing. (Kellogg's corn flakes taste like corn only because chemical flavouring is added while making the cereal.) Growing to attain yield per hectare above any other seed quality erases the importance of other seed characteristics.

The Southern African seed communities are working with a new measure to challenge the exclusivity of "yield per hectare" as a measure, by introducing "nutrition density" per hectare. When one plants a hectare with 20 to 25 different crops in one season, versus the industrial agriculture field of one variety of one crop, it is quickly clear who is the "successful" farmer. Nutrition density per hectare values biodiversity of production, with the crops using different water availability and plant maturation, deterring pests, attracting pollinators, and providing food even if one or two crops fail because of a sudden hail storm or other acts of nature. Biodiverse production on one hectare reduces vulnerability of all kinds: genetic, weather, pests, and even local market prices, if a crop matures earlier or later than most. A project in process (2014 – 2016) asks the smallholder farmersin Africa, South America, and Asiato specify the measure. It will be not specified by an academic sitting in an office, but by farmers on the ground, who will choose the indicators that will comprise the measure of nutrition density per hectare. The measure comes from the ground up from their practices. Smallholder farmers are asking that those who engage in formulating international agricultural policies to notice and use "nutrition density per hectare" as a measure of food production success.

The project has a second component that will specify the nutrition of the food eaten by the smallholder farmers. It is anticipated that their foods are more biodiverse than most urban dwellers, who eat processed and fast foods containing much sugar, fat and salt. The future of food is biodiverse food consumption, for better health, for more appropriate use of nature. Working with nature, many food products, differing by locales, will better feed future populations. Those of us living in a desert do not need tropical fruits as a daily fare-the many species of cactus provide much nutrition.

A second measure that will transform international agricultural policies expands the meaning of investment beyond the narrow measure of cash flow or finance capital. Smallholder farmers are always "cash deficit" and therefore are denigrated because they are "poor. " Cash, however, is the narrowest measure of investment, and smallholders cleverly employ other forms of capital to improve production methods and crop outcomes. Natural capital is more precious to food production than any cash and smallholders, as described briefly above, excel in mobilizing natural capital, from attracting pollinators, to slowing water flow, to adding organic fertiliser to the soil. They enhance natural capital investment by intercropping but also, mixing animal husbandry with planting, with bee keeping, or with fisheries. While industrial agriculture tries to direct and control nature, often treating it as harmful, the smallholders plan and employ natural interactions to enhance production. Social capital, a third measure of investment added to cash and natural capital, refers to activities like the participatory plant breeding-human interactions that result in innovations or organising that best mobilise the resources available. Farming is a collective activity, enhanced by participation and sharing. Human capital as a fourth measure acknowledges human labour in farming, and agroecology is more labour intensive than industrial farming. Often the labour-be it family or collective-is an efficient replacement for cash because those in the fields know their jobs and teach each other. Finally, intellectual capital is a fifth measure of investment and again, the community is rich or wealthy in the intellectual capital of their indigenous knowledge, about seeds, crops, weather patterns (often more accurate than the official meteorological forecasts), eradication of pests, and much more.

Every farmer, large scale and smallholder, always needs more cash, but to use money as the only measure of investment erases all the other forms of capital: natural, social, human, and intellectual. The smallholders are changing the measurement and correctly saying, they are the source of over 85 percent of food production investment, a figure now recognised by FAO. Investment directs the future of food and international agricultural policies need to count all its five capital measures (finance, natural, social, human and intellectual), not just one. If all five measures are tabulated, then the diversified wealth (similar to a diversified portfolio of securities) of the smallholder farmers easily becomes evident. They are only "cash poor" -in all the other ways, they are rich, very rich.

Transforming International Agricultural Policies III: Activating International Treaties

While working the ground, smallholder farmers know well from experience how high-level international policies can seriously impact their work. Not only in

Southern Africa, but across the globe, the farmers' networks are key to advancing the International Treaty for Plant Genetic Resources for Food and Agriculture (IT) and the Nagoya Protocol that has been in force sinceOctober 2014. ① Both elaborate the principle of access and benefit sharing (ABS) that facilitates obtaining a genetic resource, while requiring acknowledgement and benefit sharing back from any profits made by cross-breeding the genes accessed.

Corporations continue to access plant genetic materials without benefit sharing back to those who developed the earlier cultivars. Although the IT has a standard material transfer agreement (MTA), a contract binding the corporation or person accessing genetic materials to sharing back the benefits gained, implementation of this MTA is not working. After almost a decade of the MTA, it is not enforced for lack of contributions to the operational fund. More than one government, therefore, began refusing access to genetic materials in their national gene banks, withdrawing them, not formally from the treaty (IT), but simply not making the materials available. Changing the "access" side of the treaty until "benefit sharing" is also honoured, works toward fulfiling the treaties, transforming them from principles on paper to practices recognizing and compensating those who originally bred the parent genetic materials. The treaties acknowledge smallholder contributions, over centuries, to the genetic wealth of biodiverse foods, and the farmer networks are demanding new "best practices" of benefit sharing as reciprocity for the access, turning the acronym from ABS, access with benefit sharing, into BSA: benefit sharing contracts (enforced MTAs) before access.

Although focusing on sharing of benefits between states, the Nagoya Protocol also enshrines prior informed consent (PIC), a requirement to consult with,

① Food and Agriculture Organization of the United Nations (FAO), *International Treaty on PlantGenetic Resources for Food and Agriculture*, Rome: FAO, 2004, http: //www. planttreaty. org/content/texts-treaty-official-versions, accessed 5 August 2014; Convention on Biological Diversity, *Nagoya Protocol on Access to Genetic Resources and the Fair and Equitable Sharing of Benefits Arising from their Utilization to the Convention on Biological Diversity*, Montreal: Secretariat on the Convention of Biological Diversity, 2011, http: //www. cbd. int/abs/doc/protocol/nagoya-protocol-en. pdf, accessed 2 February 2015.

and receive consent from, local communities before removing any genetic resources. The protocol legitimizes community participation, beyond national governments, in decisions about the use of indigenous knowledge and about local plant or animal genetic materials. It provides the means for communities, who bred the cultivar in the first place, to retain power over its biodiverse resources. In 2009, Zimbabwe passed a national law "Statutory Instrument 61" which both regulates access to genetic resources and requires prior informed consent from local communities before any removal of genetic resources. It is the first statue of its kind on the continent. With this experience, southern Africans were key in writing the 2011 Nagoya Protocol. Workshops continue to train others how Southern African governments can adapt this Zimbabwean model law. [1]

Conclusion

Smallholder farmers in Southern Africa are working to change international policies toward food production. Given that their production currently provides about 80 per cent of food consumed and their seeds bred from indigenous knowledge provide new varieties ready to adapt to climate change, they are highly qualified to be full participants in the discourses to transform these policies. However, current processes for formulating international agricultural policies generally ignore these Southern African farmers, but not their genetic resources and knowledge, which are often taken without recognition to the farmer breeder. Such access without benefit sharing violates international laws.

The measureable achievements of smallholder farmers emphasise the urgency in bringing them to the conference tables and workshops to fully participate in devising new international policies. As discussed, Southern African smallholder farmers bring new concepts and new measures, which could be widely adopted for understanding biodiverse food production. The farmer networks also engage in pro-

---

① Chishakwe, Nyasha and Regis Mafuratidze, *Access to Genetic Resources, and the Sharing of Benefits Arising from their Use (ABS)*, *Trainers' Manual*, Harare: Southern Africa Biodiversity Policy Initiative, 2010.

moting two international treaties that sustain and protect their genetic treasures and their indigenous knowledge. Full enforcement of these treaties would give these farmers their rightful recognition as innovative breeders, who continue to share their genetic wealth by sharing their seeds. In many ways, therefore, Southern African smallholder farmers are leaders in sustaining biodiverse food production for the twenty-first century.

Urban Agriculture in Africa: A Missed Opportunity?

Diana Lee – Smith

Policy v. Reality: The urban food dimension

Most analysis of international agriculture policy ignores the urban dimension, thus missing the opportunity to fully articulate policy. Urban populations create enormous demand for food but there are other aspects of the urban question that need to be taken on board for agriculture to effectively address food and nutrition security. This chapter sets them out systematically, and in doing so reveals the importance of the Committee on Food Security contributions to the debate, especially because these incorporate the perspectives of farmers through a global process involving civil society voices.

Urban food – supply, consumption and even production – has been under – conceptualised in the development of international agriculture policy. This chapter tries to fill the gap and help policy catch up with the realties on the ground in Africa. There has already been some criticism from civil society organizations worldwide, concerning both the New Alliance for Food Security and Nutrition and the model proposed by the Africa Progress Panel (APP) . These general criticisms are important but need to be elaborated in the urban context.

New Alliance was proposed in 2012 to end hunger using giant agribusiness, while APP, chaired by Kofi Annan, attempts to do the same by redressing the growing inequality between rich and poor in Africa. The essence of the criticisms is thatboth models, in their strategies and subsequent investments, do not adequately address issues of nutrition security as opposed to just food production. An examination of the factors that affect nutrition security directs attention to the small family farm sector, which predominates in African agriculture. Many of the concerns raised were subsequently adopted in the United Nations Second International Conference on Nutrition in October 2014. ①However, the urban dimension remains to be addressed in international agriculture policy.

Here we go into that aspect which frequently escapes attention, namely African urban agriculture (UA) . As the data will suggest, UA contributes to the nutrition security of urban Africans and this can be crucial to the vulnerable urban poor. Again, the focus is on small household farming enterprises which are found in urban and peri – urban areas, but a wider focus is also required to encompass how African urban citizens access food, and whether it is easily available and affordable.

Availability and affordability are well – defined aspects of food and nutrition security that are still often overlooked in the over simplifications entailed in international agriculture policy – making at the level of the region. Further, the urban is usually a category sharply distinguished from the rural and identified with consumers and not agricultural production. The reality is a continuum from rural to peri – urban to urban in which African households pursue a mix of livelihood strategies that often include food production.

The chapter describes the realities of UA as well as urban hunger in Africa. The issue of sustainable development is covered because it has a particular relation to UA that needs to be conceptualised fully even as it needs to be addressed in poli-

---

① Food and Agriculture Organization of the United Nations (FAO) and the World Health Organization (WHO), "Conference Outcome Document: Rome Declaration on Nutrition", in FAO and WHO, *SecondInternational Conference on Nutrition*, Rome, 19 – 21 November 2014; Public interest civil society organizations, "Public interest civil society organizations statement to the ICN 2 Open Ended Working Group", in FAO and WHO, *SecondInternational Conference on Nutrition*, Geneva, 22 September 2014; Sandrine Dury and Anne Bichard, "Identifier et limiter les risques des interventions agricoles sur la nutrition", Working – Paper – CIRAD, UMR MOISA, France, 2014.

cy and practice. Briefly, there is a nutrient surplus available in urban areas, and this surplus acts as a resource for agriculture. The chapter ends by examining ongoing shifts in African urban food policy, presenting a case of one city, Nairobi. It is concluded that these policy shifts ought to impact on international cooperation on agriculture as well.

The Scope and Impact of UA in Africa

About 40 per cent of urban households in Sub – Saharan Africa, around 200 million persons, are expected to depend partly on UA by 2020. [1]Data are patchy and hard to interpret but about 22 per cent of poor urban households were estimated to be farming in 11 cities in Southern Africa in 2008 and 20 – 50 percent of households in 21 West African cities in 2006. [2]Figures vary a lot between cities and this is thought to depend partly on the size of the urban area but also on policy. For example, over 90 per cent of households were farming in two towns in Tanzania with 200 – 300 thousand population in 2002, [3] but only 36 per cent in the capital, Dar es Salaam with an estimated population of 2.5 million in 1995. [4]Tanzania was considered to have favourable policies towards UA at both those times.

[1] Denninger Mats, Bertil Egero, and Diana Lee-Smith, "Urban Food Production; A Survival Strategy of Urban Households", in Regional Land Management Unit (RELMA) and Mazingira Institute, *Workshop series.* vol. 1. 1998, Nairobi; S. Staal and D. Lee-Smith, "Livestock and Environment in Peri-urban Ruminant Systems", presented to seminar on Livestock, Environment and Development (LEAD) /International Livestock Research Institute (ILRI), Nairobi, 2002; Food and Agriculture Organization (FAO), "Growing Greener Cities in Africa. First Status Report on Urban and Peri-urban Horticulture in Africa", FAO, Rome, 2012.

[2] Bruce Frayne, et al. , "The state of urban food insecurity in southern Africa", *Urban Food Security Series*, no. 2, Queen's University and AFSUN, Kingston and Cape Town, 2010.

[3] Dick Foeken, Malongo Mlozi, and Michael Sofer, "Urban agriculture in Tanzania: issues of sustainability", *ASC Research Report*, vol. 75/2004, ASC, Leiden, 2004.

[4] Ophelia Mascarenhas, "Kigogo and Hananasif in Dar-es-Salaam, Tanzania: gender aspects of urbanization and natural resource management", in D Lee-Smith. ed, *Women Managing Resources: African Research on Gender, Urbanization and Environment*, Mazingira Institute, Nairobi, pp. 52 – 79.

Kampala, the capital of Uganda, is the only city where two estimates have been made over time, and there UA appears to be increasing, with 30 per cent in 1991 and 49 per cent in 2003. [1]However, the difference may also mask how the surveys were done, with the later one focusing on measuring and comparing peri – urban to urban. The proportion of households farming and the area farmed are known to increase from urban to peri – urban[2]1.

Regarding hunger, over three quarters of the urban poor were found to be food insecure in a study of multiple cities in Southern Africa, while people living in urban slums have been identified as belonging to the most malnourished groups. [3]Inability to pay for food due to lack of employment is the key factor affecting malnourishment. Some poor people practise subsistence food production as a stop – gap measure.

Most people assume that it is predominantly the poor who practise urban farming, but in fact more high and middle income do so than the poor, in relation to their overall numbers in the population. [4]All income groups engage in UA, primarily for their own food supply, but also as a form of saving on expenses and also for sale. It appears that the poor are food insecure mainly due to their lack of space for food production, living in high density slums. In fact, two distinct groups of urban farmers are distinguishable, backyard farmers, who have space and security of tenure, and open space farmers, who are generally poor and lack

① D. Lee-Smith; G. Prain; O. Cofie; R. van Veenhuizen; N. Karanja, (forthcoming) "Urban and Peri-Urban Farming Systems (UPUFS): feeding cities and enhancing resilience", in *Farming Systems and Food Security in Sub-Saharan Africa: Priorities for Science and Policy under Global Change*, eds. by John Dixon, Dennis Garrity, Jean-Marc Boffa, Tim Williams and Tilahun Amede, London, Earthscan Serial, London: Routledge, 2019.

② Sonii David et al., "Changing trends in urban agriculture in Kampala", in G. Prain, N. K. Karanja and D. Lee-Smith, eds., *African Urban Harvest: Agriculture in the Cities of Cameroon, Kenya and Uganda*, Springer, New York, NY, 2010, pp. 97 – 122.

③ African Population and Health Research Center, "Urban Health in Kenya, Key Findings: The 2000 Nairobi Cross-Sectional Slum Survey", in APHRC, *Fact Sheet*, Nairobi, June 2012; Bruce Frayne et al., "The state of urban food insecurity in southern Africa".

④ Dick Foeken and Samuel Ouma Owuor, *To Subsidize my Income: Urban Farming in an East African Town*, University of Nairobi, 2006.

such security. ①

Conversely, UA has been shown to have significant benefits to those who practise it. The benefits are in the form of wealth as well as food security and better nutrition. Even though most urban farmers produce for household use and even commercial producers consume part of their production, such households also make significant incomes. Farmers in most cities have higher than average incomes and some who use irrigation (mostly waste water) can earn up to ten times official minimum salaries. ②

A positive relationship has been established statistically between UA and household food security, as well as nutrition security. Consumption of animal – source foods by children has also been associated with better child health and nutrition levels, suggesting that keeping urban livestock increases both food and nutrition security and should be encouraged. ③However, UA contributes to household food security mostly in terms of fresh produce and not much in calories, as staples which support the daily calorie intake are purchased and derive mostly from rural cereal or tuber production. ④

Dairy cattle and poultry are common urban livestock in East Africa. There are thriving small – scale dairy industries in Kampala and Nairobi, where children and adults get much of their protein and micronutrient needs from milk, usually taken for breakfast in the form of tea. This pattern is not common in West Africa. For example in Yaoundé, the capital of Cameroon, although poultry and pigs are common livestock, the city's poor meet much of their protein and micronutrient needs, especially calcium, by eating groundnuts with fresh leafy vegeta-

① Lee – Smith et al. forthcoming.
② René Van Veenhuizen and George Danso, *Profitability and sustainability of urban and periurban agriculture*, Food & Agriculture Org., vol. 19, 2007.
③ Donald Cole, Diana Lee – Smith and George Nasinyama, eds., *Healthy City Harvests: Generating Evidence to Guide Policy on Urban Agriculture*, CIP/Urban Harvest and Makerere University Press, Kampala, Uganda and Lima, Peru, 2008.
④ Pay Drechsel, Sophie Graefe, and Michael Fink, *Rural – urban food, nutrient and virtual water flows in selected West African cities*, International Water Management Institute (IWMI) Research Report, No. 115, Colombo, Sri Lanka, 2007.

bles. Low – income households grow 27 per cent of the traditional vegetables they consume. Some households also earn income from selling these vegetables, while all households obtained over 20 per cent of the vegetables they ate as gifts from family and friends. UA provides a very high proportion of Dar es Salaam's needs for fresh perishables foods, 90 per cent of the city's leafy vegetables and at least 60 per cent of its milk. ①

Twenty percent of Nairobi's population grew crops in the city, worth \$8 million p. a. , in 1985. Around 30 per cent used organic inputs, mainly from waste. ②Over 200000 households were estimated to be farming in the city in 2013 and there were 55000 cattle; 35000 sheep; 47000 goats counted there in the 2009 census. Although, as in other cities, Nairobi farm households produce food to feed themselves, many also sell the surplus, especially livestock products such as milk, eggs and meat. For the last decade, the Nairobi and Environs Food Security, Agriculture and Livestock Forum (NEFSALF) has been training and supporting farmers to add value, collaborating with Government extension services③.

Sustainability: Using Waste as Nutrients

African urban areas are immense producers of nutrient surpluses in the form of solid and liquid waste materials containing nitrogen, potassium and phosphorus (NPK) . This has to be contrasted with the fact that soil fertility is the main constraint on agricultural productivity in the region. Thus UA has a comparative advantage in terms of agricultural productivity and, as long as it is

---

① Gordon Prainand Diana Lee-Smith, eds. , *African Urban Harvest: Agriculture in the Cities of Cameroon, Kenya and Uganda*, Springer, New York and International Development Research Center (IDRC), Ottawa, 2010

② Diana Lee-Smith and Pyar Ali Memon, "Urban agriculture in Kenya", in A. G. Egziabher et al. , *Cities Feeding People: An Examination of Urban Agriculture in East Africa*, International Development Research Center (IDRC), Ottawa, 1994.

③ Mazingira Institute, *Nairobi and Environs Food Security, Agriculture and Livestock Forum*, NEFSALF Bulletin, Nairobi, Issue no. 2, March 2005.

done safely, nutrient cycling has implications for sustainability through soil a-
mendment. ①

Large areas of African cities are currently used for open space waste – water irrigation and may produce three to ten crops per year. With regard to solid wastes
however, although millions of tonnes are produced annually in African urban
areas, suggesting high nutrient – cycling potential, these are currently not
much used. Nairobi for example generates an estimated 2223 tonnes of nitrogen,
2223 tonnes of phosphorus and 3700 tonnes of potassiumin its solid waste every
year, worth about $2 million, but this is not well used. ②Exporting the nutri-
ent surplus to rural farming systems is not really feasible. It would require an organised market, value addition, and probably subsidies to make it as economically viable to transport waste as it is to transport the food it comes from. ③

Nevertheless, urban farmers do use these nutrients on a small scale, and this
is especially true of the backyard farms. Where these are crop – livestock farms,
they could in fact be described as ideal ecological recycling units. Studies in East
and Central Africa suggest as much as 90 per cent of food wastes are recycled as
livestock feed within such urban backyard farms, the other 10 per cent being
used as compost. ④

There are three levels where the use of the urban nutrient surplus can be addressed: the city level, the neighbourhood level, and the household level. Each
has implications for agricultural policy. At present, although small – scale backyard crop – livestock farmers make use of cities' wastes, this is outside the

① Lee-Smith et al. , "Urban and Peri – Urban Farming Systems (UPUFS): feeding cities and enhancing resilience" .

② Mary Njenga et al. , "Recycling nutrients from organic wastes in Kenya's capital city," in
G. Prain, N. K. Karanja and D. Lee – Smith, eds. , *African Urban Harvest: Agriculture in the
Cities of Cameroon, Kenya and Uganda*, Springer, New York and International Development Re-
search Center (IDRC) , Ottawa, 2010.

③ Pay Drechsel, Olufunke Cofie, and George Danso, "Closing the rural – urban food and nutrient
loops in West Africa: A reality check", *Urban Agriculture Magazine*, vol. 23, 2010, pp. 8 –
10.

④ G. Prain, N. K. Karanja and D. Lee – Smith, eds. , *African Urban Harvest: Agriculture in the
Cities of Cameroon, Kenya and Uganda.*

framework of policy or planning either by the urban or agriculture sectors. ①

Cities and agriculture are linked in human history from the dawn of civilization, and the use of nutrient deposits in fertilizing crops has been intrinsic to this. Cities such as Mexico, Kolkata and many in China incorporated natural resource flows including wastewater agriculture in their mode of operation. ②Western cities, however, did not respond to ecological processes in the design of their infrastructure during the one hundred years after the Industrial Revolution (1850 – 1950), a time of explosive urban growth. Urban infrastructure designed then, which African cities have tended to emulate, focussed on elimination of diseases carried by micro – organisms, their removal being a public health priority. It was only in the mid – twentieth century that the environmental movement focussed attention on the need to understand ecosystem functioning in designing urban management systems. ③

Ways of linking the nutrients available in urban waste to agricultural production have regained currency in the twenty – first century. Indeed, sewage was widely used for food production around European cities earlier, until other sources of fertilizer became more economic,④ and it is returning as a practice today. Although the River Nile in Africa is almost the prototype of cities and civilization using the "gift" of nutrients for agriculture, not enough is done in this regard in the region's cities today. However, research is in progress, and cities such as Cotonourecycle significant amounts of household waste and animal excrement through urban horticulture. In 2006, the World Health Organization, in

---

① Nancy Karanja et al. , "Crop – livestock – waste interactions in Nakuru's urban agriculture", in G. Prain, N. K. Karanja and Diana Lee – Smith eds. , *African Urban Harvest: Agriculture in the Cities of Cameroon, Kenya and Uganda*, Springer, New York and International Development Research Center (IDRC), Ottawa, 2010.

② Jac Smit and Joe Nasr, "Urban agriculture for sustainable cities: using wastes and idle land and water bodies as resources," *Environment and Urbanization*, vol. 4, no. 2, October, 1992, pp. 141 – 152.

③ Donald Cole, Diana Lee-Smith and George Nasinyama eds. , *Healthy City Harvests: Generating Evidence to Guide Policy on Urban Agriculture*; Carolyn Steel, *Hungry City: How Food Shapes our Lives*, Random House, 2013.

④ Ibid.

collaboration with FAO and UNEP, published guidelines for the safe use of waste in agriculture including human waste. ①

At the level of communities, organic waste collected and mixed with manure can be used to produce enriched co – compost, keep neighbourhoods clean and grow food through community mobilisation as is done in some Nairobi slums. Planners can assist urban farmers with depots where crop farmers can collect manure while community clean – ups can provide compost.

At the household level, studies in Nakuru, Kenya, found that not only did urban farm households use nearly all their organic domestic waste as livestock fodder and that almost half the livestock manure was reused productively. But, while middle-income backyard farms achieved a very high reuse rate of 88 per cent, those in high density areas who farm in open spaces only achieved a 17 per cent reuse rate.

This is a clear – cut example of how local policies can intervene to manage the flow of nutrients by simply moving manure from livestock to crop farmer households. ②In fact this is done by some local urban authorities, including Cape Town and now Nakuru. There is an earlier model of such a policy intervention, enforced during World War II in UK. Households had to separate all food waste and take it to the end of the street to the 'pig bin' where it was collected by livestock farmers.

Shifts in African Urban Food Policy

Just as the urban dimension has not been included in agriculture policy, UA was likewise not a part of urban policies and institutions worldwide in the 20th century, even though the "garden city" concept is at the root of modern urban planning. ③But by the 1990s the impact on employment of Structural Adjustment Poli-

---

① World Health Organization (WHO) and United Nations Environemnt Programme (UNEP), "Wastewater use in agriculture", in World Health Organization (WHO), *WHO Guidelines for the safe use of wastewater, excreta and grey water*, Volume 2, Geneva, 2006.

② Nancy Karanja et al. , "Crop – livestock – waste interactions in Nakuru's urban agriculture".

③ Jac Smit, Joe Nasr, and AnnuRatta, *Urban agriculture: food, jobs and sustainable cities*, New York, The Urban Agriculture Network, Inc. , 1996.

cies (SAPs) in Africa meant UA was more visible and research publications such as those supported by the International Development Research Centre (IDRC) showed it was a significant phenomenon the region. ①

A few countries supported urban gardens, for example Tanzania with its self-sufficiency movement dating from the 1960s, but less as an official policy and more as a form of benign tolerance of peasant behaviour in cities. Civil wars frequently encouraged this kind of unofficial policy response to UA, as in Sierra Leone and Liberia at the turn of the century and earlier in Uganda and Mozambique, which encouraged 'green zones' around the capital, Maputo.

It was only in the 21st century that there were moves towards development of formal policies and institutions on UA in the region. In 2002 there was a Declaration on Feeding Cities in the Horn of Africa and then in 2003 the Harare Declaration on Urban and Peri – urban Agriculture Policy, guiding governments towards this new area of policy. Places such as Kampala, Uganda, were more inclined to take the idea up, due to the decentralisation of the administrative structure throughout the 1990s, which meant that all local authorities inherited previouslycentralized powers, and thus Kampala City Council had an Agriculture Department. ②

This led to some interesting developments in Kampala, including a system of classification of areas of urban and peri – urban agriculture, outreach of extension services to farmers in collaboration with civil society organizations, and then the development of new legislation on urban agriculture and livestock in 2006. ③However, the city was not able to sustain these institutional innovations effectively through subsequent political changes affecting local government in the capital. Also, there was no pressure from below as there was no organization of urban farmers in Kampala. Studies of effective legal and institutional frameworks

① AG. Egziabher, *Cities Feeding People: An Examination of Urban Agriculture in East Africa*, International Development Research Center (IDRC), Ottawa, 2014.
② Gordon Prain and Diana Lee – Smith, "Urban agriculture in Africa: What has been learnt?" in G. Prain, N. K. Karanja and D. Lee – Smith eds., *African Urban Harvest: Agriculture in the Cities of Cameroon, Kenya and Uganda*, Springer, New York and International Development Research Center (IDRC), Ottawa, 2010.
③ Ibid.

for UA found that institutions incorporating farmers and their associations in active debate with local government, such as those in Accra, Ghana, and Freetown, Sierra Leone, have greater impact in institution – building. ①

Nairobi is another capital city where devolution of powers from central to local government has brought changes in UA policy and administration. Before 2013, Nairobi City Council was opposed to UA, but urban agriculture became part of the city's mandate under the new constitution. The fact that the new Nairobi City County supports UA is a result that came about mostly because it took over its administration, but also in part due to political pressure from citizens, including farmers themselves. Not least has been pressure from the Nairobi and Environs Food Security, Agriculture and Livestock Forum (NEFSALF), a platform and network of urban farmers, which collaborated with the agriculture extension services of central government for a full decade before the administrative changes. ②

Citizen pressure also led to a new constitution being promulgated in Kenya in 2010, including moves towards more public participation in law – making. As a result of this more general political reform, UA began to emerge in a number of policy documents and pieces of legislation, including the Land Policy of 2009 and the Urban Areas and Cities Act of 2011. The latter requires every urban area to have a plan for UA.

Such changes are still in progress and it remains to be seen if the inclusion of UA in public policy and planning in Nairobi and other Kenyan towns and cities succeeds better than it has so far in Kampala. Beginning in 2013, Nairobi City County government has taken over all agriculture and livestock extension staff previously under the central government and has set up a Directorate of Agriculture, Livestock and Fisheries. There is a County Coordinating Unit that convenes all stakeholders, including NEFSALF, which continues its training programs. The county's agricultural priorities are institutional and capacity development, envi-

---

① Yves Cabannes, *Pro – poor Legal and Institutional Frameworks for Urban and Peri – urban Agriculture*, Rome, Food and Agriculture Organization of the United Nations, 2012; Prain et al., *African Urban Harvest: Agriculture in the Cities of Cameroon, Kenya and Uganda*.

② Mazingira Institute, *Nairobi and Environs Food Security, Agriculture and Livestock Forum*.

ronmental resilience and social inclusion, as well as value chain development.

The trends and initiatives described here are currently receiving insufficient attention from the arena of international cooperation on agriculture. The International Council of Local Environmental Initiatives (ICLEI) has had a sustained focus on UA in its policy work on creating environmentally resilient cities, and there are numerous other national, regional, and international civil society organizations actively researching, advocating, and educating the public on aspects of urban food security – including UA. Several of these involve exchanges of experiences between cities.

The global Committee on Food Security has a linked Civil Society Mechanism with a system of representation from groups in all regions of the world of the different sectors of food security (http: //www. fao. org/cfs/cfs – home/cfs – about/en/) . These include peasant farmers, artisanal fisher folk, women farmers, and others. Urban is also one of the sectors represented, through the Habitat International Coalition (HIC) which addresses food security as an aspect of housing and human settlements, and including urban food production (UA). These are the civil society groups that have been able to formally influence the global decision – making process including international declarations, as mentioned at the beginning of this chapter (http: //www. csm4cfs. org/) .

Thus both at the international and the local (city) levels, a bottom – up process coming from urban farmers has managed to influence policy on UA and urban food and nutrition security. These processes and institutions need also to be able to influence the mainstream of international cooperation on agricultural policy. These policies should be supportive of and responsive to the urban poor and their nutritional needs. UA has not been taken seriously enough by international development agencies, with exception of research support by IDRC in the 1990s and early 2000s. Almost all initiatives on UA and urban food security have come from bottom up. Likewise nutrition has not been a priority, only food production, driven by business. It is time for the models used in international agriculture policy to involve the Committee on Food Security and its International Food Security and Nutrition Civil Society Mechanism (CSM) .

Zimbabwe's Land Reform: Increasing Production and Reducing Poverty

Jeanette Manjengwa [*]

Introduction

Zimbabwe has a population of just over 13 million, and over 67 per cent live in rural areas, where poverty levels are relatively high, at over 70 per cent. [①] Farming dominates people's lives and plays a key role in the national economy. Thus it is not surprising that land has been such a contested issue in Zimbabwe. Land has attracted the interest of scholars in Zimbabwe and beyond. This chapter draws on the book *Zimbabwe Takes Back its Land*, [②] and the article *Who will make the "best" use of Africa's land? Lessons from Zimbabwe*, [③] as well as the large body of academic research on land reform in Zimbabwe. The chapter presents a picture of what is happening on the ground more than a decade after the most recent land reform, the Fast Track Land Reform and Resettlement Programme launched in 2000, and explores how land is being used to increase agri-

---

[*] Jeanette Manjengwa, Deputy Director, Institute for Environmental Studies, University of Zimbabwe.

① ZIMSTAT, *National Census Report*, ZIMSTAT, Harare, 2013a; ZIMSTAT, *Poverty Analysis Poverty Datum Lines*, Harare: ZIMSTAT, 2013b.

② Joseph Hanlon, Jeanette Manjengwa, and Teresa Smart, *Zimbabwe Takes Back its Land*, Kumarian Press, VA 2013.

③ Jeanette Manjengwa, Joseph Hanlon, and Teresa Smart, "Who will make the 'best' use of Africa's land? Lessons from Zimbabwe", *Third World Quarterly*, 35: 6, (2014), pp. 980-995.

cultural production and reduce poverty.

indigenization of the land was necessary, but not sufficient. Land is a valuable resource and an important national asset and should be used sustainably for economic growth and social equity. Putting the land issue in a broader context the chapter begins by looking at the struggles over land throughout the past 120 years. Then the chapter looks at what is actually happening on the ground regarding ownership, production, and labour on the resettled land. Finally, the chapter looks at land reform in the broader Zimbabwean and international context, and asks what needs to be done to promote an agriculture-based growth in Zimbabwe.

History of Land Struggles

In the 1890s, Cecil Rhodes captured much of what is now Zimbabwe. He recognized the agricultural potential, and gave large tracts of land to victorious European soldiers-evicting the African occupants.

White control of southern Rhodesia was cemented with the 1930 Land Apportionment Act, which explicitly defined European and native land areas. The 1930 law granted 51 per cent of the land – naturally the best land with the highest agricultural potential – to 11000 Europeans. The colonial law then allowed 30 per cent of the land-the poorer, drier, and less fertile land-to be divided among one million Africans. [1]

Prime Minister Hugginswrote in 1935 that " [t] he passing of the Land Apportionment Act, 1930, was a definite milestone in the history of Southern Rhodesia. It marks the first attempt in Southern Africa to effect a measure of segregation between the European and African peoples. " [2] This was more than a decade before formal apartheid was introduced in South Africa.

For the next 20 years, there were not enough white farmers to actually use the land constituting half of the country, and many thousands of black Zimbabweans

---

[1] Arthur Cyril Jennings, "Land Apportionment in Southern Rhodesia", *African Affairs*, (1935), pp. 308 – 311.

[2] Jennings, Land Apportionment, p. 296.

still farmed and lived on their ancestral lands. After the Second World War, this land was given to white Rhodesian war veterans and white European war veterans were encouraged to settle with a range of inducements, including two years of free training in farming. To clear land for the new farmers, in just one decade, 1945 – 1955, more than 100000 Africans were moved, often forcibly, into reserves and/or inhospitable, tsetse fly ridden unassigned areas. [1] People could not take their cattle, houses were burnt, and they lost all investments that had been made on their farms.

One of the new white farmers was Ian Smith, a veteran Spitfire pilot from the Second World War, who recalls in his memories how he evicted black farmers from his land. [2] Smith went on to rule Rhodesia, announce the Unilateral Declaration of Independence from Britain in 1965, and then fight a brutal war to keep Rhodesia under white rule. His war was unsuccessful because the children of those evicted by the white veterans in the decade after the Second World War became the core of the liberation movement in the 1970s-fighting not just for independence but also for land. Whereas neighbouring Mozambique and South Africa had liberation movements led by an urbanized elite, Zimbabwe's movement was led by people for whom land and farming were personally important. And when they won the war and independence came in 1980, the victorious liberation fighters expected land. [3]

The initial land reform was launched in the early 1980s, shortly after independence had been gained. In the decade after independence, 75000 families received 11 per cent of the total farmland of Zimbabwe. But this land reform was hindered in two ways. First, the Lancaster House peace agreement said that land could only be transferred from white to black farmers on a "willing-seller, will-

---

[1] Robin Palmer, *Land and Racial Domination in Rhodesia*, Berkeley: University of California Press, 1977.

[2] Ian Douglas Smith, *The Great Betrayal: The Memoirs of Ian Douglas Smith*, London, UK: Blake, 1997. Hanlon, *et al.*, *Zimbabwe Takes Back its Land*.

[3] Zvakanyorwa Wilbert Sadomba, *War Veterans in Zimbabwe's Revolution*, Woodbridge, Suffolk, UK: James Currey, 2011.

ing-buyer basis. " The land offered to the Government at an affordable price was primarily poorer land with less successful farmers. Second, Zimbabwe was under international pressure. In the 1980s, apartheid destabilization and open military attacks disrupted transport and the economy ① and Zimbabwe built up international debts, which in turn led to World Bank imposed economic structural adjustment, which squeezed the economy. Poverty levels increased from 26 per cent in 1990 to 55 per cent in 1995. War veterans became increasingly restless and began to take action; there were more than 1000 farm occupations between March and April 2000. ② The occupations were known as *jambanja* ("force" or "action in anger" in Shona), a term that was immediately popularized by the occupiers, the media, and the general public, as well as a term used by academics when writing about the fast track land reform. The former liberation soldiers used their military skills to organise unemployed people from towns and landless people from the over-crowded communal areas, and then structuring the occupation of the farm in an orderly, military way.

When Bishop Donal Lamont was convicted of treating guerrillas in church hospitals, he warned in his 1976 speech: "Were there to be an African government in this country-and indeed that seems inevitable, and very soon-and if the present laws which have been enacted and applied to create and preserve privilege-if these were retained and applied in reverse against the European, what a protest their would be! ··· Thousands of whites could be driven from their homes and farms without compensation. "③ Exactly that happened, and as the Bishop predicted, what a protest there has been.

This sort of organised land occupation is not unique to Zimbabwe. In Brazil,

① Collin Stoneman, "Zimbabwe: The Private Sector and South Africa", in Joseph Hanlon, *Beggar Your Neighbours*, London, UK: James Currey, 1986.
② Government of Zimbabwe, *Zimbabwe* 2003 *Poverty Assessment Study Survey Main Report*, Harare: Ministry of Public Service, Labour and Social Welfare, 2006; Admos Chimhowu, Jeanette Manjengwa, and Sara Feresu, *Moving Forward in Zimbabwe: Reducing Poverty and Promoting Growth*, Harare: Brooks World Poverty Institute, the University of Manchester, UK and the Institute of Environmental Studies, University of Zimbabwe, 2012.
③ Donal Lamont, *Speech from the Dock*, Leigh-on-Sea, Essex, UK: Keven Mayhew, 1997.

the Landless People's Movement works in the same way, first recruiting and organising people who want to farm, and then on a set day doing a land invasion.

Half of Zimbabwe's farmland and 80 per cent of its farmers are still in the traditional communal areas, practicing subsistence agriculture. Forty per cent has now
been resettled by 244000 families. Table 1 shows Sam Moyo's estimate of the 2010
land pattern: 75000 families received land in the 1980s. [1]For the new land reform, a fast track system was created, with two types of farms. There are A1
farms, where each former white farm was broken up into 40 to 45 smaller farms,
each with 6 to 10 hectares of arable land. There are 146000 A1 farms, and most
are held by people who occupied the land; many came from urban areas or the
communal lands. The other model is A2, where each white farm was broken up
into 3 to 5 farms. There are 23000 A2 farms. These required a formal application
with evidence that the person had farming knowledge and sufficient money to start
the farm. That requirement meant that most A2 farmers came from the elite, and
often had government jobs or other businesses.

Table 1   Zimbabwe's farmland in 2010

	Number of farms 2010		Area 2010	
	Number	%	Million hectares	%
Smallholders				
Communal	1100000	81	16. 4	50
1980s resettlement	75000	6	3. 7	11
A1	145800	11	5. 8	18
Sub total	1321000	98	25. 8	79
Middle farms				
African purchase	8500	0. 6	1. 4	4. 3
Small A2	22700	1. 7	3	9. 1
Sub Total	31200	2. 3	4. 4	13
Large farms				
Large A2	217		0. 5	1. 6

[1]   Sam Moyo, "Three Decades of Agrarian Reform in Zimbabwe", *Journal of Peasant Studies*, 38,
no. 3, 2011, pp. 493 – 531.

	Number of farms 2010		Area 2010	
	Number	%	Million hectares	%
Black large scale	956	0. 1	0. 5	1. 6
White large scale	198		0. 1	0. 4
Sub Total	1371	0. 1	1. 2	3. 5
Agro-estates	296		1. 5	4. 5
TOTAL	1354000	100	32. 9	100
Total land reform	243717	18	13	40

Source: SamMoyo, "Three Decades of Agrarian Reform in Zimbabwe", *Journal of Peasant Studies*, 38, no.3, (2011), p.512.

A common criticism of the fast track land reform is that much of the land went to so-called cronies of the ruling party leadership. And it is clear that there was some political bias in the allocation of A2 farms and whole large farms, although not for A1 farms[1]. There are also some people with multiple farms or with farms larger than the stipulated maximum size. It is estimated that of land transferred in 2000 – 2004, less than 10 per cent of land went to people who might be called cronies, that is, people perceived to be connected to the ruling party, ZANU-PF; senior civil servants; and senior military personnel. [2] This is not considered a high percentage, but it does underline the importance of a land audit.

The Importance of Land

The amount of land is limited and demand often exceeds supply, so there must be a system to allocate land to some people and not others. In many countries it is market price, but in colonial Rhodesia it was race. Such land alienation and dispossession often invoke land as a potent symbol of historic injustice and oppression, especially

---

[1] Joseph Hanlon, Jeanette Manjengwa, and Teresa Smart, *Zimbabwe Takes Back its Land*, Kumarian Press, VA 2013.

[2] Joseph Hanlon, Jeanette Manjengwa, and Teresa Smart, *Zimbabwe Takes Back its Land*, Kumarian Press, VA 2013.

where poverty and inequity prevails. ①

Land has different values and meanings, and while it is conventionally perceived as means of agricultural production, it has symbolic value as well. Economic dimensions of land go beyond economic empowerment and food security, as land is also regarded as a place to reside safely and a source of livelihood. For the majority of rural people, and increasingly for more urban people engaged in urban agriculture, land is primarily a means of generating a livelihood.

Tension runs through all land reforms between production and welfare. Should land be given to the poorest and most in need to provide immediate help to them? Or should the land be given to those who have the means to increase production and create jobs, and economic growth through multiplier effects, as new production is sold and the earnings used to buy more goods locally, thus creating jobs, both on the farm and in town. Zimbabwe's land reform model has the potential to do both, that is increase productivity and reduce poverty.

Production and Productivity

Farm production and productivity is a major criterion for measuring success. In the case of Zimbabwe, the only practical basis of comparison is with the white farmers who were replaced by the land reform farmers. The context here is that it takes a generation for new farmers to dominate the land and reach high levels of productivity. This applies to both the white farmers after the Second World War and the 1980s land reform farmers. The fast track land reform farmers have been in place for 10 to 12 years, and were badly hit by the 2006 – 2008 hyperinflation during the economic crisis-as was everyone else in Zimbabwe. ②So we would ex-

---

① Bridget O'Laughlin, Henry Bernstein, Ben Cousins and Pauline E. Peters, "Introduction: Agrarian Change, Rural Poverty and Land Reform in South Africa since 1994", *Journal of Agrarian Change*, vol. 13 no. 1, January 2013, pp. 1 – 15.

② Joseph Hanlon, Jeanette Manjengwa, and Teresa Smart, *Zimbabwe Takes Back its Land*, Kumarian Press, VA 2013.

pect the fast track farmers to be less than halfway to peak productivity. ①

Support also matters. The 1980s and fast tract land reform farmers received relatively little government support, and thus their growth has been bootstrapped or what is known as "accumulation from below", which entails reinvesting profits or using income from wages of other family members. ② By contrast, new white farmers were given free training, and from 1940 the Rhodesian government made huge investments to increase their productivity and production. Extensive research developed modern hybrid seeds, there were guaranteed markets paying white farmers more for the same crop than black farmers, and a range of other support including subsidy and credit. ③

The first step is simply to look at use of land, and it is appropriate to start with a quote about the Mashonaland provinces, where 75 percent of Zimbabwe's prime farmland is situated:

> Just get into an aeroplane and fly over Mashonaland's European farming areas. On practically every farm you will see acres of land lying idle ··· It is a national disgrace that so much land is lying idle and not being used.

This is not a quote criticizing the land reform, it was spoken in 1965 by the chairman of the Rural Land Board. ④ Later on, in 1976, Roger Riddell calculated that only 15 per cent of potentially arable European land was being cultivated. ⑤ Zimbabwe's Transitional National Development Plan in 1982 said "utilization of potential arable land in the large-scale and small-scale commercial sectors

① Joseph Hanlon, Jeanette Manjengwa, and Teresa Smart, *Zimbabwe Takes Back its Land*, Kumarian Press, VA 2013.
② Ian Scoones, Nelson Marongwe, Blasio Mavedzenge, Jacob Mahenehene, Felix Murimbarimba and Chrispen Sukume, *Zimbabwe's Land Reform, Myths and Realities*, Woodbridge, Suffolk, UK and Harare: James Currey and Weaver Press, 2010.
③ Joseph Hanlon, Jeanette Manjengwa, and Teresa Smart, *Zimbabwe Takes Back its Land*, Kumarian Press, VA 2013.
④ Malcolm Rifkind, "The Politics of Land in Rhodesia", MSc thesis, Edinburgh University, 1968.
⑤ Roger Riddell, *The Land Question, From Rhodesia to Zimbabwe*, Pamphlet 2, Gwelo: Mambo Press, 1978.

is about 21 per cent and 18 per cent respectively. "① The Rhodesian National Farmers' Union in 1977 found that 30 per cent of all farms were insolvent-kept a-live by loans, price supports, and subsidies. In the 1975 – 1976 season, 60 per cent of white farms were not profitable enough to qualify for income tax, while 52 per cent of all taxable income was accounted for by just 271 white farms. ②Starting from very little and with huge support over several decades, some farmers were spectacularly successful. But these were not many. The white farmers never succeeded in occupying their half of Southern Rhodesia.

The land reform farmers are not yet using all their land, nor are they using it intensively enough mainly due to resource constraints, but significantly more land is being used now than by the former farmers.

Production on resettled farms continues to improve. Table 2 shows average production in the 1990s, which includes the large white commercial farms, the decade before the fast track land reform, as well as the 2014 harvest from mainly smaller farms. Overall, Zimbabwe is close to the average food production in the decade before the land reform and in 2014 exceeded its estimated grain requirements (Table 2). Tobacco and cotton are up to pre-land reform exports.

Table 2　Zimbabwe agricultural production

Crop	Agricultural production (000 tonnes)		2013/14 as % of (%)	
	1990s average	2013/14	1990s average	2013/14 needs
Food				
Maize	1686	1456	86	118
Small grains	165	224	136	
Groundnuts	86	135	157	145
Soya beans	93	84	90	
Export				
Tobacco	198	193	97	
Cotton	207	200 *	97	

---

① Government of Zimbabwe, *Transitional National Development Plan 1982/83 – 1984/85*, vol. 1, Harare: 1982, p. 65.

② Roger Riddell, *The Land Question*, pp. 11 – 13.

Crop	Agricultural production (000 tonnes)		2013/14 as % of (%)	
	1990s average	2013/14	1990s average	2013/14 needs
Estate				
Sugar	439	488 *	111	
Tea	11	24	218	

Sources: For 1990s statistics-Sam Moyo, "Three Decades of Agrarian Reform in Zimbabwe", *Journal of Peasant Studies*, 38, no.3, (2011), p.519; 2013/14 statistic – Ministry of Agriculture Mechanisation and Irrigation Development (2014); except * = industry estimates.

Table 3 gives the share of 2014 maize and tobacco production. More than one half of maize and 63 per cent of tobacco was produced by resettlement farmers (Table 3).

Table 3　Sectorial share of maize and tobacco production

	Maize			Tobacco
	2014 (000 t)		% share	% share 2014
Resettlement	739		51	63
of which				
A1		323	22	28
A2		285	20	35
Old Resettlement		131	9	
Communal Areas	636		44	27
Commercial	47		3	10
Peri-Urban	19		1	
Total	1441			

Sources: Ministry of Agriculture, Mechanisation and Irrigation Development (2014); Tobacco Industry and Marketing Board (TIMB) (2014).

Land reform farmers are getting more productive and yields are going up. Compared to the predecessors, they are using more of the land, but still using it less intensively. In particular, there is much less use of irrigation. Nevertheless, the resettlement farmers are now reaching the production levels of their predecessors, and after another decade should be well ahead-especially with more irrigation and improved mechanisation.

Reducing Poverty and Creating Jobs

Land reform can reduce poverty and create jobs. Land reform has an obvious and immediate poverty reduction effect, simply because more people have land and can grow food. But there is a much broader increase in incomes and living standards. Bill Kinsey has been following 400 of the 1980s resettlement families for nearly three decades, which gives him a unique perspective. By 1997 Kinsey and colleagues concluded that there had been a "dramatic increase in crop incomes observed in these households" and "an impressive accumulation of assets by these households."[1] Ian Scoones and his research team saw a similar growth in income and asset accumulation among the 2000 resettlement farmers.[2]

Equally important, however, is the issue of jobs. Agriculture was Zimbabwe's largest source of employment, consisting of 26 per cent of the wage labour force in 1999. Walter Chambati of the African Institute for Agrarian Studies estimates that by 2011, the total number of people working full time on resettlement land had increased five-fold, from 167000 to over one million.[3] This is because resettlement farms are less mechanised and much more labour intensive than the farms they replaced.

The 2000 land reform was immensely disruptive, and tens of thousands of workers did lose jobs and homes. This is similar to the large number that were displaced by economic structural adjustment in the 1990s. Throughout the first two post-independence decades, the number of permanent, full time farm workers remained steady at 167000. Numbers are very hard to determine, but one survey showed that of the permanent workers, 98000 were still employed on plantation estates and the remaining big farms in 2006. Thus it appears that between 75000 and 100000 full time workers retained their jobs on the remaining plantations,

---

[1] Bill Kinsey, "Zimbabwe's Land Reform Program: Underinvestment in Post-Conflict Transformation", *World Development*, 32, no. 10, 2004, p. 1682.

[2] Scoones, *et al.*, *Zimbabwe's Land Reform*.

[3] Walter Chambati, "Restructuring of agrarian labour relations after Fast Track Land Reform in Zimbabwe", *The Journal of Peasant Studies*, 38, no. 5 (2011), pp. 1047 – 1068.

large estates, and large farms, while 75000 to 100000 lost full time jobs and often their homes. Of those displaced, perhaps 15 per cent gained land; some
went back to the communal lands; and others are working on farms or doing gold
panning. ① This is a serious and very disruptive job loss.

However, Chambati estimated that by 2011, 240000 people were full time employed on A1 farms and 115000 on A2 farms. ② But equally important, 510000 people from the A1 farmers' families were self-employed full time and 55000 from extended
families on A2 farms. Most of these self-employed farmers are not simple subsistence
producers, but small-scale commercial farmers. With nearly 100000 still employed on
corporate and other large scale commercial farms, this means more than one million
people are now working full time on this land, compared to 167000 before land reform.

The 2012 census unexpectedly showed a migration back to rural areas, surely
triggered in part by land reform and in part by the lack of urban jobs caused by
structural adjustment and hyperinflation. ③ Tobacco is labor intensive and its rapid
growth since Chambati's study suggests that numbers of seasonal agricultural la-
bourers must be increasing.

Hidden within these statistics are some dramatic changes. For example, prior to
2000, just 1500 white commercial farmers produced 97 percent of the tobacco.
Now there are more than 106000 registered tobacco growers. Women have made
important gains from tobacco and from the land reform in general. According to
the Zimbabwe Association of Women Tobacco Farmers, one-third of the new tobacco producers are women, who produce about a quarter of the crop. Indeed, of
the 170000 families that received land during the land reform of 2000, 18 percent of the A1 farms were allocated to women-headed households compared to
four per cent of white farms owned by women, and five per cent of 1980s land-

① Scoones, et al. , Zimbabwe's Land Reform; Chambati, "Restructuring of agrarian labour relations", pp. 1047 – 1068; Sam Moyo, "Three Decades of Agrarian Reform in Zimbabwe", Journal of Peasant Studies, 38, no. 3, 2011, pp. 493 – 531; Hanlon, et al. , Zimbabwe Takes
Back its Land.

② Chambati, "Restructuring of agrarian labour relations", pp. 1047 – 1068.

③ ZIMSTAT, 2012 National Census.

reform farms that were given to women. Women are now increasingly inheriting land, which follows directly from campaigns to ensure that married couples had both names on the letters granting them their farms. Thus land reform is reducing poverty, creating jobs, and improving the status of women.

These land reform farmers could be much more productive and create many more jobs, if they were supported with inputs, irrigation, mechanisation and better markets.

Capital, Credit and Promoting Growth

Most land reform farmers are commercial farmers growing for the market. Commercial maize production is increasing-but not as fast as might be expected. One reason is that tens of thousands of the new farmers are growing tobacco instead of maize. So Zimbabwe exports tobacco and imports maize. And therein lies an important lesson.

Zimbabwe practices high-tech agriculture, with hybrid seeds, fertiliser, pesticides, mechanical ploughing, and hired labour. Minimum input costs are $100 per hectare, but to get high maize yields inputs cost rise to $500 per hectare and $800 per hectare in the case of tobacco. Maize yields are directly proportional to fertilizer use: not buying a $40 bag of fertiliser can reduce production by 500 kilograms, with a loss of $200. [1]

Where there was huge support for the white farmers and Second World War veterans, there has been relatively little support for the 1980s or 2000 resettlement farmers. As noted above, most resettlement farmers can only accumulate and build up their farm by reinvesting profits. The most successful land reform farmers buy their inputs for the next year as soon as they sell their crop and come home with sacks of fertilizer instead of wads of $10 bills. But harsh choices must be made on spending money on fertilizer or shoes for the children or to fix a leaking roof-many farmers simply cannot pull together several thousand dollars at the start of the season.

More than half of the tobacco farmers are now working on contract. [2]The tobac-

---

[1] Joseph Hanlon, Jeanette Manjengwa, and Teresa Smart, *Zimbabwe Takes Back its Land*, Kumarian Press, VA 2013.

[2] Joseph Hanlon, Jeanette Manjengwa, and Teresa Smart, *Zimbabwe Takes Back its Land*, Kumarian Press, VA 2013.

co company provides seed fertiliser and other inputs as well as technical support, all on credit. The farmer has to sell to the contract company, but that is usually acceptable because it is a guaranteed market. A 2012 World Bank study noted a dramatic rise in contract farming of export crops, with more than 280000 cotton contract farmers, 15000 in horticulture, and smaller numbers for tea, coffee, sugar, beef, and sugar beans. [1]

The World Bank points out that yields are rising fastest for the export crops where access to credit is easier due to the contract farming. In contrast, "in maize and other commodities, yields remain far below potential." And it continues: "It does not appear that yields are limited by poor farming skills, insecurity of tenure, or lack of land as collateral. Rather it is capital scarcity that lies behind the low yields."[2]

World maize prices are low so the current $390 per tonne of maize seems less profitable than tobacco, which adds another incentive for farmers to move to tobacco. In practice, the two can be equally profitable. A six hectare farmer could concentrate on one hectare of tobacco, but would get a similar income by growing five hectares of maize at 3 tonnes per hectare. Both require farming skills and similar inputs, but there is support for tobacco and not for maize.

The dynamism of the land reform farmers should not be underestimated. One factor makes Zimbabwe unusual. The liberation war was fought for land and Zimbabweans have a real passion for farming. In 2000, the occupiers were people who wanted to farm and had the initiative to occupy land and make it flourish. This has created an entirely new rural marketing structure which is totally different for that which existed decades ago, and which has exploded since dollarization in 2009. At the top end are the big contract companies, while thousands of small dealers and traders occupy the bottom. Often they are farmers themselves, who rent out cattle to their neighbours for ploughing and perhaps buy crops from their neighbours. Agro-dealers are setting up shop in the resettlement areas. Former white farmers have moved to trading and become important

---

① Hans Binswanger-Mkhize, and Sam Moyo, *Zimbabwe from Economic Rebound to Sustained Growth: Note II: Recovery and Growth of Zimbabwe Agriculture*, Harare: World Bank, 2012.
② Binswanger-Mkhize and Moyo, *Zimbabwe from Economic Rebound.*

intermediaries, and they are also doing some processing, such as slaughtering cattle. In addition, there is a growth of chicken production.

Credit and technical support are particularly important. Credit for traders to open small processing facilities, buy trucks, and have working capital. Credit for farmers to buy fertilizer, small tractors, and small scale irrigation that can cover the dry periods as rain becomes increasingly erratic due to climate change. And technical support from Agricultural Research and Extension Services (AGRI-TEX) and industry to help the credit to be well used.

European Union sanctions have been removed from most of Zimbabwe's political leaders, but they are still imposed on the 174000 fast track land reform farmers, who cannot receive assistance by any non-governmental organisation working with European funding. So it will have to be private capital such as money from contract farming of export crops, or the increasing funding from the diaspora-or the Zimbabwean government will have to use some of its mineral revenues to support land reform farmers.

Land reform farmers should now be able to stand on their own, and many are doing this by growing tobacco instead of maize-as growing tobacco is considered to be more lucrative than maize.

Food production is more complex, and normally requires subsidy. Zimbabwe has done this successfully in the past:

- Shortly after the independence in the 1980s, the government made a policy decision to switch maize production from white commercial farmers to communal farmers. This was done by a high guaranteed purchase price for maize, backed up with seed, fertiliser, and technical assistance from AGRITEX. The result was a spectacular success, turning some communal farmers into serious small commercial farmers. [1]

- The Grain Marketing Board in recent years has traded subsidized fertiliser and seeds for maize. [2]

---

[1] Mette Masst, "The Harvest of Independence: Commodity Boom and Socio-economic Differentiation among Peasants in Zimbabwe", PhD. thesis, Roskilde University, 1996, available at http://www.open.ac.uk/technology/mozambique, accessed November 1, 2011.

[2] John Kachembere, "Legal instrument stalls grain exchange", *Daily News*, 13 December 2013, Harare.

- For the 2013-2014 season, 1. 6 million households, including A1 and communal farmers, received 10 kg of cereal seed and 100 kg of fertilizers from government. [1] This might explain the following year's high production outcomes.

In one respect, Ian Smith and the white Rhodesian regime were right: new farmers need substantial subsidy, and without subsidy they cannot be expected to produce food. It is estimated that the average subsidy to white farms before independence was the equivalent of $40000 per year in current money. [2] This does not include the support for marketing boards and research. The United States of America and Europe heavily subsidise food production. After the Second World War, the new European Community developed a Common Agricultural Policy, and the goal was to make Europe self-sufficient in terms of food production. It was built on two pillars: subsidy for small farmers and a guaranteed market, and became so successful that Europe became a food exporter. Even now, the European Union subsidises its farms at the rate of $750 per arable hectare. Extensive support for farmers in north-east Thailand turned that country into one of the world's biggest rice exporters. Zimbabwe, too, could feed itself and become a major exporter of maize produced by land reform farmers.

There is talk of farm subsidies creating what is called a dependency syndrome in the country. But in the United States and in Europe, farmers have been subsidized for generations. From Thailand to white Rhodesia, subsidy has been the norm. There is no talk of a dependence syndrome because policy makers know that food self-sufficiency depends on subsidizing small commercial farmers.

Thus, the success of the land reform depends on a political decision. The government would need to seriously scale up spending of mineral revenue to support agriculture. Credit and subsidies for the land reform farmers, and credit and technical support for the traders and processors.

---

[1] Government of Zimbabwe, *National Budget Statement for* 2014. *Towards an Empowered Society and a Growing Economy*, Harare: Ministry of Finance and Economic Development, 2013.
[2] Joseph Hanlon, Jeanette Manjengwa, and Teresa Smart, *Zimbabwe Takes Back its Land*, Kumarian Press, VA 2013.

The Zimbabwe land reform shows what can happen-that small scale commercial farmers with a passion for farming can be more productive and can create more jobs than the big farmers they replaced. But it requires a major investment by the government.

An Investigation into Zambia's Agriculture Development Framework and Its Impact on Smallholder Farmers

Simon Ng'ona

This chapter highlights outcomes from a research study undertaken in Zambia which assessed Zambia's Agricultural Growth Framework and its contribution to the improvement of Small Scale Farmer's Livelihoods by Oxfam. The structure of the agriculture sector in Zambia country was examined, including the challenges that prevent small-scale farmers from developing into large-scale farmers. This chapter presents various policy recommendations to improve the situation.

1. Introduction

As agriculture provides the main support for Zambia's rural economy, growth in the agricultural sector is one avenue through which poverty reduction can be a-chieved in Zambia. However, despite widespread recognition of the strong connection between agricultural development and poverty reduction, under-provision of public investments has persisted for over a decade and small-scale farmers have continued to wallow in poverty. Zambia's primary policy objective of achieving accelerated growth and competitiveness in the agricultural sector cannot be achieved unless adequate public resources are committed towards catalyzing the desired growth. Long-term public investment in research and development, extension services, rural infrastructure, and food safety and quality systems have high pay-offs and are among the most important drivers of agricultural growth and competitiveness. Mostly, it is the small-scale farmers who are highly affected by the challenges inhibiting the commercialisation of their production. In this regard, there is a need to understand the extent to which Zambia's agriculture development framework is involving and helping small farmers and producers to improve their production and eventually their livelihood.

Agriculture has been contributing positively to the national income and presently contributes about 21 per cent to the GDP. It is really a concern that despite the country experiencing good rainfall in the recent past, the performance has been static compared to its potential. Sustained growth in the agriculture sector enables the farmers to enjoy better incomes, and hence improved their livelihoods. The majority of the population are involved in agriculture, but despite the agriculture sector being a positive contributor to the GDP, poverty levels still remain high. This can be attested by the UNDP Human Development Report of 2011 for Zambia, which indicates that:

- 58. 3 per cent of the Zambian population lived in poor households in 2006, compared to 56. 3 per cent in 2004;
- the average poor person was deprived in 44 per cent of the weighted indicators in 2006, compared to 42. 8 per cent in 2004;
- the share of the population that is multi dimensionally poor[1] (adjusted by the intensity of the deprivations suffered) was 0. 257 in 2006, compared to 0. 241 in 2004.

This shows that the agriculture sector has not performed very well due to its failure to significantly create employment opportunities and assure food security. This failure is mirrored by high poverty levels, especially in rural areas, where most people derive their incomes from farming. This is an indication that there is a lot that is needed to be done to improve the rate of equitable growth for the Zambian economy.

---

[1] Multi dimensionally poor index (MPI) is a measure that identifies multiple deprivations at the individual level in health, education and standard of living.

Table 1 Breakdown of allocations under the poverty reduction
programmes by per cent, 2006 – 2010

Category	2006	2007	2008	2009	2010
Irrigation support	0. 7	2. 4	2	1	0. 1
Commercialization of farm blocks	2. 2	2. 6	2. 2	0	0
Animal disease control	1. 5	1. 6	3. 3	4. 2	2. 5
Livestock development	0	0. 9	0. 6	0. 6	0. 4
Fertilizer Support Programme	74	38. 2	62. 2	75. 6	78
Strategic Food Reserves	18. 6	52. 1	26. 9	17. 4	18. 1
Cooperative education and training	0. 3	0. 7	0. 2	0	0
Others	2. 2	0. 7	2. 7	0	0. 9
Total	100	99. 2	100. 1	98. 8	100
Total ZK billion	198. 8	196	198. 2	196. 6	199. 9

Source: *Agricultural Consultative Forum/Food Security Research Project* 2006 – 2010.

The table above illustrates that, on average, the allocation to poverty reduction programmes (irrigation support, land development, and FISP among other items detailed in the table above) have maintained an upward trend between 2006 and 2010. Much of the allocation went to FISP and Strategic Food Reserves which when combined in the year 2010, accounts for 92. 1 per cent while the five others remaining with 7. 4 per cent.

Although the country has experienced growth in the production of maize, this may have come at the cost of increased inequality, since pricing policies may represent a *de facto* transfer of rent from the maize-consuming population to the big commercial farmers. Areas critical for enhancing productivity, such as crop science, extension programmes, infrastructure development, and a stable and supportive policy environment have not received the needed support.

In terms of the contribution of the sector to food security and nutritional status, the recent gains in crop production Zambia has experienced have been matched with improved food security, at least at the macro-level. On the other hand, the micro-level food security was dependent on other factors, such as rural household involvement in food and non-food crop production, the inclination to export, and the gender distribution of power at the household level. These factors have combined to make micro-level food insecurity a major concern.

2. Engagement and Contribution of Small-scale Producers

Small scale farmers in Zambia account for a higher percentage in terms of production field and a few cash crops. According to the crop forecast survey of 2011/2012, a majority of small-scale farmers are engaged in the production of maize, seed cotton, sorghum, rice, millet, sunflower, groundnuts, cowpeas, sweet potatoes, Bambara nuts, paprika and mixed beans as compared to the production of tobacco, Irish potatoes, wheat and soya beans which are heavily dominated by large-scale producers. This shows that opportunities are there for the small holder farmers as they are the one feeding the nation.

Small scale farmers account for about 70 per cent of the farmers involved in agriculture. According to the crop forecast survey of 2011/2012, small holder farmers have dominated the farming of maize (95 per cent), millet (99. 9 per cent), sorghum (93 per cent), groundnuts (99. 5 per cent) and seed cotton (99. 4 per cent) in terms of crop production, which proves that the small-scale farmers are contributing substantially to the entire agricultural production.

In addition, the crop forecast survey, 2011/2012 shows that small-scale farmers account for 100 per cent production of rice, 98 per cent and 99 per cent production of sunflower and mixed beans respectively. The large-scale farmers have dominated the production of tobacco, wheat and soybeans accounting for 74100, and 93 per cent respectively.

Despite this vast potential to produce and increase sales by the farmers, the agriculture sector still remains under developed. Different government and donor funded programmes have failed to graduate small-scale farmers into medium scale farmers in terms of their production and productivity due to the fact that essential factors to exacerbate growth among the small-scale farmers still remain underdeveloped. Small scale farmers will only see noticeable growth when Zambia manages to ease the access to inputs, training and extension services, post-harvest management, and markets. In addition to this, the government should provide for the needed infrastructure (feeder roads among others) to facilitate the reduction of cost in farming among the rural community.

3. Zambia Agriculture Growth Framework

3. 1   Main Policies

National Agriculture Policy (**2004 – 2015**) – The overall objective of the National Agriculture Policy (NAP) is to facilitate and support the development of a sustainable and competitive agricultural sector that assures food security in Zambia.

At the input stage, one of the provisions aims at preventing and controlling pests, crop and livestock diseases. To achieve this, the policy provides that the monitoring, regulation and facilitation of disease and vector control implementation programmes for diseases of economic importance would be intensified in priority areas. Ensuring that the crops and livestock are protected against diseases is critical as this affects the extent to which agriculture activities could turn out to be productive.

The promotion of irrigation is also a key strategy identified under the policy which would help transform agriculture at the input stage. Given thatreduced crop yields and livestock losses in Zambia can also be attributed to severe droughts suffered from time to time, the policy provides for Government to embark on full and efficient exploitation of the country's abundant water resources, both underground and surface, and promoting irrigation to ensure all year round agricultural production. This is particularly with reference to small-scale farmers, who would be prioritised to improve household food security and incomes.

Irrigation Policy (**2004**) – The overall objective of the irrigation policy is to have a well regulated and profitable irrigation sector that is attractive to both private investors and Zambia's development partners. This objective would be achieved by addressing a myriad of challenges, many of which have a bearing on small-scale producers. For example, the policy notes that Zambia has a poorly enforced legal framework that neither regulates nor allocates water in an equitable or economically advantageous fashion hence making it difficult for small-scale

278

producers to actively participate in the system as they could benefit a lot from participating in irrigation farming if there is a good enforced legal framework for the policy in question.

To achieve the overall objective of having a well regulated and profitable irrigation sector, the irrigation policy also has some intermediate objectives that would help attain this main target. These include having accessible, demand-driven institutions characterized by efficient, transparent procedures, and a service oriented ethos. One of the major challenges for small-scale producers is the challenge in having access to institutions that readily respond to their needs. Thus, if demand driven institutions are established, they would be largely those that would be able to respond to the demands from small-scale producers as they constitute the majority of farmers in Zambia.

National Seed Industry Policy (**1999**) – The availability of seed is critical, not only for the attainment of the policy targets but also for the attainment of food security in Zambia. In that regard, the National Seed Policy of Zambia was developed. Their overall policy objective is to ensure that quality seed of various crops is made available to farmers in an efficient and convenient manner to increase crop productivity and agricultural production. This would be achieved through the attainment of other intermediate objectives with benefit the small-scale producers. These include ensuring the development of an effective, efficient and sustainable system of producing, and supplying high quality seeds of crops to satisfy the national seed requirements. Given that shortage of seed, which results in high prices of seeds and high levels of use of traditional sources, is a major concern to farmers, implementation of this strategy would help in ensuring increased produce in Zambia.

The policy is also aimed at promoting an integrated seed industry involving both the formal and informal system. The recognition of the informal system in the seed industry is a good strategy in trying to ensure seed availability, as the use of seeds saved from previous harvest and borrowing among other farmers are common informal systems used by farmers.

National Cooperative Development Policy (**2011**) – The formation of co-

279

operatives can be a critical strategy, as through this, small-scale producers in the agriculture sector could be transformed. The establishment of the following types of service cooperatives for example, which are identified under the policy, might go a long way in helping small-scale farmers across the supply chain:

• Marketing and Supply Cooperatives, which are cooperatives that sell crops produced by the members. These are critical as they would increase the bargaining power of the farmers, compared to a situation where each farmer would sell individually and be at the mercy of middlemen that can easily exploit them.

• Transport Cooperatives, which would be cooperatives running transport facilities for transporting members' produce. Given the poor infrastructure networks, farmers often face challenges in transporting their produce, and are forced to part with significant amount of money as transport costs. Utilising transport from cooperatives would significantly eliminate costs due to the mutual understanding among farmers as well as the eliminated middlemen charges which often inflate the costs.

• Savings and Credit Cooperatives, where members pool their savings and make loans to each other. Given the need for some level of investment into agriculture, farmers should have access to credit to finance agricultural activities. Many farmers often fail to produce on a large-scale due to inability to meet costs related to agriculture inputs. Thus, these cooperatives would go a long way in ensuring easy access to cheaper lines of credit for farmers.

This makes it important that strategies be developed to encourage the formation of cooperatives as well as regulating their operations. The Ministry of Agriculture and Livestock thus established the National Cooperative Development Policy in November 2011 with the overall objective of creating an enabling institutional and legal environment for the development of autonomous, transparent, viable and demand-driven co-operatives that contribute to socio-economic development and poverty reduction.

The strategies laid out under the all these policies above can go a long way in uplifting the living standards of the small-scale producers if successfully implemented. Thus, there is a lot of scope for all these policies to benefit small-scale and traditional farmers if they are well implemented and amended to the current needs of small-scale farmers. There also remain some serious challenges that need to be addressed to make the policy more effective in achieving its enshrined objectives.

3. 2　Institutional Framework

The Ministry of Agriculture and Livestock (MAL) is the implementing agency for the policies identified above. Many other institutions are needed to complement government efforts. Among them include:

- Seed Control and Certification Institute (SCCI) which complement MAL in the provision of quality seeds to farmers as well as quality control, monitoring seed trade, and providing coordination of the sector;
- The National Plant Genetic Resource Centre; also has to come in for collection and preservation of genetic resources, while other research institutions are also responsible for variety development and improvement. Private seed companies, NGOs and CBOs are also heavily involved as they are responsible for production, marketing, and distribution of seed.
- The National Plant Genetic Resource Centre; for collection and preservation of genetic resources;
- Soil and Crops Research Branch of the MAL for purposes of conducting soil and crops research on the basis of crop comparative advantage in line with agro-ecological regions;
- Private sector and NGOs; the existing policy framework gives space to these organisations to chip in the provision of services such as extension services and production, marketing, and distribution of seed.
- Other key players are Research Trusts, the University of Zambia, the Ministry of Science, Technology and Vocational Training through the National Science and Technology Council (NSTC) and the National Institute of Scientific and Industrial Research (NISIR) and seed companies for purposes of in crops research.

These institutions generally form the key players in ensuring that agriculture development objectives identified under the various agriculture oriented policies are met. Thus, their capacity to deliver in a coordinated manner is also important in booting the agriculture sector.

4. Policy Constraints Impacting Negatively on Small-scale Farmers

There seem to be a number of policies with ambitious strategies aimed at improving the performance of the agriculture sector broadly. However, the co-relationship between the content and strategies in these policies and the impact on the performance of the agriculture sector especially for small-scale farmers seem to be distant. For example, irrigation seems to be one of the major challenges most farmers are facing in Copperbelt, Chipata, and Southern Provinces. Tapping subsurface water is still a pipe dream among most small-scale farmers in these provinces and most of the farmers who produce cotton, groundnuts, and maize in these provinces depended on the rains for good yields as well as the use of watering can system.

The majority of farmers in the three provinces have no access to any form of irrigation. Only few small-scale farmers in the Southern Provinces use Treddle pumps to irrigate their farms. This form of irrigation is specifically for their horticultural crops, thus these farmers do not use any form of irrigation for the cotton, groundnuts, and maize crops.

What is interesting is that the present irrigation policy does acknowledge these and other challenges and provides remedies thereof in the quest to achieve the overall objective of having a well regulated and profitable irrigation sector. Implementation of the irrigation policy would go a long way in solving the plight of small-scale farmers. However, what is of worry is that the policy has been in place since 2004 yet only limited efforts have been made in ensuring that the policy measures are thoroughly implemented-as it is evident that the challenge of irrigation is still persistent. This could be attributed to lack of capacity in the MAL or lack of government commitment in ensuring that such measures are implemented.

Having skills re-orientation trainings for MAL staff, increased budgetary resource allocation to the agriculture sector, and political will would go a long way in addressing the implementation challenge.

Another key policy issue that constrains small-scale farmers' performance is access to credit. The NAP have several strategies in place to help farmers get access to funding, such as a fund which farmers can access through appropriate financial institutions and NGOs. In addition, the policy encourages group lending to ensure good recovery rates as well as the promotion of private/public sector partnership in credit provision and savings mobilization. Although these proposals and strategies are articulated in the policy, the implementation is yet to start in earnest, hence access to credit is still a challenge. Although there could be some level of group lending among farmers which seem to be unsustainable and on a minority scale, the study establishes that all farmers have difficulties in having access to credit schemes offered by financial institution due to collateral requirements. Besides the stringent requirements by some financial institutions, the cost of borrowing in Zambia is high and not favourable to the small-scale farmers.

Another area of concern was on access to extension services and inputs. The provision of extension services to the farming population through the extension workers of is an important responsibility of the government and is reflected in the NAP. Although the NAP does recognise the limitations of the government in the provision of extension services, nothing much seems to have been done about it. For example, on the Copperbelt, Eastern and Southern provinces, on average, one extension officer covers 1000 farmers. The study establishes that, on average, extension officers only visited farmers three times in a year. The findings indicate that distance has an effect in delivery and access of extension services. The District Agriculture Coordinators (DACOs) indicated that they are very understaffed and could not meet the growing demand to provide extension services on a frequent basis.

5. Challenges Faced by Small-scale Farmers

The study establishes a lot of challenges faced by the small-scale farmers. Both goat and beef producers rely on nature to feed their animals due to high cost of inputs (feed). They use free scavenging methods and available pastures to feed their animals without any formalised feeding scheme. Most of the farmers do have knowledge on preservation methods of pasture but the study observes that there is a challenge on the quality of the pasture they preserve due to poor storing techniques. Therefore, as good management of improved pasture is the basis of better dairy feeding, it is important that these farmers are trained in pasture quality and preservation.

As acknowledged by the NAP, there are some limitations on the ability of government to provide extension services on its own. Thus the policy encourages the involvement of the private sector and NGOs in the provision of extension services, although it does not include the harmonization and regulation of the initiatives. In cotton farming ginnery companies offer inputs at a credit and provide extension and marketing services. This is a positive development and there is every need to support such interventions which are working. However, the relationship between ginnery companies and farmers needs to be closely monitored as in most cases, going by the recent strife between the farmers and the ginners, farmers tend to lose out. A good example is on the standoff that was experienced in 2012 over cotton prices between farmer and the ginner:

> There was a heated standoff over price between farmers and the Zambia Cotton Ginners Association (ZCGA), which represents the main cotton buyers. Farmers are reported to have been demanding a price of close to K4000 a kilogram, but the ginners were said to be offering only half that. For its part, the ZCGA insisted that the world price of cotton had plummeted and its members were therefore unable to offer more.
>
> The price of cotton on the international market measured on the Liverpool index had shot to record highs the previous year and was well in excess of £ 150 (K1.2 million), which

farmers believe should have translated into a better price than they received.

Although international price of cotton were no longer at those levels, farmers felt it was still trading at reasonable levels which should have been reflected in the local price. ①

What is clear from this is that there is a lack of an effective regulatory oversight by the MAL and other statutory bodies such as the Competition and Consumer Protection Commission (CCPC). Price discussions and agreements are supposed to be tightly monitored by such institutions to avoid situations like the one mentioned above from recurring and to avoid market distortions and failure necessitated by such perceived collusive actions from a competition policy perspective.

The other challenge facing farmers is lack of knowledge and capacity in understanding the broad varieties of groundnuts. The study establishes that farmers use recycled seed and are very reluctant in adopting new and improved varieties. For maize, most farmers receive inputs through the Farmers Input Support Programme, although the amount of inputs received by most farmers under FISP is not enough. Hence they buy fertilizer and weed killers from the agro dealers in order to supplement the subsidized inputs they receive.

Overall, the productivity level on various crops in Zambia still leaves a lot to be desired. There is need to integrate appropriate technologies that will enhance crop productivity. With regards to productivity (yield/ha), Copperbelt is performing better than the Eastern and Southern province hence the need to assess the scope of replicating the practices being implored Copperbelt to improve the productivity of the other provinces. Eastern province performed better in cotton and groundnuts production compared to Copperbelt and Eastern province (Table 2).

---

① Cotton News: "Zambia cotton farmers burn lint as local prices dip by 50%", http://cottonmarketnews.com/2012/07/03/zambia-cotton-farmers-burn-lint-as-local-prices-dip-by-50/, Last visit, 03-07-18.

Table 2   2011/2012 Crop Forecasting Survey

Crop	Province	Area Planted (Ha)	Area Harvested (Ha)	Expected Production(MT)	Yield (MT/Ha)	Expected Sales (MT)
Maize	Copperbelt	89501	79329	205542	2. 30	122306
	Eastern	276288	245319	572760	2. 07	214265
	Southern	303429	227076	554275	1. 83	257126
Groundnuts	Copperbelt	8709	8447	5399	0. 62	2892
	Eastern	56903	54793	30895	0. 54	10223
	Southern	22874	20420	9514	0. 42	2040
Cotton	Copperbelt	605	605	785	1. 30	—
	Eastern	190607	184472	160956	0. 84	—
	Southern	40380	36460	33417	0. 83	—

Source: Crop Forecast Survey, 2011/2012.

According to the Zambia Central Statistics Office, by 2010 the cattle population was 3038000 and the goat population was 758501 in the country. It is undeniable that goats are second from pigs in terms of value. There was need to look at goat production from commercialization side, as this is a product that has a huge and specialised export market through Kasumbalesa and Nakonde border posts. An increasing demand for livestock products such goat meat can offer small-scale farmers opportunities for increased market participation. However, existing goat markets are largely informal, with poorly developed inputs and services.

Storage facilities being used by farmers are not well developed and this has led to the increases in the post harvest losses being incurred by farmers. The farmers who have traditional storage facilities have challenges on pest control related issues, stacking, record keeping and fire safety arrangements and above all limited storage space.

Marketing Issues

The biggest market player in the maize sector is the governmental Food Reserve Agency (FRA). Though FRA provides a ready market, farmers are generally not satisfied with the operations of FRA because of delays in payment. This hinders their effective planning for the subsequent seasons. The government of Zambia through the MAL determines the floor price of maize which some farmers do not find attractive. However, the strong message coming from the famers was for government to also allow the private sector players to participate in the purchasing chain as this will offer an alternative market. Lifting the export ban on maize could also allow the farmers to tap in the regional markets like Congo DRC and Malawi.

The cotton sector is heavily under the control of the private sector who offer out grower schemes to small-scale farmers. Ginners pre-finance the production of cotton by providing the farmers with inputs and farmers are tied to sell their produce to the Ginners. The study learns that Dunavant, Cargill, and Alliance remain the main players in this sector. Under the out-grower scheme farmers are given inputs at a credit, normally considered during the setting of the market price. The major challenge remains on the pricing as farmers are tied to a pre-arranged price which many farmers end up complaining about.

Groundnutmarketing channels are not well developed as this market is mainly informal. The problem in this sector is that farmers are unable to sort groundnuts according to varieties and grades and if they had this capacity they would have been able to maximize their returns. There is also a problem with post-harvest handling of groundnuts by these farmers which increases the level of *aflatoxin* in groundnuts, hence preventing the crop from meeting international standards.

Another challenge hinges on lack of knowledge on the lucrative nature of livestock business among most farmers. Most of the farmers do not consider livestock rearing as a lucrative business. The NAP policy also recognises the importance of livestock farming and its demand both nationally and internationally and provides strategies to ensure that animal production and marketing is enhanced. But it is clear from the findings on the ground that there is a disconnection between the intentions of the policy and the ground realities. It is only hoped that the NAP, after been reviewed, will offer better strategies on how to ensure that whatever is contained is easy to implement.

6. Agriculture Investment

According to Zambia investor guide of 2012, the Zambian government has put in place several incentives to encourage investment in the agriculture sector and these incentives are as follows:

* Guaranteed input tax claim for four years prior to commencement of production for agricultural businesses.
* Zero rating agricultural products and supplies when exported.
* VAT deferment on importation some agricultural equipment and machinery.
* Income tax rate of ten per cent.
* Farm improvement allowance at 100 per cent on fencing, brick or stone wall and an allowance of K10 million for farm occupied by farm workers.
* Farm works allowance at 100 per cent for the full cost of stumping and clearing, works for prevention of soil erosion, boreholes, wells, aerial and geophysical surveys, and water conservation.
* Dividends paid out of farming profit are exempt from tax for the first five years the distributing company commences farming.

It is clear from the above incentives and exemptions, which are mainly given to large-scale investors, that these incentives give large-scale farmers opportunities for greater economies of scale. Ensuring that small-scale farmers also benefit from such incentives, of which most of them date back to the investment Act of 1993 (amended in 1996), would be a great boost to small-scale farmers. An attempt to do so is reflected in the 2012 budget speech which notes that while committed to FDI development and an incentive programme, the Zambian government needs to re-assess the incentive policy, to make it more cost effective and allow it to benefit a broader spectrum of the Zambia population. This could also benefit small-scale farmers.

There are different ways through which investors can acquire land in Zambia, depending on whether the land is state land or customary land. For state land, they can contact ZDA, which would guide the investors by pointing out available land that is ready for investment. In addition, potential investors can also approach existing owners of state land and negotiate on commercial basis for the transfer of the land. Investors can also end up owning customary land by approaching village headmen and chiefs directly in searching for land. However, customary land has to be converted into state land first before it is acquired.

7. Recommendations

Irrigation and productivity – This study has identified some issues that need urgent attention to ensure that small-scale farmers' productivity is enhanced. Small-scale farmers account for more than 70 per cent of Zambia's farmers and they dominate the farming of maize, millet, sorghum, groundnuts, and cotton. For instance, access to irrigation is poor, which can be attested by the use of buckets and watering can system deployed by small-scale farmers. Productivity of their produce can be increased if farmers use alternative sources of irrigation such as installation of pumps, have provisions of harvesting rain water and its storage.

There are apparent gaps in the implementation of the irrigation policy. Although updating the standards and guidelines for the planning, design, and construction of irrigation schemes to benefit small-scale farmers is provided for, this is yet to commence on a large-scale. The fact that about 76, 62, and 50 per cent of the farmers had no access to any form of irrigation in Copperbelt, Eastern, and Southern Province respectively is worrisome. It is necessary to scale up the implementation of the irrigation policy to enhance agriculture productivity by small-scale farmers.

Seed usage – The National Agriculture Policy provides that there would be regularisation of the seed sector through seed testing, seed crop inspection, variety registration, variety protection and enforcement of seed quality standards to facilitate seed trade, quarantine, and other seed related issues. Although cotton farmers indicated that they receive quality seeds through grower schemes offered by the ginnery companies, the groundnut sector still has challenges. The groundnuts farmers indicated that they use recycled seeds, largely available from informal sources-hence the policy is not being effectively implemented. Although the NAP provides for the development of the informal seed sector by providing accessibility of the sector to breeders/basic seed from research, findings reveal that farmers are unable to sort groundnuts according to varieties and grades due to lack of capacity in sorting techniques. In addition groundnut farmers are reluctant in adopting new and improved varieties-this may be due to information asymmetry and hence the need to organise training programmes at ground level regarding the use of new and improved varieties, which will enhance productivity and also improve the delivery of effective extension services. There is also need to open seed banks at provincial level. This is also something that the implementation of the policy would have gone a long way in addressing.

Extension service – Although farmer groups and farmer field schools and the use of electronic and print media as communication tools to support extension information delivery are strategies identified by the NAP, the implementation is yet to kick off in earnest. As reported in the study, farmers indicated that they were only visited by extension officers three times a year, and only about 71, 78, and 84 per cent of the farmers in Copperbelt, Eastern and Southern Province, respectively, indicated that they had access to extension services. Since the District Agriculture Coordinators confirmed this and attributed it to under-staffing, it is quite apparent that the implementation of the policy needs to be enhanced to increase access to extension services. In order to have an effective and efficient extension service delivery, there is need to build capacity in terms of adequate staffing and operation efficiency, and increasing access to extension services requires the office of the DACOs to open sub-branches within a ten kilometre radius.

Access to Finance – The NAP is also yet to deal with the issue of access to finance, despite the fact that the NAP proposes to create a fund for access by farmers through appropriate financial institutions and to encourage group lending. All the farmers who were interviewed indicated that they lack access to credit schemes offered by financial institution. This can be attributed to the fact that the cost of borrowing in Zambia is high and not favourable to the small-scale farmers.

Thus, it is recommended that the government should facilitate measures that ensure that access to credit by small-scale farmers is enhanced, in line with the NAP. The government should promote the provision of micro finance through co-operative system and encouraging the establishment of self help groups. There is need to encourage contract farming with the private sector while government plays the regulatory role.

Marketing support – Although NAP promises strategies that facilitate market information flow among stakeholders in various regions, including facilitating the provision of rural infrastructure such as roads, rural storage infrastructure, and developing market centres, marketing is still a challenge for small-scale farmers. The groundnut sector's marketing channels are largely informal. Findings also reveal that in the three provinces, the storage facilities being used by farmers are not well developed, leading to post harvest losses. Challenges with regards to pest control, record keeping, and fire safety arrangements and so on compound matters. In the livestock sector, the farmers face challenges due to non-existent cold storage facilities (government should take initiations and encourage private investment to build storage facilities), making it difficult for the small-scale farmers to continuously produce goat meat and beef. As such, the provisions on marketing in the NAP call for urgent implementation. In amplifying implementation, there is need to establish provincial call centres/information cells. There is also need of capacity building workshops to disseminate market information that are arranged by the state and other key stakeholders to disseminate market information.

Cooperative Development – The strategies identified by the National Cooperative Development Policy would also enhance the performance of small-scale farmers. The development of a legal and institutional framework to facilitate the re-orientation and reforming of the co-operative organisation and ensuring that the Ministry responsible for cooperatives has a physical presence in all the districts of the country through field staff directly dealing with co-operative matters is provided for. Cooperative farming should be encouraged to ensure productive returns to the farmers. Restructuring of existing cooperative organisations is required in terms of its staffing and operational efficiency.

Livestock Development – There is also need for a change of attitude if goat and beef production are to be enhanced in Zambia. All the farmers indicated that they use free scavenging methods to feed the goats-with no formalised feeding schemes in place. The same is equally true for beef production, which is largely reliant on traditional pastures as inputs into the farming activity. There is need for orientation of small-scale farmers as well as capacity building support to ensure that the need to treat both goat and beef farming as a business, which would also call for some investments. Government support towards this would also go a long way in enhancing productivity. The current extension policy does not cover livestock, thus there is also need to have a clear extension policy that covers both the crop and livestock sector comprehensively with effective implementation.

Investment and land acquisition by investors – There are also some issues that need attention to ensure that the investment is in line with the PRAI. There is need to ensure that the existing rights to land and associated natural resources are recognized and respected by ensuring that some households do not lose land against their will. There is also need to ensure that full information is disclosed to the farmers when land is being acquired as a way of respecting rights to land. Instances where uptake by the displaced farmers is too low in newly invested areas might imply that the investment is jeopardizing food security as farmers' production would become lower than the situation before the investment. Efforts should also be enhanced to ensure that all those materially affected by the huge investments are consulted, and that agreements from consultations are recorded and enforced.

One challenge that is also apparent is the weak land tenure system among the farmers. As described in the report, the predominant form of land ownership is customary land ownership, with only 37. 5 per cent of the respondents indicating that they had title deeds. Among these, about 70 per cent were from Copperbelt province, an urban province. Having title deeds would go a long way in helping the farmers to unlock credit, as these could be used as collateral. There is need for a re-evaluation of the land tenure system to ensure that more farmers have title deeds to their land.

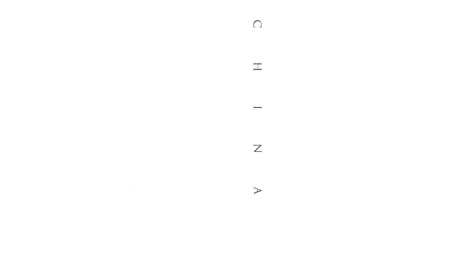

C
H
I
N
A

New Emerging Powers in African Agriculture

A
F
R
I
C
A

Solidarity Among Brothers? Brazil in Africa: Trade, Investment and Cooperation[*]

Paolo de Renzio, Jurek Seifert,

Geovana Zoccal Gomes and Manaíra Assunção[**]

Introduction

South-South cooperation (SSC) emerged as a key Brazilian foreign policy instrument in the beginning of Lula's presidency in 2003 and has generally been sustained by the government of President Dilma Rousseff. From the beginning, Brazil has emphasized SSC in Africa despite not having articulated an explicit foreign policy towards the region. The reconfiguration of Brazil's international relations, shifting towards an emphasis on the African continent over the past decade, has manifested itself in increased trade and a growing presence of Brazilian businesses on the continent, both of which have occurred alongside development cooperation. While development cooperation has been highlighted as a "horizontal" approach

---

[*] This chapter is a slightly altered version of an article previously published by the BRICS Policy Centre (BPC) as part of the research project "Brazilian South-South Cooperation and the BRICS: Changing Strategies in Africa" (SSC Project), a partnership between the UK Department for International Development and the Institute for International Relations of the Pontific University of Rio de Janeiro (PUC-Rio). Please visit www. bricspolicycenter. org for further information.

[**] Paolo de Renziois a Professor at the Institute of International Relations (IRI) at the Pontifical Catholic University of Rio de Janeiro (PUC-Rio), Jurek Seifert & Geovana Zoccal Gomes are doctoral candidates at the same Institute, and Manaíra Assunção is a master student in the institute.

based on "solidarity", the economic interaction between Brazil and its African partners appears to be based on other motivations and practices. This policy brief discusses the different strands of Brazilian intervention in Africa, noting some specific challenges and contradictions. It highlights the necessity of opening a debate regarding the reform of the institutional and regulatory framework guiding Brazilian intervention, in order to guarantee better coherence and efficacy of the country's foreign policy in the region.

The Acceleration of the Brazilian Insertion in Africa

Due to its historic ties and shared colonial past, Brazil has traditionally maintained a strong relationship with Africa, principally the Portuguese-speaking countries in the region. With the advent of African decolonization following the Second World War, relations between Brazil and African countries have grown more intense and more relevant. This dynamic formally began after 1974 with the fall of Portugal's colonial regime. In 2003, during the beginning of the Lula government, an increase in interaction between Brazil and Africa was not only promoted by the incumbent president and his "presidential diplomacy", but also evident in the expanded volume of trade, political dialogue, and cooperation between the two parties.

The Brazilian presence on the continent (whether through businesses, government bodies, or public-private partnerships) is embedded in a discourse of promoting major social and economic development in African countries. Brazil promotes the exchange of successful experiences, increased trade and cultural initiatives, increased diplomacy, and the export of technical knowledge in areas such as agriculture and health. At the same time, the growing relationship between Brazil and Africa was guided by the former's desire to increase its international presence, a theme characteristic of Brazil's diplomacy during the period. [1] The

---

① J. F. S. Saraiva, (2010), "The new Africa and Brazil in the Lula era: the rebirth of Brazilian Atlantic Policy", *Revista Brasileira de Política Internacional*, vol. 53, pp. 169–182.

personal engagement of the president and his emphasis on South-South cooperation as a form of horizontal cooperation gave origin to what has been termed the
"diplomacy of solidarity"① in the foreign policy of Brazil-with a specific focus on
African countries.

Since the beginning of her term in 2011, the current president Dilma Rousseff
has not demonstrated the same personal engagement in Brazil's relations with Africa as former president Lula. After her first visit to the region in October of 2011
(visiting South Africa, Mozambique, and Angola), President Dilma did not return to the continent for more than a year, when in February of 2013 she
travelled to the South America-Africa summit in Equatorial Guinea and also visited Nigeria. In March, she attended the BRICS Summit in Durban, South Africa, and in May she traveled to Ethiopia to participate in the ceremony celebra-
ting the 50th year anniversary of the African Union. Although these trips may be
interpreted as a significant increase in the president's attention to Africa, there
remains a noticeable pragmatism in the president's treatment of the African continent relative to her predecessor. While this may be attributed to Dilma's personal
preferences, which emphasize domestic politics, it is also true that promises
made by Lula to his African partners represent a significant challenge relative to
resources currently available for cooperation. Nonetheless, Dilma maintains the
same discourse of South-South cooperation established by the Lula government,
highlighting the importance of Africa as an equal partner of Brazilian foreign
policy:

> Brazil sees the African continent as a brother and close neighbor (⋯) [o] ur mutual
> interests are many: we seek development, which requires the promotion of inclusion of
> our population to the benefits and riches of our countries. ②

However, President Dilma has simultaneously continued to encourage Brazilian

---

① Inoue, C. Y. A. e A. C. Vaz (2012), "Brazil as 'Southern donor': beyond hierarchy and national interests in development cooperation?" *Cambridge Review of International Affairs*, 25 (4),
pp. 507 – 534.

② http://noticias. band. uol. com. br/mundo/noticia/? id = 100000601265&t = .

businesses to increase their presence in Africa. During the same visit to Ethiopia, the president also announced debt forgiveness of $897.7 million for 12 African countries. [1] Although this debt forgiveness was presented as an act of solidarity, it has been criticized for its trade and investment related motivations. Brazil's National Bank for Social and Economic Development (BNDES), it was noted, can only support corporate action in countries that do not have debts with the Brazilian government.

The Growth of Trade between Brazil and Africa

As a consequence of Brazil's foreign policy emphasis on Africa, trade between Brazil and the African continent grew consistently over the past decade. According to the think tank *Chatham House*, the volume of trade grew from $4.2 billion in 2001 to $27.6 billion in 2011, with a rate of growth of 16 per cent per year since 1990. [2] This growth led Brazil to become the third largest trading partner among the BRICS, after China (with a volume of $107 billion) and India ($32 billion), and ahead of Russia (with only $3.5 billion). [3]

In Africa, the most important partner countries are Nigeria (with 32 per cent of the volume of trade in 2009), Angola (16 per cent), Algeria (12 per cent), and South Africa (7 per cent). [4] In terms of the total volume of trade, however, Africa continues to be an average partner for Brazil. Exports to the region varied between 4 and 5.7 per cent of total Brazilian exports in the past dec-

---

[1] Congo, Tanzania, Zambia, Senegal, Ivory Coast, Democratic Republic of Congo, Gabon, Guinea, Mauritania, Sudan, São Tomé e Príncipe and Guinea-Bissau. With Angola and Moçambique, two of the most important partners for Brazil in the region, separate agréments were signed: forgiveness of US $ 315 million in debt for the Angolan government, and of US $ 330 million for Mozambique. http://www.revistaconstrucaoenegocios.com.br/materias.php? FhId-Materia = 277.

[2] C. Stolte, (2012), "Brazil in Africa: Just Another BRICS Country Seeking Resources?" Briefing Paper, London: Chatham House.

[3] H. B. Barka, (2011), "Brazil's Economic Engagement with Africa", Africa Economic Brief no. 5, Tunis: African Development Bank.

[4] Barka (2011), "Brazil's Economic Engagement with Africa".

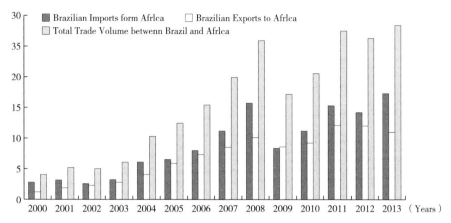

Figure 1　Evolution of Trade between Brazil-Africa in millions USD

Source: MRE (2012) . ①

ade and imports between ①5. 7 and 9. 8 per cent of the total. ② More than half of total exports from Brazil to Africa are manufactured products. The primary products exported are sugars and confectionery (26. 4 per cent in 2008 – 2010) and meats (12. 2 per cent), although exports of capital goods (machines and equipment, buses, trucks and light commercial vehicles) have also seen a significant increase over the past decade. Imports to Brazil from Africa are largely composed of primary commodities, of which the largest share (85. 4 per cent of total imports in 2008 – 2010) is composed of mineral fuels. This data demonstrates the disequilibrium that exists in the commercial agenda between the two parties and, at the same time, how Brazil has continually increased its relevance as an economic actor in Africa over the past decade, thereby increasing its economic influence in the region.

Brazilian Businesses in Africa

An important part of the changes in the economic relations between Brazil and Af-

---

① MRE (2012) Comércio Brasil-África, "Brasilia: Ministério das Relações Exteriores", available at: http: //www. brasilglobalnet. gov. br/ARQUIVOS/IndicadoresEconomicos/ComExtBrasilAfrica. pdf.

② MRE (2012), Comércio Brasil-África.

rica, particularly since 2003, is related to the internationalisation of Brazilian businesses. Although the presence of the Brazilian private sector in Africa has existed since the 1980s, the second phase of insertion of major corporations on the continent over the past decade stemmed largely from the growth of African economies and the relationship between demand for both raw materials and the infrastructure necessary for their extraction. [1] Generally, there are two types of Brazilian companies in Africa: the first includes some of the largest corporations of the Brazilian economy, and the second small and medium enterprises (SMEs) who have expanded to Africa more recently. [2]

The large corporations (Petrobras, Andrade Gutierrez, Vale do Rio Doce, Camargo Correia, and Odebrecht) are the dominant actors of Brazilian investment in Africa. Smaller investments aimed at African consumer markets, however, are incipient and involve SMEs like Marcopolo (Egypt and South Africa), Boticário and Nobel (both in Angola). In total, Brazilian companies operate in 22 African countries.

There does not appear to be a strategy of clear localization when comparing commercial flows and investment: cases in which high investment is coupled with low trade exist alongside others with reasonable trade volumes but without the presence of Brazilian businesses. There is a clear concentration of investment in Southern Africa, where three countries are highlighted as the primary destination of Brazilian companies: South Africa, Angola, and Mozambique. In terms of the public's perception of Brazilian companies, there is recognition that they tend to use local labor, such as with Odebrecht, the largest employer in Angola. [3] Despite this, there are criticisms of differential treatment, for example regarding wages of Brazilian and African laborers of the same level. Another major critique

---

[1] Iglesias and Costa, Investimento Estrangeiro Direto na A'frica. Rio de Janeiro, Brazil, 2011, Retrieved from http://www.cebri.org/midia/documentos/katarinacosta.pdf.

[2] Banco Mundial/IPEA (2011) Ponte sobre o Atlântico. Brasil e África Subsaariana: Parceria Sul-Sul para o Crescimento. Washington: World Bank. The Brazilian Export Agency (APEX) has also contributed to this recent development, for instance by organizing business fares.

[3] Banco Mundial/IPEA (2011).

is the lack of transparency in the manner by which relations between African governments and Brazilian companies are articulated. In the case of Vale's "megaproject" of coal extraction in Mozambique, the company has been the target of harsh criticism and protest, specifically regarding the relocation of several communities previously living close to the mining areas. ①

Brazilian businesses in the region are supported by their own direct investment (totaling US $ 10 billion in 2009) as well as with assistance from major financial institutions that have focused on large, international corporations. In 2008, the *Política de Desenvolvimento Produtivo* (Productive Development Policy) was implemented by the federal government and then substituted by the *Plano Brasil Maior* (Bigger Brazil Plan) in 2011, both with the objective of increasing the international competitiveness of Brazilian industry. ② These policies provided a target warranting a greater international role of BNDES. As a result, BNDES established a new directorate for Latin America and Africa that year, and sought to open a new office in Johannesburg, South Africa to administer its growing presence on the continent. ③ The Bank has provided substantial lines of credit to Brazilian businesses in Africa since 2007. For example, Angola, the largest recipient of Brazilian investment on the continent, received a line of credit of $ 5 billion. In addition to BNDES, other Brazilian financial institutions that are active in Africa include Caixa Econômica Federal, Banco do Brasil, and Bradesco.

The financial support and growing emphasis of these institutions on Africa serve as critical factors in the significant growth of economic relations between Brazil and Africa. The presence of large public financing projects demonstrates that Brazilian foreign policy actively supports the expansion of Brazilian businesses on the

---

① http://www.bbc.co.uk/news/world-africa-22646243 and http://www1.folha.uol.com.br/mundo/2013/04/1266520-megaprojeto-da-vale-e-alvo-de-protestos-em-mocambique.shtml.

② The *Política de Desenvolvimento Produtivo* (PDP) was established in 2008 with the aim of promoting and maintaining the cycle of domestic economic expansion, even during the global financial crisis, and provided the guidelines and the structure of the international intervention of BNDES, for example by creating practical means for strengthening commercial relations and direct investment flows from Brazil to Africa.

③ http://brazilafrica.com/negocios/bndes-tera-escritorio-na-africa/.

African continent and reflects the major interests of Brazil in the region, shown by the focus on financing large corporations that act in the areas of infrastructure, natural resource extraction, and energy.

Brazilian Cooperation for the Development of Africa

Undeniably, over the past few years, South-South cooperation, a product of transformations in Brazilian foreign policy, has surged as never seen before in Brazil. [1] Recognizing the capability of spurring international development, emerging countries articulated a discourse distinct from traditional (North-South) cooperation. In this context, the model of technical cooperation articulated by Brazil claims to be driven by the demands of the recipient countries and highlights the absence of conditionalities, its horizontal approach, and the non-intervention in domestic affairs.

Africa and Latin America have been the regions that benefited the most from the noticeable growth in the portfolio of Brazilian cooperation, both in terms of the number of projects and of their financial volume. The focus of Brazilian technical cooperation in Africa has been on the Lusophone countries (Mozambique, São Tomé and Príncipe, Angola, and Cape Verde). Brazil has emphasized cultural proximity and shared colonial history as important factors for the realization of cooperation with such partners. Mozambique, with 14 undergoing projects in 2013, is one of the principal recipients of Brazilian cooperation, followed by São Tomé e Príncipe and Cape Verde (with 12 and 11 projects respectively). [2] In addition to Portuguese-speaking countries, other beneficiaries of Brazilian cooperation are Algeria, Benin, Botswana, and Tanzania. Brazilian technical cooperation has demonstrated substantial diversity. The African continent has witnessed the most emphasis on health (22 per cent), agriculture (19 per cent), and education

---

[1] See also another Policy Brief recently published by the BRICS Policy Center: O Brasil e a Cooperação Sul-Sul: Como Responder aos Desafios Correntes, Maio de 2013, available at: http://bricspolicycenter.org/homolog/Job/Interna/5992.

[2] Fernando de Abreu, Diretor da Agência Brasileira de Cooperação (ABC), Presentation at the BRICS Policy Center, July 28th, 2013, http://bricspolicycenter.org/homolog/Event/Evento/596.

(14 per cent), but has also seen cooperation over matters related to the environment, public administration, cities, social development, defense, sport, culture, and others. [1]

As shown in Figure 2, the financial resources available for projects in Africa grew significantly between 2003 and 2010, but have also decreased dramatically in the past years due to the recent policy of budget cuts in Brazil. According to the current director of the Brazilian Cooperation Agency (ABC), Ambassador Fernando de Abreu, the budget of the agency has allocated $36 million for activities in Africa in 2012 – 2015. [2]

Health

With regard to health, Brazilian cooperation with Africa has occurred largely through professional education and training, specifically through the sending of Brazilian health professionals, structural assistance and institutional capacity building, transfer of Brazilian experiences with public policy in health, and donation of medicines and supplies. The primary emphasis of cooperation projects with African countries is related to HIV/AIDS. One example of an ongoing project is capacity building for anti-retroviral drug production, through which ABC and the Oswaldo Cruz Foundation (FIOCRUZ) have worked together to establish a pharmaceutical factory in Mozambique-where one in ten are infected with the virus-with the goal of strengthening the capacity of local professionals to participate in factory operations in the fight against the epidemic. Further, with the objective of establishing a clinical, epidemiologic, laboratorial, and health diagnostic research center, FIOCRUZ has established a Master's Program in Public Health in Mozambique and Angola, beginning in 2009. African students, with resources

---

[1] IPEA (2013) Cooperação Brasileira para o Desenvolvimento Internacional-2010, Brasília: IPEA, available at: http://www.ipea.gov.br/portal/images/stories/PDFs/livros/livros/livro_cooperacao_brasileira02.pdf.

[2] Abreu, Presentation at the BRICS Policy Center, July 28th, 2013, available at: http://bricspolicycenter.org/homolog/arquivos/e.pdf.

from CAPES, a federal institution supporting higher education in Brazil, travel to Brazil to complete their Masters studies at FIOCRUZ.

Agriculture

Given the expertise of EMBRAPA, a state-owned research organization affiliated with the Ministry of Agriculture, tropical agriculture has become a primary area of cooperation with Africa over the past few decades. In 2010, the organization had a presence in 11 African countries, conducting 12 projects and one isolated activity. ProSavana is the largest, current cooperation project of the ABC. Through trilateral or triangular cooperation with Japan and Mozambique, the project seeks to improve seed cultivation in the Nacala corridor, which largely consists of Mozambican tropical savanna, basing its efforts on the development of the Brazilian *cerrado*. Another example is the Cotton – 4 program. Encompassing four African countries-Benin, Burkina Faso, Chad, and Mali-the project began 2009 and has received great international attention. With the goal of increasing productivity, genetic diversity, and improved quality of the cotton sector, critical to the economy of these countries, EMBRAPA aims to strengthen and develop the production capabilities and economies of the Cotton – 4.

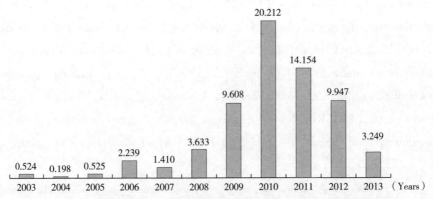

Figure 2 Evolution of Annual Budgetary Execution of Brazilian Cooperation in Africa (in millions of USD)

Source: Presentation to the Ambassador F. Abreu at the BRICS Policy Center, June 28, 2013.

Despite its emphasis on a horizontal approach and on solidarity, Brazilian technical cooperation with African countries is not free of criticism. One of the common critiques of Prosavana, the largest Brazilian cooperation project in Africa, is that it has reproduced the Brazilian experience of agricultural development in the Mozambican savannah, and as such has exported to the country a large-scale agriculture industry of soy and corn that brings environmental degradation and extinction of local communities.[1] Nonetheless, ABC argues that the establishment of priorities in the agriculture sector is a responsibility of the government's domestic policy and of the interplay of forces between civil society and the state of Mozambique, and that such priorities should not be subject to Brazilian or Japanese intervention-the providers of cooperation in this project.

Therefore, it remains important that Brazilian cooperation does not fall into the trap of ignoring tensions with local actors and develops the capacity to adapt to different social and political contexts in order to promote effective cooperation and sustainable projects. As recent comments highlight,[2] a "technical" approach to the challenges faced by developing countries, joined with a lack of experience acting in international contexts among Brazilian professionals, represents generally limiting factors for Brazilian cooperation.

The Future of Brazil-Africa Relations?

Both development cooperation and the promotion of trade and investment of Brazilian companies in Africa continue on the path initially outlined by the Lula gov-

---

[1] Open Letter of the UNAC on the ProSavana Program. National Farmers Union (UNAC). Maputo, October 11th, 2012, available at: http://www.unac.org.mz/index.php/documentos-de-posicao/38-pronunciamento-da-unac-sobre-o-programa-prosavana.

[2] I. Leite, et al. (2013), Para além do tecnicismo: a Cooperação Brasileira para o Desenvolvimento Internacional e caminhos para sua efetividade e democratização, policy Brief. São Paulo: Articulação Sul, available at: http://blogbrasilnomundo.files.wordpress.com/2013/08/policy_briefing_para-alec2b4m-do-tecnicismo.pdf. L. Cabral, et al. (2013), Brazil-Africa Agricultural Cooperation Encounters: Drivers, Narratives and Imaginaries of Africa and Development, *IDS Bulletin*, 44 (4), pp. 53 – 68.

ernment. Although President Dilma Roussef has continued such dynamic, the enthusiastic and personal approach of the previous government has been substituted by a policy that is more pragmatic and sometimes contradictory.

The Brazilian government continues to promote technical cooperation as part of its broader international strategy to position itself as a global actor that belongs to the South and maintains intense solidarity with developing countries. At the same time, however, the Brazilian Cooperation Agency (ABC), like other public bodies, has experienced a drastic budget reduction.

On the other hand, the expansion of Brazilian companies in Africa continues to be supported by the government through BNDES and brings concrete benefits in terms of trade and access to natural resources. The necessity to more clearly define the role that Brazil plays in Africa, and the relationship between cooperation, trade, and investment has become more acute in the past months, particularly through debates regarding the possible institutional restructuring of the ABC.

During her last trip to Ethiopia, the president announced the creation of a new agency that would not be part of the Ministry of Foreign Relations. According to the president, the new agency would be "a trade agency, encouraging cooperation and investment in Latin America and Africa," but she did not provide a clear specification of how such agency would contribute to the objectives of Brazilian foreign policy or of its institutional structure. Although the president alluded to an independent agency, the director of the ABC defended its continuation within Itamaraty, the Ministry of Foreign Relations. He also indicated that there is a team studying models of agencies of other countries to establish an adequate regulatory framework that would provide greater independence and technical capacity to the agency.

Independent of the institutional reforms currently being discussed, the greatest challenge for the future of Brazilian engagement with Africa will be the reconciliation of objectives and practices of development cooperation and economic cooperation (trade and investment), and the promotion of an approach that considers the priorities and necessities of the African countries in which Brazil intervenes. As discussed above, both technical cooperation and the actions of Brazilian companies, despite being apparently well-received by African countries, have been the target of criticism-primarily from civil society, as the cases of Pro-Savana and of Vale in Mozambique demonstrate. A first step in the right direction could be the definition of a regulatory framework for international cooperation-which could include the creation of a new agency-and the establishment of a specific strategy regarding Brazilian intervention in Africa in its various forms.

Brazilian Health and Agricultural South-South Cooperation in Angola [*]

João Moura Fonseca, Geovana Zoccal Gomes and Paulo Esteves [**]

Angola and Development Cooperation: Before and after the Civil War

Vast fluxes of development cooperation provided by United Nations agencies, bilateral donors, INGOs, and religious organizations shifted towards Angola during the civil war. Those were primarily geared towards emergency and humanitarian objectives, and often got to places virtually unreachable by government actors. The availability of funds enabled a mix of international and national civil society organizations to emerge and grow in Angola. Besides providing funding, international agencies played a significant role in facilitating safe mobility of development workers within war zones. [③]

[*] This article is an adapted and updated version of the working paper "Brazilian South-South Cooperation in Health and Agriculture in Angola", previously published at the BRICS Policy Centre (BPC) by the research project "Brazilian South-South Cooperation and the BRICS: Changing Strategies in Africa" (SSC Project), a partnership between the UK Department for International Development and the Institute for International Relations of the Pontific University of Rio de Janeiro (PUC-Rio). Please visit www. bricspolicycenter. org for further information.

[**] Researchers at the BRICS Policy Center, Rio de Janeiro, Brazil. Respectively, Master in International Relations from the Institute of International Relations at PUC-RJ in 2014 (joaomouraf@gmail. com); Ph. D. Candidate in the Institute of International Relations at PUC-RJ (geovana@bricspolicycenter. org) and Ph. D. in Political Science from IUPERJ in 2003 (esteves_paulo@puc-rio. br).

[③] Interview carried out in Luanda in September 2014.

After the end of the war, the organization of a donors' conference, aimed at raising and aligning funds, as well establishing commitments for reconstruction of Angola's infrastructure and economy, represented one of the national government's priority initiatives. The inability of the IMF and the GoA to reach a-greement over issues related to governance and transparency, and irreconcilable sets of statistics, were obstacles to the realization of the conference. [1] With no substantial concessions from each side, the conference was repeatedly delayed o-ver the years, never actually taking place. Additionally, the GoA never got the "seal of approval that could then make them eligible for debt rescheduling through the "Paris Club". [2] According to more than one informant, many of GoA's senior members to this day exhibited resentment against Northern donors for "not helping Angola when it needed it. "[3] It was at that time that Southern countries, particularly China, began to consolidate their foothold in Angola. One informant pointed out that, when trying to discuss China-Angola relations, more than once he heard from senior officials at the GoA that "when you are drow-ning, you don't care about who is throwing you the life jacket. "

The oil-backed loan that China provided to Angola in 2004 is often depicted as an alternative that enabled the African country to dismiss reforms supported by the IMF, which, allegedly, would have led to greater governance in Angola, if implemented. With some nuances, this also represented the view of most inter-viewees. Brautigam convincingly argues, however, that the Chinese government did not do anything that Western banks such as BNP Paribas, Commerzbank, Societé Générale, Barclays or Standard Chartered were not doing before or after the Chinese deal. The difference was that Chinese conditions were significantly more favourable to Angola, including smaller interest rates and larger grace and repayment periods. Moreover, Angolans later managed to pay their debts with reve-

---

[1] "No donors' conference for Angola on horizon", 2003, afrol. com/html/News2003/ang006_do-nors. htm. Oct. 6 2014.
[2] Deborah Brautigam, *The dragon's gift: the real story of China in Africa*, Oxford University Press, 2009.
[3] Interview carried out in Luanda in September 2014.

nue from the booming oil industry, increasing their transparency in the meantime. ①

Many civil society organizations disappeared with the retraction of traditional development cooperation in Angola following the end of the civil war. Not only were they
fund-starved, but they also had to cope with rising costs and more strict government
regulations. This trend was particularly evident in Luanda, where significant numbers
of people had moved in search of security during the conflict years. ② Due to especially high costs in Luanda, some NGOs also relocated their headquarters to Benguela. More manageable direct expenses came at significant operational costs and difficulties, since Luanda remained the country's administrative centre.

Additionally, Angolan interviewees often pointed out the regulatory framework
pertaining to associations, including the law of associations – "Lei n. 14/91 de
11 de Maio"③ – as another driver of the reduction in the number of civil society
organizations during the Post-War years. Related obstacles which some sources
mentioned includedthe difficulties in receiving foreign funds, as well as the substantial limitations to institutional autonomy imposed on organizations registered as
"associations of general interest". As a result, most interviewees characterized
Angolan civil society as small, with capacity concentrated in a handful of organizations, and non-independent, with many of the more vocal organizations being
linked to MPLA, the ruling party. However, the same interviewees pointed out
significant progress in the past 3-5 years, due to parallel positive developments in
democratic governance and transparency.

The GoAis increasingly active within the regions, and plays important roles in
regional bodies such as the African Union (AU), the New Partnership for
Africa's Development (NEPAD), and the Southern African Development Community (SADC). The document *Angola* 2025 establishes the country's long-term

---

① Deborah Brautigam, *The dragon's gift: the real story of China in Africa*, pp. 273 – 277.

② Interview carried out in Luanda in September 2014.

③ http://www. rjcplp. org/sections/informacao/anexos/legislacao-angola/outra-legislacao-angola/
lei-das-associacoes/downloadFile/file/Lei_das_Associacoes. pdf? nocache = 1365699390. 02, 10
October 14, 2014.

vision, being carried outin the medium-term through the National Development Plan 2013 – 2017, the first national development plan elaborated under the new Angolan Constitution (2010). The Plan defines the following six broad national objectives: 1) preserving national unity and cohesion; 2) securing the basic principles necessary for development;① 3) improving quality of life; 4) engaging youth in active life; 5) strengthening private sector development; and 6) promoting the competitive insertion of Angola in the international context.

Table 1   Angola's National Development Plan 2013 – 2017: Objectives and priorities for the agricultural and health sectors

Agriculture	
Objective	Priorities
To promote integrated and sustainable development of the agrarian sector, taking as reference the full development of the potential of productive natural resources and the competitiveness of the sector, aiming to ensure food security and domestic supply, as well as to take advantage of opportunities related to the international and regional markets	1. To develop a competitive agriculture, based on the reorientation of family production to the market and development of the business sector
	2. To rehabilitate and expand support infrastructure for agricultural and livestock production
	3. To promote associative and business-like practices under the framework of integrated strategies aimed at developing the ranks of agricultural production
	4. To reach self-sufficiency in basic food products
	5. To develop crops with prospects of profitability and tradition in the territory, aiming to promote increase in producers' income and national exports
	6. To reduce imports and contribute to the diversification of economic activity
	7. To promote irrigation practices for the increase of productivity and competitiveness of agriculture as means to effectively mitigate the effects of climate change
	8. To strengthen the system of agrarian investigation as means for scientific, technological and technical development
	9. To promote job creation and significantly contribute for the increase in income of family agriculture and for the development of the business sector

---

① Defined as the preservation of macroeconomic stability, promotion of national population policy, promotion of an active employment and national human resource valorization policy, increasing productivity and transforming, diversifying and modernizing the country's economic structure.

续表

Health		
Objective	Priorities
	1. To increase life expectancy at birth
	2. To improve the Human Development Index and the Millennium Development Goals
	3. To reduce maternal, child and youth mortality, as well as morbidity and mortality under the national nosology framework
	4. To improve the organization, management and functioning of the National Health System, through directing necessary funds and adopting norms and procedures aimed at improving the efficiency and quality of NHS' response
To sustainably promote Angolan population's sanitary state, guarantee the population's longevity, supporting less favored social groups and contributing to the fight against poverty	5. To improve health care services in the areas of promotion, prevention, treatment and rehabilitation, reinforcing the articulation between primary care and hospital care.
	6. To participate in the transformation of social determinants of health and promote national and international partnerships aimed at the reduction of maternal and child mortality and the programmes of fight against major endemics
	7. To improve health care services in the areas of promotion, prevention, treatment and rehabilitation, reinforcing the articulation between primary care and hospital care.
	8. To adequate human resources to objectives and goals, and adopt new health technologies
	9. To develop the capacity of individuals, families and communities for the promotion and protection of health
	10. To monitor and assess the performance of the sector through SIS and special studies

The National Development Plan 2013 – 2017 reveals a robust, modernist conception of development, with significant emphasis placed on economic growth. However, despite the substantial growth rates of Angola in the last few years, social indicators remain generally low. Life expectancy at birth in Angola (51 years) is below the average for sub-Saharan Africa, and 36. 6 per cent of the population still lives below the national poverty line. ①

---

① The World Bank Data: Angola, http: //data. worldbank. org/country/angola, Mar. 10th 2014.

This context points to both the potential and challenges for development cooperation. While it is safe to assume that development cooperation funds will continue to play a marginal role in the country's Gross National Income-the current total of USD 200 million of net ODA (2011) encompasses less than 0. 3 per centof the country's GNI-it could also play an important role in improving social indicators as well as reducing poverty and inequality.

Among DAC-donors, the United States is by far the largest in terms of gross ODA (totalling approximately $63 million between 2010 and 2011). European Union institutions ($26 million), Japan ($25 million), Korea[1] ($18 million) and Portugal (USD 18 million) are also significant donors. Donor's ODA is primarily directed to Angola's social sectors, particularly education, health and population. [2]

As with civil society organizations and official donors, budgets of United Nations agencies in Angola were significantly reduced over the past decade, which contributed to a redefinition of scope of action in light of the GoA's demands and needs. Initiatives of UN agencies are based on the UN Development Assistance Framework in Angola (UNDAF-Angola). UNDAF-Angola (2009 – 2013) aims to harmonize and integrate the UN system at a country level. The new UN-DAF has not yet come to fruition. The World Bank Group (WBG) has similarly redefined its strategic engagement in Angola. Followinga decade of ill-established relations with the GoA, the International Bank for Reconstruction and Development (IBRD), International Development Association (IDA), International Finance Corporation (IFC) and the Multilateral Investment Guarantee Agency (MIGA) have released in August 2013 a joint country partnership strategy for 2014 – 1016.

As it has appeared in the World Bank's Country Partnership Strategy 2014 – 2016, the general perception among interviewees was that the GoA has been

---

① It is noteworthy that, although a DAC member, South Korea considers itself a South-South provider.
② According to the OECD, population sector activities typically include population/development policies, census work, vital registration, migration data, demographic research/analysis, reproductive health research, as well as other unspecified population activities.

maintaining a "strong record of own-management of its development agenda". As such, both bilateral and multilateral development partners, with few niche-related exceptions, have to play by the GoA's rules if they wish to participate in development policy formulation and implementation. This is in many ways a result of GoA's not so "new-found sense of political and economic leverage", which has been intrinsically linked with the development of the oil and extractive industries in the country. [1]Moreover, the oil and extractive industries have attracted both traditional and emerging powers willing to take part in the expansion of these economic sectors. Even though the GoA is still highly dependent on natural resources and international commodities prices, when compared to other settings, such as Mozambique, oil and natural resources dependency has distinctive effects on how the actors posit themselves within the development field. Hence, while aid dependency in Mozambique has been contributing to limiting national ownership, oil dependency in Angola has enabled the Government to take over its development agenda, despite the negative short and medium-term effects on wealth concentration and democratic consolidation. Furthermore, as discussed below, the growing emerging powers' foothold in Angola has enhanced the GoA's capacity to carry out development policies and programs. [2]

Brazil-Angola Development Relations

Relations between the regions that would, eventually, become Brazil and Angola date back to the 17th century. Both were Portuguese colonies and the second provided slaves to the first. Brazil was the first Western nation to recognize Angola as a sovereign state, in 1975, a fact that is regularly remembered by Angolan sen-

---

[1] Lucy Corkin, Christopher Burke and Martyn Davies. "China's Role in the Development of Africa's Infrastructure", *Documents de travail du SAIS dans African Studies* 04 – 08, 2008.

[2] This contextual analysis does not imply, however, that Angola is achieving better development outcomes than aid dependent countries like Mozambique. Rather, the oil and natural resources dependency very often stresses the negative impacts of focusing on static comparative advantages and the consequent economic concentration around specific sectors.

ior officials in mid and high-level meetings. The Brazilian embassy to Angola was formally created in the same year.

Brazil's national development bank (BNDES) funds several projects carried out by Brazilian companies in Angola, particularly in the infrastructure sector. Banks such as Caixa Econômica Federal, Banco do Brasil and Bradesco are also present in the country. Like China, the Brazilian government also uses commodities and raw material as credit guarantees. ①

Angola is the main target of Brazilian investments in Africa. Currently, Brazil ranks 4th in Angola's top import countries and 19th as Angola's top export destinations. ②For Brazil, trade with Angola represents 0. 4 per cent of its total foreign trade. According to APEX, Brazil has been benefiting significantly from Angola's growth. Bilateral trade between Brazil and Angola grew significantly between 2000 and 2010, reaching an all-time high in 2008 of $4. 21 billion. Brazil's leading export sectors to Angola in 2010 were production and packing of meat and fish (23. 7 per cent) and the manufacturing and refining of sugar (13. 0 per cent). Main Brazilian imports from Angola in the same year were oil and natural gas (73. 7 per cent) and oil-derived products (25. 9 per cent). ③ From 2009 – 2013, Brazilian exports to Angola were reduced by 4. 6 per cent and imports increased by 427. 6 per cent, which indicates a transformation of the trade balance in favour of Angola. ④

Angola is also a relevant destination for Brazilian private companies' investment. In fact, Angola concentrates the highest number of Brazilian Small and medium-sized enterprises in Africa. Furthermore, BNDES has disbursed $2. 8 billion for private investments in Africa since 2007, of which Angola has received

---

① Ana Saggioro Garcia, Karina Kato and Camila FONTES, "A história contada pela caça ou pelo caçador", *Perspectivas do Brasil em Angola e Moçambique. Rio de Janeiro*: *PACS*, 2013.
② Victoria Waldersee, "Chinese and Brazilian Private Firms in Africa", *BRICS Policy Center*, 2015.
③ http://www2. apexbrasil. com. br/exportar-produtos-brasileiros/inteligencia-de-mercado/estudos-sobre-paises/perfil-e-oportunidades-comerciais – angola – 2012. Nov. 15th 2014.
④ http://www. brasilglobalnet. gov. br/ARQUIVOS/IndicadoresEconomicos/INDAngola. pdf. Dec. 18th 2014.

96 per cent. ① Figure 1 presents some of the main projects carried out by Brazilian transnational companies in Angola.

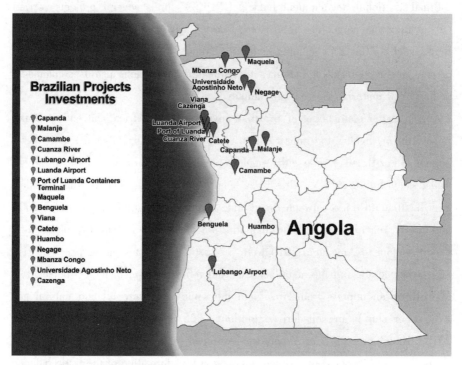

Figure 1 Mapping Brazilian Investments in Angola

Source: Waldersee, 2015.

Table 2 Brazilian Investments in Angola

Company	Present since	Sector	Activities
Petrobras	1980	Energy/Oil & Gas	Exploration of petroleum and biofuels. Partner in 6 petroleum blocks and operator in 4. Since June 2013, Petrobras acts in a joint venture with BTG Pactual Bank (50 per cent each) worth $1.5 million for oil and gas exploration in several African countries, including Angola
Vale	2005	Mining	Joint venture with Genius for mineral excavation (primarily nickel and copper) and research

---

① Victoria Waldersee, "Chinese and Brazilian Private Firms in Africa".

续表

Company	Present since	Sector	Activities
Andrade Guiterrez	2005	Construction/Infrastructure	Works in partnership with Zagope Construções e Engenharia, a Portuguese subsidiary, to gain access EU finances. Has constructed various roads and the express highway between Luanda and Viana to the International Airport of Luanda. Renovation of the International Airport of Lubango. Extended contracts for rehabilitation of Container Terminal in Luanda Port in 2011
Camargo Corrêa	2005	Construction/Infrastructure	Construction of Uige-Maquela road. Partners with Escom, a Portuguese firm, and Gema, an Angolan firm, in constructing a cement factory in Benguela
Odebrecht	1984	Construction/Infrastructure/Agriculture/Energy/Retail/Real State	Holds 25 contracts in the country in real estate, biofuels, minerals, agribusiness, and energy. Highlighted examples: Construction of Capanda Hydroelectric Dam in Malange. Hydroelectric project in Cambambe. Owns 40 per cent of Biocom, Angolan bioenergy firm (ethanol), and 20 per cent of Sonangol. SENAI does training programs for Biocom, for example. Runs Nosso Super supermarket chain in joint venture with Angolan government, with 37 shops in the country. An agribusiness project that may be highlighted is the Farm Pungo a Ndongo (or Pungo Andongo). Odebrecht is responsible for the management of agroindustrial production, construction of factories and capacity building. Embrapa-Africa participated in experiments with varieties of corn, black beans, rice and soy
Engevix	2005	Energy	Works in partnership with Angolan group Genius. Environmental engineering, electricity generation and distribution, involved in Cambambe hydroelectric project in Cuanza Norte
Fidens	2009	Construction/Infrastructure	Construction of runways at Catoca airport, Luanda Sul
Asperbras	2007	Real State/Infrastructure	Involved in Special Economic Zones in Viana, Catete, Huambo, Negage, M'Banza Congo. Construction of real estate and residential condominiums, irrigation systems, and commercial vehicles
Queiroz Galvão	2005	Real State/Infrastructure	Real estate, roadwork construction and renovation
Stefanini	2004	ICTs	Technology and information industries

Source: Vieitas e Aboim (n. d.); Institutional websites.

Brazil's development cooperation with Angola dated back to the civil war period, focused then on professional development and vocational training. Inaugurated in 1998 with support from Brazil's SENAI (*Serviço Nacional de Aprendizagem Industrial*-National Service for Industrial Training), the CFPC (*Centro de Formação Profissional do Cazenga*-Cazenga Center for Professional Training), located on the outskirts of Luanda, trains around 2500 professionals yearly. Today cooperation sectors range from sports to fire fighting. [1] Embrapa and Fiocruz also respectively implement agricultural and health projects in the country.

In 2012, Angola occupied the 5th position in terms of volume of technical cooperation received from Brazil, and it received the least when compared to other developing countries in the Community of Portuguese Language Countries (CPLP). According to documents from ABC, Brazil's bilateral cooperation with Angola would be characterized by low performance, allegedly related with factors such as difficulties in dialogue with Angolan counterparts, low decision-making power of executing agencies, and high rates of turnover among local coordinators. [2]

Brazilian Development Cooperation in the Health Sector of Angola

Brazilian-Angolan development cooperation in the health sector begun in 1996 when ABC organized a mission with health experts to discuss prospective projects in strategic areas already defined within the Community of Portuguese Language Speaking Countries (CPLP). Since then, governments from Portuguese speaking countries in Africa, Angola included, have demanded support for their own national health systems. During the 1990's the emphasis was on training and capacity building. After ten years, CPLP health ministries were able to set up a strategic plan (2009-2012) for the health sector. The strategic plan had as its main objective strengthening national health systems in order to assure universal access

---

[1] http: //luanda. itamaraty. gov. br/pt-br/cooperacao_tecnica_e_cientifica. xml.

[2] Available at a 2013 document from ABC secured at the Embassy of Brazil in Angola.

to quality health services. [1] The plan encompassed seven strategic axes and four structuring networks. Besides the structuring networks established within CPLP's health plan, Brazilian Health Ministry and FIOCRUZ expanded to African countries the Human Milk Bank Network. Table 3 presents CPLP's strategic axes, and a comparison between Angola and Mozambique, both in terms of projects developed with Brazilian agencies in these two countries, and their participation within the structuring networks.

Table 3 CPLP's Strategic Axes and structuring networks and Brazilian SSC projects in Angola and Mozambique

CPLP's strategic axes (SA) and structuring networks (SN)	Brazilian SSC projects within CPLP's Strategic Axes		Engagement in Structuring Networks	
	Angola	Mozambique	Angola	Mozambique
SA1-Training and development of health workforce	X	X		
SA2-information and communication in health		X		
SA3-research in health		X		
SA4-development of the health-industrial complex		X		
SA5-epidemiological surveillance and monitoring of health situation		X		
SA6-emergences and natural disasters				
SA7-promotion and protection of health	X	X		
SN1-national health institutes				X
SN2-national schools of public health			X	X
SN3-health technical schools			X	X
SN4-technical centers of installation and maintenance of equipment				X

Fonte: Paulo Buss, "Brazil: structuring cooperation for health", *The Lancet*, 377: 9779, pp. 1722 – 3, 2011.

According to a document provided by the Embassy of Brazil in Luanda, refer-

---

[1] COMUNIDADE DOS PAÍSES DE LÍNGUA PORTUGUESA (CPLP), "Plano Estratégico de Cooperação em Saúde da CPLP (PECS/CPLP) Reunião Técnica de Avaliação do PECS – 2009 – 2012", *Secretariado Executivo da CPLP Lisboa*, *Relato Resumido da Reunião*, 17 e 18 de Abril de 2013.

ring to July 2013, there were only two bilateral cooperation projects being executed in Angola in the health sector, namely: "Pilot Project in Sickle Cell Disease" and "Capacity Development for Angola's Health System". The "Pilot Project in Sickle Cell Disease" aims to support the reduction of morbidity and mortality from sickle cell disease in Angola by contributing to the consolidation of public policies to fight the disease, and deployment of neonatal laboratory screening and diagnostic imaging. The "Capacity Development for Angola's Health System" intends to strengthen the capacity of training in public health in Angola in the scientific, technological and educational fields, including communication and information. [1] As per the former, informants have reported many difficulties during the implementation period[2] while the later is considered a successful experience enabling 30 Angolan professionals to obtain a Master's in Public Health. [3]

Additionally, it is not unlikely that, as in many other countries, technical cooperation projects under negotiation in Angola were stopped due to the severe budget cuts of both Brazil's Ministry of Foreign Affairs and the Brazilian Cooperation Agency. The following subsection discusses specifically.

Brazil's most well-known health project in Angola is PROFORSA a 3-year triangular cooperation initiative involving Brazil, Japan and Angola aimed at strengthening individual, institutional and systemic capacity in the Angolan health sector (already concluded). Even though PROFORSA has been recognized as the most

---

[1] The actions undertaken by the project aim to support the Ministry of Health in the training of professionals to work in teaching, research and technical cooperation in Angola's Public Health School. The project also targets the structuring of a network of health libraries in Angola, the restructuring of technical health schools, and the strengthening of Angola's National Public Health Institute.

[2] Brazilian health workers report that, despite their full collaboration, recurrent problems related to dialogue with Angolan counterparts have led to several delays and inconsistencies in project execution. The research team was not able to track the actual status of the project, although according to informants the project may have been finalized in 2013 without complete implementation of activities.

[3] The project's first phase faced significant implementing difficulties, including incomplete/delayed activities linked to the Master's in Public Health. Nevertheless, the Master's in Public Health course was deemed very successful and important by the GoA, which, subsequently, manifested its own interest in supporting a second edition of the project.

well known among Brazil's health cooperation projects in Angola, specific knowledge about the project varied significantly across health stakeholders. The origins
of PROFORSA are related to the intersection between University of Campinas'
(UNICAMP) cooperation-ongoing since 2004 in the area of capacity development for Angolan tertiary health workers-and JICA's efforts to develop capacity at
Hospital Josina Machel in Luanda. JICA's project involved both the infrastructural
rehabilitation of the Hospital, and targeted health trainings activities for employees. Japan's bilateral agency engaged Brazilian teams to carry out trainings, including through its Third Country Training Program (JICA-TCTP), due to the
extensive benefits related to improved communication in the Portuguese language.
Both formal and informal assessments of such initiatives highlighted access to and
quality of primary health care as key issues to be addressed in improving Angola's
health system and indicators. These issues manifested themselves in the vast number of unnecessary referrals of patients to central hospitals, which, consequently, overloaded central parts of Angola's health system. This overarching diagnosis
served as basis for the design of PROFORSA.

Table 4　PROFORSA's initial budget

Country	Share (USD/per cent)	
Brazil	970415	24 per cent
Japan	2500000	61 per cent
Angola	630000	15 per cent
Total	4100415	100 per cent

With the formulation of PROFORSA as a triangular cooperation project in 2011,
Fiocruz, through Escola Politécnica em Saúde Joaquim Venâncio (EPSJV/Fio-
cruz) and Escola Nacional de Saúde Pública (ENSP), became the lead institution in the project's primary health component. The project targeted capacity development at four health reference centres[1] in Luanda, chosen due to their stra-

---

[1]　The health centers in Samba, Ingobota, Rangel and Ilha. According to interviews, JICA had also
previously donated equipment to those same health centers.

tegic location and high number of referrals to central hospitals. The tertiary component, led by UNICAMP, particularly through Hospital Sumaré in Brazil, and JICA, focused on improving the organization of hospital services and nursing care, in areas such as neonatal and women's health, at both Hospital Josina Machel and Maternidade Lucrécia Paim.

Given that PROFORSA identified primary care and health management as the main issues to be addressed, a capacity development programme divided in 10 modules, as well as a course for specialization in management of primary health units, was designed and implemented during the three years of the project. During the research team's visit to Luanda, PROFORSA's Angolan counterparts were implementing recommendations that responded to participatory assessments conducted during PROFORSA's execution. Interviews pointed out that these recommendations have been generally well accepted, pertaining to basic structural issues such as the integration of registry and record systems of clinical processes. In fact, the need for integration was reemphasized by 2010 decree issued by Angola's Ministry of Health. However, informants pointed out that the decree hadnot been implemented systematically, due in part to lack of capacity and understanding by health workers who were supposed to implement those changes about the fundamental issues at hand.

In that sense, PROFORSA was a jointly developed structuring project. The project strived to provide capacity and knowledge needed for the implementation of basic public policies across the entire health sector, including through trainings on management and organization of health and clinical process records. Its design was guided by a consensual diagnosis of systemic yet context-specific issues within Angola's health system, which had already been identified and, sometimes, targeted by public policies shown to be largely ineffective.

According to interviewees, the models of management and processes implemented were guided by decrees issued by Angola's Ministry of Health, which were regularly discussed with regulatory authorities such as the National Directorate of Public Health and the Provincial Directorate of Health of Luanda. "On the job" training with key managers was also conducted in Brazil. The informants frequently stressed that all information used as evidence for diagnosis and implementation of solutions was locally collected. Altogether, such practices would guarantee the project's national ownership and context sensitivity.

One of the informants emphasized how Fiocruz had been very apt in promoting understanding of basic issues related to Angola's health system among sectorial stakeholders. The same informant criticized other top-down initiatives, including the ones implemented through private health consultancy firms, some of which were from Brazil, which would impose new management rules, directives and practices without discussion with health workers. The same was said to be true in relation to PROFORSA's tertiary health component. While a management system had recently been implanted in Hospital Josina Machel by a health consultancy, UNICAMP and JICA found it necessary to develop a simpler management system, discussing it with health workers at the Hospital. While interviews pointed to the potentially significant and sustainable impact of gains from PROFORSA, many of the respondents also had a sizable stake in its success. Nonetheless, interviews exposed substantial challenges in the execution of PROFORSA either in terms of implementation, financing or political/cultural context.

Brazilian Development Cooperation in the Agricultural Sector

As discussed above, Angola has been a relevant destination for Brazilian private-investments. In the agricultural sector, the Pungo Andongo farm, with 36000 hectare located in the Malanje Province, is one of the highlights in Embrapa-Africa's engagement in Angola. The farm is an agribusiness project where Odebrecht is the main responsible for the construction and operationalization of maize flour and animal feed plants, capacity building and the management of the agro-industrial production. Under the project, Odebrecht signed, in 2007, an agreement with Embrapa-Africa to give technical support in the experiments with maize, beans, rice and soybeans. Interviews with Angolan civil society evaluates the participation of the Brazilian private sector in Angola's agriculture sector as positive and the Pungo Andongo farm as an example of the development that can come from learning with the Brazilian experience.

In terms of technical cooperation within the field of agriculture, according to a document provided by the Embassy of Brazil in Luanda, referring to July 2013, there was only one bilateral project being executed in Angola, namely, "Support for Rural Professional Training and Social Promotion in Angola". Agricultural projects listed as being under execution on the ABC website also include a course on sustainable production of vegetables, enabled by a triangular partnership ABC, JICA and Embrapa. The project is aimed at bettering the food security of Portuguese-speaking African countries through the improvement of vegetable production enabled by knowledge and capacity development.

Interviews with Brasília and Luanda-based agricultural stakeholders also pointed out to the existence of other co-operation initiatives with the participation of Brazilian public servants in Angola's agricultural and food security sectors. One of them fits in the grey area of Brazilian official co-operation, and it concerns institutional support to Angola's agricultural research and innovation system. Brazilian informants contacted consider it a *sui generis* international cooperation project for Embrapa, possibly because it will depend on the mobilization of consultants for significant part of the activities envisaged. One of the informants pointed out that the project will be mainly funded by the Government of Angola through and Food and Agriculture Organization (FAO) Unilateral Trust Fund (UTF), and will not involve technology transfer or validation assessments.

According to an extract published in the Government of Brazil's official diary, the project's global budget is $ 3071140. Angola's counterparts are Instituto de Investigação Agronómica (IIA) and Instituto de Investigação Veterinária (IIV), both located in Huambo, a province in Angola's Midwest. In the first phase, the project's main objective is to facilitate a programmatic alignment between both institutes, also enabling better articulation between research, diffusion activities and technology transfer. This includes, for example, support to the elaboration of a strategic management and human resources plan for the institutions.

Informants also mentioned the project "Building Capacity in Food Security in

Brazil and Angola", a partnership led by the Centre for Studies in Food Security (CSFS) of the Ryerson University in Canada, and the Reference Centre for Food and Nutrition Security (Centro de Referência em Segurança Alimentar e nutricional-CERESAN) of the Federal Rural University of Rio de Janeiro (UFR-RJ). The Canadian International Development Agency (CIDA) was supporting the 6-year project which started in 2004. Its main goal was to catalyse international collaboration among Portuguese speaking countries in food security education. The project encompasses capacity building activities throughout the design of on-line courses offered, in Portuguese, to students in Brazil and Angola, and also workshops and seminars.

Two other initiatives within the field of food security are noteworthy, though they may not be classified as an official technical cooperation. The first initiative is aimed at supporting the creation of multi-sectorial and participatory mechanisms for the management of food and nutrition security issues in Angola. While not official development cooperation, in the sense that it does not stem from a formal commitment of the Government of Brazil, this cooperation initiative is due to the central role of Brazilian professionals involved with Brazil's National Food and Nutrition Security Council (Conselho Nacional de Segurança Alimentar e Nutricional-CONSEA). Created more than 10 years ago, CONSEA is the main institutional apparatus for articulation of government and civil society in regards to guiding principles and structuring initiatives related to food and nutrition security in Brazil. Though of consultative nature, CONSEA has significant influence over public policies in this field, and is linked directly to the highest levels of the executive branch in Brazil.

According to Brazilian informants involved in the initiative, their participation came as a request from FAO's headquarters in Rome. The initiative was related to FAO's first official strategic objective-help eliminate hunger, food insecurity and malnutrition. FAO hired a Brazilian consultant to conduct the project, together with the involvement of Embrapa and the Ministry of Agrarian Development (MDA) in this process. The main governmental counterpart in Angola is the Ministry of Agriculture, through the Cabinet of Food Security, currently headed by Mr. David Tunga. The NGO Action for Rural Development and Environment (Acção para Desenvolvimento Rural e Ambiente-ADRA), which was one of the Angolan organizations to participate in the already mentioned co-operation project between Brazil, Canada and Angola, is the main responsible for the dialogue with Angolan civil society. This initiative started in 2013, with a meeting in Angola, where the parts involved elaborated the initial work plan. Throughout 2014 some meetings took place, although without the participation of the Brazilian agencies.

While most of the preparatory work appears to have been finalized, the mechanism is yet to be formalized. According to one informant, the process has been deflated in the last few months, and will hardly reach any level of relevance in food security policies in Angola comparable to that of CONSEA in Brazil. Another informant pointed out that one of the problems with the mechanism in process of consolidation is that it is currently linked to the Ministry of Trade (MINCO). [1] According to the same informant, the change of institutional affiliation would have "transformed the vertical process into a horizontal one", alluding to the fact that the mechanism is now less capable of influencing public policies designed by line ministries.

The second initiative is the establishment of the Zero Hunger Africa (Fome Zero África), in 2013, at African Union's meeting in Addis Ababa-Ethiopia. The programme is a partnership between the African Union, the Brazilian Instituto Lula and FAO, under the scope of the Declaration on Renewed Partnership for Unified Approach to End Hunger in Africa. The principal aim of the programme is to eliminate hunger and poverty by 2025 along with five other goals before that, as reducing hunger by 40 per cent by 2017, in countries of full implementation of the programme and reducing, within 10 years, the need of external food aid to provide access to food all year round. Part of the resources for the programme comes from the Africa Solidarity Trust Fund for Food Security (launched in 2012

---

[1] According to local informants, this development was due to the fact that Mrs. Rosa Escórcio Pacavira de Matos, who previously spearheaded the process as Secretary for Social Issues of the President of the Republic, became the head of MINCO.

during the FAO Africa Regional Conference), to which many African countries contribute, including Angola. Interviews showed that the main concern on the implementation of the programme in Angola is the capacity to real adaptation of the Brazilian Zero Hunger programme to the Angolan domestic context.

Final Considerations

Economic and political dependence tend to be associated with higher vulnerability and lower resiliency. While tapping on their respective comparative advantages, as well as the country's natural and developed resource endowments, governments frequently strive to improve the sustainability of their socioeconomic systems by mitigating dependency-related risks. Yet, dependency on different resources, institutions or foreign aid, also has diverse implications to formulation, ownership and implementation of national development policies. In that sense, administrating dependencies is an important aspect of the management of development, particularly for governments of developing countries.

Angola's socioeconomic trajectory since the late 1990s shows GoA's prioritization of the extractive and oil industries over the attraction of foreign aid. Strict political conditionalities attached to North-South cooperation, as well the knowledge of extensive natural resources in Angola, contributed to GoA's decision.

The project's field research indicates that development cooperation is better harmonized, aligned and results-based managed in the Angolan context. The GoA clearly "owns", for better or worse, its development agenda, even though ownership in Angola could be described better as top-down than bottom-up. The increasing engagement of the BRICS countries in Angola has been certainly impacting oil and aid dependency in complex ways.

When attention is devoted to Brazilian health and agricultural cooperation, Brazilian development cooperation is much smaller in volume and number of projects in Angola in term of traditional form's aid; while Brazil's most recent and important projects in both countries are either based on Brazilian domestic experiences, or emphasize a "structuring" dimension. Additionally, issues linked with Brazil's lacking development cooperation system consistently appear. This move must be seen not only in light of Brazil's government more general foreign policy, but also as way to strengthen their particular institutional positions and principles that underlie their work within international and domestic fields. This further points out to the need of advancing bottom-up and top-down research agendas in regards to Brazilian South-South cooperation, analysing not only the role of ABC in Brazil's development cooperation system, but also the stakes that each implementing agent holds while engaging in South-South cooperation.

Domestic Structures and South-South Interests: A Comparison of Brazil's Relations with Malawi and Mozambique

Carolina Milhorance de Castro [*]

The growing foreign public and private sector presence in emerging economies in Africa has captured the attention of scholars and policy makers worldwide. These countries have assumed a proactive role in several multilateral contexts aiming to promote normative and operational changes with the political support of African countries[①] and have turned themselves into significant outward investors in the continent. [②] China has been a notable player in foreign direct investment (FDI), but it is not the sole protagonist. Sustained by a rising political-economic presence, Brazilian actors have been fostering ties with African countries in the past decade. Many recent studies have provided important insights about the interests and strategies of these countries in amplifying their presence, as well as some of the consequences of this engagement in the con-

---

[*] Carolina Milhorance de Castro, POST-Ph. D. of the Center for Sustainable Development, University of Brasilia.

① Monica Hirst, "Emerging Powers and Global Governance" (Universidad San Andrés, Buenos Aires, 2012), http://www.udesa.edu.ar/files/UAHUMANIDADES/EVENTOS/PAPERHIRST 11112.PDF.

② Marin A. Marinov and Svetla T. Marinova, "International Business and Emerging Economies", in *Impacts of Emerging Economies and Firms on International Business*, eds. Marin Marinov and Svetla Marinova, Basingstoke: Palgrave Macmillan, 2012.

tinent. ① A widely diffused notion about the increasing engagement in Africa by countries like Brazil stems from the idea that partners from the emerging world are familiar with similar development challenges and, hence, are well placed to propose solutions formulated on their own experiences. ②

However, not much light has been shed on the role of African domestic institutional framework and political interests in transforming these relations and influencing development trajectories. This article aims to discuss how domestic structures interact with and alter some of the effects of emerging foreign aid and investments. Drawing upon the Brazilian private and public engagement with African countries, particularly Mozambique and Malawi, the study provides an appraisal of the interaction of domestic structures and international institutions in regard to FDI and technical cooperation. It is based on the case study of a development cooperation project in the rural sector-the PAA Africa-supported by Brazil in the two neighbour countries and also the Nacala Corridor Railway infrastructure development project executed by the mining company Vale SA. The article provides insights on the capacity of Brazilian governmental and private actors in fostering territorial and economic integration in the region. The notion of "domestic structures" refers to institutional features of the state, of society, and of state-society relations established separately from specific policies③.

---

① Chris Alden, *China in Africa: Partner, Competitor or Hegemon?* London, New York, Capetown, South Africa, New York: Zed Books, 2007; Jean-Jacques Gabas and Jean-Raphaeël Chaponnieére, *Le Temps de La Chine En Afrique: Enjeux et Réalités Au Sud Du Sahara*, GEMDEV (Group), Hommes et Sociétés, GEMDEV, 2012; Lidia Cabral, *Cooperação Brasil-África Para O Desenvolvimento: Caracterização, Tendências E Desafios*, Texto Cindes 26, Rio de Janeiro: Cindes, 2011.
② Iara Costa Leite, Bianca Suyama, and Melissa Pomeroy, *Africa-Brazil Co-Operation in Social Protection: Drivers, Lessons and Shifts in the Engagement of the Brazilian Ministry of Social Development*, WIDER Working Paper, 2013.
③ Thomas Risse-Kappen, *Bringing Transnational Relations Back In: Non-State Actors, Domestic Structures and International Institutions*, Cambridge, New York, NY, USA: Cambridge University Press, 1995.

Contextualizing Brazilian Relations with Malawi and Mozambique

Brazil-Africa relations strengthened significantly during the LuizInacio Lula da
Silva presidency (2003-2010). Political dialogue, technical cooperation, investment, and trade have been complementary factors to deepening relations during the two mandates of the Lula administration. [1]Technical co-operation has received increasing financial resources. Several new embassies have been established, making Brazil the fifth most represented country on the African continent. Moreover, Lula's administration launched a strategy of reinforcement of economic relations, strengthening not only trade relations, but also the performance
of Brazilian companies. [2]This drive goes hand in hand with Brazilian domestic efforts to fight agains thunger and poverty, supporting the diplomatic focus on social issues and the sharing of experiences. [3]In 2011, Brazil elected President
Dilma Rousseff, a candidate from Lula's party, but some changes in terms of
diplomatic style and foreign policy priorities were observed despite the continuity
of most directives from the previous Government. The new President has faced a
less favourable international economic context, where economic agendas have become a priority in the post-financial crisis years.

As noted earlier, the rise of emerging economies has not only made the countries more attractive for inward FDI but has also provided domestic companies
with the means to become competitive enough in the global outward FDI market. [4]Brazil has consolidated its position in this process through a high degree of

---

① Carolina Milhorance de Castro and Frédéric Goulet, "L'essor Des Coopérations Sud-Sud: Le
Brésil En Afrique et Le Cas Du Secteur Agricole", *Techniques Financières et Développement*, no.
105, December 2011.

② Matthew Flynn, "Between Subimperialism and Globalization A Case Study in the Internationalization of Brazilian Capital," *Latin American Perspectives* 34, no. 6, November 1, 2007: 9 –
27.

③ Costa Leite, Suyama and Pomeroy, *Africa-Brazil Co-Operation in Social Protection*.

④ Marinov and Marinova, "International Business and Emerging Economies."

internationalisation among Brazilian companies. ① The Brazilian Government sought to establish a strategy to make the country more competitive in the export of goods and services, linking political commitment and a long term-vision, as evidenced by the initiative to cancel the debt of several African countries in 2013. ② Mechanisms of public funding of exports have been recognized as major instruments of Brazil's commercial policy towards Africa. The Brazilian Development ment Bank (BNDES) is the most active public institution in the concession of export credits. These mechanisms tend to favour export of goods but also services from large national companies. The implementation of this programme has been followed by the establishment of the Working Group "GTEX Africa" within the Ministry of Development, Industry and Trade (MDIC), in order to discuss and surpass bottlenecks in the consolidation of economic relations. BNDES has established stronger relations with African financial and multilateral institutions aiming to establish co-funding mechanisms as well as facilitating information exchange. In addition, the Bank has gone through important institutional reforms since 2007 in order to create conditions for more flexible support to foreign investment and export.

Portuguese-speaking countries, specifically Mozambique and Angola, are Brazil's main partners in Africa. Linguistic and historical ties are key arguments favouring diplomatic discourse regarding the Continent. Mozambique is Brazil's leading partner in terms of technical cooperation and an important destination in the internationalisation of Brazilian companies, particularly relating to mining and infrastructure construction. Although diplomatic relations date back to post-Independence period, it is only since the 2000s that these ties have deepened. Trade relations between the two countries have also increased significantly. Between 2008 and 2012, trade exchange between Brazil and Mozambique increased

---

① Flynn, "Between Subimperialism and Globalization A Case Study in the Internationalization of Brazilian Capital".

② Alessandra Scangarelli Brites et al. , "Os BRICS na África: a diversificação das parcerias e a contribuição da cooperação sul-sul para o desenvolvimento do continente", *Século XXI* 3, no. 2, January 14, 2013: 95 – 116.

by more than 300% , impulse by the expansion Brazilian imports of more than 1000%. The number of official co-operation staff and international partners in the country, note scholars, attests to the importance of Mozambique in Brazil's co-operation efforts which focus on agriculture, education and health. ① Further, the ties are now stronger and deeper in the sense that the co-operation efforts have moved from one-off training initiatives towards programmes with longer tenures and "structural" objectives.

Neighbouring countries in the Continent, such as Malawi, have established more recent relations with Brazil, in the context of Lula's approximation with Africa. The Brazilian Embassy in Malawi was inaugurated in June 2013, respecting the commitment made during the visit of former President of Malawi, Bingu wa Mutharika to Brazil, in 2009, and the increase of Brazilian interest in the region. Bilateral relations comprise mutual interest in exploring potential in the bio-fuels sector, experience-sharing of policies to fight hunger, and the private investments of Vale SA (Interview, May 2014). The company is rehabilitating the railway that connects mining investments in Tete, Mozambique, to the Nacala port on the Indian Ocean, through Malawian territory. The former Malawian Minister of Foreign Affairs, Ephraim Chiume, has also mentioned the country's interest in being included in on-going co-operation projects in Mozambique such as ProSavana, a trilateral initiative between Japan-Brazil-Mozambique to develop commercial agriculture in the Nacala Corridor, North of Mozambique. Other initiatives, which present trilateral co-operation opportunities such as the programme to support the Cotton sector in Malawi and Mozambique, went through a prospecting phase even before the establishment of the Brazilian Embassy in the country. ②

Despite being neighbours and sharing extensive socio-economic ties the relationship between Mozambique and Malawi has been historically characterized by ani-

---

① Sérgio Chichava et al. , "Brazil and China in Mozambican Agriculture: Emerging Insights from the Field", *Ids Bulletin* 44, no. 4 (2013): 101 – 15. Ibid.

② SERE/MRE, "Encontro com o Ministro de Negócios Estrangeiros do Malaui. Entrega de cópias figuradas. Relato", Circular Telegráfica, April 7, 2013, Itamaraty.

mosity, even in the face of recent efforts to increase bilateral co-operation, as synthetized by Lalbahadur. ① She points out that the origins of this difficult relations are often associated with Malawi's support for the opposition guerrilla movement during the Mozambican civil war of the late 1970s and early 1980s. Malawi-Mozambique's Nacala railway was already subject of regional debate in the 1960s, when South African Apartheid government provided financial assistance to Malawi in the form of "soft loans" for the construction of the railway. In this context, the Malawian government has opposed Frelimo's combat to independence of Portuguese colonization and it remained suspicious of Mozambican leaders afterwards.

However, the president Banda's pragmatic approach to regional integration helped lead to the rapprochement between the two countries during the 1970s. ② The impact of the Mozambican Civil War on Malawi from Renamo's disruption of the country's transport corridors were very deep. ③ The Nacala railway remained open, however, its poor condition placed heavy limitations of traffic. Despite efforts to normalise relations after their democratization in the 1990s, the relationship has remained cold. In the 2000s, the two countries reached a number of key agreements aimed at enhancing trade and infrastructure such as theBilateral Preferential Trade Agreement (2005), a memorandum of understanding (MoU) on the development of the Shire-Zambezi Waterway (2007), and another MoU on the Nacala Development Corridor (2010).

According to Lalbahadur, both countries face pressing infrastructural challenges and integrated power and transport projects are seen by investors and development agencies as steps to address these challenges. ④ Furthermore, access to the sea is critical to Malawi and recent infrastructure projects have contributed to in-

① Aditi Lalbahadur, *Mozambique and Malawi: Recalibrating a Difficult Relationship*, Policy Briefing, SAIIA Policy Briefings, Johannesburg: South African Institute of International Affairs, June 2013.
② David Robinson, "Renamo, Malawi and the Struggle to Succeed Banda", *Eras*, no. 11, November 2009.
③ David Robinson, "Renamo, Malawi and the Struggle to Succeed Banda", *Eras*, no. 11, November 2009.
④ Lalbahadur, *Mozambique and Malawi: Recalibrating a Difficult Relationship*.

crease interdependency between the two countries. A number of border and diplomatic incidents, including an impoundment of a barge destined for the inaugura-
tion of the Nsanje Port in Malawi by the Mozambican authorities, served to deteriorate the fragile reconciliatory efforts. The port was constructed as part of the
Shire-Zambezi Waterway Project, to allow navigation of the Shire-Zambezi River
as far as the Indian Ocean. Since 2012, Malawi's former President, Joyce Banda, has given a positive push to the relationship, signalling the importance given
to the strategic nature of bilateral relations with Mozambique and opening up possibilities for collaboration in areas where both countries face developmental challenges.

Sharing Rural Public Policies: Building Context-Based Initiatives

Brazilian technical co-operation has relied on the narrative that partners from the
emerging world have faced similar development challenges and are consequently
well placed to propose solutions formulated on their own experiences. [1] The
country's development trajectory led to a decrease in poverty and inequality levels, which has drawn the world's attention, particularly during the onset of the
international food and economic crisis in 2007-2008. Having successfully naviga-
ted the crisis, Brazil found itself endowed with diplomatic, technological and
policy credentials to become a prominent actor for policy dialogue and co-operation on agriculture and food security. [2]The food crisis from the perspective of population growth has contributed to the re-emergence of agriculture and food security
at the top of international agenda. Brazilian co-operation policy for SSA in the rural sector was discussed with African leaders during the 2010 Brazil-Africa Dialogue on Food Security, the Fight against Hunger and Rural Development (Brasilia, May 2010). The Zero Hunger Strategy is one of the most internationally

---

[1]   ABC/MRE, *Manual de Gestão Da Cooperação Técnica Sul-Sul*, Versão externa, Brasília:
      Agência Brasileira de Cooperação/Ministério das Relações Exteriores, 2013; Costa Leite, Suya-
      ma, and Pomeroy, *Africa-Brazil Co-Operation in Social Protection*.
[2]   F. Pierri, "How Brazil's Agrarian Dynamics Shape Development Cooperation in Africa", 2013.

recognized Brazilian experiences, and both international and domestic drives have led to the intent of sharing this framework with Sub-Saharan countries. Inspired by the Brazilian experience of the Food Purchase Programme (*Programa Aquisição de Alimentos*-PAA), the PAA Africa became the main channel of this co-operation initiative. [1] The programmes a joint initiative by the Brazilian government, the Food and Agriculture Organisation of the United Nations (FAO), the World Food Programme (WFP), to "promote food and nutrition security and income generation for farmers and vulnerable communities in African countries." [2] Other partner such as the UK Department for International Development (DFID) support knowledge-sharing activities.

The Brazilian PAA showcases a new agricultural policy model for boosting incomes of smallholders while supporting the food-insecure population. Implemented with resources from the Ministry of Social Development (MDS) and the Ministry of Agrarian Development (MDA), in partnership with the National Food Supply Company (CONAB), states, and municipalities, the programme created a new market for the commercialization of family farm products which are purchased for distribution to social assistance networks, for the establishment of public stocks and price regulation as well as institutional procurement for food-based safety net programmes without the need for a public bidding process. Although there is a lack of research on the concrete results national programmes have achieved and their impacts on people's lives, the PAA has demonstrated the creation of a state-driven structured demand for small farms. [3] The National School Feeding Programme (PNAE) is another major source of structured demand, considering that 30 per cent of these resources must be used to purchase food from family farmers. [4]

---

[1] Costa Leite, Suyama and Pomeroy, *Africa-Brazil Co-Operation in Social Protection*.

[2] PAA Africa, "PAA Africa: Purchase from Africans for Africa", PAA Africa Website, 2013.

[3] Fabio Veras et al. , *Structured Demand and Smallholder Farmers in Brazil: The Case of PAA and PNAE*, IPC Technical Paper, Brasília: International Policy Centre for Inclusive Growth (IPC-IG) /WFP Centre of Excellence Against Hunge, October 2013.

[4] Jose Graziano da Silva et al. , *The Fome Zero (Zero Hunger) Program: The Brazilian Experience*, Brasília: Ministry of Agrarian Development, 2011.

PAA-Africa Programme comprises five small-scale projects in Ethiopia, Malawi, Mozambique, Niger, and Senegal. The projects combine emergency actions for agricultural recovery and food assistance with development strategies to link smallholder farmers with structured demand. [1] The Programme aims at contributing to the dialogue on advocacy and government policy on longer transition strategy toward public procurement for food assistance. In Mozambique, the pilot project targets three districts in Tete Province (Angonia, CahoraBassa and Changara) and includes distribution of agricultural inputs and trainingon production systems and post-harvest handling. Given the different local procurement projects underway in the country, PAA Africa has sought to support school feeding national programme (PRONAE) and provide the opportunity to implement a model of local procurement that can provide lessons learned to the implementation nationwide. Further efforts will be followed in the second phase in order to put in place diversification of production including horticulture. Moreover, local procurement done by district authorities will be tested in order to complement WFP direct procurement and strengthen government capacities of procurement.

A number of challenges have been identified during the pilot's first phase. A five-month participant-observation research within the FAO Mozambique office, field work in the implementation zones of Tete, individual interviews, and debate within the PAA's working group contributed to attest some of the information presented here. Productive zones in Tete province are localized and remote from the more food insecure districts (around 400 kilometers). This implies high logistical costs to deliver maize to schools and raises the question of the capacity of local structures in continuing the initiative once the pilot project will be closed. Other institutional bottlenecks exist, particularly concerning the Mozambican framework of procurement. It demands a bureaucratic process for legalizing, attributing fiscal register, and creating a bank account to farmers' organizations which creates a stumbling block given the high rate of illiteracy and low resources condition among target farmers.

---

[1] PAA Africa, "PAA Africa: Purchase from Africans for Africa".

Moreover, the required bidding process does not enable smallholder farmers' participation and competition with medium/big farmers and local merchants. In addition, the insufficient dialogue with other social policies highlights the challenge for implementing an intersectoral policy. However, in Mozambique the project has counted on a participative process of inception and collaboration with civil society organizations continues to deepen in creating a policy dialogue with national institutions and contributing to advance the local procurement concept. This collaboration also stems from the relationship Mozambican organizations built with Brazilian organizations that participated in the construction of PAA in Brazil and also benefited from the programme and agree on PAA's role in promoting family farming sector.

Pierri (2013) recognizes that Brazil's family farming policy framework has been based on a state-led process for the delivery of the specific public policies and regulation. Thus, factors such as financial capacity, the role of civil society and the (dis) similarities between African peasants and Brazilian family farmers have to be taken into account in the sharing of experiences. Agricultural and food security strategies depend on strong institutionalisation processes and hinge on the fiscal capacity to pursue a trajectory that requires financial sustainability. [1] Likewise, cash transfer programmes are perceived as costly and as demanding a complex delivery structure. [2] Even in Brazil, the Programme still faces several challenges incorporating the most vulnerable producers and addressing operational obstacles such as transportation, payment mechanisms and up-scaling, [3] apart from the risks of political misuse.

In this context, understanding the political and economic dynamics of owner-

---

[1] Pierri, "How Brazil's Agrarian Dynamics Shape Development Cooperation in Africa".

[2] Costa Leite, Suyama and Pomeroy, *Africa-Brazil Co-Operation in Social Protection*.

[3] Maya Takagi, "Food and Nutrition Security and Cash Transfer Programs", in *The Fome Zero (Zero Hunger) Program: The Brazilian Experience*, by Jose Graziano da Silva et al., Brasília: Ministry of Agrarian Development, 2011; Ryan Nehring and Ben McKay, *Scaling up Local Development Initiatives: Brazil's Food Acquisition Programme*, Working Paper, International Policy Centre for Inclusive Growth, 2013.

ship in international projects is crucial, as stated by Castel-Branco. [1] According
to the author, ownership is the result of the dynamics of competition and influence on options, priorities, contents, and opportunities of development. Social
and economic development implies a continuous dispute for ownership-or for the
influence on development dynamics, institutions and economic and social. Consequently, the ownership in itself means less than social and political interactions
under which the power of influence on political options is built. Perceptions of the
concept of ownership differ among social actors according to each one's agenda
and interests; on social, economic and political contexts; and on the history of
the interactions of those social agents. For instance, the practice of ownership re-
nunciation has been recurrent in recipient countries, making it possible to attrib-
ute the responsibility of the high social costs of reforms to donors.

In the case of institutional markets and school feeding programmes, the level of
State-led investments required is very high as well as in social protection policies.
This could discourage Government from undertaking this kind of initiative. On the
other hand, Mozambican Government give priority to public investments for areas
with high agricultural potential, including promotion of active private sector in
both production and service provision, with focus on the large-scale use of animal
traction, adoption of technical packages, promotion of mechanisation, processing and marketing. [2]

Conversely, the pilot project in Malawi relies on strong support from Government authorities. It intends to expand the implementation of Home-Grown School
Feeding approach and is being implemented in the areas of Mangochi and Pha-
lombe, in Southern Malawi. The procurement is undertaken directly by the
Schools. The farmers' organizations identified to provide products are located with-

---

[1] Carlos Nuno Castel-Branco, *Aid Dependency and Development: A Question of Ownership? A Criti-cal View*, Working Paper, Colecção de Workin G Papers Do IESE, Maputo: IESE, February 2008.

[2] Ministry of Agriculture, *Strategic Plan for Agriculture Development-PEDSA* 2010-2019, Republic of Mozambique, 2010, http://www.safi-research.org/wp-content/uploads/2015/10/2010_PEDSA_FI-NAL-English_22_Nov.pdf.

in the school's catchment area (30 kilometers average), which reduces the distances for transport of food and subsequent logistical costs. ① It is worth noting that Malawi is a densely populated country with an estimated 15 million people, wherein 85 per cent of the population lives in rural areas and derives its livelihood from agriculture. In contrast with Mozambique, the majority of the population and production is concentrated in central and southern regions, where the project is localized. ②Since 2010, the Malawian Government has been allocating funds to a number of public policies that support school feeding programmes.

Some of the factors that facilitated smooth PAA implementation in Malawi include the concentration of productive and consumer zones; the national interest in Home-Grown School Feeding initiatives already in place which assured the leadership of an institution with budget and mandate; and the simplification of procurement rules in order to adequate it to smallholder participation and procurement directly by the schools. Furthermore, some decentralisation policy initiatives in the target districts contributed to quick mobilisation of public and non-governmental actors on the field to find adaptable implementation solutions. However, certain barriers to sustained success of the programme exist. For example, Malawi's policy of chemical fertilizers and hybrid seeds restrict possibilities to effectively discuss sustainable agricultural systems like those in Mozambique.

A weakness in extension services, particularly in terms of mobility, is a limiting factor in increasing production and productivity in Malawi as well as Mozambique. Likewise, both face the constraint of aid dependency and the challenge posed by social protection policies in this kind of context. But Mozambique presents some strategic advantages regarding its partners such as its geographic localization, the size of its territory and its mineral resources. Such factors influence a country's position in negotiations with the donor community.

School feeding programmes in Malawi started in 1999. The WFP has provided

① PAA Africa, "PAA Africa: Purchase from Africans for Africa".

② Jacob Ricker-Gilbert, Charles Jumbe and Jordan Chamberlin, "How Does Population Density Influence Agricultural Intensification and Productivity? Evidence from Malawi", *Food Policy* 48, October 2014: 114 – 28.

funds to support 24 schools. In 2007 the Cabinet decided to scale up this programme and determined that a strategy should be built in order to assure this expansion. On the Brazilian side, the Centre of Excellence against Hunger had an important role in providing information about the Brazilian experience (Interviews, May 2014). School feeding programmes were a priority on the agenda during official visit of former Malawian President to Brazil. Discussions contributed to the objective of producing a proposal of national public policy for a sustainable school feeding programme. The formulation of national plans and policies is essential to raise and attract funds from donors and even Government budget. The draft proposal was supposed to be summited to Cabinet after the 2014 Presidential Elections (Interview, May 2014). Besides PAA Africa, the country has been implementing other pilot programmes based on three different models for procurement, promotion of school gardens, and access to markets.

Additionally, an autonomous inter-sectorial department chaired by the Minister of Education is leading the process in the country and has committed budget and mandate to scale up school health and nutrition in Malawi. But in terms of implementation of initiatives, the authority rests with the District level while local staff from different ministries is directly involved. These efforts appear smoother in Malawi than Mozambique as the needs in terms of scale of production are much lower. The zones chosen for the implementation of the pilot project comprise a larger number of legalized and reinforced farmers associations and enough production for school markets.

PAA in Malawi found the procurement structure already initiated. Because of the programme of support to schools they were already empowered in procuring school material and PAA decided to take advantage of the same structure to build capacity in procuring food items. The local food procurement directly from schools is an innovative concept in the country. The process has been simplified and is based on the direct purchase and negotiation as the amounts are not considerable and accountability rests with of the District Council. Despite such enabling factors, marketing in Malawi is challenging in terms of produced amounts and price instability. The impact a broader project of institutional markets would have in these dynamics would require a deeper analysis.

Risse-Kappen[1] has looked the interaction between states and transnational relations in various issue-areas and concluded that domestic structures and international institutions mediate the influence of networks among non-state actors in international society. Domestic structures are likely to determine both the availability of channels for transnational actors into the political systems and the requirements for winning coalitions to change policies. Drawing upon this literature, we argue that domestic structures mediate, filter and refract the efforts by international actors, in this case Brazilian public and private alliances, to influence policies in the various issue-areas. Their ability to influence policy changes depends on the domestic coalition-building processes and on the built institutional structure, as observed in the case of implementation of local procurement for school feeding initiatives in Malawi and in Mozambique. The same countries will be taken as an example to show that besides domestic coalition-building processes, regulatory framework and dialogue mechanisms may also alter the impacts of foreign investments and influence policy change.

Infrastructure Investments: Regional Integration Opportunities and Land Challenges

The geographic diversification of Brazilian exports of goods and services towards Africa is highly dependent on public support, even for large companies. Brazilian investments in the continent are concentrated on infrastructure construction and engineering, energy and mining, which makes economic flows sensitive to intergovernmental decisions. [2] The visibility of Brazilian investments in Mozambique rose in the 2000s and Vale SA has played an important role in this increment. In Mozambique, the company has invested in mineral research, operation of the Moatize Coal Mine and the Sena Corridor while the Moatize Mine II and Nacala

---

① Risse-Kappen, *Bringing Transnational Relations Back In*.

② World Bank and IPEA, *Ponte Sobre O Atlântico: Brasil E Africa Subsaariana-Parceria Sul-Sul Para O Crescimento*, Brasilia, 2011.

Corridor projects are currently underway.

This presence has been widely discussed in media, civil society fora and academia, particularly with respect to the resettlements of population in the coal mine sites in Moatize I. ① The railway line along which coal will be transported by Vale in the Nacala Corridor is being restored and expanded for an investment of $4. 4 billion and it passes through Mozambique and Malawi. ② The 912 kilometer line will lead to new maritime terminal in Nacala-à-Velha, where a deep-water sea port is being built. The project will acquire transport capacity of 18 million metric tons of coal per year.

In Malawi, the company is building 137 kilometers of the Nacala railway. Its subsidiary Vale Logistic Ltd entered in 2011 into a concession agreement with the Republic of Malawi for the Chicwawa-Nkaya Junction railroad. The railroads existing in Mozambique and Malawi are owned by Corredor de Desenvolvimento do Norte (CDN) and the Central East African Railway Company (CEAR), respectively, each a 51 per cent owned subsidiary of sociedad de Desenvolvimento Corredor Nacala (SCDN). The railroad would play an important role in the transport of copper produced at the Lubambe copper mine in the Zambian copper belt, a project started in 2012 through a joint venture with TEAL Exploration & Mining Inc.

The Mozambican Government's expectationisthat, in addition to loads, the trains canalsocarry passengers. On the Malawian side, the expectation is that the railroad represents an alternative for the import and export of goods and passengers' transport taking into account the landlocked nature of the country. These expectations have not yet shown signs of accomplishment or concrete discussions. It is worth noting that in a context of decrease of international prices of mineral commodities, Vale SA has found itself obliged to sell part of the assets of its investments in the Nacala Corridor. The company has recently announced the

---

① Chichava et al. , "Brazil and China in Mozambican Agriculture". Ibid.

② VALE, "Vale Highlights Its Projects in Mozambique at an Event in Africa", *VALE*, February 17, 2014, http: //www. vale. com/mozambique/EN/aboutvale/news/Pages/vale-destaca-projetos-em-mocambique-em-feira-na-africa. aspx.

participation of the Japanese trading, Mitsui, in the investments of the complex mine-railway.

An international network of Brazilian, Canadian, Chilean, and Mozambican NGOs has given rise to International Articulation of those Affected by Vale, criticizing the company's corporate sustainability policy. In sequence to the realm of critiques around Vale investments in Mozambique, as well as the accused inability of the extractive sector in the country to produce social development, particularly in rural areas, ① the Government has developed a new mining code proposal. This includes introducing national preference for procurement, subjecting transfers of mining rights and share capital participation to Mozambican Law and Governmental approval.

In addition, a new Resettlement Regulation enacted in 2012 contains, according to Vale Annual Report 2012, "stricter requirement that may result in increased costs and delays in the implementation of (the company's) projects"②. The decrease of fiscal incentives to the mining companies in Mozambique has meant increase of production costs, almost making the investments unfeasible in a context of low international prices of mineral commodities. Vale's strategy of controlling logistical infrastructure in the Nacala Corridor has maintained the company's interest in the investments, even though part of the assets has been negotiated. Other companies such as Rio Tinto have decided to sell at a price that is lower than the current market price their project in Tete to an Indian group (DW Notícias, 2014).

While Vale SA has made efforts to change its approach to resettlement in the Nacala corridor work, following the criticism it faced for the Moatize project, it would be important to observe the company's operations in the next steps because of persistent issues regarding local communities. Recent steps in public awareness and legal frame-

① João Mosca and Tomas Selemane, "Mega-Projectos No Meio Rural, Desenvolvimento Do Territorio E Pobreza", in *Desafios Para Moçambique* 2012, Maputo: IESE, 2012, 231 – 55, http: //www. iese. ac. mz/lib/publication/livros/des2012/IESE_Des2012_12. MegRur. pdf. Ibid.
② VALE, *Delivering Value through Capital Efficiency: Annual Report* 2012 (VALE SA, 2013), 74. Ibid.

works in Mozambique, particularly concerning land laws, would have an influence in this aspect. In Mozambique, land issues have acquired political interest, especially following the boom of the extractive sector in recent years and the debate of how to adequate communities' land rights and private investments.

The Mozambican Land Law (Law 19/97) was passed by Parliament in July 1997, followed by the Land Law Regulations for rural areas (Decree 66/98). This dual objectives progressive land law aims at supporting rural community land-rights and encouraging private investment. The legal framework provides local communities with some degree of tenure security over their land, however the majority of peasants and rural residents is still unaware of their rights or lack financial and technical support to demarcate and register land rights. According to Mosca,[1] there has not been significant changes in terms of distribution of cultivated land since the colonial period. In this context, civil society organizations (CSO) have since the approval of Land Law specialised in diffusing peasants' rights and empowering communities to exercise these rights.

The railway construction throughout the Nacala corridor should use a different approach for resettlement compared to the Moatize mine. A lower number of families will be displaced per square kilometers operations are executed on a linear axis. There has been consultations to address the type of compensation the communities would chose, and most have opted for financial compensation. Some of the conflicts of interest raised between the companies and communities are at first addressed by local leaders who often receive subsidies from the companies to deal with communities' expectations. Local traditional leadership is very strong in most of the zones affected by the development of the railway. Besides, in cases where farmers did not have the land title (DUAT) they received the agreed financial compensation, pertaining to what is "above" the land: the houses and facilities, some fruit trees, and not the whole property. This remuneration pattern has been observed in Nacala-à-Velha district, where the Vale railway construction is

---

[1] João Mosca, *Políticas Agrarias de (em) Moçambique* (1975-2009), 1ª ed., Lisboa: Maputo: Escolar, 2010.

underway. However, in the absence of DUATs, this approach is valid according to national legislation.

In Malawi, the land issue does not attain the same degree of awareness. Vale SA has just started resettlements in the country and the process is expected to be led by the Government. The Malawi land tenure system is based on the Land Act (1967), adopted during the colonial period and inspired by the English framework. This Act divided land into three statutory categories namely customary, private, and public. The first does not recognize freehold ownership rights but user rights which are not inalienable. Private land is exclusively owned, held and occupied by an individual or institution. And public land is acquired by government for public use. Therefore, independence did not lead to significant changes in the institutional arrangements governing land access and rights nor the inherent objectives of land governance.

In this context, private ownership and statutory security represent desired trajectory and customary land is perceived as a reserve from which private and public land ownership should be created. ① But only few investors can bear the high land acquisition and processing costs and it is the duty of the local communities to prove that land targeted for lease is not productively utilized or gathered under community consultations. Local chiefs are often divided over supporting or opposing land lease, resulting in highly polarized views about whether customary land can be deemed occupied or vacant. ② Matrilineal descent and devolution of land rights are the traditional norms for the majority of the population in Malawi, particularly in the central and southern regions, whereas the formal landholding system is modelled on patrilineal English legislation. Land-tenure relations finish by being governed by local customs for most Malawians, especially smallholders. ③

---

① Blessings Chinsinga, "Seeds and Subsidies: The Political Economy of Input Programmes in Malawi", *IDS Bulletin* 42, no. 4 (2011): 59 – 68. Ibid.
② Chinsinga, "Seeds and Subsidies."
③ Erling Berge et al., "Lineage and Land Reforms in Malawi: Do Matrilineal and Patrilineal Landholding Systems Represent a Problem for Land Reforms in Malawi?", *Land Use Policy* 41, November 2014: 61 – 69.

Despite installation challenges in the country, Vale SA envisions a number of differences regarding Mozambique and a strong participation of the Government, taking into account the expectations of increasing investments in the country and of creating an alternative route to the Indian Ocean. Land availability remains an important issue, particularly in the southern region where population density in rural areas is very high. Population density affects agricultural intensification and household through supply and demand forces such as increased information flow, development of markets and institutions, and reductions in transaction costs. But studies demonstrate that in Malawi areas of high rural population density are associated with reduction in farm sizes, lower real agricultural wage rates, and higher real maize prices, as well as intensification of fertilizer use per hectare. [1] So although the number of families to be resettled is relatively low, sustainability of communities should be taken into account in the progression of operations.

Another issue of local importance to be addressed is the impact of some of these security-led displacements on the commercialization of local products along the train line. This is an important source of resources to rural communities and is not yet being fully addressed in the feasibility projects. Malawi Government has not regulated any resettlement plan. There are no clear guidelines and legislation concerning the sector as it does in Mozambique which ultimately hampers the negotiation process. Local Governments end up having more autonomy in conducting the resettlement activities, together with local leaders. The access the company has to district administrations and communities is considered by the company's staff more open in Malawi than in Mozambique. For other aspects, the company can consult a full time focal point in the Ministry of Mining, which attests the interest of rapidly accomplishing the project. The government is hoping to benefit greatly from a reduction in transportation costs, but the possibility of agreeing with Malawi Government the use of the railway to transport country's production has not yet been subject of discussion with the company.

---

[1] Ricker-Gilbert, Jumbe, and Chamberlin, "How Does Population Density Influence Agricultural Intensification and Productivity?".

The Vale SA logistical project fulfils the regional parts of physical integration, which are underway through other projects such as the Nacala Corridor Development Project led by the World Bank and other partners. The objectives are to contribute to improving road transportation and trade facilitation along the Nacala Road Corridor from Zambia to Mozambique and improving the transport services in these countries. Long distance to the sea ports escalate transportation costs in Malawi and is a major impediment to regional and international trade. Similarly in Mozambique, the AfDB, JICA, and Korea Exim Bank are co-financing sections of the road from Nampula to Lichinga through Chiponde, the border between Malawi and Mozambique. When questioned if these initiatives underpin an expansion of the trilateral (Japan-Brazil-Mozambique) agricultural programme in Nacala corridor, ProSavana, agencies' staffs affirm that efforts of integration have been made only in transport infrastructure.

National organizations in Malawi which are internationally networked have experience in advocacy work regarding mining projects. For instance, Mzembe and Meaton[1] suggested that corporate social responsibility (CSR) agenda pursued by Paladin Africa, a subsidiary of an Australian multinational mining company operating the first uranium mine in Malawi, has been strongly influenced by externally generated pressures such as CSOs and community expectations. For investors, such cases in Malawi showcase the country's "juridical insecurity". In Malawi as well as in Mozambique, the mining communities, neighbours as well as some CSOs expect such international companies to perform some roles of the national government. However, although national legal frameworks are complex and not always take into fully account communities land rights and wellbeing, these multinational companies should address these issues without creating prejudice for communities and taking the role of state.

Finally, the Nacala Corridor railway is being suggested by Brazilian diplomacy

---

① Andrew Ngawenja Mzembe and Julia Meaton, "Driving Corporate Social Responsibility in the Malawian Mining Industry: A Stakeholder Perspective: Driving CSR in the Malawian Mining Industry: A Stakeholder Perspective", *Corporate Social Responsibility and Environmental Management* 21, no. 4。 July 2014: 189 – 201.

as a tool of reinforcing regional integration. Brazil is involved in other trilateral a-
greements connecting both countries. The first is a MoU, currently under final-
ization, aimed at supporting the establishment of economic, trade and investment projects between Malawi and Mozambique in the areas of mining, transport, logistics, energy, agriculture and forestry. It is an umbrella cooperation
arrangement and not a Free Trade Area. According to Malawian officials, this a-
greement does not address specific needs of the country and the officials are unable to foresee gains from the agreement. Apart from the areas noted earlier in the
text, Malawi has significant interest in issues related to agriculture development
and ethanol regulation. For mining, research has been conducted but no justifia-
ble sites of investments have been found according to sector's officials.

Therefore, bilateral agreements with Brazil are allocated priority status in these
two countries. Currently there is a Brazil-Mozambique MoU under negotiation, re-
presenting an agreement proposed by the Brazilian Government in the fields of cooperation and investments. It has been negotiated by MDIC and aims at facilitating
investments through, for instance, the simplification of mobility of business men
and capital transfers. It is important to notethat mobility agreements often benefit
informal Mozambican merchants travelling to Brazil for goods.

Final Considerations

The ties emerging economies have been fostering with African countries for the
past decade has stimulated dynamic debate in academia, political set-ups and the
media about the motivations, approaches and consequences of these recent relations. Brazil has played a key role in this international move, particularly towards
countries such as Mozambique. But since the Lula Administration, governmental
and private efforts have diversified, extending to partners beyond Portuguese-
speaking countries or those with historical ties such as Malawi. However, the role
played by domestic structures has been identified as an important complementary
agenda of research. With the aim of contributing preliminary results to this debate, this paper has sought to shed light on the differences in domestic structures

found by similar Brazilian interventions and their responses following the interaction with public and private actors. Two bordering countries have been chosen, in which Brazil held some similar and integrated projects despite an unlike history of relations.

The analysed projects and agreements have been proposed by the same Brazilian actors in both countries and the paper has evaluated the diversity of responses and concern of appropriation. The PAA Africa as a pilot project aimed to share the Brazilian experience of fighting hunger and reinforcing the family farming sector. Mozambique and Malawi defined school feeding as the priority for the institutional markets agenda. But the institutional conditions and the policy line each one presented in implementing the pilot and amplifying the discussion towards the consolidation of public policies has been different. Some agricultural, political and institutional conditions have facilitated the implementation of PAA Africa in Malawi, as well as the higher flexibility of procurement process. These conditions can be combined with the political interest in school feeding attested to by the District authorities and the strong involvement of communities and allocation of Government budget to the initiatives.

In Mozambique, the enterprise took a different path, starting with the elaboration of a national programme which is also testing pilot models. Agricultural policies intend to increasingly connect the farmers to the market and promote the private sector, but the efforts of preparing these farmers to deal with markets and the profile of social protection policy demand high costs and human resources which have not been made available by Mozambican government. On the other hand, in Mozambique the project has counted on a participative process of inception and collaboration with CSO which stems from the relationship Mozambican organizations built with Brazilian organizations and is contributing to advance the institutional markets initiatives in the country.

Specific to Vale SA, the Nacala Corridor railway project is promising for regional integration efforts, and transport of passengers and goods. Malawi is one of the most affected and interested countries given its landlocked nature and difficult historical relations with its neighbours. Challenges in land governance and use should be taken into serious account. Mozambique has been facing challenges with mega projects for many years now and institutional conditions have been gradually built to deal with these investments. Moreover, social control mechanisms have been created in the country in response to efforts made by civil society articulations.

In the case of Malawi, land rights have not been actualized since the colonial period and communities' rights are not very clear. The possibility and conditions of using the railway for national interests have not yet been addressed. Brazil is also increasing its engagements through other triangular initiatives. However, the integrated engagement contradict the partners' preference for leading the relations bilaterally, raising the question of full implementation of such agreements. Therefore, despite some analogous political strategies or asymmetric position of African countries regarding Brazilian capital, the role of African domestic structures, which includes regulatory framework, institutional structure, social dynamics and political interests, should not be ignored in analysing the effects of this interaction.

The Africa Rising Narrative and Agriculture Development in Africa: Deepening China-Africa Relations

Said Adejumobi   Gedion G. Jalata *

The African Continent demonstrated impressive growth rates in the decade 2000-2010; however, growth has since decelerated in recent years due largely to the decline in commodity prices. In scaling up agricultural productivity as part of the "Africa rising" narrative, the Continent in 2003 adopted the Maputo declaration aiming at boosting agricultural productivity through increased funding and policy priority, yet, enormous challenges exist, militating against the process of agricultural transformation.

In posting its recent growth trends, Africa's trade and development assistance were diversified to extend beyond the traditional Western countries, to include the emerging industrial nations of China, Brazil, Russia and India. For instance, China's resource-intensive growth model encouraged a boom in the commodity sector which African countries benefited from, and China's investments and support in the agricultural sector, though still very limited, is contributing to enhanced agricultural productivity in Africa.

* Prof. Said Adejumobi is Director, United Nations Economic Commission for Africa (UNECA), Sub-Regional Office for Southern Africa Lusaka, Zambia. Mr. Gedion G. Jalata is Programme Manager, Africa-China Dialogue Platform (ACDP), Oxfam International Liaison Office to the African Union, Addis Ababa, Ethiopia and is a PhD candidate at Erasmus University, The Netherlands. The views expressed herein are personal and do not reflect that of the UNECA, UN generally or OXFAM.

The article reflects on the recent "Africa rising" narrative and the role of China in Africa's agricultural sector as part of the narrative. The chapter argues that the agricultural sector in Africa has not demonstrated any transformative capacity, hence, its stunted growth; and China's agricultural development assistance to Africa is marginal, compared to other sectors of the economy, albeit on the increase. While China's investments in the agriculture sector in Africa would be desirable, of greater importance is the comparative experience and lessons learned from China in the process of its agricultural transformation, which is one of the most remarkable in the World.

The Africa Rising Narrative: Story and Evidence

Since the mid-1980s, however, African countries have increasingly taken measures aimed at revitalizing their economies. The measures include better economic management through budgetary and fiscal discipline, control of inflation, sale and privatization of inefficient and wasteful public enterprises, and boost in exports of commodity products, oil and minerals. Although the Structural Adjustment Programmes (SAP) with its unabashed commitment to market fundamentalism and the neo-liberal ideology of economic liberalization had negative consequences for many African countries in the 1980s to 1990s, however, this trend was soon to be reversed as the state took control in directing the economy better and steering it to recovery and growth in many African countries. [1]

The growth recovery that started within a few African countries soon spread to most of them since the mid-1990s. For instance, GDP growth rate on the continent from 1995 to 1997 was 4.5 per cent compared to 1.5 per cent from 1990 to 1994. Export growth also doubled from an annual average of 3.9 per cent from 1990 to 1994, to 7.8 per cent from 1995 – 1997. However, the average growth rate in Africa was only to 3.4 per cent from 1998 – 2002.

---

[1] Said Adejumobi, "Adjustment Reforms and its Impact on Economy and Society" in S. Adejumobi and A. Momoh, eds., *The Political Economy of Nigeria under Military Rule: 1986 – 1993*, 1995, Harare: SAPES Trust.

In 2007, over 39 African countries were growing persistently for more than three years at an annual real growth rate of three per cent. Of these, 15 had growth rates at five per cent or more. But from 1998-2014 the continent wide average growth rate increased to 4. 7 per cent. (See figure 1 below on real GDP growth in Africa from 1998 – 2014).

This made the continent the second-fastest growing region in the world following East and South Asia. Improvements were also observed in the (a) tax system and revenue mobilization, (b) improved budgetary management, (c) a more conducive macroeconomic environment for private investment and private-sector growth, (d) consumer price inflation was in single digits, (e) improved government budget balances and current account performance, and (f) debt-GDP ratio significantly reduced for many African countries.

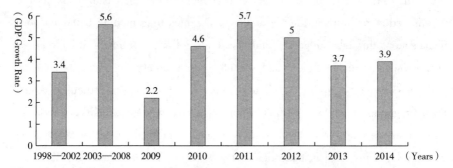

Figure 1   Real GDP Growth in Africa from 1998 to 2014

Source: UNECA, *Economic Report on Africa*, Addis Ababa: ECA Printing Press, 2015.

The growth pattern in Africa has been skewed towards commodity boom rather than economic diversification or transformation. Hence, it is vulnerable, fragile, and susceptible to external shocks. This is what some refer to as " growth without prosperity". Also, there is a challenge at ensuring improvements in economic and social conditions for marginalized groups such as the rural population, women, the youth, and the disabled. In comparison with other regions, Africa lags behind in all indicators of social development. Currently, half of the population of Africa – 48 per cent-is living in poverty and if the trend is not reversed, the number maylikelyincrease in the future. There has also been insufficient progress

towards meeting international food security targets; at present more than one in
four people remain undernourished in Africa-the highest prevalence of any region
in the world①.

Also, economic growth in Africa has not been job promoting, especially for
young people, which some refer to as "jobless growth". For instance, an extra
450 million jobs must be created in the next two decades in the continent in order
to match expansion in the number of working age people in the region. ② The
challenge therefore is in ensuring that the sources of growth are diversified
through industrialization, value-addition and structural transformation.

Slow growth, and high levels of unemployment and poverty are the triple challenges
facing many African countries presently. Added to this is the problem of corruption. The
devastating impact of Human Immunodeficiency Virus (HIV/AIDs) is receding but remains of concern. The recent Ebola crisis also impacted negatively on the economies of
three African countries affected-Liberia, Sierra Leone and Guinea. ③

It is against this backdrop that in recent years, there has been emerging con-
sensus in Africa that economic transformation is imperative if African countries
are to squarely address the problem of underdevelopment. In conclusion, Africa
needs not only growth but also growth with DEPTH④, which encompasses Diversification of production and exports, Export competitiveness and gains, Productivity increase, Technological upgrading, and Human economic well-being
improvements through formal employment and raising income. ⑤

---

① Food and Agriculture organization of the United Nations (FAO), International Fund for Agricultural Development (IFAD), World Food Programme (WFP), *The State of Food insecurity in the
world*: *Strengthening the Enabling Environment for FoodSecurity and Nutrition*, Rome, FAO,
IFAD and WFP, 2014.

② Pauline Bax, "From Burkina Faso to Burundi, Jobless Young Africans Rise Against Corrupt and
Failed Rule", *fahamu*: *networks for social justice*, 05. 14. 2015.

③ United Nations, Economic Commission for Africa (ECA), *Socio-Economic Impacts of Ebola on
Africa*, ECA, 2015-01.

④ This is the acronym used by the African Centre for Economiv Transformation (ACET) based in
Accra, Ghana to describe, Diversification, Export competitiveness, enhanced Productivity,
Technological upgrading, and Human well-being (DEPTH).

⑤ African Centre for Economic Transformation (ACET), 2014 *African Transformation Report*:
Growth with Depth, ACET, 2014.

Deficit Agricultural Development in Africa

Africa is endowed with abundant natural resources. The continent has about 12 per cent of the world's arable land, of which 60 per cent is uncultivated. Moreover, only 7 per cent of the arable land is irrigated compared to 40 per cent in Asia. In 2013, 183 million hectares of land was under cultivation in Sub-Saharan Africa, and approximately 452 million hectares of additional suitable land was not cultivated. Smallholder farmers account for most of the cultivated land and a sizable share of agriculture production. For instance, more than 75 per cent of the total agriculture outputs in Kenya, Tanzania, Ethiopia, and Uganda are produced by smallholder farmers with average farm sizes of about 2.5 hectares[1].

As Sub-Saharan African countries are heavily dependent on agriculture, the sector has a positive relationship to national GDP. The contribution of agriculture to the GDP of countries in Sub-Saharan Africa countriesvaries widely but relatively predictable. Agriculture accounts for average 30 per cent of Africa's total GDP, while agriculture contributes less than 8 per cent per cent for Southern African countries. Moreover, on the average about 65-70 per cent of Africa's labor force is employed in the agriculture sector. See figure II below on GDP, employment and relative productivity level of the agriculture sector for 11 African countries (1960, 1990, and 2010). The countries are Botswana, Ethiopia, Ghana, Kenya, Malawi, Mauritius, Nigeria, Senegal, South Africa, Tanzania, and Zambia.

As figure 2 above indicates, the agriculture sector's contribution to the 11 African countries indicated has been declining – 37.6, 24.9, 22.4 per cent in 1960, 1990, and 2010 respectively. While productivity of the sector declined from 0.5 in 1960 to 0.4 in 2010. The sector is also losing labor incrementally from 72.7 per cent, 61.6 per cent, and 49.8 per cent in 1960, 1990, and

---

① United Nations, Economic Commission for Africa (ECA), *Frontier Markets in Africa-Misperception in a Sea of Opportunities*, ECA, July18, 2014.

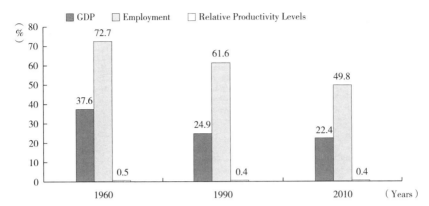

**Figure 2   GDP, Employment and Relative Productivity Levels of the agriculture
sector for 11 African countries (1960, 1990, and 2010)**

Source: Gaaitzende Vries, Marcel Timmer, and Klaas de Vries, "Structural Transformation in Africa: Static Gains, Dynamic losses." *Research Memorandum* 136, University of Groningen, Groningen Growth and development Centre, The Netherlands, 2013: 6, p. 11.

2010 respectively. However, agriculture still has the potential to contribute greatly to economic growth and transformation in Africa. It remains the key sector for food security, employment, and growth, and development in most African countries. Agriculture has the potential of increasing rural income, foreign exchange earnings and releasing labour for industrial growth in African economies. It can also expand the markets for inputs and consumption goods and services for other sectors of the economy. [1]

Furthermore, agriculture-led growth has a strong potential of reducing the depth and breadth of poverty. This is possible because food staples have strong growth linkages. Growth in food staples is considered generally as pro-poor but export crop may have higher value and growth potential. However, initially before the value chains develop, food crops are more effective for economy wide growth and poverty reduction. Africa's agricultural development target was to achieve an annual 6 percent growth rate in the sector in order to meet the set MDG goal in

---

[1] Henley David, "The Agrarian Roots of Industrial Growth: Rural development in South-East Asia and Sub-Saharan Africa", *Development Policy Review*, 30 (1), pp. 25 – 47; African Centre for Economic Transformation (ACET), 2014 *African Transformation Report: Growth with Depth*, p. 107.

that regard. ①But only eight African countries were able to achieve the six per cent agriculture sector annual growth ratebefore the close of the MDG in 2015. These were Angola, Ethiopia, Burkina Faso, the Republic of Congo, Gambia, Guinea-Bissau, Nigeria, Senegal, and Tanzania. The impressive economic growth and rapid reduction in rural poverty in Ethiopia, Rwanda, and Ghana were largely made possible by growth in the agricultural sector. However, productivity in the sector remains low in Africa and lags considerably behind that of other continents. ②

In scaling up agricultural production in Africa, regional policy initiatives have been launched. This includes the 2003 Maputo Declaration on Comprehensive African Agriculture Development Programme (CAADP) and the SADC Agricultural Policy. CAADP is "Africa's policy framework for agricultural transformation, wealth creation, food security and nutrition, economic growth and prosperity for all". ③CAADP prescribes that African countries should allocate at least 10 percent of their national budget to the agricultural sector, raise agricultural productivity by at least 6 percent annually and make agricultural transformation a major priority of government policy in Africa. As such, the number of countries spending more than 10% of their national budget on agriculture increased from 11 per cent in 2003 to 22 per cent in 2006. Moreover, 50 per cent of the countries spent 4. 6 per cent of their national expenditure on agriculture development, showing a decrease from 57 per cent in 2003. ④ Countries like Niger, Ethiopia and Mali

---

① Economic Commission for Africa (ECA), The Organization for Economic Co-operation and Development (OECD), *The Mutual Review of Development Effectiveness in Africa: Promises and Performance*, ECA and OECD, November, 2014.

② Economic Commission for Africa (ECA), African Union (AU), African Development Bank Group (AfDB), *MDG 2104 Report: assessing progress in Africa toward the Millennium Development Goals: Analysis of the Common African Position on the Post-2015 Development Agenda*. ECA, AU, AfDB and UNDP, 2014, pp. 13 – 17.

③ NEPAD. 2015. Available at http: www. nepad. org/foodsecurity/agriculture/about, last visit on Oct. 6, 2016.

④ Economic Commission for Africa (ECA), The Organization for Economic Co-operation and Development (OECD), *The Mutual Review of Development Effectiveness in Africa: Promises and Performance*, 2014, pp. 14 – 15.

have consistently over a period allocated 10 per cent and above of their national
budget to the agricultural sector.

**Table 1 Share of agriculture expenditure (% of total expenditure)
in selected countries in Africa.**

Country	Year												
	2000	2001	2002	2003	2004	2005	2006	2007	2008	2009	2010	2011	2012
Burkina Faso	25.0	18.0	23.0	33.0	20.0	12.0	20.0	16.0	14.0	9.0	11.0	–	–
Ethiopia	10.4	4.0	5.6	8.4	13.6	16.5	17.5	14.6	11.7	17.5	21.2	–	–
Ghana	3.2	4.7	6.9	5.8	8.8	9.8	10.3	9.9	10.2	9.0	9.1	–	–
Kenya	6.8	6.6	5.4	4.1	5.1	6.6	5.9	4.4	4.8	3.9	4.6	8.7	6.8
Liberia	–	–	–	–	–	–	4.0	5.5	8.6	2.3	2.9	–	–
Malawi	8.8	4.9	8.7	6.6	7.0	11.1	11	13.2	31.6	24.7	28.9	–	–
Mali	8.9	12.8	8.9	9.6	11.4	15.5	10.6	11.0	12.7	16.9	13.9	23.9	–
Mozambique	–	–	–	–	6.2	4.4	3.4	3.9	5.4	5.8	5.5	–	–
Niger	–	15.8	16.6	16.4	19.5	14.5	15.1	15.4	12.2	13.9	12.7	–	–
Nigeria	1.6	6.0	3.5	1.9	3.1	3.4	4.1	4.4	4.6	5.3	5.7	–	–
Rwanda	–	6.2	8.6	3.9	4.0	3.4	3.3	5.5	5.6	6.4	6.6	–	–
Sierra Leone	–	2.4	2.3	3.1	3.0	2.3	2.9	2.5	2.2	2.0	1.7	0.2	–
South Sudan	–	–	–	–	–	–	–	–	1.4	1.9	1.4	1.9	–
Tanzania	–	–	4.5	6.8	5.7	4.7	5.8	5.7	2.5	6.7	6.8	6.8	–
Uganda	2.6	1.6	2.6	2.3	2.1	2.0	3.9	3.0	3.2	4.5	3.8	3.1	4.5
Zambia	8.6	6.2	5.2	6.1	6.1	7.2	9.3	13.2	12.5	9.3	10.2	–	–

Source: Regional Strategic Analysis and Knowledge Support System (ReSAKSS, 2015) . Available
athttp: //www. resakss. org.

Challenges to Agricultural Development in Africa

Agriculture is the mainstay of most economies in Africa, accounting for more than
30 per cent of Gross Domestic Product (GDP). Nonetheless, the sector has not
witnessed impressive growth due to a combination of factors such as weak political
will to support agriculture, price risk and non-conducive policies, inadequate investments in modern agricultural inputs, technology and infrastructure, limited

market access and poor access to credit and financial services, rural-urban migration, the vagaries of climate change, and increase in soil degradation.

Internal seed regulatory policies in many Africa countries, for instance, are weak undermining the functioning of the entire seed value chains. As measured by cereal productivity, growth remains low, averaging one metric tonne per hectare. This is one-fourth of the global average. Per capita food production has been declining even though aggregate production has been increasing through expansion of cultivated areas. This, coupled with the recent food crisis, has resulted in Africa becoming a net food-importing region-except South Africa. Africa's imported cereal increased dramatically from less than five million metric tonnes a year in the early 1960s to more than 50 million metric tonnes per year by mid 2000s. This is direct opposite to the situation in Asia where per capita food production almost doubled between the early 1960s and the mid-2000s. ①This happened as a result of rapid uptake of high-yielding wheat and rice varieties and the use of fertilizers and irrigation combined with subsidies. This in turn reduced the unit cost of production inputs and raised land and labor productivities.

Evidence from research suggest that "a 10 per cent drop in transport cost as a result of improved road infrastructure is likely to generate a 25 per cent increase in trade and drive down distribution margins to the benefit of producers and consumers". ②Low human skills development, land management capabilities, and limited institutions to support the use of technology are important factors in explaining the relatively sluggish progress of the agriculture sectoring many African countries. ③There is also low agricultural research and development in Sub-Saha-

① Economic Commission for Africa (ECA), African Union (AU), *Economic Report on Africa* 2007: *Accelerating Africa's Development through Diversification Africa*, Addis Ababa, Ethiopia, 2007, pp. 48; Deborah A. Brautigam and Xiaoyang Tang, "China's Engagement in African Agriculture: Down to the Countryside", *In China Quarterly*, Number 199, 2009, pp. 686-706.

② Alliance for a Green Revolution in Africa (AGRA), *Africa Agriculture Status Report: Focus on Staple Crops*, Smart Printers, 2013, p. 86.

③ Hans P. Binswanger-Mkhize, "Challenges and opportunities for African agriculture and food security: High Food Process, Climate Change, Population Growth, and HIV and AIDS", *Expert Meeting on How to feed the World in*, vol. 2050, 2009.

ran Africa (SSA). Only five African countries are paying the recurrent budget of their national agricultural research system from national resources. These are Nigeria, South Africa, Botswana, Ethiopia, and Mauritius. [1] For instance, only Kenya and Uganda consistently spend more than 1 per cent of their GDP on agricultural research and development. Increasing the budget allocation to research and development by each country to attain at least one per cent of agricultural GDP is recommended. [2]

Financing also constitutes another major challenge. As noted above, agriculture accounts more than 30 per cent of the GDP of most countries, yet government expenditure on agriculture is less than a third of that. Estimates by FAO in 2009 indicated that global food production needs to grow by 70 per cent to feed 9.1 billion people in 2050. This expansion of agriculture output will require average annual net investments of $11 billion in SSA, where the majority of farmers are smallholders. Given the huge financing requirements for smallholder agriculture, it is unlikely that African countries will be able to raise the needed funds. [3]

The challenge of illicit financial flows also depletes the resources available for development in Africa. According to the ECA and AU report on Illicit Financial Flows (IFFs), trade mispricing alone is causing Africa to lose $50 billion per year. In the years from 1970 to 2008, the continent lost around $854 billion in IFFs. The total outflows from 2000 to 2010 were equivalent to nearly all the official development assistance (ODA) received by the continent. This is a massive financial haemorrhage that could have been used to finance development on the continent.

---

[1] Hans P. Binswanger-Mkhize, "Challenges and opportunities for African agriculture and food security: High Food Process, Climate Change, Population Growth, and HIV and AIDS", *Expert Meeting on How to feed the World in*, vol. 2050, 2009.

[2] Alliance for a Green Revolution in Africa (AGRA), *Africa Agriculture Status Report: Focus on Staple Crops*, Smart Printers, 2013, pp. 25. Xiayun Li, et al., "What Can Africa Learn from China's Experience in Agriculture Development?" *IDS Bulletin.* 44 (4), 2013, pp. 31 –41.

[3] Alliance for a Green Revolution in Africa (AGRA), *Africa Agriculture Status Report: Focus on Staple Crops*, Smart Printers, 2013, p. 23.

China-Africa Collaboration on Agricultural Development

At a policy level, the Chinese government proclaims to give great importance to agricultural cooperation with African countries. As indicated in the 2013 white paper on China-Africa Economic and Trade Cooperation, "the Chinese government attaches great importance to its mutually beneficial agricultural cooperation with Africa, and works hard to help African countries turn resource advantages into developmental ones and sustainably develop their agricultural capacities". [1] It is important to note that China has been involved in African agriculture for almost half a century. Since China adopted a zero-tariff policy for the least developed African countries along with certain products, agriculture export from Africa to China increased from $1.16 billion in 2009 to $2.86 billion in 2012. Meanwhile, China's agriculture exports to Africa grew from $1.58 billion to $2.49 billion. The most notable agricultural exports from Africa to China are non-food items such as cotton, hemps, silk, and oilseeds. Especially after the introduction of this policy, sesame imports into China grew from $97 million in 2005 to $441 million in 2011.

China's direct investment in Africa's agriculture is also increasing rapidly. From 2009 to 2012 it almost tripled from $30 million to $82.47 million. This was a result of Chinese enterprise investment in Africa inter alia in breeding improved seeds, planting grain and cash crops, and processing agricultural products. [2]

Alongside monetary support, Chinese agriculture aidconsists of sending Chinese senior agricultural experts and technicians to help with food production, breeding, storage and transport, infrastructure development, training, and constructing agricultural technology demonstration centres. Financing services for the agri-

---

① Information Office of the State Council, The People's Republic of China, *White Paper on China-Africa Economic and Trade Cooperation*, 2013.

② Information Office of the State Council, The People's Republic of China, *White Paper on China-Africa Economic and Trade Cooperation*; Lila Buckley, "Chinese agriculture development cooperation in Africa: Narratives and politics." *IDS bulletin* 44.4, 2013, pp. 42 – 52.

culture sector comes from Chinese banks. Since 2006, China has built more than
40 agricultural demonstration centres in Rwanda, the Republic of Congo, Mozambique, Ethiopia, and some other countries. The country has also sent 50 agricultural technology teams to African countries to provide policy consulting,
teach practical techniques and train local staff. Chad is one of the beneficiaries of
this aid. The country benefited from China's agriculture development assistance to
breed high-yield and quality crop varieties, and several thousand farmers were
trained as well. Consequently, the country reap over 25 per cent increase of crop
yield. [1]

Agriculture played a central role in China's own economic development and sharing these experiences has been a consistent priority in China's engagement with
Africa. Chinese cooperation with the sector in Africa focused on technology and
capacity building as well as providing hybrid seeds. It is also influenced by
China's own domestic development experience. For instance, since 2012 China
has provided training opportunities for more than 20000 Africans. China also provided scholarships to more than 14000 African Students in 2012 and 2013 alone.
China and African countries as well collaborated to launch 30 agricultural technology cooperation projects. In addition, China has sent more than 500 agricultural experts and technicians to Africa. [2]

Country Case Studies in China-Africa Agricultural Development: Ethiopia

China's ties with Ethiopia is historic as both countries are the oldest nations in the
world. Yet the Sino-Ethiopian economic cooperation including aid officially began

---

[1] Information Office of the State Council, The People's Republic of China, *White Paper on China-Africa Economic and Trade Cooperation*; Lila Buckley, "Chinese agriculture development cooperation in Africa: Narratives and politics." *IDS bulletin* 44. 4 (2013), pp. 42 –45.

[2] ChinAfrica, "A Good Story to Tell: China-South Africa Relations Reach Strategic Milestone", *Africa Report*, vol. 7, 2015; Lila Buckley. "Chinese agriculture development cooperation in Africa: Narratives and politics." *IDS bulletin* 44. 4 (2013), p. 45.

in the early 1970's and remained low until 1995. The Sino-Ethiopian economic cooperation's were restored with the coming of Ethiopian People Revolutionary Democratic Front (EPRDF), the incumbent ruling party, to power in Ethiopia since 1991. Especially after 1995, the bilateral economic cooperation witnessed marked progress and rapid development in different areas. During the late Prime Minister MelesZenawi's visit to China in 1995, the two countries signed economic and technical cooperation agreements. Meles also reached a good understanding with prominent Chinese enterprises and corporations. On the other hand, when the Chinese President, Jiang Zemin, made an official visit to Ethiopia in 1997, the two countries signed agreements on trade, investment and joint commercial ventures, and science and technology. [1]

In Ethiopia about 92% of Chinese development assistance goes to two sectors namely energy generation and supply (65%), transport and storage (27%) while the remaining constitute: industry (3%), agriculture (3%) and education (2%). Accordingly, the agriculture sector constitute only 3 % out of the total Chinese development assistance to Ethiopia. It was since 2008 China started to support the agriculture sector in Ethiopia. In this regards, in the years from 2008 to 2015 China disbursed concessional loan for the agriculture sector in Ethiopia equivalent to 11 million USD (11, 374, and 700, precise figure). Furthermore, China disbursed grants on the agriculture projects in 2013and 14 worthy of 97 thousand USD (97, 355 USD precise figure). Sino-Ethiopia agricultural cooperation do have two principal features, which the above mentioned loans and grants disbursed for. The first feature is establishing agricultural technology demonstration centre. The second feature is dispatching agricultural technologists to work in in agricultural technology demonstration centre and teach at agricultural technical vocational education and training (AT-VET) in Ethiopia. See figure 3 below on China's aid to Ethiopia by sectors (actual disbursement) from 2005 to 2015 (April).

---

[1] Gamora Gedion and M. Venkataraman, "An analysis of Ethio-China relations during the Cold War." *China Report at Siege Publications in New Delhi* 45, 2009, pp. 17-22; Dawit Alemu and Ian Scoones, "Negotiating new relationships: How the Ethiopian State in Involving China and Brazil in Agriculture and Rural development," *IDS Bulletin.* 44 (4), 2013, pp. 91 – 100.

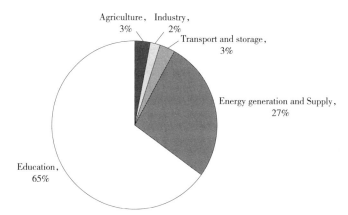

**Figure 3　China's aid to Ethiopia by sectors（actual disbursement）
from 2005 to 2015（April）**

Source: Ministry of Finance and Economic Development of Ethiopia（MOFED, 2015）.

The Ethiopian government is promoting investment in the country by offering diverse incentives for public and private investors. China's agriculture sector foreign direct investment to Ethiopia's, however, like development assistance is very minimal. Chinese total investment in Ethiopia is equivalent to 16 billion USD in 2015 while the actual investment is equivalent to over 2 billion USD. Out of which agriculture constitute 0. 024 %. The largest Chinese foreign direct investment in Ethiopia respectively are in transport, energy, technology, real state and agriculture. [1]The total number of registeredinvestments by China since 2008 are over 32. Out of these: （i）18 are in the area of vegetablefarming; ii）4 are in edible oil production and processing including a major investment in palm oil plantation; iii）3 companies are licenced in sugar cane production and processingand iv）3 have received permits to operate in pig farming and processing. V）Another 2 companies have got permits for poultry farming, vii）1 in mushroom farming, viii）1 in a rubber plantation. Although Chinese investment in agriculture is smaller in Ethiopia, it has been growing incrementally. For instance, a decade ago Chinese investment in the sector was almost nil.

---

[1]　American Enterprise Institute（AEI）and the Heritage Foundation, *The China Global Investment Tracker（CGIT）*, 2015.

Ethiopia also adopted some lessons from emerging economies such as India (restructuring agricultural research system), Brazil (promotion of a bio-energy strategy), and from the South Korea (group action approaches for organizing farmers). Ethiopia also took some agricultural policy lessons and measures from China: [1]

1. The introduction of Agricultural technical and Vocational School (TVET);
2. The introduction of agro-industry zones near major towns;
3. Adaptation of group action approaches for organising farmers.

Country Case Studies in China-Africa Agricultural Development: Mozambique

Formal diplomatic relationship between China and Mozambique was established in 1975 immediately after the country gained independence from Portugal. The country is one of the top emerging destination for Chinese development cooperation, trade and investment. In February 2007 Hu Jintao, the then president of China, made an official visit to Mozambique. He and the then president of Mozambique, Mr. Armando Guebuza, pledged cooperation in technology, agriculture, and education among others. Accordingly, till 2012 there had been 53 Chinese development cooperation projects in Mozambique. China also built public buildings and facilities. The EXIM Bank of China provided 50 million USD. Out of this 30 million disbursed for rehabilitating and developing important agricultural infrastructure, and used to build three agro-processing factories for cotton, rice and maize. While the remaining 20 million used to import agricultural equipment from China. Mozambique signed another concessional loan in 2012 of 60 million USD to develop agro-processing complex. The complex planned to develop diverse activities such as processing, packing, conservation unit, and rice processing factories. China also cancelled debt of 52 million USD for Mozambique. In the years

---

[1] Future Agricultures, "Can China and Brazil help Africa feed itself?" in Future Agricultures, *Comprehensive Africa Agriculture Development Programme (CAADP) policy brief.*

1992 to 2003, 22 Mozambicans got scholarship from China. ①

Following the 2006 FOCAC pledge, china built agriculture technology demonstration centre in southwest of Maputo, Mozambique. The principal objectives are to perform agricultural demonstrations, rural extension and technical training to boost productivity of agricultural sector and secure food security. The centre with its operation coasted the Chinese government around 186. ②

Investment by Chinese enterprises in Mozambique has been rapidly increasing. For instance, China investedaround 200 million USD while other source reflected 95 million USD in investment in Regadio do Baixo Limpopo, otherwise the place is well known by the name Xai-Xai irrigation scheme. The project aimed to increase a rice production through irrigation scheme and transfer rice production technology to local farmers. As a result, local farmers see their paddy fields yield five tons per hectare, two tons more than previous yields. Critics, however, argue that technology transfer has failed as Mozambican farmers lack commitment to agriculture. The investment also regard as ' land grabbing' and reported that several local people were displaced from their land. Critics further argues that there was no local consultation when the project was implemented. ③

The Chinese government, however, indicated that the agricultural investment happened through the request of Mozambican government with the aim of increasing the country's rice production from 100000 to 500000 tons Chinese enterprises and the China-Africa Development Fund also jointly invested in a cotton planting and processing project modelled on having enterprises work with farming households in Mozambique. The project was able to involve tens of thousands of local growers, effectively enhancing local capabilities in cotton processing. This pro-

---

① Sergio Chichava, et al. , "Brazil and China in Mozambican Agriculture: Emerging Insights from the Field", *IDS Bulletin*. 44 (4), 2013, pp. 101-115.

② Sergio Chichava, et al. , "Brazil and China in Mozambican Agriculture: Emerging Insights from the Field", *IDS Bulletin*. 44 (4), 2013, pp. 106 – 107.

③ Cecilia Anesi and Andrea Fama. "China accused of stealth land grab over Mozambique's great rice project", *The Ecologist* 30, 2013.

ject is also extended to Malawi and Zambia. ①

Country Case Studies in China-Africa Agricultural Development: Ghana

China and Ghana established diplomatic relations in 1960. Since then Ghana provided diplomatic support to China in quid pro quo China provided different material support, loans and grant to Ghana. For instance, Ghana gave diplomatic support to China in its attempt for a permanent seat in the UN and for its policy on one China Policy, which note that Taiwan is an integral part of China. During Wen Jiabao's visit to China in 2007 the two countries signed agreements on different areas of economic cooperation. The principal China-Africa cooperation areas include infrastructure, energy, communications, agriculture, trade, education and training. In this context, China gave 66 million USD as a loan to Ghana to upgrade the telecommunications network. China also offered 6 billion USD as concessionary loan from Exim Bank for Ghana's rail network. It also written off 25 USD debt for Ghana among others. China also extended development cooperation for hydro-electric dam, road construction. Chinese funded training courses in education trading, communication, energy, and auditing, agriculture and fisheries operation were given to 700 Ghanaian. Within the context of oil industry Chinese development cooperation to Ghana has been ever increasing. Very recently Ghana signed over 13 billion USD with the Chinese Exim Bank. ②

In the agriculture sector, China provided support for fishing and rice project of

① Jean-JacquesGabas and Frederic Goulet, "South-South cooperation and new agricultural development aid actors in western and southern Africa, China and Brazil Case Studies", in Agence Française de Développement and Agricultural Research for Development (CIRAD), *Working Paper*, No. 134, May. 2013.

② Austin Strangeet al., "China's Development Finance to Africa: A Media-Based Approach to Data Collection", in Center for Global Development (CGD), *Working Paper* 323, Washington DC, 2013; Kojo Sebastian Amanor, "South-South Cooperation in Africa: Historically, Geopolitical and Political Economy Dimensions of International Development", *IDS Bulletin*, 44 (4), 1013, pp. 80 – 90.

99 million USD interest free loan. Moreover, exchanges have been facilitated in
the areas of irrigation, agro processing, agricultural technology and infrastructure development. Volunteers sponsored by Chinese government have been teaching agriculture at the University of Ghana. China also established the West African
regional office of China-Africa development Fund (CAD Fund) in Accra to facilitate Chinese investment in the sub region. Chinese investments in the agricultural
sector, however, is very small-it constitute only 4% of the total investment in
Ghana. Out of which the largest agriculture investment is on irrigation projects. The
project is known as the Afife or Weta project and it occupies an area of 880 acres
and is the largest irrigation on rice-growing project in Ghana. There are also other
Chinese companies' investments on fertiliser plant and on agrochemicals. This may
be developed in relation to emerging petroleum resources in Ghana. ①

Deepening Agriculture Cooperation: Challenges & Mutual Benefits

Despite attempts to promote China-Africa collaboration on agricultural development, collaboration in the agriculture sector remains at a low level. As indicated
above, Chinese support to the agriculture sector by trade relations, investment,
and development cooperation is very low. There are concerns that Chinese agricultural investments in Africa may have deleterious consequences for food security in
certain respects in Africa. Chinese investments in food crops like rice destined for
Chinese market may create food shortages especially of the product in Africa. Although Chinese farms in Africa currently produce both for local and export markets, the fear is that as land pressure mounts in China given the size of her population, the country may opt for producing greater quantities of food abroad as Japan and South Korea are doing.

---

①   Austin Strangeet al. , "China's Development Finance to Africa: A Media-Based Approach to Data
Collection", in Center for Global Development (CGD), *Working Paper* 323, Washington DC,
2013; Kojo Sebastian Amanor, "South-South Cooperation in Africa: Historically, Geopolitical
and Political Economy Dimensions of International Development", *IDS Bulletin*, 44 (4), 1013,
pp. 80 – 90.

Associated with the above, is the incipient phenomenon of "land grabbing" which is also of concern in Africa. ① Given the fact that Africa has considerable arable land, there appears to be a scramble for land in Africa for agricultural and other purposes, which both advanced and emerging industrialized economies including China are alleged to be engaged in. Land grabbing will likely displace small local farmers, stunt or retard rural livelihoods, increase poverty and deteriorate standard of living in rural communities.

There are questions around technology and skills transfer in the agricultural sector from China to Africa. For instance, the hybrid rice technology which is quite common in China's technology demonstration parks in Africa does not lend itself to local domestication. The seeds, which are mainly imported, are controlled by the multionational corporations (MNCs) and local breeding is hardly encouraged. Also, Chinese expertise deployment is largely on short term contracts, which affects skills and technology transfer. Indeed, China like the West appears protective of its technology since it is the source of her emerging power.

Another challenge is the cultural differences between China and Africa, which can create barriers. For instance, not all experts coming from China speak English very well-rather they are employing "teaching-by-doing" to transfer practical skills. This creates a challenge in communication between the Chinese experts and their African counterparts. Moreover, there is a huge gap in agricultural practices between China and Africa. Chinese farmers use intensive agriculture while African farmers use shifting cultivation and depend on fallow systems, further increasing the likelihood of creating misunderstandings. This phenomenon leads to the popular perception that Africa does not understand China and vice versa. This is further fuelled by Chinese tendency to segregate themselves from local populations when implementing development assistance projects. ②

---

① Cecilia Anesi and Andrea Fama. *China accused of stealth land grab over Mozambique's great rice project.*

② Sérgio Chichava, et al. , "Brazil and China in Mozambican agriculture: Emerging insights from the field", pp. 101 – 112; Lila Buckley, "Chinese agriculture development cooperation in Africa: Narratives and politics", *IDS bulletin* 44. 4, 2013, p. 48.

Despite the challenges of agricultural development in the current China-Africa relations, agriculture remains an emerging area for China's engagement with Africa. Agriculture engagement in Africa today is framed as "South-South Cooperation," emphasizing reciprocal relationships with mutual benefits. It seems there is a bright future ahead for the following reasons. First, just as Africa needs China, China also needs Africa due to the latter's abundance of resources, labor force, and market connections, which are vital for agri-business and trade plans. Africa's large uncultivated arable land is also critical as well for longer-term global food security-particularly for a populous country like China.

Second, China-Africa relationships have deepened and will continue to do so, which will have positive implicationsforfuture agricultural cooperation between the two. As the Chinese White Paper (2013) noted, "In the future, China will advance agricultural cooperation with Africa in all respects while ensuring that this cooperation puts both parties on an equal footing, is mutually beneficial, and advances common development".

Third, there is improved political commitment from African countries on agricultural development. This is demonstrated in rising African countries' commitments toformulatingappropriate policies and budgetaryallocationstothe agricultural sector, but more still needs to be done. African countries can learn from the experience of Chinese smallholder agricultural policy and institutional capacity through development cooperation efforts. China's agricultural cooperation in the future may also be extended to building irrigationsystems, dams, supply of farm machinery, inputs, and agrochemicals rather than the current assistance on farm management and seeds and inputs provision. ①

Fourth, agricultural development assistance is considered as complementary to China's growing interest in energy and mineral projects. This is based on China'sdiplomaticprinciples known as "getting and giving." As the director of China farm Agribusiness Corporation commented: "China's growing interest in

---

① Kojo Sebastian Amanor, "South-South Cooperation in African Agriculture: China, Brazil and International Agribusiness", *Great Insights* 4. 3, 2014, pp. 53 – 55.

energy and mineral projects in Africa is likely to trigger some negative reactions," and to counter these, he suggested that "China should offer to combine exploitation of other countries' resources with the help for their agriculture". ①

Finally, there are other emerging powers engaged in agriculture development in Africa. The most notable one is Brazil. Both China and Brazil have an interest in supporting the agriculture sector in Africa. The competition between China and Brazil in Africa is vividly seen in their involvement in the agriculture sector in Ghana and Mozambique. Thismay influence China to enhance its agriculture sector support to Africa. African countries thus need to leverage this advantage as the two emerging powers are competing to support the agriculture sector in Africa. Furthermore, it is important to note that the emerging economies do have different focus and achievements in their agriculture support to African countries. For instance, China focuses onintensive small-scale agriculture whereas Brazil has been providing technology to assist in transforming the Cerrado (savannah) into the top grain, beef-producing, and dairy cattle regions. ②

Conclusion: Way Forward

Africa's agriculture is at a turning point with growing momentum of transformation. Scaling up agricultural productivity is of imperative necessity for Africa not only in ensuring food security for its teeming population but also to promote increased exports of processed agricultural products rather than raw materials, in facilitating increased revenue and foreign earnings for developmental purposes. Transforming and modernizing Africa's agriculture will require greater political commitment with increased state funding, investments in agricultural research, science and technology, improved rural infrastructure, entrepreneurial skills,

---

① Deborah A. Bräutigam and Tang Xiaoyang. "China's engagement in African agriculture: Down to the countryside", *The China Quarterly* 199, 2009, pp. 686 – 706.

② Kojo SebastianAmanor, "South-South Cooperation in African Agriculture: China, Brazil and International Agribusiness", pp. 53-55; Kojo Sebastian Amanor, "Expanding Agri - business: China and Brazil in Ghanaian Agriculture", *IDS Bulletin* 44. 4, 2013, pp. 80-90.

capacity and finance in agro-processing small scale enterprises, climate change mitigation, higher quality yields, better market access and halting the rural-urban drift especially of young people, who could provide the needed labour and innovation for such transformation.

While the responsibility to transform Africa's agriculture is that of Africans themselves, China like the other emerging industrialized countries like Brazil, and India can provide development assistance in the areas of modern agricultural knowledge, training and education, technology transfer, rural infrastructure, and demand based investments in the agricultural sector. Lessons learned and experience sharing of China's agricultural transformation may prove more useful in supporting African countries in navigating their path to such transformation.

It is important to recognise that the agriculture sector in China was not developed through development assistance but rather through a combination of market reforms, trade, and controlled foreign direct investment. Various kinds of development assistance, likewise, have so far not facilitated the transformation of Africa's agricultural sector. In this regard, African countries must look inwards, prioritize the agricultural sector in national planning, and develop sound agricultural policies and strategies with good implementation machinery, monitoring and evaluation.

Africa must have clear objectives and strategies of how it wants to tap into the agricultural resources and gains of China, and this would require having an Africa China Policy. China has an Africa Policy that guides and directs its engagement with Africa on what her interests are, in Africa in all sectors of the economy; Africa must do the same and be clear about what it wants from China and the means and processes of achieving them. ①

---

① Said Adejumobi, "China-Africa: Beyond the Money and Infrastructure", *New African Magazine*, March, 2015, pp. 1 – 12.

C
H
I
N
A

China's Agricultural Cooperation with African Countries

A
F
R
I
C
A

Angola's Agricultural Development and China's Role

Zhou Jinyan [*]

Angola is one of China's four strategic partners in Africa. The current cooperation between China and Angolais multifaceted and covers trade, agriculture, education, health, science, and technology as well as personnel training. In 2014, the Chinese navy fleet visits Angola for the first time. In 2015, the first Confucius Institute was established in Angola. However, outsiders still tend to observe the Sino-Angola strategic partnershipwith doubt. Academic research has mainly focused on the oil cooperation and classified it as the "Angola model". The defects of the simple narrative of "oil-for-loan" are two folded: on the one hand, it ignores other dimensions in China-Angola cooperation and overlooks the transforming and deepening development of China-Angola strategic partnership. On the other hand, the simple narrative has trapped the story of Angola's growth in the conventional analysis framework of "resource curse" and "resource boom". It leads the outside world to neglect Angola's efforts in diversifying its oil-dependent economy and diplomatic partners.

Through more than one decade of post-war reconstruction, Angola, with its fast economic growth and political stability, is becoming an important player in the region. A keyword in Angola's economic and diplomatic strategy is diversification. In response to the recent slackening oil-dominated economy, the Angolan government committed to diversify its economy into new sectors, especially agri-

---

* Dr. Zhou Jinyan, Institute of West Asian and African Studies, Academy of Social Sciences.

culture. Inits foreign relations, Angola continues to develop a strategic partnership with China, but also attempts to diversify diplomatic partnersto maximize its national interests. In the past decade, Angola not only expanded cooperation with the U. S. and Europe, but also gradually improved relations with the World Bank and IMF. While seeking a balance between Eastern and Western partners, Angola showed a strong sense of ownership in international cooperation.

Economic strength serves as the foundation for political and diplomatic ambitions. Agriculture not only helps Angola to achieve poverty reduction and food security, but also holds the key to the government's strategy of economic diversification. The Angolan government has already realised the importance of agriculture and set up a series of policies to foster international agricultural cooperation. As Angola's strategic partner, China has been playing an important role in agriculture cooperation.

Agriculture Key to Economic Diversification

The dramatic falling of global oil prices alarmed Angola to its vulnerabilitydue to its high dependence on oil. Dueto oil price volatility, Angola's GDP growth plummeted from 13. 8 per cent to 2. 4 per cent in 2009. [1]The government was aware of the need for economic diversification and importance ofredistributing the oil wealth into the society. The Angolan government thus prioritized the growth of non-oil sectors, and especially the development of agriculture, in its economic strategy.

Before the war, Angola was the world's fourth largest producer of coffee and a top exporter of sugar cane, banana, sisal, and cotton. War-induced infrastructure destruction and lack of investment and technology resulted in slowdevelopment of Angola's agriculture. Less than 30 percent of its arable land has been cultivated, mostly by small-scale farmers lacking basic skills. Angola is heavily dependenton food imports, which account for half of the food supply and 15 percent

---

① "IMF data mapper", April 2011, http: //www. imf. org/external/data-mapper/index. php.

of the country's total imports. ①

After the war, Angola's agriculture had a 10-year-average growth rateof 13 percent, although it dropped to 7. 3 percent in 2012 after a severe drought. ② Angola
has vast agricultural potential, with favorable climate and 6. 7 million hectares of
cultivated land and over 30 million hectares of land to be developed. ③In June
2015, Angola was awarded by FAO for having achieved the first of the Millennium Development Goals of halving the prevalence of malnutrition by 2015. ④

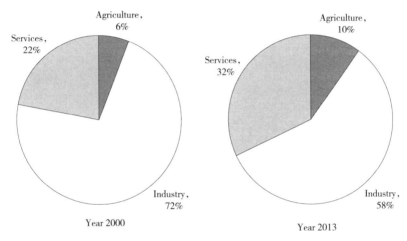

**Figure 1　Change of oil and non-oil sector contribution toAngola's
GDP（Year 2000 and 2013）**

Source: compiled by author using data from World Bank 2015, "World development indicators: structure of output," http://wdi. worldbank. org/table/4. 2.

Since the government embarked on reforms towards economic diversification, the contribution of industry to GDP—mainly the oil sector—fell from 72
per cent to 58 per cent（see Figure 1）. Agriculture generated around 10 per-

① World Bank, "Doing Business 2015: going beyond efficiency-Angola", Doing Business
　2015. Washington, DC: World Bank Group.
② World Bank, "Angola economic update", June 2013. http://www. worldbank. org/content/
　dam/Worldbank/document/Africa/Angola/angola-economic-update-june-2013. pdf.
③ MOFCOM, "Gao Hucheng: Booming and Promising China-Angola Economic and Trade Cooperation",
　May 2014, http://gaohucheng2. mofcom. gov. cn/article/speech/201411/20141100797857. shtml.
④ "Angola Distinguished With FAO Award", http://allafrica. com/stories/201506090286. html.

cent of GDP in 2013, which is a rapid increase compared with the 6 percent in 2010. Manufacturing increased itsshare of the GDP from 3 percent to 7 percent.

Despite of the rapid growth of the agricultural sector, the gap between food production and food demandis still large. Moreover, it is worrying that the output growth is mainly due to the expanded arable land, but not the improvement of productivity. Angola's per-hectare productivity is among the lowest in the region[1] (see Table 1).

Table 1　Cereal yields of Angola in regional comparison (kg per hectare)

Cereal yield	2000	2005	2010
Angola	572	599	644
Kenya	1375	1646	1613
Malawi	1676	778	2206
Mozambique	868	741	1006
Nigeria	1172	1422	1413
South Africa	2755	3315	4162
Zambia	1682	1902	2547
Sub-Saharan Africa	1131	1174	1336

Source: World Bank (2013), "Angola economic update," June 2013.

Angola's Agricultural Policy Framework

After the end of war, poverty reduction has been one of the Angola government's priorities. Since 2003, the "Strategy for Fight against Poverty 2003-2005" and "Global Strategy for Poverty Reduction 2006-2010" have been launched. In 2009, the "National Food Security and Nutrition Strategy", supported by FAO, was approved. In 2010, the above mentioned strategies were merged into an "Integrated Municipal Program for Rural Development and the Fight Against Poverty" with the general objective of reducing levels of extreme poverty in Angola, particularly in rural areas, promoting access to basic public services, and turn-

---

① World Bank, "Angola economic update", June 2013. http: //www. worldbank. org/content/ dam/Worldbank/document/Africa/Angola/angola-economic-update-june-2013. pdf.

ing Angola into a prosperous country with social justice. ①

The government of Angola also formulateda series of programs for people's liveli-hood, such as "Water for all", "Education for all", and "Energy for all", showing the government's willingness tobring the oil wealth to ordinary people. In the early period of post-war reconstruction, the government focused on supportin-gex-combatants, displaced families, and people elsewise affected by the war. ②
Now, the government shifted the priority to wider social sectors, especially food security, in order toassistpoor and vulnerable groups.

The government of Angola recognizedthe importance of agricultureand placedit as a top priority in all government strategies. In 2009, the government put food security on the list of the top national strategy. ③With two-thirds of the employed population engaged in agriculture, agriculture and rural development does not only help reduce poverty and improve food security but alsohold the key to stimu-lating growth. The government summarised the reasons for the impediment of agri-cultural development: The many years of war, urban-rural migration, destruc-tion of economic and social infrastructure, failureof macro-policies, insufficiency of the health and welfare system, and the lack of human resources. ④

These agricultural policies are in line with the government's long-term goals of equitable and inclusive development. The economic policy framework is envisaged in three main policy documents: The "2025 Vision", the "National Develop-ment Strategy (2013 – 2017)", and the "Poverty Reduction Plan (2010 – 2015)."⑤ After the 2012 election, MPLA introduced the "National Develop-

---

① UNFAO, *Angola Country Programming Framework* 2013 – 2017, ftp: //ftp. fao. org/TC/CPF/ Countries/Angola/CPFAngola_FirstDraftNov2012. doc.

② World Bank, "Country partnership strategy (FY 14-FY16) for the Republic of Angola", Au-gust 15, 2013.

③ Liu Haifang, "From resource curse to resource boom: research of Angola's development", in Li Anshan (eds), *The African dream: in search of the road to modernization*, Jiangsu People's Publishing House, p. 744.

④ Liu Haifang, "From resource curse to resource boom: research of Angola's development", in Li Anshan (eds), *The African dream: in search of the road to modernization*, Jiangsu People's Publishing House, p. 740.

⑤ Estrategia de Combate a Pobreza, ECP, 2010 – 2015.

ment Strategy (2013 – 2017)", which sets the goal of income growth and rational distribution. ① Concrete measures include poverty reduction, promoting economic diversification, fair distribution of wealth, providing better public service, helping young entrepreneurs, as well as improving education and vocational training.

The government endeavors to address the agriculture problem through production, processing, funding, and the market mechanism. In May 2015 Angola startedconstruction of a mill with capacity to process 1200 tons of wheat per day—a breakthrough for a country which itself does not produce wheat flour. ②

The National Medium-term Development Plan for the Agricultural sector 2013 – 2017, established the following strategic objectives:

> *Objective* 1: To promote a wider campaign of professional training and transfer of technology to optimize agricultural production and productivity;
> *Objective* 2: To implement a process of agrarian transformation and rural development based on family farming, cooperatives, and public-private partnerships;
> *Objective* 3: To establish a mechanism for tight coordination and synergies between different sectors and other stakeholders in rural areas, emphasizing society participation in the national development process;
> *Objective* 4: To contribute to the process of industrialization of the country. ③

The Ministry of Agriculture and Rural development has accordingly identified five major tasks: (1) increasing overall agricultural production and productivity; (2) linking farmers (particularly smallholders) to markets to raise farmers' income; (3) building rural infrastructure (e. g. irrigation, transportation, e-

---

① *Angola National Development Plan* 2013 – 2017, http://www. embangola-can. org/en/national_development_plan. html.
② Macauhub news, "Angola's Minister of Industry announces construction of wheat mill", April 24, 2015.
③ UNFAO, Angola Country Programming Framework, 2013 – 2017, ftp://ftp. fao. org/TC/CPF/Countries/Angola/CPFAngola_FirstDraftNov2012. doc.

lectrification, land quality improvement, etc.); (4) creating non-farm job opportunities; and (5) strengthening the capacity of rural community-based organizations. [1]

Angola's Multiple Partners in the Agricultural sector

Dueto the government's diversified diplomacy, Angola's strategy of agriculture development and economic diversification has been supported by various governments and international organisations. Angola has already designed good policy frameworks for agricultural development. Financial and technology support from both bilateral and multilateral partners add potential to the development of agriculture. What hampers the agricultural growth is poor infrastructure, low productivity, lack of technology, as well as the gap between the government's capacities and ambitions. Further so, the safety and security situation in Angola is deteriorating due to the devaluation of Kwangza and excessive inflation.

Since 2011, the UNFAO has contributed around $3 million every year to Angola to help establish an agricultural framework and follow up agricultural policies, as well as to assist poverty reduction. The EU planned a 5-year budget of 220 million euros to help improve the country's land registration system and assist smallholder farmers with agricultural technology training and nutrition education.

The UNFAO and World Bank tend to give priority to smallholders when giving advice to the government of Angola on making agriculture and rural development strategies. The World Bank's projects in Angola mainly focus on capacity-building for smallholder farmers to enhance their outputs in order to improve food security and increase rural income and eliminate extreme poverty. The Bank's "Market O-riented Smallholder Agriculture Project (MOSAP)" is structured to linkAngola's rural smallholders directly with markets.

Besides multilateral organizations, Angola's agricultural development also at-

---

[1] World Bank, "Country partnership strategy (FY 14-FY16) for the Republic of Angola", August 15, 2013, p. 21.

tracted lots of financial and technical support from bilateral partners. Argentina opened up a $100 million credit in 2013 to finance agricultural projects in Angola. [1] In 2014, the United States' Export-Import Bank announced that it would provide unlimited amounts of funding to business projects in Angola, with agriculture, energy, and other sectors as priorities. [2] The British government also showed support to Angola's economic diversification strategy, with a focus on the agricultural sector.

While Western countries and international organizations put more emphasis on smallholder famers, southern countries like Brazil and China focus on large agribusiness projects. Odebrecht, a Brazilian company, is taking part in an agro-industrial project on a 36000-hectare farm in Pungo Andongo in Malanje province. [3] Odbrecht's role includes constructing infrastructure, managing production, building and operating maize flour and animal feed plants, as well as training farmers.

China's Role in Angola's Agricultural Development

Sino-Angolan cooperation hasfrequentlybeen portrayed by western media and academia as oil-centered, a misperception ignoring the big picture of the current China-Angola relationship. Starting from the comprehensive package model (resources, credit, and infrastructure), cooperation between Angola and China has deepened into agriculture and other livelihood sectors. The bilateral trade has experienced a steady growth since 2002. Angola is now China's second-largest trading partner in Africa (after South Africa). [4] China is Angola's largest trading

① Macauhub news (2013), "Argentina opens up US $100 million credit line to Angola", http://www.macauhub.com.mo/en/2013/07/26/argentina-opens-up-us100-million-credit-line-to-angola/.

② Macauhub news (2014), "United States' Ex-Im bank announces unlimited funding for Angola", http://www.macauhub.com.mo/en/2014/02/14/united-states% E2% 80% 99-ex-im-bank-announces-unlimited-funding-for-angola/.

③ Odebrecht online, http://www.odebrechtonline.com.br/complementos/01801-01900/1815/.

④ Economic review of Angola (updated in October 2015), MoFCOM website, http://ao.mofcom.gov.cn/article/ddgk/201411/20141100804585.shtml.

partner, largest export destination, and second largest source of imports, with the bilateral trade volume accounting for about 37. 6 percent of Angola's foreign trade. ①Since 2006, Angola became the second largest supplier of crude oil to China, second only to Saudi Arabia. China gave duty-free access to 95 per cent of Angola imports in 2012. ②

Since China and Angola established a strategic partnership in 2010, bilateral relations have strengthened in the sectors of agriculture, industry, infrastructure, energy, etc. China Development bank (CDB), for the first time, provided a commercial loanof $ 1. 5 billion to Angola in 2009. Without future oil as guarantee, ③ the CDBloan mainly supports the development of agriculture in Angola. In May 2014, during his first ever visit to Angola, Chinese Premier Li Keqiang signed a new financing agreement with Angola. CDB will provide a new credit line with $ 2. 5 billion to support Angola's housing, transportation, agriculture, hospitals, schools, water, electricity, etc. ④ Gao Hucheng, China's Minister of Commerce vowed to increaseagricultural investment to Angola and launch an agricultural demonstration center as soon as possible. ⑤

Both China and Angola are facing economic challenges domestically and promoting transformation now. Thedrop in the price of crude oil plunged Angola into crisis. A positive aspect is that this provides pressure for the Angolan government to carry out serious diversification strategy. In the meantime, China's economy is heading for a slowdown in growth and embracing green and low-carbon development alongside with the transition from an investment-driven to consumption-driven economy. Under the current circumstances, agricultural cooperation

---

① Economic review of Angola (updated in October 2015), MoFCOM website, http: //ao. mofcom. gov. cn/article/ddgk/201411/20141100804585. shtml.

② Economic review of Angola (updated in October 2015), MoFCOM website, http: //ao. mofcom. gov. cn/article/ddgk/201411/20141100804585. shtml.

③ Yao Guimei," Main models and challenges of Sino-Africa investment cooperation", Xiyafeizhou, Volume 5, 2013, p. 109.

④ MOFCOM (2014), http: //ao. mofcom. gov. cn/article/sqfb/.

⑤ "Gao Hucheng: Booming and Promising China-Angola Economic and Trade Cooperation", MOFCOM, May 13, 2014, http: //english. mofcom. gov. cn/article/newsrelease/significantnews/201405/20140500591202. shtml.

brings opportunity for the transformation and upgrading of the Sino-Angolan partnership.

China as one of Angola's Foreign Partners

Plagued by wars for more than 40 years, Angolais facing an enormous task of reconstruction. Reluctant to accept strict conditions imposed by the IMF and Paris club, Angola's negotiations with Western lenders failed to reach an agreement. Instead, China stepped in with an oil-backed financing without strings attached, which met Angola's urgent needs. In November 2003, China's Ministry of Commerce and Angola's Ministry of Finance signed the first "Framework Agreement on Special Arrangement of Economic and Trade Cooperation", a package combining oil, credit, economic, and trade cooperation. Under the Framework Cooperation Agreement, Chinaprovidesan oil-backed loan worth of $2 billion and large infrastructure construction to Angola. In 2007, Angola and China signed two similar package agreements worth $500 million and $2 billion respectively. The lending for the fourth framework agreement signed in 2011 was $3 billion. Under the framework cooperation, China constructed more than 130 infrastructure and livelihood projects, such as schools, hospitals, roads, water supply, irrigation, power transmission, and so on—a strong support for the post-war reconstruction and development of Angola. The improvement of infrastructure created favorable conditions for developmentinmore diversified areas, for example, agricultural development. More importantly, cooperation with China enhanced the credibility of Angola and helped Angola'sgovernment gain "international space with more power to convince others." [1]

However, reading between the lines of the Angolan government's statement, China's comprehensive cooperation with Angola is submerged in the "simple nar-

---

[1] Liu Haifang, "From resource advantage to development advantage: The research on Angola's post-war development", in Wang Chengan (eds), *Research of Portuguese Speaking Countries*, 2013, p.71.

rative" and China's innovative way of cooperation has been "normalized."① Goingthrough post-war reconstruction and the financial crisis, Angola not only madeefforts to diversify its economy, but also endeavors to diversify its diplomacy partners. While first pursuinga strategic partnership with China, today Angola is also actively "looking West" to develop multiple partnerships in order to improve the country's credit rating, expand itsinternational space, and maximize its own national interests.

Contrary to the outside perception that Angola has a special relationship with China, China is only one of Angola's diversified foreign partners. Angola's relationswith Western countries and organizations, such as the IMF and World Bank have been gradually improved since 2009. The Angolan government constantly receives guidance on macroeconomics from Bretton Wood organisations. From 2009 to 2012, Angola implemented $1.4 billion Standby Arrangement (SBA) program from IMF, which was followed by a post program monitoring that ended in May 2014. The IMF representative office in Luanda not only supervises the Angolan government on macroeconomic policy through formal channels, but also maintains daily communication with different levels of Angolan officials. The IMF resident representative to Angola believes that the considerable improvement of external perceptions about Angola's macroeconomic management is partly due to the successful implementation of IMF's SBA program.②In 2006, the government has requested support from IMF for a three-year Extended Fund Facility (EFF) program to help recover the economy. An IMF team visited Luanda from 1-14 June 2016 to negotiate the deal.

Similar to the IMF, the World Bank's cooperation with Angolahas focused on providing advice and guidance. Before the 21st century, the World Bank had made only one national strategy report for Angola, namely "Country Assistance

---

① Liu Haifang, "From resource advantage to development advantage: The research on Angola's post-war development", in Wang Chengan (eds), *Research of Portuguese Speaking Countries*, 2013, p. 71.

② Interview with Nicholas Staines, IMF Resident Representative, December 9, 2014, www. imf. org/external/country/AGO/rr/2014/120914. pdf, accessed 27 May 2015.

Strategy" published in 1991. However, entering the second decade of the 21st century, Angola's attitude has witnessed gradual changes. The Angolan government explicitly expressed strong will to strengthen cooperation with the World Bank Group in 2013. [1] The bank, for the first time, developeda new strategy for its partnership with Angola, namely the "Country Partnership Strategy (FY 14-FY16)". The evolution of titles from "assistance" to "partnership" hints at a changing attitude towards Angola. When preparing and writing the strategy report for Angola 2013, the World Bank also changed the top-down approach and wrote the report jointly with the Angolan government. The consultation and discussion process during the report writing was taken by the World Bank as an opportunity to strengthen its relationship with Angola.

The development financing now constitutes less than 0. 5 percent of Angolan government's expenditure. [2] The World Bank is aware of the declining role of development finance to the Angolan government. Therefore it exerts influence mainly by providing strategic advice and technical assistance to Angola's long-term development goal, as well as to build up the government's capacity in institution building. The World Bank's strategy towards Angola is thus in transition from providing preferential development loans to a more strategic way of offering consultation and sharing knowledge and experience.

For today's Angola, experience, technical, and policy guidance is far more important than sole financial support. The Angolan government has been constantly saying to the World Bankthat " (we) need your brains and not your money. " [3] The changing role of the World Bank in Angola indicates the future direction of China-Angola relationship. China's cooperation with Angola in the first ten years, a simple model of oil-for-credit-and-infrastructure, met the needs and

① World Bank (2013), "Country partnership strategy (FY 14-FY16) for the Republic of Angola", August 15, 2013.

② World Bank (2013), "Country partnership strategy (FY 14-FY16) for the Republic of Angola", August 15, 2013, p. 17.

③ World Bank (2013), "Country partnership strategy (FY 14-FY16) for the Republic of Angola", August 15, 2013, p. 53.

interests of both sides and thus was successful in this particular period of Angola's post-war reconstruction. However, as Angola began to diversify its economy, the enthusiasm of Angola's government to cooperate with Chinese enterprises has been decreasing. The Angola model itself thus came to a standstill. ①Agricultural cooperation between China and Angola will explore new ways of cooperation and contribute to the strengthening and transformation of the strategic partnership between China and Angola.

Features of China-Angola Agricultural Cooperation

The main forms of China's agricultural cooperation with Angola are agricultural infrastructure construction, technical training, and credit support. Since 2009, with the credit line supported by China Development Bank and China Exim Bank, China has begun the construction of seven comprehensive agricultural projects in Angola (table 2). All seven farms are managed under a similar model based on a five-year contract signed by Chinese partner companies and the Angolan Ministry of Agriculture, represented by its state-owned enterprise Gesterra. Under the one-stop farm style, China not only constructs farms, irrigation facilities, grain drying, food storage, and processing plants, but also helps Angola trainskilled personnel and farm managers. All the farms plant rice, corn, and soybeans to meet the needs of local markets in Angola. The size of each farm ranges from 1500 hectares to 12000 hectares. All the land belongs to Angola and will be given back to Gesterra after the five-year project period. Among the current seven farms, Guimba is funded by Exim Bank, while the other six farms are supported by the CDB loan.

Pedras Negras, the largest farm among the seven, has been developed jointly by CITIC Construction and Xinjiang Production and Construction Corps since 2010. Covering an area of 12000 hectares, the total value of this contract is more than $120 million. Pedras Negras is the first non-engineering project signed by

---

① Yao Guimei, "Main models and challenges of Sino-Africa investment cooperation", Xiyafeizhou, Volume 5, 2013, p. 109.

CITIC Construction in this region and marks a new era of Chinese companies in Angola that go beyond construction and explore cooperation in new fields such as agriculture. Main products at Pedras Negras are corn and soybean. Under the five-year contract, CITIC Construction shall be responsible for land clearing, infrastructure construction, planting tests in the first three years, and formal operation and personnel training in the last two years. All harvests shall be handed over to Gesterra. After the five-year contract terminates, all land, farms, and equipment will also be transferredto Gesterra.

Table 2   Seven agro-farming projects supported by CDB and Exim Bank in Angola

Farm	Location	CN partner	Enterprise type	Starting year	Bank	Credit (US $ m)	Size (ha)	Products
Pedras Negras	Melange	CITIC Construction	SOE	2011	CDB	160/117	12580	Corn, soybean
Sanza Pombo	Uige	CITIC Construction	SOE	2012	CDB	87. 5/129	1050	Rice, cattle keeping
Longa	Cuando Cubango	CAMC	SOE	May 2012	CDB	76. 6	1500	rice
Camacupa	Bie	CAMC	SOE	2012	CDB	88. 64	4500	corn
Guimba	Zaire	CEIEC	SOE	Starting soon	Exim Bank	68	3000	Corn, soybean & cultivation
Camaiangala	Moxico	CEIEC	SOE	2013	CDB	79	16000	Corn, soybean
Manquete	Cunene	CEIEC	SOE	2014	CDB	85. 5	45000	rice

Source: Zhou Jinyan, "Neither friendship farm nor land grab: Chinese agricultural engagement in Angola", Policy brief of SAIS China Africa Research Initiative at Johns Hopkins University.

China-Angola agriculture cooperation at its current stage has the following features: First, Chinese state capital and state-owned enterprises are playing a leading role in the cooperation, while private capital and investment in agriculture is still at its initial stage. The situation is different in other African countries, e. g. Tanzania and Mozambique, where private capital and companies are playinga dominant role in agriculture cooperation. The reasons of "strong state, weak market" can be explained fromtwo aspects. On one hand, during Angola's post-war reconstruction, a large number of China's state-owned enterprises entered the country through the Framework Cooperation Agreement. These included Sinohydro, China National Machinery and Equipment Import and Export Corporation (CMEC), China Railway 20th Bureau Group, and more. Initially engaged in the construction sector, these companies continued to seek other business opportunities uponcompletion of infrastructure projects. The Chinese state-owned enterprises that accumulated years of experience in Angola are familiar with local conditions. Coupled with policy preference and credit support from the Chinese government, state-owned enterprises have more advantages in agricultural cooperation with Angola. On the other hand, the infrastructure conditions and investment environment of Angolahas restricted Chinese private enterprises from investing in agriculture.

Taking the year of 2016 as a dividing line, China's agricultural cooperation model with Angola is gradually changing in two aspects. First, China's agriculture projects in Angola are shifting from large-scale agricultural farm construction to market-oriented agricultural investment. When the projects listed above (see Table 2) were begun, China had not yet become a main investor in Angola's agriculture sector, but was mainly anengineering contractor. The intention of China's agricultural cooperation with Angola was primarily to maintain China's national image and strengthening the strategic partnership. However, the current agricultural cooperation is gradually shifting cooperation towards a market-oriented model in which enterprises (both state-owned and private) play the dominant role. There are increasingly more Chinese private enterprises seeingbusiness opportunities in Angola's agriculture. For example, Zong Qinghou, chairmanof Wahaha Group toldbusinessmen from Zhejiang province: "Angola covers 1.2 million square kilometers and has 35 million hectares of arable land. Industry there is barely developed and all necessities rely on import. It is in desperate need to attract foreign investment to develop its agriculture, fishery, and other industries."[1] The

---

[1] China Daily, "Wahaha eyes African market", http://www.chinadaily.com.cn/world/2014-10/22/content_18786452.htm.

company had already signed a memorandum of cooperation with the Angolan government for investment, which got support from the China-Africa Development Fund and CDB's branch in Zhejiang.

Chinese contractors and subcontractors, by participating in the construction of the seven farm projects (see Table 2), have gained valuable experience in operating agriculture in Angola. Approaching the completion of the five-year contract, some Chinese enterprises are initiating new agricultural investment projects. Jiangsu Jiangzhou Agriculture Scientific Development Company, a sub-contractor of CAMC for the construction of Camacupa farm in 2012, sees great potentialin Angola's agriculture. In 2014, the company decided to shift its business from engineering contracting to agriculture investment. In 2016, Jiangsu Jiangzhou Group was awardeda project to develop 10000 hectares at the Caala farm in Huambo Province. Another progress in China-Angola agriculture cooperation is that provinces are playing a more active role now. A recent example is how the province of Jiangsu intends to carry out several projects for agricultural cooperation with the provinces of Cunene and Huambo. The idea was based on mutual visits of provincial leaders between both countries. Fifteen Angolese students will soon come to the Jiangsu Agri-animal Husbandry Vocational College to complete three years' study programs. Besides bilateral cooperation, China also engages in multilateral agriculture cooperation by sending experts to Angola through the UNFAO South-South Cooperation Framework and contributing to South-South Cooperation Trust Fund.

The Effects of China-Angola Agricultural Cooperation

China's agricultural projects in Angola can improve the agricultural infrastructure of Angola, boost their technology, and enhance their production, which helps Angola achieve the goal of poverty reduction and food security. First, China has great advantages in improving Angola's infrastructure, which is crucial for Angola's strategy to diversify its economy and attract foreign investment. Angola has now become China's third largest contracting market in Africa. Under the

Framework Cooperation Agreement, Chinese enterpriseshavebuilt traffic network and public facilities for Angola, which effectively improve the conditions of industrial and agricultural development. The improvement of infrastructure has long-term positive impact on investment environment and the competitiveness of private sectors. China's construction of infrastructure and public utilities has not only laid a solid foundation for the two countries to expand cooperation from oil to the agricultural sector, but also helped reduce the cost of other countries to invest in Angolaand thuscreate a more favourable environment for private investment.

Under the Framework Cooperation Agreement, the Chinese company Hydropower has built four irrigation projects for Angola in the agricultural areas of Caxio, Gandjelas, Luena, and Wako-Kungo. The Benguela railway, restored by the 20th Bureau of China Railway Corporation, starts in the port of Lobito, continues to Benguela, reaching the border of DRC in the city of Luau. The railway will bring huge business opportunity for Angola's agricultural trade. The connection from landlocked Zambia and DRC to the sea will reduce transportation costs and encourage agricultural trade in the region.

Angola's 35 million hectares arable land only comprises one fifth of the total land area, which means that Angola has great potential for agriculture, but huge reclamation and investment is needed. Since 2010, China has implemented seven comprehensive farming projects across Angola and plan to clear nearly 100000 hectares of land. Through construction of farms, agricultural training centers, agricultural product processing plants, and storage facilities, China is assisting Angola in improving agricultural infrastructure, increase productivity, and connect agricultural products to the market.

Second, China helps Angola to improve agricultural technology and extends the valuechain. For example, trickle irrigation, a water-saving irrigation method, was promoted by Xinjiang Production and Construction Corps in Angola. Besides, the agriculture production of Angolan has been enhanced. A highlight of China's agriculture cooperation in Angola is the construction of agricultural processing plants. The purpose is to help Angola extend its agricultural industrial value chain and improve the added value of agricultural products. For example, atPedras

Negras farm, the corn processing plant produces 12 tonnes of corn flour each hour.

Besides the infrastructure problem, shortage of skilled personnel is the biggest barrier for improving Angola's agricultural productivity. If farmers in Angola grasped modern farming techniques, agriculture outputs would double or even quadruple. To meet Angola's needs, China puts emphasis on "training the trainers" to build Angolans' capacity of agriculturaltechniques and farm management. China Electronics Import and Export Corporation (CEIEC) sent 17 Angolans to China's Heilongjiang province for training. CITIC Construction funded 19 Angolans to study at Xinjiang Shihezi University for a year. After training in China, they will be dispatched by the Angolan Ministry of Agriculture to other farms in the country as managers and trainers.

On land issues, some outsiders accuse China for grabbing land in Angola or use land as security for cooperation. This is against the fact. China will nerve grab land overseas, but will continue to "hold the rice bowl in our own hands. "① If Angola and other African countries could achieve food security, world food prices will be stable. It is beneficiary for China to buy food from the world market with stable prices and indirectly promotes China's own food safety.

Conclusion and Policy Recommendations

Under the guidance of the World Bank and other international organizations, the Angolan government has already made a lot of good strategies. However, the problem lies in implementation of policies. Angola has a huge potential in agriculture, but poor infrastructure and personnel shortages are bottlenecks that restrict the development. Especially for non-oil sectors, infrastructure improvement is the key. It is hard to make profit from agricultural investment in the short term in Angola, thus most of the private enterprises are reluctant to bear the cost of land

① "Angolanmedia interview with Li Chong, Chinese diplomat in Angola". http: //ao. china-embassy. org/chn/sghd/t1274791. htm.

clearing and farming preparation. The World Bank, the European Union, and other Western organizations' agriculture cooperation focus on two aspects: (1) supporting smallholder farmers through training and by improving market linkages and (2) influence the government's agricultural policy making through consulting. Policy advice and the sharing of knowledge are as important as credit lines

During President Dos Santos's visit to Beijing, Chinese President Xi Jinping pointed out that China and Angola are good brothers and long-term strategic partners. China is willing to work with Angola to transform the advantage of bilateral traditional friendship into "win-win" cooperation, comprehensively deepen mutually beneficial cooperation, help Angola turn the advantage of abundant natural and human resources into development outcomes that benefit the people, and provide comprehensive cooperation for Angola to achieve independent and sustainable development. He believes that Angolan President's visit will inject new impetus to the China-Angola strategic partnership. The cooperation between China and Angola is transforming from government-led trade and engineering contracting into enterprise-led investment. Agricultural cooperation can be a pioneer for the ongoing transformation and upgrading of Sino-Angola cooperation.

The plunge of international oil prices forced the government of Angola to pursue economic diversification. Agriculture and rural development is taken as top priority by the Angolan government. Agriculturaldevelopment can help Angola to reduce poverty, improve food security, and is crucial for Angola's strategy of economic diversification. For China, the agricultural cooperation with Angola is part of China's "going out" strategy for agricultural enterprises and a key to movingthe strategic partnership with Angola to a new stage. With government credit support, China's state-owned enterprises are the biggest infrastructure partner for Angola's agricultural sector. However, there is still large room for the agricultural cooperation between China and Angola. At its current stage, Chinese companies are making efforts to shift their role as infrastructure contractors to real investors. The cooperation in the future should be gradually transformed to a market-oriented model by attracting more private investment from China. The Angolan government should mitigate structural risks, improve the investment environment, and simplify the procedures to provide one-stop service for foreign investors. More preferential policies for agriculture investment, such as tax cuts are expected.

The implication for China is to increase its influence on the policy level on the basis of existing agricultural technical training and infrastructure projects. For China and Angola, the "Angola model" was the special choice under special conditions. [1]When Angola developed to a certain level, the model of resources for large-scale infrastructure was bound to be replaced by a market-oriented model. Now China-Angola relations are going beyond the resource-centered cooperation and stretch into agricultural and other non-oil sectors.

China should step up efforts to promote Chinese enterprises (including state-owned enterprises and private enterprises) to invest in Angola's agriculture. Besides the current large-scale farming projects, more attention should be paid to Angola's small scale agriculture, where China can provide technology and years of experience. Through training smallholder farmers and connecting farmers to the market, it will help more ordinary people to benefit from China-Angola cooperation and change the perception that China only focus on resources without caring about the trickle down of wealth.

① Shen Chen, "China's investment in South Africa should go beyond Angola model", http://www.thepaper.cn/newsDetail_forward_1322028, accessed 17 April, 2015.

Agricultural International Cooperation in Zimbabwe and Food Crops Cultivation of Chinese Agribusinesses

Shen Xiaolei*

When Zimbabwe's Fast Track Land Reform was launched in 2000, it turned the country's land resources into a controversial issue among the international community. And a subsequent dramatic reduction of Zimbabwe's agricultural production led many scholars to think the land reform represented a threat to the country's food security. [1]After *Zimbabwe's Land Reform: Myths and Realities*[2]and *Zimbabwe Takes Back Its Land*[3]were published in 2010 and 2012, the international community changed its attitudes on Zimbabwe's land reform and accepted the argument that land reform farmers can help to increase agricultural production and reduce poverty. But the land reform has caused international actors to cut aid and investment into Zimbabwean agriculture and this situation cannot be changed in the short term. Due to the sanctions imposed by the United States and European Union, Zimbabwe implemented the "Looking East" policy in 2003, seeking

---

* Shen Xiaolei, Research Fellow from Institute of West – Asian and African Studies, Chinese Academy of Social Sciences.

[1] See International Crisis Group, *Blood and Soil: Land, Politics and Conflict Prevention in Zimbabwe and South Africa*, 2004; African all party parliamentary group, *Land in Zimbabwe: past mistakes, future prospects*, 2009.

[2] Ian Scoones, Nelson Marongwe, Blasio Mavedzenge, et al. , *Zimbabwe's Land Reform: Myths and Realities*, James Currey, 2010.

[3] J. Hanlon, J. Manjengwa & T. Smart, *Zimbabwe Takes Back Its Land*, Jacana Media (Pty) Ltd. , 2013.

397

help from eastern countries, such as Malaysia, Singapore, India, Russia, and especially China. Simultaneously, China had been enhancing its cooperation with African countries since 2000. Under this background, the agricultural cooperation between China and Zimbabwe was carried out in different sectors step by step. In 2010 and 2013 respectively, two Chinese agribusinesses, Anhui State Farms Agribusiness Corporation (AHSFAC) and Anhui Tianrui Environment Technology Co., Ltd. (ATETC) came to Zimbabwe to plant food crops. This opened up a new area of agricultural cooperation between China and Zimbabwe, and demonstrates an important difference between China and other international stakeholders.

Overview of Agricultural Development in Zimbabwe

Agriculture plays a very important role in the Zimbabwean economy. According to Zimbabwe's Ministry of Agriculture, Mechanisation and Irrigation Development, Zimbabwe's agriculture provides livelihoods for 80 per cent of the population, accounts for 23 per cent of formal employment, and contributes 14 – 18.5 per cent to Zimbabwe's GDP. [1] The contribution of different agricultural products accounts as follows: tobacco 25 per cent, livestock (excluding beef) 24 per cent, maize 14 per cent, cotton 12.5 per cent, beef and fish 10 per cent, sugar and horticulture 7 per cent, and subsistence crops 0.5 per cent. [2]

Zimbabwe's arable land is classified into five agro – ecological regions based on soil types and precipitation (see Table 1) Further classifications are based on the land ownership and use patterns, and farms are classified as communal farms, 1980s resettlement farms, A1 farms, A2 farms, small – scale commercial farms, large – scale commercial farms, and agricultural estates (see Table 2) .

---

[1] See the website of Zimbabwe's Ministry of Agriculture, Mechanisation and Irrigation Development, http://www.moa.gov.zw/.

[2] "Zimbabwe Agricultural Investment Plan (ZAIP) 2013 –2017: A Comprehensive Framework for the Development of Zimbabwe's Agriculture Sector", p. 14.

Table 1　Zimbabwe's Agro – Ecological Regions

Nature region	Province Spread	Average Rainfall (mm)	Total Land (%)	Characteristics	Agricultural Activity
I	Manicaland	Greater than 1050	2	High rainfall, specialized and diversity	Forestry, tea, coffee, fruit, intensive livestock
II	Mashonaland, Central, Mashonaland East, Mashonaland West, Manicaland, Harare	750 – 1000	15	High rainfall	Maize, flue cured tobacco, sugar beans, horticulture, intensive animal husbandry, coffee, irrigated wheat and barley, sorghum, groundnuts
III	Manicaland, Midlands	450 – 650	19	Periodic droughts, unreliable start to rain season, mid – term dry spells	Semi – intensive farming, extensive beef ranching, marginal maize, millet, sorghum
IV	Masvingo, Matebeland South, Matebeland North, Manicaland, Midlands, Bulawayo	450 – 650	37	Too dry for successful crop production without irrigation, prolonged midterm dry spells	Marginal millet, sorghum, extensive beef ranching, game ranching
V	Masvingo, Matebeland South, Manicaland, Midlands, Bulawayo	Less than 450	27	Too dry for successful crop production without irrigation, prolonged midterm dry spells	Marginal millet, sorghum, extensive beef ranching, game ranching

Source: Ministry of Agriculture, Mechanization and Irrigation Development, "Zimbabwe Agricultural Investment Plan (ZAIP) 2013 – 2017", p. 15.

Table 2　Agricultural land inventory as of 2011

Land pattern	Area (ha)	Number
A1	5759153. 89	145775
A2	2978334. 08	16387
Communal areas	16000000	1200000
Old Resettlement Areas	3667708	75569
Large – scale commercial farms	648041. 27	1154
Small – scale commercial farms	1400000	8000
Others	1695220. 93	630
Total	32148517. 17	1447523

Source: Prosper B. Matondi, *Zimbabwe's Fast Track Land Reform*, Zed Book Ltd. , 2012, p. 9.

Zimbabwe was once was considered Southern Africa's breadbasket, but since the Fast Track Land Reform in 2000 it has suffered a serious decline in agricultural production. This decline has mostly been blamed on the government's poor policies on market and price controls, inadequate agricultural investment, hyperinflation, international sanctions, and lack of skills and management experiences among the new farmers. [1] Compared to the average production in the 1990s, the production of two of the most important crops, maize and tobacco, dropped 65. 8 per centin the 2007/2008 season and 72. 2 per cent in the 2005/2006 season. [2] From then on, food insecurity became a serious problem in Zimbabwe. [3]

In order to rejuvenate crop production and increase agricultural productivity, the Government of Zimbabwe (GoZ) initiated a series of agriculture policy papers, including the "Agricultural Sector and Medium Term Plan" (MTP 2011 – 2015) and the "Zimbabwe Agricultural Investment Plan" (ZAIP2013 – 2017),

[1] Prosper B. Matondi, *Zimbabwe's Fast Track Land Reform*, Zed Book, 2012, p. 134; Hanlon, et al. , *Zimbabwe's Fast Track Land Reform*, pp. 93 – 96

[2] Sam Moyo & Walter Chambati, eds. , *Land and Agrarian Reform in Zimbabwe: Beyond White – Settler Capitalism*, CPDESROA 2013, p. 212.

[3] T. S. Jayne, etc. , "Zimbabwe's food insecurity paradox: hunger amid potential", in MandivambaRukni, etc. , *Zimbabwe's Agricultural Revolution Revisited*, University of Zimbabwe Publications, 2006, pp. 525 – 541.

to guide the agricultural development atmacro – level. The government adopted a series of measures to achieve this goal, which included introducing a contract farming scheme in tobacco in 2004, and allowing the contracting company to sign contracts with tobacco farmers directly, which contributed to the restoration of tobacco production greatly. The government then opened the cereal market to private traders,[1] and set up a minimum protection purchase price, and further allowed farmers to trade maize for fertilizer to increase food crops production. Contract farming of soya bean, sweet bean, peanut, sorghum, millet, popcorn, and sunflower was expanded. The government also encouraged investments into agriculture by providing tax and non – tax incentives to both domestic and foreign investors, such as lowered income taxation for agriculture processing companies that export 50 per cent or more of their output, special initial allowance for farm improvements and tobacco barns, zerovalue – added tax for agriculture inputs such as fertilizer, seeds, pesticides, agricultural machinery, and deferment of collection of VAT on imported agricultural goods. [2]

These policies have led to some improvement. Zimbabwe's agricultural production began to increase in 2009 and the growth rate in 2010 reached 33 per cent. [3] Up to the 2013/2014 season, the yields of maize, cereal, tobacco, and cotton reached and even exceeded the average production of the 1990s. [4]The rejuvenation of agricultural production not only proves that the Fast Track Land Reform was necessary and right, but also demonstrates that smallholder farming is more suitable for Zimbabwe in the current situation and can increase its agricultural productivity and create more employment. [5]

---

[1] "ZIMBABWE: No winds of change at the Grain Marketing Board", http://www.irinnews.org/report/85092/zimbabwe – no – winds – of – change – at – the – grain – marketing – board, accessed 2005 – 04 – 26.

[2] ZAIP, pp. 54 – 56.

[3] ZAIP, p. 3.

[4] Jeanette Manjengwa, Joseph Hanlon and Teresa Smart, "Who will make the 'best' use of Africa's Land? Lessons from Zimbabwe," *Third World Quarterly*, Vol. 35, No. 6, 2014, pp. 980 – 995.

[5] Jeanette Manjengwa, Joseph Hanlon & Teresa Smart, "Who will make the 'best' use of Africa's Land? Lessons from Zimbabwe", *Third World Quarterly*, Vol. 35, No. 6, 2014, pp. 980 – 995.

However, there still remain disadvantages in the agricultural development in Zimbabwe, which includes low rate of mechanisation, poor irrigation infrastructure, and lack of basic agricultural inputs such as fertilizers and pesticides. In order to solve these problems, the GoZ needs to increase financial support to the agricultural sector and attract more foreign and domestic investments in agriculture. But with a stagnant economy and insufficient revenue it is unrealistic to expect the government to increase financial support. Therefore, the most urgent thing for the Go Z to do is to secure more aid and investment through international agricultural cooperation. ①

International agricultural cooperation

After independence in 1980, the Western countries headed by UK donated a large sum of money to Zimbabwe to help it with land resettlement and agricultural development. But since 2000, because of the Fast Track Land Reform and the violence in the following elections, the United States, the European Union, and Australia have imposed sanctions on Zimbabwe. As a result, the agricultural aid from the international community to Zimbabwe has dropped dramatically. The land – reform farmers were affected most severely, as both the EU and the United States discontinued aid programs targeting these farmers. ② Nevertheless, the international community still carry out some agricultural cooperation with Zimbabwe in two aspects: Agricultural aid and investment in cash crops.

---

① In order to guide the investment in agricultural sectors, Zimbabwe Investment Authority listed 18 projects as investment opportunities on its official website, the sectors of which include irrigation rehabilitation and development, livestock (includes cattle, pig and poultry), meat and dairy development, agro – processing, cold storage, inshore fisheries development, cotton and potato farming, ground nuts and popcorn contract farming, and farm mechanization. See, "Opportunities in the Agricultural Sector", http: //www. investzim. com/index. php? option = com_content&view = article&id = 251&Itemid = 688, accessed 2005 – 04 – 26.

② J. Hanlon, *Zimbabwe Takes Back Its Land*, p. 92.

Agricultural Aid

The stakeholders who provide agricultural aid to Zimbabwe are mainly the UK, the United States, Switzerland, UN agencies, and other traditional donors. In recent years, the new emerging economies such as Brazil has joined in. Agricultural aid covers food assistance, rehabilitating and building irrigation facilities, as well as recovering agricultural production. The fundamental aim of the aid is to help Zimbabwe solve its massive problem of food insecurity.

Food Assistance

In 2011, the Swiss Agency for Development and Cooperation (SDC) allocated about CHF 2. 3 million for food assistance. In 2012, SDC denoted CHF 1 million to WFP which could distribute cash and food products to poor and destitute people. [1] The Canadian International Development Agency allocated $7 million for food aid to Zimbabwe between 2009 and 2010. [2] The World Food Programme provided some food assistance through the Food Assistance Working Group. [3]

Rehabilitating and Building Irrigation Facilities

In October 2013, the Brazilian government supplied $98 million in loans to Zimbabwe to fund the mechanisation of the agricultural sector and the rehabilitation of irrigation schemes. [4] At the end of 2014, Switzerland committed $6. 3 million for the rehabilitation of eight irrigation schemes in Zimbabwe's Masvin go

---

[1] China – DAC Study Group, "Effective Support for Agricultural Development", pp. 8 – 9.

[2] Zhang Jun, "On the method and characteristic of agricultural development aid by western countries to Zimbabwe" (QiantanXifangGuojiaYuanzhuJinbabuweiNongyeFazhan de FangshiyuTedian), *YuanjianJinbabuweiNongyeJishuHezuoJianbao*, No. 12, 2014, p. 17.

[3] ZAIP, p. 40

[4] "US $ 98m loan for mechanization, irrigation development", http: //www. herald. co. zw/ us98m – loan – for – mechanisation – irrigation – development/, accessed 2005 – 04 – 27.

province, covering more than 700 hectares. ①The Japan International Cooperation Agency built an irrigation facility in Gutu, Masvingo. ②

Recovering Agricultural Production

The United States' Agency for International Development launched the "Zimbabwe Agricultural Income and Employment Development" project in October 2010 with the overall goal of increasing the incomes and food security of 150000 rural Zimbabwean households. It ran until September 2015. ③ Another project is the "Protracted Relief Programme" launched by the British Department for International Development and implemented through 17 partners. The aim of this project is to stabilize food security, improve agricultural investment, and increase crop production in Zimbabwe. Until now, it has concluded two phases—first from 2003 to 2007, and then 2008 to 2012—and has made some good progress. ④Some UN agencies, especially the Food and Agriculture Organization and the World Food Programme, have provided support through alternative delivery channels to Zimbabwe's agriculture. Through coordination with donors and NGOs, they have formed a series of donor working groups that encompass agriculture coordination, market linkage, food assistance, livestock and conservation agriculture, and so on. Initially, their support focused on providing emergency food aid, but it later shifted towards agricultural recovery and transition aid. The support from these groups increased from $25 million in the 2008/2009 season to $74 million for the 2009/2010 season. ⑤ Moreover, in 2011 Brazil and Zimbabwe signed a memorandum of understanding on the "More Food for Africa" pro-

---

① "Zimbabwe: Switzerland Avails U. S. $6, 3 Million for Irrigation", http://allafrica.com/stories/201412190556.html, accessed 2005 – 04 – 27.

② Zhang Jun, "On the method and characteristic of agricultural development aid by western countries to Zimbabwe", p. 17.

③ See the website of Zimbabwe Agricultural Income and Employment Development, http://www.zim – aied.org/。

④ Mary Jennings, Agnes Kayondo, et al, *Impact Evaluation of the Protracted Relief Programme II*, Zimbabwe, April 22, 2013.

⑤ ZAIP, pp. 40 – 41.

gramme, which aims to increase Zimbabwe's food crops production through provision of agricultural machinery, training, and technical support. [1]

Agricultural Investment

The sanctions by the United Stated and EU also affected the foreign investment flow into Zimbabwean agriculture. According to the statistics published by the Zimbabwe Investment Authority, the number of agricultural foreign investment projects in 2009, 2010, 2012 and 2013 was only seven, [2] and officials from the Ministry of Agriculture, Mechanisation and Irrigation Development said that most of them were not successful projects.

Until now, the main sectors attracting foreign investors are cash crops, especially tobacco and cotton. In 2014, more than 50 countries and regions carried out tobacco contract farming or bought tobacco on auction floors. Besides China, other countries that list among the top are Belgium, South Africa, U. A. E, Russia, Indonesia, Sudan, German, UK, and France. [3]Some big tobacco companies, such as British American Tobacco and Universal Corporation Alliance One, have invested in Zimbabwe's tobacco sector for a long time and carried out contract farming through their local subsidiaries. As for the cotton sector, South Africa is the single largest buyer of Zimbabwe's lint. They accounted for 39. 9 percent and 36. 4 percent of Zimbabwe's total lint exports in 2007 and 2008 respectively. [4]

It needs to be pointed out that there are no international stakeholders coming to Zimbabwe to buy or lease land, which means that there is no "land – grabbing" in Zimbabwe at present.

---

[1] Langton Mukwereza, "Zimbabwe – Brazil cooperation through the More Food Africa programme", China and Brazil in Africa Agriculture Project Working Paper, No. 116, p. 5.

[2] Zimbabwe Investment Authority, 2009 *Annual Report*, p. 17, 2010 *Annual Report*, p. 24, 2013 *Annual Report*, pp. 33 – 34.

[3] Tobacco Industry and Marketing Board, *Annual Statistical Report* 2014, p. 18.

[4] Langton Mukwereza, *Chinese and Brazilian Cooperation with African Agriculture: The Case of Zimbabwe*, China and Brazil in Africa Agriculture Project Working Paper 048, March 2013, p. 7.

Agricultural Cooperation between China and Zimbabwe: Food Crops Cultivation①

The agricultural cooperation between China and Zimbabwe began in 1980s and is currently carried out in three aspects: agricultural aid, which includes dispatching agricultural experts,② building an Agricultural Technology Demonstration Centre③ and donating agricultural machineries, and cooperation on cash crops such as tobacco and cotton. The main companies involved in cash crops production are Tianze Tobacco Company (Private) Limited (Tianze)④ and China – Africa Cotton Zimbabwe (PVT) Limited (CACZ). ⑤Food crops cultivation has been carried out by AHSFAC and ATETC since 2010. There are both similarities and differences between China's and other international stakeholders' in terms of agricultural cooperation with Zimbabwe. As for the similarities, there is a com-

① The data cited in this sector are mainly from the interview conducted by author in Zimbabwe.
② China began to dispatch its agricultural experts to Zimbabwe in 2009. Up to now, it has dispatched three teams made up of 25 experts, whose areas of expertise include livestock, horticulture, aquaculture, crops, veterinarian, and agricultural machinery service.
③ The Agricultural Technology Demonstration Centre is located at Gwebi Agricultural College and has an area of 109 hectares (90 hectares are used for cultivation). It was put into use in June 2012 and has 7 agricultural experts now. The key objectives of the experts are cultivation of crops, processing of agricultural products, demonstration and promotion of livestock farming technology, research and experiment, and training local experts.
④ Founded on April 1st, 2005, Tianze is a wholly – owned subsidiary of China National Tobacco Corporation. Through providing interest – free loan to tobacco contract farmers and increasing the purchase price of tobacco, Tianze became one of the biggest tobacco merchants from 2008 onwards and played a pivotal role in the recovery of Zimbabwe's tobacco industry. See Longton Mukwereza, "Situating Tian Ze's role in reviving Zimbabwe's Flue – Cured Tobacco sector in the wider discourse on Zimbabwe – China cooperation: Will the scorecard remain Win – Win?", China and Brazil in Africa Agriculture Project Working Paper, No. 115, February 2015, p. 8.
⑤ CACZ was founded by China – Africa Cotton Development Limited (CACD) through merging two cotton companies in Zimbabwe in 2014. So far, CACZ has established two ginneries with annual production being more than 80000 tonnes. It is the second largest cotton company in Zimbabwe, see "China – Africa Cotton Zimbabwe (PVT) Limited – the pioneer of the spanning development of China – Africa Agriculture", http: //zimbabwe. ca – cotton. com/Index. asp? id = 10, accessed 2015 – 04 – 28.

mon emphasis on agricultural aid and investment in cash crops like tobacco. The difference is that while other international stakeholders put a large emphasis on improving agricultural infrastructure and providing food assistance in the process of solving Zimbabwe's food insecurity, the Chinese agribusinesses mainly came to Zimbabwe to cultivate food crops. That is to say, other international stakeholders are still focusing on "giving a man a fish", while Chinese agribusinesses are starting to "teach a man to fish".

But there is a contradiction behind the Chinese agribusinesses coming to Zimbabwe to cultivate food crops. On one hand, after the Fast Track Land Reform, due to lack of fund, technology and infrastructure, a vast amount of Zimbabwe's arable land remainedunused or underused. ①This provided a good opportunity for foreigners to invest in Zimbabwe's farms and grow food crops. On the other hand, GoZ forbids farmers from leasing and selling land to others. If investors want to get lands for agricultural cultivation, they have to have joint venture with land owners who use their lands as investments, and according to indigenization policy, the land owners must held 50 per cent of the shares. This in particular has discouraged foreign investment. ②It was within this background that AHSFAC and ATETC came to Zimbabwe and established Zim – China Wanjin Agricultural Development Limit Company (ZCWA) and Zim – China WanjinTianrui Food Processing (Private) Limited (ZCWT) in 2010 and 2013, respectively, to grow food crops.

---

① It is estimated by Chinese agricultural expert that arable land utilization rate is only about 10%; In its 2006 research, Sam Moyo's team also found that the rate has not reached optimum level. See Zhang Anping, "On how to improve arable land utilization rate in Zimbabwe" (Shilun Jinbabuwei Tudi Gehuang de Jiejue Fangan), *Yuanjian Jinbabuwei Nongye Jishu Hezuo Jianbao*, No. 12, 2014, p. 18; Sam Moyo, et al, *Fast Track Land Reform Baseline Survey in Zimbabwe: Trends and Tendencies*, 2005/06, Harare: African Institute for Agrarian Studies, 2009, p. 55.

② According to Indigenization and Economic Empowerment Act enacted in 2007, at least 51% of the shares of every existed company or now company shall be owned by indigenous Zimbabweans. Many high government officials, including vice president E. D. Mnangagwa, have realized this policy is an obstacle to foreign investment and told the media that they would adjust it at the end of 2014, but up to now, they didn't take any action.

ZCWA

Following the national "going out" policy and under the support of the Anhui provincial government and GoZ, ZCWA was created by AHSFAC in January 2010 as a joint venture with Zimbabwe's Ministry of Defence (ZMD) . According to their contract, AHSFAC and ZMD each hold 50 percent of the shares and provide 50 percent of the investments. The profits of ZCWA were divided in 50 – 50, but ZMD should repay 70 percent of its profits to ACWADLC. ZCWA appoints a chairman and a general manager and supplies funds and equipment, while ZMD provides land with a tenure of 99 years.

ZCWA finished its first project phase covering 1800 hectares of land in 2011 and are now carrying out the second phase which will span 10000 hectares. The plots of the second phase are located in Mashonaland West, Harare, Mashonaland Middle, and Mashonaland East, which are all in the areas of Natural Region II. In the 2014/2015 season, ZCWA planted 3000 hectares of maize, 500 hectares of soya bean, 700 hectares of wheat, and 150 hectares of sorghum.

In the process of cultivation, ZCWA takes "unified planning, gradually implementing, sustained developing and steadily promoting" as its basic principle and "making sure every plot they develop will be successful and profitable and play an exemplary role" as its main goal. In order to achieve this goal, ZCWA places emphasis on the following things: Prioritising farm infrastructure, especially irrigation facilities, using the proper kinds of crops and agricultural machineries on the basis of soil conditions and cultivation systems, preparing a practical agricultural production program, and promoting technical training and implementation of technical solutions.

As for investments, in order to save money ZCWA imported agriculture machinery from China and bought seeds, fertilizers, pesticides, and fuel in Zimbabwe. Food products from the plots were not exported to China to help solve its own problem of "food security" but sold to National Foods Limited, the biggest food processing company in Zimbabwe. Due to the high quality of the produce, the price of their products per ton was $20 higher than local market.

In 2014 average yields of maize, soya bean, and wheat was 6 tonnes, 2.5 tonnes and 6 tonnes, respectively, with a per tonnes price of $390, $520, and $430. Not including inputs, profits on each crop was $1040, $400, and $880 respectively.

In order to carry out the Anhui provincial government's "go out" policy collectively, AHSFAC set up the "Cooperative Association of Anhui Enterprises for Developing in Zimbabwe" in June 2013. Based on the platform of ZCWA, the Association aims to attract other Chinese enterprises to collectively invest and develop in Zimbabwe. Up to now, three enterprises have joined the Association and their investment have focused on building materials, food processing, and logistics and transport. Moreover, in order to increase the profits and establish an agricultural production chain led by the agricultural products storage and food processing enterprises, ZCWA is preparing to establish an economic trade zone for agriculture products processing in Chinoyi. If the zone is established, it will make a great contribution towards the development of Zimbabwe's modern agriculture.

ZCWT

On the recommendation of AHSFAC and at the invitation of ZMD, ATETC visited Zimbabwe to explore investment opportunities in mineral, building materials, agriculture, and food processing in January 2013. Through comprehensive research on local politics, economy, culture, population and geography, and based on its own capabilities, ATETC signed a strategic agreement with ZCWA in May 2013. According to this agreement, ATETC took over three farms named Kassama, Chivero and Eureka from ZCWA in the Chegutu district. The total area of the three farmsis 3228 hectares and will be used for developing modern agriculture, wood processing, and food processing. In July 2013, ATETC set up ZCW-Tas a joint venture with ZCWALC. Both ATETC and ZCWALC hold 50 percent of the shares of ZCWT, but ATETC alone provides capital and operates the farms independently.

On the three farms, only a very small part of landis arable and most of the land had remained idle for a couple of decades. After overcoming initial difficulties, ZCWT planted 320 hectares of maize in the 2013/2014 season. In the 2014/2015 season, ZCWT expanded the total areas of maize to 600 hectares by continued reclaiming.

Because ZCWT lacks agricultural skills, and the land is unsuited for cultivation due to lying idle for so long and need at least three years to become arable, the total yields of maize was only about 800 tonnes in the 2013/2014 season, which means that it was less than 3 tonnes per hectare—far below the yields of neigh-bouringlarge-scale farms. Due to the failure of fertilizing and weeding, the maize on one plot were so small that they were not even harvested as local ZCWT personnel were afraid that the sales would not be enough to cover costs of renting a reaper. Nevertheless, they gained some experiences from the failure. For example, in 2014/2015 season, they sowed the seeds before the delayed rain season coming and did a good job in fertilizing and weeding. When the author visited their farms in January 2015 it was evident that their maize was much better than the neighbouring farms. Zhang Hengxi, the general manager of ZCMTFPL, said during interviews that if the rain were enough and regular, the yield of maize would be about five tonnes per hectare that year.

ZCWT has bought more than 20 large scale agricultural machineries from China and South Africa, and are continuing land clearing to expand the areas of recla-mation. In the 2015/2016 season, their total planting areas will be about 1000 hectares. But reclamation will cause another problem. Since the farms are located in areas of sandy soil, it is necessary to carefully protect the reclaimed areas from the danger of desertification. When the author visited the farms, ZCWT had rec-ognized this issue and reserved 10 to 30 meters of windbreaks around every re-claimed plot in order to keep the sand at bay.

Achievements and Difficulties

Both ZCWA and ZCWT have managed some achievements in growing food crops in Zimbabwe, but they are still facing some difficulties and obstacles. Achievements have been made in the following three aspects.

Contributions to Zimbabwe's Food Security

Zimbabwe has experienced food shortages in recent years and thus relied on importing several hundred thousand tonnes of food from other countries. Taking maize, the most important food crop, for example, because of drought and water – logging since the beginning of the 2014 rain season, the output of maize was expected to drop by 35 percent in 2015. This meant that Zimbabwe needed to import 700000 tonnes of maize to cover the deficit. [1]Although ZCWA and ZCWT have not been operating in Zimbabwe long, they have made contributions to Zimbabwe's food security in three aspects. First, if the yields of their maize could reach 5 tonnes this year, then the total output will be 18000 tonnes, which is equivalent to 3 percent of the amount of planned imports. This contribution will continue to increase their production and expand areas of cultivation. Second, all the crops they produced were not transported to China but were sold to local food companies to be used by local people directly. Third, since most of the food crops production took place on reclaimed land this in itself is a contribution to food security.

Promotion of Regional Development

ZCWA and ZCWT have formed a kind of demonstration effect to local regions and promoted the development of them with their advanced management skills and modern cultivation methods. As for the agricultural skills training, one of

---

[1] "Zimbabwe to import 700000 tons of maize after poor harvest", http: //thezimbabwemail. com/zimbabwe – to – import – 700000 – tonnes – of – maize – after – poor – harvest/, accessed 2015 – 05 – 08.

ZCWA's farms is being used by the University of Chinoyi for teaching and experimentation and by neighboring farmers for technical exchange and agricultural products demonstration. ZCWT has trained more than ten drivers and machinists with its own agricultural machineries. As for job creation, they employ more than 1000 farm workers altogether. Salaries are enough to cover for a family of four. When the author visited a village near Kassama farm, most of the young men there were working on the farm. It was obvious that some houses were newly built or repaired. ZCWT also rent their farm machinery to neighboring farmers and sell them seeds, fertilizers, and pesticides at wholesale prices. Moreover, they have promoted the development of other industries in local regions and since ZCWT came to Chegutu in 2013, some of its local industries including building materials, services, and banking have all achieved a great development.

Relationship with Local Communities

ZCWA paid much attention on corporate social responsibility and has fulfilled it in many ways, which include: Solving the issues concerning people's livelihood, such as lack of electricity and drinking water; donating funds to neighbouring schools; and building roads for remote areas. These activities have created a good relationship between ZCWA and local communities. As for ZCWT, it has allocated a plot on the farm where each farm worker are allowed to grow their own foods. It also set up a soccer team for the dropout children from neighboring villages and allowed them to play on the vacant area of the farm compound. It also rent tractors to the locals. When the author visited Kassama farm, a villager came there to rent a tractor to transport building materials, which indicates that the relationship between ZCWT and the locals is good.

The two Chinese companies are also facing some problems in Zimbabwe. These are mainly related to land policies, investments and outputs, and natural conditions.

Unfavourable Land Policies

Because the GoZ forbids farmers from leasing and selling land to others and according to the indigenization policy, AHSFAC and ATETC only hold 50 per cent of the shares of ZCWA and ZCWT. This results in some risks to them in terms of recouping their investments and making profits. Moreover, after the Fast Track Land Reform, most of previously "white – owned" large commercial farms were divided into A1 and A2 farms. As for the size of them, the largest A1 farm is only 20 hectares. ①A2 farms are more complicated, but even for the large commercial farms, the largest is only 400 hectares. ②This means that if they want to expand their businesses, they have no choice but to get land from GoZ. If they want to cooperate with A1 or A2 farmers directly, they will face more difficulties in operation and management because the farms are very small and there are too many stakeholders involved. Up to now, a lot of farmers near Chinese – invested farms have told them that they want to cooperate with them, but because of the two restrictions, they have been unable to take any actions.

Investments are very large but the period of return is too long

Because the agricultural infrastructures in Zimbabwe are very poor, ZCWA and ZCWT have to clear lands, build roads, storage rooms, and irrigation facilities. They also need to purchase agricultural machineries, seeds, fertilizers, and pesticides. As a result, the total amount of their investments is very large. ③As of 2014, ZCWA has invested $20 million in the second phase of its project while ZCWT has invested $4 million in total. However, compared with economic crops, such as tobacco and cotton, the profit from food crops is very low. Taking tobacco planted by ZCWA in the 2013/2014 season as an example, the yield per hectare was 2.5 tonnes and the price per tonne was $3000. Deducting the production cost of $4000, total profit per hectare was $3500, which is at least three times higher than maize or wheat (table 3) . As for maize planted by ZCWT in the 2013/2014 season, because the yields were very low, they only re-

---

① Matondi, *Zimbabwe's Fast Track Land Reform*, p. X.

② J. Hanlon, *Zimbabwe Takes Back Its Land*, p. 140.

③ Take land – clearing for example, the cost of clearing bushes and anthills per hectare is $600 – 800.

covered their costs. In order to make the most of the farms, ZCWA decided to perform a modern agricultural structure based on food crops, aquaculture, tobacco, and other highly profitable economic crops in 2014 and has planted 100 hectares of tobacco in the same year. ZWTFPL also planted 15 hectares of tobacco in the 2014/2015 season and they are preparing to expand to tobacco cultivation and plant potato, onion, along with other cash crops in the 2015/2016 season.

Table 3 Profit of maize, wheat, soy bean and tobacco of ZCWA (2013/2014 season)

Crop	Yeild (ton/hec)	Price (ton)	Cost ($)	Profit ($)
Maize	6	390	1300	1040
Wheat	6	430	1700	880
Soy bean	2.5	520	900	400
Tobacco	2.5	3000	4000	3500

Natural Factors

Zimbabwe has rich water resources but because of lacking irrigation facilities and poor management, the lands that can be irrigated are only 135000 hectares as of 2009. [1]Food crops are highly dependent on natural factors, so the rain season can have a huge impact on yields. Both ZCWA and ZCWT have begun to build or repair irrigation facilities, but because of lack of capital and electrical supply, it will take a long time before dependency on natural factors can be circumvented. In the 2014/2015 season, due to the delayed rain season, too much rainfall during the New Year festival and a subsequent drought, both ZCWA and ZCWT's yields of food crops we predicted to be affected heavily. A manager estimated that the yields of ZCWA's farms would be reduced by 20 per cent. [2] The yield per hectare at ZCWT was only two tonnes, which is far below the five tonnes initially predicted. [3]Due to global warming, Zimbabwe's rainy season is expected to become shorter and shorter or even disappear—to be displaced by unpredictable and

---

[1] ZAIP, p. 19.

[2] Email from He Hongshun, general manager of ZCWA to the author, April 26, 2015.

[3] WeChat interview with Zhang Hengxi, general manager of ZCWT, Beijing, July 30, 2015.

freakish weather year by year, which will bring great challenges to food crops growers, such as ZCWA and ZCWT. Moreover, there are some other factors that could reduce their output, such as sparrow, termite, baboons, or even stealing by neighboring villagers.

Conclusion

Food crops (mainly maize) cultivation carried out by ZCWA and ZCWT in Zimbabwe facilitates new areas of agricultural cooperation between China and Zimbabwe, and provides experiences and platforms for other Chinese agribusinesses coming to Zimbabwe to invest. Although having made some achievements already, they are still facing many difficulties. Both He Hongshun, general manager of ZCWA, and Zhang Hengxi, general manager of ZCWT, told the author during interviews that they are investing in Zimbabwe's agricultural sector without support and help—and unlike domestic farmers, they are cut off from benefiting agricultural policies. Therefore, they suggested that Chinese government should put forward some policies to support "going out" agribusinesses, such as reducing tariff for exporting agriculture machinery and fertilizers, providing concessional loan for creating agribusiness or building agricultural infrastructure, such as irrigation facilities, and help them set up a modern agricultural economic trade zone. I want to end this article with an insightful argument made by Zhang Hengxi from ZCWT: "In order to solve the problem of Zimbabwe's food crisis, the Chinese government has provided food assistance to Zimbabwe many times, and has also taken many other methods to aid Zimbabwe, but if it can increase its support to those agribusinesses that grow food crops in Zimbabwe on funds and policies, it would get more with less. Because in order to make more profits, those agribusiness will use this support to cultivate more lands and improve their production, which is the way to solve the problem of Zimbabwe's food insecurity."

China's Agriculture Investments in Zambia and Suggestion

Wan Ru [*]

Because of the importance of Zambia in China's political and diplomatic strategy, Zambia has been a major destination for China's aid and investment since the last half of 20th century. With the liberalisation of Zambia's economy and the implementation of China's agriculture "going – out" policy, a growing number of Chinese companies entered Zambia to invest its agriculture. This article will first briefly introduce the agriculturaldevelopment of Zambia and the incentives provided for foreign investors, then introduce China's agriculture investment in Zambia. After a comparison between three different Chinese farms in Zambia, the author will end with a reflection oncurrent issues and provide suggestions for further development.

I. Zambia's Agriculture Development and its Investment EncouragementIncentives

i. Zambia's Agriculture Development

Zambia locates in the plateau of southern Africa, and its average altitude is 1000 to 1500 meters. With great natural conditions, Zambia is very suitable to conduct

* Wan Ru, Graduated with MA degree from School of International Studies, PEKING University, now serves as Compliance Manager, Industrial and Commercial Bank of China, Dubai (DIFC) Branch.

416

agricultural activities, however, over the years its agriculture development level has remained low. During the British colonisation period, copper was discovered in the mid – north of the country, which proceeded to become its pillar industry and the main source of financial revenue. For a long time, agriculture only functioned asa complement to mining and support for mining workers and the urban population, and its productivity was relatively low. After gaining control over Zambia's land, the colonial authority sorted the land according to race and utility into four kinds: Crown Land, White Habitat, Native Reserve Land, and Native Trust Land. For different kinds of land, the land authority had different plans and policies. However, this distinction of land became a hidden danger for future agriculture development.

Gaining its dependency in 1964, the Kaunda administration was faced with pressures to swiftly recover Zambia'seconomy and improve people's livelihood, so Kuanda chose to focus on the mining which had already proven an economic pillar of Zambia. As for agriculture, Kaunda launched the "fair price" policy for corns, which sought to increase the income of local farmers by having a nationally fixed market price. However, his plan did not go as he wished. The government supported policy encouraged areas that were not suitable for corns to increase their production. When the financial crises caused by the oil crisis in the 1970s hit Zambia, the government lost most of its revenue due to a drop in international copper price, and became unable to maintain the corn production subsidy. Farmers lost interests to grow corns and huge drops in corn production followed.

To ensure the food security, Kaunda tried several methods to boost agricultural production. On the land aspect, Kaunda launched the Land Conversion of Title Act of 1975, which nationalised all land and put it under government control. The land acquired by white settlers in colonial times was changed to tenures of 99 years duration. The 1975 Land Act kept the jurisdiction of local chiefs over their land, however, they were prohibited from selling or renting the land. [1] In

---

① LIU Jing, "Zambia's Agriculture and Its Problems", "West Asia and Africa", Issue 3, 1988, p. 36.

1985 an amendment to the Land Act was passed, prohibiting foreigners from attaining land in Zambia without first getting the approval of the president. The purpose of the Land Act was to change the colonial legacy of white people owning vast lands while local people had no land to farm. However, such radical policies hampered the interests of foreign capital. ①In terms of agriculture, Kaunda pursuedvarious economic strategies but had a clear focus on developing state – owned farms and production groups. It was clear that the motivation for the government to support agriculture development was to provide for the domestic market consumption, to secure food production, instead of to export more food. However, despite of Kuanda's endeavors, the roaring price of food (especially corn) led to social instability and demands for multi – party – rule, and eventually Chiluba won the presidential elections on October 31ˢᵗ 1991.

As the new president, Chiluba decided to rejuvenate the agriculture sector by liberalising agriculture markets, reforming the land policy, and providing favorable investment environments to attract more foreign investors. Zambia had until then used a land system under both customary law and state civil lawd, in which 93 per cent of Zambia's land was classified ascustomary land and only the remaining 7 per cent open for rental. The new Land Act in 1995 opened the door for foreigners and saw the creation of the Land Tribunal and Land Development Fund to settle disputes and support the utilisation of the newly rented land.

Other than the Land Act 1995, Zambia has passed many other policies and action plans to ensure the growth and development in the agricultural sector. The National Agriculture Policy 2004 – 2015, ② the Zambia Vision 2030③, and the-

---

① Bastiaan van Loenen, "Land Tenure in Zambia", University of Maine, http: //www. spatial. maine. edu/ ~ onsrud/Landtenure/CountryReport/Zambia. pdf

② Ministry of Commerece, Trade and Industry, Policy Documents, "National Agriculture Policy (2004 – 2015)", http: //www. mcti. gov. zm/index. php/quarterly – newsletters/cat_view/37 – policy – documents, accessed 2015 – 4 – 21.

③ "Zambia Vision 2030", http: //www. mcti. gov. zm/index. php/quarterly – newsletters/cat_view/ 37 – policy – documents, accessed 2015 – 4 – 21.

National Agriculture Investment Plan 2014 – 2018① all addressed the importance of developing agriculture and set plans for the future on different levels.

ii. Zambia's Investment Encouragement Incentives

Agriculture plays an important role for the Zambian government. First, the livelihood of Zambian people is strongly related to agriculture. According to a census done by the United Nations Food and Agriculture Organization, 8. 72 million out of Zambia's total population of 14. 54 million lived in rural areas in 2013② and 3. 54 million people were economically active in the agricultural sector, taking up 61. 37 per cent of the total economically active population. Second, vast number of rural residents form the "ticket bunker" for Zambian politicians, making agriculture policy an important part of their political platform. Third, developing agriculture will help Zambia movingaway fromits dependency on the mining sector and could help build economic diversification. Lastly, agricultural development is clearly linked with national food security. For the above reasons, the Zambian government is keen on agricultural growth and prosperity.

However, there are many obstacles for local agricultural production. First of all, the majority of the rural population is poor (83 per cent), and 71 per cent of them live in extreme poverty. Therefore their agricultural production primarily consists of – subsistence farming and/or rely on subsidies from the Zambian government. Secondly, although the arable land in Zambia makes up 58 per cent of the country, only 14 per cent is actually utilised for agricultural production. Households only cultivate small pieces of lands and 72. 7 per cent of these are less than two hectares.

Smallholder farming like this means limited use of farming machinery and that yields are more linked with the weather. Thirdly, rural areas are generally far a-

① Ministry of Agriculture and Livestock, Government of the Republic of Zambia, National Agriculture Investment Plan (NAIP) 2014 – 2018, http: //www. gafspfund. org/sites/gafspfund. org/files/Documents/6. %20Zambia_investment%20plan. pdf, accessed 2015 – 4 – 28.

② Rural Poverty Portal, IFAD, Rural poverty in Zambia, http: //www. ruralpovertyportal. org/country/home/tags/zambia, accessed 2014 – 4 – 28.

way from markets (urban areas) and the infrastructure for transportation, irrigation, and power supply is scarce. It is also hard for smallholder farmers to access loans, so they cannot enlarge their production when they want. Therefore, whether from the perspective of cultivating more farmland and raising productivity or from the perspective of ensuring domestic food supply and security, facilitating large scale commercial farming is a fast way to boost Zambia's agricultural production and commercial crops market.

Due to limited funds and technology, the Zambian government chose to open the agricultural sector to foreign investors and facilitate the investment process by creating a number of agencies and supporting policies. The most important agency is the Zambia Development Agency (ZDA) established in 2006. ZDA is responsible for promoting investments in Zambia and deepening economic development through facilitating key areas such as "trade development, investment promotion, enterprise restructuring, development of green fields' projects, small and enterprise development, trade and industry fund management, and contributing to skills training development. "[1] By gathering investment information and procedures, ZDA allows investors to enter Zambia's agricultural sector faster and easier. Although there is no policy in place that requires foreign investments to move through ZDA, its convenience has persuaded many investors to do so.

II. China's Investment in Zambia's Agriculture and Case Studies of Three Chinese Farms in Zambia

i. China's Investment in Zambia's Agriculture

In 1949, the newly founded People's Republic of China faced an international environment dominated by the Cold War, making a "lean to one side" (Soviet Union) policy its only choice. In order to gain supports from the newly dependent African countries and build the Communist Bloc, China launched its agricultural

---

① Zambia Development Agency, Backgrounds, http: //www. zda. org. zm/? q = content/background, 2015 - 4 - 28.

cooperation with African countries in the early years. When the Cold War ended, the cooperation shifted alongside China's changing policy. The Third Plenary Session of the 14th Central Committee of the Communist Party of China established the socialist market economy as its new regime and introduced the "going – out" policy. Many Chinese companies grabbed the opportunity and went abroad, and large state – owned – companies such as China State Farms Agribusiness (Group) Corporation and China National Fisheries Corp went to invest in Africa.

Among the 54countries in Africa, Zambia has long been an important partner of China, and the two countries' friendship dates back to the 1960's when Zambia was newly independent. China and Zambia soon established diplomatic relations and Zambia became the first of the southern African countries to do so. In the disputes of the right to use the rail between Zambia and South Rhodesia (now Zimbabwe), China supported Zambia's bid – and decided to build a new railway to connect Zambia and Tanzania so that the cooper mine of this land – locked country could be transported out. Up till today, the Tanzania – Zambia Railway (TANZAM) is still regarded as the symbol of China – Africa and China – Zambia friendship.

Aside from the TANZAMrailway, China aided Zambia for a long period of time. With China's – opening – up policy and Zambia's economic reform in 1991, the economic ties between the two countries were no longer only about aid and trade. Zambia became an early destination of China's investment. Generally speaking, China's investments flows to the mining sector. Between 1993 and 2009, China's investments into the mining sector made up 88 per cent of total investment. Meanwhile agricultural sector only received 0. 2 per cent. This figure also shows that the potential for China to invest in Zambia's agriculture is huge.

According to a business surveyfrom the Economy and Commercial Counsellor's Office of the Embassy of China in Zambia there are 36 Chinese companies and farms in Zambia. [1]

---

[1] Embassy of China in Zambia, there are 36 Chinese companies and farms in Zambia, http: // zm. mofcom. gov. cn/article/jmxw/201504/20150400955561. shtml, accessed 2015 – 05 – 22.

Table 1 Business Directory of Chinese Agriculture Investment in Zambia

Company (in Pinyin)	Manager	English Name (If registered)
Zhongken Farm	DuanChanglong	Johnken Estates LTD
ZhongzanYouyi Farm	Song Guoqiang	China Zambia Friendship Farm
Xiyangyang Farm	Jiang Jian	
Yangguang Farm	Si Su	Sunlight Farms
Qiuhua Farm	Huang Xianggao	
Dongyang Co.	Yang, Qingxian	
Weima Farm Ltd.	Hu, Hongyi	
Zhongyi Farm	Feng, Kehong	
Baixin Agriculture Co. Ltd.	Zhou, Bin	
Zhonghua Farm	Tian, Wenxi	
Teji Agriculture Development Co. Ltd.	Han, Zhiwei	
Longping Xinxi Agriculture Co. Ltd	Jiang, Qingwen	
Zanqin Farm	Zhou, Shunsheng	
Huafeng Farm	Tian, Xiufeng	China Harvest Farm
Xingda Investment Co. Ltd.	Li, Gang	
Ronghe Co. (Lao Hu Farm)	Hu, Herong	
Zambia Agriculture Science and Technology Limited (AST)	Du, Dan	Agriculture Science and Technology Limited
SUNUP AGRIFARMS AND INVESTMENTS	Huo, Shuren	Sunup Agrifarms And Investments
Tianxiang Farm	Liu, Changming	
Luyao Farm (Lu Mingli Farm)	Lu, Mingli	
Zhang Zhensheng Farm	Zhang, Zhensheng	
HuashenDongfang Farm (LZ EASTER)	Liu, Qinghua	
Kaifeng Agriculture Investment Co. Ltd.		
Huafei Livestock and Poultry Limited Company	Sun, Dejin	
Huaxing Co.	Zhang, Zhensheng	
Danhui Farm	Wang, An	
Jilin Agricultural University (Agriculture Demonstration Center)	Bao, Heping	

Company (in Pinyin)	Manager	English Name (If registered)
Jiangquan International Co.		
Xinghua Agriculture Investmen Co.		
Zanrong Co.	Zhai, Guanghua	
Anya Agriculture Investment Co. Ltd.	Li, Zhijie	Agriyana investment ltd
KuaileXiongdi Farm Co. Ltd.	Huang, Jianhua	
Atlantic Wood Industry Co. Ltd.	Wei, Zhibin	
Zambian Jihai Agriculture Co. Ltd	Yao, Yunwu	Zambian Jihai Agriculture Co. Ltd
Pristine Ecological Products Co. Ltd.	Yuan, Guangjie	Pristine Ecological Products
Shinuo Agriculture Development Co. Ltd.	Yang, Jin	

Although the Economy and Commercial Counsellor's Office of the Embassy of China in Zambia posted a notice on their website and asked managers of Chinese companies in Zambia to complete the survey, it is obvious that the table lacks information, and the actual sub – sectors they invested in and their business situation and such are missing. Therefore, more specific studies of Chinese farms are needed.

ii. Case Studies of Three Chinese Farms in Zambia

From the field experiencesin September 2013, the author found that the Chinese farms in Zambia vary greatly and therefore it is impossible to perceive the Chinese farms as an indistinctive whole. When looking at Chinese farms in Zambia, individual differences need to be addressed. Due to limited time and mobility, the author chose to conduct interviews with three different Chinese farms: Johnken Estates Ltd. , (hereafter as Johnken Farm), Yangyang Farm, and Kaifeng Agriculture Investment Co. Ltd. (hereafter as Kaifeng Farm). According to the author's field observations and interviews on these farms, the author compiled the following table to show the general situation of each of these farms.

According to Table 2, the ownership, skill levels of managers, and scale of these three farms varies a lot, and the preferential policies from both China and Zambia that they actually used are also different. Farms faced different problems too, but generally speaking, they encounter issues from the market, management, technology, and funds.

Table 2　A Comparision between Johnken Farm, Yangyang Farm and Kaifeng Farm

Name	Ownership of the Farm	Scale	Reason of Entry	Preferential Policy Used		Problems faced
				Chinese	Zambian	
Johnken Farm	State – owned	4000 ha	– responded to China's going – out policy – dispatched by the mother company – had relevant agriculture knowledge (e. g. WANG Chi, the former manager, worked in China Agriculture University before.)	– National loan – attentions from the Embassy	– Joined the ZN-FU	– Jurisdiction of Chinese management level is unclear – Restrictions on large amount of money spent – Decision – making chain in state-owned company is too long, so responses are slow – Disputes with local employees on salary
Yangyang Farm	Contract, originally state – owned	40 ha	– responded to Jiangsu's provincial going-out policy – dispatched by mother company – Processed agriculture knowledge – had done agriculture in Zambia		– joined the ZN-FU – ZDA's tax preference – ZDA's preferential policy on imported agriculture machinery	– market prices fluctuate too much – old equipment and the repair cost is high – difficult to access loans
Kaifeng Farm	Private farm	10 ha	– responded to Kaifeng's municipal going – out policy – Subsidies from the Bureau of Agriculture and Forestry in Kaifeng – Had been to Zambia	– Subsidies from the Bureau of Agriculture and Forestry in Kaifeng	– ZDA's visa support	– hard to enter market – lack of breeding and disease preventing skills – social instability – inefficient government – difficult to access loans

III. Problems with China's Investment in Zambia

i. The Insufficiency of China's Policies

First of all, many of the – alluring policies that encourage agricultural companies to "go – out" in China are actually hard to achievein reality, especially for private companies. The problems companies may face include:

(1) In the "Beijing Action Plan" (2013 – 2015) launched on the 5th Ministerial Meetings of Forum on China – Africa Cooperation (FOCAC), the topic of encourage Chinese companies to invest in Africa was re-addressed, and encouraging "Chinese financial institutions to support cooperation between Chinese and African companies in agricultural planting, processing of agricultural products, animal husbandry, fishery, and aquaculture" was mentioned for the first time. However, the Beijing Action Plan also included a criteria to only support companies that were "capable and reputable,"[1] making it rather ambiguous who was to receive the support. One thing is for certain, state – owned farms with state – company backgrounds and national loans are more likely to receive such supports and encouragements than privately invested and small – scale farms.

(2) Although special funds were provided to Chinese investment in Africa, the application for funding also holds barriers. Not only does the company have to fulfill a series of investment and registration qualifications in both China and Zambia, the scale of investment also needs to reach a certain level, which is no less than one million US dollars. That means that most private small farms are excluded from applying to this special fund.

(3) According to the objectives of the China-Africa Development Fund (CAD Fund) and the requirements of many FOCAC Action Plans, it can be a source of loans and financing service for Chinese companies. However, CAD Fund's partner re-

---

[1] The Fifth Ministerial Conference Of The Forum On China – Africa Cooperation Beijing Action Plan (2013 – 2015), http://www.focac.org/chn/ltda/dwjbzzjh/hywj/t954617.htm, accessed 2015 – 5 – 1.

quirement states that companies should "have advantages, investment experience in Africa, good human resources, strong management capability and team advantages in the industry," and the projects seeking funds should "have a promising market prospect and rapid and steady growth potential" and be "able to generate good cash flow."① Obviously, the agricultural sector is greatly influenced by the fluctuating market and small companies are hard to reach the potential and cash flow goal set by CAD Fund, thus hard to get the loan or investment. One of the major agriculture projects that CAD Fund invested in is the China – Africa Cotton Zambia Ltd. , and clearly most of the Chinese farms in Zambia cannot compare with this giant company that controls more than 100000 hectares and 90000 households.

Therefore, it is important for the Chinese government and relevant departments to generate more "on the ground" policies with not only good intentions, but also good execution. More business service agencies should be encouraged to go abroad and facilitate Chinese companies' investment so that all the preferential policies and encouragement methods are easier to access by the Chinese companies in Africa. Secondly, many incentive policies for the agricultural sector that have proven effective domestically are not extended to going – abroad companies. For example, the Chinese government subsidises 30 per cent of agriculture machinery purchasing costs for domestic agriculture companies. During the author interviews with the Chinese farms in Zambia, farm managers stated that they lacked money for purchasing new machinery. It was a common wish from the farm management that the incentives provided for domestic agriculture producers should be extended to overseas companies to encourage the investment abroad. Thirdly, even for large state – owned companies (such as Johnken Farm) that receive plenty of incentives and preferential policies, these benefits mean more restrictions. These government issued funds requires managers to report to their superiors in China for every major decision concerning capital spendingand operation management.

---

① China – Africa Development Fund, http: //www. cad fund. com/en/ Article_List. aspx? columnID = 185, accessed 2015 – 5 – 6.

This processcan be long and ineffective, and it is hard for local managers to keep up with the changing Zambian and international environment. Private or contract farms may lack Chinese government funds, but they have more freedom in their management and operation and can therefore more easily set goals and change production methods according to the actual situation. The Chinese government may want to research on how to balance fund providing and autonomous operation. - While Chinese small - scale private farms are the most vulnerable among all types and always neglected by Chinese government policies, they are also the businesses most connected with local people—and to a great extent responsible for defining the perception of Chinese and China's image in local minds. Therefore, future policies for agricultural "going out" should place an emphasis on small and medium scale farms, as well as bring more flexibility to the larger state-owned farms.

ii. The Deficiencies of Managers

Although incentives provided by both originand host countries will encouragecompanies to enter the agricultural sector, the longevity of a certain companies depends hugely on the operation and management skills of the manager. If the manager is familiar with Zambia's agricultural conditions, incentives and facilitating policies provided by ZDA, and has previous experience or knowledge in agriculture, then it will definitely help the company's performance. Besides, mastering the local official language (English for Zambia) definitely helps managers to effectively communicate with their employees, traditional authorities and government officials, and push forward their productivity. From the case of Yangyang Farm, speaking fluent English definitely helped the manager and his family to benefit from local incentive policies. "Going out" to Zambia and invest in agriculture means that Chinese companies will be exposed to theenvironment of Zambia's economy. For each company, it is generally hard to change the ownership status, but easy to adjust the management skills. Other than understanding the incentives provided, and overcoming language barriers, managers can work to understandand make up for their deficiencies. Subjectively, managers can pay more attention to the changing market and economy and consult with agriculture expert or partners to sum up lessons and improve management skill. Second, the author noticed that most companies investing in Zambia went into primary product sector (e. g. , agriculture and mining), and the production type is too unified. When these Chinese companies entered Zambia's agricultural sector for the first time in the 1990's, such cautious movement is understandable. However, more than twenty years have passed and these companies have grown in size, but not in type and scope. Many companies appeared to hesitate in face of opportunities to localizing production and shorten their value chain. This is despite the fact that operating farms that produce only primary crop products not only costs more, but is highly competitive and have longer production cycles while the final product can only be sold at a relatively low price hugely influenced by fluctuating global and domestic markets. Kaifeng farm's owner mentioned during interviews that because he lacked butchering equipment and refrigeration equipment, he could only sell live chicken on the – nearby local market instead of selling butchered chicken meat to supermarkets.

Chinese companies investing in Zambia's agriculture should consider adding more value chains, entering higher and vaster agriculture markets, and diversifying production to avoid being too affected by fluctuating market prices. The author noted that communication between Chinese companies islow. As the most famous Chinese farms in Zambia, Johnken farm is well known among Chinese and Zambians, and the story of its first managers WangChi and LiLi have been popularised in both countries' media. However, few people know about other Chinese farms. For example, both managers from Yangyang farm and Johnken farm were ignorant of Kaifeng farm, but Kaifeng farm's manager was familiar with the names of the other two. At the same time, market and policy information has trouble reaching Chinese farmers.

To address this issue, Chinese farms could form an association or union so all farms or agriculture companies can be united and share information and experiences. The Economy and Commercial Counsellor's Office of the Embassy of China in Zambia should also facilitate such demands and provide more information, resources, and guidance. Establishing platforms and channels as well as increasing communications between Chinese companies are also effective way to overcome difficulties caused by lack of competence from the managers. This would be especially beneficial for information flow so Chinese companies can gain better access to local policies and market information.

IV. Conclusion and Suggestions

After three decades of "going – out" policy, the focus point of both the Chinese government and investors should shift away from merely constructing channels for businesses and encouraging investment in Africa, and towards helping the investments to prosper. The cases of Chinese farms indicated that after 20 years or more in Zambia, a range of challenges remain to be solved. These include, but are not limited to, domestic challenges from within Zambia, external challenges from China and the global environment, as well as institutional barriers from the parent company, the difficulty of funds securement, and capacity building. The Chinese government and companies have to work together to guide them onto the road of becoming blooming transnational agriculture companies. As mentioned above, companies should change their mind – set, diversify their investment, and create their own production value chain.

As for the Chinese government, it should realise that after many years of "going out", the objective at this stage is to support companies "settledown". In order to achieve this, the government should adjust their policy making process from a perspective of top level design and strategic planning, and instead pursue policies that will help overseas companies to set roots and develop sustainably in the local economies. At the same time, reforms should be made in related departments to tackle specific problems encountered by the overseas investment companies. For example, the government should improve financial services to these companies and build overseas agriculture investment insurance to provide funds and safeguards for the Chinese companies investing in foreign agricultural sectors.

The Status Quo of China-Kenya Agricultural Cooperation: A Case Study of the Pyrethrum Project

Hu (Annie) Jiao *,　　Dr. Wang Duanyong **

Brief Introduction of Kenya Economic Development

After independence, Kenya implemented a mixed market economy, in which the private sector dominates and accounts for 70 per cent of the GDP. [1] Agriculture is the backbone of Kenya's economy. About 70 per cent of the population is directly or indirectly engaged in agricultural industry. The share of agriculture in Kenya's GPD is on the rise. The total output value of agriculture in Kenya climbed from 26.2 per cent in 2012 to 32.6 per cent in 2016 as a percentage of overall GDP, which undoubtedly made it the No.1 industry. [2]

---

* Hu (Annie) Jiao is a Nairobi-based social entrepreneur and researcher. She is a graduate of Sun Yat-sen University and a Harvard SEED fellow in 2014. She has traveled repeatedly to Ethiopia, Tanzania, Rwanda and other African countries and currently lives in Nairobi working with Chinese communities/companies. Annie's research focuses on sustainable investment of China in Africa, including CSR practice, localization and skill transfer, job creation and entrepreneurship.

** Dr. Wang Duanyong is an associate professor at Shanghai International Studies University, China, the founder and director of the Center for Chinese Overseas Interests Studies affiliated to Shanghai International Studies University. Prof. Wang received his Ph.D. in Economics from Wuhan University in 2007.

① Official website of the Economic & Commercial Counsellor's Office of Chinese Embassy in Kenya, http://www.fmprc.gov.cn/web/dszlsjt_673036/t1337078.shtml.

② Kenya National Bureau of Statistics, Economic Survey 2017, https://www.knbs.or.ke/download/economic-survey-2017/

Table 1 Kenya's agricultural output and contribution to GDP①

(Unit: Million Kenya Shilling)

Year / Industry	2012	2013	2014	2015
Agricultural output	1115198	1254813	1482840	1900965
Gross output value of GDP	4261370	4745143	5402410	6260646
Growth rate of GDP (per cent)	4. 5	5. 9	5. 4	5. 7
Agriculture as a percentage of GDP (per cent)	26. 2	26. 4	27. 4	30. 4
Growth rate of agriculture (per cent)	2. 8	5. 4	4. 3	5. 5
The contribution of agriculture to GDP growth (%)	14. 3	20. 9	18. 2	21. 2

Kenya is the world's largest exporter of black tea and the third largest supplier of flowers to Europe. Agricultural products account for 65 per cent of Kenya's total exports. Tea, horticultural products (mainly flowers and vegetables) and coffee are the three main foreign exchange earners. Corn crops are mainly grown in Kenya, while others include wheat, rice, millet, beans and potatoes. Corn is basically self-sufficient innormal years, while wheat and rice are heavily dependent on imports. Economic crops include tea, horticultural products and coffeeas well as pyrethrum, sugarcane, sisal, cotton, macadamia (Hawaiian fruit) and more.

Agriculture is identified as one of the six key industries in *Vision* 2030. The primary goal articulated is to boost income through added value agriculture. The government has adopted policies that are designed to increase major crop outputs and encourage farmers to be more specialized in management. The highest priority is a series of reforms to incentivize the farmers and improve agricultural productivity. *Agricultural Sector Development Strategy* 2010 – 2020, an amendment of the earlier influential guideline *Kenya's Strategy For Revitalizing Agriculture* 2004 – 2015 in accordance with *Vision* 2030. ②According to incomplete statistics, Kenya has put forward at least 19rules, regulations and policies to conduct and guide

---

① Kenya National Bureau of Statistics, Economic Survey 2017, pp. 45 – 46.
② Ministry of Agriculture, Livestock and Fisheries of Kenya, Strategic Plan 2013-2017, Revised 2015, p. 10. http: //www. kilimo. go. ke/wp-content/uploads/2015/05/MoALF_Strategic-Plan_2013-2017. pdf.

agricultural development in various areas, with most of them oriented towards crop farming. ①In order to promote agriculture, the Kenyan government has strived to fuel the productivity and global competitiveness of mid-and-small sized farm owners by amending the production system of rural cooperatives, expanding production scales, popularizing agricultural techniques, and providing financial support. It is also determined to draw more non-governmental and global capital into Kenya's agriculture by improving traffic and transportation, facilitating rural infrastructure construction and formulating relevant regulations. In the past, the production and distribution of agricultural products was rigidly planed within a monopolized management system. Now supporting export-oriented agriculture has become the government's major function.

However, Kenya's agricultural infrastructure is weak, lacking of capital, technology and management talent, and the information exchange is not smooth and the added value of agricultural products is low. Overall, the extensive agricultural production basically depends on the weather for eating. Many small and medium-sized farmers and ordinary peasants is especially prevalent. Ordinary individual farmer is facing challenge for investing in pesticides, seeds and other basic agricultural inputs, due to the limited funding. ②On the other hand, agricultural development is greatly affected by the external environment. For example, the growth rate of agriculture industry in Kenya in 2016 was 4.4 per cent,③ lower than the growth rate of 5.6 per cent in 2015. ④The main reason for the poor performance of the industry was drought, especially in the second half of the year. The change of external environment has a great impact on ordinary farmers. Owing to a single source of income, the overall risk-resistance capability of farmers is relatively low.

---

① Carol N. Kamau, "Kenya's Agricultural Sector Reforms", *Global Agricultural Information Network Report*, USAID, Foreign Agricultural Service, 1/7/2013.

② Based on interviews our research team conducted over local Chinese agricultural experts on 2015-08-13 at Egerton University, Nakuru, Kenya.

③ Kenya National Bureau of Statistics. Economic Survey 2017, p. 24 and p. 27.

④ Kenya National Bureau of Statistics. Economic Survey 2017, p. 59.

Existing China-Kenya Agricultural Cooperation: Trade, Aid and Investment

The bilateral investment and economic and trade relations between China and Kenya have begun since the establishment of diplomatic relations in 1963. At present, China is the largest source of direct investment in Kenya and the largest construction contractor in Kenya thanks to rapid development of bilateral investment and trade. [①] According to the data from the Kenya National Bureau of Statistics. China has become Kenya's largest trading partner for two consecutive years in 2015 and 2016 respectively. [②]According to Chinese Customs' statistics, important categories of Chinese imports from Kenya are agricultural products, including hides and skins (except fur) and leather, coffee, tea, mate, seasonings, plant fibers and flowers etc. In May 2017, President Xi Jinping met with Kenyan President Kenyatta during the Leaders' Roundtable Summit at the Belt and Road Forum (BRF) for International Cooperation. He proposed upgrading the bilateral relations to a comprehensive strategic partnership and deepening China-Kenya cooperation in various fields including agriculture. The Chinese government has also organized foreign-aid training and planned to train 534 Kenyans in 2015 in programs covering sustainable rural development. [③]In addition, bilateral agricultural delegations visits are also actively, and as the bilateral relations have been strengthened in recent years, the frequency of visits has also been increasing.

According to the author's fieldwork in Kenya, Chinese agricultural investment is still in phase one. Contrary to the situation in Mozambique, Tanzania, Zambia, and Ethiopia, the Chinese state-owned enterprises rarely invest in Kenya's

---

① Official website of the Chinese embassy in Kenya, http://www.fmprc.gov.cn/ce/ceke/chn/xw/t1493715.htm.

② Official website of the Chinese embassy in Kenya, http://www.fmprc.gov.cn/web/dszlsjt_673036/t1337078.shtml.

③ CRI international online, "Human resources training cooperation between China and Kenya is getting closer", online available: http://gb.cri.cn/42071/2015/09/16/3245s5104976.

agriculture and only a few private companies have started to show interestsand invested. A list from the Ministry of Commerce showed that the earliest large-and-mid sized Chinese enterprises to conduct agricultural investment in Kenya was registered in 2012. So far there are only five enterprises, or 3. 1 per cent of the entire registered amount. According to interviews in Kenya, individual Chinese private enterprises in Kenya begin to pay close attention to agricultural investment. Those enterprises who invested in agriculture, mostly of them started from agricultural trade. For example, Julong Group in Tianjin entered the market in Kenya in May 2014, by setting up an branch office in Nairobi. Initially the company started with trade and exporting olive oil, but have not invested in an official agriculture project yet. Kenya's total export of flowers ranked first in Africa, there are a handful of Chinese enterprises engaged in direct trade in selling the flowers to China. Kai King International Flowers (Africa) Co. , Ltd. is one of the them. It has sold more than 320 tons flower to Chinese market since 2016, with roses, narcissus lily, hydrangea, big swallow, dragon ball and other cut flowers mainly. [1]According to field visits, Chinese businessman invested in donkey slaughterhouse in in Nakuru County, trading donkey related products, exporting donkey meat to countries such as China and Vietnam, and processing donkey skins, providing raw materials for the production of ejiao in China. In addition, there are a number of individual businessmen operate Chinese farms in Kenya to grow Chinese vegetables such as spinach, beans, cucumbers and peppers, and supply them to Chinese companies, Chinese supermarkets and Chinese restaurants in Kenya. Besides, private investors are also investing cash crops such as moringa seeds and pyrethrum. One of the largest Chinese private projects in Kenya is the pyrethrum project, which will be discussed in detail below.

Chinese Agriculture Investment in Kenya: The Pyrethrum Project

According to senior Chinese agricultural experts who reside in Kenya, the East Af-

---

① Xinhua Net, "Kenyan rose fragrance floating to China", online available: http: //news. xinhuanet. com/world/2017 - 09/17/c_1121676990. htm.

rican nation has limited land for agricultural development, with the northeastern and northwestern parts of the country-two thirds of its territory-suffer from perennial drought. In the south, there are very few concentrated areas favorable for traditional agriculture since large parts of the land are plateaus. As a result, crops and other bulky agricultural products are not capable of competing with large-scale foreign investment and therefore lack global competitiveness. Those with a competitive edge and in fact a proper place in the global market are mainly foreign-exchange-earning economic crops. [1]Pyrethrum used to be one of these major products.

Pyrethrin is an internationally recognized green bio-insecticide made from the extract of pyrethrum (Chrysanthemum). In 2005, the Ministry of Agriculture of China classified pyrethrin as the most preferred substitute for previously used high-toxic insecticides. Pyrethrin cannot be synthesized and has no harm on warm-blooded animals although it is known to narcotize cold-blooded animals' nerve systems. It decomposes in rain, which means that there will be no remains left on the harvested fruit. Demand for pyrethrin has been growing by a steady 15 per cent every year since 2002. 2013 alone saw pyrethrin's global demand reaching 450 tons, meaning around 24000 ton of dried pyrethrums were consumed. Pyrethrum is currently being cultivated in countries such as China, Kenya, Australia, Tanzania and Rwanda. Kenya was the country with the largest area of suitable species for pyrethrum in the world.

Kenya has the largest area of land suitable for pyrethrum growth of any country in the world. As such, it has been a major pyrethrum producer since the 1930s. From the 1960s to the end of the 1990s, Kenya's pyrethrum production amounted to more than 90 per cent of the global market share. The amount of dried pyrethrum provided by Kenya reached more than 10000 tons in 2003. [2]For a long time, pyrethrum not only served as the most important source of foreign exchange

---

① Interview to Chinese agricultural experts residing in the area, University of Egerton, Nakuru, Kenya, 2015 – 08 – 13.

② Justus M. Monda (Chairman of Pyrethrum Growers Association of Kenya), *Pyrethrum Sector in Kenya: Current Status*, Oct. 30th, 2014, http://projects.nri.org/options/images/Current_status_of_pyrethrum_sector_in_Kenya.pdf.

revenue for Kenya, but also became vital to the livelihood of ordinary Kenyan farmers. In a normal year, there are usually as many as 200000 rural families planting pyrethrum, creating direct or indirect income for about one million people. For a typical pyrethrum-growing family, half of the farmland (about two to four acres) is used to grow pyrethrum in exchange for cash. The income gained by a pyrethrum-growing family, equal to that of a primary-school teacher, is often enough to support the expenses of all the family members, including tuition fees from primary school, college, medical care, retirement and other daily expenses. There is no denying the fact that with the immense returns brought about by moderate investment, pyrethrum is playing a significant part in Kenya's rural economy. It was so important that in as early as the colonial 1934, an official organization named the "Pyrethrum Board of Kenya" was established to administrate the affairs of the industry①and has become a state-owned enterprise that monopolized the entire pyrethrum production chain.

However, since 2004, Kenya's pyrethrum production has experienced an abrupt plunge, with its output decreasing by 50 per cent compared with 2003. It has gone downhill ever since. In 2011, the pyrethrum output dropped by 98 per cent in eight years to 250 tons, occupying less than 2 per cent of the global market share. ②To make matters worse, the output value of pyrethrum dropped by a larger margin than its output alone. One imagine that those who stay behind are earning far less than they did, which means that the breakdown of the pyrethrum industry is not only incurring a huge economic blow to the entire country and all its farmers in terms of their absolute returns, but also cut down the relative returns of those who stay in the industry. The Kenyan government on the one hand attributes the breakdown of the industry to the oversupply of the global market, and on the other hand to the administrative organization, the Pyrethrum Board of Kenya, for its payment delays. ③In fact, according to small-and-mid-sized farm owners who undertake almost all the direct losses and appoint themselves repre-

---

① Pyrethrum Board of Kenya's official website: http://www.kenya-pyrethrum.com/.

② Justus M. Monda, *Pyrethrum Sector in Kenya: Current Status.*

③ Justus M. Monda, *Pyrethrum Sector in Kenya: Current Status.*

sentatives of the Pyrethrum Board of Kenya, payment delays are a major factor. They point out that in some areas, farmers received no payment at all for as
long as four years. ①Some third-party local agricultural departments also hold similar views. ②Given that Tasmania and Tanzania have now replaced Kenya as leading producers, ③ Kenya's biggest limitation appears to be the highly monopolized
governance, which explains why its management has become reluctant and indif-
ferent. On the one hand, governance has ignored changes in the global market,
and been reluctant to adjust policies; on the other hand, by paying absolutely no
attention to the benefits of the farmers, it shows no respect to the industry's ecol-
ogy and the basic rules of its value chain. In any event, to revitalize the pyrethrum industry is not only necessary to Kenya's agricultural development and economic growth, but also effective in poverty alleviation. China's agricultural investment enterprises play a role in participating in the process of rejuvenation of the
pyrethrum industry in Kenya According to the information released by the Chinese
Ministry of Foreign Affairs official website, at least two Chinese-funded enterprises in Kenya specialize in the production and trading of pyrethrum. ④Among
them, UNEP and Tongji University conducted pyrethrum planting projects in
East African countries such as Kenya and produced organic chemical pesticides. An environmental company from Yunnan province participated in this project. According to Bloomberg, a Chinese company help Kenyan farmers grow 43
percent pyrethrum over the previous year. ⑤

---

① Justus M. Monda, *Pyrethrum Sector in Kenya: Current Status.*

② Barnabas Bii, "Farmers in Rift Valley return to pyrethrum production", June 29, 2014, http://
www. nation. co. ke/counties/eldoret/Rift-Valley-pyrethrum-farming/-/1954186/2365558/-/e93hea/-/
index. html.

③ In 2012, the market share of pyrethrum produced in Tasmania accounted for 65%, while that of Tanzania,
Rwanda and China together accounted for 33%, For more information: Justus M. Monda. (Chairman of
Pyrethrum Growers Association Of Kenya), Pyrethrum Sector in Kenya: Current Status. 30th October,
2014, http://projects. nri. org/options/images/Current_status_of_pyr ethrum_sector_in_Kenya. pdf.

④ Official website of China's Ministry of Foreign Affairs, Beautiful China and Green Africa look forward to shaking hands again, http://www. fmprc. gov. cn/zflt/chn/jlydh/dfwl/t1316403. htm.

⑤ Samuel Gebre, "Kenya Plans Pyrethrum Industry Comeback with Chinese Help", March 4,
2016, https://www. bloomberg. com/news/articles/2016-03-04/kenya-plans-pyrethrum-indus-
try-comeback-with-chinese-help.

After 2013, there has been a sharp rebound in the production and output of pyrethrum in Kenya, and the overall industry is gradually recovering.

Table 2 Annual sales and value table of pyrethrum industry in Kenya for 2012 – 2016①

	Unit	2012	2013	2014	2015	2016
Sales volume of finished pyrethrum	Ton	1. 0	4. 2	3. 6	3. 7	3. 3
Gross production value of pyrethrum	Million Kenya Shilling	17. 0	52. 6	61. 6	51. 0	37. 9

Dingli, the company we will mention following, entered to the market when the pyrethrum industry in Kenya was in a downturn.

In 2009, a Chinese entrepreneur Mr. L founded a trading company in Kenya that mainly conducted businesses in the purchase and export of agricultural products, with the Chinese mainland as its major export destination, while new markets were also being explored in the U. S. and Europe. As his businesses expanded, Mr. L established another agricultural company in 2012 in order to avoid risks brought about by instable purchases and to lower transaction costs. Namely, by growing and processing relevant agricultural products, the company was able to form a relatively complete industrial chain and internalized the market. While the company was registered with one million shillings (about $10000 as of late 2015) of capital, it now fully owns two plantations in Kijabe and Kilome by renting land with a gross investment of RMB 15 million.

After signing a 45-year lease contract with the Kenyan forestry department, Mr. L's company leased about 800 hectares of bare hills and land to test-grow cash crops like pyrethrum so that arable, profitable and alternate varieties of crops emerged. So far about 67 hectares of land have been developed. In terms of pyrethrum production, the company adopts a system that involves the company, the government and the farmers-with the government playing an intermediary role (under Kenya's pyrethrum regulation system, interference from the Pyrethrum Board of Kenya is inevitable), the company and the farm owners sign contracts that run through the entire growing procedures. However, for an agricultural en-

---

① Kenya National Bureau of Statistics, Economic Survey 2017, pp. 170, 175.

terprise that runs in an foreign-invested industrial manner, the company has always been confronted with two issues: Management localization and the creation of the value chain.

Localized Management

According to Mr. L, the limited development of Kenya's human resources market poses as the major problem in his company management. First of all, it is difficult for him to find enough middle-and-high-level managers. In addition, as the growth and processing of pyrethrum both require techniques, local farmers need to go through a long process of professional skills training, given the difference between entrepreneurial management designed to increase added value and traditional individual farming. While both costs and management localization are impractical if management at all levels is dependent upon Chinese, there are perceived risks in employing exclusively locals in management position, not to mention risks of information asymmetry between management and investor. Given however the necessity of localization, whether harmonious relations can be established between Chinese managers and local staff often seems to determine the life or death of an enterprise. Meanwhile, it is still an issue of top priority for a company's day-to-day management that employees adjust themselves well enough to its management so that cultural conflicts are avoided. By then can the management be effective.

Mr. L's company started to grow pyrethrum beginning from 2011. It began by carrying out campaigns among the farmers, providing free seeds for them, and collectingtheir harvest at designated places – a form that resembles cooperatives. However, since 2012, as farms began to undertake scientific research, the company has gradually enlarged its local employment to grow seedlings on a trial basis. In July 2013, the company began to promote self-planting and therefore needed more farm laborers. In accordance with the seasonal characteristic of agriculture, farm owners invariably adopted a flexible employment model, with more than 200 people being employed at the busiest time and at least 30 during off-season. Most of those people are local farmers whose habits of production were at odds with the company's requirement. Therefore it took a while for both sides to get used to the technical training and staff management. According to Mr. L, after two years, both sides had adjusted to the other. Regular labor issues like strikes have never occurred.

Mr. L summed up his management experience as follows: to reduce management conflicts, shorten the feedback process, make management transparent, and bring management incentives into full play.

Very few Chinese staff work on the management level, instead, managerial or mid-level managerial positions are held by the locals. Top-level Chinese executives usually keep themselves out of detailed basic daily routines, and pass on such affairs to local managers. For top-level managers, their task is to focus on the final result on the one hand and on building the company on the other. It is often the case that when procedural hiccups occur, something must be wrong with the management localization. Such an incident so fundamental to the company's management that adjustment in either positions or their functions must be proceeded with at any cost.

For Chinese who work in Kenya, language is a common obstacle that can only be overcome through intensified face-to-face communication with staff on the ground. Experience has demonstrated that the most effective way to mitigate miscommunication is to gather relevant staff for consultation, coordination, and resolution the instant a problem takes place. Such direct and sufficient problem-solving method may not be sensible to all the staff, yet some of the local staff may first become reasonable to influence and instruct fellow colleagues through personal examples. This is better than pure verbal instruction in principles.

Serious legal relations bind the company and the farmers, as well as management level and the staff. Purchase agreements and labor contracts are signed. Therefore pre-negotiations and agreements, including business contents and work plans, require respect, determination and execution. Mr. L believes that the company's management level has provided full respect for the locals' work style, customs and beliefs, and that the best way to show respect inside the company is to exercise mutual understanding, mutual trust and full support through the managerial process. While the management level keeps itself updated on a weekly basis by tracking, controlling, and coordinating operations to set work goals and examine progress, meetings with mid-level managers and basic-level team leaders are also held once a week on site to verify progress and communicate further plans and ideas. As a result, work plans for the following week are often reached among the management levels. Such a transparent and engaging management style is an attempt to make local managers feel fully respected and provide them space utilizes their own initiatives. Given that farming requires little of the staff's technical ability but much of operational norms and standards, managerial principles must also be safeguarded and respected. Therefore, according to Mr. L, effective management requires a system of rewards and punishments. For "violators" that destroy management, the company will provide several chances for rectification before it has to fire them to avoid "broken windows"; meanwhile, rewards are also be given to hardworking contributors on appropriate occasions. It has taken two years of mutual adjustment, talent cultivation and management localization, but now Mr. L's plantations are now enjoying smooth management, with communication problems often troubling Chinese overseas enterprises mostly resolved. Successful integration during the early stage has made it possible to accelerate plantation-building for future cooperators, and also shortened the investment cycle.

Value Chain Creation and Extension

The development of agriculture requires relevant infrastructure to reduce costs; export-oriented farming hasan even higher requirements. Mr. L's plantation is located within an hour's drive of the capital, Nairobi. Given Kenya's power shortages, Chinese companies helped build up a geothermal power plant located about 30 km from the plantation, therefore the electricity supply is more stable than Nairobi. However, since agriculture relies on water, and uniform irrigation cannot be provided, rainwater has become extremely important. After detailed inspection and research analysis, Mr. L picked one of Kenya's most rainy regions as the site for his plantation. Kenya's rainy regions, mostly still occupied by traditional farming, provide sufficient labor force with sound farming skills and experiences.

By adopting the business model of order agriculture, the company is able to cut local labor management costs, while having farmers conduct processes like seedling growing, transplanting, harvesting, and crop drying. To make sure the crops meet the standards, the company begins provides free pyrethrum seeds to the farmers; during the planting process, it also sends technicians to instruct the farmers how to grow, transplant, harvest and dry the crops; finally, contracts are signed with the farmers to secure the lowest price before its agents are sent to purchase the crops. At this time, farmers are paid in cash instead of IOUs, to avoid payment delays. The company also uses its plantation as a base for breeding and technical training, while conducting R&D in technical transfer to local farmers. It is alsodispatched by the company to the farms are more often than not locals who have received training at the base.

Kenya has long monopolized the management of pyrethrum in the country when it comes to export and sale. Before 2012, businesses relevant to pyrethrum are all required to hold licenses that were impossible for them to attain, except for the state-owned enterprise Pyrethrum Board of Kenya (PBK). After the pyrethrum market was partially opened in 2012, Mr. L's company spent immense efforts over a course of three years to gain the processing and export license for pyrethrum. Until now, Kenya has only issued such certificate to three companies, among which Mr. L's is the only one with a Chinese background. As the Kenyan government still imposes strict regulations on pyrethrum export, Mr. L's has designed a step-by-step plan for processing and export. Kenya's pyrethrum policy is such that no dried flowers but powder can be exported, so Mr. L's current strategy is to simply process dried flowers into powder before the export. In the next phase, he plans on establishing factories in Kenya to process products like pyrethrum essential oil and then have them exported. In order to do so, Mr. L has strived hard to extend his value chain into the global market. To do so, he has made a joint-investment with its company in China in establishing a high-tech enterprise in Shanghai that conducts R&D in pyrethrum processing and global trade.

Prospects for pyrethrum growing in Kenya are bright, according to Mr. L. With policy support from the government, Mr. L's company succeeded in stimulating the farmers to start growing, and can harvest more than 3000 ton of dried flowers each year. If this occurs, the company will become the world's second largest pyrethrum supplier after Australia.

Conclusion

The collapse of the pyrethrum industry in Kenya was the result of changes in the global market demand and the Pyrethrum Board of Kenya's payment delays and the difficulties inflicted on the farmers. To revitalize the pyrethrum industry, and to push the healthy development of the national economy generally, basic individual economic units (individual farmers) should become the very starting point. In other words, the improvement of living conditions and sustainable development are the first steps to be taken. Only in this way can poverty alleviation serves as a solid foundation for the country's development.

In our case study, Mr. L and his company had an understanding of Kenya's industrial set-up, economic traditions and direction of development, and made worthwhile attempts to try out possible market opportunities on that basis. The collapse of Kenya's pyrethrum industry seems to have been caused by risks from outside the industry rather than a significant change in factor endowment or comparative advantage. On the one hand, the core competitiveness of the industry is not yet lost, since traditional advantages can be restored after more resources are put in; on the other hand, as traditional forces of monopoly that once controlled the industry begin to fade out, private sectors will have more market space to breathe.

Therefore, for foreign enterprises ready to exercise long-term operation, confidence must be injected in the belief that long-term returns will eventually exceed immediate returns, so that they are willing to transform immediate returns into long-term investment, or to interpret interest transfer as risk discounts. What's more, in order to lower immediate risks and reinforce trade cooperation, the better solution is to establish a risk-sharing relationship with partners in the host country. Given such, foreign enterprises will likely turn their immediate returns into investment in their host partners or stakeholders. For developing countries, a close relationship between foreign investment and development cooperation is hence formed. From this point of view, the issue of social responsibility for foreign enterprises can be better approached.

As the case in this chapter has shown, Mr. L first built up confidence in revitalizing Kenya's pyrethrum industry by focusing on long-term returns, and undertook practices that transferred part of his immediate returns, such as injecting funds, carrying out order agriculture, and providing human resource training, to either invest in the long run or to avoid risks. Overall, Mr. L's operational model is one built upon the symbiotic relationship with the farmers. By binding shared interests to incentivize cooperation, the company has not only lent independence to its local partners, but also achieved survival and growth – a classical cooperative game model, which strives to rebuild the pyrethrum value chain by integrating the industrial value chain.

致　谢

与乐施会的合作开始于 2012 年，我和 2 个研究生一起翻译出版了赞比亚学者的《赞比亚农业发展及其对小农生计的影响》一书。2013 年，国际上关于中国在非洲的负面认知有增无减；在 BBC 的视频《中国人来了(The Chinese are coming)》发表后，关于中国在非洲农业领域里面"圈地"、用廉价产品抢夺和霸占非洲市场的各种失实的指摘也开始满天飞。我们开始酝酿，针对农业合作中国应该有自己的实地调研，但是单纯地看中国自己在非洲国家农业领域的作为，难以有客观的评价标准，于是我们和乐施会同仁共同商讨邀请来自印度、巴西、南非的学者，共同调研不同新兴国家的方法，在比较中看不同国际合作伙伴（特别是新兴市场国家）在非洲农业领域中的优势和劣势并进而评价其对非洲发展的贡献。赞比亚是我们选择的开始调研的国别。共同的调研报告，已经发表在《赞比亚农业外国直接投资：减贫和发展的机会与挑战》（中英双语版，社会科学文献出版社，2017），特别是印度国别的完整报告收录在这本书。

2014 年 10 月，在乐施会的大力支持下，北京大学非洲研究中心召开了大型国际合作会议"非洲农业国际合作与包容性、可持续发展：机遇和挑战"，会议除了邀请我们课题组发言，更广泛邀请国内和国际学者、企业商会、中资企业代表以及非政府机构及国际组织的代表参会发言、讨论互动。本书正是当时与会专家学者在发言基础上的进一步深入分析。全书设计为非洲农业的最新发展与内生动力（大陆内的政策和激励机制、外来援助、投资与商贸合作分析以及不同层面的创新实践）、新兴市场国家对非洲农业的南南合作以及中国对非洲农业合作的新型实践（国别案例：赞比亚、津巴布韦、肯尼亚、安哥拉、坦桑尼亚）三章。笔者认为，中国在非洲开展跨境农业援助、投资和贸易，都存在知识准备不足、战略布局有待深入调整的问题，最重要的问题在于研究严重不足——对非洲本土、中国已有实践经验以及以"他山之石可以攻玉"来作为学习参照的其他国际合作伙伴的研究都嫌不足；决策者和相关实务工作人士无法获得充足的信息用于设计、指导当下日益增加的大规模展开的对非农业合作实践。农村农业部国际合作中心 2017 年开始的非洲重点国别资料招标和政府购买服务工作正是明证。这也成为本书设计的初衷，即在当前对非合作实际工作需要的大背景下，提供有用的知识，深入研究非洲农业发展和自身的政策激励机制，同时参考其他相似经济体的对非合作实践经验，并且收集整理和分析中国已经开展的新型农业合作实践案例，从学理上深入分析中国对非农业合作的性质、特征和发展趋势等。

这本中英文论文集历经 5 年的酝酿、沟通、开会、写作、翻译、中英文校对整理，直至今天即将付梓，我不禁感激涕零，多位同仁参与了这项漫长的工作，感谢大家跟我一起携手走过这段时间。在几个国别调研中，二十多年来奋斗在坦桑尼亚的汪路生先生、管善远先生、侯世元先生、中非基金在一线工作的李俊先生、李东升先生、赞比亚农业示范中心的包和平主任、津巴布韦的赵科先生、南非的姒海先生以及在中国使馆工作的苟皓东公使、孙丽华老师等给予了课题组太多的无私帮助、指导。特别是经营农场的管总和汪总，身为国有企业的经理人，在非洲工作多年，热爱非洲更对中非关系充满着热情，因此，他们经营的剑麻农场与当地人社区总能够共度时艰，其中不乏被当地人保护、赞扬、爱护的故事。管总对于同样作为在非洲的第一批农业投资者、几年前已经长眠在赞比亚的王驰经理的评价也同样适用于自己："他的专业、专注、理想、情怀……使他在同等条件下干出非同一般的业绩！"我们在调研中遇到的这些充满真爱的"老非洲"，令我和学生们感动。我们认为他们是建设牢固、光明的中非关系的"民族脊梁"。

对于所有为本书提供精彩内容的作者，不一一赘述他们的名字，谨致以衷心的感谢！感谢萨利（Salih）教授邀约联合国非洲经济委员会总干事洛佩斯博士，我们得以用中文发表他关于农业在非洲经济转型中作用的作品。

感谢研究团队的每一位成员，宛如、马婕和马平岩（Alphonce Maya-la）、柯文卿（Kristian Secher）、天佑（Luyolo Sijake）曾经和我长时间在非洲不同国家、在相对艰苦的环境中调研。每每回忆和同学生们在调研生活中的点点滴滴，难免唏嘘他们对于我这个笨拙师长的巨大帮助，调研中反而是我往往要向他们学习。很多在非洲一线工作、接受我们采访的同仁都赞扬道："这一代青年人一直生活、成长在优厚的环境中，却跟我们在坦桑尼亚、赞比亚、津巴布韦和南非的艰苦环境中进行田野调查，并且甘之如饴，太令人震撼了！"

长期担任杂志专职英文编辑的柯文卿为本书所有的英文稿件做了一丝不苟的校对和编辑工作；刘均在博士就读的这几年里做了大量的资料整理工作，也担任本书中文文稿的翻译和第一次校对工作；已经在中国社会科学院西亚非洲研究所承担重要研究工作的沈晓雷博士，因为我们的课题而开始了他在津巴布韦的第一次长达5个月的调研工作，他对于中资农业公司的调研报告和关于津巴布韦土改的博士论文都是精彩作品；另一位在我们的团队中的优秀毕业生贾丁，因为跟我研究安哥拉而开始对葡语非洲国家产生浓厚兴趣，并承担了这本书三篇有关巴西对非合作英语文章的翻译工作；已经远在塞内加尔学习和生活了半年的杨逸凡、从哥伦比亚大学硕士毕业后在中美非三地创业的王筱稚和沈东普、聂晓、李家福等同学在本科和硕士研究生学习期间参与了本书相关文章的翻译工作，并且耐心地一遍遍打磨，付出了很多时间和精力。孙威、邹雨君同学虽然还没有正式开始他们的博士学习，但已经承担了本书部分文章的翻译和校对工作。

最后再次感谢乐施会同仁的督促、协作配合和耐心的等待！也要特别感谢社会科学文献出版社的编辑，常常督促、鼓励我们，对此我感激不尽。

是为记。

刘海方

2018 年 9 月 9 日于奥斯陆大学

图书在版编目（CIP）数据

非洲农业的转型发展与南南合作 / 刘海方等主编
. -- 北京：社会科学文献出版社，2018.12
ISBN 978 - 7 - 5201 - 3686 - 0

Ⅰ.①非…　Ⅱ.①刘…　Ⅲ.①农业发展 - 研究 - 非洲
②南南合作 - 研究　Ⅳ.①F34 ②F114.4

中国版本图书馆 CIP 数据核字（2018）第 240223 号

非洲农业的转型发展与南南合作

主　　编／刘海方　宛　如　刘　均　柯文卿

出 版 人／谢寿光
项目统筹／高明秀
责任编辑／吕　剑

出　　版／社会科学文献出版社·当代世界出版分社（010）59367004
　　　　　地址：北京市北三环中路甲 29 号院华龙大厦　邮编：100029
　　　　　网址：www.ssap.com.cn
发　　行／市场营销中心（010）59367081　59367083
印　　装／三河市龙林印务有限公司

规　　格／开 本：787mm × 1092mm　1/16
　　　　　印 张：29.25　字 数：471 千字
版　　次／2018 年 12 月第 1 版　2018 年 12 月第 1 次印刷
书　　号／ISBN 978 - 7 - 5201 - 3686 - 0
定　　价／98.00 元

本书如有印装质量问题，请与读者服务中心（010 - 59367028）联系